Dear Images
Art, Copyright and Culture

This publication has been made possible
by an Arts Council of England
National Visual Arts Publishing Grant
and an anonymous contribution

First published in 2002 by
Institute of Contemporary Arts
The Mall London SW1Y 5AH
and
Ridinghouse
47 Lexington Street London W1R 3LG
Distributed by
Cornerhouse Manchester
70 Oxford Street Manchester M15NH
Tel 0161 200 1501

British Library Cataloguing-in-Publication Data
A catalogue record for this book is available from the British Library

ISBN 1 – 900300 – 37 – 0 (Institute of Contemporary Arts, London)
ISBN 0 – 9541710 – 2 – 0 (Ridinghouse, London)

Copy-edited by Roger Denson, New York
Special thanks to Adam Gahlin
Designed and typeset by Marit Münzberg, London
Coverdesign by Richard Hollis and Marit Münzberg, London
Printed and bound in the United Kingdom by Short Run Press, Exeter

Coverillustration: Andy Warhol, Flowers, 1964
Collection Bruno Bischofberger, Zurich
© Andy Warhol Foundation For the Visual Arts/ARS, New York and DACS, London
Photograph courtesy Galerie Bruno Bischofberger, Zurich

Dear Images
Art, Copyright and Culture

Edited by
Daniel McClean and
Karsten Schubert

Ridinghouse
ICA

Foreword

Philip Dodd

In one of Jorge Luis Borges' great stories, the hero Pierre Menard wishes to write, not re-write, Cervantes' Don Quixote. He copies each word of Don Quixote as it is in the original but finds when he has finished that the story is somehow different. The implication of the narrative is of course that even the idea of an absolute copy is comic. It's impossible.

Borges' acute and witty scepticism notwithstanding, it's hard to argue with the proposition that the idea of the copy and even more of copyright are at the centre of a great deal of contemporary debate. The reasons for this are legion, some of passing interest, some more weighty. They might include the emergence of appropriation art in the 80s; the unravelling in the last quarter of the last century of certain Enlightenment notions of originality; the development of new kinds of digital technology which throw into doubt traditional ideas of ownership, production and distribution; and the increasing commercial exploitation of artworks and artists by a whole range of institutions and individuals. This book therefore, is very welcome. It reminds us that ownership is a historically variable matter. One only has to read Michael Baxandall's *Painting and Experience in Fifteenth-Century Italy*, his account of the power of the patron in 15th century Florence to see that; or to look at Orson Welles' melancholy struggles with Hollywood studios over who could do what with 'Welles's pictures'.

But this volume also reminds us just how careful we have to be in discussions of copyright. All artists are, of course, acutely aware that art is unimaginable without a shared language – and that this complicates all discussions of copyright. Absolute originality is, in short, as impossible as the 'private language' that the Wittgenstein's demonstrated was a myth. The artists recognise, too, that certain forms of appropriation are acceptable. After all, if we let a whiff of history into the arguments about 'ownership' we can see that 'theft' isn't always a matter of the 'bad' commercial guys stealing from artists. James Joyce's great novel *Ulysses* is unimaginable outside its dialogue with advertising, as recent scholarship has shown. And if we are talking about the exploitation of brands, then the art museum-world itself would be a candidate for salesman of the year. No blockbuster exhibition is complete without the exploitation of an artist's name in terms of merchandise. What Artists rightly object to is the unjust exploitation of their work – and the inability, given the nature of English law, to seek redress.

The arguments over copyright in the cultural domain are just one sign that issues over intellectual property are becoming more extensive and intense, not less, in the new knowledge economy. In a world where corporations such as AOL/Time Warner and Microsoft seem to own an increasing amount of the world's cultural heritage, we need a sophisticated guide through issues of copyright, which Time Warner is just as keen on as is any solo artist. The ICA is delighted to be co-publisher of a volume that provides more than a little intelligence about such a key contemporary issue.

Introduction[i]

Daniel McClean

Copyright has become a deeply contested issue within the art world: an issue that artists, gallery owners, curators and museum staff are forced to confront every day. During the 1990s there has been an abundance of copyright disputes involving leading contemporary artists and artists' estates[ii]. In highly publicised cases, Glenn Brown,[iii] Damien Hirst,[iv] Barbara Kruger,[v] Elizabeth Peyton,[vi] Cai Guo Qiang[vii] and the Andy Warhol Estate,[viii] have all faced legal action from commercial artists, photographers and designers for copyright infringement of their work. Many of these disputes have been settled out of court or are in the process of litigation, but such disputes not only cost artists heavy damages and legal fees, they take up much time and stifle creativity.

The famous 1992 case of *Art Rogers v. Jeff Koons*[ix] was watched closely by the international art world and has since informed artists of how copyright restrictions must from now on be weighed in the production and dissemination of their work. The claim brought against Koons was that his fabricated sculpture of a smiling suburban couple holding a litter of puppies was illegitimately 'copied' from a photograph taken by Rogers. Koons lost the case and was forced to pay Rogers damages. This opened the door to a wave of further copyright infringement suits against Koons for similarly 'appropriated' sculpture made during the 1980s[x] with the burden of litigation against the artist becoming so great that it effectively forced Koons to abandon this line of cultural enquiry altogether. For defenders of copyright, the purpose of copyright is to protect artists from acts of intellectual 'theft' by others. However, for many artists and curators, the 'intrusion' of law into the hallowed sphere of artistic production is perceived to be, at the least, nothing short of perverse and, more ominously, to set a precedent for state restrictions on artistic freedom and individual creativity.[xi]

Absolute originality is an untenable ideal, it is clear that all ideas are based upon existing ones. Critics of copyright law argue that it is in the nature of art to copy, quote and gather from all visual sources, including art itself and popular culture, and that the current law unfairly restricts and regulates the activities of artists: a problem exemplified where copyright holders refuse to allow their material to be used or seek to demand unreasonable fees.[xii] They also point out that the law is perilously out of step with the 'post-modern' practices of contemporary artists who use and re-contextualise the readymade imagery and materials of our culture, thereby calling into question the values of originality and authorship upon which both modernist aesthetics and copyright law are seemingly built.

Yet as artists have found themselves to be the victims of copyright disputes, copyright law has also become commercially exploited by artists and museums – a consequence of the circulation of images throughout society. Licensing agreements for the reproduction of artists' works have become increasingly common in the spheres of advertising and publishing, and copyright collection societies like DACS (in the U.K.) and SPADEM (in France) have been formed with the specific purpose of enforcing copyright licences. As Peter Wienand and Naomi Korn show in their essay, income derived from copyright fees has become in many cases, a significant source of revenue for artists and their estates as well as for museums.

Imagery and ideas taken from artists abound within the advertising and design industries, as seen in the repeated references to the grids and motifs found in the work of Gilbert & George. [xiii] A recurrent cause of complaint for artists has been finding their ideas exploited in a commercial context without the offer of financial reward or authorial acknowledgement (though Gilbert & George view such 'appropriations' as acts of homage). Gillian Wearing's outspoken criticisms of the exploitation of her series, *Signs*,[xiv] in an advertising campaign commissioned by Volkswagen, and her film *10-16*,[xv] in an advertisement produced by M&C Saatchi, typify this reaction. Artists are often reluctant to embark upon litigation when they think that their rights have been infringed because of the expense and uncertainty involved in protracted legal cases. Yet the case of *Lebbeus Woods v. Universal City Studios*[xvi] illustrates that when artists do litigate against major players in a commercial context, the economic rewards can be considerable. In this case the visionary architect, Lebbeus Woods, discovered that his drawing of a chair suspended in an antechamber had been closely modelled in a sequence of the film, *Twelve Monkeys*. The artist successfully sued the production studio and was awarded a substantial, undisclosed figure in compensation.

But copyright actions are not only embarked upon by artists for financial reasons; they are also pursued to uphold the moral rights of artists to control the context in which their work is reproduced and presented, with the intent of protecting the original from being 'degraded' by undesirable commercial associations. This is particularly true of the numerous copyright suits brought by the painter, Bridget Riley, against fashion and interior designers for imitating her instantly recognisable 'Op' abstractions[xvii]. Another well-known example is the

Damien Hirst, *Hymn*, 1999

2000 case in the U.K. won by the Cuban photographer Alberto Diaz Guiterrez against an advertising agency [xviii]. The court upheld the photographer's legal right to prevent his iconic photograph of the Cuban revolutionary leader, Che Guevara, from being further exploited in an advertisement for a brand of vodka and he settled for out of court damages paid to a charity.

Cases like these illustrate that copyright law has important ramifications on both sides of the art world fence, with artists being both protected as creators and charged as plagiarisers of copyrighted material. Yet the relationship of contemporary art to copyright connects to much wider debates about the nature and legitimacy of copyright as a form of intellectual property law and its impact upon society in the light of vast cultural, economic and technological changes.[xix] On this, Johnson Okpaluba notes: 'The debate as to the form that copyright law should take in the digital era has led to a polarisation of viewpoints between those who wish to see more rights granted to authors to protect their works and greater enforcement of these rights and those who believe that copyright is already 'over-strength' and that users' rights need to be considered so that creativity and creation of cultural products are not stifled'.

Copyright is a form of intellectual property law alongside patent and trade-mark law regulating cultural creation and reproduction.[xx] Broadly speaking, copyright seeks to protect the creative mental processes embodied or materially expressed in different types of cultural media including artistic, literary, dramatic and musical works by giving owners (usually the author) the right to control and exploit the work in which the right subsists. This includes the right to copy the work and perform it in public. Other users must obtain the consent of the copyright owner to undertake these acts in relation to the work, otherwise they risk infringing the copyright. Civil and criminal remedies exist for the owner when the right is infringed. The rights of copyright owners, in most jurisdictions, last for the lifetime of the author plus seventy years post-mortem.

Copyright ownership is distinct from physical ownership of the work because copyright protects what is intangible in the work. In addition, multiple copyrights can exist in a single work. For example, in a film, individual copyrights may protect the film itself (the artistic work), the spoken words (the literary work), the script (the dramatic work), and the soundtrack (the musical work).

In addition to copyright, moral rights exist to protect authors. These rights include the right to be identified as author (paternity), to prevent false attribution (attribution) and to prevent derogatory treatment of the work (integrity), see Ruth Redmond-Cooper's essay. In contrast to copyright, moral rights are unassignable and under some jurisdictions, like France, perpetual. Derogatory treatment encompasses both mistreatment of the original work, including vandalism (as seen in the attack on Marcus Harvey's painting of Myra Hindley during the exhibition *Sensation*, held at the Royal Academy (1997)), and acts of copying which are prejudicial to the honour of the author, including distortions and caricatures[xxi]. Moral rights imply that an indissoluble bond exists between author and work and that in damaging a work or failing to ascribe proper recognition, the creator is somehow harmed, see Anthony Julius' essay.

It is clear that copyright raises complex cultural, philosophical, political and ethical questions regarding both its assumptions of 'authorship' and 'work', and its justification as a property right: in particular, the premise that ideas can be owned as private property when disseminated in the public domain and that legally enforceable restrictions can be placed upon other users.[xxii] For critics of copyright law, as Kathy Bowrey points out in her contribution, these restrictions are seen as unjustifiable in constraining creative cultural practices.[xxiii] They are also considered realistically unsustainable, as the proliferation of reproduction in the digital environment renders legal mechanisms for controlling information redundant.[xxiv]

The need to balance private authorial rights with wider public rights (e.g. free expression) is key to the shape of copyright law which can be seen as an uneasy compromise between these two competing principles. Copyright laws recognise that new cultural creations are inevitably inspired by existing forms, they do not give authors unfettered rights over their ideas. These limits are encoded in devices such as the so-called 'idea-expression' dichotomy, which implies that copyright cannot apply to ideas alone, but only to their material expression. They are also reflected in fair use exemptions. Where the limits should be drawn, however, is a matter for continuous debate and revision.

In his essay, Michael Spence distinguishes two broad groups of justification. In the first group, copyright is justified on economic grounds as a benefit to the community: copyright rewards authors for their creative endeavours and discourages plagiarism by assigning authors property rights over the products of their mental labour. In this way, it is argued, copyright encourages cultural production to the benefit of society. In the second group, copyright is conceived in individualistic terms as a moral or 'deontological' right. Here, copyright is validated on different grounds: from rewarding authors for the 'fruits of their labour' and preventing theft by others (a man may only reap what he sows), to the notion that copyright exists to protect the creative expression of the author's 'personality'. Different legal systems make use of different arguments. The U.S., for instance, favours the first model, where the constitution justifies copyright in so far as it 'promotes progress in the sciences and the arts'.[xxv] By contrast, French law tends to emphasise the rights of the author in a moral sense, as an imprint of the author's self (*droit d'auteur*).

The shape and territory of copyright law are fluid, changing in response to developments in technology.[xxvi] From its inception as a literary property right granted to English authors and publishers in the Statute of Anne 1710, which was intended to regulate the uncontrolled copying of books facilitated by the new printing press, copyright law has evolved to accommodate both technological developments and wider categories of cultural media, including mechanical reproduction (photography and film) and more recently, digital reproduction (the internet). As Gregor Claude illustrates in relation to the internet, copyright law has, alongside other techniques of control (such as the encryption and the digital watermarking of images), expanded, strengthened and harmonised over the last decade: a response to the threat posed by digital technology for unregulated copying and distribution.

Copyright is both a right of authorship and a property right. Inscribed within its structure is a tension between its existence as a right to protect authorial expression and its locus as a commodity that can be assigned, sold and licensed to others, including publishers. Paradoxically, as Jane Gaines has observed,[xxvii] the growth of copyright law has witnessed the disappearance of the individual author as copyright holder and the emergence of the corporation as owner – exploiting its economic benefits long after the death of the author. This emergence of corporations as owners of copyrighted photographic images is reflected in the spectacular growth of image libraries like Corbis Inc. and Getty Images in the U.S., organisations that have acquired nearly all of North America's major collections (see Carla Shapreau's essay). In a globalised capitalist society predicated upon the rapid reproduction, dissemination and consumption of information and images, it may seem inevitable that copyright law should assume this central role as a mechanism in exploiting what are valuable, intangible commodities. But to copyright sceptics like Peter Drahos,[xxviii] the corporate ownership of copyright is further evidence of its negative influence as a constraint upon communication and its role in the erosion of the public domain. This is reflected in some alarming cases, as for example when the Walt Disney Corporation demanded that the artist, Dennis Oppenheim remove his public sculpture, incorporating the figures of Mickey Mouse and Donald Duck.[xxix]

On close inspection, copyright emerges as a complex constellation of legal, cultural, economic and technological forces raising a multitude of demanding questions. How are we, for example, to measure originality and creativity? How do we differentiate between inspiration, interpretation and plagiarism? How do we balance intellectual ownership with the rights of others to free expression? Despite its growing importance both within the art world and within culture at large, there is a remarkable lack of understanding of the basic structure of copyright, as well as of the relationships implicated between the law, culture and art.

This anthology of essays brings together contributors from different disciplines – art historians, cultural theorists, lawyers and legal theorists – to address some of these issues.

The first purpose of this anthology is to provide a legal overview of the architecture of copyright law as it applies to the visual arts. It analyses the basic conceptual framework of copyright as an intellectual property right. It also considers the important and related subject of moral rights (see below). The second purpose is to consider the problems that emerge when contemporary art confronts copyright law. On the one hand, copyright laws appear to fail to confer sufficient protection upon many contemporary art forms and practices including Appropriation, Conceptual, Minimal and Installation Art.

On the other hand, there is the problem of infringement: what happens when modern and contemporary artists make use of copyrighted material and seemingly infringe the rights of copyright owners? Here criticism is levelled at the criteria of infringement and the limited defences available to artists when they find themselves on the wrong side of the law. In addition to the problems faced by artists, contributors consider the problems which confront publishers and museums who seek to reproduce copyrighted art works in the absence of fair-dealing exemptions.[xxx]

Thirdly, in examining the extent to which art and copyright law are in conflict, this anthology analyses the values of authorship underpinning both models of cultural production. Just as copyright law provides rules for demarcating intellectual ownership and for regulating 'copies', so 'art', as a system of authorship, defines works of aesthetic originality by separating and privileging them over works of reproduction. In the words of Man Ray, 'to create is to divine, to reproduce is human'. In this regard, the essays collected here explore the respective roles that the original and copy have played within art since the Renaissance, particularly during the era of modernity, and ask to what extent these relationships are mirrored in copyright law. The question of protecting the arts, in particular, revolves around the importance of the 'creative subject' to copyright law, and to what extent, if any, copyright law is imbued with Romantic aesthetics.

Finally, by considering the evolution of copyright law in the light of the dilemmas raised, the essays focus on the question of infringement and whether fair use exemptions (as on the grounds of parody) can be extended to accommodate artistic practices that incorporate copyrighted visual material. Reflecting on the possible changes in the structure of copyright law in relation to the specific legal systems in which laws are made (primarily in the U.K.), the essays assess two general points about the constraints and directions these systems support. First, how we envisage the shape and direction of copyright law largely emanates from our view of what we believe the purpose of copyright to be. The second, at a residual level, is how there may be fundamental and insurmountable differences in the way that legal and aesthetic judgements are made and enforced. An example of this is the aspiration for legal certainty, which in copyright terms is expressed by creativity being measured, ideally, in an aesthetically neutral, value-free way; a judgement that is always inherently unstable. [xxxi]

I. Legal Sources
What does Copyright protect?

Copyright does not protect all works, nor does it prohibit all copies. In order for copyright to subsist in an artwork, various conditions must be satisfied: most notably, the work must fit within a recognised category of artistic subject matter and be original in a legal sense. There are additional jurisdictional requirements that the author or production of the work be connected to the country of the copyright law invoked. Such requirements can be bewilderingly complex as Brett Rowlands, Mervyn Flatt and Samantha McGonigle reveal. Even when a protected work is copied, this may not amount to an infringement; it all depends on what part of the original work is copied, in what form, and how much the copy takes from the original. Last, there are defences against infringement.

Authorship

Generally, copyright vests automatically in the author of the work, though there may be registration requirements as in the U.S. (see Donn Zaretsky's essay). However, if a work is made during the course of employment then the copyright will vest in the employer, not in the employee, (note this does not apply to commissions). The question of who the author is, legally speaking, has moral rights implications. It has become a cause of dispute for 'conceptual' artists who have arranged for other artists to execute work on their behalf. Notably, the artist Gavin Turk was involved in a dispute with a photographer over a 'self-portrait' which he had arranged, for which he claimed exclusive authorship.[xxxii]

Categories of Artistic Work

The various copyright statutes do not seek to define art; instead, they provide lists of categories within which works have to fall to be protected. As Karen Sanig shows in her analysis of U.K. copyright law, the Copyright, Designs and Patents Act 1988 (CDPA) [xxxiii] divides artistic works into various abstract categories, including graphic works, sculptures and photographs, whose meaning is fleshed out through case law. The categories are not fixed but have been added to over time, as the law has sought to register developments that have occurred in art. Copyright protects most traditional art forms, but has a more problematic relationship to some contemporary artistic practices (see below).

Aesthetic Neutrality

The artistic categories under copyright law at first sight appear strange as they do not seem to hinge on aesthetic criteria. Indeed, in the U.K., the CDPA explicitly states that artistic works (with the exception of works of architecture and artistic craftsmanship) are not to be considered in terms of their artistic quality.[xxxiv] In case law, these artistic categories have been interpreted primarily in terms of the visual techniques deployed rather than by reference to the intention of the artist or the end result. Broader groups of works are protected as 'artistic' than are traditionally associated with fine art, including works of industrial design. For example, an electric circuit diagram has been held to be a drawing, placing it in the same category of graphic works as a sketch by Picasso.[xxxv]

Fixation

It is generally a requirement for copyright protection that the work be recorded. In the U.K., this requirement is not stated, but has been assumed by the courts in various cases. It has been held that artistic works lacking permanence such as sand drawings or a face painting will not qualify for protection, thus posing problems for works of an ephemeral nature.[xxxvi]

Originality

In contrast to aesthetic discourse, copyright legislators and judges try to avoid using originality in an evaluative sense to describe the creative nature of artistic works; i.e. in relation to their quality, inventiveness or merit. Instead, the originality requirement focuses on the causal relationship between an author and the work: that the author is distinctively the originator of the work in question; in other words, that the work is not copied from someone else.[xxxvii]

De Minimis

In addition to the work originating from the author, something creative has to be contributed. All copyright laws adopt a minimal approach when it comes to measuring the creative mental substance of originality, though, as Brad Sherman points out, precisely how this elusive substance or something else is to be measured oscillates within and between legal cultures. In the U.K., originality is seen as the embodiment of the author's mental labour and tests rotate around minimal standards of skill, judgement and effort.[xxxviii] In France, on the other hand, where originality is seen to be the imprint of the author's personality, the creative threshold is higher, as it is in the U.S.[xxxix] In the U.K., tests for originality have excluded only the very trivial. A basic drawing of a hand pointing to a square on a ballot paper was held in one case to be an original graphic work.[xl] There are limits though. Protection may be extended to works which derive from existing works, but a slavish copy, however much effort or skill is applied, will not be original: nor is a work likely to be protected if its elements are too basic, for example, a drawing of a straight line. It has been said that only certain kinds of skill, labour and judgement confer originality. Mental labour must be appropriate and bring about some material change: in artistic works this is measured in terms of whether there has been an embellishment of visual significance to the materials used.[xli]

Mechanical Acts

Photographs are protected as original on the basis that though the medium is mechanical, a photographer exercises skill, judgement and effort in the lighting, composing, taking and printing of the photograph. Simon Stokes and Carla Shapreau discuss the shifting threshold of originality here, addressing the topical issue of whether photographs and digitised images of artworks are capable of being granted copyright protection. Traditionally, these types of photographs have been construed as 'original', however, a recent U.S. judgement, *Bridgeman v. Corel*,[xlii] applying U.K. law, questioned whether such 'copies' do exhibit sufficient creative effort. Stokes concludes that this judgement misapplies U.K. law and that the threshold under U.K. law remains unchanged. Shapreau, from a U.S. perspective, draws the opposite conclusion, though she notes that artistic originality may subsist in the compilation of digital images of artworks.

The Work

Copyright divides all artworks into protected elements, which are the property of the author, and non-protected elements, which can be used freely by others.[xliii] The scope of protection varies between works depending on such considerations as the type of work in question, the 'originality' of the author's contribution, and the nature of the idea. It is difficult to determine the scope of protection in a work as this is only established in law when the work is copied.

The Idea-Expression Dichotomy

It is a presumption stated in certain copyright statutes and developed by the courts in other jurisdictions that copyright cannot exist in an idea but only in its material expression. This means that copyright tends to protect the form of a work rather than its content. In reality, as many commentators have pointed out, there is no clear dividing line between ideas and their expression and it is up to judges to determine on the facts which ideas are protected. [xliv] According to U.K. judge, Hugh Laddie, the dichotomy describes the expression of ideas encoded in a work in terms of different levels of abstraction: from detailed to general expressions.[xlv] For example, in a painting, the application of brush strokes onto canvas is a more detailed idea than the style of the painting or the idea behind the painting: e.g. to paint a monochrome or a landscape.

Beyond the Surface

Ideas beneath the surface of a work may be protected as original expressions providing they are sufficiently detailed. The less detailed ideas become, however, the further they move from being the property of the artist to belonging in the public domain. How much beyond the visual surface of an artwork will copyright protect? This is a tricky question and one that depends upon the analysis of infringement. Bently and Sherman have distinguished between the ideas used in the preparatory stages of a work and in its execution.[xlvi] They suggest that protection may extend to such mental acts as arranging a view or composition within a painting or a photograph, even if they are copied in a very different visual form. More general ideas, however, will not be protected.

Artistic Style and Technique

On the whole, copyright laws tend not to protect an artistic style or a technique. Nadia Walravens gives the example of two similar infringement actions brought by the French artist, Christo (famous for his large-scale wrapping of public monuments) against different photographers. In the first case, concerning photographs of the wrapping of the Pont-Neuf Bridge, the Paris Court of Appeal held that this was an original work whose form had been copied. In the second case, concerning an advertising agency which had produced photographs of a swimming pool covered in a pink cloth closely resembling one of Christo's works, protection was denied on the grounds that the law protects 'only creations of a particular, individualised object and not a category or a family of forms that have features in common; only because they all correspond to a style or a process arising from an idea'.

Infringement

A copyright infringement takes place when a person, without the copyright owner's consent, performs a restricted act in relation to the copyright work. The law distinguishes between primary infringements: including copying, adapting, translating and performing the work, which do not depend upon knowledge, and secondary infringements such as publicly disseminating infringing copies, which do. Galleries, museums and publishers should take note that in displaying and distributing infringing works they may also be liable as secondary infringers and may be joined to proceedings. [xlvii]

Copyright laws do not place absolute restrictions on artistic copying: they are limited in their scope and in their duration. However, copyright laws take a wide view of copying, to use the terminology of Hillel Schwartz, covering acts of *re-enactment* (manual copies) and acts of *appropriation* (mechanical copies).[xlviii] Legal restrictions, therefore, are clearly of significance to contemporary artists whose practice is to copy and borrow substantial parts of their imagery (restrictions which they rarely consider), whether through traditional techniques like painting (note the difficulties encountered by Glenn Brown and Elizabeth Peyton) or mechanical techniques of mass reproduction, as seen in the work of many Pop artists (note the difficulties encountered by Andy Warhol). This diversity gives us reason here to collect criticisms of copyright that focus on different areas of inadequacy. We examine, for instance, how the law substantively misunderstands the complex process of copying within art, a problem encountered in the law's criteria of infringement and its apparent miscasting of the diverse impulses and purposes that motivate artistic copying.

Copying

Copying means reproducing the work in any material form, including all artistic media. All copies are translations in which something of the original is both added to and erased in the copy.[xlix] In law a copy need not, be identical in order to amount to an infringement. It may be enough to reproduce an essential feature or a significant extract.

Substantial Part

The general test is whether the amount taken is the whole or a substantial part of the original, and as such it is qualitative rather than quantitative, i.e. depending on the degree of importance of what is taken from the original rather than on the amount. For example, a collage, in which a fragment of a protected work is reproduced, may be an infringement, and given the extensiveness of this technique in art, this is a major area of potential difficulty (see Johnson Okpaluba's essay, referring to the difficulties faced by appropriation artists).[1] The law takes an expansive view of what constitutes the copying of a substantial part of an artwork, allowing for changes across media and dimensions. *Rogers v. Koons* illustrates how infringement extends to changes from two to three dimensions. In this case, Koons' wooden sculptures were held by a U.S. court to infringe the copyright in Rogers' black and white photograph.[li]

Measuring a Substantial Part

How is the copying of a substantial part measured? The approach followed by the House of Lords in a recent case [lii] suggests that it lies in taking both works as 'wholes' and considering the cumulative copying of ideas, rather than in dissecting the original work into individual parts and looking to see which expressions have been reproduced (see Karen Sanig's discussion). In the words of Lord Hoffmann, 'a substantial part can be a feature or combination of features of the work, abstracted from it rather than forming a discrete part'. This decision entrenches the scope of protection under U.K. law. In the light of this case, it is likely for example, that Glenn Brown's controversial *The Loves of Shepherds (after Double Star by Tony Roberts)* 2000, based on a science-fiction illustration by Anthony Roberts and displayed during the Tate Gallery's Turner Prize 2000 exhibition, amounts to an infringement. Comparing both images as 'wholes', Brown's painting reproduces the essential features of Roberts' composition (the skeletal structure of the spacecraft and the configuration of orbiting planets), despite the creative and skilful alteration of the image in terms of its scale, colour and detail.[liii]

Defences

Defences to copyright infringement vary considerably between jurisdictions. In the U.K., they are relatively narrow. The exemptions are specific rather than general, and confined to activities such as fair dealing for the purposes of criticism, review and news reporting [liv] and fair dealing for research and private study.[lv] Under these provisions, an artist will have no defence in an infringement action if producing a work for public view or sale, though private preparatory studies may be exempted. For publishers of copyright-protected imagery the exemptions provide uncertain refuge. They have been confirmed as too narrow to cover commercial art historical publications (see Suzanne Garben and Ruth Hoy's essay addressing the implications of the action brought by the Matisse Estate against Phaidon).

By contrast, in the U.S., the fair use defence is wider.[lvi] The U.S. Copyright Act 1976 creates a general fair use defence, listing four factors to be taken into consideration: the purpose and character of the use, the nature of the copyrighted work, the amount and substantiality of the portion used and the effect upon the potential market for the value of the copyrighted work (see Donn Zaretsky's discussion). Significantly and in contrast to the U.K., parody of the original work is permitted as a possible ground for fair use.

II. Copyright and Art

The second purpose of the anthology is to examine some of the main differences and points of conflict that have arisen between art and copyright law. On examination, two areas emerge: the apparent limits to the legal protection of contemporary art forms and, conversely, the legal restrictions that copyright imposes upon artistic practices.[lvii] Paradoxically, these problems are often interrelated, as an artwork that is based upon appropriation might fail to be ascribed protection as original. These problems have been attributed to the way in which copyright law conceives the author, the work and their inter-relationships, though they can also be seen as a manifestation of a general tension that exists between art and the law.

The Scope of Protection

Defenders of copyright argue that its goal is to promote progress in the visual arts in a neutral way. However, if copyright gives protection to conventional art forms, it also excludes others. Martha Woodmansee and Peter Jaszi [lviii] as cited by Anne Barron have observed that 'no copyright can exist in a work produced as a true collective enterprise (rather than by one or more identifiable or anonymous authors); a work cannot be copyrighted unless it is 'fixed' (which excludes body art, land art and performance art in general); copyright does not extend to works that are not 'original' (which rules out the readymade and appropriation art in general); and copyright does not protect 'basic' components of cultural productions (and so radically limits the protection awarded to minimalist and conceptual art).' According to this line of argument, many 'works' accepted as art by the institutions of the art world, its museums, galleries, critical journals and auction houses, lack (at least hypothetically) judicial recognition. Critics have also pointed to the closures implicit in the judicial interpretation of non-western art forms such as aboriginal paintings, which based upon the repetition of existing designs in the depiction of creation and dreaming stories, lack the requisite originality. [lix]

Authorship

Many of the contributors address the authorship requirements of copyright law: in particular, how the legal conception of originality diverges from its understanding and practice within the field of art. The tendency of much twentieth-century art has been to question prevailing conceptions of artistic originality (particularly modernist) and to suggest other models of authorship (often ironically), as embodied in Marcel Duchamp's readymades. In turn, the readymade, essentially a functional object chosen and designated by an artist as 'this is art', has been accepted in the very context of display (the museum) that it was proposed to question.[lx]

In her essay, Nadia Walravens analyses how the 'vague and ill-defined' prerequisite of originality that underpins French copyright law is shaped by a 'subjective vision of authorship', through which the work must express, in a concrete visual form, the personality of the artist. In addition, under French copyright law, the work must be personally executed by the artist (though note that this second requirement is not necessary in other jurisdictions like the U.S. and U.K.). In Walraven's view, it is unlikely that the readymade can be ascribed copyright protection under extant French law because being derivative, it will not be deemed an original work of form. This would seem to apply under other copyright jurisdictions where artists have similarly reproduced existing objects and images to transform their meanings without substantially changing their material nature: for example, Damien Hirst's *Hymn* (2000), a twenty-foot, magnified reproduction of a child's small anatomical toy.

Celia Lury argues that the 'author-function' has been transformed so greatly within contemporary culture that existing copyright law provides an inadequate legal framework for artistic protection. Addressing the work of Damien Hirst, and in particular his *Spot Paintings*, she argues that the components of his work that authenticate and designate authorship, namely Hirst's artistic style and signature, make trademark law a more appropriate legal register of protection for his works than copyright law. To quote, 'Hirst says that he is a brand name, and thus implies that what he 'does' should be protected by the laws of trademark as much as, or rather than, by those of copyright'.

Categories of Work

Other contributors place greater emphasis on the categories of work through which copyright law interprets art. In Anne Barron's analysis, it is the taxonomic, medium-specific approach embedded in copyright that is particularly problematic. Anglo-American copyright law divides and separates artistic works into discrete categories of media; for example, painting and sculpture based on characteristics attributed to that medium. In this way, she argues, it reflects an essentialist tradition of thinking about the arts that first emerged in eighteenth century aesthetic discourse through which artworks are separated according to their mode of sensory perception and whether they are perceived in space or time. This discourse was resuscitated with much acclaim in the modernist art criticism of Clement Greenberg and Michael Fried,[lxi] in the 1940s and 1950s, and became the framework for modernist art. In Barron's view, it is the collapse of modernism and the rise of new art practices that are critical to the present encounter between copyright law and art. Copyright, reflecting modernist aesthetic prejudices, is unable to accommodate these practices. She refers to the rise of theatrical art in the wake of minimalism – art that co-exists in the time of the spectator and is completed by the audience – while also highlighting 'generic' art: art that encompasses hybrid media, installation, video and readymade objects, as posing difficulties.[lxii]

The problem of artistic works lying in between categories and marked by temporality can be seen in relation to Gillian Wearing's *Signs* (1993).[lxiii] In this series, the artist asked people on a street to write down what they were feeling onto boards shown to a camera (an example being a young businessman holding a sign with the words 'I'm Desperate'). Wearing's idea was later re-enacted in a Volkswagen advertisement, but with different characters, locations and signs. Despite the apparent plagiarism of her idea, the artist would, it seems, be left with little protection under U.K. law. Whilst the image in each of the artist's photographs would be protected, it is submitted that she would be unable to protect the underlying ideas of the event and documentation as they do not fit into existing artistic categories. Protection would also be limited by the idea-expression dichotomy.

The Copy

To quote the German painter Gerhard Richter, who painted extensively from 'found' photographs during the 1960s (both from those that are 'private' in photo-albums and 'public' in newspapers): 'Perhaps because I'm sorry for the photograph, because it has such a miserable existence even though it is a perfect picture, I would like to make it valid, make it visible – just make it'.[lxiv]

In one sense, Richter's sentiment echoes the entire history of western art, or at least that part of it that is based around 'copying': through classicism, romanticism, modernism, and postmodernism, artists have interpreted and transformed the works of their predecessors, contemporaries, and frequently even themselves, (as in the work of Marcel Duchamp and Giorgio de Chirico) by imitating, borrowing and repeating motifs and compositions.[lxv] In classical painting, as Richard Shone illuminates here, the copy has a complex typology. At one pole lies the faithful 'replica', at the other lies the errant 'forgery'. Within this typology, the 'imitation' of 'masters' is a creative tradition amounting to the construction of forms analogous to those of the 'original'; indeed such acts reinforce the very prestige of the 'original'. Karsten Schubert traces the creative transformations embedded in one of the most famous and seminal sequences of copying in western art, from Raimondi's etching of Raphael's lost drawing, *The Judgement of Paris*, to Manet's *Le Déjeuner sur l'herbe* and beyond.

This tradition is not necessarily at odds with copyright law, but when the copied sources are under protection then problems may arise. Paul Edward Geller identifies the courts' analysis of infringement as being one of the main defects of copyright law. He argues that the courts apply tests which are far too rigid, failing to distinguish between 'creative' copies that build on the original and literal or 'close' copies which do not.

He suggests that there is a spectrum of copying: starting with mechanical or rote copying, graduating to knowledgeable reworking and culminating in innovative recasting. He proposes that the courts, with the assistance of art experts, refer to this spectrum when analysing the infringing work and tailor their remedies to suit.

Appropriation

Johnson Okpaluba identifies three types of appropriation. First, the copying of whole images with or without attribution to the copyright owner. Here, the original may be altered, as in *L.H.O.O.Q.* (or 'she's got a hot arse'), Marcel Duchamp's famous addition of a moustache to a postcard of the *Mona Lisa*; or it may be copied in unaltered form as in Sherrie Levine's reproductions of iconic photographs by Walker Evans and Edward Weston. Second, the practice of montage that involves incorporating images from several sources into a new work, as seen in the screen prints of Robert Rauschenberg. Third, the practice of simulationism: the appropriation of whole genres and styles. As Okpaluba elucidates, appropriation practices pervade the avant-garde movements of the early twentieth century such as Dada and Surrealism, coming to fruition with Pop Art in the 1960s, where commodity images and the techniques of mechanical reproduction coincide and continue to the present day.

It is important to distinguish the movement 'appropriation' art of the 1980s from current contemporary art practices. Appropriation art (as reflected in its pejorative name) has an iconoclastic and polemical dimension. This is perhaps

seen most visibly in the work of Sherrie Levine who, by repeating reproductions of twentieth-century photographic masterpieces, according to Rosalind Krauss, deconstructs modernist notions of authorship and originality to 'open the print from behind to the series of models from which it, in turn, has stolen, of which it is itself the reproduction'.[lxvi] Strategies of appropriation are evident in the work of artists of the 1990s, but often to different, less direct ends as seen in the wide-spread re-working of cinematic images. In Douglas Gordon's 're-presentations' of classic cinematic works, such as Alfred Hitchcock's *Psycho* (which he slowed down over a twenty-four hour period), the object is less to question the status of the original than to reveal, as it unfolds in real time, its inner memory.[lxvii]

Appropriation appears to pose a particular type of challenge to copyright law (though see Brad Sherman's sceptical essay here). In the words of one critic, 'it rebels against the traditional norms of ownership, originality and expression that define copyright protection'.[lxviii] In terms of ownership, images that belong to copyright owners are 'taken' without their consent; in terms of originality, images are copied without visual embellishment therefore failing to creatively 'transform' the original. Finally, in terms of expression, the meaning of the work resides in the ideas that underlie it rather than in its form, thus once again failing to transform the original source. This 'challenge', for many critics stems from the failure of the law to recognise the 'intertextuality' of cultural production: that artists in playing with images, originality and identity are caught within a game of representation in which to repeat is to produce something new.[lxix] The law's distance from culture here would seem to be inscribed in the often repeated dictum of U.S. Judge Wendell Holmes: 'Others may be free to copy the original (*nature*), but they are not free to copy the copy (*culture*)' (my italics).[lxx]

In a wider sense, for critics such as John Carlin in *Culture Vultures*,[lxxi] copyright law constrains the impulse of modern artists to use, refer, quote, challenge and praise the imagery that pervades the visual environment, thus placing unacceptable limitations upon artistic activity and free expression. In addition to coming into conflict with copyright laws artists also fall foul of trademark law (outside the scope of this book), particularly where their work is politically charged and comments upon corporate power, as in the case of the German artist, Hans Haacke.[lxxii]

Fair Use

A major criticism of copyright law raised by appropriation art is the absence of wide and flexible fair use exemptions capable of accommodating infringement. Whilst some jurisdictions like the U.S. allow for parody, appropriation art still seems to fall on the side of plagiarism rather than on the side of legitimate comment.[lxxiii] Johnson Okpaluba discusses the relationship between appropriation art and fair use in the light of *Rogers v. Koons*.[lxxiv] In this case, Koons, sought to justify his work, *A String of Puppies* contending that it was a parody of society: by invoking Rogers' 'kitsch' image, Koons argued that he was commenting upon the deterioration in the quality of society and the artistic tradition engendered through mass consumerism. Whilst the court accepted the artistic heritage of Koons' work, they held that it could not be considered as a parody of Rogers' photograph because it did not comment upon it directly. In addition they noted a further difficulty, that, even if Koons had intended to parody the image, it is unlikely that an audience would have understood this purpose because they would have been unaware of the original.

For Okpaluba, Koons' failure to successfully establish the parody defence, exposes the limits of the fair use doctrine in tolerating appropriation art. He points out how the courts decision might now decide differently, following the later case of *Acuff-Rose v. Campbell* (which exempted the copying of elements of Roy Orbison's song *Pretty Woman* by the rap-group, 2 Live-Crew as a parody),[lxxv] but he still doubts that this would be the case. In any event, however far it is stretched, *Acuff-Rose v. Campbell* will not accommodate literal copies because the courts do not recognise that original works can be transformed through change in context alone.

III. Authorship

The third objective of this book is to examine the complex values of authorship which underpin both art and copyright law and to address to what extent they conflict or coincide. The question arises, if 'originality' means to 'originate' within copyright law, what does this share with the Romantic notion of originality (to give birth to) that informs art during the modernist era? [lxxvi] Two observations become apparent: just as it is a misunderstanding to assume that copyright and art are necessarily in tension, so the legal protection of the artist or creative subject is not a natural objective of copyright law.

Art as Property

As Susan Lambert has illustrated in graphic detail in her extensive study of the reproduction *The Image Multiplied*,[lxxvii] art is a system of authorship and property relations in which 'originality' is constructed via differentiation and control over copying. A synonym for 'authentic' or 'genuine' (the sign of the artist's presence), the original has been distinguished from the copy through devices such as the signature. For Lambert, this is embodied in artists' prints: an inherently multiple process in which selected prints are stabilised as original by being restricted in edition and inscribed with the artist's name.

There are parallels here between the way in which art and copyright law as systems delineate mental property and control reproduction. Yet, because many of the conventions and property relations that define the art market exist independently of legal norms, copyright has not always been a necessary mechanism for artists.[lxxviii] It is clear however, that when the economic interests of artists and dealers are threatened, then they will have recourse to and may even help to develop copyright law. Lionel Bently reveals in his essay on the 1862 Copyright Act in the U.K. (a statute that extended copyright protection for the first time to 'paintings' and 'drawings') how instrumental Victorian 'fine' artists and publishers were to its passage. The development of photography at this time meant that engravers could now produce engravings of paintings without having to gain access to the original painting, hence undermining the control that fine artists had hitherto exerted over their works. For 'fine' artists, copyright – as during later moments of mechanical reproduction – was a necessary solution to this crisis.

Copyright and Romantic Authorship

As Kathy Bowrey elucidates, recent accounts of copyright, particularly those indebted to the analysis of Michel Foucault,[lxxix] have examined its dynamic role in the construction of authorship from the 18th century onwards. These accounts, questioning the assumption that it is the necessary purpose of copyright to protect the arts, have addressed the way in which copyright law has helped to culturally shape the link between 'authors' and their 'works'.

Paradoxically, certain critics like Martha Woodmansee and Peter Jaszi,[lxxx] while indebted to these methodologies, have claimed nonetheless that copyright law is imbued with Romantic values of authorship (see Anne Barron's essay). The Romantic thesis sees copyright law as embodying in its conceptual structure the notion of the author as 'self-creative' genius and the 'work' as the unique template of individual artistry. According to the Romantic thesis, it is because the structure of copyright law is imbued with Romantic aesthetics that it is unable to accommodate practices such as appropriation art, which question modernist notions of originality and expression. The Romantic thesis is attractive. Rosalind Krauss,[lxxxi] for one, has pointed to the correlation between the modernist cult of originality ('modernism is based on the repression of copying') and copyright law, as seen in her discussion of the restrictions imposed on the casting of Rodin's sculpture *The Gates of Hell*.[lxxxii] De-constructivists like Rosemary Coombe [lxxxiii] have also pointed to the correspondence between the sovereign subject posited by the law and the Romantic author arguing that in its reaction to the intertexuality displayed within appropriation art, copyright reveals its commitment to both models.

Focusing on the 'work' rather than on the 'author' as the subject of her inquiry, Anne Barron disputes the Romantic thesis, pointing out how copyright's artistic categories are better understood as reflecting the internal logic of intellectual property law, 'the logic of property that is simply not reducible to the logic of aesthetic judgement'. Brad Sherman also questions the tendency to focus on the author rather than on the work. Addressing the work, Sherman reveals the contingent presence of the author rather than a unified Romantic subject, visible in the fact that law invents authors where necessary (as in computer programs)[lxxxiv] and is indifferent to qualitative distinctions between high and low. Rather than being a closed, stable system of laws, copyright, Sherman argues, is on inspection, a series of unstable judgements. This is reflected in the indeterminacy of its various examinations of originality.

'High' and 'Low'

The realm of 'high' art is composed of a corpus of unwritten conventions and practices with its own scale of values. Art is ambivalent to the practices of copying that nourish and sustain it: valuing the homage, prohibiting the fake and exhibiting relative indifference to plagiarism (a literary crime).[lxxxv] Copyright laws in contrast to those preventing forgery have not been a significant feature in the realm of 'high' art production.

So far, artists have rarely pursued similar artists for copyright infringement, though artists' estates (notably that of Salvador Dali)[lxxxvi] have been aggressive in ensuring compliance by both artists and publishers as well as commercial users. The increasing importance of copyright in art would seem to be bound up with the demise of the autonomy of art: a response to the crisis in the art object precipitated by mechanical reproduction as diagnosed by Walter Benjamin.[lxxxvii]

In a prescient article, Martha Buskirk[lxxxviii] located the emergence of copyright as a problem for 'high' artists in the collapsing interstice between art and mass culture. She observes how it is often the same artists who use reproductive techniques to incorporate mass-media and related imagery into their work in order to question the boundaries between 'high' and 'low' aesthetics, that have been sued by 'commercial' artists (particularly photographers) from whom they have borrowed. Litigation has grown as art has become more widely disseminated throughout society and as photographers, designers, and commercial artists have discovered that their work has been appropriated. A recent example is the highly publicised action brought by photographer, Thomas Hoepker against the artist Barbara Kruger.[lxxxix] Yet just as many artists have incorporated techniques of mass-production and reproduction into their work as reflected in the factory-style creations of Andy Warhol and Damien Hirst, so the artist's signature – that traditional mark of authenticity and creativity – has retained its significance in differentiating the special type of commodity that is art. Indeed, it is this difference that has made the artist's signature a source of inversion and play. As Andrew Wilson reflects in his essay on Andy Warhol, 'the signature becomes a form of creative activity as well as of ownership, and that this should take place in the context of copying and the making of fakes burdens the signature even more, it says what the work is, as much as it hides what it is not'.

IV. Bridging the Gap

The fourth objective of this book is to examine possible future directions the law might take in response to the problems defined. Paradoxically, the strengthening of copyright law implied in the demand for increased protection of contemporary art forms would seem to push the law in an opposite direction from the weakening implicit in the accommodation of artistic infringement.

Extending Protection?

Nadia Walravens argues that in order to extend protection to avant-garde art forms the courts should, where necessary, deploy experts from the art world to enable them to assess what is original art. The U.S. courts did this in the famous Brancusi case of 1928, where the artist successfully sued the U.S. customs, following the seizure of his *Bird in Space* and their refusal to recognise it as an artwork.[xc] Walravens' proposal seems to alleviate the problem of the courts having to arbitrate aesthetically whilst allowing for developments in art. However, it still leaves questions: first, there may not be a stable consensus within the art world as to whether something is an artwork; second, it does not resolve what degree of protection should be afforded to novel art works. If a readymade like Duchamp's *Fountain* is judicially recognised as art (which does not seem implausible), it may be protected from narrow acts of reproduction such as being photographed. But would it be protected from wider acts, such as Sherrie Levine's recasting. In the light of the idea-expression dichotomy and the reluctance of the law to give monopoly in ideas, it is difficult to envisage how.

Resolving Infringement

Arguments about resolving the problem of infringement embrace an array of complex positions.[xci] Robert Burrell highlights two main trajectories in the debate: the widening of fair use provisions or the introduction of a system of compulsory licensing. Common to both is the notion that copyrighted material may be used permissibly without consent, thus circumventing censorship; licensing models differs from fair use models however, in that copyright owners are financially compensated. These arguments hinge on theories of copyright and authorship as well as upon concepts of art. Furthermore, as Burrell stresses, these debates should be located within the realities and constraints of the law-making process, i.e., existing laws, judicial practices and legislative expectations. For example, the move to implement the EC Directive within the U.K., makes the possibility of widening existing fair use exemptions to include parody a realistic possibility.[xcii]

Extending Fair Use?

Fair use provisions are an implicit recognition within the law that other rights (for example, critical comment) can and should prevail over copyright laws in certain circumstances. The difficult question is how widely they should be drawn and how much flexibility the judiciary should be given in their interpretation. The problem with fair use exemptions from a legal point of view is that they seem to introduce elements of legal uncertainty, by making use of indeterminate, non-legal criteria (ethical, literary, aesthetic) in helping to determine the character and purpose of use.[xciii] This is reflected in judgements regarding the parody defence which can produce startlingly erratic results.[xciv]

Common to all legal systems is the cardinal, if illusory principle, of aesthetic neutrality, that legislators and judges should not seek to define art or to make value judgements between competing types of work. In the words of U.S. Judge Holmes: 'it would be a dangerous undertaking for persons trained only to the law to constitute themselves final judges of the worth of pictorial illustrations, outside of the narrowest and most obvious limits'.[xcv] Whilst it might seem attractive to many in the art world for the activities of artists or certain types of artists to be exempted on grounds of their being art, it clearly conflicts with this principle. It furthermore begs the question of whose interpretation of art is to count, 'art's or the 'law's' (assuming either to be unified entities)? As mentioned, copyright in many respects recognises a broader range of artworks than the art world, seeking to eschew distinctions between 'high' and 'low'.

Paradoxically, the suggestion that the law should exempt the activities of 'high' artists over those of 'low' would seem to reflect a modernist notion of art as 'autonomous': placed outside the tainted, commercial sphere of mass culture. This paradox is particularly striking given the fact that an artist can become a celebrity on the basis of use of copyrighted images and mass media-derived strategies while at the same time claiming exemption from the legal limits inherent in the original conditions of their production'.[xcvi] The point perhaps is that some forms of artistic activity may deserve to be exempted from copyright laws, but this should be justified on non-circular grounds, appealing to wider ethical criteria such as the desirability of communication, democracy, justice and free speech.[xcvii]

A plausible approach adopted by many who favour the extension of fair use (including those who justify copyright on economic grounds), is to distinguish between types of commercial use. Artworks are different type of goods from other cultural works; it is argued in that their economic value derives primarily from the uniqueness or singularity of the artwork rather than from the exploitation of the right of reproduction, as with novels or films. Hence, in copying images of mass-reproduction, artists are neither competing with copyright owners of these images nor undermining incentives. William Landes has argued that artists might be exempted when 'appropriating' images from the mass domain providing they do not seek to make multiple copies when using the copyright owners work.[xcviii] Likewise, U.S. Judge Leval has argued that in applying fair use tests, the courts should

Pierre Huyghe, *2 Minutes out of Time, 2000*

take into account the damage suffered by the claimant in terms of his market.[xcix] The argument is attractive, though there are problems: the most obvious is that it does not resolve competition between fine artists whose market is similar. Furthermore, it neglects the fact that fine art is increasingly bound up with reproduction.[c]

Compulsory Licensing

Those in favour of licences argue that fair use provisions are problematic, in that they fail to remunerate copyright owners and that they suffer from legal uncertainty. For artists and publishers who wish to copy protected works, the problem with existing licensing arrangements (whether they be direct or through collection societies like DACS) is that the copyright owner might either refuse to license the work or charge a prohibitively high sum for doing so, a particular problem with collection societies. Compulsory licensing, it is argued, resolves these problems by allowing users to use copyrighted material at an equitable rate either defined by statute or by independent third parties. It also promotes efficiency in that it reduces transaction costs and ensures that owners are compensated where they might otherwise not have been.[ci] These arguments make assumptions about measurement and administration which have yet to be tested.

Both the fair use and licensing models have a tendency to overlook the ethical rights of authors in controlling their 'work' once it has entered the public domain, though fair use provisions can give weight to authorial rights depending on how widely they are drafted. The licensing model is the more radical in that it effectively severs authors from the works of their creation to value them as products alone. Whether we accept this depends once again on our view of authorship. According to Marcia Hamilton, compulsory licensing is, 'intuitively fair in a post-modern era that no longer buys into the notion that works are the conduits of their authors' personalities'.[cii]

The Future

The growing significance of copyright mechanisms for contemporary artists and for the art world in general reflect the way in which art is moving closer to the conditions of mass-reproduction. If the reproduction and dissemination of artistic imagery is an increasingly valuable commodity for artists and museums to exploit, then copyright owners from other spheres of culture have become more aware of the infringement of their work (as it has been reproduced) by artists resorting to the law, in order to enforce their rights. This commodification of art perhaps suggests that licensing will increasingly become a model for artists in the future, both in securing copyright clearance and exploiting copyright as a tool, despite the anxieties of artists and curators. Indeed, licensing arrangements have almost become the norm in particular areas of artistic production, such as the securing of film copyright by artists like Douglas Gordon and Pierre Huyghe from major film studios i.e. Warner Brothers and MGM.

It is timely to note how certain artists in the late 1990s moved away from the position of appropriation artists of the 1980s, to play with the inscription of art within legal and commercial codes. This difference can be seen in an ongoing project by the artists, Pierre Huyghe and Philipe Parreno.[ciii] *Annalee* is a cartoon character of a young girl created by a Japanese animation (manga) company, who produce thousands of basic shelf characters to be sold to other animators. The artists purchased the exclusive copyright in the character and have used it in their own work as well as franchising it to other artists in turn. When acquired, *Annalee* was a nameless, generic character with minimal facial expressions, waiting in the words of the artists, to be 'dropped into a story'. In rescuing this deviant sign, the artists in their own projects have created a fictional life, both adding animating features and the recorded voice of a little girl. In this work-in-progress, the copyright status of the sign is part of its meaning as a 'readymade'. Yet, rather than copying the sign in order to transgress legal and artistic ownership, the artists have played with the real yet fictitious nature of its legal identity, making the process of copyright acquisition part of the work itself.

Conclusion

We might question the premise that occupies much of this book: that 'art' and 'law' can or should be reconciled. As Anthony Julius reflects in his essay here, *Art Crimes*, 'Artists will always force the boundaries of what is lawful. Just as aesthetics lags behind art, so law lags behind aesthetics. This does not mean that there is no aesthetics implicit in law. Quite to the contrary. It is the existence of such an implicit aesthetics that both produces and then validates law's proscriptions'. Art has a contingent relationship to law, morality and social sentiment and it often 'offends' these regimes just as it transgresses aesthetic boundaries. Julius identifies three types of 'art crime' (or crimes made by artists): crimes committed against art works (offences of reproduction or destruction), crimes made in the preparation of artistic works (illegal actions) and crimes of art (works that are crimes). Art crimes involve artists in different arguments with the law. With 'strong crimes' the law seeks to prohibit certain forms of art as not being art (plagiarism) in order to protect what it perceives as true art; with 'weak crimes' the law is indifferent to the work's status as art (blasphemy) refusing to allow it special exemption. Both arguments imply an unbridgeable antimony between art and the law, which will be the subject of continuous debate.

i   With thanks to Professor Lionel Bently and Simon Stokes.

ii   Public disputes are a visible manifestation of a growing problem. Many complaints are settled prior to litigation and out of court, because of confidentiality agreements they often go unreported.

iii   Glenn Brown's painting, *The Loves of Shepherds 2000 (after Double Star by Tony Roberts)* exhibited in the Tate's Turner Prize 2000, is based on a science-fiction book cover illustration by Anthony Roberts. The illustrator began proceedings (U.K.) in 2001 against Brown for copyright infringement which are still going on, see 'Copycat row as The Times reveals Turner Prize artist's inspiration' *The Times*, 28 November 2000 and 'Sci-fi artist sues over Turner 'plagiarism'', *The Times*, 11 April 2001.

iv   Damien Hirst's *Hymn* (1999), a 20ft bronze reproduction of a child's anatomical toy led the toy manufacturer Humbrol, to sue Hirst for copyright infringement (U.K.). The case was eventually settled out of court with Hirst paying undisclosed damages to a charity, see 'Hirst pays up for Hymn that wasn't his' *The Guardian*, 19 May 2000.

v   The photographer, Thomas Hoepker filed a lawsuit in 2001 (U.S.) against Barbara Kruger, the Whitney Museum of American Art and the Los Angeles Museum of Contemporary Art alleging infringement of his image '*Charlotte as seen by Thomas*' (1960) in two of Kruger's collages; and further alleging secondary infringement by the museums. See '"Appropriation" art may land museums in hot water', *The Art Newspaper*, June 2002.

vi   Elizabeth Peyton was sued by the photographer, Harry Benson (U.S.) for using his photograph of John Lennon as the source of a painting, it was settled out of court, see 'Copyright woes for Peyton painting', *Art in America*, November 1997.

vii   Cai Guo Qiang provoked furor in China for his partial recreation of a series of sculptures, *Rent Collection Yard* at the Venice Biennale, 1999. The sculptures were iconic works from the Cultural Revolution made by the Sichuan Academy who threatened legal action, see 'Cultural Revolution, Chapter 2; Expatriate Artist Updates Maoist Icon and Angers Old Guard', *New York Times*, 17 August 2000.

viii   Amongst numerous actions, the Andy Warhol Estate was sued by the French photographer, Henri Dauman and Time Inc in 1997 for copyright infringement of his photograph of Jackie Kennedy (*Life Magazine*, 6 December 1963) used by Warhol in his *Jackie* series, see 'Warhol estate sued over Jackie Photo', *Art in America*, February 1997.

ix   The sculpture *A String of Puppies* was exhibited as part of Koons' exhibition, *Ushering in Banality*, Sonnabend Gallery, New York, 1988. Rogers successfully sued Koons, *Rogers v. Koons* 751 F. Supp. 474 - 476 (S.D.N.Y. 1990). On appeal this judgement was affirmed, *Rogers v. Koons* 960 F.2d 301, 309 (2nd Cir. 1992) Koons was held liable and ordered to pay an appropriate amount of damages (settled out of court), see Inde, R. Villis, *Art in The Courtroom*, Praeger, Westport, 1998, pp. 1- 47.

x   Koons was also successfully sued for reproducing the cartoon character, *Odie*, in the sculpture, *Wild Boy and Puppy* displayed in the same exhibition, see *United Feature Syndicate v. Koons*,17 F. Supp. 370, 383-384 (D.N.Y. 1993). He was also successfully sued by the photographer, Barbara Campbell, for using her *Boys with Pig* in the sculpture *Ushering in Banality*, see *Campbell v. Koons*, unreported, S.D.N.Y., (1993 U.S. Dist LEXIS 3957).

xi   For an example of vocal criticism of copyright law from an artist, see the website of Miltos Manetas, 'I AM GOING TO COPY' *www.manetas.com/iamgonnacopy*.

xii   See Carlin, John, 'Culture Vultures: Artistic Appropriation and Intellectual Property Law', *13 Colum.-Vla J.L. & Arts*, (1988) and Buskirk, Martha, 'Commodification as Censor: Copyrights and Fair Use', *October 60* (1992).

xiii   Gilbert & George in private conversation with the author.

xiv   Gillian Wearing considered taking legal action against BMP DDB, the producers of a television advertisement for the Volkswagen'Golf', see 'VW ad rips off my work, says artist', *The Times*, 12 June 1998.

xv   Wearing also contemplated bringing legal proceedings against the advertising agency, M & C Saatchi, for using the idea in her video installation *10-16*, see 'Gillian Wearing v. Saatchi', *The Art Newspaper*, No. 91, April 1999.

xvi   The architect, Lebbeus Woods, successfully sued Universal City Studios after discovering that his drawing *Neo-mechanical Tower (Upper) Chamber (1987)* depicting a suspended chair in an ante chamber had been reproduced in a scene from the film *Twelve Monkeys* (1995), see *Woods v. Universal City Studios*, Inc., 920 F.Supp. 62 (1996).

xvii   Bridget Riley has regularly pursued copyright actions. This followed the traumatic experience of seeing her paintings reproduced in fashion designs in boutiques along Madison Avenue following her first major group exhibition in New York, *The Responsive*

Eye, MOMA, 1965. She discovered that copyright legislation in the U.S. was insufficient at that time to protect artists and with the aid of lawyers she was instrumental in the passing of new copyright legislation, 1967. See *Bridget Riley: Selected Paintings 1961-1999* (exh. catalogue, Dusseldorf), Hatje Cantz, 1999, p. 133.

xviii See 'Che Guevara photographer wins damages from Lowe Lintas', *The Guardian*, 15 September 2000.

xix See, Laddie, Mr. Justice, 'Copyright: Over-strength, Over-regulated, Over-rated?' *5 European Intellectual Property Review 253* (1996).

xx For a detailed analysis of U.K. copyright law, see Bently, Lionel and Sherman, Brad, *Intellectual Property Law*, Oxford University Press, 2001. For a detailed analysis of U.S. copyright law see M.B Nimmer and D. Nimmer, *Nimmer on Copyright*, M.Bender, New York, 1998. For international copyright law, see Sterling, J.A.L., *World Copyright Law*, Sweet & Maxwell, London, 1999.

xxi Reproducing an art work and adding satirical features may amount to a violation of the integrity right, for an interesting hypothetical discussion of Marcel Duchamp's famous addition of a drawn moustache to a postcard reproduction of the *Mona Lisa* see, Yonover, Geri J., 'The "Dissing" of Da Vinci', *29 Valparaiso University Law Review*, 1995.

xxii For a superb account of these dilemmas see, Waldron, Jeremy, 'From Authors to Copiers', *Chicago-Kent Law Review (vol 68)* (1993) pp.841-887.

xxiii Coombes, Rosemary J, *The Cultural Life of Intellectual Properties. Authorship, Appropriation and the Law*, Durham, London: Duke University Press, 1998.

xxiv Barlow, John Perry,'The Economy of Ideas: A Framework for rethinking patents and copyrights in the Digital Age', *Wired*, March, 1994,'The Next Economy of Ideas: Will Copyright Survive the Napster Bomb?', *Wired*, August 2000.

xxv U.S. Const. Art 1, S.8, Cl.8.

xxvi For an excellent anthology of essays on copyright's development see Sherman, Brad & Strowel, Alain (eds), *Of Authors and Origins: Essays on Copyright Law*, Oxford: Clarendon Press, 1994.

xxvii Gaines, Jane' *Contested Culture. The Image, The Voice and The Law*, Chapel Hill: University of North Carolina Press, 1991, pp. 1-81.

xxviii Drahos, Peter, 'Decentring Communication: The Dark Side of Intellectual Property' in T. Campbell and W. Sidurski (eds.), *Freedom of Communication*, 1994, pp.249-279.

xxix See, 'Disney Demands Removal of Sculpture' Los Angeles Times, Oct 16, 1992, also c.f. Buskirk, Martha, refers to the Walt Disney Corporation's legal efforts to remove murals depicting pictures of their cartoon characters from the walls of a Florida children's day-care centre, op.cit.12, p.83.

xxx Publishers seeking to use images of art works in art historical publications have come into conflict with artists' estates and collection societies (like DACS) on numerous occasions in the U.K., a result in part of ambiguities in the fair use provisions under the CDPA 1988. Criticism has been made of the exorbitant fees charged by collection societies for reproducing images in art historical books, see Copyright Threat to Modern Art Books, *The Sunday Telegraph*, 26 February 1995.

xxxi For a discussion of the contingent nature of legal judgement and its relationship to aesthetics see Douzinas Costas, Nead, Lynda (eds) Law and Image: The Authority of Art and the Aesthetics of Law, University of Chicago Press, 1999. See 'The Case of the Missing Credits', *The Guardian*, 1 April 1999. S.1(1)(a) CDPA 1988. s.4(1) CDPA 1988.

xxxv *Anacon Corporation v. Environmental Research Technology Ltd* (1994) FSR 659.

xxxvi   A mobile device producing sand patterns was denied protection as a sculpture in *Komeraroff v. Mickle* (1988) RPC 2204 and the face make-up on the pop star Adam Ant was denied protection as a painting in *Merchandising v Harpbond*, (1983) FSR 32.

xxxvii   Peterson. J, *University of London Press v. University Tutorial Press* (1916) 2 Ch 601.

xxxviii   Reid, Lord, *Ladbroke v. William Hill* (1964) 1 ALL ER 465 (U.K.) and *Feist Publications v. Rural Telephone* Service Co. 499 U.S. 340 113 L Ed 358 (1991)(U.S.).

xxxix   *Kenrick v. Lawrence* (1890) 25 QBD 93.

xl   Oliver, Lord, *Interlego v. Tyco Industries* (1989) AC 217 (PC).

xli   *Ibid.*, AC 217 (PC).

xlii   *TThe Bridgeman Art Library, Ltd. v Corel Corp* (S.D.N.Y. 1998) 25 F.Supp.2d 421.

xliii   Bently & Sherman, *op.cit.*, 20. p.165.

xliv   See Jones, Richard H.,'The Myth of the Idea-Expression Dichotomy In Copyright Law', *Pace Law Review, Volume 10*, Summer 1990, Number 3, pp.551-607.

xlv   Laddie, Hugh in (Laddie, Prescott,Vitoria *et al*) *The Modern Law of Copyright and Design, 3rd edn.* Butterworths, London, 2000, p.138.

xlvi   Bently & Sherman, refer to the case of *Krisarts SA v. Briarfine* (1977) FSR 557 in which it was considered, *obiter*, whether a view could be protected in a painting, *op.cit.*, 20, p.164.

xlvii   See *Rogers v. Koons* in which the Sonnabend Gallery was a co-defendant, *op.cit.*,9.

xlviii   Schwartz, Hillel, *The Culture of the Copy: Striking Likenesses, Unreasonable Facsimiles*, New York: Zone Books, 1996, p.229.

xlix   The origin of the artist is the work of art, the origin of the work of art is the artist, neither is without the other', Derrida, Jacques, *The Truth in Painting*, tr. Bennington and McLeod, Chicago: Chicago Uni Press (1987), pp.31-32.

l   It is important to distinguish between collages which reproduce fragments of existing works and which may thus potentially infringe copyright and those which directly incorporate material, as in many Cubist works, and therefore do not infringe copyright, though they may conflict with other intellectual property rights such as trademark law.

li   *Op.cit.*, 9.

lii   *Designer Guild Ltd v. Russell Williams (Textiles) Ltd* (2000) FSR 121 (CA); (2001) FSR 113 (HL)

liii   *C.f.* Stokes, Simon, *Art & Copyright*, Hart Publishing, Oxford and Portland, Oregon, 2001, p134 in which he draws the same conclusion.

liv   S.30(1) CDPA 1988.

lv   S.29(1) CDPA 1988.

lvi   S.107 U.S. Copyright Act 1976.

lvii   See Petruzzelli, Lori, 'Copyright Problems in Post-Modern Art', *Journal of Art and Entertainment Law*, (Winter,1994/Spring, 1995).

lviii   Jaszi, Peter and Woodmansee, Martha, 'The Ethical Reaches of Authorship' (1996) 95:4 *South Atlantic Quarterly*, 947-977, 948.

lix   For example, see Sherman, Brad, 'From the Non-Original to the Ab-original: A. History' in Sherman, Brad and Strouwel, Alan (eds), *Of Authors and Origins*, Clarendon Press, Oxford, 1994.

lx   de Duve, Thierry, 'Echoes of the Readymade: Critique of Pure Modernism' in M. Buskirk and M. Nixon (eds.) *The Duchamp Effect*, Cambridge, Mass. and London: MIT Press, 1996, pp. 93-130.

lxi   See Greenberg, Clement, *Art and Culture: Critical Essays*, Beacon Press, S.F., 1978 and Fried, Michael, Fried, *Art and Objecthood: Essays and Reviews by Michael Fried*, University of Chicago Press, 1978.

lxii For the rise of 'post-medium' art, see Krauss, Rosalind, *A Voyage on Art in the Age of the North Sea: Post-Medium Condition*, Thames & Hudson, 1999.

lxiii For an account of Gillian Wearing's work 'Signs' see Ferguson, Russell, 'Show Your Emotions', *Gillian Wearing*, Phaidon, London, 1999, pp.34-68. Regarding her complaint, *op.cit.*,14.

lxiv Richter, Gerhard, *The Daily Practice of Painting: 1962-1993*, MIT Press, 1995, p.31.

lxv For an overview of how originality has functioned historically within art, see Shiff, Richard in Shiff and Nelson (ed), *Critical Terms in Art History*, Univ. of Chicago Press, 1998.

lxvi On Sherrie Levine see Krauss, Rosalind E., 'The Originality of the Avant Garde' in *The Originality of the Avant Garde and Other Modernist Myths*, MIT Press, 1985, p.165.

lxvii See Nash, Mark, 'Art and Cinema: Some Critical Reflections', *Documenta XI — Platform 5: Exhibition Catalogue*, Hatje Canz, Germany, 2002, pp. 129-136. For the work of Douglas Gordon, see *Douglas Gordon*, (exh cat) MOCA LA, MIT Press, 2001.

lxviii Petruzzelli, Lori, *op.cit.*, 57.

lxix See Barthes, Roland, 'to depict is to . . . refer, not from language to a referent, but from one code to another' in *S/Z*, trans. Richard Miller, New York, Hill and Wang, 1974, p.55.

lxx Holmes, Judge Oliver Wendell, *Bleistein v. Donaldson Lithographing Co*, 188 U.S. 239 (1903).

lxxi Carlin, John, *op.cit.*,12.

lxxii The radical German conceptual artist was threatened with trade mark infringement by the multi-national, Mobil for using their trade mark in his work, *Metromobilitan* in order to criticise its activities in South Africa during the Apartheid era, see Coombes, Rosemary, *op.cit.*, 23. pp.73-74.

lxxiii For discussions of the fair use doctrine in the U.S. see Ames, K. E, 'Beyond Rogers v. Koons: A Fair Use Standard For Appropriation', 93 *Colum. L. Rev.* (1993) pp. 1473, 1477-1478 and Badin, Roxanna, 'An Appropriate (d) Place in Transformative Value: Appropriation Art's Exclusion From Campbell v. Acuff-Rose Music Inc.', 60 *Brook. L. Rev.* pp.1653.

lxxiv Rogers v Koons, *op.cit.*, 9.

lxxv Campbell v. Acuff-Rose Music, Inc. 127 L Ed 2d 500, 523 n. 21 (1994).

lxxvi On the double etymological meaning of originality, see, Gaines, Jane, *op. cit.*, 27, pp.63, 64.

lxxvii Lambert, Susan, 'The Status of the Reproduction', *The Image Multiplied: Five Centuries of Printed Reproductions of Paintings and Drawings*, Abaris Books, London, 1988, pp.14-33.

lxxviii Foucault, Michel, 'What is an Author?' in Harai V Josue (ed), *Textual Strategies: Perspectives in Post-Structuralist Criticism* (Ithaca, NY, 1979), p.141.

lxxix See Jaszi, Peter, 'Towards a theory of copyright: the metamorphosis of 'authorship'' (1991) *Duke L. Jnl.*, p.445 and Woodmansee, Martha, *The Author, Art and the Market* (New York: Columbia University Press, 1994).

lxxx The ability of copyright to invent 'authors' is embodied strikingly in the ascription of authorship to companies and to computer programs.

lxxxi *Op.cit.*,66, pp.175-194, particularly on the role of Rodin's estate.

lxxxii *Op.cit.*, 66, p.168.

lxxxiii *Op.cit.*, 23.

lxxxiv For the invention of authors see Rose, Mark, *Authors and Owners: The Invention of Copyright*, Cambridge, Mass: Harvard University Press 1993.

lxxxv *Op.cit.*, 5.

lxxxvi see Jones, Mark the Fake, British Museum Catalogue

lxxxvii The Salvador Dali Estate has actively pursued artists for infringement including Glenn Brown.

lxxxviii See, Benjamin, Walter, The Work of Art in the Age of Mechanical Reproduction' in Arendt, Hannah (eds) *Illuminations*, Schocken Books, 1985 and Crow, Thomas, 'Modernism and Mass Culture in the Visual Arts' in *Modern Art in a Common Culture* (New Haven: Yale University Press 1996).

lxxxix *Op.cit.*, 5.

xc For an account of the Brancusi case see Adams, Laurie, *Art on Trial*, New York, 1977, ch. 2.

xci The positions are too complex to be summarised here, but supervene upon different ethical, political and legal theories.

xcii The scope of the U.K. fair dealing provisions, e.g. parody, will soon change following the implementation of the EC Directive 2001/29/EC (22nd May 2001) ('Information Society Directive').

xciii See, Gredley, E., Maniaits, S., 'Parody: A Fatal Attraction? Part 1: The Nature of Parody and its Treatment in Copyright', *7 European Intellectual Property Review*, p. 339, 1997.

xciv Contrast the judgement in *Rogers v Koons* with *Leibovitz v. Paramount*, 137 F.3d 109 (2nd Cir. 1998) in which the film production studio successfully invoked parody as part of a fair use defence to defeat the photographer, Annie Leibovitz's copyright infringement action. Leibovitz claimed that Paramount had infringed her well-known photograph of the pregnant nude body of Demi Moore, by commissioning a photograph to be taken with the head of actor, Leslie Nielsen superimposed over the pregnant body as an advertisement for the film, *Naked Gun 33 1/2*.

xcv Holmes, Judge Oliver Wendell, *Bleistein v. Donaldson Lithographing Co*, 188 U.S. 239 (1903).

xcvi *Op.cit.*, 12.

xcvii For a compelling grounding of fair use in wider ethical notions related to the community, see Netantel, Neil W., 'Copyright and a Democratic Civil Society' *106 Yale Law Journal 283* (1996).

xcviii Landes, William 'Copyright, Borrowed Images and Appropriation Art: An Economic Approach' John M. Olin Law & Economics Working Paper No. 113, (2nd series) Chicago.

xcix Leval, Pierre, 'Toward A Fair Use Standard', 103 *Harv. L. Rev.* 1105, 1125-1130 (1990). John Carlin proposes a two stage test in 'Culture Vultures' to avoid this problem. The first stage, identifies the type of use, inquiring who is copying and why: if a work is being copied by a fine artist as a unique work or small edition, then there is a presumption of fair use. The second stage addresses what is being copied: if the work copied is part of popular culture and within the public domain, then the use will be fair. If, however, the work derives from protected artistic imagery, then the test becomes more complicated. The use of artistic imagery will be more limited to prevent competition between artists, depending on the stature of the artist.

c See Hamilton, Marci A: 'Appropriation Art and the Imminent Decline in Authorial Control Over Copyright Protected Works' *42 J. Copyright Society. 93* (1994), pp. 93-126.

ci *Ibid.*, p. 125.

cii On the 'Annalee' project see *No Ghost Just A Shell*, (Pierre Huyghe) Kunsthalle Zurich, San Fransisco MOMA, 2002. It is as if the artists have grasped the notion that copyright protects the empty shell of origination over authorial expression.

Part 1
Legal Sources

Protection of Copyright in Art under the *Copyright, Designs and Patents Act 1988*

Karen Sanig

Introduction

Intellectual property is the legal term for intangible rights attaching to abstract creations of the mind. Copyright is a form of intellectual property. It does not create a monopoly. Concepts, which are protected by copyright, can be used by more than one person provided each source is independent. Yet, copyright gives a degree of control to its owner to prevent others copying or exploiting works without prior agreement.

Many, but not all, artworks are protected by copyright in the U.K. under the Copyright, Designs and Patents Act of 1988 ('the Act'). No one, least of all legislators in a statute, is able to stipulate what constitutes 'art'. Consequently the protection afforded by the Act is somewhat artificial and limited. It leads to complicated cases where the judges are forced to analyse concepts to determine whether they fit the terms of the Act.

Accordingly, the owner of copyright has exclusive rights to perform certain acts in relation to the copyright work or to authorise others to do certain acts in relation to the work in the U.K. These exclusive rights are defined in the Act[i] and last for the artist's lifetime, plus seventy years after death. They include, for example, a right to produce a copy of the artist's own painting or to licence someone else to do so. Copyright in an artwork is infringed by a person who without the authority of the copyright owner carries out, or authorises another to carry out, any of the acts restricted by the copyright, either in relation to the whole or any substantial part of it.

There are, however, some aspects which the owner of the copyright cannot control. The Act balances the owner's rights with public interest providing certain 'permitted acts' in relation to copyright works. A copyright owner does not have a remedy under the Act if his work is used in a fair manner for research, private study, criticism, review, and reporting current events. [ii]

What Art is protected by the Act?

Copyright subsists in various 'original artistic works', defined by the Act and in some cases irrespective of artistic quality. The only qualitative test is contained in section 4(1)(c), which confers copyright protection on works of 'artistic craftsmanship'. Artistic works are defined by s.4(1) of the Act as follows: '(a) a graphic work, photograph, sculpture or collage, *irrespective of artistic quality*. (author's italics) (b) a work of architecture being a building or a model for a building, or (c) a work of artistic craftsmanship. A 'building' includes any fixed structure, and a part of a building or fixed structure; 'graphic work' includes (a) any painting, drawing, diagram, map, chart or plan, and (b) any engraving, etching, lithograph, woodcut or similar work; 'photograph' means a recording of light or other radiation on any medium on which an image is produced or from which an image may by any means be produced, and which is not part of a film; and 'sculpture' includes a cast or model made for purposes of sculpture. Art not falling within one of the above categories will not be protected by copyright.

Other works afforded protection under s.1(1) of the Act are: (a) original literary, dramatic, or musical works; (b) sound recordings, films, broadcasts, or cable programmes; (c) the typographical arrangement of published editions. These too have specific definitions too detailed for this chapter but relevant outside the realms of fine art. They are highlighted for the benefit of contemporary artists whose works often comprise of more than paint on canvas. One example, is film. The most recent case *Norowzian v. (1) Arks Ltd (2) Guinness Brewing Worldwide Ltd (3) Guinness plc (no. 2) (1999) (2000) FSR 363*[iii] decided that in certain cases a film would be protected not merely under s.5B of the Act as 'a recording on any medium from which a moving image may be produced' but also under s.1(1)(a) as an 'original dramatic work'. There follows a brief analysis of how some of the definitions of 'original artistic works'[iv] have been applied or could be applied.

'Graphic works': The s.4(2)(a) and (b) definition of graphic works is so wide, it is hard to envisage a conventional form of fine art falling outside it. The difficulty lies with unconventional art forms. These cannot always be slotted into existing statutory definitions of artistic works. Consequently, no copyright protection exists. For example, *Merchandising Corporation of America Inc and Others v. Harpbond Ltd and Others [1983] FSR 32* considered the distinctive face paint of Adam Ant (a 1980's pop star) was not protected by copyright because 'painting', the Court decided, had to be on a surface to attract copyright. The paint marks on Adam Ant's face, without the face itself, were not a 'painting'. Lawton LJ said that 'a painting is not an idea: it is an object, and paint without a surface is not a painting'. This does not necessarily apply to permanent body art, but according to this case temporary body art does not attract copyright.

Other forms of modern and contemporary art may not attract copyright according to the strict definitions of the Act. Examples of artworks which do not fall obviously into the statutory definitions include installation art or readymades. In this respect, original pieces like Tracy Emin's 'unmade bed' are impossible to categorise within existing statutory definitions. This artwork uses a readymade object, a bed, which by her own admission is nothing special. Could the work therefore attract copyright? And would it be categorised as a collage, sculpture, or a work of artistic craftsmanship?

Is the 'Unmade Bed' a Collage?

The current law would not treat the 'unmade bed' as a 'collage' because there has to be an element of sticking two or more things together. The case of *Creation Records Ltd v. Newsgroup Newspapers Ltd. The Times April 29 [1997] E.M.L.R 444* decided that the collation of random, unfixed elements is not a collage even if done with artistic intent. The case concerned a scene of assembled objects in a swimming pool with members of the Oasis pop group prepared as the subjects of a photograph for an album cover. The scene had no permanence to it. It was not made up of glued objects.– and therefore it was not itself a 'collage' under the Act.

Is the 'Unmade Bed' a Sculpture?

The definition of a sculpture can be found in *Metix Ltd v. GH Maughan (Plastics) Limited [1997] F.S.R 718*. In this case Laddie J. states that the term sculpture bears the meaning which ordinary members of the public would understand: 'a three dimensional work made by an artist's hand'. This explanation does not identify the base material of a 'sculpture', but traditionally it would be stone, wood, clay, or marble. Other substances, such as ice or papier-mache, could be the basis of 'sculpture' for copyright purposes. 'Sculpture' may also include objects not traditionally associated with artistic skill due to the Act's inclusion of sculpture 'irrespective of artistic quality'[v]. In some cases, arguments have been raised to suggest mouldings for industrial objects, such as frisbees, are sculptures. However, in Metix, the Court held there was no arguable case for subsistence of sculpture copyright in moulds used for making cartridges for mixing chemicals. The reason was that the makers of the moulds were not considered, nor did they consider themselves, 'artists.'

The bed in 'unmade bed', although three dimensional, is not itself made by the artist's hand. However Tracy Emin's intention was artistic, and she is an artist. This may help to clarify its status as a 'sculpture', and as such it would attract copyright protection under the Act. Still, the case is not clear-cut.

Is 'the Unmade Bed' a Work of Artistic Craftsmanship?

Unlike fine art, a work of craftsmanship needs to possess artistic and aesthetic qualities. Typical works in this category would be hand-painted tiles or stained glass windows. The position of mass-produced crafts is not so clear. To qualify for copyright protection, work must demonstrate an exercise of craftsmanship and be a work of art, or at least perceived as such by the public.

This category creates difficulty for the courts. It was designed to cover the situation of artist-craftspeople, which Tracy Emin does not claim to be. The leading case in this respect *is George Hensher Ltd v. Restawile Upholstery (Lancs) Ltd [1975] R.P.C.31*, which was decided in the House of Lords. This case held that there was no copyright protection for a particular prototype model of a furniture suite. Copyright of the 'unmade bed' (were it to fall into this category, which it does not) would not attach to the bed itself, but to the whole piece. The type of work envisaged by this section was defined by Lord Simon as 'applied or decorative arts'. Lord Simon asks, 'Was the work by an artist craftsman? What was the intent of the creator?'

Sample patchwork bedspreads were not considered works of 'artistic craftsmanship' in the recent case of *Vermaat v. Boncrest Ltd (2001) FSR 43 June 2000*. The making of the samples was considered craftsmanship, but the result was not sufficiently artistic. It did not display the necessary requirement of creativity. The New Zealand case of *Bonz (Pty Ltd) v. Croke 1994 3 NZLR 216*, on the other hand, held that jumpers showing dancing lambs and golfing kiwis did display the requisite creativity!

The 'unmade bed' is certainly original, but perhaps it is so out of the ordinary there is no clear cut copyright protection under the Act. Although originality is not enough of a defining criterion, it is definitely an essential element for protection under the Act.

Originality

The benchmark for originality in copyright works in the U.K. is fairly low. The work must be the artist's own creation and should emanate from, and be capable of being traced directly to, the artist in question. It is possible (although improbable) that two artists will paint identical paintings. Provided each painting was produced independently, both artists will be regarded as the authors of their respective works and be entitled to full copyright protection. As both had the same original idea, there is no problem in them expressing it identically as long as such expression is totally independent.

Lord Bingham, in *Designers Guild Ltd v. Russell Williams (Textiles) Ltd 2001 1 All ER*, stated 'the law of copyright rests on a very clear principle: that anyone who by his or her own skill and labour shall create an original work of whatever character shall, for a limited period, enjoy an exclusive right to copy that work.' Copyright protection may extend to an original work even if the work relies on existing work – provided the new work has sufficient elements of originality. Appropriation art is an example of this. To secure copyright for a particular work, it is necessary that labour, skill, and capital were expended sufficiently to impart to the work some quality or character which the raw material had not possessed and then differentiates the said work from the raw materials. The case of *Interlego AG v. Tyco Industries Inc and Others [1988] RPC 343* established that there must be some 'material alteration or embellishment which suffices to make the totality of the work an original work'. Changes must be visually significant for the work to attract copyright protection. A separate copyright protection may also be available to any work related to another work, such as preparatory sketches.[vi]

Idea versus Expression

Ideas themselves are not capable of attracting copyright, but the expression of them is. This quandary appears often in cases where style, technique, or other aspects of a design or painting have been reproduced but there has been no complete copying. Lord Hoffmann, in *Designers Guild Ltd v. Russell Williams Ltd [2001] 1 All ER*, offers that 'in cases of artistic copyright, the more abstract and simple the copied idea, the less likely it is to constitute a substantial part. Originality, in the sense of the contribution of the author's skill and labour, tends to lie in the detail with which the basic idea is presented.'

Infringement – Restricted and Permitted Acts

The Act envisages that copyright can be infringed by way of primary and secondary infringement.[vii] Primary infringement occurs when a restricted act defined by the Act is carried out. Restricted acts comprise copying,[viii] renting, lending, issuing copies to the public, and broadcasting the work. The restricted act may relate to the whole or part of a protected work to constitute an infringement of copyright. The Court assesses whether an alleged infringing copy, for example, is sufficiently similar visually to the original work or a substantial part of it: the degree of substantiality is qualitative, not quantitative. Copying the eyes of Leonardo da Vinci's 'Mona Lisa' for example, a central characteristic of the work, would amount to an infringement of the work as a whole were the painting still in copyright. However an overall visual similarity is not necessary if it is possible to establish that the alleged copy incorporated elements of an existing work.

Designers Guild Ltd v. Russell Williams Ltd [2001] 1 All ER analysed whether a simple pattern of stripes and flowers in textile design could attract copyright. The design of the fabric itself was not original. Its creator had based it on works by Matisse. But her creation as an ensemble was original and accepted as an original artistic work. A number of artistic ideas therefore joined together to make one design which attracted copyright and could not be copied. It is not a breach of copyright to 'borrow' an idea, according to Lord Scott, and translate that idea into new work. However, there is a difference between 'borrowing' and what he termed 'impermissible piracy' of the artistic creation of another. The conclusion to be drawn from this case is that not only are there degrees of copying the whole or the part, but it is their expression which counts too. The House of Lords finally ruled that there was an infringement of the painting on which the Designers Guild material was based. This overruled the Court of Appeal, which had concluded that although the defendants had copied the idea of the copyright work (stripes and flowers produced together on fabric design), they had not copied a substantial part of the expression of that idea.

The artist's original work is an embodiment of the skill and labour used to create an original work. An infringement can occur if a substantial part of that is copied. The simpler the idea, the more closely it will have to be copied before an infringement is judged to have taken place. Liability is strict. A work may be infringed subconsciously, where the infringing party is unaware that it has based a work on an earlier one, but the Court has the power to reflect the gravity of the infringement and its circumstances in the damages awarded.

Renting or lending artistic works to the public are also restricted acts. Rental is the making of a work or a copy of the work, on terms that it will or may be returned, and making it available for use directly or indirectly for commercial advantage. Lending artwork does not entail commercial advantage, and to infringe, it must be lent to an establishment which is accessible to the public. Meanwhile, the inclusion of artistic works in a broadcast or in a cable programme service is a restricted act. Secondary infringement requires an element of knowledge (i.e., a dealer knowingly selling copies or giving others reason to believe he is). Secondary infringement may also arise from the providing of means for making infringing copies.

Finally, permitted acts are only those expressly allowed by the Act. They can be carried out without a licence. The right to freedom of expression pursuant to Article 10 of the *European Convention of Human Rights and Fundamental Freedom* could not be relied on recently to create defences to alleged infringement of copyright over those which appeared in the Act.[ix] The most relevant 'permitted acts' in relation to art are:

- S.62 of the Act: artistic works 'permanently situated in a public place or in premises open to the public'. The public may draw, photograph or make two-dimensional copies of buildings, sculptures, models of buildings, and works of artistic craftsmanship (if in public places).
- S.63 of the Act: advertisement of sale of artistic work; for example, paintings reproduced in an auction house sale catalogue.
- S.64 of the Act: embodies the right of artists to repeat subsidiary features of their own works; for example, an artist is commissioned and agrees not to retain the copyright. When s/he wishes to use original sketches for another artwork, there is no copyright infringement, provided s/he does not repeat the main design of the earlier work (i.e., use of minor parts of the work only). S/he can therefore authorise commercialisation of that minor part incorporating the same features as the original. If you purchase copyright, you only get copyright of the main design and not subsidiary parts.
- S.31 of the Act: incidental inclusion in a broadcast or cable service programme will not constitute an infringement. This is not confined to an accidental use, as long as such use is not made for the purpose of a direct comparison between two works in furtherance of the infringing party's commercial purposes.
- S.19 of the Act: the public showing of films is an infringement, but not the public exhibition of artistic works.

Authorship, Ownership and Exploitation

Section 9(1) of the Act states that the author of a work is the person who creates it. It is, however, possible to have joint authorship, for example, a mural which is the result of the artistic efforts of more than one person. S.9(2) of the Act states that the author of computer generated work is the one by whom the arrangements necessary for the creation of the work were undertaken, and the copyright in such work expires fifty years from the end of the calendar year in which it was made.

Ownership

The artist/author is generally the first owner of copyright in his work. This can vary as follows:

· The artist employee: where an artist is employed to create works the presumption is that the employer owns the copyright unless expressly agreed otherwise.[x]

· The commissioned artist: the general rule is that the creator retains copyright unless there is an expressly agreed assignment of copyright to the commissioner. Written agreements between commissioner and artist avoid ambiguity if there is a dispute.

Economic Exploitation

There are two main ways of economically exploiting copyright other than by the artist selling reproductions: these are assignment and licensing. Mere physical possession of an object containing or representing a work of copyright or a copy of such a work does not, in itself, transfer the copyright. For example, the sale of a painting, no matter how expensive, is unlikely to assign the copyright in it. The purchaser obtains a property right in the physical object but in the absence of a specific assignment of the copyright in the painting, no interest in the copyright is obtained.

An assignment is by definition a disposal of the copyright by way of sale or hire, or by will, usually in writing. An assignment not in writing and signed by the owner may take effect as an equitable assignment. The person to whom the painting is assigned (the assignee) will have to go to court to substantiate his ownership. Such an assignment is particularly unsafe. It will not protect the assignee from the possibility of the person who assigns (the assignor), further assigning the right to an 'innocent' third party, this time opting to comply with the statutory requirements of writing and signature. It is possible to have an assignment of copyright in work that has not yet come into existence. Such prospective ownership of copyright and its assignment is provided for under the Act at Section 91(1) as a 'future copyright'.

A licence, on the other hand, is an agreement (not necessarily in writing) between the owner of the copyright (the licensor) and another person (the licensee). The licensee can do certain acts in connection with the artistic work that would otherwise infringe the copyright in the artistic work, for which s/he pays either a lump sum or royalties. A licence may be exclusive – to the exclusion of all others, even the owner. A prospective owner can also license future copyright. Like an assignment, a licence can be limited either in the scope or duration of the copyright, or both. A licence granted by a copyright owner, is normally binding on successors in title of the licensor.

Legal Remedies

If copyright in an artistic work is infringed, civil law offers remedy by means of damages, account of profits, and injunction.

In order to succeed with a claim for damages, it must be shown that the infringement is the effective cause of loss. If there has been a depreciation in the value of the copyright work caused by the infringement, damages aim at putting the copyright owner in the position he would have been in had the infringement never occurred. For example, if the infringing party marketed the infringing copies to markets unavailable to the owner, such profits might not be included in the assessment of damages, in which case the Court may award a notional licence fee [xi]. Consideration will be given to the flagrancy of the infringement in awarding additional damages.

An account of profits is within the Court's discretion to award. But because it is complicated and expensive to administer and entails a detailed demonstration of all profits obtained by the infringing party, it is the least likely remedy.

An injunction, on the other hand, can be obtained on a short term basis. In it, a Court order prevents further copying to halt imminent damage to exploitable rights in a work. The Court can also order a permanent injunction to ensure that no copying is ever carried out by the infringing party again. The order may take different forms depending on the case. Those options include:

- an order for immediate delivery, seizure, or destruction of the infringing work;
- freezing the assets of the infringing party;
- searching the infringing party's property to look for the infringing goods.

Conclusion

This chapter is only a brief overview of the Act and its application to art. Its application is enormously complex and we have here only highlighted some of the legislation in relation to copyright. Each case, while applying the law, will nevertheless be decided on its own facts while considering (1) whether art is protected by copyright under one of the Act's categories; (2) whether a restricted act has been carried out, or if it is permitted within the exceptions; and (3) if there is an infringement and to what degree (first or second). If all of the above apply, an appropriate remedy is awarded.

i   Section 16 of the Act 'The acts restricted by copyright in a work' (a) to copy the work (see section 17); (b) to issue copies of the work to the public (see section 18); (c) to perform, show, or play the work in public (see section 19); (d) to broadcast the work or include it in a cable programme service (see section 20); (e) to make an adaptation of the work or do any of the above in relation to an adaptation (see section 21).

ii   Known as 'fair dealing' ss.29-30 of the Act. Of particular interest is s.30(1) of the Act which states 'fair dealing with a work for the purpose of criticism and review ... does not infringe copyright ... provided it is accompanied by a sufficient acknowledgment'. It is questionable whether art publishers can reproduce entire works of art without paying appropriate royalties. Such factors as the proportion of the artwork reproduced compared to the proportion of the work consisting of criticism and review are considered. If an entire work is reproduced and there is no criticism and review, then this would constitute an infringement of the artist's copyright. It is even arguable that reproduction of the entire piece with criticism and review is not permissible. It is customary for authors to seek permission for publication of such artworks.

iii   Mr Norowzian had made a short film called 'Joy' with no dialogue. (Nourse LJ described it as a work of action, with or without words or music, which is capable of being performed before an audience). He used a technique called 'Jump cutting' to create a man dancing to music with surreal qualities. The defendants made a film called 'Anticipation' which showed a man dancing and a barman. This was used in a Guinness advert. 'Joy' as a whole was protected by copyright under Section 1(1)(a) as an original dramatic work, but the case decided there was no infringement because merely the style and technique of the filming had been copied. 'Joy' as a whole attracted copyright protection: its particular style did not.

iv   Section 4(1) and Section 4(2) of the Act.

v   Section 4(1)(a) of the Act.

vi   CA in *LA Gear v. Hitec [1992] FSR 121.*

vii   Sections 16-21 and Sections 22-27 of the Act, respectively.

viii   Copying includes Section 17(3) of the Act – the making of a copy in three dimensions of a two-dimensional work and the making of a copy in two dimensions of a three-dimensional work.

ix   See the Case of *Ashdown v. Telegraph Group Ltd (2001) CA.*

x   Section 11(2) of the Act.

xi   As per Hutchison LJ in *Gerber Garment Technology Inc v. Lectra Systems Ltd and Another (1997) RPC 443.*

Overview of U.S. Copyright Law

Donn Zaretsky

Copyright law in the U.S. begins with the Constitution. Article I, Section 8 provides that Congress shall have the power 'To promote the Progress of Science and useful Arts, by securing for limited Times to Authors and Inventors the exclusive Right to their respective Writings and Discoveries.' The nation's first federal copyright statute was enacted in 1791; it was applicable to books, maps, and charts and provided protection for an initial fourteen-year term, plus a renewal term of the same length. The categories of covered works have been gradually expanded, as has the length of protection: for a work created today, the term of protection is the life of the author plus 70 years. Two copyright statutes are primarily relevant today in the U.S.: the 1909 Copyright Act and the 1976 Copyright Act, which for the most part replaced the 1909 Act but left certain provisions in place as they apply to pre-1978 works. This essay will focus largely on the 1976 Act and will give particular attention to its application to the visual arts.

Requirements for Copyright Protection: Idea vs. Expression and Originality

A key concept of U.S. copyright law is the distinction between the *expression* of an idea and the idea itself. Only the former is protected. No one can 'own' the *idea* of, for example, photographs of floating naked babies,[i] or combining a series of brass rings,[ii] or photographing a particular statue in a particular cemetery.[iii] But an artist may obtain protection for a particular expression of such an idea – including, as one court put it in a case involving photographs, 'the photographer's selection of background, lights, shading, positioning and timing'[iv] – so that, if someone else produces a floating baby photograph that looks too much like (or *expresses the idea* too much in the same way as) the original, then an infringement claim may be possible.

   To be protected, an expression must also be 'original' – which perhaps will sound like more of a limitation than it is. It certainly does not mean the same thing as it might to an art critic; the originality necessary to support a copyright merely requires *independent creation*, and not the slightest degree of novelty. Originality in the copyright sense is meant quite literally: it means only that the work owes its *origin* to the author. Indeed, it is possible to imagine two separate works, each qualified for protection, which are identical by coincidence. As a well-known American judge ruled: 'If by some magic a man who had never known it were to compose anew Keats' *Ode On a Grecian Urn*, he would be an 'author' [that is, he would among other things have satisfied the 'originality' requirement] and, if he copyrighted it, others might not copy that poem, though they might of course copy Keats [because Keats copyrights would have long ago expired].' [v] So the originality requirement rarely makes much of a difference in practice, although it was central to an important recent U.S. court decision involving a United Kingdom-based company that marketed CD-ROMs of photographic reproductions of public domain artworks,[vi] and where the court denied copyright protection to such a project:

> In this case, plaintiff by its own admission has labored to create 'slavish copies' of public domain works of art. While it may be assumed that this required both skill and effort, there was no spark of originality. Indeed, the point of the exercise was to reproduce the underlying works with absolute fidelity. Copyright is not available in these circumstances.[vii]

What the Copyright Holder controls

When the standards of copyright-ability are met, what exactly does the holder of the copyright have? Basically, the work's creator has the exclusive rights:

1. To *reproduce* the work.
2. To *distribute* those reproductions.
3. To *display* and *perform* the work publicly.
4. To *adapt* the work (or make so-called 'derivative works').
5. To *authorize* others to do any of these things.

These are fairly straightforward, but a couple of points are perhaps in order. first, while the performance right does not apply to pictorial, graphic, or sculptural works, it does apply to literary, dramatic, and choreographic works, as well as pantomimes, motion pictures, and other audiovisual works. Since the display right does not apply against someone who has acquired ownership of a lawfully made copy (or the original) of the work, the owner of a painting, for example, could publicly exhibit it in a museum or gallery (and, of course, in the privacy of his home, because then there is no 'public' display at all). The owner of a video work, on the other hand, probably needs the artist's permission to show the work in a public setting, such as a museum or gallery.

Second, while it is true that the copyright owner has the exclusive right to prepare derivative works based on the copyrighted work (a classic example being a film version of a novel, the *Harry Potter* film, for example), this does not mean the copyright holder can prevent others from making works 'inspired by' or 'based on' copyrighted works. So an artist ought to be free to make a painting 'inspired by' a particular poem, or piece of music, or even another painting. Only if the later work is 'substantially similar' (on which more later) to the work that inspired it will there be an infringement.

How Copyright is obtained

Nothing special need be done to obtain a copyright in a work. The moment a work is created and 'fixed in a tangible form,' it enjoys copyright protection whether or not it has been published and whether or not it has been registered with the Copyright Office. The statute says a work is 'fixed' when it is embodied 'in a tangible medium of expression . . . sufficiently permanent or stable to permit it to be perceived, reproduced, or otherwise communicated for a period of more than transitory duration.' [viii] Similarly, there is no requirement that a copyright notice be affixed to a work (or to copies) – although this is true only for works first published after March 1, 1989. For works first published before 1978, there is a notice requirement, and an omission of the notice, or an error in it, could result in forfeiture of the copyright. For works published between January 1, 1978 and March 1, 1989, there is a modified notice requirement that allows defects to be 'cured' under certain conditions. Although for works published after March 1, 1989 there is no notice requirement at all, the presence of a copyright notice can preclude a defence of 'innocent infringement' (which can affect the amount of money a plaintiff can recover in an infringement lawsuit).

In the same way, although failure to register the copyright in a work does not invalidate it, there are several advantages to prompt registration:

- Registration is a prerequisite to suing an infringer
  (at least a U.S. infringer).
- To be eligible to recover 'statutory damages' or attorney's fees for an infringement, the work must have been registered prior to commencement of the infringement for which such remedies are sought.
- Registration conveys certain presumptions of ownership and authorship which can be helpful in a dispute.

The second point – that registration opens the door to statutory damages and attorney's fees – can be especially important to artists. One practical difficulty an artist will face in encountering any particular infringement is establishing the financial damage caused by the infringement. If an artist's work is used without permission in a print ad, or on an invitation to an event, or an article of clothing, it is often hard to determine the economic cost to the artist (or, in many cases, the infringing party's profits 'from' the infringing use). If the work was registered prior to the infringement, however, the artist can avoid that burden by electing to recover 'statutory damages' rather than actual damages and the defendant's profits. The Copyright Act allows an award of statutory damages in such amount 'as the court considers just,' within a range of mandatory minimum and maximum limits (currently, from $750 to $30,000 for knowing infringement). The avail-ability of such damages and, equally important, an award of attorney's fees, will at a minimum put an artist in a much better bargaining position in any settlement discussions. (The mechanics of registration are relatively simple: essentially all that's required is to deposit in the Copyright Office two complete copies of the best edition of the work (and one is enough in some cases) along with an application and a small fee ($30 currently).

Copyright Ownership

The question of how long a copyright lasts turns out to be a surprisingly compli-cated one because the answer largely depends on when the work was first pub-lished and whether or not the copyright was registered or renewed. The general rule for a work created on or after January 1, 1978 is that the copyright lasts for the author's life plus 70 years. (Until recently, the term was life of the author plus 50 years. The Sonny Bono Copyright Term Extension Act, which went into effect in late 1998, extended the term an additional 20 years.)

With respect to 'works made for hire,' anonymous works, and pseudony-mous works, copyright lasts for 95 years from publication or 120 years from creation, whichever is shorter.[ix] A 'work made for hire' consists either of 'a work prepared by an employee within the scope of his or her employment,' or of certain works specially ordered or commissioned – namely, (1) a contribution to a collective work, (2) a part of a motion picture or other audiovisual work, (3) a translation, (4) a supplementary work (a work designed to supplement another work, such as a forward or afterward, or illustrations), (5) a compilation, (6) an instructional text, (7) a test, (8) answer material for a test, (9) a sound recording, and (10) an atlas.[x] If the parties are not in an employment relationship, and the work at issue does not fall within one of the enumerated categories, it cannot be a work made for hire.

With respect to joint works, the duration of copyright is the life of the last surviving author plus 70 years.[xi] Joint authorship results when a work is prepared by two or more authors '*with the intention that* their contributions be merged into inseparable or interdependent parts of a unitary whole.'[xii] Each joint owner may, without obtaining the consent of the other joint owners, exploit the work herself or grant a non-exclusive license to do so to third parties (subject only to a duty to account to the other joint owners of the work for their share of the profits realized from her use of the work).

Infringement

There are two elements to a copyright infringement: (1) ownership of the copyright by one person and (2) copying by someone else. As a practical matter, since proving actual copying is often difficult, the copyright owner typically attempts to prove access (generally *the opportunity* to copy) and 'substantial similarity' as substitutes for direct proof of copying. Determining whether two works are 'substantially similar' (as opposed to just similar) is one of the toughest questions in copyright law. It has been said that this line 'wherever it is drawn will seem arbitrary'[xiii] and that 'the test for infringement of a copyright is of necessity vague.'[xiv] The traditional formulation of it has been by reference to an 'ordinary observer':

> The question really involved in such comparison is to ascertain the effect of the alleged infringing play upon the public, that is, upon *the average reasonable man*. If an ordinary person who has recently read the story sits through the presentation of the picture, if there had been literary piracy of the story, he should detect that fact *without any aid or suggestion or critical analysis by others*. The reaction of the public to the matter should be spontaneous and immediate.[xv]

If, however, the work at issue is directed to a particular audience, then the 'spontaneous and immediate' reaction of that particular audience is what counts.[xvi] Indeed, at least one U.S. court has proposed swapping the 'intended audience' for the 'ordinary observer' as the appropriate name for the test.[xvii]

If a plaintiff fails to establish the required elements of ownership and copying (either directly, or by substituting access plus substantial similarity), the defendant will prevail in the lawsuit. A defendant may also have various other defenses (including joint ownership of the work, or the statute of limitations), but perhaps the most important of these is that the copying was a 'fair use.' One could devote an entire treatise to the concept of fair use (in fact, someone has[xviii]); the following is meant only as a brief summary. The Copyright Act's treatment of fair use begins with an enumeration of certain *contexts* in which a finding of fair use would be most appropriate (although it may be considered in other contexts as well): 'criticism, comment, news reporting, teaching (including multiple copies for classroom use), scholarship or research.'[xix] It then sets out four factors courts are to consider in determining whether the use made of a work in any particular case is a fair use:

1. the purpose and character of the use, including whether such use is of a commercial nature or is for non-profit educational purposes;
2. the nature of the copyrighted work (basically, the more creative a work, the more protection it should be given; likewise, the more informational or functional the work, the broader the application of the fair use defence);
3. the amount and substantiality of the portion used in relation to the copyrighted work as a whole;
4. the effect of the use upon the potential market for, or value of, the copyrighted work.

One common fair use argument that defendants make is that their work is a 'parody' of the underlying work. (It was the argument Jeff Koons made, and the court rejected, in the *String of Puppies* case.[xx]) An important limitation on this line of argument is that, to qualify for fair use, the parody must comment (at least partially) on the work that it is copying: one cannot make use of another's copyrighted work solely to make a point about something other than that copyrighted work. Thus, the U.S. Supreme Court held 2 Live Crew's rap version of Roy Orbison's 'Pretty Woman' was a parody (at least in part) of the Orbison song itself, and so qualified it as a fair use.[xxi] Another federal court held that an advertisement for one of the *Naked Gun* movies, with a photo of actor Leslie Nielsen's head superimposed on the naked body of a pregnant woman, was a parody of the Annie Leibovitz photograph of Demi Moore that it was conjuring up ('the ad may reasonably be perceived as commenting on the seriousness, even the pretentiousness, of the original,' it said).[xxii] On the other hand, a different federal court ruled that a book about the O.J. Simpson murder trial, called *The Cat Not In The Hat*, did not qualify as a parody of Dr. Seuss's *The Cat in the Hat* because it was not making any comment on the Seuss book (the court noted that although it may have broadly mimicked 'Dr. Seuss' characteristic style, it does not hold *his style* up to ridicule'), but, rather, was using it to make points about something else.[xxiii]

Another defence that is sometimes offered up is that the use was 'de minimis' and therefore not an infringement. In one case, a television sitcom used a Faith Ringgold work as part of a set decoration: a poster of the work was used as a wall-hanging in a scene and was fully or partly visible a total of nine times for an aggregate duration under 30 seconds. The court denied fair use, rather sharply:

> It is not difficult to imagine a television program that uses a copyrighted visual work for a purpose that heavily favours fair use. If a TV news program produced a feature on Faith Ringgold and included camera shots of her story quilts, the case for a fair use defence would be extremely strong. The same would be true of a news feature on the High Museum that included a shot of 'Church Picnic.' However, it must be recognized that visual works are created, in significant part, for their decorative value, and, just as members of the public expect to pay to obtain a painting or a poster to decorate their homes, producers of plays, films, and television programs should generally expect to pay a license fee when they conclude that a particular work of copyrighted art is an appropriate component of the decoration of a set.[xxiv]

On the other hand, another case, decided right around the same time as the Ringgold case, did accept an incidental reproduction as a fair use. In that case, background shots in a movie, each ranging from one to six seconds for an aggregate total of 30 seconds, showed the plaintiff's photographs, but the images were out-of-focus.[xxv] Interestingly, both cases involved about 30 seconds of depiction of the plaintiff's work, and while the difference in result can perhaps be explained by the different levels of 'recognizability' (the Ringgold work was 'plainly observable, even though not in exact focus,' while in the other case only 'careful scrutiny' would permit one to recognize the images), it is perhaps best that the industry practice, among most studios at least, is to obtain clearance before using, even in the background, images of any clearly recognizable copyrighted work.

Remedies

Various civil remedies are available for copyright infringement, including:
- · An injunction against future infringement;
- · Impounding and destruction or other disposition of infringing reproductions;
- · The actual damages suffered by the copyright owner;
- · The profits earned from the infringement by the defendant;
- · Instead of actual damages and profits, statutory damages (if available); and
- · Costs and attorney's fees (if available).

Certain civil infringements of copyright also constitute federal criminal infringements, the penalties for which depend on the number of copies involved and whether it is a first or subsequent offense.

i *Gentieu v. Muller & Co.*, 712 F. Supp. 740 (W.D. Mo. 1989).

ii *Arthur v. ABC*, 633 F. Supp. 146 (S.D.N.Y. 1985).

iii *Leigh v. Warner Bros.*, 10 F. Supp. 2d 1371 (S.D. Ga. 1998) (involving the Clint Eastwood movie *Midnight in the Garden of Good and Evil*).

iv Gentieu, supra, 712 F. Supp. at 743.

v *Sheldon v. Metro-Goldwyn Pictures Corp.*, 81 F.2d 49, 54 (2d Cir. 1936) (Learned Hand, J.).

vi *Bridgeman Art Library, Ltd. v. Corel Corp.*, 36 F. Supp. 2d 191 (S.D.N.Y. 1999).

vii Id. at 196.

viii 17 U.S.C. § 101.

ix 17 U.S.C. § 302(c).

x 17 U.S.C. § 101.

xi 17 U.S.C. § 302(b).

xii 17 U.S.C. § 101.

xiii *Nichols v. Universal Pictures Co.*, 45 F.2d 119, 122 (2d Cir. 1930).

xiv *Peter Pan Fabrics, Inc. v. Martin Weiner Corp.*, 274 F.2d 487, 489 (2d Cir. 1960).

xv *Harold Lloyd Corp. v. Witwer*, 65 F.2d 1, 18 (9th Cir. 1933) (emphasis added).

xvi See, e.g., *Dawson v. Hinshaw Music, Inc.*, 905 F.2d 731 (4th Cir.); Sid & Marty Krofft *Television Prods., Inc. v. McDonald's Corp.*, 562 F.2d 1157 (9th Cir. 1977).

xvii *Dawson v. Hinshaw Music, Inc.*, supra, 905 F.2d, at 737.

xviii William F. Patry, The Fair Use Privilege in Copyright Law (1985).

xix 17 U.S.C. § 107.

xx *Rogers v. Koons*, 960 F.2d 301 (2d Cir. 1992).

xxi *Campbell v. Acuff-Rose Music*, Inc., 114 S. Ct. 1164 (1994).

xxiii *Leibovitz v. Paramount Pictures Corp.*, 137 F.3d 109, 114 (2d Cir. 1998).

xxii *Dr. Seuss Enters., L.P. v. Penguin Books USA, Inc.*, 109 F.3d 1394, 1401 (9th Cir. 1996) (emphasis in original).

xxiv *Ringgold v. Black Entertainment Television, Inc.*, 126 F.3d 70 (2d Cir. 1997).

xxv *Sandoval v. New Line Cinema Corp.*, 147 F.3d 215, 218 (2d Cir. 1998).

Moral Rights

Ruth Redmond-Cooper [i]

When droit moral fanatics discuss moral rights, they take the attitude of a religious zealot talking of sacred things, or a Girondin reading the Declaration of the Rights of Man.
  Pierre Recht

The desire of an artist to control the way in which his or her work is used or displayed stems not always from economic considerations, but also very often from an emotional urge to be recognised as the creator or to protect a creation from perceived disfigurement. The traditional law of copyright, based merely on controlling the copying of a work, does not take account of the intimate, emotional involvement between an artist and his or her creation. This is the domain of moral rights, an area of law, which originated in France: *le droit moral*. 'Moral' in this context implies not a superior ethical standpoint, but rather an intellectual or emotional right, as opposed to the commercial and tangible right, which is copyright.

For example, in Canada in the early 1980s, the artist Michael Snow relied on his moral rights as established in that country to force a shopping centre to remove red ribbons which it had tied at Christmas around the necks of his sculptures of geese. The geese had been bought by the centre, but Snow retained his moral rights: he claimed that the ribbons made the sculptures look ridiculous and prejudiced his reputation as an artist – he likened it to putting earrings on the Venus de Milo.[ii] The composer Shostakovitch also relied on his moral rights when he objected to the use of a faithful recording of his work as the background to a documentary critical of the Soviet regime: he was successful in an action brought in France,[iii] but he failed in the U.S.,[iv] as moral rights had yet to be legally introduced there. Similarly, Charles Chaplin was successful in an action complaining that a film distributor had without permission added a musical accompaniment to the film, *The Kid*.[v]

Where do Moral Rights come from?

Common law countries (the U.K., the U.S., Canada, Australia, etc.) have tended to stress the economic or proprietary rights arising out of the creation of artworks: that the artist has the right to control the issue of copies of the works but, until recently, did not have specific rights to object to modifications to the work which might be carried out by persons who had purchased it. Civil law countries have always taken a wider view of the rights attached to authorship, taking the view that such rights carry with them an intellectual element which transcends the purely economic aspects of copyright.

The Berne Convention, as revised at Paris in 1971, now provides for limited moral rights, in the form of a right of paternity (the right to be identified as the author of a work) and a right of integrity (the right to object to certain forms of derogatory treatment of the work). Article 6 bis provides:

1. Independently of the author's economic rights, and even after the transfer of the said rights, the author shall have the right to claim authorship of the work and to object to any distortion, mutilation, or other modification of, or other derogatory action in relation to, the said work, which would be prejudicial to his honour or reputation.

2. The rights granted to the author in accordance with the preceding paragraph shall, after his death, be maintained, at least until the expiry of the economic rights, and shall be exercisable by the persons or institutions authorised by the legislation of the country where protection is claimed . . .

3. The means of redress for safeguarding the rights granted by this Article shall be governed by the legislation of the country where protection is claimed.

Countries implementing the revision contained in article 6 bis are confronted with a series of choices as to the scope of the protection to be accorded to moral rights. Should the rights be limited to those enumerated in 6 bis, or should they be wider (as in France and other civil law countries)? Who and what should be protected? (The U.S. has opted to accord protection only to the creators of visual art.) For how long should such protection extend? Should it be coterminous with copyright (as in the U.K.), or indefinite (as in France), or cease upon death (as in the U.S.)? Who exercises such rights after the death of the artist? Does the right of integrity extend to destruction of the work (as it does in certain situations in France and the U.S., but not in the U.K.)? Should we talk of protection of the artist or of art generally? (Are there wider policy issues to be addressed, which would ensure protection of all art, rather than merely allowing the creator of a work to object to alterations or destruction?) In the discussion, which follows, consideration will be given primarily to the laws of the U.K., France, and the U.S., three jurisdictions which demonstrate widely differing conceptions of the term 'moral rights'.

Differing Jurisdictional approaches:
U.K.

In the U.K., the concept of moral rights is a relatively recent one, dating back only to the 1988 Copyright, Designs, and Patents Act. Sections 77-89 of the Act, contained in Chapter IV, divided into four kinds of moral rights, the first two of which were introduced in order to fulfil the U.K.'s obligations under article 6bis of the Berne Convention:

1. The right to be identified as author or director of a work: the paternity right, or the right to be identified.
2. The right to object to derogatory treatment: the integrity right.
3. The right to object to false attribution of work: the false attribution right.
4. The right to privacy of certain photographs and films: the privacy right.

France

It is to France that we owe the concept of moral rights. These rights include; the right of disclosure (*droit de divulgation*); the right to withdraw from publication or to make modifications (*droit de retrait ou de repentir*); the paternity or authorship right (*droit au respect du nom* or *droit à la paternité*); and the right of integrity (*droit au respect de l'oeuvre*). The various rights are now laid down in article L. 121 of the French Intellectual Property Code (which derives from the Law of 11th March 1957, having been established by the case law of the nineteenth and early twentieth centuries.

U.S.

Moral rights existed at the state level[vi] for a number of years before the enactment of the federal Visual Artists Rights Act in 1990. VARA (which amends the Copyright Act 1976 and came into force on 1 June 1991) will pre-empt state laws which grant legal or equitable rights equivalent to those recognised by VARA where the cause of action arose after 1 June 1991. Where the state law grants protection which is wider than that granted under VARA, it will not be pre-empted by VARA. VARA grants to the author of a 'work of visual art' the rights of attribution and integrity and has been described by Lerner and Bresler as 'a victory for artistic principle, particularly when viewed in the historical context of U.S. copyright doctrine, which has consistently subordinated the sensibilities of the artist to the advancement of commerce'.[vii]

Duration of Moral Rights

If moral rights were concerned purely with protecting the reputation of the artist or author, it could be expected that they might expire at death. However, more is at issue here, and this is recognised by the fact that, while in some jurisdictions moral rights die with the author (as is the case under the U.S. Visual Artists Rights Act for works created on or after 1 June 1991), in others (for example, the U.K.) they expire at the same time as copyright[viii] (the life of the author plus 70 years, though the right to object to false attribution extends for a period of just twenty years after a person's death[ix]), and in others (most notably France) such rights survive without limitation.

Who may assert Moral Rights?

The rights of paternity and integrity apply to the authors of copyrighted works: while copyright and moral rights will often be owned at least initially by the same person, it is quite possible for copyright to pass to a third party while the author or artist retains his or her moral rights in relation to the work. However, where the work was created in the course of employment, special rules will apply. In such a case, if the copyright in the work is vested in the employer, the right to be identified as author or artist will not apply if the act was done by or with the authority of the copyright owner.[x] The artist or author will not have the right to complain of derogatory treatment of a work where such treatment has been done with the authority of the copyright owner, unless the artist or author was identified at the time either of the relevant act or previously.[xi] The right to object to false attribution of work may be exercised by anyone, whether an artist or author or not.

It is a common feature of all the legal systems under scrutiny that moral rights, unlike copyright, are regarded as falling outside the normal rules of commerce. In France, this is taken to its furthest extreme, with moral rights being inalienable and neither ably waived nor assigned. A leading academic has stated that, unlike economic rights, moral rights cling to the author 'as light does to phosphorus'.[xii] Under the CDPA 1988, moral rights are viewed as personal and are not assignable.[xiii] However, they may be waived by an instrument in writing signed by the person entitled to the right[xiv] (although a waiver by one joint author will not affect the rights of the other joint authors[xv]); the position is similar under VARA.

The right of paternity, the right of integrity, and the right of privacy are transferable on death, and the person entitled to the rights may stipulate in a last will and testament the person to whom such rights should pass.[xvi] However, if s/he fails to make any such express stipulation, the passing of the right will depend on whether or not the work in question forms part of the transferable estate, and if it does, then the moral rights will pass to the person to whom the copyright passes.[xvii] But if copyright in the work does not form part of the estate, the moral right will pass to the deceased owner's personal representatives.[xviii]

What is covered?

The moral rights provisions of the U.K. CDPA cover the creators of copyright literary, dramatic, musical, and artistic works, as well as the directors of copyrighted films. Since 'artistic merit' is not generally a prerequisite under English law for copyright protection, it will not be a prerequisite for moral rights protection either. The right to be identified (the paternity right) will not be infringed by an act which would not infringe copyright in the work by virtue of the fair dealing provision (section 30 of the 1988 Act) or the incidental inclusion exception (section 31).[xix] These exceptions do not, however, apply in the case of derogatory treatment of the work.

While moral rights go hand-in-hand with copyright in France, the scope of the U.S. federal moral rights protection is far narrower and covers only 'works of visual art', which themselves are fairly narrowly defined, excluding, for example, posters, maps, charts, technical drawings, diagrams, advertising, promotional and packaging materials, etc. In *Gegenhuber v. Hystopolis Productions Inc.*,[xx] the plaintiffs were professional puppeteers who sought to rely on the attribution right contained in VARA following the discovery that their role in adapting a play for puppets was not being given appropriate credit. The Illinois federal district court held that, although VARA grants an attribution right, this right does not extend to puppets, costumes, and sets.

The Right of Paternity

The paternity right, the right to be identified as the author of a work, which is one of the two moral rights contained in article 6bis of the Berne Convention, is the right most frequently encountered (together with the right of integrity). In many ways it takes a form which is economic as much as moral: paternity must be established in order to reap the financial benefits which come from exploitation of a work of art. In some countries, the paternity right encompasses rights which are dealt with separately elsewhere, most notably the right of authors or artists to object to others claiming authorship of their work or to prevent their names appearing on works for which they are not the author (false attribution, as to which, see below).

In the U.K., the paternity right is defined as a right to be identified as the artist whenever the work is published commercially or exhibited in public, or a visual image of the work is broadcast or included in a cable programme service.[xxi] The identification must in each case be clear and reasonably prominent.[xxii] In order to rely on the right of paternity, it is first necessary under U.K. law to have asserted authorship of the work: there is no infringement in the absence of any assertion by the artist or author of his or her rights in relation to the work.[xxiii] In relation to artistic works, the requirement of assertion of authorship may be fulfilled by indicating the name of the artist on the original or authorised copy, or on the frame to which the artistic work is attached.[xxiv] Then again, this requirement has been criticised, as authors and artists may not know of the need to assert their authorship – many newer forms of artistic creativity do not fit easily with the concept of a signature or other traditional assertion of authorship, and indeed, is not required by the Berne Convention to do so. However, those who justify the rule do so on the ground that it is necessary in order to protect publishers and others who may deal with copyright material so that they know to whom requests to copy must be made.

In France, the paternity right extends not only to acknowledgement of the artist's identity whenever a work is exhibited or reproduced, but also permits the artist to deny works which s/he did not create, or to remain anonymous, should s/he so choose. The right to deny authorship is one which is fraught with difficulty, particularly where an artist has died and the estate acquires control of the right effectively to determine authenticity: it has been argued that in some instances decisions have been made based on the fear that prices may be depressed if the market is 'flooded' with works by a particular artist.

False Attribution of Authorship

This is not a right provided for under the Berne Convention, and in the U.K. it was previously contained in the 1956 legislation.[xxv] The law of tort, in particular the torts of passing off and defamation, may also assist plaintiffs here.[xxvi] Under the 1988 Act, a person has the right not to have a literary, dramatic, musical, or artistic work falsely attributed to him or her as author, and not to have a film falsely attributed to him or her as director.[xxvii] It is not necessary that the name of the person be used expressly: an implied statement that s/he is the author will suffice, provided s/he is identifiable. In the case of an artistic work, the right will be infringed where a person, dealing with the work in the course of a business, alters the work after the artist has parted possession of it and presents it as the unaltered work of the artist.[xxviii] In France, the right is not separately enumerated, but forms part of the right of paternity.

The Right of Integrity

Unlike other contracts of sale, the contract for the sale of a work of art does not give the purchaser an unfettered right to deal with the work as s/he wishes, even if s/he acquires the copyright under the contract. The right of integrity gives artists a degree of control over the use which is made of their work even after they have parted with physical control. However, the scope of this right varies greatly from one jurisdiction to another.

In France, the right (known as *le droit au respect de l'œuvre*) is commonly invoked by artists in an attempt to prevent their work from being distorted or damaged. When the artist Bernard Buffet discovered that a refrigerator which he had painted in six panels for a charity auction (three on the door, one on the top, and one on each side) had been dismantled by the buyer who was selling each panel separately, he asserted his right of integrity to prevent this 'mutilation' and to force the buyer to maintain the work as a whole.[xxix] However, the courts have accorded to themselves a not-inconsiderable power of determination of the concept of 'distortion' in the context of moral rights: when Salvador Dali attempted to rely on the right of integrity in relation to certain modifications which had been made to some costumes which he had designed, the Cour de Cassation qualified the right by stating that the artist's right to object to modifications is limited to those modifications as a result of which an inaccurate view of the work is given.[xxx] However, in contrast to certain other jurisdictions, including the U.K., and to the Berne Convention itself, the artists or authors who seek to rely on this right before the French courts is not required to demonstrate that their honour or reputation has been damaged: the right exists in order to protect the artist's personal and emotional involvement with the work, and as such, questions of honour and reputation are irrelevant. What matters to artists is whether or not the work is being exhibited in a manner which accords with their artistic expectations.

It has been said, in a case brought by the author Samuel Beckett, that 'respect is owed to the work as the author wished it to be, [and] that it is not for either third parties or the judge to impose a value judgement on the wishes of the author, [and] that the holder of the moral right is the sole master of its exercise'.[xxxi] In that case, Becket complained that his moral rights had been infringed in relation to the production of his play, *Waiting for Godot*, in that it went against his clearly expressed wish not to have women acting in it.

Under the CDPA, the author or artist has the right not to have his or her work subjected to derogatory treatment.[xxxii] Treatment of a work is derogatory if it amounts to distortion or mutilation of the work or is otherwise prejudicial to the honour or reputation of the artist. 'Treatment' is restrictively defined as any 'addition to, deletion from, or alteration to or adaptation of the work'.[xxxiii] The limits of the protection accorded to artists under this provision, as compared with certain other jurisdictions, were highlighted by the case of *Tidy v. The Trustees of the Natural History Museum*,[xxxiv] in which cartoons that had been drawn by the applicant for the purposes of display at the museum alongside exhibits were then reproduced, without the consent of the applicant, in far smaller dimensions in a book. The applicant argued that the reduced size constituted a distortion of the drawings in that it detracted from the visual impact of the originals and, further, that the reproduction of the reduced size drawings was prejudicial to his honour or reputation since it might lead readers to assume that he could not be bothered to redraw the cartoons for the book. However, the judge, Rattee J., interpreting the phrase in section 80(2)(b) 'prejudicial to his honour or reputation', rejected the subjective test of the Canadian courts [xxxv] where O'Brien J. had stated that the words 'prejudicial to his honour or reputation . . . involve a certain subjective element or judgement on the part of the author so long as it is reasonably arrived at'. Instead, Rattee J. adopted an objective approach, stating that 'before accepting the plaintiff's view that the reproduction in the book complained of is prejudicial to his honour or reputation, I have to be satisfied that that view is one which is reasonably held, which inevitably involves the application of an objective test of reasonableness'. [xxxvi]

A vexed question in relation to the right of integrity is that of determining whether or not the right accords protection against destruction of the work. In the U.K., it would appear that destruction, as opposed to distortion or mutilation, is not protected: 'treatment' is defined as any 'addition to, deletion from, or alteration to or adaptation of the work', [xxxvii] and, since the purpose of the right is to protect the honour and reputation of the artist, it is argued that there is no need to protect against destruction.

However, in France, the destruction of a work of art may, in the absence of any justification, give rise to an obligation to compensate the artist for breach of his right to respect for his work: destruction will be permitted only in the case of *force majeure* – an external, unforeseeable, and unpredictable event which makes destruction necessary. [xxxviii] In the case of architectural works, compromise is clearly necessary: the owner cannot be obliged to keep the building unaltered indefinitely. The courts have tended to judge public bodies more harshly in relation to protection of the integrity of a work of art: public bodies who allow a work to deteriorate with the result that it has to be removed or destroyed may be liable to a fine on the grounds that the artist's right to respect for his or her work has been infringed.[xxxix]

With U.S. law, an intermediate position is reached: under VARA, the artist has the right to prevent any 'intentional or grossly negligent destruction of a work of recognised stature', thereby raising the question of what is meant by 'recognised stature'. The 1979 California Art Preservation Act prohibits 'defacement, mutilation, alteration, or destruction' of 'fine art' and was relied on to prevent, in 1988, the removal of a David Hockney mural of a swimming pool painted on a hotel wall. It was argued that removal was necessary since the mural violated a local safety regulation, but the response of the California legislature was to specifically exempt the mural from the regulatory provisions that would have required its destruction, stating 'To allow needless destruction of this unique work of art would be a great tragedy and inconsistent with the intent of the California Art Preservation Act, which establishes a public interest in preserving the integrity of cultural and artistic creations'. Mere negligent destruction of a work of art is not, however, covered, as was shown when the City of Los Angeles was not liable when one of its dustcarts rolled down a hill into a vehicle containing artworks by the plaintiff.

The Right of Disclosure (*Le Droit de Divulgation*)

In France, article L.121-2, para 2 of the CPI provides that the author has the sole right to disclose his or her work. As early as the turn of the century, James McNeill Whistler exercised his *droit de divulgation* before the French courts when sued for breach of contract after failing to deliver to Lord Eden a portrait he had commissioned from Whistler of Lord Eden's wife when a dispute arose over payment. Whistler claimed to be unhappy with the work and argued that he should not be compelled to hand it over. The French courts held in his favour, holding that the artist should not be forced to make public a painting with which he was not happy. He was, however, obliged to pay damages to Lord Eden.[xl] The scope of the right of disclosure has not been fully resolved by the French courts and the question remains: is the right limited to permitting the artist to control the first publication of the work, or does it give the artist a much wider degree of control over display of the work even after it has been exhibited? It appears that the right of disclosure gives the artist a limited degree of control following publication, particularly where it may be inferred that a subsequent publication has occurred in circumstances other than those for which publication was originally authorised.[xli] However, the artist will not be permitted to exercise this right, where to do so would constitute an abuse: for example, to prevent the copyright owner from making legitimate reproductions of the work.

The Right to Withdraw or to Repent
(*Le Droit de Repentir ou de Retrait*)

French law gives artists the right to 'repent' of their earlier work: they may, as a result of a change in style or ideas, decide that certain works are no longer representative of their talent and wish to withdraw or alter the work. The CPI grants this right in article 121- 4, but subjects it to an obligation to indemnify the owner of the copyright in respect of any losses s/he may suffer as a result of this. In practice, the right is almost never used.

Conclusion

The term 'moral rights' is one which encompasses a wide range of rights. Publishers and organisers of exhibitions should take care to ensure that they comply with the law of any country in which they operate, as in many instances the level of protection to artists and authors will be considerably greater than it is in the U.K.

i   Ruth Redmond-Cooper is the Director of the Institute of Art and Law, London

ii   *Snow v. Eaton Centre Ltd* (1982) 70 C.P.R. (2d) p.105.

iii   *Soc. Le Chant de Monde v. Soc. Fox Europe et Soc. Fox Américaine Twentieth Century* (1953)
     Gaz. Pal. 191 (judgment of 13 January 1953).

iv   *Shostakovitch v. Twentieth Century Fox Film Corp.*, 196 Misc. 67, 80 N.Y.S. 2d 575
     (Sup. Ct. 1948), aff'd., 275 App. Div. 695, 87 N.Y.S. 2d 430 (1st Dept. 1949).

v   Paris Court of Appeal, 29 April 1959, J.C.P. 1159.402.

vi   States which have moral rights legislation include California, New York, Maine, New Jersey, Louisiana, Pennsylvania and others. The scope of this legislation differs from state to state: see R. Lerner and J. Bresler, *Art Law*, (2nd edn, Practicing Law Institute, 1998), vol.2, p.959 *et seq.* for further details.

vii   Lerner and Bresler, above note 5, at p.949.

viii   Section 86(1) CDPA.

ix   Section 86(2) CDPA.

x   Section 79(3)(a).

xi   Section 82(2) CDPA.

xii   C. Colombet, *Propriété Littéraire et Artistique et Droits Voisins*, (8th edn, Dalloz, 1997), p.113.

xiii   Section 94, CDPA.

xiv   Section 87(2) CDPA.

xv   Section 88(3) CDPA.

xvi   Section 95(1)(a) CDPA.

xvii   Section 95(1)(b) CDPA.

xviii   Section 95(1)(c).

  xix   Section 79(4) CDPA.

   xx   No.92-C1055, 1992 U.S. Dist. Lexis 10156 (N.D. Ill. July 10, 1992),
        cited in Lerner and Bresler, *Art Law*, p.973.

  xxi   S.77(4)(b).

  xxii S.77(7).

 xxiii Section 78(1) CDPA.

 xxiv   Section 78(3) CDPA.

  xxv   Section 43 Copyright Act 1956.

 xxvi   See *Moore v. News of the World* [1972] 1 Q.B. 441.

xxvii   Section 84(1) CDPA.

xxviii Section 84(6) CDPA.

 xxix   Gaz. Pal. 1965.2.126, Cass. 6 July 1965.

  xxx   *L'affaire Salvador Dali* D.1968.382, Cass. 1re Civ. 5 March 1968: 'l'auteur a le pouvoir
        de s'opposer à toute correction ou modification susceptible d'altérer le caractère de
        son oeuvre' and there is no question of invocation of moral rights where 'les adjonctions
        n'ont pas pour conséquence de donner une idée inexacte de l'œuvre'.

 xxxi   Paris Tribunal de Grande Instance, 3rd Chamber, 15 October 1992
        (RIDA January 1993) n.155, p.225.

xxxii   S.80(1) CDPA 1988.

xxxiii Ibid., section 80(2).

xxxiv   [1995] 39 IPR 501.

 xxxv   *Snow v. Eaton Shopping Centre* (1982) 70 CPR 105 at 106.

xxxvi   Ibid., p.504.

xxxvii S.80(1) CDPA 1988.

xxxviii *L'affaire Scrive* T.G.I. R.I.D.A. April 1975, 219, Paris, judgment of 14 May 1974.

xxxix   *L'affaire de la fontaine du Roussillon* D.1936.3.57, Conseil d'Etat 3 April 1936.

   xl   *Whistler v. Eden* [1900] D.P. 1 5000, Cass. Civ. Judgment of May 14 1900.

  xli   Cass. 1re Civ. 13 December 1989, *Leprêtre v. Société Bovida*, RIDA April 1990, n.144, p.199.

Breaking Down the Borders: International Copyright Conventions and Jurisdiction

Brett Rowland, Mervyn Flatt and Samantha McGonigle

The Global Village: the 48th Venice Biennale

In the spring of 2000, the Chinese Art World was thrust into a debate about the place of appropriation in artistic creation. The catalyst was the work of the Chinese artist Cai Guo Qiang, created for the 48th Venice Biennale. This work was a recreation of a 1960's Communist-influenced work entitled *Rent Collection Yard*, but both unfinished and left to decay to reflect the passage of time and its ravages on ideology. This new work offended the original sculptors from the Sichuan Academy of Art to such a degree that they contemplated legal action against Cai Guo Qiang. Much of the debate concerned the degree to which plagiarism should be permitted in art from a creative point of view, but other important facets of this case are more political and legal. The work that was allegedly infringed was created at a time when China was relatively isolated and had substantial antipathy towards intellectual property rights. Despite this, the creators of this work still contemplated legal action for breach of their intellectual property rights. More than this, they contemplated bringing these legal proceedings in another jurisdiction more sympathetic to the protection of intellectual property rights.

Two observations may be made from this. The first is that even countries such as China, which once had little or no interest in intellectual property rights, are becoming aware of the growing importance of copyright.[i] Secondly, cultural changes are weakening international borders so that uses of art and transactions in art (for example, art exhibitions) are increasingly becoming globally oriented with the result that disputes about intellectual property rights are more often focused on resolving complicated problems concerning conflicting laws and treaty obligations. This chapter explores the means by which copyright protects artistic endeavour on an international level in the context of a discussion of the effects of Cai Guo Qiang's reproduction of *Rent Collection Yard*.

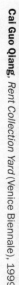

Cai Guo Qiang, *Rent Collection Yard* (Venice Biennale), 1999

Setting the Scene: the Biennale and Rent Collection Yard

The Venice Biennale has been described as the world's oldest, biggest, and most prestigious exhibition of contemporary art, dating back to 1895, and has a long history of controversy. Artists from Renoir and van Gogh to Pollock and Chagall to Hirst and Löwenberg have all presented their works to the world from the stage of the Biennale. Hirst's decaying carcass and Löwenberg's installation of military surveillance images, computers, and details of U.S. nuclear plants are but two examples of the artistic creations exhibited at the Biennale over the last 20 years. The director and curator for the 48th Biennale in 1999 was Harald Szeemann, who presided over a Biennale that dwelled extensively on the contribution of Chinese artists and on the influence of politics on art. Szeemann reportedly acknowledged this influence in his preface to the Biennale catalogue by alluding to Venice as the 'gateway to the Orient'. One of the artists providing this Asian connection in the 48th Biennale was Cai Guo Qiang.

Cai Guo Qiang was born in China in 1957 in the town of Quanzhou and studied at the Shanghai Drama Institute, graduating in 1985. He moved to Japan in 1986 and following that to New York in 1995 to take up a grant from the Asian Cultural Council. His artistic career has been punctuated by statements on a generous and spectacular scale, as exemplified by his works entitled *Project for Extraterrestrials No. 10: Project to Extend the Great Wall of China by 10,000 Meters* (1993), in which he extended and lit a fuse from the Great Wall for 10,000 metres into the desert, and *No Construction, No Destruction: Bombing the Taiwan Museum of Art* (1998), where he again placed and lit a gunpowder fuse, this time laid throughout the Taiwan Museum. His work has been described by critics as 'rich and varied' and the artist himself as 'one of the most important artists of the late 20th Century'.[ii] One critic said that he 'seeks to transform Oriental aesthetics and concepts associated with mystery and philosophy into a concrete modernity with new cultural implications'[iii] and in December 1999, New York's Daily News listed him as one of the Top 50 'Most Noticeable New Yorkers'; he was both the only artist and the only person of Chinese origin on the list.[iv] However, one of Cai Guo Qiang's most controversial works was that exhibited at the 48th Biennale, which embodied Cai's interpretation and reconstruction of the famous Chinese Sculpture, *Rent Collection Courtyard*.

The original *Rent Collection Courtyard* was an installation of more than 100 life-sized clay figures, created in 1965 in the south western Sichuan Province of China and representing not only a piece of art, but a powerful political statement. Its creators are said to have been a team of students from the Sichuan Academy of Fine Arts in Chongqing, directed by Wang Guanyi. The work was designed to contrast the life of the people under Mao and Communism with their life under the old feudal system by depicting the collection of rent from peasants by their feudal landlord. In all, the original work comprises 114 characters with 108 props (farm implements, tables, chairs, etc.) collected by the artists and can be divided into elements representing the different stages of the rent collection process and draws attention to the sheer magnitude of the oppression suffered by the peasants. The work features the dispassionate, tyrannical landlord overseeing the suffering of his bedraggled debtors, as rag-clad babies are snatched from their mothers and peasants beg for their lives. Several copies of the work were made or authorised by the Chinese Authorities for display in other parts of China but the original work was installed on the property of Liu Wencai, who was the landlord of Sichuan's Dayi District in the years before the Communist Revolution in 1949.[v] The location of the work added to the political impact given the onset of the Cultural Revolution in China, and it remains one of the most important artworks in Chinese history. It is reported that, in 1972, Harald Szeemann issued an invitation for the *Rent Collection Courtyard* to be exhibited at the Kassel Documenta Exhibition.[vi] This exhibition did not occur as China was in the midst of the Cultural Revolution, but when Szeemann presented the 48th Biennale in 1999, he procured Cai Guo Qiang to present his own unique interpretation of this classic work.

Cai's work was created in the period leading up to and during the 48th Biennale at Venice's Arsenale, the immense naval and ship building area on the fringe of Venice, where it filled an entire 'barn-sized' room. It was constructed by nearly two dozen sculptors, one of whom was Lone Xu Xi, who had worked on the original *Rent Collection Courtyard* some 34 years before. The work itself consisted of around 100 life sized figures of which approximately half were completed, the others constituting only wire and wooden frames and the props were drawn from whatever could be collected by the artists from the surrounding area, repeating the process undertaken by the original artists. The figures (or at least those that were completed) were created from clay but were not kiln fired, as a result of which they crumbled during the course of the exhibition, even as other figures were constructed, enabling Cai to point to the impermanence of physical and societal constructions. However, because of the open-ended nature of the work, it may be argued that no two people will derive the same meaning from the installation. Perhaps it is appropriate to refer to a report from the Jury's citation in granting the International Award at the 48th Biennale, in which Cai was said to 'question the history, function, and epic of art through temporal and physical contextual isolation'.[vii] Ultimately, it may be a futile exercise to speculate on Cai's precise intent and more profitable to concentrate on the impact of the work on the artistic community and on the original work's creators.

As stated above, Cai's work won him the International Award at the 48th Biennale, regarded as a supreme honour in one of the world's most important exhibitions of contemporary art, and Cai was the first Chinese artist to receive such an accolade. Indeed, Emma Bedgod, curator at the South African National Gallery[viii], supports the Biennale jury's comment that Cai's *Rent Collection Yard* is 'strong and surprising and perfectly balanced in its space'. Britta Erickson[ix] has also commented that '[w]ith such powerful and multivalent meanings, it is a rare and wonderful creation'.

However, not all reactions to Cai's work were so positive. In academic circles there was a furore that Cai, Szeemann, and the Biennale had seemingly ignored international copyright law. The question raised by Cai's work is the place of appropriation in art and the legal protection of original works. More specifically for the purposes of this essay, the question is how copyright law can transcend borders and national laws. Wang Guanyi, a professor at the Sichma Academy, who reportedly directed the construction of the original *Rent Collection Yard*, stated that 'Cai Guo Qiang has violated [their] creative rights', claiming that Cai did so '[w]ithout [their] approval'. Wang, in the magazine *Sculpture*, wrote that 'This is different from Duchamp painting a moustache on the '*Mona Lisa*', because in that case the copyright protection time had expired. If daVinci and Duchamp were both alive today, they would surely end up in a copyright suit'.

In the case of Cai's remodelling of *Rent Collection Yard*, it was announced in spring 2000 that some of the original sculptors planned to bring legal action against Cai, Szeemann, and the Biennale for copyright infringement. It was reported shortly thereafter[x] that lawyers were working to build a case although they had 'not yet decided in what legal venue, if any, they can proceed'. In the latter half of 2000 it was reported[xi] that it no longer appeared likely that the legal action would progress, but the initial deliberations of the Academy's lawyers demonstrated that the international dimension of copyright law and the interrelationship of national copyright frameworks can be a difficult area.

From here we turn to look at the international legal framework within which Cai's work and the original *Rent Collection Courtyard* were enmeshed. The provisions of the major international conventions and treaties relating to the protection of copyright in works of art are highlighted as are their aims, weaknesses, and the way in which they interact. Also discussed is the choice of governing law in disputes, such as the outrage generated by the reconstruction of *Rent Collection Yard* and the location of proceedings where actions are brought. Unfortunately, the legal framework governing international copyright treaties in some ways resembles Cai's work in that it is a work in progress with levels of impermanence from which it seems no two people derive the same meaning.

Global Problems: Influences on the Development of Copyright

Prior to the late nineteenth century, various countries had developed and maintained their own systems of copyright causing a divergence of national approaches. The recent shift in emphasis from domestic to international protection is the result of the increasingly global nature of international trade. The Internet is the latest in a line of technological advances that has increased globalisation of content distribution and caused problems for copyright owners due to the divergence of national copyright systems. Intellectual property rights, of which copyright, moral rights, and resale rights are parts, are valuable commodities. The digitisation and international movement of materials protected by copyright (for example, text, music and film) that is facilitated by the Internet has highlighted the need for countries to harmonise their copyright laws. In fact, pressure has been exerted over the past few decades by the leading producers of copyright materials[xii] on countries with poor levels of protection,[xiii] with the aim of getting them to strengthen their copyright laws. This pressure is driven by the massive amounts of money generated by the publishing, music, movie and software industries, the influence of their lobby groups on the policies of the major copyright producing nations and the influence of those nations in world affairs. The result of this influence was a series of international treaties culminating in 1994 with the General Agreement on Tariffs and Trade (GATT).

Global Solutions: International Conventions

One major problem facing many nations was how to deal with disputes over copyright where the copyright owner and the alleged infringer were resident in different jurisdictions or where the infringing act occurred out of the copyright owner's jurisdiction. To deal with this, various countries entered into international agreements setting out the approach to be taken to these cross-border disputes. The earliest of these agreements were bilateral treaties governing how each country would deal with cross-border copyright disputes involving the other country.

These agreements often set out mechanisms for dealing with straightforward situations involving nationals of the two contracting countries. One problem was that no two treaties contained the same terms because the mechanics of how copyright was protected between countries diverged. Further, bilateral treaties only regulated the affairs of those countries that signed up to them and, therefore, more complex situations – for example situations involving infringement in two different states of copyright held by a resident of a third state – could not satisfactorily be addressed. A solution to this problem was for states to enter into multilateral agreements, establishing common rules regarding the protection of copyright and enabling multinational co-operation. The aim of these agreements was to protect copyright more effectively, to reduce disparities between national and bilateral copyright protection, and to reduce the risk of piracy being carried out from 'safe haven' countries with low thresholds of copyright protection.[xiv] There have been four important such conventions:

- Berne Convention for the Protection of Literary and Artistic Works (1886)
- Universal Copyright Convention (1952-1971)
- Agreement on Trade Related Aspects of Intellectual Property Rights (TRIPs) (1994)
- World Intellectual Property Organisation Copyright Treaty (1996).

In the Beginning: the Berne Convention

The Berne Convention was adopted in 1886 and has been revised on several occasions.[xv] The original signatories were Belgium, France, Germany, Haiti, Italy, Liberia, Spain, Switzerland, Tunisia, and the United Kingdom, and there are now 149 members.[xvi] The Convention created a Union of Member Countries which is open to all countries that satisfy its conditions. Authors who are nationals of Berne Union countries are granted protection for their published and unpublished works, whereas authors who are not nationals of a Berne Union country are only granted protection for works first published or simultaneously published in a Berne Union country. Authors who are habitually resident in a Berne Union country are treated as nationals of that country.

Basic Principles

The Berne Convention is founded on two principles. The first, 'National Treatment', means that all countries of the Berne Union afford nationals of the other members of the Union the same treatment as they grant their own citizens. The second, all countries of the Berne Union are to provide the owner of a work in which copyright subsists with the minimum set of exclusive rights set out in the Berne Convention. Beyond these minimum rights, the members are free to implement their individual copyright laws so long as these laws apply to citizens of all countries in the Union.

The minimum rights that all countries of the Berne Union must provide[xvii] to authors are:

- The right of reproduction: the right to authorise the copying of the work in any manner or form;
- the right to adapt or translate works;
- a limited right of distribution;
- rights of communication: the public performance of dramatic, dramatico-musical and musical works, and the public recitation of literary works, the broadcasting (whether by television or radio) of literary and artistic works and the recording of musical works;
- rights of resale: authors of artistic works (or their estates after their death) have a right of interest in any sale of their works, so that they are entitled to royalties every time the work in question is sold; and
- moral rights: these remain with the author of the work even if the author has transferred the physical work and the copyright to another party as moral rights are designed to protect the author's reputation.[xviii]

The number of countries that signed up to the Berne Convention was limited by the stipulation that copyright protection is not to be dependent on any formalities. Some countries found this provision to be unattractive. The most notable example was the United States, which declined to join the Union on the basis, at least in part, that the stipulation was in conflict with the United States' registration system (the United States did not adopt the Convention until 1989). The result was that Berne's geographical scope was limited, because some countries that granted a substantial level of protection did not satisfy the criteria for membership of the Berne Union and because several less developed countries did not offer protection above the threshold required under the minimum protection principle of Berne, the effect being that they were not permitted to enter the Union.[xix] As a consequence, other conventions were introduced with terms designed to entice states that objected to, or did not meet, the criteria for membership of Berne into joining the international copyright community.

Safety in Numbers: the Universal Copyright Convention

In the years following World War II, the United Nations Educational, Scientific, and Cultural Organisation (UNESCO) developed a new international convention. It was aimed at widening the scope of international co-operation relating to copyright to attract membership by a broader base of nations (most notably, perhaps, by attracting the membership of the U.S.). Originally adopted in 1952, this was the Universal Copyright Convention (UCC).[xx]

Like the Berne Convention, the UCC provides that Contracting States must afford the same copyright protection to nationals of other Contracting States as to its own residents. Also, as with Berne, the UCC states that a copyright owner need not be granted copyright protection for a period longer than that provided for in either of the copyright owner's home country or the country where the work was first published. However, the UCC does not set out a list of specific minimum rights that must be protected by its members, rather it merely stipulates that Contracting States must provide 'adequate and effective' protection for the rights of copyright owners. Member states are permitted to carve out exceptions from copyright protection, but the only guidance as to the nature of these exceptions given by the UCC is that they must not counteract its spirit. Unlike the Berne Convention, the UCC makes no provision for the protection of moral rights.[xxi]

Talking Trade: the TRIPs Agreements

The Berne Convention and the UCC went some way to ensuring that a certain minimum level of rights were granted on an international level.[xxii] However, the rise of the importance and value of intellectual property rights, together with the increasing ease of copyright piracy, resulted in pressure for measures to be introduced regarding the enforcement of copyright and methods for resolving disputes that extend across borders. The negotiations in Uruguay for the revision of the General Agreement on Tariffs and Trade (GATT) in 1994 resulted in the conclusion of the World Trade Organisation Agreement. The signing of this agreement by the contracting states created the World Trade Organisation (WTO), the members of which adopted and agreed to be bound by the Agreement on Trade Related Aspects of Intellectual Property Rights (TRIPs). The key feature of TRIPs in relation to copyright protection of artistic works is that it compels all members of the WTO to comply with most of the substantive provisions of the Berne Convention.[xxiii]

The major difference between TRIPs and the Berne Convention is that TRIPs is a trade agreement, based on the premise that wrongful trade discrimination may occur if a country provides inadequate protection for copyright works or fails to sufficiently enforce these rights. With this in mind, TRIPs aims to impose the rights set out in Berne to ensure that these rights are sufficiently enforceable and to provide mechanisms for resolving disputes. As far as enforcement is concerned, TRIPs stipulates that all WTO members must ensure the provision of effective and appropriate means for the enforcement of intellectual property rights. This includes the availability of effective remedies to prevent and deter infringement.[xxiv]

The Electronic Age: the WIPO Copyright Treaty

Recent technological developments permit the increasingly easy dissemination of copyright works on a global scale and create complexities in copyright law. The task of addressing these issues was taken on by the World Intellectual Property Organisation (WIPO).[xxv] One of the results of its labours was the WIPO Copyright Treaty (WCT), adopted in 1996.

The WCT grants protection to authors of literary and artistic works. Under the WCT, signatories are to adhere to the terms of the Berne Convention, including its principle of national treatment. The WCT also extends Berne (and reiterates TRIPs) by specifically bringing computer programs and compilations of data under its protection and by providing additional rights to copyright owners in order to meet the challenges posed by technological advances.[xxvi]

The first additional right is the exclusive right of distribution of a work to the public.[xxvii] However, this applies only to tangible works, such as hard copies of works. In addition, this right is exhausted once the author sells or transfers a copy of the work in question. The second additional right is the exclusive right to rent or lend to the public originals or copies of computer programs, cinematographic works, and works embodied in phonograms.[xxviii] The third additional right, is a general right of communication to the public, extending and clarifying the rights in this area protected under the Berne Convention.

In addition, the WCT states that member countries must introduce adequate protection and effective remedies against the unauthorised circumvention of effective technological measures employed by copyright owners to protect the rights granted by the Berne Convention and the WCT. Further, the WCT stipulates that contracting parties must provide adequate and effective protection against interference with rights management information.[xxix]

Horses for Courses: other Conventions and Treaties

The discussion above identifies the major international agreements that impact upon the international treatment of copyright in the field of the visual arts. There are several other treaties and conventions that deal with issues relating to copyrights subsisting in performances, phonograms, wireless broadcasts, and satellite transmitted programme-carrying signals.[xxx] In addition, there are European Directives[xxxi] that address copyright issues arising in EU Member States.

Getting from A to B: Incorporation into Domestic Law

The provisions of conventions and treaties make their way into countries' domestic laws in different ways. The key question is whether a particular country treats the convention or treaty as having direct effect, or whether that country does not recognise the provisions as being binding on its courts until they have been implemented by domestic legislation. The difference is that in some countries residents may be able to claim protection under a convention or treaty as soon as it has been adopted, while residents of other countries cannot claim protection until that country has enacted a law implementing the relevant convention or treaty. For instance, when France enters into a convention or treaty it will usually be considered to form part of France's legal code. On the other hand, English courts do not recognise convention or treaty provisions on their own. Rather, they look to any domestic legislation that has been enacted to give effect to such provisions. There is, of course, a third way: a country may recognise convention or treaty obligations as having direct effect, but also introduce domestic legislation that enforces the obligations of a particular international agreement.[xxxii]

First among Equals: Conflicts of Conventions

When trying to determine the rights of foreign copyright owners in a country's legal system, it is necessary to consider conventions and treaties and any unilateral protection or bilateral arrangements outside the scope of multinational conventions as well as domestic legislation implementing them.

A problem arises because many countries are party to more than one international agreement. Accordingly, when there is a conflict between conventions or treaties, it is necessary to determine which takes precedence. There appears to be an order of precedence of conventions that can be summarised in the following way[xxxiii]:

- The Berne Convention provides that minimum levels of protection must be granted by Member Countries and that members of the Union may only enter into other agreements if they impose more extensive protection and do not conflict with the Berne Convention.
- As TRIPs incorporates many of Berne provisions, including its statement of precedence, it may be said that TRIPs is next in order of precedence after Berne.[xxxiv]
- Next probably comes the UCC, which supersedes all its predecessors except the Berne Convention (it actually states that Berne takes precedence for works originating in another Berne Member State).
- The WCT explicitly states[xxxv] that it satisfies the provision in the Berne Convention that members may enter into international agreements that are compatible with Berne and grant extended protection to copyright owners' use; the WCT also specifically provides that it does not prejudice rights and obligations under other treaties.
- The ranking of other conventions and treaties is debatable, but there may be a tenable argument that the one to be applied is that which grants the copyright owner the greatest protection as this would accord with the spirit of the Berne Convention.

For countries that are members of the European Union (EU) it is also possible that EU law may clash with a convention or treaty. The method of resolving such problems is not entirely clear, but it appears at least arguable that the standard to be applied in cases of conflict is that of the Member State that grants the greatest protection.[xxxvi] Accordingly, it appears likely that EU law will often be in accordance with provisions that are more generous than those in the Berne Convention as Berne Member States have to at least meet the minimum standards of the Berne Convention but are likely to exceed these rather than providing exactly the bare minimum. Where there is a conflict between EU law and the Berne Convention involving two states, only one of which is a member of the EU, Berne prevails.[xxxvii]

Home Advantage: Issues of Jurisdiction

Despite some degree of harmonisation of copyright law throughout the world, it is clear that copyright is given greater protection in some countries than in others. Naturally, a copyright owner involved in a cross-border copyright dispute will wish to take advantage of the laws that provide the most generous protection. To do this, the copyright owner will have to decide in what country the work is protected, where the infringement occurred, and whether the work is protected, under one of the Conventions. Once this has been done and it has been decided that the work is protected, the effect of domestic implementing legislation has to be considered and only then can the principles of copyright law be applied to the facts. The principle of national treatment under the Berne Convention means that where the copyright of a foreign national has been infringed in a Member Country, that Member Country must treat the foreign national in the same way as one of its own nationals. Accordingly, the law of that country can govern the decision as to whether infringement has occurred and, if so, what remedy is available.

There are two issues to look at – the territorial limitations of national copyright acts and the jurisdictional limitations of national courts in applying foreign copyright laws to claims. This analysis is relatively easy to apply in the straightforward situation where, for example, the copyright of a German national is subject to a single infringing act by an Italian national in Italy. The Protecting Country is the country where the infringement occurs.[xxxviii] This is Italy and Italian copyright protection will be granted to the German copyright owner. But there can be more complicated cases of infringement, with many infringing acts occurring in the course of a single transaction and each infringing act occurring in a different country. For example, copyright in a photograph may be held by a French national. The photograph may be published in the Netherlands, where an infringing reproduction taken and distributed to a resident of Italy. That Italian resident may copy the photograph and send that copy to a resident of England who in turn copies and posts the image on a web site, the server for which is in the United States and from which the image is downloaded or printed by a user in Belgium.

In this example, there is a series of acts that constitute separate infringements (e.g. the reproduction in Italy and the publication in England). The French copyright holder may consider claiming for infringement separately with regard to each act, the law of the jurisdiction in which the relevant infringement occurs applying in each case. The problem for the copyright owner is that it would have to bring separate infringement actions against each party involved in each different jurisdiction.[xxxix] This means that the copyright owner would have to go to substantial effort and incur substantial cost, as it would face the prospect of instructing lawyers and initiating legal proceedings in a handful of different countries. Even more complicated scenarios can easily be imagined, for instance, involving publication in South American, Asian, and Pacific countries where the levels of copyright protection are low and the enforcement processes uncertain and inconsistent.

Cai Guo Qiang's work is an example of an alleged infringement occurring in one jurisdiction, the original work having been created in a second jurisdiction and the copyright owners residing in that second jurisdiction. The original work and its authors were Chinese, but the display of the alleged infringement by Cai Guo Qiang took place in Italy. The question is, therefore, which law to apply to any claim – Chinese or Italian? Added to this, the creator of the new work was a resident of the United States and the applicability of U.S. Copyright Law was apparently considered by the copyright owners. Italy had higher levels of copyright protection than China, which would have made a claim more desirable under Italian law. However, to take advantage of Italian law, the original work, *Rent Collection Yard*, had to be protected under copyright law in Italy. China and Italy had no bilateral conventions relating to copyright. However, China and Italy were both signatories to the Berne Convention, so copyright would be available in Italy under the terms of Berne. A possible reason for the copyright owners of *Rent Collection Yard* to consider the applicability of U.S. Copyright Law is due to the high levels of protection it affords to copyright owners.

In any event, for a resident of one country to claim for infringement of a copyright work under the laws of another it is necessary for there to be some link between the work to be protected and the foreign country called on to protect it. The eligibility criteria for a work to be subject to a Protecting Country's system are commonly known as 'connecting factors'. The relevant considerations here include the nationality of the author and the place where the work was first published. In all cases, once the Protecting Country has been identified, it is necessary for at least one of the connecting factors to be present so that the copyright owner is able to take advantage of the protection of that country's laws. However, a full discussion of the connecting factors in China, Italy, and the U.S. is outside the scope of this essay.

Once the applicable law has been identified, the copyright owner must decide where to sue. Conventions address the level of protection to be granted to copyright owners and what law is to apply, but not where such protection can be enforced. This will be governed by the rules of jurisdiction applying to the courts in each country. For instance, in the European Union the Brussels Convention applies.[xl] In the case of Cai Guo Qiang, had Italian copyright law provided redress, it would have been necessary to decide in which country's courts the claim, based on Italian law, should be brought. The infringed work was of Chinese origin; the infringement occurred in Italy; and the artist was a resident in the U.S. There were therefore three states in which it seems that a claim could potentially be brought, and a decision would have to be made as to which is the appropriate territory in which to take action.

The sculptors at the Sichuan Academy who created the original work and therefore owned the copyright in it considered that Cai Guo Qiang 'violated [their] creative rights'.[xli] The problem for the creators was where and how to get redress for what they perceived to be the infringement of their rights. For several reasons, it would have been difficult for the creators to bring an action in China. China became a member of the Universal Copyright and Berne Conventions in 1992, however the nation's minimal levels of protection for intellectual property at the time would have discouraged taking proceedings there. There are also the jurisdictional difficulties: there would have to be a basis for the creators/owners to bring an action in China. Currently there is no provision under Chinese law that provides for extra-territorial jurisdiction over civil actions, such as a breach of copyright, and China has not entered any treaties for the enforcement of Chinese court judgements, though its Criminal Law does have extraterritorial effect against Chinese citizens. Cai could theoretically be prosecuted for copyright infringement in China for infringement of copyright in the statute, however this is highly unlikely. Even if an action could be brought to court in China, and even if the action was successful, there would still be the hurdle of obtaining an order (such as an injunction) that could be enforceable in Italy. On the other hand, a judgement for an injunction to prevent exhibition in Italy could have been immediately enforced because the art work was located in Venice. Thus, on the face of it, bringing an action in Italy would be far more attractive than in China. As a result, any judgement made by a Chinese Civil Court would have to be recognised and enforced under private Italian-International law.

In Italy, the procedure for the recognition and the enforcement of any decision given by a foreign court outside the EU, (such as Chinese or U.S. courts) is governed by Law no. 218/1995 on private international law. This sets out the requirements for the direct recognition of a foreign judgement in Italy. Such recognition of a foreign judgement is automatic (without the need for any formalities) when:

1. the decision was given by a court considered to have jurisdiction according to Italian law;

2. the writ of summons has been served and the action has been instituted or the failure to appear has been declared in compliance with the law of the state of origin and the fundamental rights of defence have not been violated; and .

3. the judgement is final or conclusive (*res judicata*) in the State of origin.

Alternatively, the copyright owners may have sought damages against Cai in the U.S., where he was residing. In the U.S., the enforcement of judgements is a matter of state law. Many States have enacted the Uniform Foreign Country Money-Judgements Recognition Act of 1962, which covers any judgement of a foreign state granting or denying recovery of a sum of money.[xlii] The judgement may be enforced if it is final and conclusive (*res judicata*). Where the Uniform Act does not apply, the enforcement of a foreign judgement is governed by the common law.[xliii] However, a judgement will not be enforced if the foreign court lacked jurisdiction over the defendant, which is to be determined by the principles of the state of origin. A foreign judgement may be impeached on a number of grounds, the most notable being breach of natural justice. A judgement is not impeachable on grounds that the foreign court misapplied either the *lex fori* or some other body of law.[xliv]

The likely result is that it may have been possible, but certainly very expensive and time consuming, for the creators/owners to try to prevent the exhibition of the new work, or seek damages for copyright; by first bringing a civil action in China and then enforcing this in either Italy or the U.S. It is worth considering the question of what the creators/owners would want to achieve from such an action. To prevent the exhibition of the work at the Biennale, they would have to obtain an order against, at least, those responsible for organising the Biennale. To prevent the exhibition being shown anywhere else, they would have to obtain an order against Cai and, for safety's sake, against anyone involved in exhibiting the reproduction. Finally, to obtain damages, the creators/owners could again consider suing the potential defendants referred to above. The problem in each case, however, is that the potential defendants reside in different locations, again raising the spectre of multiple proceedings in different jurisdictions and of the need to serve Cai in the U.S. with the Italian Court's initiating documentation, a measure that increases both the complexity and cost of the action for the claimants.

Fair Use, the Protection of Artistic Works, and Harmonisation of Rights and Defences

As indicated at the start of the last section, when faced with a potentially infringing work in a cross-border copyright dispute, copyright owners will need to consider the jurisdictional issues. In addition, they will also need to consider whether the relevant copyright legislation provides protection for the type of work in question, whether a copyright has expired, whether the act carried out in a foreign country constitutes infringement, and whether any defences are available. Depending on the country, a person who has copied a work may be able to claim 'fair use' of the work and, as such, there is no infringement. On this last point, there are some differences among countries as to what and how much use of a work is deemed fair. For instance, the fair use provisions of the U.S. Copyright Act are less favourable to the copyright owner than in some jurisdictions (such as the U.K. and Australia). By way of illustration, a comparison of Chinese, Italian, and U.S. fair use law in the context of *Rent Collection Courtyard* follows. It illustrates the extent to which countries which are all members of the Berne Convention can have laws that differ.

The Copyright Law of the People's Republic of China was adopted on 7 September 1990 and most recently amended on 27 October 2001. Section 4 of the Copyright Law is entitled 'Restrictions on Rights' and deals with fair use and use by the State. Article 22 provides that the copyright holder's permission is not required, remuneration does not need to be paid and while there must be attribution the copyright holder's rights are not infringed in twelve defined circumstances ranging from using the published work of another for personal study, research or appreciation (paragraph (1)) to copying, painting, photographing or video-filming art works installed or displayed outside in public places (paragraph (10)).

Of the twelve defined circumstances only the two above seem to have even some remote applicability to the circumstances surrounding Cai's reproduction of Rent Collection Yard. The lack of extensive case law in China and relative lack of sophistication of Chinese Copyright Law means that there is limited scope for interpretation. Having said that, it appears unlikely that Cai's reproduction would fall within these exceptions. Accordingly, it is difficult to maintain that the reproduction would not infringe copyright.

Under the Italian Copyright Act (Law no. 633/1941) the reproduction of a fine art work is one of the exclusive rights of the author. Any modification or reproduction, in whole or in part, of the work must be authorised by the author. Article 70 of the Italian Copyright Act is dedicated to the principle of the 'fair use'. Among other things, the reproduction of works is permitted:

1. when it is made for critical purposes, as an expression of idea; and
2. where there is not an unfair, economic and competitive use of the original work.

Accordingly, in the context of the reproduction of *Rent Collection Courtyard*, it is relevant to analyse the purposes as well as the use made of the original work. In the production of fine art works, the use of precedent works from previous cases can be considered and interpreted under the conditions required for 'fair use'. In one interpretation, the exhibition of *Rent Collection Courtyard* at the 48th Venice Biennale could be interpreted as the free and creative recreation and reinterpretation of the original work. It may also be said that Cai's work may amount to a new and original creation, the rationale being that the original work is recognisable by the public as an independent work and the paternity of the original work was not appropriated. The proviso to this is that there is not an unfair economic advantage gained by Cai in connection with the reproduction of the original work.

These interpretations could be criticised on the basis of a stricter application of the Italian Copyright Act (i.e., the exclusive rights of the artist and the inapplicability of the fair use principle). However, at present, there is not any case law in Italy in relation to the fine art sector so it is impossible to draw any conclusions based on precedent.

In the U.S., the fair use defence is governed by section 109 of the Copyright Act 1976. It sets out factors that can be considered in determining whether a use is 'fair'. However, these factors are only meant to be a guide and, as a result, are not exhaustive. They were mostly drawn from U.S. case decided prior to the introduction of the 1976 Act. They are:

1. the purpose and character of the use, including whether such use is of a commercial nature or is for non profit educational purposes;
2. the nature of the copyrighted work;
3. the amount and substantiality of the portion used in relation to the copyrighted work as a whole; and
4. the effect of the use upon the potential market for or value of the copyrighted work.

It is obvious that these factors are only stated in the most general terms; furthermore, the statute does leave courts free to consider additional factors with almost complete discretion. In *Universal Studios Inc v. Sony Corporation of America*,[xlv] the Ninth Circuit Court of Appeal held that, for a use to be considered fair, it must be productive – i.e., the activity must result in the creation of another work of authorship or clearly benefit society in some other way. The requirement for a 'productive use' was rejected by the Supreme Court in this case, although the majority observed that it may be a useful consideration in striking a balance in fair use cases. One way in which the use of a copyright work can be described as fair is where the use can be described as a 'transformation use'. In *Benny v. Loew's Inc.*,[xlvi] the central issue was the proportion of the original work that had been copied and, therefore, the lack of independent work by the defendant. It was stated that:

> The fact that a serious dramatic work is copied practically verbatim, and then presented with actors walking on their hands or with other grotesqueries, does not avoid infringement of the copyright. Counsel have not disclosed a single authority, nor have we been able to find one which lends any support to the proposition that the wholesale copying and publication of copyrighted material can ever be fair use.

Even though the statutory factors are only a guide it is still useful to consider them in relation to the work created by Cai Guo Qiang:

· The purpose and character of the use: it may be possible to argue either that Cai Guo Qiang's work is for a commercial purpose and intended for financial gain and the enhancement of his reputation, or that it is for an educational purpose depending upon certain factors, including the audience who saw the creation of the sculpture, the financial remuneration received, and the future location and purpose of the sculpture.

· The nature of the copyrighted work: arguably this is a case of the appropriation of the creative imaginings of the author, rather than any factual information.

· The amount and substantiality of the portion used: Cai Guo Qiang used a large portion, if not all, of the original work. Courts in the United States have held that the fair use defence is not available where the copying has been excessive. The rationale is that the fair use defence should not be available where there has been complete copying, as this should not be required if the new user 'is truly pursuing a different functional milieu'.[xlvii] Despite this, there is support for the proposition that if the copying has been for a different functional purpose, then even complete copying may come within the fair use defence.[xlviii] As discussed in Section 2, there could be said to be some differences between the two works. The degradation of Cai's work during the Biennale may form the base of an argument that there has been copying for a different functional purpose.

· The effect upon the potential market for or the value of the copyrighted work: arguably the work of Cai Guo Qiang is aimed at a different market from the original work and may be able to be considered a parody. The foundation for the argument that Cai Guo Qiang's work is a parody is the 'transformative use' that is made of the original work. Cai has stated that the actual work ceases to be of such importance and the focus is upon the process of creation and the life of the sculpture. There may however be an analogy with the case of *Benny v. Loew Inc* in that Cai has arguably copied the original work verbatim and merely altered the presentation.

Accordingly, it can be seen that there may be a certain similarity between the law in Italy and the United States on fair use in this case. It is difficult to draw any firm conclusions because Italian law appears less developed than U.S. law. However, despite this, it seems possible that Cai and the Biennale may just be able to avail themselves of these defences if proceedings are instituted in either the U.S. or Italy. In comparison, the doctrine of fair use is not really available to the same degree in China, the result being that the protection that may be granted to the copyright owners under U.S. and Italian laws is limited by the potential availability of the fair use defence. Whereas there is limited availability of the defence in China, there is less extensive or, at least, less sophisticated copyright protection. The copyright owners appear to be left in an unfortunate lacuna.

This problem has to be added to all of the other issues that the copyright owners have to take into consideration, for instance proving ownership, subsistence of copyright, infringement, assessing the law that applies to the particular act of infringement, resolving the complications concerning jurisdiction and determining which parties to sue. These barriers confronting the copyright owners may in part explain their decision not to pursue proceedings against Cai and the Biennale. Given all these difficulties, it is little wonder that few copyright owners apart from the most sophisticated rights holders have the desire or financial ability to protect their rights. It is also unsurprising that contemporary artists find copyright laws to be a straightjacket on creativity and freedom of expression and often tend to ignore its structures.

Harmonisation of world copyright laws is increasing as is the overall level of copyright protection. In the mid 1980s, there were only about 80 members of the Berne Convention. Many countries in Asia, Latin America, South America, Africa and the Middle East failed to protect copyright or failed to enforce their existing copyright laws. By 1 January 1996 there were almost 120 members of the Berne Convention, and as at May 2002 there are 149 members. As mentioned in section 3 of this chapter, substantial forces in driving this increase in the level of protection and in the degree of harmonisation have been the copyright-rich nations, arguably under the influence of the entertainment, publishing, and software industries. The copyright-rich nations of the European Union and particularly the United States have been at the forefront of this movement.

The process was accelerated by the TRIPs Agreement from the 1993 Uruguay Round of GATT and by the WIPO Copyright Treaties. Despite all this activity there are still significant differences in the countries' national copyright laws. Divergence is caused by under-regulation in some countries and by inadequate enforcement in others. Differences also arise between the Anglo-American system, which places more emphasis on economic rights, and the Franco-Continental Europe system, which focuses more on the moral and resale and other authors' rights. For instance, moral rights have not been realistically harmonised across Europe, let alone the rest of the world.

In the same vein, a criticism of the Digital Copyright Directive is that it does not harmonise exceptions to copyright infringement in the European Union. Member States are able to choose their own exceptions within the limits set out in Article 5 of the Directive. It is illustrative to consider the Directive in the context of the lack of harmonisation of copyright law, as even under this Directive the exceptions to the exclusive rights remain out of harmony.

One obvious area where this can present problems is in the distribution of copyright works over the Internet. A problematic example is arts catalogues, where auctioneers or galleries make available catalogues for downloading or distribute them to recipients via e-mail. The auctioneers and galleries need to be made aware that what constitutes an exception to copyright infringement, for instance by way of fair use, in one jurisdiction may not be exempted from infringement in another. The simplest way to avoid an action for breach of copyright is to obtain the copyright holder's consent to the desired use. In the case of auction and gallery catalogues, this should often not cause a problem. The necessary copyright should have passed with the physical possession of the work in question under the original agreement to transfer the work. Where sufficient copyright has not passed, one way to attempt to limit the risk of copyright infringement is to limit the ambit of the distribution. This may often not be a practical solution. One approach is to limit distribution to those countries that have sophisticated, developed copyright laws with broad fair use defences and specifically tailored exemptions to copyright infringement, copyright laws that are not enforced, or little or no copyright laws at all. The rationale is that the first type of country is more likely to have fair use exemptions that will permit such distribution. In the second and third types of country, the risk of any action for infringement is minimal.

Of course, this offers no more than a general rule and, unfortunately, may not prove useful. For example, under U.S. and Italian fair use law the distribution of such catalogues may possibly be permitted. In some countries, there are specific provisions in their copyright laws dealing with this issue. There is a specific provision in the U.K. copyright legislation[xlix] dealing with the advertising of a sale of artistic works which provides that it is not an infringement of copyright in an artistic work to copy it or to issue copies to the public for the purpose of advertising the sale of the work. There are, however, limits placed on subsequent dealings with the copy. Similarly, according to section 58 of the Germany Copyright Act, the representation of copyright protected items in exhibition and auction catalogues is exempted provided that the work at issue is displayed in an exhibition or is for sale at auction.

The position is also similar in France. Article L.122-5 3° (d) of the French Intellectual property Code provides that on the condition the name of the author and the source is clearly indicated, the author may not prevent full or partial reproductions of graphic or plastic art works designed to be published in a catalogue for an auction sale taking place in France. The reproductions must be made for the sole purpose of describing the art works put on sale and displayed to the public shortly before the auction. This exemption applies only for catalogues of auction sales; it does not apply to catalogue issued by galleries or to catalogues related to a sale organised through the Internet. Moreover, in France it should be noted that only 'second-hand' art works may be sold by auctions. Therefore, for example, reproductions of works coming directly from the artist's studio or from an engraver are not allowed to be published in an auction catalogue. In comparison, use of this type is far less likely to be permitted under Chinese copyright law, but any infringement is less likely to be the subject of a successful action.

Conclusion: 2002 and Beyond

Much was made at the time of the Biennale of the importance of appropriation in contemporary art and the ability of a later work to have a meaning different from its source. The New York Times[l] referred to Wang Mingxian, who described the creation of the installation as 'a work of performance art in itself' and who called it 'a projective transformation'. In essence, copyright is a bundle of rights that protects the form that expresses an idea and not the idea itself.[li] Copyright looks to the appropriation and only in limited circumstances considers the rationale for it.[lii] In this sense, there is an argument that copyright does not allow sufficient scope for factors relevant to contemporary art and in this way can act to stifle, rather than encourage, the development of contemporary art and the appropriation it can entail. For example, copyright fails to recognise the rationale for the appropriation and the ability to convey new meanings by the use of old forms in different contexts. Those comments have to be read in the light of the fair use/fair dealing defences to copyright infringement discussed above. They do allow some limited scope for appropriation artists such as Cai Guo Qiang. Artists who use these methods would probably like to see a reduction in the levels of copyright protection to enable them to ply their trade with greater freedom.

Prescience is a difficult art form. But what appears most likely is the ongoing introduction and widespread use of new technology – of which the Broadband Internet is a prime example – that will increase the opportunities for the legitimate and illegitimate appropriation and distribution of copyrighted works throughout the world. The complications introduced by divergent copyright laws and treaties pose as barriers to the enforcement of copyright protection. What is needed is effective and cost efficient enforcement mechanisms, the kind that can only be achieved by supranational solutions to these cross-jurisdictional problems. The possibility that different territories will introduce new and divergent laws to cater for copyright issues arising from evolving technology must be avoided to avoid further disparity.[liii]

As copyright works are distributed with increasing ease and better quality of reproduction, and as the value of intellectual property appreciates, there will be a growing call from the copyright industries in developed nations to allow national laws to give way to international standardisation of copyright protection. This is unlikely to be in the interests of less-developed nations that have a scarcity of copyright material. It is also unlikely to be in the interests of appropriation artists who face the prospect of increased copyright protection for the very materials they wish to appropriate.

i   This can be attributed in part to the Chinese desire to join the World Trade Organisation.

ii   Britta Erickson, www.chinese-art.com.

iii   Huang Du, as quoted by Yang Yingshi at www.china-gallery.com.

iv   Reference: Yang Yingshi at www.china-gallery.com

v   For additional detail refer to the report at:
www.chineseart.com/art.com/Contemporary/volume3issuef/press.htm.

vi   *Los Angeles Times*, July 18, 1999.

vii   *The New York Times*, August 17, 2000.

viii   www.arthrob.co.za.

ix   www.chinese-art.com

x   *The New York Times*, August 17, 2000.

xi   Britta Erickson.

xii   Most notably the U.S.

xiii   For example, countries in Asia, including mainland China.

xiv   In addition, each convention was shaped by its own individual aims.
These are discussed later in this essay in the context of each convention.

xv   Paris Act and Interpretative Declaration, 4 May 1896; Berlin Act, 13 November 1908;
Berne Additional Protocol, 20 March 1914; Rome Act, 2 June 1928; Brussels Act
26 June 1948; Stockholm Act, 14 July 1967; Paris Act, 24 July 1971.

xvi   Including Albania, Argentina, Australia, the Bahamas, Bahrain, Belarus, Cameroon, China,
Denmark, Egypt, Greece, Hungary, Iceland, Indonesia, Korea, Malaysia, Mexico,
New Zealand, Pakistan, Sweden, Thailand, Turkey, the Ukraine and Zambia.
See www.wipo.org/members/index.html.

xvii   There are exceptions available to countries that do not want to comply with or implement
the full rigour of the Berne Convention. Note Article 14 ter (2) that enables countries
to escape the need to provide for the droit de suite (the right of resale).

xviii   Only the rights of paternity and integrity are referred to in the Berne Convention. The right
of publication is a feature of some countries' domestic legislation, as is the right to withdraw
a work from publication on the grounds of change of opinion (the right of retraction).
The Berne Convention provides that the legislation of member countries of the Berne Union
must provide redress for infringement of moral rights. It can be said that 'moral rights'
encompass the rights to decide where and when a work should first be published or divulged
(the right of publication or dissemination); be identified as the author of a work (the right
of paternity or attribution); and object to the distortion, mutilation, alteration, or derogatory
treatment of a work that adversely affects the reputation of the author (the right of integrity).
Most Civil Law countries and some Common Law countries recognise moral rights within
their legislation. However, many Common Law countries do not provide recognition for
moral rights as such, although redress for their infringement can in some cases be based
on other causes of action. These causes of action include: breach of confidence, which
provides an alternative action to the moral right of publication; passing off and unfair
trade practices, legislation for which can provide an alternative action to the moral right
of paternity; and the right to prevent unauthorised amendments which provides an
alternative action to the moral right of integrity.

xix   Berne specified the threshold of membership by dictating that certain rights must
be granted by prospective member states. In this sense Berne could be said to have
been pitched too high, imposing a minimum standard of protection that was not
attainable by developing countries whose copyright laws and commercial markets
were not sufficiently advanced to support such copyright protection.

xx   The objections of the United States to the Berne Convention related to the duration of copy right and to the U.S. requirement of satisfaction with formalities for registration. The UCC states that formalities are not to be a requirement for the protection of copyright. The concern of the United States in this regard was addressed by stipulating that any required formalities in a member state are to be treated as satisfied by a foreign national if the work in question bears the '©' symbol, the author's name, and the year of first publication.

xxi   The UCC succeeded in gaining the support of the United States (in 1976, when the U.S. adopted life of the author plus 50 years as the minimum duration of copyright) and the Soviet Union (in 1973), which had previously rejected Berne. A minimum period for protection (life of the author plus 25 years or 25 years from the date of first publication) is set out by the UCC, but Contracting States are free to extend protection for longer periods.

xxii   Although there were countries who were not members of either Convention, including Botswana, Ethiopia, Hong Kong, Iraq, Korea, Mongolia, Myanmar, Mozambique, Oman, Singapore and Vietnam.

xxiii   The substantive provisions set out the guaranteed rights and the rules on limitations and exceptions. The most notable exception is that concerning moral rights. TRIPs also brings computer programs and data compilations under the protection of Berne and makes provision for the prevention of the unauthorised recording of live audio or visual performances.

xxiv   TRIPs provides for the settlement of inter-country disputes regarding copyright under the system established by the GATT as applied by the Dispute Settlement Understanding. Under this system, disputes are addressed in the first instance by consultation between the Member States concerned. If this does not resolve the dispute, it is heard by a TRIPs panel. The ruling of the panel is final and non-compliance by a Member State may lead to the imposition of trade sanctions. Note that some countries, including the People's Republic of China, Iraq, the Russian Federation, Saudi Arabia, and Vietnam are not members of the WTO and are there fore not subject to these enforcement provisions nor to the need to comply with the other substantive provisions.

xxv   WIPO promotes the protection of intellectual property and the cooperation of all international copyright conventions.

xxvi   Article 10 of TRIPs, which extends the definition of literary works in the Berne Convention to include computer programs and compilations of data.

xxvii   'Works' are literary and artistic works within the meaning of Berne.

xxviii   These terms are as defined under the relevant national laws.

xxix   Information that identifies the work, the author, the copyright owner, or the terms of use of the work, together with codes representing such information, where this is attached to the work. The rationale for protecting rights management information is that it is simply better to enable rights owners to protect their copyright. The reason for this is twofold: to encourage and reward creative expression, and to balance the rights of the author against the rights of the public for access to the work.

xxx   Including: the Rome Convention (1971), which provides protection for performances, phonograms and wireless broadcasts; the Phonograms Convention (1971), which protects phonograms; the Satellites Convention (1974), which protects programme-carrying signals transmitted by satellite; and the WIPO Performances and Phonograms Treaty (1996), which protects phonograms and performances.

xxxi   Including: Council Directive No 92/100/EEC on the rental right and lending right and on rights related to copyright; Council Directive No 93/83EEC on the coordination of rules and rights related to copyright applicable to satellite broadcasting and cable transmission; Council Directive 93/98/EEC harmonising the term of protection of copyright and certain related rights; Directive of the European Parliament and of the Council 96/9/EC on the legal protection of databases; Directive of the European Parliament and the Council of the European Union 2001/29/EC on the harmonisation of aspects of copyright and related rights in the information society.

xxxii   When domestic legislation is enacted to give effect to convention or treaty provisions, there is room for discrepancies between the implementing domestic legislation and the international convention or treaty. Additionally, it is also necessary to consider whether there is any existing domestic legislation that impacts on the convention or treaty or on the implementing legislation.

xxxiii   See the discussion in Gellar & Nimmer, International Copyright Law and Practice, Int-150 to Int-157.

xxxiv   Article 2 of TRIPs states that nothing in Parts I to IV shall derogate from existing obligations under the Paris Convention, the Berne Convention, the Rome Convention, and the Treaty on Intellectual Property Rights in respect of Integrated Circuits.

xxxv   Article 1.

xxxvi   See Geller & Nimmer, International Copyright Law and Practice, Int-157 to Int-159.

xxxvii   This is because the EU Treaty preserves the dominance in such situations of treaties and conventions that, like Berne, predate the EU Treaty. Refer to the Treaty of the European Union, Article M. See also Geller & Nimmer, International Copyright Law and Practice, Int-159.

xxxviii   This does not necessarily refer to the country in which the copyright holder actually sues for infringement, as to which, see below.

xxxix   Note that this does not take the operation of Brussels Convention into account.

xl   The Convention on Jurisdiction and the Enforcement of Judgments in Civil and Commercial Matters, 27 September 1968.

xli   Erik Eckholm, Expatriate Artist Updates Maoist Icon and Angers Old Guard.

xlii   Except taxes, fines or other penalties, or a judgement for support in matrimonial or family matters.

xliii   *Hilton v. Guyot*, 159 U.S.113, (1895).

xliv   See WIPO Forum on Private International Law and Intellectual Property, Geneva, 30 - 31 January 2001: Private International Law and Intellectual Property Rights a Common Law Overview by Prof. Graeme Austin, Faculty of Law, University of Auckland, New Zealand.

xlv   639 F 2d 963 (9th Cir 1981)

xlvi   (1956) 239 F 2d 532

xlvii   Nimmer on Copyright at 13.05 [D] [1] referring to, among other cases, Walt Disney Prods. v. Air Pirates, 581 F.2d 751 (9th Cir. 1978).

xlviii   Ibid referring to Update Art, Inc v. Maariv Israel Newspaper, Inc, 635 F. Supp. 228, 231 (SDNY 1986).

xlix   Copyright, Designs and Patents Act 1988, section 63.

l   17 August, 2000.

li   Ideas as such are not protected by copyright laws. Copyright protects the form in which the ideas are presented. For example, the text of a literary work, the visual aspects of an artistic work, and the aural component of a musical work.

lii For instance, in cases involving fair use.

liii For instance, refer to the Directive 2001/29/EC of the European Parliament and
of the council of 22 May 2001 on the harmonisation of certain aspects of copyright
and related rights in the information society, which makes provision for the
protection of rights management information.

Bibliography

Geller and Nimmer, 'International Copyright Law' and '*Practice*';

Nimmer and Nimmer, '*Nimmer on Copyright*';

Sterling, '*World Copyright Law*';

Stewart, '*International Copyright and Neighbouring Rights*' (2nd edition);

Blakeney, 'The Impact of the TRIPs Agreement in the Asia Pacific Region' [1996]
10 EIPR S44.

Graves' Case and Copyright in Photographs: *Bridgeman v. Corel (USA)* [i]

Simon Stokes

Photography has had a difficult passage to the status of 'art'. The mechanical nature of photography was commented on early in the history of the subject. John Ruskin, himself a pioneer in the use and appreciation of photography, made the following observations in *The Stones of Venice*:

> Art is valuable or otherwise, only as it expresses the personality, activity, and living perception of a good and human soul; that it may express and contain this with little help from execution, and less from science; and that if it have not this, if it show not the vigour, perception, and invention of a mighty human spirit, it is worthless . . .
>
> For . . . a photograph is not a work of art, though it requires certain delicate manipulations of paper and acid, and subtle calculations of time, in order to bring out a good result.[ii]

Photography also poses problems for copyright law: in a sense, every photograph is a 'copy' of something. Unlike drawing, engraving, or painting, the actual recording of the image can require no skill or labour beyond the operation of a 'point and shoot' camera. So the question naturally arises: Can photographs be 'original' in order to qualify for copyright protection? Can the notions of authorship and personal creativity that are so embedded in how copyright treats paintings, drawings, engravings, and sculpture be applied to the 'mechanical' art of photography?

In U.K. law, under the Copyright, Designs, and Patents Act of 1988 (CDPA), section 4, photographs are included within the category of 'artistic works' for copyright protection. This protection dates back to the Fine Arts Copyright Act of 1862. A 'photograph' is defined under the CDPA as 'a recording of light or other radiation on any medium on which an image is produced or from which an image may by any means be produced, and which is not part of a film'.[iii] The Berne Convention also includes 'photographic works to which are assimilated works expressed by a process analogous to photography' within the expression 'literary and artistic works'.[iv]

U.K. law is more generous in its protection of photographs than is typically the case in continental authors' rights (*droit d'auteur*) copyright systems. In the authors' rights systems, the stamp of the author's 'personality' on a work is generally crucial. However, only a low level of originality is required in U.K. law – that some, albeit limited, work or effort has gone into the creation of the work is enough. In the U.K., a photograph of an engraving from a picture, for example, was held to be an 'original' photograph worthy of copyright protection as early as 1869.[v]

The *droit d'auteur* approach to the copyright protection for photographs is reflected in Article 6 of the Copyright and Related Rights Directive (Council Directive 93/98/EEC), which extended the term of copyright protection across the EU to life plus 70 years:[vi]

> Photographs which are original in the sense they are the author's own intellectual creation shall be protected in accordance with Article 1.
> No other criteria shall be applied to determine their eligibility for protection. Member States may provide for the protection of other photographs.

Despite the fact that U.K. law protects the humble snap shot and high art photograph alike, it is still a matter of debate in the copyright law itself as to the standard of originality required for photographs to benefit from copyright protection. In particular, to what extent should photographs that are simply reproductions in two dimensions of three – or two-dimensional artistic works be protected? This question is of special importance to picture publishers, libraries, museums and galleries, which exploit photographs of artistic works for commercial gain or fund-raising purposes. The widespread use of digitised photographs of artistic works on Internet websites also means that the question is of increased importance.

There is surprisingly little U.K. authority on this issue – the leading case, *Graves' Case*,[vii] dates back to 1869. However, recently a U.S. District Court reconsidered *Graves' Case* in a surprising series of decisions in *The Bridgeman Art Library Ltd v. Corel Corporation*[viii] and the High Court in London also considered the matter in the context of photographs of (three dimensional) antiques in July 2000.[ix]

Background

Graves' Case was argued under the Fine Arts Copyright Act, 1862. This Act was the first U.K. statute to accord photographs copyright protection. Section 1 of the Act afforded to the author (being a British subject or resident within the dominions of the Crown) of every original painting, drawing, and photograph *inter alia*, the sole and exclusive right of copying, engraving, reproducing, and multiplying such painting or drawing, and the design thereof, or such photograph and negative thereof, by any means and of any size. In this case, one J.B. Walker was charged with infringing Henry Graves' copyright in a number of paintings and three photographs. Of particular relevance were the photographs that were taken from three engravings made for Graves. The copyright in the engravings belonged exclusively to Graves, and they were the first and only photographs of the subjects. One of the points at issue in the case was whether the photographs were protected by copyright.

The Counsel in support of Graves argued there is a copyright by reason that a photograph from an engraving of a picture is an original photograph, hence by implication protected by the Act. In opposition, it was stated that the photographs were not originals, as they were taken from a work of art. They were mere copies of the engraving, and not original in the sense intended in section 1 of the Act.

The relevant part of Blackburn J's judgement (to which the other two judges agreed) states:

> It has been argued that the word 'original' is to be taken as applying to a photograph. The distinction between an original painting and its copy is well understood, but it is difficult to say what can be meant by an original photograph. All photographs are copies of some object, such as a painting or a statue. And it seems to me that a photograph taken from a picture is an original photograph, in so far as to copy it is an infringement of this statute.[x]

Indeed Blackburn J's judgement hits on the central issue: all photographs are a copy of something. In this sense, they are different from other artistic works. So what is the standard of originality required by English law? The prevailing view is that expressed in the leading copyright text, *Copinger*[xi]:

> Provided that the author can demonstrate that he expended some small degree of time, skill and labour in producing the photograph, (which may be demonstrated by the exercise of judgement as to such matters as the angle from which to take the photograph, the lighting, the correct film speed, what filter to use, etc.) the photograph ought to be entitled to copyright protection, irrespective of its subject matter.

It is also worth noting a case predating *Graves*, that of *Newton v. Cowie and Another*[xii], which concerned the piracy of nine engraved copies of drawings and the reproduction by mechanical means of another artistic work. What copyright protected in an engraving, according to Best CJ, was not the picture from which the engraving was taken – another engraver could copy that equally well; rather the labour of the engraver was protected.[xiii]

> The engraver, although a copyist, produces the resemblance by means very different from the painter or draftsman from whom he copies; means which require great labour and talent . . . The . . . engraver does not claim the monopoly of the use of the picture from which the engraving is made; he says, take the trouble of going to the picture yourself, but do not avail yourself of my labour, who have been to the picture, and have executed the engraving. [xiv]

The view that copyright protects photographs of artistic works that are not in copyright (i.e., in the public domain) had gained general acceptance by those exploiting photograph libraries and using photographs, although the application of *Graves' Case* as authority for establishing the standard of originality to be used today was questioned in the 1995 (second) edition of another major U.K. copyright text, *Laddie*.[xv] So it was with surprise that, at the end of 1998, the Bridgeman Art Library found that a U.S. district court denied copyright protection to their picture library images when they attempted to sue Corel for copyright infringement, the Court citing English law as authority for their decision.

The Bridgeman Case

The plaintiff was the leading British art library founded by Lady Bridgeman, which has a large collection of photographs (both transparencies and digital image files) taken of art works that are out of copyright (i.e., in the public domain) but to which Bridgeman claims copyright in the photographs. Corel is a leading Canadian software house that recently started to market a CD-ROM collection reproducing European master paintings in the U.S., U.K., and Canada, called Professional Photos CD Rom Masters. The images were brought from Off the Wall Images, a company which no longer exists. Bridgeman claimed that Corel had infringed 120 of its images of paintings in the public domain by including these images on its CD-ROM. It was claimed that Corel's digital images must have been copied from the Bridgeman reproductions because no other authorised reproductions of those works existed. Bridgeman sued in the New York federal court, alleging copyright infringement and other claims. Both parties moved for summary judgement.

On 13 November 1998, the Southern District Court of New York granted the defendant's motion for summary judgement, dismissing the plaintiff's copyright infringement claim on the alternative grounds that the allegedly infringed works

– colour transparencies of paintings which themselves are in the public domain – were not original and therefore not permissible subjects of valid copyright and, in any case, were not infringed.[xvi] The Court applied United Kingdom law in determining whether the plaintiff's transparencies were protected by copyright and applied U.S. law to determine if there was infringement. The Court noted, however, that it would have reached the same result under United States law. Additionally, the Court held that even if the photographs were protected by copyright, they could not be infringed by Corel's photographs as the only similarity between them is that 'both are exact reproductions of public domain works of art'. According to the Judge under well-settled U.S. law, where the only similarity between two works relates to 'uncopyrightable' elements, there can be no infringement as a matter of law.

Following the entry of final judgement, the Court, in the words of the Judge, 'was bombarded with additional submissions'. On 23 November 1998, the plaintiff moved for re-argument and reconsideration, arguing that the Court erred on the issue of originality. It asserted that the Court had ignored the U.S. Register of Copyright's issue of a certificate of (copyright) registration for one of the plaintiff's transparencies, *The Laughing Cavalier*, which it took as establishing the subsistence of copyright. Furthermore, the Court had misconstrued British copyright law in that it failed to follow *Graves' Case*. At about the same time, the Court received an unsolicited letter from Professor William Patry, author of a U.S. copyright law treatise, which argued that the Court erred in applying the law of the U.K. to the issue of copyright protection. The plaintiff then moved for an order permitting the filing of an *amicus* brief by one of its associates, The Wallace Collection, to address the United Kingdom law issue. The Court granted leave for the submission of the *amicus* brief and invited the parties to respond to Professor Patry's letter. Accordingly, the case was re-argued and reconsidered, and a judgement was given by Judge Kaplan on 26 February 1999. At the outset of his second judgement, Judge Kaplan made clear that:

> It is worth noting that the post-judgement flurry was occasioned chiefly by the fact that the plaintiff failed competently to address most of the issues raised by this interesting case prior to the entry of final judgement. In particular, while plaintiff urged the application of U.K. law, it made no serious effort to address the choice of law issue and no effort at all (apart from citing the British copyright act) to bring pertinent U.K. authority to the Court's attention before plaintiff lost the case. Indeed, it did not even cite *Graves' case*, the supposedly controlling authority that the Court is said to have overlooked.

Nevertheless, as the Judge felt the issues were significant beyond the immediate interests of the parties, he was prepared to allow a re-argument and reconsideration of the case.

Choice of Law

The Judge considered Professor Patry's arguments and U.S. law generally, especially in relation to the Copyright Clause of the Constitution[xvii] (which permits Congress to enact legislation protecting only original works, with originality determined in accordance with the meaning of the Copyright Clause) and the Copyright Clause's relation to the Berne Convention, the Universal Copyright Convention, and the U.S. Berne Convention Implementation Act of 1988 (the 'BCIA'). After a technical review of the law relating to treaties such as the Berne Convention and their effect on the protection of foreign copyrights in the USA, the Judge considered it was quite clear that whilst U.S. copyright law (the Copyright Act 1976, as amended by the BCIA), extended certain copyright protection to the holders of copyright in Berne Convention works, the Copyright Act was the exclusive source of that protection. Accordingly, in the case of the photographs in issue, the subsistence of copyright in them was properly a question of U.S. law, which limits such copyright protection to 'original works of authorship'.[xviii]

Originality and Copyright
United States Law

The Court's previous opinion was that the plaintiff's exact photographic copies of public domain art works would not be protected by copyright under United States law because they were not original. In view of the Court's conclusion that U.S. law governs on this issue, the Judge considered it appropriate to give a somewhat fuller statement of the Court's reasoning. Stating that U.S. law has photographs as 'writings' within the meaning of the Copyright Clause of the U.S. Constitution,[xix] the Judge ruled 'there is broad scope for copyright in photographs because 'a very modest expression of personality will constitute sufficient originality'.[xx] Citing a leading U.S. copyright text, *Nimmer*, to the effect that there 'appear to be at least two situations in which a photograph should be denied copyright for lack of originality', the Judge considered directly relevant one 'where a photograph of a photograph or other printed matter is made that amounts to nothing more than slavish copying'.[xxi] The Judge therefore held that *Nimmer* concluded that a slavish photographic copy of a painting would lack originality.

The Judge was also of the view that there was little doubt that many photographs, probably the overwhelming majority, reflected at least the modest amount of originality required for copyright protection. This could include posing the subjects, lighting, angle, selection of film and camera, evoking the desired expression, and almost any other variant involved,[xxii] but the Judge held that 'slavish copying', though without a doubt requiring technical skill and effort, does not qualify.[xxiii] He also referred to the Supreme Court in *Feist*, where 'sweat of the brow' alone was *not* the 'creative spark' which is the *sine qua non* of originality under U.S. copyright law.[xxiv]

The Judge thus found that in this case the plaintiff, by its own admission, had laboured to create 'slavish copies' of public domain works of art. Thus he had no difficulty in finding that, 'while it may be assumed that this required both skill and effort, there was no spark of originality – indeed, the point of the exercise was to reproduce the underlying works with absolute fidelity'. He therefore found that the works were not original and not protected by copyright.

In discussing the plaintiff's technical defence that the U.S. Register of Copyright issued a certificate of registration for one of the plaintiff's transparencies, *The Laughing Cavalier*, and that this demonstrated its photographs were protected by copyright under U.S. law, the Judge countered, saying this argument was misguided. Rather, he said, while the certificate was *prima facie* evidence of the validity of the copyright,[xxv] including the originality of the work, the presumption was not irrebuttable.[xxvi] Here, the Judge was of the view that the facts pertinent to the issue of originality were undisputed. The Court held, as a matter of law, that the plaintiff's works were not original under either U.K. or U.S. law and therefore was not entitled to copyright protection.

United Kingdom Law

Although the Judge concluded that his decision as to the law governing the subsistence of copyright rendered the point moot, it is surprising that he nevertheless felt able to state that the plaintiff's copyright claim would fail even if the governing law were that of the U.K., as opposed to the U.S. According to the Judge, the plaintiff's attack on the Court's previous conclusion – that its colour transparencies were not original and therefore not protected by copyright under U.K. law – depended primarily on its claim that the Court failed to apply *Graves' Case*, the supposedly controlling authority that the plaintiff did not even cite in its opposition to the defendant's motion for summary judgement. In particular, the judgement of Blackburn J quoted above was cited. The plaintiff and the *amicus* in its brief argued that the plaintiff's photographs of public domain paintings were protected by copyright under U.K. law on the clear authority of *Graves' Case*.

The Judge, however, was of the view that the antiquity of *Graves' Case* was overlooked, as well as the subsequent development of the law of originality in the United Kingdom. In particular, one of the leading U.K. copyright texts, the second edition of *Laddie* noted earlier, was cited in detail by the Judge to the effect that originality presupposes the exercise of substantial independent skill, labour, judgement, and so forth. According to *Laddie*, there was room for originality in three respects. First, there can be originality which does not depend on the creation of the scene or object to be photographed – this includes the angle of the shot, the light and shade, the exposure, the effects achieved by means of filters, developing techniques, etc. Second, there may be creation of the scene or subject to be photographed, such as the arrangement or posing of a group. And, third, a person may create a worthwhile photograph by being at the right place at the right time and capturing and recording a scene unlikely to recur.

The Judge then discussed *Laddie*'s questioning of the continued authority of *Graves' Case* under the above analysis. *Laddie* states:

> It is submitted that *Graves' Case* . . . does not decide the contrary, since there may have been special skill or labour in setting up the equipment to get a good photograph, especially with the rather primitive materials available in those days. Although the judgements do not discuss this aspect it may have been self-evident to any contemporary so as not to require any discussion. If this is wrong it is submitted that *Graves' Case* is no longer good law and in that case is to be explained as a decision made before the subject of originality had been fully developed by the courts.[xxvii]

This analysis, according to the Judge, was quite pertinent in this case. Most photographs, according to the Judge, are 'original' in one if not more of the three respects set out in *Laddie* and therefore are protected by copyright. But the plaintiff's difficulty here is that it is seeking protection 'for the exception that proves the rule': photographs of existing two-dimensional articles (in this case works of art), each of which reproduces the article in the photographic medium as precisely as technology permits. As the Judge noted, 'Its transparencies stand in the same relation to the original works of art as a photocopy stands to a page of typescript, a doodle, or a Michelangelo drawing'.

Although the plaintiff argued that the photocopier analogy was inapt because taking a photograph requires greater skill than making a photocopy and the transparencies involved a change in medium, according to Judge Kaplan, 'the argument is as unpersuasive under British as under U.S. law . . . The allegedly greater skill required to make an exact photographic, as opposed to Xerographic or comparable, copy is immaterial'. The Judge then went on to refer to the Privy Council case of *Interlego AG v. Tyco Industries, Inc.*[xxviii], which held that 'Skill, labour, or judgement merely in the process of copying cannot confer originality.'[xxix] This point, according to the Judge, was exactly the same as the lack of protection under U.S. law for a 'slavish copy'. Nor was the change in medium (i.e., from painting to photograph) significant:

> A copy in a new medium is copyrightable only where, as often but not always is the case, the copier makes some identifiable original contribution. In the words of the Privy Council in *Interlego*, 'There must . . . be some element of material alteration or embellishment which suffices to make the totality of the work an original work.[xxx]

Indeed, the Judge considered the plaintiff's expert witness effectively conceded the same point, noting that copyright 'may' subsist in a photograph of a work of art because 'change of medium is likely to amount to a material alteration from the original work, unless the change of medium is so insignificant as not to confer originality'.

The Judge was of the view, as the Court noted in its earlier opinion, that 'it is uncontested that Bridgeman's images are substantially exact reproductions of public domain works, albeit in a different medium'.[xxxi] There was no suggestion that they varied significantly from the underlying works. In consequence, the change of medium was immaterial and they were not original enough to be protected by copyright.

Conclusion

The seriousness of the issues raised in *Bridgeman* caused the U.K. Museums Copyright Group, which assists museums with copyright matters, to both commission an in-depth report on the case and also seek a written opinion from the leading copyright barrister, Jonathan Rayner James Q.C. (one of the authors of *Copinger*). According to the Group, Mr Rayner James has no doubt that U.K. copyright law protects photographs of works of art, citing him as follows:

> As a matter of principle, a photograph of an artistic work can qualify for copyright protection in English law, and that is irrespective of whether . . . the subject of the photographs is more obviously a three dimensional work, such as a sculpture, or is perceived as a two dimensional artistic work, such as a drawing or a painting'.[xxxii]

Bridgeman is not, of course, binding in the U.K. courts. It can also be argued that the picture library images in question, by virtue of the careful photography and lighting involved in order to show artistic works to their best effect (better probably than most gallery visitors would see), in no way compare to a mere photocopy or slavish copy. Nevertheless, Judge Kaplan's careful review of the English authorities in his second decision, in particular the important Privy Council case of *Interlego v. Tyco*, is of considerable interest.

It is at least arguable that the antiquity of *Graves' Case* and the particular facts in issue (the owner of the copyright in the photographs and the engravings was the same person and they were the first and only photographs of these subjects) mean that this case is now less than persuasive. The following comments of Lord Oliver in *Interlego v. Tyco* (cited in part by Judge Kaplan) about what the test of originality should be also seem particularly relevant:

> Originality in the context of literary copyright has been said in several well known cases to depend on the degree of skill, labour, and judgement involved in preparing a compilation . . . the amount of skill, judgement, or labour is likely to be decisive in the case of compilations. To apply that, however, as a universal test of originality in all copyright cases is not only unwarranted by the context in which the observations were made but palpably erroneous. Take the simplest case of artistic copyright, a painting or a photograph. It takes great skill, judgement, and labour to produce a good copy by painting or to produce an enlarged photograph from a positive print, but no one would reasonably contend that the copy painting or enlargement was an 'original' artistic work in which the copier is entitled to claim copyright. Skill, labour or judgement merely in the process of copying cannot confer originality.[xxxiii]

It is therefore submitted that following *Bridgeman*, there is some doubt about the copyright protection of photographs which are themselves simply copies of other artistic works. *Graves' Case* may no longer be good law. Having said that, there are contrary arguments, with these and a recent case now to be considered before reaching a final conclusion.

Bridgeman: the Aftermath

Bridgeman has been criticised by another leading copyright barrister, Kevin Garnett Q.C.[xxxiv] and this has occasioned a debate in a leading U.K. journal, *The European Intellectual Property Review*.[xxxv] Kevin Garnett, Q.C., sees the reasoning in the case as flawed. In particular, he views Lord Oliver's speech in *Interlego* as clearly *obiter* – as not addressing the specific issue – and furthermore, as not taking into account *Graves' Case* or the House of Lords in the later case of *Walter v. Lane*.[xxxvi]

Walter v. Lane concerned literary copyright: the House of Lords held that an independent reporter's copyright subsisted in the verbatim report of a public speech. Now, it is clear that photographs are protected by copyright irrespective of their artistic quality, and the skill of the photographer is often to faithfully reproduce what is in front of the camera. In many ways, according to Garnett, such a skill is analogous to the reporter who faithfully reproduces the spoken words of a speaker, as in *Walter v. Lane*. Mere photocopies are also different in kind from the photographs in *Bridgeman*; photocopying is usually a wholly mechanical process. Although it is a copy of a painting, such a photograph is nevertheless different in character and quality from the painting and therefore is sufficiently different to secure copyright protection, even though the photograph is derived from the painting.

Certainly a consideration of other authorities and the context of *Interlego* can be used to challenge *Bridgeman*. A case similar to, but by no means the same as *Bridgeman, Antiquesportfolio v. Fitch*,[xxxvii] was heard by the High Court in London in July 2000 in an application for summary judgement. This case concerned *inter alia* whether copyright could subsist in photographs of antiques (i.e., of *three dimensional* items as opposed to the photographs of paintings considered in *Bridgeman*). The authorities discussed earlier (namely *Bridgeman, Copinger*, and *Laddie* (second edition) as well as the U.S. text *Nimmer on Copyright*,[xxxviii] but not *Graves' Case*) were all considered by the Judge, Mr Justice Neuberger. He was of the view that the positioning of the three dimensional object in question (unless it was a sphere), the angle at which it was taken, the lighting and focus, and similar matters, could all be matters of aesthetic or even commercial judgement, albeit at a very basic level. In particular in this case, the photographs appeared to have been taken with a view to showing specific aspects and features of the items, such as their colour, the glaze (in the case of pottery), and other details. He also thought a relevant factor may be that the photographer had chosen particular items as either typical or especially fine examples of the artefact in question. Taking all these factors together, he held that the photographs were protected by copyright.

Nevertheless, the Judge expressly did *not* decide whether copyright could subsist in photographs of paintings – this was not a matter he needed to decide. However, he did observe that, as was suggested in *Nimmer on Copyright,* such photographs could well be protected by copyright if the photographer could show he had used some degree of skill and care in taking the photograph – this would be sufficient to make them 'original' for copyright purposes.

In light of *Antiquesportfolio*, it is submitted that in the U.K., the *Bridgeman* photographs would still be likely to benefit from copyright protection despite the uncertainties surrounding the application of *Graves' Case*. It is hard to see how a court could make a distinction between photographs of two and three dimensional items: the labour and skill in aspects of selection, focus, angle, shutter speed, lighting, etc., are common to both sorts of photograph. There may be more choice in how to photograph a three dimensional object in terms of aspect, positioning, and background, but sufficient skill and labour will arguably be involved in photographing a picture as well. The protection of the author's skill and labour from misappropriation remains the fundamental objective of U.K. copyright law. [xxxix]

Whether, of course, it is in the public interest that the photographer or his assigns should acquire a life plus 70 year copyright monopoly in the image is another matter. Museums and galleries will no doubt argue they require such protection to help secure much-needed revenue. They might also argue that the 'fair dealing/fair use' exceptions to copyright law and their reasonable copyright licensing policies mean that any concerns here are unfounded. But with the exception of databases and the difficult area of industrial design, U.K. law (as opposed, say, to Germany) has traditionally not sought a lesser copyright term or more limited *sui generis* rights to protect works of dubious originality or artistic merit. So any U.K. developments along these lines appear unlikely without the European Commission forcing change in this area, which it shows no sign of wishing to do at present. The 1993 Term Directive (93/98/EEC), which extended the duration of copyright protection for original photographs (in the sense that they are the author's own intellectual creation) to life plus 70 years, in effect left Member States free to decide how to protect other photographs of lesser originality. [xl]

i   This chapter is an expanded and revised version of Simon Stokes',
    Art and Copyright (Hart Publishing, Oxford 2001), Chapter 6.
ii John Ruskin, *The Stones of Venice* (fourth edition, George Allen, Orpington, Kent 1886
    (first published 1851-53)) Volume III, Chapter III at paragraph vi; Tim Hilton,
    John Ruskin: The Later Years (Yale University Press, New Haven and London 2000),
    pp.196-198.

iii s4(2).

iv Article 2(1).

v *Graves' Case* (1869) LR 4 QB 715.

vi Previously the term was generally life plus 50 years.

vii (1869) LR 4 QB 715

viii February 26, 1999, U.S. District Court, Southern District Of New York; Lewis A. Kaplan J, 97 Cir.6232 (LAK).

ix *Antiquesportfolio.com plc v. Rodney Fitch and Co Ltd, The Times* 21 July, 2000 (Chancery Division; Neuberger J).

x P. 723.

xi Kevin Garnett Q.C. et al. (eds), *Copinger and Skone James on Copyright*, (fourteenth edition, Sweet & Maxwell, London 1999) ('Copinger') para.3-104. *Antiquesportfolio.com plc v. Rodney Fitch and Co Ltd, The Times* 21 July, 2000.

xii [1827] 4 Bing 234, 130 ER 759

xiii P. 246.

xiv Pp. 245-246.

xv Laddie, Prescott and Vitoria, *The Modern Law of Copyright and Designs* (second edition, Butterworths, London 1995) ('Laddie') 3.56.

xvi *The Bridgeman Art Library, Ltd. v. Corel Corp.*, 25 F.Supp.2d 421 (S.D.N.Y. 1998)

xvii U.S. Const. Art. I,§8, Cl.8.

xviii Copyright Act 1976 (s102(a))

xix *Burrow-Giles Lithographic Co v. Sarony* 111 U.S. 53 (1884).

xx Nimmer §2.08[E][1], Melville B. Nimmer & David Nimmer, *Nimmer on Copyright* (1998) (cited as 'Nimmer'), para.2-130.

xxi Nimmer at 208[E][1] 2-131.

xxii *Rogers v. Koons*, 960 F.2d 301, 307 (2d Cir.), 506 U.S. 934 (1992), and *Leibovitz v. Paramount Pictures Corp.*, 137 F. 3d 109, 116 (2d Cir. 1998).

xxiii *Hearn v. Meyer*, 664 F. Supp 832 (S.D.N.Y. 1987).

xxiv 499 U.S. 340.

xxv s410(c) Copyright Act 1976.

xxvi *Lakedreax v. Taylor*, 932 F.2d 1103, 1108 (5th Cir. 1991).

xxvii at 239 n.3.

xxviii (1988) 3 All E.R. 949, 970 (appeal taken from Hong Kong).

xxix At 971 per Lord Oliver

xxx At 972 (per Lord Oliver)

xxxi 25 F. Supp. 2d, 426.

xxxii Museums Copyright Group Press Release of December 1999. The author is grateful to Emma Williams of the Museums Copyright Group for this information.

xxxiii P. 971.

xxxiv Kevin Garnett, 'Copyright in Photographs' [2000] E.I.P.R., p.229

xxxv From Ronan Deazley, 'Photographing Paintings in the Public Domain: A response to Garnett' [2001] E.I.P.R. 179; Simon Stokes, Letter to the Editor, [2001] E.I.P.R., p.354; Ronan Deazley, Letter to Editor, 'In response to Simon Stokes' [2001] E.I.P.R. p.60

xxxvi [1900] A.C., p.539.

xxxvii *Antiquesportfolio.com plc v. Rodney Fitch and Co Ltd, The Times* 21 July, 2000.

xxxviii At 2.130.

xxxix *Designers Guild v. Russell Williams* [2001] 1 W.L.R. 2416 (House of Lords).

xl Recital 17 and Article 6

Fair Dealing: Section 30(1) of the *Copyright, Designs and Patents Act 1988* and the Case of *Matisse v. Phaidon*

Suzanne Garben and Ruth Hoy

It is a defence to copyright infringement that the use made of a copyright work is, for the purposes of criticism and review, one of the so-called 'fair dealing' defences. This article examines the scope of that defence as it was pleaded in a case brought by the Matisse Estate. The case was recently resolved following undertakings by the publisher, Phaidon Press Limited, not to use the Matisse works without a license and an agreement to pay past royalties, plus interest and legal costs.

The Facts of the Case

The Claimants, Les Heritiers Matisse, are members of the family of Henri Matisse, one of the giants of twentieth-century art, and other beneficiaries of his estate. Matisse's formidable estate includes the copyright in his works, certain of which are included in well known books such as *The 20th Century Art Book*, *The Art Book*, and *Minimum*, published by the Defendant, Phaidon Press Limited. These works, and the works of other artists, were included without permission and without payment of an appropriate licence fee. The Claimants claimed breaches by the Defendant of, *inter alia*, section 16 (copying the works) and section 17 (issu-ing copies of the works to the public) of the Copyright, Designs and Patents Act 1988 (the 'Act').

Phaidon Press Limited did not deny that it had used Matisse's works in these books but, rather, relied on two defences: namely, that the Matisse works had been included in its books for the purpose of criticism and/or review of the works (pursuant to section 30(1) of the Act) and, alternatively, that the Defendant was entitled to use the works because of a prior licence. The licence relied on was granted to a corporate predecessor of the Defendant by Société de la Propriété Artistique et Dessins et Modèles (the Claimants' French copyright agents) in 1977.

The Matisse Estate worked closely with the Design & Artists Copyright Society (DACS) in the U.K., which acts as agent for the Matisse family in respect of the exploitation of its U.K. copyright. DACS also acts as the U.K. agent for the estates of other artists. Each book complained of in the Statement of Claim contained a considerable number of reproductions, not just of Matisse works, but of the works of other artists as well. For example, *The Art Book* and *The 20th Century Artbook* both contain 500 or more reproductions of artists' work. DACS and the Matisse Estate hoped the case would establish a point of principle that the use did not fall within the defence claimed and which would apply equally to the other artists they represent whose works are included in the books. The Defendant, Phaidon Press Limited, has enjoyed a great deal of commercial success from the books, which is borne out by the fact that it has more recently introduced a series of 'mini' editions of some of the books.

The Claim and the Law

The Claimants' asked for an injunction restraining the Defendant from including the Matisse works in its books, an order for delivery up of any books in the Defendant's possession, custody, or control in order that they might be destroyed, and an inquiry as to damages, together with interest and costs. The primary defence relied on by the Defendant was section 30(1) of the Act, which states: 'Fair dealing with a work for the purpose of criticism and review, of that or another work or of a performance of a work, does not infringe any copyright in the work provided that it is accompanied by a sufficient acknowledgment'. It embodies the principle that there will be no breach of copyright where an otherwise infringing act can be said to be 'fair dealing for the purpose of criticism and review'. The test is a two stage test: (1) is the work 'criticism' or 'review' of either the copyright work or another work? And (2) is the use that has been made of the work 'fair'?

There was no issue in this case relating to the fact or sufficiency of an acknowledgement. Each work which had been reproduced was clearly labelled as the work of a particular artist.

'Criticism or Review'

When considering whether an act is for 'criticism' or 'review', judges have consistently had regard to the dictionary definitions of these terms. It is accepted that 'criticism' is the act of passing judgement on the quality of a particular work, whilst 'review' is the resulting critical article or report. In the case of *The 20th Century Artbook*, each page is dedicated to a different twentieth-century artist. Approximately 80 to 90% of each page is taken up with a reproduction of a particular artist's work. In small print at the top of each page are some details about the particular work reproduced. *The Dance* by Matisse is featured in *The 20th Century Artbook*, and at the top of the page it reads:

'Set against a blue and green background, five pink figures dance joy-
ously in a circle. They twist and turn their bodies with feeling as they
lose themselves in the rhythm of the dance. They seem to be moving
so fast that the woman in the centre of the picture in the foreground
has lost her grip on the hand of the figure to her left. The vivid colour
scheme and the expressive freedom of the women are characteristic
of the bold palette and uncompromising hedonism of the Fauves, of
whom Matisse was the leading exponent. 'Fauve' means 'wild beast',
a term which was derogatively applied to Matisse's work by an outraged critic because of his use of wild colour. His fascination with
Near Eastern art and textiles spawned a decorative, exotic style
which often incorporated highly patterned surfaces. Along with
Picasso, Matisse is widely held to be the greatest genius of the twentieth century, his revolutionary use of colour to evoke emotion inspir-
ing subsequent generations of painters.'

The Claimants argued that this text could not fall within the scope of the meaning
of 'criticism and review' for, *inter alia*, the following reasons:

(1) Most of the so-called 'criticism' was merely descriptive of the work (see
by way of example the two sections of the works *The Dance* and *The Dinner Table
(Harmony in Red)*, quoted in this article and which the Claimant would argue
could not be said to be 'passing judgement on the quality of a particular work' (the
dictionary definition of 'criticism'); (2) The text itself is very general, and does not
relate to 'that work', i.e., *The Dance*, or, the Claimants' argued to 'another work'. In
this regard, it is telling that *The Artbook* (another of the books which was the subject of the action), in which a different Matisse work is reproduced (*The Dinner
Table (Harmony in Red)*) along with the purported 'criticism', Matisse's bold use
of colour and the fact that he was known as a 'Fauve' is again referred:

A flurry of primary colours dominates this dazzling painting of the
interior of a room with a woman laying a table. The entire surface is
harmonized into a vibrant, unified pattern of pure colour which has
been skilfully integrated into the structural composition, saturating
the room. The tablecloth merges with the wall, and the forms have
been completely flattened, distorted and simplified. This enhances
the lyrical flow of the ornamental forms and iridescent colours.
Matisse has used colour as a means of expression rather than description and has deliberately flouted the conventional rules of drawing
and perspective. He and his followers were called 'Fauves', or wild

beasts, due to the primitive savagery of their style. Matisse's Fauvist manner spanned the years 1905-8 and his style continued to develop throughout his long career. Colour always played a central role in his work, however, as can be seen in the vibrant paper collages he produced in his last years.

(3) Finally, the book was clearly intended to be a glossy 'coffee table' book, and it was the reproduction of the works of art that would lure customers to purchase a copy of the book, rather than the content of the text. The text was so small and incidental to each page taken as a whole that it could not be the case that it amounted to 'criticism' or 'review' of the work.

'Fair Dealing' and the Concept of 'Fairness'

The concept of 'fairness' applies to the other 'fair dealing' defences to copyright infringement actions, in particular, the 'research and private study' defence (section 29 of the Act) and the use of a work 'for the purpose of reporting current events' (section 30(2) of the Act). It has most famously been considered recently in the case of *Pro Sieben Media AG – v. – Carlton U.K. Television Limited*, in which the Court of Appeal confirmed that the test of fairness is an objective test, in that the views of the person making the copy, whilst important, should not be decisive of the issue. In the early authority of *Hubbard –v.- Vosper*, Lord Denning said that three factors should be considered in determining whether a work was fair: (1) the number and extent of the reproductions; (2) the use made of the reproductions; and (3) the proportion of the work consisting of reproductions compared to the proportion of the work consisting of comment and analysis.

In the Claimants' view, use of the Matisse works in the Defendant's books could not be considered to be fair, particularly when considering these factors. In particular the Claimants relied on the fact that the purported criticism was small and occupied a relatively small section of the page compared to the reproduction itself. It is interesting to note that at the case management conference, the Claimants were given permission to adduce expert evidence from an art industry expert concerning whether the use of the Matisse works was fair, but that it was decided by the Master that whether a work amounted to 'criticism or review' was a matter of fact to be decided by the judge alone, without reference to expert evidence.

The Outcome

The case did not go to trial but settled on terms which included an injunction preventing the Defendant publishing the books in question in the future without a licence. And the payment to the Matisse Estate of a sum representing payment for past royalties together with interest and payment of its legal costs. The issue of whether inclusion of the Matisse works in the Defendant's books amounted to fair dealing with the Matisse works for the purposes of criticism and review did not therefore fall to be decided by a Court. However, it may be considered implicit in the fact that the Defendant accepted that a fair licence fee should be paid for the use of the work, and that the Defendant did not believe that the section 30(1) defence would be successful.

The settlement is obviously good news for the Matisse Estate, as their right to a royalty for use of the Matisse works has been upheld. In addition, it is hoped that it will have wide ranging consequences for other artists whose works have been included in the Defendant's books without payment of licence fees.

First published as 'Coffee Table Art Books-Unfair Dealing?', 2000 Entertainment Law Review, Issue 1, (Sweet & Maxwell).

Copyright, Art and Digitisation: European & U.K. Perspectives [i]

Simon Stokes

The modern law of copyright can be considered to represent a balance between conflicting interests: the author's economic/monopoly rights and the need in a liberal society for access to information. Digital technology poses challenges to this balance. It is also unclear what place moral rights have in the digital environment.

But before announcing the imminent death of copyright it is worth bearing in mind that copyright has grown out of the development of mechanical reproduction technologies: printing, engraving, and so on. Through a process of incremental change, it has adapted in large part to protect the new digital technologies. The U.K. Copyright statute (the Copyright, Designs, and Patents Act 1988 (CDPA)) makes clear, for example, that:

 i copying in relation to a literary, dramatic, musical or artistic work
     means reproducing the work in any material form and this includes
     storing the work in any medium by electronic means;[ii] and

 ii copying in relation to any description of work includes the making
     of copies which are transitory or are incidental to some other use of
     the work.[iii]

Therefore, digitising a copyrighted work and storing the digitised image in a computer memory (whether in hard, permanent form, on hard disk, or in more transitory form in computer random access memory (RAM)) would amount to copying under the CDPA. Nevertheless, there has been a debate about the extent to which copyright properly protects digital works. Also is copyright outdated? Will encryption or technical protection measures now dominate, as without them digital copying is just too easy? This chapter explores the current debate from a European perspective centred on U.K. law.

Copyright in Digitised Works

Is it the case that a separate copyright can subsist in a digitised work, distinct from the copyright in the original work, just as there can be a separate copyright in a photograph of a painting distinct from the copyright in the painting itself?

It is submitted that if the digitised image is taken using a digital camera, then the skill and labour used by the photographer would appear to qualify the digital image as an 'original' photograph for copyright purposes, and therefore it ought to qualify for copyright protection. This is clearly no different than using an ordinary camera – the only difference is in the technology of reproduction.[iv]

However, if the digitised image is simply made by scanning a photograph using a digital scanner it is hard to see how the image can itself benefit from copyright protection, as no originality at all is expended in creating the scanned image, which is analogous to a Xerox copy.[v] However, if the scanned image were then to be digitally enhanced or manipulated, this may well qualify the digitised image for separate copyright protection.

An issue here will be whether the enhancement was carried out by a person using, for example, a mouse button and relevant software – in this case, provided that person used sufficient originality (i.e. some independent skill and labour), the copyright in the enhanced image should vest in that person: i.e., we are talking here about a computer-aided or assisted work rather than a computer-generated work. Alternatively, the digital image may have been created automatically without manual intervention and is therefore a computer-generated work, which U.K. copyright law will also protect, as discussed below.

Copyright and Computer-generated Works

Interesting questions arise in the context of computer-generated artworks. It is important, first, to distinguish between 'computer-generated' and 'computer-aided' works. Computer-aided works do not receive special treatment under the CDPA. This would be the case where the work is largely generated by a human author, though a computer is used incidentally in order to facilitate the task. An example would be a book written on a word processor. The computer is a labour-saving tool.

Section 178 of the CDPA defines a computer-generated work as one generated by a computer in circumstances such that there is no human author of it. Provided it is original and satisfies the other relevant criteria for copyright protection discussed earlier, a computer-generated work can benefit from copyright protection. However, the interesting question is who the author of the work for copyright purposes is – section 9(3) of the CDPA provides that in the case of a computer-generated work, the author shall be taken to be 'the person by whom the arrangements necessary for the creation of the work are undertaken.' It is a point of debate as to what precisely is meant by the ambiguous words 'the person by whom the arrangements necessary for the creation of the work are undertaken'.

It is certainly not clear how any conflicting claims between programmers, data providers, and computer operators can be resolved. In a decision under the predecessor to the 1988 Act, *Express Newspapers plc v. Liverpool Daily Post & Echo plc*,[vi] the court ruled that the author of grids of letters produced with the aid of a computer for use in prize draws was the programmer who wrote the relevant software. Contrary arguments were rejected by Whitford J, who said:

> The computer was no more than a tool. It is as unrealistic (to suggest that the programmer was not the author) as it would be to suggest that, if you write your work with a pen, it is the pen which is the author of the work rather than the person who drives the pen.

In *Express Newspapers* the nexus between one person and the finished work was close, as the programmer was also the person who ran the program and checked the results. If the nexus is less close, disputes are likely to arise where a number of competing individuals claim to have 'made arrangements necessary for the creation of the work'.

Transitory copying and the Internet

When a copyright work, let us say a photograph of a painting ('Work'), is scanned into computer memory using a digital scanner, the Work will be copied, and if the Work is in copyright, this is likely to amount to an infringement.[vii] Once it is in electronic form, numerous further copies of the Work can be made, for example onto a floppy or hard disk, which would also infringe copyright under the CDPA. Also, transitory copies of the work will be made – for example, as the work is viewed on-screen a copy of it will be made in the computer RAM memory – both this copy and perhaps the on-screen 'copy' will infringe copyright. Furthermore, if the electronic copy of the Work is loaded onto a computer server (itself an act of copying) that is then accessible on the world wide web, a person browsing the web would download a copy of the work onto that person's computer, making yet another copy. Indeed, as one author has succinctly put it: 'the Internet works by copying'.[viii]

The Internet is a global computer network which allows computers worldwide to talk to each other. The viewer's ('browser's') computer transmits a request to the server computer holding the website which is being browsed to forward a copy of some particular material that it is storing. This material is not passed directly to the browser's computer. It is broken into packets, each with an address, and sent across the Internet. It is then passed from one computer on the Internet to another, all of which could be said to make a copy, until all the packets are received at the browser's computer. (Figure 1 illustrates this in greater detail.)

Figure 1.

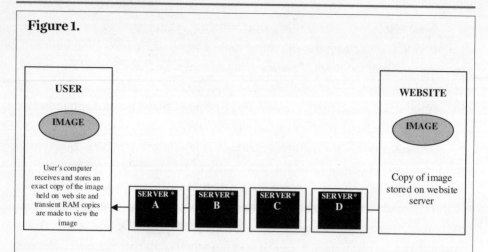

How the Internet works: the route of an image downloaded from a website †

* The image is broken down into small packets of information (digital data), and this data is passed along a chain of servers and networks to the user (multiple transitory copies are made in the process).

† Note: this diagram has been simplified for the purposes of clarity. In practice, when messages are sent via an Internet network, they are broken into individual packets of bits that are sent separately. All the packets will not follow the same linear path to the user; each packet is likely to take a different path, although some of the same servers may be used. (This figure is taken from Simon Stokes, 'The Internet and Copying: Copyright Principles Challenged,' *Electronic Business Law*, June 1999 (courtesy of Butterworths Tolley)).

Thus the exploitation of works in digital form is likely to involve the generation of a number of potentially infringing copies. Copying may also take place in several countries, for example, if the server in question is located in Country Y and the person browsing is in Country X. In practice, provided the digital copy of the work is lawfully made available for browsing, those browsing ought to benefit from an implied licence – i.e. the law will imply a licence from the circumstances. But query the scope of this licence. Also if the copyright laws of X and Y differ, this may lead to a different degree of protection between countries.

Caching

A cache is a computer (generally a server) which holds copies of information (e.g., the most popular pages on the world wide web) so that users do not have to return to the original server. In general terms, cached material can be stored in three ways: at a geographically closer site; on a more powerful computer; and on a computer with a less congested path to the user.

Typically internet service providers (ISPs) store ('cache') frequently-accessed web pages onto their own servers to speed up users' connection times. A cache is also created by web browsers (such as Microsoft's Internet Explorer software), which can create a cache on the hard disk of the user's computer in addition to the transient RAM copies created whilst browsing. This means that users have easier and quicker access to particular websites. Thus caching can occur both on the user's computer and at server level (so-called 'proxy caching').

Caching clearly involves copying a substantial part of a copyright work and (assuming the work is protected by copyright) would appear to require a licence from the copyright owner to avoid a claim of infringement. Although convenient for users, caching is by no means necessary and therefore it can be argued that no licence will be implied from the circumstances. But regardless of its legal status, caching facilitates the copying of entire websites, throwing up obvious copyright issues. The cache site may not be updated as frequently as the original site, and infringing information may have been removed from the original site but not the cache, rendering the website owner and/or the person operating the cache still potentially liable for any infringement actions.

Linking and Framing

Hypertext links enable a website browser to jump from one website to another, facilitating the accessing of related information. Viewers are often unaware that having clicked onto a particular word or phrase (usually highlighted and underlined) that they have accessed another website. Cases have highlighted that when providing hypertext links, care must be taken to prevent the copying of protected materials from another's website without a licence.[ix]

There is still much debate about the extent to which the use of hypertext links requires the consent of the person whose site is being linked and/or of the copyright owner. This is especially true where such linking is defamatory, harmful to that person's reputation, – misleading (e.g. by 'framing' someone else's content so that it appears on-screen as your own, though in fact it is from a hypertext linked site with no connection to your site), or facilitates copying in circumstances such that a licence permitting such copying cannot be implied from the copyright owner.

Liability of ISPs and Others

Internet service providers may charge subscribers for the right to access the Internet, for the use of their bulletin boards, and for the rental of pages on their server on which they host content on behalf of third parties: they are intermediaries in the sense they do not themselves determine what appears on the websites they host. A much debated question is whether an ISP can be held liable for copyright infringement occurring on its site and, if so, what (if any) knowledge of, or participation in, the infringement must the ISP have to be liable?

So far the U.K. courts have not given detailed consideration to an ISP's liability for copyright infringement, though the defamation case of *Godfrey v. Demon Internet Ltd*[x] provides food for thought here. Whilst defamation law is clearly different from copyright, once Demon Internet knew of the defamatory posting on a news group Demon Internet carried, they could not avail themselves of a defence that they were innocently hosting defamatory content.[xi] It certainly seems unfair that an ISP could be liable for copyright infringement without knowledge that the content it was hosting was infringing (whether actual knowledge or 'constructive' knowledge, i.e. implied from the circumstances).

Various other intermediaries are involved in facilitating the transmission of content over the Internet: telecommunications operators may provide the backbone/pipe (in this case they may be said to be acting as a 'mere conduit') and may (or others may) provide the intermediate servers and proxy caches. It is debatable to what extent such activities may infringe copyright. ISPs and other intermediaries are concerned that their activities may be held to infringe copyright and such persons (including the Internet Service Providers' Association in the U.K.) have been vociferous in seeking to ensure that copyright law does not impose liability on them unfairly. As discussed later in this chapter, there have been European initiatives in this area.

Transmission Right

A current issue regarding the Internet is to what extent 'transmissions' via the Internet are protected by copyright. When a person browses a website, as discussed above, instructions sent from the browser's computer will arrive at the computer (server) which is the physical location of the website and will set in motion the transmission of the relevant text or image in digitised packets over the Internet. These packets are received by the browser's computer and are then converted into on-screen images. Such 'on-demand', interactive, access to copyright material is considered by some to represent a challenge to existing copyright laws.

In the U.K., at least, for the act of transmission to potentially infringe copyright, the transmission would have to amount to either a broadcast (which it clearly is not) or a cable programme service. However, the interactive nature of the Internet would appear to rule out cable programme protection, though in certain cases such protection might apply.[xii]

International concerns about the level of protection for on-line transmissions were addressed in the 1996 WIPO Copyright Treaty [xiii] and in the EC Copyright Directive ('Digital Copyright Directive') of 22 May 2001, discussed below. The WIPO Treaty provides for a new right of communication to the public for authors of literary and artistic works, who shall:

> enjoy the exclusive right of authorising any communication to the public of their works, by wire or wireless means, including the making available to the public of their works in such a way that members of the public may access these works from a place and at a time individually chosen by them.[xiv]

Once implemented, this 'communication to the public right' will give artists (and other rights holders) clear control over the use made of digitised images of their works over the Internet. Museums and others who wish to make use of the Internet will need to bear this right in mind when exploiting images of artworks in their collections.

Publication Right

Publication right (which protects unpublished works no longer in copyright) applies just as much to the electronic publication of a work (e.g., by putting a copy on a CD-ROM issued to the public or by putting a digitised copy on a website and making it available by means of an electronic retrieval system) as it does to more traditional publishing. Furthermore, it can be infringed in an analogous manner to copyright, and this includes making electronic copies. This right cannot therefore be ignored in the digital environment.

Database Right

A right analogous to copyright is the database right, which was introduced on 1 January 1998 by the Copyright and Rights in Databases Regulations 1997 ('Regulations').[xv] The Regulations also attempt to harmonise what copyright protection applies to 'databases' following an earlier EC Directive. A database is defined to mean 'a collection of independent works, data or other materials which: (a) are arranged in a systematic or methodical way, and (b) are individually accessible by electronic or other means.'

The Regulations provide that a database can be protected by database right from the unfair extraction of its contents, regardless of whether the individual contents (text, images, moving pictures, etc.) are themselves protected by copyright. This is an issue in particular for collections of pure data (whether or not in electronic form) which are not selected or arranged in an original manner (for example, a telephone directory). Given the definition of 'database', the Regulations potentially apply to CD-ROMs, digital video discs (DVDs), and other collections of text, images, websites, etc. They therefore strengthen the protection afforded to those who produce and compile CD-ROMs, DVDs, etc., as opposed to those (such as artists, museums, and galleries) who may own the copyright in their content.

Implications of Moral Rights for the Digital Environment

The moral rights of paternity and integrity do not apply to computer programs or computer-generated works, though surprisingly the right to object to false attribution could theoretically apply to computer programs or computer-generated works. However, moral rights can still be relevant to the Internet. It is clear that making digital copies of a work of art ('Work') available on a server for public access over the Internet does amount to 'publication': s175(1)(b) of the CDPA makes clear that publication includes making a work 'available to the public by means of an electronic retrieval system.' And, as the Internet is one enormous electronic retrieval system, it can be argued that putting a copy of the Work on a website can also amount to commercial publication. It could also be argued that showing a copy of the Work on a website is tantamount to exhibiting the copy of the Work in public. Thus moral rights could be infringed by making a digitised copy of the Work available for browsing on a server over the Internet as the following examples illustrate:

(a) A digitised copy of a Work in which the right of paternity has been asserted is put on a server available for browsing over the Internet. The artist is not identified in relation to the image made available over the Internet: *prima facie*, this would be an infringement of the artist's right of paternity. Also, as discussed earlier, there would be an issue regarding copyright infringement as well.

(b) The digitised copy referred to (a) is manipulated electronically, for example, the colour tones are altered, and this may amount to derogatory treatment.[xvi] Indeed, in the context of authors' rights systems of moral rights protection, it has been discussed whether simply digitising a work could infringe the 'right of respect' under French law.[xvii]

(c) A derogatory hypertext link is placed on one website linking to an image of an artistic work on another website: could this be derogatory treatment? Moral rights laws vary substantially in scope from state to state in particular as to who possesses such rights and their scope. This has led to arguments that the global nature of the Internet requires a harmonisation of moral rights laws.[xviii]

But it has also been argued that the very notion of moral rights is under threat from digitisation. The possibility of both perfect and distorted copies seems to fly in the face of the Romantic 'eighteenth-century idea of a work as a perfect, static, and self-contained unit, linked to the author as a projection of his personality.'[xix] On the other hand, the 'strong' inalienable nature of moral rights (especially in authors' rights systems) means that an aggressive assertion of moral rights could stifle the exploitation of artistic and other copyrighted works on the Internet. This has led to calls for a more flexible moral rights system internationally together with collective schemes for moral rights management.[xx]

Copyright Legislation and the Digital Future

Legislative activity in this area has tended to address two issues:

(a) The implementation of the World Intellectual Property Organisation (WIPO) Treaties of 1996, which deal with the challenges of copyright and digitisation generally and which prompts us to ask, does existing copyright law adequately protect authors and others involved in exploiting copyright works over the internet?

(b) Clarifying the liability of ISPs and other intermediaries. In Europe two main pieces of legislation are particularly relevant: the Electronic Commerce Directive, dealing, among other things, with the liability of intermediaries; and the Digital Copyright Directive, which implements the WIPO Treaties and follows on from the 1995 EU Copyright Green Paper. The U.S. is already ahead of Europe in this area, with the enactment in 1998 of the Digital Millennium Copyright Act that deals with the implementation of the WIPO Treaties and includes the liability of intermediaries.

Digital Copyright Directive

The main copyright issues addressed by the Digital Copyright Directive (the 'Copyright and Related Rights in the Information Society Directive') are:

(a) Clarification of the extent to which the reproduction and distribution rights apply in the digital environment including the scope of fair use/fair dealing exceptions.[xxi] The reproduction right (subject to limited exceptions) is that authors shall have the exclusive right to authorise or prohibit 'direct or indirect, temporary or permanent reproduction by any means and in any form in whole or in part ... of their works.'[xxii] However, temporary acts of reproduction that are transient or incidental and an integral and essential part of a technological process to enable transmission in a network (but without independent economic significance themselves) are expressly excepted from copyright protection. Hence, the activities of internet intermediaries may not necessarily infringe copyright.[xxiii]

(b) A new right of communication to the public (as part of an on-demand service on the Internet) is to be added to the rights of authors, reflecting the discussion above on the need for a 'transmission right' for the Internet:

> Member states shall provide authors with the exclusive right to authorise or prohibit any communication to the public of their works, by wire or wireless means, including the making available to the public of their works in such a way that members of the public may access them from a place and at a time individually chosen by them.[xxiv]

(c) Legal protection of anti-copying and rights management systems.[xxv]

Electronic Commerce Directive [xxvi]

Among other things, this Directive clarifies that an intermediary such as an ISP would not be liable for acting as a 'mere conduit', 'caching', or 'hosting', nor is it under a general obligation to monitor information it transmits or stores. The U.K. was required to implement the Electronic Commerce Directive before 17 January 2002, while the Digital Copyright Directive had to be implemented before 22 December 2002.

Technical Protection Measures, Rights Management, and Copyright Alternatives

Rights owners have been lobbying both for stronger copyright protection and the power to take effective legal steps against those who try to circumvent the use of anti-copying technologies (such as encryption) and rights management information (such as copyright notices and digital watermarks). The Digital Millennium Copyright Act 1998 in the USA and the new EC (digital) Copyright Directive of May 2001 are among the outcomes of this lobbying.

In addition, rights owners and consultants are promoting the use of digital content management systems, (voluntary) copyright registration schemes for digital works, and the use of digital technology to scour the web for infringing images. Collective schemes for clearing digital rights are also under development, as is the related technology of 'micro-payments' for the use of digital content.

Artists have also been looking to the Open Source software movement as a possible model for dealing with digital rights. A 'Free Art Licence' similar to the Open Source public licences used for open source software has been developed (www.artlibre.org). This recognises both the communal nature of much digital art but also seeks to ensure the originators of the work are acknowledged.

Conclusion

Initiatives such as the Digital Copyright Directive have substantially strengthened the hand of rights owners to prevent digital piracy. But so far the European Commission has not sought to harmonise moral rights protection across Europe, whether with the digital environment in mind or otherwise. This is regrettable as far as artists are concerned.

It can also be questioned how far the fair use/fair dealing exceptions to copyright will survive in a world of technical protection measures. The Digital Copyright Directive does not harmonise these exceptions, though Member States may permit some or all of those exceptions expressly listed in the Directive to apply in the digital environment. It is as yet unclear to what extent the Directive permits any fair use/fair dealing exceptions under national law to survive attempts to negate these exceptions by contract (e.g., website terms excluding any fair use rights) or technology, such as encryption. Certainly the European Commission was not seeking to foreclose the public domain. How Member States such as the U.K. implement the Directive will therefore be crucial.

i   For a further discussion of art and digitisation, see Simon Stokes, *Art, Digitisation, and Copyright: Some Current Issues* (1998) ARTL 361, and Simon Stokes, *Art and Copyright* (Hart Publishing: Oxford, 2001), upon which part of this article is based. The author also looks in detail at the current digitisation and copyright debate in his recent book *Digital Copyright: Law and Practice* (Butterworths: London, 2002).

ii   S.17(2) CDPA.

iii   S.17(6) CDPA.

iv   *Antiquesportfolio.com v. Fitch* (2001) FSR, 345.

v   *The Reject Shop v. Manners* (1995) FSR, 870.

vi   (1985) 1 WLR, 1089.

vii   S.16 CDPA.

viii   Clive Gringras, *The Laws of the Internet* (Butterworths: London, 1997) p.163.

ix   *Shetland Times v. Wills* (1997) FSR, 604.

x   (1999) 4 All ER, 342.

xi   Section 1, Defamation Act, 1996.

xii   *Shetland Times v. Wills* (1997) FSR, 604.

xiii   Adopted by Diplomatic Conference on 20 December 1996.

xiv   Article 8 (Right of Communication to the Public).

xv   SI. 1997/3032.

xvi   *Houston (Angelica) v. Turner Entertainment* (1992) ECC 334.

xvii   A. Francon, 'Protection of Artists' Moral Rights on the Internet' in Poullaud-Dulian (ed.), *The Internet and Authors' Rights* (Sweet & Maxwell: London, 1999).

xviii   Paul Torremans, 'Moral Rights in the Digital Age,' Stamatoudi and Torremans (eds), *Copyright in the New Digital Environment* (Sweet & Maxwell: London, 2000).

xix   Lea, 'Moral Rights and the Internet: Some Thoughts From a Common Law Perspective', Poullaud-Dulian (ed.), *The Internet and Authors' Rights* (Sweet & Maxwell: London, 1999).

xx   Lea, ibid.

xxi   Articles 5 and 6(4). See Directive 2001/29/EC, OJ L167, 22 June 2001, p.10.

xxii   Article 2.

xxiii   Article 5 (1).

xxiv   Article 3.

xxv   Chapter III.

xxvi   Directive 2000/31/EC (2000) OJ L178/1.

Art, Internet, and U.S. Copyright Law

Carla J. Shapreau [i]

'Deep linking', 'metatags', 'hypertext links', 'spiders', and 'thumbnails', describe just a few of the Internet tools encountered in the new and rapidly evolving body of copyright law involving art and the Internet. Courts and legislators struggle as they stretch to apply traditional copyright law to factual scenarios born of the digital revolution never before encountered, or even imaginable. Balancing the benefits of immediate global access to copyrighted works on the Internet against the risk to copyright owners of a loss of control over their copyrighted works is one of the challenges that must be met in the somewhat uncharted territory of the World Wide Web.

In the Internet context, images of digitised visual art may be uploaded, viewed, copied, downloaded, forwarded and otherwise distributed, manipulated, altered, and printed. The sender and receiver are unlimited in volume, age, sex, and ethnicity. The speed is instantaneous. The geographic distribution is global. In 0.12 seconds, an Internet search on www.google.com fetches 55,800,000 hits on the topic of art relating to virtually every sector of the art community, including artists, galleries, and other dealers, auction houses, appraisers, experts in authentication, insurers, theft victims, and related entities maintaining stolen art databases, law enforcement, students, museums, educators, collectors, commercial merchandisers, and more. It has been estimated that 112 million computers were connected to the global information system by the year 2001. [ii]

The collection, digitisation, and licensing of digitised images for some, such as Corbis Inc. and Getty Images Inc. is a nearly $2 billion-a-year industry. The New York Times reports that, 'in the last few years, Corbis and Getty Images have gobbled up nearly all of North America's major collections'.[iii] They currently fulfil more than half of their orders online, delivering licensed images over digital networks. Getty Images believes that 100% of its sales in North America will be on the Internet by mid-2004.[iv] Corbis is said to have a collection of about 70 million photographic and fine arts images, 3 million of which are available online,[v] including the rights to license digital reproductions from the archives of some of the world's most prominent museums as well as the photographic archive of the United Press International, the Bettman Archive, Saba Press, and Sygma. Getty Images has bought more than two dozen collections, including Europe's largest historical assemblage of photographs, the Hulton. In addition, several non-profit entities are engaged in digital image licensing, including the Museum Educational Site Licensing Project, commenced in 1995 by Getty Information Institute and MUSE Educational Media, the Art Museum Image Consortium, a project of the Association of Art Museum Directors, and the Museum Digital Library Collection Inc. These vast archives of digital images controlled both by commercial and non-profit sectors fuel the tremendous growth of electronic publishing and the Internet.

Just as the Statute of Anne, enacted in England in 1710, was the modern worlds first copyright statute, the digital revolution has given rise to the need for a new legal rubric within which to address cyberspace copyright conflict. In the United States, legislators have attempted to meet this challenge by the recent enactment of the Digital Millennium Copyright Act. The judiciary is only in the beginning stages of interpreting and applying this new law, as well as traditional copyright law, in order to resolve copyright disputes in the Internet context. This chapter examines art on the Internet and how U.S. copyright law is being applied to disputes arising in this new digital environment.

What is a Digital Image?

Art protected by copyright law and which appears on the Internet is in digital format. Digitisation of two and three dimensional art forms, as well as audio-visual materials, involves conversion of an image into electronic signals in a series of one and zero digits. The result can be translated into a digital or binary computer code that a computer can read and produce on a screen. This electronic version of the artwork is made up of a set of picture elements called pixels. Each pixel is assigned a tonal value and is represented digitally in binary code.[vi] The pixels, resulting from the work of a scanner or digital camera, are arranged in columns and rows that denote the visual elements of the image, which may then be manipulated by modifying these elements, thus changing the characteristics of the image. The resulting digital files can be stored in a variety of formats that may be accessed on the Internet, and since digitisation is a universal language, digital technology has changed forever the nature and process of reproduction and distribution of art the world over.

Common file formats for visual images include Graphic Interchange Format (GIF) and Joint Photographic Experts Group (JPEG); several other formats are also in use. If you are not a 'Netizen' or a 'Digerati' and you want to know what a 'GIF', 'JPEG', or 'Cookie' is, then you may find the answers to these burning questions in the many glossaries available on the Internet, such as www.pcwebopedio.com, www/matisse.net/files/glossary, or Guides/Internet/Glossary.html.

A Summary of Copyright Basics on the Internet

The original source of copyright law in the U.S. arises from the U.S. constitution, which provides that Congress shall have the power 'To promote the progress of science and useful arts, by securing for limited times to authors and inventors the exclusive right to his/her respective writings and discoveries'.[vii] The goal underlying this provision is to balance the tension between the artist and the public. Artists are granted several exclusive rights for their creative efforts during the term of the copyright, and society, in turn, obtains the unfettered right to access and use the creative contributions only after the expiration of the copyright term, at which time the copyrighted work passes into the public domain.

The Elements of a Copyright

Copyrightable content on the Internet, as with all copyrightable material, subsists in 'Original works of authorship fixed in any tangible medium of expression, now known, or later developed, from which they can be perceived, reproduced, or otherwise communicated, either directly or with the aid of a machine or device'.[viii] Therefore, for art on the Internet to qualify for copyright protection, the art must be original, consist of expression and not ideas, and be fixed in a tangible medium of expression.

A work is 'original' if it has not been copied from another source and possesses some minimal degree of creativity. The U.S. Copyright Act protects expression; it does not, however, protect 'any idea, procedure, process, system, method of operation, concept, or discovery, regardless of the form in which it is described, explained, illustrated, or embodied'.[ix] In the context of the Internet, issues such as functionality, compatibility, industry standardisation, and external constraints may limit the scope of what is due protection under copyright law.[x]

A work is 'fixed' in a tangible medium of expression when its embodiment in a copy (by or under authority of the author) 'is sufficiently permanent or stable to permit it to be perceived, reproduced, or otherwise communicated for a period of more than transitory duration'.[xi] The traditional copyright concept of 'fixed' becomes more complicated when digitised images often appear to be only transitory.[xii]

Under the U.S. Copyright Act of 1976, all works created on or after January 1, 1978 are protected from the moment of creation regardless of whether registration has been obtained or the work has been published with a copyright notice. However, obtaining a registration provides many benefits, including the right to file an infringement action, the possible recovery of attorney's fees, and the right to statutory damages, which may be a significant remedy in the absence of actual damages, or where actual damages are nominal. Although not required, it is certainly prudent to affix a copyright notice to any copyrighted work.

Are Digital Copies worthy of Copyright Protection?

In order to qualify for copyright protection, art must have some level of originality. If a digital image is a mere reproduction of a non-digital work of art, the digital version will, in most instances, not be worthy of copyright protection separate from the work copied. This is so because digitised copies of art generally involve mechanical acts and do not require any human judgement or originality,[xiii] although there is a dearth of legal authority on this issue to date.

Public Domain Art and Digitisation

Digitised versions of art that are in the public domain (art that may be freely copied) cannot be monopolised via copyright law by one who creates a digitised version if that digitised image lacks the requisite degree of originality for copyright protection. *Bridgeman Art Library, Ltd. v. Corel Corp.*,[xiv] provides guidance on the issue of under what circumstances copyright protection may exist for public domain art converted to a new medium. The case involved the issue of whether colour transparencies of paintings in the public domain were entitled to copyright protection. The goal of the photographs was to reproduce the paintings with absolute fidelity.

Because the copyright law in both the U.S. and England require some degree of originality, the court concluded that a slavish photographic copy of a painting lacked the necessary originality to warrant copyright protection under either British or U.S. law. The court pointed out that a change of medium alone will not be sufficient to render the work original and copyrightable. There must be some element of original and material alteration or embellishment. For example, in photography such originality may arise from the angle of a shot, the choice of lighting, exposure, or visual effects derived through the use of filters or developing techniques. The requisite degree of originality might also be created through the artist's creation of a scene or capturing a scene unlikely to reoccur.

Although an individual digitised image may not have the requisite degree of originality to warrant copyright protection, the collection of many such images may warrant copyright protection under U.S. law as a 'compilation' (discussed further below), which is defined as a work 'formed by the collection and assembling of pre-existing materials or of data that are selected, coordinated, or arranged in such a way that the resulting work as a whole constitutes an original work of authorship'.[xv]

An Internet dispute over public domain art that was digitised recently arose involving the Internet gallery, www.vangoghgallery.com, which took David Brooks five years to create. Brooks scanned and digitally reproduced all of Van Gogh's 2,200 paintings, sketches, watercolours, and drawings, posting them on his Web site. Another Internet site, www.about-van-gogh-art.com, which engages in the commercial sale of Van Gogh merchandise, copied all of Brooks' Van Gogh digital images in only two hours and re-posted those images to its Internet site.[xvi] The digitised copies that Brooks created of public domain art would, in all probability, not be worthy of copyright protection under the rationale set forth above in the *Bridgeman* case. However, Brooks may have a viable claim under U.S. law for copyright infringement of his database as a 'compilation' if his selection and arrangement of the images is sufficiently original to warrant copyright protection.

The Copyright Owner's Exclusive Rights

In the U.S., one who owns the copyright in a work of art has the following bundle of exclusive rights: to reproduce the copyrighted work; to prepare 'derivative works' based on the copyrighted work (discussed below); to distribute copies of the copyrighted work to the public by sale or other transfer of ownership, or by rental, lease, or lending; to perform the copyrighted work publicly; and to display the copyrighted work publicly. Any or all of these exclusive rights may be licensed or assigned.

When a copyrighted work is digitised and uploaded to the Internet without the copyright holder's consent, several of the copyright holder's exclusive rights may be violated in the process, such as the right of reproduction, the right to make derivative works (if the work is altered or recast), the right to distribute the work, and the right to publicly display the work.

Copyright Ownership

Initial ownership of a copyright vests in the work's author. If two or more authors create a joint work, the copyright vests in each of the co-authors. To qualify as a joint work, the co-authors must have intended to merge their contributions into one integrated work at the time the contributions were made. A work created by an employee in the course of his or her employment – a work made for hire – generally vests in the employer.

Ownership of the copyright in artwork is distinct from ownership of the material object in which the copyrighted work is embodied under present U.S. copyright law. When one purchases a work of art, one does not automatically obtain the copyright in the art. Under the U.S. Copyright Act of 1976, transfers of ownership in a copyright made on or after January 1, 1978 were henceforth required to be in writing and signed by the transferor in order to be valid and enforceable. The U.S. Copyright Act of 1909 contained similar requirements for the transfer of statutory copyrights. However, prior to enactment of the 1976 Act, some courts applying common law copyright to unpublished works held that the common law copyright flowed with the sale of the material object. The 1976 Act eliminated the need for common law copyright protection, since all copyrightable works were protected under the 1976 Act from the time of creation, regardless of whether those works were registered, published, or bore a copyright notice.

When an artist or other copyright holder enters into a contract with a publisher to have his copyrighted work published in a book, magazine, catalogue, or other hard copy media, unless the digital or electronic publication rights are explicitly included in the agreement to publish, the copyright holder may retain ownership in the copyright of the digitised version and the right to license or assign it.

For example, in *Random House Inc. v. Rosetta Books LLC, et al.*,[xvii] the court held that Random House could not block the Internet start-up Rosetta Books from selling digital files containing the contents of eight novels Random House publishes in print. Rosetta Books signed new contracts with the authors for the rights to republish their novels as electronic books to be bought, downloaded, and read on a screen. Random House filed suit against Rosetta Books for copyright infringement, arguing that the new publications violated its pre-existing contracts to publish the novels 'in book form'. The court held that digital publication constituted a different medium with different features, like the ability to search and annotate the text. 'In this case, the "new use" – the electronic digital signals went over the Internet – is a separate medium from the original use – printed words on paper'.

Categories of Copyrightable Subject Matter

U.S. copyright law provides copyright protection to a non-exclusive list of works, including literary works; musical works, including and accompanying words; dramatic works, including any accompanying music; pantomimes and choreographic works; pictorial, graphic, and sculptural works; motion picture and other audio-visual works; sound recordings; and architectural works.

Compilations

The U.S. Copyright Act protects 'compilations' under section 201(c), such as a digitised database of art. A 'compilation' results from a process of selecting, organising, and arranging previously existing materials of all kinds, regardless of whether the individual items in the material have been or ever could have been subject to copyright.

An example of this would be a museum collection or gallery catalogue of an art show that contains multiple images of different works of art. The catalogue would constitute a 'compilation' separately copyrightable by the party that created it if the selection and arrangement of the art contained in the catalogue is sufficiently original. The copyright in the specific art works, included in the catalogue, continue to belong to the copyright holder in the individual works that are contained in the compilation. The term 'collective work' is defined by copyright law as 'a work, such as a periodical issue, anthology, or encyclopaedia, in which a number of contributions constituting separate and independent works in themselves are assembled into a collective whole'. Collective works are included in the broader category of 'compilations'.

The U.S. Supreme Court recently decided a hotly debated copyright dispute regarding the circumstances under which a copyrighted work lawfully included in a collective work (such as a newspaper, magazine, or book) pursuant to contract, may also be included in a computerised database, in which the work may be viewed, printed, or downloaded standing alone and not in its original context without the consent of, and compensation to, the holder of the copyright. The contracts at issue did not include the authors' specific consent to place their copyrighted works in an electronic database. In June, 2001, the Supreme Court held in *New York Times Co. Inc. v. Tasini* [xviii] that the print publishers New York Times Company, Newsday Inc. and Time Inc. as well as the electronic publishers LEXIS/NEXIS, University Microfilms International, New York Times OnDisc, and General Periodicals OnDisc, had infringed the copyrights of the authors whose works were included in the various electronic databases.

The print and electronic publishers in *Tasini* argued that they had a valid right to electronically reproduce and distribute the articles under the privilege accorded collective work copyright owners under section 201(c) of the U.S. Copyright Act, but the Supreme Court rejected that argument concluding that if there is a demand for a copyright holder's work standing alone, or in a new collection, the Copyright Act allows the copyright holder (here the freelance writer) to benefit from that demand; after authorising initial publication, the author may also sell the copyrighted work to others.[xix]

Derivative Works

The right to create a 'derivative work' is one of the exclusive rights that U.S. law grants to copyright owners. A 'derivative work' is a work based on one or more pre-existing works, in which the pre-existing work is recast, transformed, or adapted.[xx] Only the copyright owner, or one acting with his or her consent, may create a derivative work.

In contrast, art in the public domain may be modified or altered by an artist and the new work may be copyrightable as a derivative work belonging to the artist that created the modifications, if sufficiently original. However, the copyright in such a derivative work only protects the artist's new and original portion of the art and does not protect the underlying public domain elements upon which the derivative work is based. An image of public domain art altered on the Internet in an interactive gallery by one or many artists would be an example of a derivative work if the image derived from the public domain art was sufficiently original.

Copyright Infringement – Direct, Contributory, and Vicarious

Violation of any of the exclusive rights of the copyright owner may constitute copyright infringement. The copyright owner as well as the 'legal or beneficial owner of any exclusive right under copyright',[xxi] which includes exclusive licensees and assignees, has standing to file an infringement action. The test for direct infringement consists of proof of two elements: (1) ownership of a valid copyright and (2) copying by the defendant of an element of the copyrighted work that is original.

Copying may be proved by direct evidence of copying or by circumstantial evidence that (1) the defendant had access to the copyrighted work and (2) that the defendant's work is 'substantially similar' to the plaintiff's copyrighted work. A defendant's intent or knowledge is not itself an element of infringement under the U.S. Copyright Act.

In addition to direct infringement, one may be sued for contributory or vicarious infringement. One who, with knowledge of the infringing activity, induces, causes, or materially contributes to the infringing conduct of another, may be held liable as a contributory infringer. Vicarious liability may arise, even in the absence of an employer-employee relationship, if the party alleged to have vicariously infringed one's copyright has the right and ability to supervise the infringing activity and also has a direct financial interest in such activities.

All three types of infringing conduct were alleged in *A & M Records Inc. et al., v. Napster Inc.*, in which the Ninth Circuit Court of Appeals affirmed the trial court's injunction against Napster's alleged direct, contributory, and vicarious infringement in connection with its Internet system, which enabled online users to locate and download copyrighted sound recordings employing a digital format called MPEG-3. The court, speaking of Napster's alleged contributory infringement, pointed out that 'if a computer system operator learns of specific infringing material available on his system and fails to purge such material from the system, the operator knows of and contributes to direct infringement'.[xxii] The Ninth Circuit also found that Napster's right and ability to control access to its system and exchange of copyrighted material combined with Napster's financial benefit from the availability of infringing files on its system gave rise to a likelihood of liability for vicarious infringement.

The 'Fair Use' Defence

There are many possible defences to a claim of copyright infringement, but one of the most important in the Internet arena is the doctrine of 'fair use', which includes parody. Under this doctrine, copying for the purpose of criticism, comment, news reporting, teaching, scholarship, or research, is a defence to copyright infringement.

In determining whether the use made of a work in a particular case is a fair use, courts consider, among other things, the following four factors: (1) the purpose and character of the use, including whether such use is of a commercial nature or is for non-profit educational purposes; (2) the nature of the copyrighted work; (3) the amount and substantiality of the portion used in relation to the copyrighted work as a whole; and (4) the effect of the use upon the potential market for, or value of, the copyrighted work.

In the Internet environment, issues such as functional requirements, technical compatibility, computer industry standardisation, external constraints, or the need for technical efficiency may give rise to viable fair use arguments. If, for example, the alleged infringing conduct is the only means of gaining access to unprotected aspects of a copyrighted work (ideas, procedures, processes, systems, methods of operation, concepts, and other forms of non-expression) and there is a legitimate functional reason for use of the copyrighted work, a court may find that the infringement is excused under the fair use doctrine.

A fair use Internet dispute recently ruled on by the Ninth Circuit Court of Appeals in *Kelly v. Arriba Soft Corp.*[xxiii] involved an artist's claim that an Internet search engine, which scanned the Internet for images using Web searching tools called 'spiders', infringed his copyrights when the spiders made copies of his photographs from the Internet. The resulting images were displayed in the search engine's listings as reduced 'thumbnail' images without the artist's approval. Although the search engine linked searchers to the Web sites from where the image was originally taken, it also enabled users to 'deep link' directly to the pages containing the retrieved images, allowing them to view and potentially download the artist's full-size image while separating it from both the surrounding content on the original Web page and the artist's copyright notice.

The Ninth Circuit ruled that creation and use of the thumbnails in the search engine was a fair use, noting that 'the thumbnails were much smaller, lower-resolution images that served an entirely different function than Kelly's original images . . . Arriba's search engine functions as a tool to help index and improve access to images on the internet and their related web sites'.[xxiv] However, the court found that the defendant's deep linking was not excused as a fair use, holding that the display of the larger image (defendant's online linking to and framing of plaintiff's images) was a violation of plaintiff's exclusive right under the Copyright Act to publicly display his work [xxv]. In contrast, in *Ticketmaster v. Tickets.com*,[xxvi] the court found hyperlinking to be lawful under the fair use doctrine in order to obtain access to non-protectible facts.

Where can you sue or be sued for Copyright Infringement on the Internet?

The issue of where an injured party may file suit for damage incurred in connection with the Internet is evolving. Generally, conduct occurring outside the U.S. will not qualify for protection under U.S. copyright law. However, when infringement occurs on the Internet, the issue of boundaries becomes blurred when Internet material is accessible to those in the U.S. In such cases, there is a substantial risk that jurisdiction for a copyright infringement lawsuit may be had in the location where infringement occurs.

For example, in *Pavlovich v. DVD Copy Control Association Inc. et al.*,[xxvii] Pavlovich owned and operated a Web site where he posted a computer program that was designed to defeat the copyright owner's encryption-based copy protection system, known as the Content Scramble System, enabling unlicensed DVD playback and copying. Pavlovich, a resident of Texas, claimed that the copyright holder could not obtain personal jurisdiction over him in California merely resulting from access to his Web site in California. The court disagreed and considering a variety of factors held that personal jurisdiction to sue Pavlovich existed in California, stating:

> Instant access provided by the Internet is the functional equivalent of personal presence of the person posting the material on the Web at the place from which the posted material is accessed and appropriated. It is as if the poster is instantaneously present in different places at the same time, and simultaneously delivering his material at those different places. In a sense, therefore, the reach of the Internet is also the reach of the extension of the poster's presence . . . It should not matter whether the delivery system used to inflict the injury is the traditional delivery system of air, land, or sea transportation, or the cutting-edge technological system of cyberspace, satellites, cable, and electro-magnetic waves.[xxviii]

At the time of this book's publication, the appeal of the *Pavlovich* decision was pending before the California Supreme Court.

The Digital Millennium Copyright Act ('DMCA')

International recognition of the enormous need to address current and future developments in the digital era gave rise to a December 1996 conference in which delegates from approximately 150 countries met in Geneva, Switzerland to negotiate the Copyright Treaty and the Performances and Phonograms Treaty under the auspices of the World Intellectual Property Organization (WIPO). In the U.S., compliance with the requirement of the WIPO Copyright Act required implementing legislation, which took form in the U.S. as the Digital Millennium Copyright Act.

Signed by President Clinton on October 28, 1998. The DMCA was enacted both to preserve copyright enforcement on the Internet and to provide immunity to service providers from copyright infringement liability for passive or automatic actions in which infringing conduct occurs through a technological process initiated by a third party without the knowledge of the service provider.

The provisions of the DMCA are complex and most have yet to be interpreted by American courts. The general outlines of the DMCA are as follows:

Protection of Copyright Owners' Rights under the DMCA

To comply with the WIPO Copyright Treaty, the DMCA makes it unlawful to circumvent a technological protection used by copyright owners to effectively control unauthorised access to works protected by U.S. copyright law.[xxix] The DMCA explains in section 1201(a)(3)(A) that to 'circumvent a technological measure' means 'to de-scramble a scrambled work, to decrypt an encrypted work, or otherwise to avoid, bypass, remove, deactivate, or impair a technological measure, without the authority of the copyright owner'.

Section 1201 of the DMCA also makes it unlawful to 'manufacture, import, offer to the public, provide, or otherwise traffic in any technology, product, service, device, component, or part thereof' that is (1) primarily designed or produced for the purpose of circumventing a technological measure that effectively controls access to copyrighted works; (2) that has only a limited commercial purpose or use other than such circumvention, or (3) that is marketed for the intended purpose of circumventing such technological measures that effectively control access to or protect copyrighted works.[xxx] Under section 1202, the DMCA makes it unlawful to provide, distribute, or import false copyright management information or to intentionally alter or remove copyright management information provided by a copyright owner, such as the copyright notice or other information that identifies a work, its owner, and the terms and conditions for use of the copyrighted work.[xxxi]

Statutory damages for violation of sections 1201 and 1202 are significant and criminal penalties including steep fines and prison terms for those who violate sections 1201 or 1202 wilfully and for the purpose of commercial advantage or private financial gain. One of the first criminal prosecutions under the DMCA, *U.S. v. Sklyarov*, was filed in July 2001 in California against the Russian cryptographer, Dimitri Sklyarov, who developed software that allegedly decrypted or circumvented Adobe eBook Reader software by converting encrypted electronic books into unprotected files that could be distributed freely. However, on December 13, 2001 the Justice Department dropped all criminal charges against Sklyarov in exchange for his testimony in the pending case against his former employer, ElcomSoft Co. Ltd.[xxxii]

A useful legal tool that the DMCA has provided to copyright owners is the right to serve a subpoena on an Internet service provider requesting the identification of an alleged infringer. The copyright owner must file with the clerk of any U.S. district court a proposed subpoena, a copy of the written notification of infringement required by section 512(c)(3)(A) (discussed below), and a sworn declaration that the purpose of the subpoena is solely to obtain the identity of an alleged infringer. Armed with this information, a copyright owner has reasonable means to obtain a meaningful remedy against copyright infringement.

DMCA Immunity for Internet Service Providers

The DMCA sets forth a detailed framework in section 512 that provides immunity for Internet service providers for innocent copyright infringement that is promptly corrected upon notice of the infringement. The DMCA contains specific immunity for non-profit educational institutions. The legislative history of the DMCA points out that

> In the ordinary course of their operations service providers must engage in all kinds of acts that expose them to potential copyright infringement liability. For example, service providers must make innumerable electronic copies by simply transmitting information over the Internet. Certain electronic copies are made to speed up the delivery of information to users. Other electronic copies are made in order to host World Wide Web sites. Many service providers engage in directing users to sites in response to inquiries by users or they volunteer sites that users may find attractive. Some of these sites might contain infringing material.[xxxiii]

Who qualifies as an Internet 'Service Provider'?

A service provider is defined broadly in the DMCA to include any provider of 'online services or network access, or the operator of facilities therefore', including any entity providing 'digital online communications, between or among points specified by user, or material of the user's choosing, without modification to the content of the material as sent or received'.[xxxiv]

The DMCA's Safe Harbours

Under the DMCA, Internet service providers (ISP) that control or operate systems or networks, may be immune from liability for copyright infringement in connection with the ISP's intermediate and transient storage of copyrighted materials. Its transmitting, routing, or providing connections for copyrighted works, or its linking users to an online location containing infringing material or activity *if* the ISP has no actual knowledge that material or an activity using material on the system or network is infringing. Or the ISP is not aware of the facts or circumstances from which infringing activity is apparent. There will be no liability if upon obtaining such knowledge or awareness, the ISP acts expeditiously to remove, or disable access to the material; the ISP does not receive financial benefit directly attributable to the infringing activity in a case in which the ISP has the right and ability to control such activity; *and* upon written notification (as described below) the ISP responds promptly to remove or disable access to the copyrighted work being infringed.[xxxv]

In order to qualify for immunity under the DMCA the ISP also must designate an agent to receive notifications of claimed infringement. The ISP also must provide to the U.S. Copyright Office, the name, address, phone number, and electronic mail address of the ISP's agent. The Register of Copyrights is required to maintain a directory of ISP agents which is available to the public for inspection in hard copy or on the Internet.

In order for a notice of copyright infringement to be effective under the DMCA the notice must: (1) be made to the ISP's agent; (2) be a written communication (it may be a physical or electronic signature); and (3) identify the copyrighted work. If multiple copyrighted works are at issue at a single online site, the notice must include a representative list of the copyrighted works [xxxvi]); (4) provide information reasonably sufficient to permit the ISP to locate the allegedly infringing material; (5) provide the complaining party's name, address, telephone number, and if available, an electronic mail address; and (6) contain a statement that the complaining party is giving such notice in a good faith belief that the use of the material is not authorised by the copyright owner, its agent, or the law, that the information in the notification is accurate, made under penalty of perjury, and that the complaining party is authorised to act on behalf of the owner of an exclusive right that is allegedly infringed.[xxxvii]

In order for ISP's to be eligible for immunity under the DMCA, they must both accommodate and not interfere with 'standard technical measures' employed by copyright holders to protect their copyrights. These technical measures must (1) 'have been developed pursuant to a broad consensus of copyright owners and service providers in an open, fair, voluntary, multi-industry standards process'; (2) be 'available to any person on reasonable and non-discriminatory terms'; and (3) 'not impose substantial costs on service providers or substantial burdens on their systems or networks'.[xxxviii]

Tools to protect Art on the Internet

Unauthorised use of copyrighted art on the Internet may be deterred or prevented through a variety of techniques, such as encryption, scrambling, authentication or some measures that require a key provided by a copyright owner in order to obtain access to a copyrighted work, such as a password. Encryption technology can keep artwork from being viewed without payment of a fee or consent to an online contract.

A digital watermark or fingerprint that is embedded directly into a computer image, imperceptible to the human eye but detectable to a computer through analysis, is another tool that may protect a copyright holder from infringement.[xxxix] Digital watermarks may survive multiple generations of copying, modification, printing, scanning, and compression.[xl] Another protective device includes the use of low-resolution images or distortion by additions or suppressions such as sectioning or superimposition of signs or words. More common are on-line notices or contracts that restrict or control downloading, use, reproduction, modification, transmission or display. Breach of such a license agreement may constitute infringement of the copyright, as well as breach of contract, for which remedies such as injunctive relief and/or damages may be available.

Conclusion

Today a 'cookie' is not just something sweet to eat. It is also an electronic tag placed on your computer by Web sites you visit without your knowledge or consent that can generate profiles of your personal information, monitoring what pages you access on the Internet.[xli] As more than one court grappling with application of copyright law to disputes in cyberspace has indicated, 'applying traditional legal principles to the Internet can be troublesome'.[xlii] The digital revolution continues to dramatically transform our world, just as the advent of the printing press in the fifteenth century resulted in a revolution in the free flow of ideas and information to a global public. But as we enter the twenty-first century, some things do not change. Copyright protection against unauthorised copying, modification, distribution, performance, and display of copyrighted works continues to be a core value that courts and legislators struggle to preserve in an effort to foster and protect creative contributions to society.

i   Carla Shapreau is an attorney with the law firm of Gnazzo Thill, P.C., San Francisco, California. Ms. Shapreau specializes in art law, cultural property, and intellectual property litigation and frequently lectures and writes on these topics.

ii   Bruce Lehman, Congressional Testimony, May 21, 1998, 1998 WL 12760310.

iii Laurie J. Flynn, 'Licensing Famous Art, Digitally', May 17, 2001, *New York Times*, at C4.

iv Laurie J. Flynn.

v   Daniel A. Shaw, 'Image is Everything for Digital-Photo Lawyer', *Recorder IP*, 30, Winter 2002.

vi http://coloradodigital.coalliance.org/glossary.html.

vii U.S. Const. art. I, §8, cl. 8.

viii 17 U.S.C. § 102.

ix 17 U.S.C. § 102(b).

x   See e.g., *Apple Computer Inc. v. Microsoft Corp.*, 35 F.3d 1435 (9th Cir. 1994); *cert. denied*, 115 S.Ct. 1176 (1995) (Microsoft windows held not to infringe Apple's operating system because of license agreement and because of a narrow array of alternative means of overlapping or tiling); *Sega Enterprises Ltd. v. Accolade Inc.*, 977 F.2d 1510 (9th Cir. 1992) (reverse engineering which involved copying permitted as 'fair use' because of insufficient alternative means to obtain interoperability); *Sony Computer Entertainment, Inc. v. Connectix Corp.*, 203 F.3d 596 (9th Cir. 2000).

xi 17 U.S.C. section 101.

xii See e.g., *MAI Systems Corp. v. Peak Computer Inc.*, 991 F.2d 511 (9th Cir. 1993), *cert. denied*, 510 U.S. 1033 (1994). The Ninth Circuit found copyright infringement for temporary copying of computer software into random access memory (RAM) by a computer maintenance consultant. The MAI ruling gave rise to the 1998 amendment of section 117 of the Copyright Act, which insulates independent service providers from copyright infringement liability when, in the course of providing maintenance and repairs to their clients' computers, service providers must by necessity make temporary copies of software by virtue of a program loading into the RAM of a computer when the computer hardware is activated. 17 U.S.C., section 117(a)(2)(c).

xiii See e.g., *Greenberg v. National Geographic Society*, 244 F.3d 1267, 1273 fn.14 (11th Cir., 2001), *cert. denied*, 122 S.Ct. 347 (2001).

xiv 36 F. Supp.2d 191 (S.D.N.Y., 1999).

xv 17 U.S.C. section 101.

xvi See Nancy Matsumoto, 'When the Art's Public, Is the Site Fair Game?' (May 17, 2001), *New York Times*.

xvii 150 F.Supp.2d 613 (S.D.N.Y., 2001), *aff'd*, 2002 U.S. App. LEXIS 3673 (2nd Cir., 2002).

xviii 121 S.Ct. 2381, 150 L.Ed.2d 500 (2001).

xix See also *Greenberg v. National Geographic Society*, 244 F.3d 1267 (11th Cir., 2001), *cert denied*, 122 S.Ct. 347 (2001).

xx 17 U.S.C. § 101.

xxi 17 U.S.C. § 501(b).

xxii 239 F.3d 1004, 1021 (9th Cir., 2001).

xxiii 280 F.3d 934 (9th Cir., 2002).

xxiv 280 F.3d 934.

xxv 280 F.3d 934.

xxvi   2000 U.S. Dist. LEXIS 12987 (C.D. Ca., 2000), *aff'd*, 248 F.3d 1173 (9th Cir., 2001) (copying in the process of hyperlinking excused by fair use doctrine since copy made only to facilitate obtaining non-protectible facts). Case can be found at http://pub.bna.com/ptcj/ticketmaster.htm.

xxvii 91 Cal.App.4th 409 (Cal.app., 2001), *petition for review granted En Banc*, 114 Cal.Rptr.2d 611 (2001).

xxviii 91 Cal.App.4th 409.

xxix   17 U.S.C. § 1201(a)(1)(A).

xxx   17 U.S.C. § 1201(a)(2). See also *Universal Studios Inc. et al. v. Corley et al*, 273 F.3d 429 (2nd Cir., 2001) and *Real Networks Inc. v. Streambox Inc.* 200 U.S. Dist. LEXIS 1889 (W.D. Wash., 2000).

xxxi   17 U.S.C. § 1202.

xxxii Jason Hoppin, 'Cracking Down on IP Crime', *The Recorder IP*, 15, Winter 2002.

xxxiii S. Rep.(DMCA), p.8.

xxxiv 17 U.S.C., section 512(k).

xxxv   See e.g., *Als Scan Inc. v. Remarq Communities Inc.*, 239 F.3d 619, 624 (4th Cir., 2001).

xxxvi See e.g., *Als Scan Inc. v. Remarq Communities Inc.*

xxxvii See e.g., *Hendrickson v. eBay Inc.*, 165 F.Supp.2d 1082 (C.D.Cal., 2001); *Costar Group Inc. v. Loopnet Inc.*, 164 F.Supp.2d 688 (D.Md., 2001).

xxxviii 17 U.S.C. Section 512 (i)(B)(2)(A-C).

xxxix See http://www.stanford.edu/~bagene/new_page_2.htm for a discussion of watermarks.

xl   See e.g., Digimarc watermark systems at http://www.digimarc.com.

xli   See http://www.cookiecentral.com.

xlii   *Ebay Inc. v. Bidder's Edge Inc.*, 100 F.Supp.2d 1058 (N.D. Cal., 2000).

Copyright and the Visual Arts: Questions and Answers

Stuart Lockyear

Copyright is an economic right that enables copyright owners to exploit commercially the fruits of their endeavour, principally by granting a monopoly over use of their copyright works. However, this does not always sit easily with the aesthetic or artistic objectives of visual artists. The purpose of this essay is to assist artists and those involved in the visual arts to establish (a) when a work is likely to attract copyright protection; (b) when a work is likely to infringe the copyright of others; and (c) what the consequences are of infringing copyright in artistic works by highlighting the questions which need to be asked.

Is the Work protected by Copyright?

Artistic works are protected by the copyright laws of specific countries or international copyright conventions, which can differ from each other. The applicable law will often depend on the nationality of the artist concerned. Artists should, therefore, always consider whether and how their work qualifies for copyright protection under the law of the country in which they wish to enforce their copyright. We are going to assume here that the artist qualifies for protection under the U.K. copyright law.

Under the 1988 Copyright Designs and Patents Act, which applies to all work created after 1 August 1989, copyright *may* subsist in original artistic works. Any work created prior to this should be considered against the transitional provisions in the 1988 Act, the 1956 Copyright Act, or the 1911 Copyright Act.

Is the Work Original?

Originality relates to the artistic representation in the work, irrespective of whether the work has an artistic 'quality', except in the case of works of artistic craftsmanship (see below). This does not mean a work has to be unique or novel, merely that the creator must have used his or her own skill or labour. In the *Reject Shop Plc v. Manners* case, it was decided that the enlargement of an image by using a photocopier did not involve sufficient skill and labour to confer copyright on the photocopy. This creates real problems in the area of so called 'appropriation art'. Does the (often careful and meticulous) copying of another visual image by an artist mean that there is no copyright in the 'copy'? I would submit that the answer is no: provided sufficient skill and labour is used in the artistic creation, there is no reason why the resulting work should be lacking in originality so as to disqualify it from copyright protection.

Is it an Artistic Work?

Copyright will protect original artistic works which are graphic works (i.e., paintings, drawings, diagrams, engravings, etchings, lithographs, or similar works), photographs, sculptures, or collages (irrespective of artistic quality), works of architecture (a building or a model of a building), and works of artistic craftsmanship. Films are not necessarily treated as artistic works under the 1988 Act but rather have their own category of film copyright, though they may also be classified as artistic works or as dramatic works.

Unless a work of visual art falls into one of these categories, it may not enjoy copyright protection. For example, it is likely that so called 'readymades', the most infamous of which is perhaps Marcel Duchamp's *Fountain*, do not enjoy copyright protection if they cannot be so classified.

When was the Work created?

Copyright does not last indefinitely – works eventually fall into public domain and lose copyright protection. This period is seventy years from the creator's death. By way of example, works by Francis Bacon will remain in copyright until 2062 (seventy years after his death), though works by Rubens are no longer protected (see Robert Rauschenberg's 1963 Silkscreen *Tracer*, which contains Vietnam war images juxtaposed with a clear reproduction of Rubens' *Venus at her Toilet* (1613)). However, it is likely (though the subject of debate) that photographs of such works have their own copyright, and so it would still be possible to infringe the copyright in a photograph of the Rubens work.

Who owns the Copyright?

The copyright owner is usually the creator or author of the work. The copyright in a commissioned work is still owned by the author. However, the copyright owner of a work created by an employee in the course of employment will be his or her employer. Difficulties can arise when a work is commissioned or produced during the course of employment. For instance, many contemporary artists pay professional photographers to execute works on their behalf (e.g., Sam Taylor Wood).

The resulting work may be commissioned and, possibly, created during the course of employment. To avoid such ambiguities, it is advisable to ensure that the copyright position is clarified in a written Assignment or Licence Agreement (see below).

As an economic right, copyright can be bought and sold. Thus, the copyright owner may not be the author but may have purchased the copyright from the author or another person (by an assignment), or may have licensed it to another, thus retaining ownership while granting the right to use the work in some way – either on an exclusive or non-exclusive basis. If an artist is seeking to use an existing work of visual art in which copyright subsists, it is advisable to identify the copyright owner and obtain permission or a licence to cover the intended use.

Does the Intended Use infringe?

An infringement of copyright takes place if the copyright work, or a substantial part of it, is copied without the consent of the owner.

What is Copying?

Copying means to reproduce the work in any material form, including storing it electronically. In relation to art, it includes changes in artistic media and dimensions.

What is a Substantial Part?

This is a qualitative rather than a quantitative test. A substantial part usually contains the essence of the earlier work and can be difficult to judge. The question can be framed in this way: does the later work reproduce the most important elements of the earlier work? Thus, a collage which uses a fragment of a copyright work may still infringe. For example, the photographer (and the photographer's model!) who owns the copyright in an image entitled *Charlotte As Seen by Thomas*, published in a German photographic magazine in 1960, recently sued Barbara Kruger (plus the Whitney Museum and others) for reproducing the photographic image in *Untitled (it's a small world but not if you have to clean it)* (1990). It was eventually decided, perhaps surprisingly, that the Kruger work did not infringe a substantial part of the image in the photograph.

However, it has often been said that it is not the 'idea' which is protected, but rather the way that idea is expressed. The tension between ideas and their expression was examined recently in *Designer's Guild Limited v. Russell Williams (Textiles) Limited*. It was held by the House of Lords that it was wrong to attempt to establish copyright infringement by submitting each of the individual elements of the competing work to an analytical comparison. The better approach was to look at each work as a whole and ask whether the later work incorporated a substantial part of the skill and labour used by the author of the earlier work. The 'substantial' part copied can in some cases be abstract elements of the work rather than immediately obvious concrete elements. So, it can be misleading to say that there is no copyright in an idea: it is more accurate to say that there is no copyright in ideas which are not expressed in a material form.

Liability for copyright infringement is not limited to the artist who reproduces the copyright work. The museum or gallery, which displays the work in public, or the magazine, which publishes it, can be equally liable. Furthermore, it is not only reproducing a copyright work which constitutes infringement; artistic works can be infringed not only by reproduction, showing to the public, broadcasting, and adaptation, amongst other things (all of which constitute 'primary' infringement) but also by someone who imports the infringing work into the U.K., possesses it in the course of business, or deals with it commercially (all of which constitute 'secondary' infringement). In the case of secondary infringement, that person is only liable if s/he knew or had reason to believe that the work was an infringement.

Is there a Defence to Infringement?

There are occasions when acts which would otherwise constitute copyright infringement are in fact permitted.

Fair Dealing

If a use constitutes fair dealing for the purpose of criticism, review, or for the purpose of reporting current events (except photographs), it will not constitute infringement. However, in the area of reporting current events, there must be a 'sufficient' acknowledgement. It should be emphasised that any dealing must be 'fair'. There is no precise definition of what constitutes 'fairness' in this context, but the following factors are important:

· Is the original author credited?
· Is the later artist in commercial competition with the author of the work taken?
· Is the taking moderate? For example, no more than what is reasonably necessary is taken?
· Is there any dishonest motive?
· Are there any other adverse factors?

A recent example of a fair dealing defence arose in the controversy over Glenn Brown's use of a science fiction book jacket in his 2000 Turner Prize nominated work *The Loves of Shepherds (After Double Star by Tony Roberts)* 2000. Although

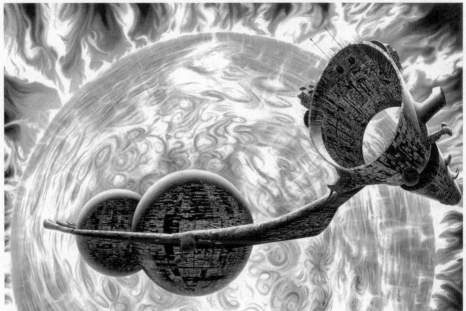

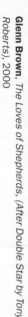

Glenn Brown. *The Loves of Shepherds, (After Double Star by Tony Roberts)*, 2000

Glenn Brown was said by the press and many commentators at the time to have committed a blatant act of copyright infringement, it is submitted that his use of the earlier artist's work, on proper examination and bearing in mind the questions outlined above, constituted a fair dealing for the purpose of criticism or review of the earlier work, though this particular example has not as yet been tested by the Courts.

The fair dealing defence does not give publishers (including museums) carte blanche to reproduce artworks simply on the basis that to do so is in their opinion to facilitate the study of art. For example, reproducing an artwork in an art history book is not a defence in itself, as the publishers of Phaidon discovered when they published several well-known Matisse works without first securing permission from the U.K. agent of the Matisse estate, DACS (The Design and Artists Copyright Society (see below)).

Incidental Inclusion

If a copyrighted work appears incidentally in a subsequent work, does the subsequent work infringe copyright in the earlier? For example, a painting, or a sculpture, which appears in a newsreel film, unintentionally would be used incidentally, and so no infringement would occur. Although the relevant circumstances are not defined, it would appear that fairness is again a crucial factor. However, it is submitted that this defence is unlikely to be of practical use to visual artists, as it may be said that, unless the artwork consists of random elements, each element of an artwork would have been carefully considered. Therefore it is very unlikely that they could properly be considered 'incidental'.

Is there an Infringement of Moral Rights?

Moral rights are not, strictly speaking, a part of copyright, but they arise only when a copyright work has been created and can be infringed in a similar way. In essence, the moral rights of artists are:

- · The right to be identified as author (provided the right has previously been asserted).
- · The right not to have one's work subjected to derogatory treatment.
- · The right not to have a work falsely attributed to the claimant.

In many cases, it might be argued that where a copyright work has been infringed, the author will have failed to credit the author of the original work and will have 'treated' (i.e. added to, deleted from, altered, or adapted) the earlier work in a 'derogatory' way (i.e. distorted or mutilated the work or prejudiced the honour or reputation of the earlier author). However, the circumstances where moral rights have been established are rather restricted.

One example occurred in 1993, when the Natural History Museum published a book which reproduced certain cartoons of the well-known cartoonist Bill Tidy. They were reduced in size, and Bill Tidy contended that this constituted a distortion of his works, or at least that the reproduction was prejudicial to his honour or reputation. The court held that it was not certain that the reduction constituted distortion or (in the absence of evidence from members of the public) that the reductions were prejudicial to his honour or reputation.

A further example would be the famous work by Rauschenberg, *De Kooning Erased*, in which the artist acquired a De Kooning drawing and literally rubbed it out – undoubtedly a derogatory treatment of the work. However, De Kooning apparently appreciated the iconoclastic gesture and no lawsuit ensued.

What Remedies are available?

There are both civil and criminal remedies available against infringers. Criminal prosecution is rare and usually reserved for cases of obvious counterfeiting and piracy. But upon conviction, an infringer can expect to receive a fine, confiscation of the infringing work, and possibly imprisonment.

Civil actions are more common, and the remedies available include an injunction to restrain future infringement, financial damages (either by means of an enquiry into the losses the Claimant has sustained or an account of the profits derived from the infringing activity), and an Order that all infringing works be delivered to the Claimant or destroyed. If the infringement is 'flagrant', then the Court can award additional damages, though there is some debate as to whether such damages are punitive or compensatory in nature.

Can Liability be avoided?

In order to avoid these pitfalls, it is advisable to seek permission of the prior artist if an artist wishes to use elements of another copyright work. A good example of such a licensing arrangement is the collaboration between Julian Opie and the pop group Blur. After Opie painted portraits of the four members of the group in a semi-abstract style, they were then licensed to the group and their record label for use on a record sleeve and in advertising. Douglas Gordon is another artist who makes extensive use of feature films works but makes Licensing Agreements with the copyright owners of all films he uses. Nevertheless, it may be expensive and time-consuming to negotiate a Licence Agreement, and the copyright owner may refuse to give permission.

Many artists and their estates are represented by DACS, and a simple enquiry to them will often secure the necessary permission and avoid these problems. Equally, in order to police the use of an artist's own images, it would be advisable to register with a society such as DACS. Without a Licence Agreement, it is necessary to evaluate the degree of risk involved and the likelihood of receiving a claim for copyright infringement. The essential questions to ask are:

· Is the work protected by copyright?

· Who owns the copyright?

· Does the intended use infringe?

· Are there any defences?

· What are the likely damages or consequences of an injunction?

Conclusion

I have tried here, at the risk of over-simplifying the issues, to highlight the essential questions an artist must ask in order to establish whether a work of art enjoys copyright protection or has infringed the copyright of another. In essence, most artworks will enjoy copyright protection from the moment they are created, that is to say from the moment when they are expressed in a material form. The more difficult question is whether there is a risk of infringement of an earlier work. To this question, there is often no right or wrong answer but only degrees of risk. By applying principles such as substantiality and fair dealing, it is possible to minimise that risk; but by entering into a proper Licence Agreement, any such risk can be eradicated.

Part 2
Copyright and Art

The Concept of Originality and Contemporary Art

Nadia Walravens[i]

Brancusi's *Bird in Space*[ii] was seized in 1927 by the U.S. Customs, who demanded that its owner pay the tax on raw materials (metal and stone) and refused to grant it the exemption applicable to original works of art. Thus *Bird in Space*, which is today recognised as being a formative Modernist work, was denied the status of art. This led to an historic lawsuit against the United States, which Brancusi won in 1928. In granting an abstract sculpture the status of a work of art, the court took account of the development of art and in particular the influence of the school of modern art.

This exceptional lawsuit[iii] illustrates the difficulty in defining a work of art,[iv] What, for instance, are the assessment criteria, and who is the judge?[v] The answers are of fundamental importance because artists can claim copyrights only in original works of art. Yet the law is not necessarily in step with the realities of contemporary artistic creation: complete synchrony between this 'truth of art' and the law still remains to be achieved.[vi] Moreover, the legislator has not given any definition of a work of art. Copyright law adopts a rather vague approach to works, a fact which can be explained by the principle of aesthetic neutrality. Article L. 112-2 of the French Intellectual Property Code contains a list of copyrightable works, which include 'works of drawing, painting, architecture, sculpture, engraving, lithography' and 'graphic works'.[vii] On the whole, legal literature defines an artistic work as a visual work that translates ideas, emotions and feelings into images and appeals directly to the viewer's senses and sensitivity.[viii]

While the approach to works of art does not appear to raise too many difficulties for legal scholars because of the principle of aesthetic neutrality, the definition of an original work of art, on the other hand, has proved to be trickier. Originality is an inescapable requirement: it determines the protection afforded by copyright. It is possible to refute a work of art's 'work' status if its originality cannot be shown by its author,[ix] yet the concept is an obscure one because it has never been defined by the legislator.[x] Although the term was mentioned in case law in the nineteenth century,[xi] 'originality' was systematised, in fact, by legal scholars –

particularly by Henri Desbois,[xii] who believed that 'any creation that is not the simple reproduction of an existing work and that expresses its author's taste, intelligence and know-how, in other words *his or her personality in its composition and expression*, is original'. A work, is then posed as the creation of a natural person – the author – whose personality it reflects. The law thus seeks to protect the author and takes account of the bond existing between the author and the work. It adopts a subjective approach to creation rather than an objective one based on novelty as existing in industrial property law. Copyright law was influenced by the liberal and individualist philosophy of the nineteenth century. The subjective approach to originality illustrates this traditional, personalist conception of literary and artistic property accepted by the majority of legal scholars.

Although the nature of copyright sheds some light on the criterion of originality, it still needs to be made clearer. Case law and legal literature have laid the foundations for marking out the contours of originality. It can be said that, for a work to be granted protection, it must be original, but not only that: its originality must also be expressed in a concrete way, in a form, so as to be capable of being perceived by the senses. Hence, copyright protection does not extend to ideas. On the other hand, other factors referred to in Article L. 112-1 of the Intellectual Property Code are not taken into consideration, namely the type of work (artistic, literary, musical, etc.), its form of expression (oral, written, drawn, painted, sculpted, etc.), its purpose (aesthetic, functional, recreational, decorative, etc.) and its merit (appraisal of the work's value). Acceptance of the originality of works of art is subject to a further precondition: personal execution, because it shows the expression of the artist's personality.

In the light of these premises, the question that must be raised is whether the choice of subjective originality for works of art is still appropriate today. Legal literature has naturally applied this conception of originality to traditional, figurative works, yet, if contemporary artistic practices are considered, it becomes apparent that the law is out of step with art.[xiii] An assessment of the stamp of the author's personality proves to be problematical in the case of contemporary works of art (I-Copyright Law's Personalist Approach Challenged by Contemporary Artistic Practices). As a result, the law's adaptation may be considered desirable through the adoption of a more realistic conception of originality (See section II: The Desirability of Adapting the Law in Response to the Development of Contemporary Art).

I. Copyright Law's Personalist Approach challenged by Contemporary Artistic Practices

The subjective conception of originality seems appropriate for figurative art. The author's personality is clearly reflected in the 'subject' represented in the work and the artist's personal execution, however, most works today do not seek to describe a situation or a feeling and have no representational function in themselves. 'Depersonalisation, the involvement of random choice, and anti-art have called into question the 'work' concept as defined in the light of the traditional creative process'.[xiv] It becomes a delicate matter, therefore, to assess the stamp of the artist's personality as required by the law and, consequently, the originality of a work.[xv] The development of contemporary artistic practices makes it necessary to consider the relevance of this requirement and that of personal execution.

The Stamp of the Personality: a Concept that needs to be rethought

As a work must be expressed in a form, it is in the form that the stamp of the author's personality is reflected. In 'The Disappearance of the Form/Idea Distinction', we shall see to what extent contemporary works of art tend to erase the boundary between form and idea. Moreover, some scholars are critical of the subjective approach to originality when dealing with certain works of art: they argue that the stamp of the artist's personality is non-existent. For works of this kind and particularly monochromes, we will ask in 'Absence of the Stamp of the Personality?', must the stamp of the artist's personality really be ruled out?

The Disappearance of the Form/Idea Distinction

As a result of the form/idea distinction, ideas are excluded from copyright protection. But today artists are laying claim to ideas as 'works' in their own right.

The Exclusion of Ideas from the Subject Matter of Copyright

Under Article L. 112-1 of the Intellectual Property Code, 'The provisions of this Code shall protect the rights of authors in all intellectual works, regardless of the kind, form of expression . . .' To enjoy copyright protection, intellectual works must be capable of being perceived by the senses and expressed in a concrete form. There is unanimous agreement in legal literature that the distinction between form and idea is a decisive factor in the field of copyright. If only the form is protected, it is because only the form reveals the personal character of the author, the stamp of his or her personality, that emerges from the work's material execution.

In the case of works of art, Henri Desbois [xvi] considered that 'ideas as such do not have access to the painter's or sculptor's studio: even if he plans to express a thought or a feeling, he must first effect a transformation, in the form of an illustration... *In the field of art, images exclude ideas.*' However, these remarks need to be qualified and must be restricted to figurative art. The development of art has led to significant changes in artistic practices. Today, many artists attach vital importance to the work's idea because, in their eyes, it is the idea in fact that constitutes the work regardless of its execution. [xvii]

While the courts are unanimous in excluding copyright protection for ideas, two cases concerning Christo's wrapping of the Pont-Neuf nevertheless reveal the difficulty in determining the boundary between form and idea in contemporary works of art. In the first case, two news companies had used photographs and films of the wrapped Pont-Neuf that had been taken and made without Christo's authorisation. The Paris Court of Appeal [xviii] sought to determine whether the work presented by Christo was indeed an original work of form, in which case an act of infringement had been committed and noted that 'The idea of accentuating the pureness of the lines of a bridge and its lampposts by means of a cloth and ropes so as to bring out the bridge's form and pure lines constitutes an original work eligible as such for protection under the law on literary and artistic property'. [xix] This language followed from the Court's finding of an 'idea that is formulated and thus defined, determined, perceptible and capable of being proved'. [xx] In the second case, Christo brought an infringement suit against an advertising agency which had disseminated photos of a swimming pool covered in a pink cloth. But this time the trial court [xxi] denied him protection on the ground that 'the law... protects only creations of particular, individualised, and perfectly identifiable objects and not a category or a family of forms that have features in common only because they all correspond to a style or a process arising from an idea'. [xxii]

These decisions illustrate the difficulty in distinguishing between form and idea, particularly in the case of contemporary works of art where the borderline may be faint, if not non-existent. Yet the outcome is of importance to artists. In the first case, the work was expressed in a concrete form that was considered original and thus enjoyed protection: any representation, reproduction, or adaptation of the work in whole or in part without the artist's consent was thus prohibited and would constitute an act of infringement. In the second case, the work's execution process was realised in an original work of form, but the process itself did not enjoy protection because it merely corresponded to the artist's style or the idea. Therefore, anyone could use that idea to create another work. Although this legal position must be endorsed having regard to the imperative of legal certainty and the preservation of creative freedom,[xxiii] a reservation can be expressed about such a lack of legal recognition where it is precisely the artist's style that constitutes 'the work'.[xxiv] This is because 'the style is inherent in the artist's work; it is through the style that the work is identifiable'.[xxv] This refusal to grant ideas copyright protection conflicts with the reality of contemporary artistic creation. Indeed, today, artists are laying claim to ideas as works.

Ideas as Creations

The exclusion of ideas from the subject matter of copyright seems questionable in the light of the development of artistic creation: the idea in itself may constitute a work and the work may be the result of a simple choice.

The Idea as such constitutes a Work: Conceptual Art

In the view of Donald Judd,[xxvi] 'the word 'form' cannot be used because the substance/form distinction is a non-problem, itself derived from the artificial separation between thinking and feeling'. In fact, most contemporary works of art place the idea at the heart of the work. Conceptual art practices provide a good example in this regard. As early as 1969, Sol LeWitt [xxvii] argued that 'ideas can be works of art. They are linked together and are sometimes expressed in material form, but not all ideas have to be expressed in material form'. Here, the completed concrete work is merely the incidental result of the mental act of creation. According to Catherine Millet,

> In the 70s, conceptual art militated – at times in a very radical way – in favour of the disappearance of the art object. As its name suggests, conceptual art sought to replace the circulation of works of art with that of ideas . . . conceptual artists thus revealed that, after all, the work of art possibly had no value in itself, contrary to what people had thought – almost obsessively – during the previous decade, and that the work was merely the residue of a vast process that had enabled it to exist. The art object was just the left-over of a thought. [xxviii]

This contemporary art movement thus challenges the legitimacy of copyright law's refusal to accept ideas as works of art. The thought or the work's idea is crucial, and its expression in concrete form is of no importance in the eyes of the artist. It is the mental act of creation that matters. Moreover, artists today seek recognition of the idea, but also the choice of an object, as a work.

The Work may be the Result of a Simple Choice: Readymades

When originality is considered from a subjective angle, the work must be 'the fruit of a conscious expression that is controlled and directed by the author'.[xxix] However, in their quest to extend the frontiers of art, artists have used manufactured objects: an ordinary functional object became a work of art. Today, readymades are presented as works and accepted as such by the actors of the art world: institutions,[xxx] artists, critics, galleries, collectors,[xxxi] etc. Arguably, these 'works' would be denied copyright protection because they are not the result of the artist's own intellectual activity.[xxxii] Yet, in the case of Marcel Duchamp, it is not the object as such which constitutes the work but rather the designation process through which the object is presented as a work of art: the idea is the most important.[xxxiii] Consequently, an assessment of the stamp of the artist's personality is problematical because the law requires not only a concrete work capable of being perceived by the senses but also an original work of form. Professors André and Henri-Jacques Lucas [xxxiv] observe in this regard that, while 'protection cannot be granted in principle, therefore, to readymades which their 'inventor' claims as works of art', it must be accepted, as Ivan Cherpillod[xxxv] has suggested, that 'creative input may nevertheless be discerned in the positioning of the object and its situation in a precise context and space'. Indeed, it does seem to us that the work's presentation is a feature of artistic creation: although the work, as an object, does not usually need anything else to exist, the context of its presentation is nevertheless inherent in it.

The characteristics of contemporary art have led some representatives of legal literature to challenge the subjective conception of originality. Might it be appropriate to abandon copyright's personalist approach towards artistic creation?

Absence of the Stamp of the Personality?

Can the subjective approach to originality be completely discarded? Is it conceivable, for example in the case of monochromes, to assess the originality of a work of art without considering the author's personality?

Are Contemporary Creation and Subjective Originality contradictory?

Contemporary artistic practices reveal a tendency on the part of artists to rid their works of their directly perceivable personal stamp. In the event of a dispute, it is possible to question the originality of a work if it does not 'show' its author's

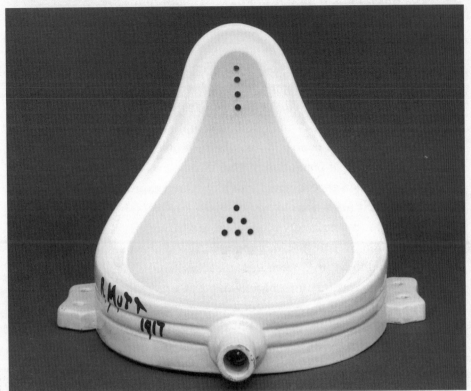

Marcel Duchamp, *Fountain*, 1917

personality.[xxxvi] This is because copyright law has remained tied to a nineteenth century approach to art as being representational or figurative in nature. Today, the factors that determine the work's recognition are above all the artist's signature, the critics, and the institutional context.[xxxvii] The increasingly anonymous appearance of works calls for artists who are unquestionably recognised as such by the artworld itself. Thus 'abstraction's impregnation of art has called into question the form/substance distinction and the subjective conception of originality'.[xxxviii]

How, then, can the courts judge the presence of the stamp of the artist's personality relevantly and with certainty when dealing with a readymade, for example? Having asked that, can and should copyright law's personalist approach be discarded for contemporary works of art? The bond between the author and the work cannot be hidden altogether. As Ghislain Mollet-Viéville[xxxix] stressed, 'It is thus the idea of the readymade that truly forms the work; the object – for its part – is nothing, it is interchangeable'. It is no longer the object as such that bears the stamp of the artist's personality, it is the idea in itself – the idea forming the work – which reveals that stamp. The same holds for monochromes.

The Subjective Originality Approach called into Question by Monochrome Painting?

The originality of a work of art was characterized by Henri Desbois as the idea/composition/expression trilogy.[xl] The composition – meaning the plan – can give rise to a work in its own right, such as a sketch, which is protected independently of the final work. The expression is reflected in the lines and colours.[xli] Legal literature agrees with Henri Desbois that, in the sphere of visual art, the work's composition and expression will be protected. The requirement of the artist's personal stamp is not questioned here.

With the emergence of new forms of pictorial expression, such as monochrome painting, it is necessary to consider the relevance of the requirement of the stamp of the author's personality. Indeed, a monochrome can be characterised as a surface painted in a single colour. Some representatives of legal literature have noted that it is difficult to discern the artist's personal stamp in contemporary paintings.[xlii] Contemporary art certainly requires a more flexible approach than was previously the case: the artist's personal stamp must be assessed differently today.[xliii] It is for the 'viewer' to consider the work differently:[xliv] the emotion felt by the viewer will depend on that view, on his or her attitude towards the painting and his or her own sensitivity. The stamp of the artist's personality has not disappeared for all that, it is just less clearly perceptible.[xlv]

Copyright law's personalist conception does not seem to have to be called into question as a result of contemporary artistic creation. It is rather the assessment of the stamp of the artist's personality that needs to be rethought. However, from copyright law's personalist conception, legal literature has inferred a further condition for works of art, namely the requirement of personal execution.

The Requirement of Personal Execution: a Superfluous Criterion

A work of art cannot be considered original if it has not been executed personally by the artist. Indeed, in the view of some representatives of legal literature, the originality of a work of art is subject to its execution by the artist. This condition was proposed by Henri Desbois, who believed that 'the expression . . . plays a major, if not exclusive, role in the genesis of works of art'.[xlvi] In contemporary art, however, some artists do not execute their works themselves and leave this to others. Moreover, this requirement is not always consistent with artistic practices of the past:[xlvii] in the 16th century, it was quite common for works to be executed jointly by masters and apprentices and even by artists of repute working together. The personal execution requirement is thus inappropriate.

In the case of a monochrome, its execution is of no importance; only the result of the intellectual representation matters. Thus Denys Riout notes:

> While the brushes of gestural painters inscribed the artist's corpore- ality straight onto the canvas, the use of a roller created a severance. Klein, who was *happy not to be an abstract painter*, laid particular stress on the virtues of this distancing. Later, the *Anthropometries* gave rise to an even more radical break between the artist, the cre- ator, and his *living brushes*, in other words the bodies of the models. Klein stresses the fact that he is then *completely detached from any physical work* . . . Happy and proud not to get dirty, he breaks with the fetishism that, by contiguity, transforms the painted object into a relic. So as to be impregnated more fully with pure sensitivity, his works are not painted masterfully.[xlviii]

The artist's approach shows clearly that what is important is to be found not in the material execution but in the whole, purely mental phase of the work's preconcep- tion, leading only at the end to its execution.[xlix]

Delegated personal execution is quite common: Reinhard claimed that his assistant could execute his paintings as well as he could. Denys Riout[l] also refers to the work of Daniel Walravens: 'We know that the painter, D.W., does not paint the works he presents under his name himself: he always has them executed by professionals. His instructions, which are precise, do not leave any possibility of interpretation where traces of personal fancy might seep through and he checks with extreme care the results which must be in keeping with his intentions in every respect.' Mere execution subject to the artist's instructions does not give rise to a copyright. Moreover, certain artists are dismissive of personal execution. Examples include Camille Pissarro: 'As to the execution we regard it as irrelevant . . . art has nothing to do with it',[li] and Gerhard Richter 'for whom *the making* is not an artistic act'. Accordingly, a painting may become 'a simple problem of men- tal projection and of implementing one's own instructions'.[lii] The absence of personal execution has no impact on the originality of the painting; the stamp of the author's personality is still present. In fact, the person who executes the work matters little; the only thing that counts is the supervision exercised over the execution.

The problem has been raised before the courts and case law [liii] has accepted a claim for copyright protection without material execution. In the case in point, Vasarely had entrusted the execution of a painting *Stri Pauk* to another painter, Valuet. However, he had not merely given the general theme of the work. He had also supervised the work's execution by making corrections, expressing criticisms, and giving his approval when he felt satisfied with the result. The trial court held that 'insofar as he reserved the right to correct and approve the work, which involved another painter's material participation, before affixing his own signature on it, the completed work thus bears the stamp of his creative personality and must be considered a joint work that required the collaboration of two painters'. The court did not refer to the criterion of personal execution; it was the artist's creative activity, his creative freedom, that was taken into consideration.

Literary and artistic property law lays stress on the stamp of the author's personality, which reveals the irreducible bond between the artist and his or her work.[liv] We have noted that this approach is fully in keeping with the specificity of artistic creation.[lv] However, if the law and art are put in perspective, it becomes apparent that the present legal conception fails to take account of the development of contemporary artistic practices. That conception is obsolete today. It is obsolete in the first place because of its refusal to protect ideas: conceptual art and readymades, among others, are relegated to a legal no-man's land. Secondly, the requirement of a visible personal stamp in the work rules out copyright protection for a sector of creation. As to the personal execution factor, it is also inappropriate for assessing the originality of a work. This discrepancy between the law and art leads to legal uncertainty due to the difficulty in determining what is a copyright work of art. The law's indifference towards contemporary creation and the resulting lack of acceptance of its 'work' status can be explained by the inflexibility of the requirement of the artist's personal stamp in the work.[lvi] The development of art thus calls for the law's adaptation.[lvii]

II. The Desirability of adapting the Law in response to the Development of Contemporary Art

Contemporary artistic creation shows the discrepancy that exists between copyright law and art. This can be explained by the development of art. Nathalie Heinich [lviii] analyses it as follows:

> After the codes of classic representation, then of figuration itself, the frontiers of art as such were to be systematically put to the test from the Second World War onwards ... These transgressions confirm the strength of art by showing that it can even incorporate what is the most alien to it. At the same time they test the artist's power in relation to the world and, in particular, the world of art, the gamble being to impose on it this extension of the frontiers of the acceptable.

The law must thus extend its own frontiers to works that are recognised by all the actors of the art world: artists, philosophers, critics, writers, collectors, galleries, and institutions. Hence a more realistic concept of originality must be considered.

Artistic Practices that cannot be ignored

The characteristics of contemporary creation will be shown through two examples: some artists enable their works to be attributed to them and authenticated not by means of their signatures but through deeds, while other artists treat the work's personal execution with complete indifference, with only the concept being important in their eyes.

Art through Deeds, the absence of the Artist's Signature: Attribution and Authentication of the Work

Today, a work of art is always linked to a name, that of its author. The art market relies on this system. As Raymonde Moulin notes,[lix] 'For the signature to be capable of marking out (labelling) a product as artistic, the author must first have been defined socially as an artist . . . Arguably, on the basis of a circular definition, the artistic world makes the artist and, accordingly, whatever the artist makes is art.' The question of attribution thus becomes a fundamental one 'because the market now buys *names and not works*'.[lx] Yet many artists do not sign their works today. Instead, a certificate of authenticity bearing the artist's signature accompanies the work and enables it to be attributed to that artist.

Sol LeWitt explained:[lxi] 'As my wall drawings are not signed, a certificate of authenticity bearing my signature accompanies them. A lot of artists have used certificates (including Carl Andre, Daniel Buren, Dan Flavin, Donald Judd and many others)'. Thus the signature is detached from the work.[lxii] Lawrence Weiner even signs notarial deeds: the purchaser of one of the phrases exhibited on the wall receives a letter from the artist stating that his or her acquisition has been registered with a notary. 'Mr so-and-so, notary, at such and such an address and telephone number . . . This short letter sent in exchange for the cheque that you yourself have signed will be the only proof you have that the little phrase is really his and that it really belongs to you and you alone . . .'[lxiii] The separation between the work and the signature authenticating it 'tends to transform the commercial transaction for a work of conceptual art into a simple exchange of signatures: the artist's signature for the purchaser's signature, the legal deed (whether it is called a 'certificate', 'documentation', 'notice', 'description', etc.) for the cheque signed by the purchaser'.[lxiv] This type of transaction provides an illustration of the development of artistic practices which challenge the traditional criteria governing the attribution and authentication of works. It requires an adaptation of the law in terms of its understanding of art and particularly the originality of works. In addition, personal execution – a precondition for accepting the originality of a work of art – does not reflect the reality of contemporary artistic creation.

The Irrelevance of Personal Execution and the Importance of the Concept

If art meant . . . *to feel and make*, it can now mean *to think up and have made*.[lxv] This sentence summarises in itself the development of art and shows clearly the change that has taken place in the creative enterprise of contemporary artists.[lxvi] Catherine Francblin [lxvii] points out that 'It is because of the secondary nature of the project's materialisation that you can make your sculpture yourself if you find the same steel plates and the same building bricks as the ones used by Carl Andre. You could also easily make a Dan Flavin with neon tubes purchased at the BHV store'. Therefore, it is necessary today to take into account the fact that, as Sol LeWitt stated, 'the concept is the most important aspect of the work. The artist is a thinker and a creator far more than a craftsman. Other persons can carry out the project'.[lxviii] Hence the work is first and foremost a product of the mental act of creation.[lxix]

The specificity of contemporary creation changes the whole basis of the law. The work may be executed by the artist, or by a person who is not predetermined. Or it may not be executed at all:[lxx] for only the concept is really important. The requirement of an original work of form is thus ill at ease.

> When you focus on the form of the work, its concrete execution, it is as though you were insensitive to the intellectual, critical aspect of the work (its 'questioning component') and reacted (stupidly) only to the plastic sensations; as though, instead of adoring the creator, you became infatuated with the craftsman; as though, by analogy with music, you preferred one of the many performers of the composer's works to the composer.[lxxi]

Contemporary works require an active attitude on the part of the viewer: he or she participates in the artist's creative enterprise, both in its purely mental phase and in its final result, the finished work.[lxxii]

Back in 1958, Yves Klein played with this idea of impalpable works, described as transfers of 'zones of immaterial, pictorial sensitivity'. Yves Klein exhibited *the Void* in Iris Clert's gallery in Paris and sold it: there were thus eight transfers of immaterial, pictorial sensitivity. The prospective purchaser of such a work had to pay in gold weight and received a certificate in exchange from Yves Klein. Klein took part of the gold to make one of his 'Monogold' works and the rest was scattered into the river Seine at Paris. 'At the same time as Yves Klein scattered the gold into the water, that is to say not only the tangible but also the precious trace of the exchange, the collector had to burn his receipt. Klein thus succeeded in creating a mechanism whereby, although there was an exchange of material goods for the transfer of the *Void*, at the end of the day nothing was left. At any rate, the purchaser was completely dispossessed of objects since even his receipt went up in smoke'.[lxxiii]

This example illustrates the uneasiness that can result from the law's requirement of an original work of form. From the viewpoint of copyright law, Klein's work, *the Void*, is not recognised and has no legal existence. Yet this work does exist for the actors of the art world: it was exhibited in a gallery and collectors bought it. Although no tangible trace remains of the work itself or the transactions relating to it, *the Void* has a place in the history of art. We share the view of Sylvie Hans [lxxiv] that 'the exclusion of ideas is likely to give rise to much debate and litigation in the years to come; the claims of contemporary creators will be at that cost'.

These examples of artistic practices show the lack of coherence between the law and art. Can the law continue to remain out of step with contemporary art? Artists should be able to claim their copyrights in their works serenely. Yet any attempt to enforce moral or economic rights in court may fail on the ground of the work's lack of originality. Moreover, attempts to claim copyrights in works that are not recognised by the law may weaken the art market. Contemporary creation invites us to consider a more appropriate definition of originality: it is desirable to adapt the law.

For a Revision of the Concept of Originality

Some representatives of legal literature propose a radical stance and advocate an objective conception of originality that implies eclipsing copyright law's personalist approach. However, in our view, the proposal to adopt an objective approach does not reflect the specificity of artistic creation. Accordingly, a refinement of the subjective conception seems more appropriate.

The Argument against an Objective Approach to Originality

The traditional subjective conception of originality views the protected work as a personal emanation of its author. However, the difficulty in assessing the stamp of the artist's personality in contemporary works of art has prompted some representatives of legal literature to propose an objective concept of originality: the work is then considered without reference to its author's personality. The criterion of novelty – already the decisive factor for industrial property protection – would replace that of the author's personal stamp. Thus, for an invention to be patented, the precondition is that it must be novel. Accordingly, the bond between the author and the work is irrelevant in the industrial property system. The objective approach to originality challenges this characteristic of authors' rights since it eliminates completely the personal nature of the creation. So, can this logic be applied to contemporary works of art?

Alain Strowel has argued that certain works of art reveal themselves in the specific creative project to a greater extent than in the work's concrete execution: 'They constitute a dramatic accentuation that differentiates the exhibited object from a simple, everyday one. What such works highlight . . . is the novelty factor's hold over the art market. The novelty factor seems to have become the only point of reference for creation, requiring increasingly refined demarcation strategies'.[lxxv] Indeed, we have noted the disruption that modern artistic practices generate in the assessment of the originality of works. Nevertheless, we believe that only the subjective approach to originality is capable of preserving the specificity of authors' rights, namely the moral rights which spring directly from the bond between the work and its author. This bond cannot disappear, whatever the form of the work, because a 'work of art amounts to being. That is its task, to be, to make the very words 'it is' present . . . there lies the whole mystery'.[lxxvi]

Even if most contemporary works of art seem less accessible today to the viewer, the bond between the work and its author has not disappeared. If an objective conception of originality is adopted, then it is no longer 'the psychological act through which the author gives birth to the work that constitutes the decisive factor for granting protection but rather the fact of providing the community with a new possession'.[lxxvii] Such an approach completely eclipses the key aspect of artistic creation. Remember the words of Yves Klein: it is from painting that the very essence of the creative being emerges.[lxxviii] Thus we share Sylvie Hans' view that an

> . . . original work originates in the mind of its author and not in anyone else's. It is in this that originality can be described as a subjective notion, i.e. one that is attached to a subject. The creative activity that it characterises is an activity of individuals and hence in its modern sense . . . it seems certain, if we refer to our own conclusions concerning novelty, that originality cannot be reduced to an objective notion, be it novelty, personal execution or merit, fame or inventiveness.[lxxix]

It appears necessary, then, to consider a refinement of the subjective conception of originality to take account of the development of art.

For a Refinement of the Subjective Conception of Originality

The subjective conception of originality requires the stamp of the author's personality in the work. In addition, for a work of art to be considered original, it must have been executed personally by the artist. Most legal scholars remain attached to the subjective conception of originality. The artist's thinking must be visible in the work and the stamp of his or her personality must be directly perceivable by the person contemplating it.

As we already noted, the development of artistic creation calls for the viewer's increasingly active involvement. The viewer is invited to follow the creative process right from the work's preconception, that is to say its purely mental stage. If some people take the view that a monochrome painting cannot express the artist's personality, the words of Yves Klein illustrate a different standpoint. It has to be accepted, therefore, that 'Whereas (self-) expression is within everyone's reach – we can all aspire to it – the ability to impregnate pictorial matter is a gift. The work's justification and credentials are no longer to be found in an analysable visible object; the work is a blank cheque and the artist is its only guarantor.'[lxxx] Indeed, even a monochrome reveals the stamp of the artist's personality, just like any other painting. Thus, when we look at monochrome paintings, if our 'emotion springs less from the paintings themselves than from what they denote',[lxxxi] the artist's personality is present nonetheless. The work is impregnated with the artist's personality, if only at the preconception stage. However, it cannot be inferred from this that the work lacks substance.[lxxxii]

Similarly, the refusal to grant readymades the status of works of art creates a legal no-man's land.[lxxxiii] The absence of the stamp of the author's personality is given as justification for this refusal: the artist's proposition, it is argued, does not reflect his or her personality. But in that case, a whole contemporary art movement is barred from copyright protection. Yet, as the artworld's 'experts'[lxxxiv] rightly explain, it is the artist's proposition as such that constitutes the work. This proposition reveals in itself the stamp of the artist's personality that emerges in the process of designating an object as a work.[lxxxv] Thus 'by shifting the problem of art from a question of form to a question of function, readymades prioritize the mental activity'.[lxxxvi] The stamp of the artist's personality, which used to be revealed only in the material object, is also visible today in the purely mental creative proposition. In sum then, it is still to be found in the work: although it seems less apparent to the viewer, at least directly, it is still present.[lxxxvii]

Like the art world's 'experts', copyright law should accept that the choice of an object may reflect the artist's personality and hence the originality of a work of art. The courts use this criterion of 'choice' already when determining the originality of photographs. In a ruling of 7 May 1996, the Court of Appeal of Dijon accepted the originality of the photographs at issue in view of 'a number of choices concerning notably the lighting and the correlative use of the equipment'.[lxxxviii] Therefore, we cannot subscribe to the opinion that contemporary artistic creation has drained itself of all substance. We need to expel the idea of the author's personality being expressed only in the work's composition and expression and accept that a work – which may be impenetrable at first sight to the 'viewer' – always springs from a person and thus reflects that person's personality. It is necessary to accept today that what is capable of being perceived by the senses is not always visible or actually perceived, particularly as that perception will be sharper or weaker depending on the viewer.[lxxxix] The courts should thus determine the originality of contemporary works of art not only by referring to their own criteria based on copyright law's personalist approach but also by seeking the opinion of experts: reference to contemporary artistic movements would thus enable them to adopt a flexible attitude in their assessment.[xc]

The Requirement of Personal Execution

The requirement of the artist's personal execution should be discarded for good because this criterion – which was added by some representatives of legal literature – is not consistent with the reality: the stamp of the artist's personality cannot be reduced to purely technical execution, know-how or craftsmanship. This criterion does not seem to be considered today by the courts. Moreover, in some contemporary works of art, the artist's individuality can be distinguished by his or her proposition more than anything else. What matters is not the execution in itself, but rather the artist's creative activity, his or her 'creative freedom'. Therefore, it seems far more relevant to accept creative freedom as the criterion for granting author status.[xci] Personal execution, whether under the artist's control or otherwise, cannot be accepted without repudiating contemporary artistic practices. For this reason, it should be completely eliminated from the concept of originality.

Indeed, we have noted that the work's execution can be left to complete chance when it is entrusted to others. This aleatoric element in the work's execution is an integral part of the work. The requisite originality is thus to be found in the person of the artist, in his or her attitude. Like Sylvie Hans,[xcii] we do not consider personal execution to be 'sufficient or necessary as evidence of the work's originality and, therefore, authorship as traditionally understood cannot follow from the definition of the studied concept [originality]. The very idea of personal execution, which is undergoing a necessary change in response to the emergence of new art forms, is tending to give way to creativity, to the point that, in our view, it should be abandoned altogether in favour of the latter and thus in favour of the concept of originality.' Therefore, consideration of the artist's creative freedom seems to be appropriate for new forms of contemporary art because the work is the result of this creative freedom, the artist's mental projection and instructions concerning the work's execution.

Conclusion

Contemporary artistic practices are acknowledged by the world of art and produce works which provide material for the art market today. The sale and international circulation of such works show that the law cannot disregard these new forms of creation for a simple reason: disputes may arise in the future. So when the question of the originality of these works arises, what will the courts do, caught between the law – in which the concept of art has not developed since the nineteenth century – and the reality of contemporary creation? If art evolves, the concept of originality, for its part, cannot remain static because the enforcement of copyright protection against any infringement of an artist's moral or economic rights depends on the assessment of originality. So it is in the acceptance of the development of art that the courts can approach the 'truth of art' that is so difficult for the law to define, as the *Brancusi* case so clearly showed. The principle of not considering the merit of the work must always be borne in mind by the courts. It is necessary today to accept that the stamp of the artist's personality is no longer clearly visible in contemporary creation. Hence the law should draw conclusions from the disappearance of 'rationalising aesthetics'. This obviously makes the task harder for the courts, which have neither the requisite expertise nor the competence of art critics. The help of 'experts' from the art world would thus enable them to make a sharper and more correct assessment. This is the attitude that was adopted in the *Brancusi* case by the court which, in granting *Bird in Space* the status of a work of art, relied on the criteria of the school of modern art.[xciii] It is always possible that new forms of artistic creation will have difficulty in establishing themselves even in artistic circles, but the risk of denying them the status of works of art is nevertheless slight. Judges who rely on these criteria show, in our view, a flexibility that the law needs to have towards art. The concept of originality would thus be more consistent with the function of literary and artistic property law to protect works and authors.

Reprinted from *Revue Internationale du Droit d'Auteur (RIDA) 181*, (1999).
English translation by Margaret Platt-Hommel

i   Nadia Walravens is a researcher at the Centre d'Etudes et de Recherche en Droit de l'Immatériel (CERDI), University of Paris XI, Sceaux.

ii   Work in bronze, slender in form and tapering, measuring 1.35 metres in height, its whole surface polished like a mirror.

iii   'For having challenged the assessment criteria of the customs authorities, but also and above all a certain vision of art, this lawsuit was a landmark case that the history of modern sculpture cannot continue to disregard. Art defied the law and the law finally bowed to the 'truth of art' and regained its flexibility. Thus this case goes far beyond the strictly legal context and can be counted as one of the best pleas for freedom and truth that are the pride of American justice', A.Paleologue, Postface et fortune critique, *Brancusi contre Etats-Unis, un procès historique, 1928* (Adam Biro, 1995) p.122.

iv   'In this lawsuit . . . what was involved was nothing less than the imposition of a fair delimitation of the cognitive frontiers of art that had been called into question as a result of the crossing of the geographical frontiers between two continents – in other words, the very definition of what can or cannot be considered artistic', N. Heinich, *Le triple jeu de l'art contemporain* (Les éditions de Minuit, 1998) p.48.

v   This question will be addressed here purely from a legal perspective, although it can and has frequently been addressed from other – notably philosophical, aesthetic and sociological – perspectives. See also W. Benjamin, 'L'œuvre d'art à l'époque de sa reproduction mécanisée', in *Ecrits Français* (Gallimard, Paris, 1991); T. de Duve, '*Réponse à côté de la question* 'Qu'est-ce que la sculpture moderne?'', in Catalogue *Qu'est-ce que la sculpture moderne?* (Centre Georges Pompidou, 1986).

vi   N. Heinich comments that 'the conservatism of the cultural institutions is not the only obstacle to the integration of aesthetic innovations: the legal . . . frameworks add their inertia or contradictions', *Le triple jeu de l'art contemporain*, ibid., p.47.

vii   J.-M. Pontier notes that 'the notion of 'work(s) of art' thus appears in [Article L. 112-2] in a fragmented manner through several sorts of creations; no overall notion of 'work(s) of art' is considered', 'La notion d'œuvre d'art', in *Revue de Droit Public* (1990) p.1408.

viii   Professor P.-Y. Gautier proposes defining works of art as 'intellectual productions essentially involving forms and aesthetics', *Propriété littéraire et artistique* (Puf, 1996) p.92. Professor Sirinelli favours a broader approach: '...not restrictively works corresponding to an aesthetic ideal, but rather, more generally, creations which are exteriorized by forms and/or colours (and which, it is said, are perceptible to the eye)', *Propriété littéraire et artistique et droits voisins* (Dalloz,1992) p.25.

ix   In which case, the author will be unable to remedy an infringement of his moral or economic rights. As this article is concerned with the concept of originality and the conditions of its recognition, it will not deal with the implications of that recognition, namely the enjoyment of protection. The crucial point is to determine in the first place whether, having regard to the criteria of substantive law, a 'work' is recognized as being original and can thus enjoy protection.

x   For example, Article L. 122-8 of the Intellectual Property Code restricts enjoyment of the *droit de suite* to original works without specifying the characteristics of such works; cf. also the amended proposal for a European Parliament and Council directive on the *droit de suite* for authors of original works of art presented by the Commission on 12 March 1998, *COM* (1998) 78 final.

xi   Civ. Ct., Seine, 20 December 1895, Ann. 1898, 52, cited by S. Hans, *L'originalité au sens du droit d'auteur : contribution à l'étude de la notion*, Thesis (Paris I, 1991) p.7.

xii   *Le Droit d'Auteur* (Dalloz, 1950) p.23.

xiii   R. Moulin thus observes that 'contemporary art . . . has challenged the accepted definition of a work of art . . . In the course of the last two decades, artists . . . have explicitly sought to *assassinate* the work, in the generally accepted sense of the term, in order to put an end to its elitist social status and its privileged economic one. They only had to continue the enterprise of art's self-destruction that was started at the beginning of the 20th century: rejection of the craftsmanship element of the artistic profession, refusal of the depictive; abandonment of the work to chance; designation of 'found' objects as art; substitution of the artist for the work', 'Remarques sur la définition sociologique de l'œuvre d'art', in *Le marché commun et le marché de l'art* (La Documentation française, 1986) p.32.

xiv   H. Cherpillod, *L'objet du droit d'auteur* (Cedidac, 1985) p.116.

xv   M. Melot thus notes that 'numerous historians have already sought to dispel the illusion that the originality of an artist is to be found in the content of his or her works and, particularly, in what is inimitable in that content. The unique character of the content is not really unique once it is understood as a process of signification that exists only if shared and becomes the sum of the interpretations that are required if the work is not to sink into absolute insignificance . . . It is the content of the work as a whole that must be evacuated as being irrelevant for the definition of an art object . . . It could be said, provocatively, that the content of the work hides the true creative enterprise of the artist in the object that he or she chooses to make', 'La notion d'originalité et son importance dans la définition des objets d'art', in *Sociologie de l'Art*, International Symposium, Marseilles, 13-14 June 1985 (La Documentation française, 1986) p.198.

xvi   *Le droit d'auteur en France* (Dalloz, 1978) p.11.

xvii   Professors A. and H.-J. Lucas note that 'the distinction between the idea and the form tends to become more blurred with the development of 'conceptual art' whose followers share Sol LeWitt's view that 'ideas can be works of art'', *Traité de la propriété littéraire et artistique* (Litec, 1994) p.72.

xviii   CA Paris, 13 March 1986 (Dalloz, 1987) summaries with comments, 150, C. Colombet obs.

xix   Professor C. Colombet criticized the use of this expression: 'The Court states that the idea is an original work, when it must be repeated constantly to avoid serious confusion that ideas cannot enjoy copyright protection; in actual fact, the idea was given concrete expression in this case through the creation of an original form . . . and it was this form that triggered off the legal protection', obs. under CA Paris 13 March 1986 (Dalloz, 1987) summaries with comments, p.150.

xx   C. Carreau, 'Mérite et droit d'auter', *RIDA* no.109 (July 1981) 207. C. Carreau notes that 'the Paris Court of Appeal doubtless yielded without hesitation for a while to the temptation to accept the protection of the idea contained in the form, against the very principles of our law', p.207.

xxi   TGI Paris, 26 May 1987 (Dalloz, 1988) summaries with comments, 201, C. Colombet obs.

xxii   Professor C. Colombet observes that 'this type of dispute is not surprising as we know that it is sometimes difficult to distinguish between the idea and the form in late 20th century visual art', obs. under TGI Paris, 26 May 1987 (Dalloz, 1988) summaries with comments, p.201.

xxiii   A. Strowel agreed with this decision because, in his view, Christo's 'land art method' cannot be appropriated. He points out that 'the collage process or the impressionist style fall outside the scope of copyright protection, unlike such and such a work by Juan Gris or Renoir', *Droit d'auteur et copyright, Divergences et convergences, Etude de droit comparé* (Bruylant-LGDJ, 1993) p.414.

xxiv   In I. Cherpillod's view, it seems 'wrong to believe that an author can be recognized through the creation. While it is true that a work by Vasarely, for example, is easily identifiable as such for a connoisseur, it is more because the author's own 'style' is recognizable in it. Yet style, as an abstract process, is not included among the protected features', *L'objet du droit d'auteur, ibid.*, p.132.

xxv   H. Braun-Vega, 'Du style et de l'image de marque, Paroles d'Artistes, Nourritures du corps et de l'esprit', *Arts et Lettres*, no.6, (Verso, 1997) p.28.

xxvi   *L'époque, la mode, la morale, la passion. Aspects de l'art d'aujourd'hui 1977-1978*, Centre Georges Pompidou, 1987, p.524, cited by A. Strowel, *Le droit et l'objet d'art, Réflexions en marge d'un colloque : Annales de droit de Louvain*, vol.L.4 (Bruylant, 1990) p.389.

xxvii   *Sentences on Conceptual Art*, (G.M.T.A.C., 1989) p.21.

xxviii   'Le montant de la rançon, Art conceptuel : l'avant et l'après', *Art Press* no.139 (Sept. 1989) p.36.

xxix   H. Cherpillod, *L'objet du droit d'auteur, ibid.*, p.128.

xxx   On several occasions, museums have exhibited Duchamp's readymades, such as the urinal baptised *Fountain* by the artist.

xxxi   'The urinal obtained its status of a work of art by means of an impeccable strategy that was both cunning and cruel ... So many books cite it that it is futile to deny that it has been recorded by the jurisprudence of modern art. Legal vocabulary is more than appropriate here because one speaks of legitimacy in general and the legitimation of *Fountain* in particular...', T. de Duve, *Résonances du Readymade, Duchamp entre avant-garde et tradition* (Editions Jacqueline Chambon, 1989) p.107.

xxxii   O. Laligant notes 'that an object that is not in any way the product of an intellectual activity on the part of the person who claims to be its 'author' cannot be considered to be an intellectual work within the meaning of the 1957 law. Indeed, the choice of the person who claims to be the 'author' – a choice in which aesthetic consideration has admittedly played a role – cannot in itself make it a copyrightable work because the object existed already as such before it was chosen and the person claiming to be its author added nothing to it', 'Problématique de la protection du parfum par le droit d'auteur', *RRJ* (1989-3) p.606.

xxxiii   'First condition: *determine the readymades*; in other words, choose them. In an unpublished interview, Duchamp, without the slightest ambiguity, lay the foundations of a syllogism: *the word 'art' means to make and, almost, to make with one's hands*, he said, and a bit later: *to make is to choose and always to choose*. All that remains is for us to conclude: the word 'art' means to choose', T. de Duve, *Résonances du Readymade, Duchamp entre avant-garde et tradition*, ibid., p.23.

xxxiv   *Traité de la propriété littéraire et artistique*, ibid., p.67.

xxxv   *L'objet du droit d'auteur, ibid.*, p.131.

xxxvi   Professor M. Vivant thus observes that 'it would be amusing to submit Duchamp's *Urinal* or Malevich's *Square on a White Background* to the traditional criterion of originality ... It is a good bet that they would have difficulty in passing the test', cited by A. Maffre-Baugé, *L'œuvre de l'esprit, empreinte de la personnalité de l'auteur?*, Thesis (Montpellier I, 1997) p.285.

xxxvii   R. Moulin rightly raises the question of the law's relevance: 'Can this modern system inherited from the 19th century still be the contemporary system? Today, by a sort of reversal of perspectives, it seems to be the artist-creator's social recognition by the public cultural institutions and/or the art and cultural goods market that constitutes the precondition for defining a work as artistic', 'Remarques sur la définition sociologique de l'œuvre d'art', in *Le marché commun et le marché de l'art, ibid.*, p.32.

xxxviii   A. Strowel, *Le droit et l'objet d'art, Réflexions en marge d'un colloque : Annales de droit de Louvain*, ibid., p.394.

xxxix   'De quelques réflexions sur l'idée d'une collection autre', in Catalogue *Passions privées, Collections particulières d'art moderne et contemporain en France* (Editions des Musées de la Ville de Paris, 1995) p.104.

xl   The idea and the composition precede the genesis of a work of art; as long as the concrete vision of the subject, transforming the idea into an image, has not been exteriorized, it is still only a prefiguration of the future work, a purely intellectual composition or, if you prefer, an internal vision, a concrete dream . . . Then, when the artist has put the finishing touches to it, the composition becomes an integral part of the completed work and is inseparable from the expression, *i.e.* the strokes and shades of the colouring . . . *Precisely because it is an integral part of the finished work, the composition is capable of appropriation and lends itself to the exercise of an exclusive right*', *Le droit d'auteur en France*, ibid., p.76.

xli   Professor C. Colombet points out that the composition of a painting will be made up of 'the form of the rectangular, square or oval picture, the place of each component and the harmony of the whole', 'L'art et l'originalité (sur quelques propos de Georges Braque)' (Dalloz, 1992) chronicle 195.

xlii   Thus A. Strowel considers that, in works such as Malevich's *Black Square* or Yves Klein's monochromes, 'it is hard to find a personal stamp (especially since some artists, such as D. Buren, explicitly adopt a strategy of eliminating all subjectivity) other than in the project or the artistic idea which, in principle, are not copyrightable', *Droit d'auteur et copyright, Divergences et convergences, Etude de droit comparé*, ibid., p.411.

xliii   Yves Klein wrote: 'I stroll about and meet states, nice things, a real or imaginary landscape, an object, a person, or simply an unknown cloud of sensitivity that I cross suddenly by chance, an atmosphere . . . The silent conversation that follows between the way things are and myself generates an impalpable affinity, an affinity that is *indefinable* as Delacroix says, It is this indefinable quality, this poetic, ineffable moment that I wish to fix on my canvas since my mode of being (note that I did not say expression) is to paint. So I paint the pictorial moment springing from an illumination by impregnation in life itself', quoted by D. Riout, *La peinture monochrome, Histoire et archéologie d'un genre* (Editions Jacqueline Chambon, 1996) p.24.

xliv   D. Riout observes in this regard that 'monochromes – and there is no reason why Klein's should be an exception to the rule – are paintings. However, torn from the problematics of painting, monochrome propositions invite the viewer to invent a new attitude that is essential if the artist's desire and the viewer's mind are to be able to meet', *La peinture monochrome, Histoire et archéologie d'un genre*, ibid., p.22.

xlv   While the lines record only moods or psychological states, colour – *materialized sensitivity*
       – catches the indefinable ... The picture that is the product of such an operation is neither
       a representation nor a construction nor even an expression and Klein can define it:
       The picture is only the witness, the sensitive plate that has seen what happened ...
       My pictures represent poetic events or rather they are still, silent and static witnesses of
       the very essence of free movement and life, a flame of poetry during the pictorial instant!',
       D. Riout, *La peinture monochrome, Histoire et archéologie d'un genre*, ibid., p.22.

xlvi   *Le Droit d'Auteur en France*, ibid., p.12.

xlvii As D. Arasse notes, 'many works today that are considered to be pictorial unities are the
       fruit of a true division of labour where several artists have collaborated in the light of their
       specific artistic abilities. This practice continues the tradition of the studio where, after
       learning to grind and mix colours and then to draw in the style of the master's works, the
       apprentice was allowed to paint the surrounds before participating in the secondary and
       perhaps even the main parts. Works made by several artists are thus in the direct tradition
       of the collective and temporary studios that were created in the 16th century ... It is not
       surprising, therefore, to learn that, in Mechelen (Malines), in the 16th century, the paintings
       were sometimes systematically collective: 'one person did the heads, another the
       extremities, a third the drapery and yet another the landscape', *Le détail, Pour une*
       histoire rapprochée de la peinture (Flammarion, 1992) p.119.

xlviii *La peinture monochrome, Histoire et archéologie d'un genre, op.cit.*, p.23.

xlix   Did not Leonardo da Vinci say that painting is '*cosa mentale*'?

l   D. Riout, 'Les peintures d'un peintre qui ne peint pas', in Daniel Walravens,
       De la peinture en général (ERSEP, 1994) p.15.

li   D. Riout, 'Les peintures d'un peintre qui ne peint pas', in Daniel Walravens,
       De la peinture en général, ibid., p.16.

lii   B. Marcadé, 'Daniel Walravens ou la peinture déléguée', in
       De la peinture en général, ibid., p.11.

liii   TGI, 21 January 1983, second case (Dalloz, 1984) Juris.
       summaries with comments, 286, C. Colombet obs.

liv   'Is a work of art not ... the very expression of the person of the artist? And is it not the case
       that the prerogatives of artistic creation are closely linked to the inviolable attributes of the
       human person?', R. Savatier, *Le droit de l'art et des lettres, les travaux des muses dans les*
       balances de la justice, (LGDJ, 1953) p.16.

lv   B. Guelton notes in connection with contemporary creation that 'the ever-growing
       importance of the artist's 'personality' as opposed to the work's material or aesthetic
       status is also found in the very conception of works as defined by copyright law',
       L'exposition, interprétation et réinterprétation, L'Harmattan, 1998, p.62.

lvi   The conflicting opinions that this requirement provokes are instructive: A. Strowel's view
       of Malevich's *Black Square* is that 'it is hard to find a personal stamp ... other than in the
       project or the artistic idea which, in principle, are not copyrightable', whereas O. Laligant
       states; 'We admit that we cannot understand why an abstract painting ... should not,
       by nature, be fit to receive the stamp of its author's personality', see notes 41 and 81.

lvii   There is no doubt in N. Heinich's mind that the law needs to evolve in response to the 'profoundly disruptive character of these new artistic practices'. Thus contemporary art puts the rules of copyright law to the test in two ways: firstly, by prompting the actors to take legal action to obtain relief for damage caused by works or acts performed in the name of art (leading to the development of case law) and, secondly, by prompting legal scholars to modify their categories to adapt them to the new situations that are created ... in both cases, contemporary artists help to make the law move', *Le triple jeu de l'art contemporain, ibid.*, p.158.

lviii   N. Heinich, *Le triple jeu de l'art contemporain, op.cit.*, p.75.

 lix   *Remarques sur la définition sociologique de l'œuvre d'art, ibid.*, p.32.

  lx   C. Francblin, 'L'art conceptuel entre les actes', *Art Press* no.139 (1989) p.45.

 lxi   Interview by A. Miller-Keller, *Consequences* no.5, 1985, quoted by C. Francblin, 'L'art conceptuel entre les actes', *ibid.*, p.45.

lxii   It is this annexed signature, separate from the object itself, that it is interesting to consider. Artists have not constructed theories about it. They have simply signed deeds, deeds that enable a piece of work to be attributed without any possibility of error – and these deeds have the value of speeches', C. Francblin, 'L'art conceptuel entre les actes', *ibid.*, p.45.

lxiii   C. Francblin, 'L'art conceptuel entre les actes', *ibid.*, p.45.

lxiv   C. Francblin, 'L'art conceptuel entre les actes', *op.cit.*, p.46.

 lxv   Vasarely, *Plasti-cité, L'œuvre plastique dans votre vie quotidienne*, coll. Mutations orientations (Casterman, 1970) p.19.

lxvi   For S. LeWitt, 'execution is a matter of no importance'.

lxvii   In 'L'art conceptuel entre les actes', *op.cit.*, p.46.

lxviii Quoted by C. Francblin, 'L'art conceptuel entre les actes', *op.cit.*, p.46.

lxix   S. LeWitt demonstrates clearly the case where the idea takes precedence over the work itself: 'when an artist uses a conceptual art form, it means that everything is planned and determined beforehand and that the execution is a matter of routine. The idea becomes a machine that makes the art', quoted by G. Mollet-Viéville, 'De quelques réflexions sur l'idée d'une collection autre', in Catalogue *Passions privées, ibid.*, p.10.

 lxx   L. Weiner thus sells works that exist only in the form of statements and have not yet been executed when acquired by a collector who is offered 'three possibilities for its exhibition':
        1) the artist can construct the work;
        2) the work can be produced (by someone else);
        3) the work can remain unexecuted; as each proposal is equal and consistent with the artist's intention, the choice of one of the conditions of display is for the receiver to make on reception ... here everything is evolving; the work becomes plural and plays with the tangible/intangible, visible/invisible ambivalence by requiring the collector, who assumes responsibility for his *Statements*, to return to the eternal question of what is the reality of the work he possesses'. Lawrence Weiner thus affirms that 'the work does not necessarily have to be executed', G. Mollet-Viéville, 'De quelques réflexions sur l'idée d'une collection autre', in Catalogue *Passions privées, ibid.*, p.106.

lxxi   C. Francblin, 'L'art conceptuel entre les actes', *op.cit.*, p.46.

lxxii   When all is said and done, the artist is not the only one to perform the act of creation because the viewer establishes the work's contact with the outside world by deciphering and interpreting its underlying qualifications and so adds his or her own contribution to the creative process', M. Duchamp, *Duchamp du signe, Ecrits* (Flammarion, 1994) p.189.

lxxiii C. Millet, 'Le montant de la rançon, Art conceptuel : l'avant et l'après', *ibid.*, p.39.

lxxiv   *L'originalité au sens du droit d'auteur : contribution à l'étude de la notion*, ibid., p.321.

lxxv   A. Strowel, *Le droit et l'objet d'art, Réflexions en marge d'un colloque :*
        Annales de droit de Louvain, ibid., p.394.

lxxvi   M. Blanchot, *L'espace littéraire*, Folio Essays (Gallimard, 1996) p.44.

lxxvii A. Strowel, *Le droit et l'objet d'art, Réflexions en marge d'un colloque :*
        Annales de droit de Louvain, op.cit., p.386.

lxxviii N. Heinich observes that while, for some, 'a rejection of self-expression accompanies the
        conceptualist dematerialization of works of art . . . By contrast, Klein expressed the desire
        to 'paint a single masterpiece: myself, constantly', writing that 'true painters and poets do
        not paint or write poems. They are quite simply painters and poets by condition. Their
        presence and the mere fact that they exist as such is their one major work.' He thus showed
        the passage from the first to the second dimension of the dematerialization of the work
        of art, detached from the object which is now only the pretext or the instrument, namely
        dematerialization through the shift not to the concept this time but to the person of the
        artist. We are dealing here with personalization in the most literal sense of the term, since
        the artist is physically implicated in his or her creation: not only through the expression
        of his or her 'hand' which signs the work's authenticity but also through the presence of his
        or her body in the work's materiality – or what remains of it.' *Le triple jeu de l'art
        contemporain, op.cit.*, p.105.

lxxix   S. Hans, *L'originalité au sens du droit d'auteur : contribution à l'étude de la notion,
        ibid.*, p.162.

lxxx   D. Riout, *La peinture monochrome, Histoire et archéologie d'un genre, op.cit.*, p.27.

lxxxi   D. Riout, La peinture monochrome, Histoire et archéologie d'un genre, op.cit., p.24.

lxxxii O. Laligant has rightly observed: 'We admit that we cannot understand why an abstract
        painting . . . should not, by nature, be fit to receive the stamp of its author's personality…',
        'Problématique de la protection du parfum par le droit d'auteur', *RRJ*, ibid., p.630.

lxxxiii However, M. Sanouillet notes that 'Fifty years on, it became clear that the appearance
        of *readymades* in 1914 represented not an evolution or even a revolution in the history
        of modern aesthetics, but a true transformation', in *Duchamp du signe, Ecrits*, ibid., p.11.

lxxxiv That is to say persons who are in a position to give an enlightened opinion: artists,
        philosophers, writers, critics, collectors, art dealers, exhibition curators...

lxxxv   'When you choose something belonging to an earlier period and adapt it to your own work,
        this process may be creative. The result is not brand new but it is new to the extent that it is
        the product of an original process.' M. Duchamp, *Duchamp du signe, Ecrits, ibid.*, p.169.

lxxxvi G. Mollet-Viéville, 'De quelques réflexions sur l'idée d'une collection autre', in Catalogue
        Passions privées, op.cit., p.104.

lxxxvii Thus for A. Bertrand, 'Is this operation in which the artist expresses his personality not
        a creative act for the purposes of copyright? Most certainly [...]: 'Whether Mutt [Marcel
        Duchamp] produced the fountain with his own hands or not is of no importance. He
        CHOSE it. He took an ordinary functional object and arranged it in such a way that its
        utilitarian significance disappears under the new title and the new viewpoint – he created
        a new way of thinking for this object' (Duchamp M., extract from an article published in
        The Blind Man, quoted in *Duchamp and his Time*, (Time Life, 1978) 39, *Le droit d'auteur
        et les droits voisins* (Masson, 1991) p.99.

lxxxviii CA, Dijon, 7 May 1996, *Dalloz* (1998) Juris. summaries with comments, 189. A. Bertrand
        points out in connection with readymades that 'the situation is similar to that of
        photography where case law considers that the work's originality does not stem from
        the photographed object but from the creative effort that is reflected in the framing, the
        play of light and the object's presentation', *Le droit d'auteur et les droits voisins*, ibid., p.99.

lxxxix O. Laligant notes that 'what is required is not that the work should be perceived by everyone's senses and intellect but only that it should be capable of being perceived by some people's senses and intellect', 'Problématique de la protection du parfum par le droit d'auteur', *ibid.*, p.623.

xc The assistance of an *amicus curiae* could help the courts to form an enlightened opinion and supplement the view of an expert. An *amicus curiae*, is neither a witness nor an expert but a person who can attend the hearing to provide legal or factual information', J. Vincent and S. Guinchard, *Procédure civile* (Dalloz, 1991) p.735.

xci C. Cass., 13 November 1973, *Dalloz*, 1974, J. 533, C. Colombet note, and TGI, 21 January 1983, second case, (Dalloz, 1984) Juris. summaries with comments, 286, C. Colombet obs.

xcii *L'originalité au sens du droit d'auteur : contribution à l'étude de la notion*, *op.cit.*, p.85.

xciii 'Thus the frontiers of art were officially extended to incorporate modern practices and, in particular, abstraction. That this extension had to be legalized by the courts and not just legitimized by the opinion of experts, the interest of collectors and the purchasing policy of museums says a lot about the profoundly disruptive character of these new artistic practices', N. Heinich, *Le triple jeu de l'art contemporain*, *op.cit.*, p.48.

Appropriation Art: Fair Use or Foul?

Johnson Okpaluba [i]

The history of art is the history of copy rites, of transformations that take place during acts of copying. [ii]

The reuse of pre-existing material in new contexts is a feature typical of modern arts practice, and is considered to be an essential component of postmodern artistic expression. This practice is generally referred to as 'deconstruction and recontextualisation.' In the visual arts, this practice is termed 'appropriation art,' [iii] and covers a wide range of artistic practices including collage, montage and simulationism. Outside of artistic circles, the term 'appropriation' bears strong negative connotations, signifying essentially theft or piracy. [iv]

Recently the so-called 'threat' posed by digital technology to copyright law and copyright owners, has been of widespread concern to legal commentators. The discussion has centred on the uncontrolled copying and distribution of digitised works that have the potential in the digital environment to make copyright law unenforceable, thereby undermining authors' incentives to create works for dissemination. The debate as to the form that copyright law should take in the digital era has led to a polarisation of viewpoints between those who wish to see more rights granted to authors to protect their works and greater enforcement of these rights and those who believe that copyright is already 'over-strength' and that users' rights need to be considered so that creativity and creation of cultural products is not stifled. The irony of this debate is that appropriation art, an essentially non-digital artistic practice, raises a question that has been at the centre of the copyright discourse ever since the invention of the printing press made it possible for the widespread dissemination of ideas, namely, how do we define the legal interest of a copyright owner in his work. Artists such as Sherrie Levine and Jeff Koons have in the last two decades pushed appropriation art to its extreme by appropriating whole images without attribution to the copyright owner, and as a consequence these artists have found themselves subject to copyright infringement suits as copyright law tends to view appropriation as tantamount to copyright infringement.

At present, courts in the U.K. and U.S. utilise three broad options to excuse an otherwise infringing copy. First, they may analyse the original work and decide that the work is not one that is subject to copyright protection.[v] Second, even if the original work is capable of being protected by copyright, courts may determine that the defendant did not in law make a 'copy.'[vi] Finally, where the original work is protected by copyright and the courts determine that the defendant has copied a substantial part of the plaintiff's work, courts have the option of deciding that the defendant's use falls within an exemption.[vii] The focus in this essay is on the third option. The most significant exemption is the fair use/fair dealing[viii] doctrine which allows users, under certain circumstances, to use the copyright protected works of others without permission.

The first part of this essay discusses the development and nature of appropriation art to provide the reader with the context in which appropriation artists work. The second part of this essay discusses appropriative practices and how copyright law impacts upon such practices with particular reference to the U.S. decision of *Rogers v. Koons*[ix] (*'Koons'*), a case involving appropriation art where the defence of fair use was invoked. This part of the essay also briefly considers the position under U.K. law and provides a brief overview of the context in which any fair dealing defence in the U.K. will have to operate following the implementation of the Information Society Directive.[x] The third part of this essay focuses on the Supreme Court decision in *Campbell v. Acuff Rose Music, Inc.*[xi] (*'Campbell'*), a case which involved a music parody of the well-known Roy Orbison song *Oh Pretty Woman*. This author uses the decision in *Campbell* to demonstrate that the fair use provisions in the U.S. are flexible enough to accommodate appropriation art practices, provided the courts are willing to recognise that appropriation of images can serve a valid artistic and critical function.[xii] The final part of this essay briefly considers an alternative to liability, namely, licensing, and focuses on the suitability of various forms of licensing from the point of view of users and right-holders.

I. Appropriation Art

Throughout the twentieth century, artists have employed the practice of appropriation both as a means of creation and for articulating social criticism. Using the work of other artists has enabled artists to comment upon or react to the presence and meaning of pervasive cultural icons. In fact, appropriation art is essentially an artistic technique not peculiar at all to the twentieth century, as it has always been used as an aid to teach drawing.[xiii]

There is a long tradition of artists who have appropriated elements of other artist's work and recycled them into their own works, starting with Picasso's cubist collages. In the early twentieth century, artists like Picasso, Braque, Gris, and Schwitters began to use 'found' objects in their work; everyday items such as newspapers, litter, string, and photographs were integrated with painting. Collage allows pre-made objects to co-exist, combining to form one new work of art. Although the individual component parts of a collage have had a previous life, a previous function, they are given new life by the new context in which they are set. The essential concept of collage is to bring into association unrelated images to form a different expressive identity.[xiv] It is interesting to note that some commentators liken digital sampling,[xv] a form of appropriation practice in the audio arts, to visual collages. For instance Christine Fellner notes:

> Collages are interesting in that they are works which will incorporate parts, substantial or otherwise, of other works which are likely to have their own copyright. It may be acceptable to cut out photographs, etc., from magazines to make a collage, but if the collage is then itself photographed or shown on television or incorporated in a film, the photographer would have grounds for complaint. In this respect, collages have a lot in common with 'megamixes' and sampling in the music industry . . . Or with 'deconstructionism' in literature . . .[xvi]

By the middle of the twentieth century, the direct incorporation of source material from pre-existing texts and popular culture became commonplace. Many of the most influential artists in their fields made collage-like appropriation a central part of their work,[xvii] with the result that today this practice has entered the mainstream and is no longer a preserve of the avant-garde.

In the 1950s, and throughout the development of Pop art, commodity images and objects were juxtaposed or run parallel with mechanically reproduced high-cultural icons by artists such as Andy Warhol, Robert Rauschenberg, and Roy Lichtenstein. Warhol is probably the best-known appropriation artist and a figurehead of the Pop art movement. Warhol appropriated the designs and trademarks of popular commercial items such as Brillo boxes and Campbell's soup cans and the images of icons such as Marilyn Monroe and Jacqueline Kennedy. These artists exalted the commonplace and put forward as icons the commercial images and personalities of their times. Integral to the Pop art movement were the appropriation of mass production techniques for creating the works and thematic presentations of Pop art in exhibitions that serve to emphasise the assembly-line characteristics of the art.[xviii] By co-opting images and strategies integral to consumer culture, Pop art undermined many of the tenets fundamental to modernism, and it is said to be responsible for providing the conceptual foundation for much of contemporary art and the transition from modernism to postmodernism.[xix]

The past three decades have witnessed several movements that involve the resurrection of previous artistic styles. The ascendancy of neo-Expressionism, neo-Minimalism, and neo-Pop, among others, can be interpreted as an admission that everything has been done before and that the avant-garde has exhausted itself. Thus artists who appropriate images question whether art can ever be original and authentic, replacing sincerity with cynicism.[xx] These so-called 'appropriationists' are said to challenge the notions of authenticity and originality, and as a practice, appropriation art serves to remind us that copyright law is unable to accommodate this new form of cultural expression.[xxi]

II. Appropriative Practices and Copyright

Some appropriation art does not implicate copyright law at all, but when the borrowed image is a copyright work, there is a risk of copyright infringement. The doctrine of fair use may provide an alternative to liability for copyright infringement. The following section looks at fair use and focuses on the decision in *Koons*.[xxii]

Three forms of appropriation practice can be identified. First, there is the practice of appropriating whole images which are often protected by copyright and used virtually unchanged in works without any attribution to the copyright owner. Second, is the practice of montage, which involves incorporating images from several sources into a new work. A third form of appropriation practice is termed 'simulationism,' and involves the appropriation not from a specific original or set of originals, but appropriation from an entire genre to produce a work that does not resemble any specific work.

> In discussions of contemporary art, appropriation is generally understood as a method that uses recontextualisation as a critical strategy. In theory, when an artist places a familiar image in a new context, the manoeuvre forces the viewer to reconsider how different contexts affect meaning and to understand that all meaning is socially constructed . . . [xxiii]

The challenge of appropriation art to copyright law is not necessarily designed to reform the law, but to implicate the viewer in the artist's critical gesture and to test 'the viewer's ability to see beyond the link between notions of originality and art's commodity status.'[xxiv] For instance, in the late 1970s, appropriation artist Sherrie Levine re-photographed well-known photographs by Edward Weston and Walker Evans without transforming or altering the original images, thus giving her photographs the semblance of being duplicates of the 'originals.' Levine thus debunks the notion of the artist as author, and invites alternative 'readings' of the work as regards originality. Levine's work, though, is not solely concerned with criticism and deconstruction; it may also be viewed as a celebration of the artists that she copies. Acceptance of Levine's pictures as her own, would require us to ignore the codification of artworks predicated on ownership, and this, it is said, would cause the very foundations of copyright law to crumble.[xxv] Proponents of appropriation art view practices such as Levine's as being distinct from plagiarism and situated within a larger movement of critical political discourse: that of 'postmodernism'.[xxvi] By recontextualising an image, the artist is said to have transformed and altered it in an attempt to force viewers to see the original work and its significance differently.[xxvii] The legacy of artists such as Levine is important because the appropriated image and the parodied image are central to contemporary art.

It is an interesting characteristic of appropriation art lawsuits that most of them tend to settle out of court.[xxviii] For instance, in 1976, photographer Morton Beebe discovered that his photograph, entitled *Diver*, had been incorporated into a Robert Rauschenberg print named *Pull*, part of the *Hoarfrost* series that is considered by many critics to be among Rauschenberg's most important. Beebe was apparently extremely upset by the unauthorised use of his work because Rauschenberg was a leader in the artists' rights movement and had spent a great deal of time bringing the needs of artists to the attention of the legislature, media, and the public. Rauschenberg was surprised at Beebe's reaction, as he had received many letters from people expressing their happiness and pride that their images were incorporated and transformed in his work. Beebe sued Rauschenberg for a minimum of $10,000 damages and the profits of the sale from Rauschenberg's print. The matter eventually settled more than a year later and four years on from Beebe's original complaint. Beebe accepted $3,000, a copy of Rauschenberg's print, and an undertaking that if the print were exhibited, Beebe would be credited in any accompanying catalogue.[xxix] Beebe was forced to settle for less than his claim because his legal costs were mounting and he did not want to risk losing the case on a technicality. However, Rauschenberg was unsympathetic in his views on the matter and stated that as he had used collage in his work since 1949, he never

Art Rogers, *Puppies*, 1986

felt that he was infringing anyone's rights, as he had consistently transformed the images to give the works the possibility of being reconsidered and viewed in a totally new context.[xxx]

More recently in the U.K., there have been two copyright infringement disputes, both of which have settled. First, Damien Hirst's appropriation of the toy company Humbrol's 10-inch high Young Scientist Anatomy Set for his 6 metre high, 20 ton, bronze anatomical sculpture, *Hymn*; and secondly, the controversial Turner Prize entry by Glenn Brown appropriated from an illustration by Anthony Roberts on a jacket cover of a book published in 1974.

The Application of the Fair Use Defence in Appropriation Art

In the U.S., *Koons*[xxxi] was a case which did not settle. In this case, Jeff Koons, an appropriation artist, bought a postcard reproduction of a black and white photograph by Art Rogers, *Puppies*, which depicted a smiling couple sitting on a park bench holding eight German Shepherd puppies in their laps. Rogers was commissioned to take the photograph and subsequently licensed the right to use the photograph on note cards and postcards for distribution.

Koons tore off the back of the postcard which bore Rogers' copyright notice and sent the image to his fabricators in Italy to make four sculptures by copying faithfully the postcard, reproducing features such as the angles, expressions and poses used in the photograph. When Rogers learnt of the sculptures, he filed for copyright infringement against Koons and the Sonnabend Gallery, which exhibited the sculptures, seeking $367,000 damages for alleged profits derived from the sale of three of the sculptures. Koons argued that his appropriation of the image was a fair use, as together with the other works in his exhibition, 'the Banality Show', the sculpture was designed to provide a critique of the conspicuous consumption, greed, and self-indulgence of modern consumer society.[xxxii]

Fair use is essentially 'a privilege in others than the owner of the copyright to use the copyrighted material in a reasonable manner without his consent.'[xxxiii] Fair use 'permits courts to avoid rigid application of the copyright statute when, on occasion, it would stifle the very creativity which that law is designed to foster.'[xxxiv] Whilst the expansion of the scope of copyright protection limited the rights of others to transform copyright protected works, fair use was used to determine whether the statutory right of the copyright owner should nevertheless be withheld for reasons of private or public benefit.

The doctrine of fair use in the U.S. is set out in section 107 of the Copyright Act 1976 as follows:

> Notwithstanding the provisions of section 106 and 106A, the fair use of a copyrighted work, including such uses by reproduction in copies or phonorecords or by any other means specified by that section, for purposes such as criticism, comment, news reporting, teaching . . . , scholarship or research, is not an infringement of copyright.[xxxv] In determining whether the use made of a work in any particular case is a fair use the factors to be considered shall include –
>
> 1. the purpose and character of the use, including whether such use is of a commercial nature or is for non-profit educational purposes;
> 2. the nature of the copyrighted work;
> 3. the amount and substantiality of the portion used in relation to the copyrighted work as a whole; and
> 4. the effect of the use upon the potential market for or value of the copyrighted work.

The District Court granted partial summary judgement in Rogers' favour ruling that the sculpture was an infringing unauthorised derivative work based on Rogers' photograph and that such use was not a fair use.[xxxvi] Koons was, however, afforded the opportunity to prove deductible expenses at trial in order to reduce his liability in damages. On appeal, the Second Circuit acknowledged the existence of the postmodern practice of appropriation, but rejected Koons' defence of fair use, believing that one's mode of artistic expression must be constrained by the traditional limits of copyright.[xxxvii] A detailed analysis of the Second Circuit's consideration of the four fair use factors is set out below.

The first fair use factor to be considered is 'the purpose and character of the use, including whether such use is of a commercial nature or is for non-profit educational purposes.'[xxxviii] This might be characterised as a question of whether the secondary use impedes what is said to be one of the goals of copyright, the stimulation of creativity. The Copyright Act 1976 does not state which purposes will make a 'use' fair, instead, section 107 lists criticism, comment, news reporting, teaching, scholarship and research as examples where a finding of fair use may be appropriate, although they are not irrebuttable.[xxxix] The listed uses may be said to enjoy a preferred status under copyright legislation and the legislation appears to have set up value judgements on the worth of these works.

In *Koons*, the court ruled that Koons' substantial profit from his 'intentionally exploitive' (*sic*) use of the plaintiff's work militated against a finding of fair use.[xl] The Second Circuit adopted the reasoning of the Supreme Court in *Sony Corp. of America v. Universal City Studios, Inc.* ('*Sony*') that copies made for commercial or profit-making purposes are presumptively unfair.[xli]

The U.S. Congress has declared that parody is a type of use to which it is appropriate to apply the fair use defence[xlii] and the courts have recognised parody as a valuable art form.[xliii] Koons argued that his work was a satire or parody of society at large and that he was a member of the school of American artists who believe the mass production of commodities and media images has caused a deterioration in the quality of society, and this artistic tradition by incorporating these images into works of art proposes to comment critically on both the incorporated object and the political and economic system that created it.[xliv] In order to make his point Koons' sculpture clearly ridiculed Rogers' photograph in that: (i) he added different colours to the dogs' noses which were navy with shiny purple tips, (ii) the dogs' collars were striped with purple and blue; and (iii) the couple were painted a garish colour with daisies sprouting from their heads.[xlv]

The Second Circuit, whilst accepting that Koons' work was part of the appropriation artist's tradition,[xlvi] ruled that his work was not a parody because it did not comment directly upon the appropriated photograph.[xlvii] Furthermore, even if Koons had claimed that he was parodying the photograph, his defence would not have been upheld, because the court ruled that by 'requiring that the copied work be an object of the parody, we merely insist that the audience be aware that underlying the parody there is an original and separate expression . . .'[xlviii] Thus, if the image had been widely known, it is more likely that this factor would have weighed in favour of Koons.[xlix]

The second fair use factor that the courts consider recognises that some works are closer to the core of intended copyright protection than others. Courts may consider, 'among other things whether the work was creative, imaginative, and original . . . and whether it represented a substantial investment of time and labour made in anticipation of a financial return.'[l] Inquiry into the nature or value of the plaintiff's work determines whether the work is of the type that copyright was intended to encourage. The Supreme Court decision in *Harper & Row, Publishers, Inc. v. Nation Enterprises*[li] ('*Nation*') suggests that more use may be permitted in relation to factual works, but only where they contain little subjective expression. The more creative a work, the more protection it is generally afforded from copying. Although Koons' work did not compete with or exploit the success of the original, the court weighed this second factor against Koons because they found that Rogers' photograph was 'creative and imaginative' and not factual in nature.[lii]

The third fair use factor focuses on the amount and substantiality of the portion used, and although wholesale copying is usually regarded as unfair, it should be noted that because the third factor is just one of four, it is possible that a court may find fair use even when an entire work is copied and the market for the original work is not impaired.[liii] Although in *Koons* the court did not acknowledge the defendant's need to appropriate an entire image in order to comment on or criticise it, it is possible that artists who appropriate whole images may successfully invoke the fair use defence.

Koons argued that he had made significant changes in the expressive elements of Rogers' work and that he had only appropriated the factual visual information in Rogers' work, namely 'two people with eight puppies, a bench and a background.'[liv] The court ruled that Koons had without authority 'copied nearly *in toto*' the very essence of Rogers' photograph and that he had taken more of the Rogers' work than would have been necessary to parody it.[lv] Given the changes made by Koons, it is not clear in what sense he copied the very essence of Rogers' work.[lvi]

The fourth fair use factor that the courts consider is the potential market for the original work. This factor is primarily concerned with the problem of market substitution for an original work and involves analysis of two markets, namely the potential market for the original work and the potential market for any derivative works.[lvii] The effect of the use upon the plaintiff's potential market for, or the value of, the copyright work has been regarded by the Supreme Court as 'undoubtedly the single most important element of fair use.'[lviii] In *Koons*, the court noted that a critical inquiry under this factor was whether Koons planned to profit from his unauthorised use of Rogers' work.[lix] The court had already found that Koons intended to profit from his work[lx] and therefore ruled that this undercut Rogers' market for his original work.[lxi] The court suggested that Rogers was likely to be harmed if Koons sold photographs of his sculpture which would then compete in the marketplace with Rogers' work.

As to the potential market for derivative works, the Second Circuit agreed with Rogers' contention that Koons' unauthorised use of his image had deprived him of the right to earn income by licensing the use of the photograph. Without enquiring whether or not the sculpture competed in the same market with Rogers' photograph, the court ruled that because Koons produced his sculpture for profit, the likelihood of future harm could be presumed and, therefore, the market for Rogers' work was prejudiced.

Whilst it is acknowledged that the defence of fair use is more readily used in cases of literary or musical parody, it should not have been beyond the court to take heed of (contemporary) artistic practice and the commercial realities of the art marketplace with a view to expanding the doctrine of fair use in the context of appropriation art. It appears from the Second Circuit's decision that it was more influenced by its distaste for Koons and his art than by any sound legal principle. It is unlikely that Koons would have benefited if the case had been heard in the U.K. The U.K. currently provides five purposes for which a work, or a substantial part thereof, can be improperly appropriated and excused as fair dealing, namely: research, private study, criticism, review, and reporting current events. In contrast to the U.S., in the U.K. there are no statutory guidelines for determining 'fair dealing', and it has sometimes been held that the statutory purposes for fair dealing are to be construed strictly.

Although the relevant purposes to which the defence of fair dealing applies are limited, the factors used to determine whether a dealing is fair under the CDPA 1988, are close to those stipulated in s. 107 Copyright Act 1976 as evidenced by the comment of Lord Denning in *Hubbard v. Vosper*: 'You must consider first the number and extent of quotations and extracts . . . Then you must consider the use made of them . . . If they are used to convey the same information as the author, for a rival purpose, that may be unfair'.[lxii]

Although no case has affirmatively decided the issue, there is scope for treating a parody as fair dealing with a work for the purposes of criticism or review of that work or of another work under section 30(1) of the CDPA 1988.[lxiii] However, to be considered fair dealing for the purposes of criticism or review, the parody must be accompanied by a sufficient acknowledgement,[lxiv] which would serve to take a lot of sting out of the parody. It is unlikely therefore that an appropriation artist would be able to claim the benefit of the fair dealing provisions if he appropriates a substantial part of a copyright protected work.[lxv]

Not all parodies, though, would be considered an infringement. Artists who practice simulationism are more likely to invoke successfully the doctrine of fair dealing where their work does not copy the recognisable expression of a copyright protected work, but merely its style or elements that are not original to the copyright author yet which an observer would readily associate with the copyright protected work.

The scope of the U.K. fair dealing provisions will soon change following the implementation of the Information Society Directive, which is designed to harmonise aspects of copyright law in the digital environment across Member States. The Directive is aimed at dealing with the digital environment but would have an impact well beyond that realm. The Directive *inter alia* limits the exceptions and limitations that Member States may make available with respect to the reproduction right. Article 5 of the Directive lists some 20 exceptions and limitations to most, if not all, of the limitations existing in national laws across the EU. The exemptions listed under Article 5 are optional, except for Article 5.1 which is mandatory.[lxvi] In any particular instance, a use will not be deemed to be fair if it prejudices the legitimate interests of the right-holder or if it conflicts with the normal exploitation of the work.[lxvii]

The current Section 30(1) fair dealing for the purpose of criticism or review, would have to be modified as the Directive gives Member States the option of enacting the following exception, 'quotation for purposes such as criticism or review.' The use has to be in accordance with fair practice and to the extent required by the specific purpose. The Directive also gives Member States the option of enacting an exception or limitation for 'use for the purpose of caricature, parody or pastiche'.[lxviii] This mirrors French law,[lxix] which despite its strong author's rights tradition, permits parody where there is no risk of it being confused with the parodied work. French law offers no definitions for 'caricature', 'parody', or 'pastiche', and thus the law is flexible and capable of affording potentially broad protection to appropriation artists. Notable also is Spanish law, where parodies are specifically exempted from infringement of the author's exclusive right of adaptation provided that they involve no risk of confusion with that work and do no harm to the original work or its author.[lxx] If the U.K. were to enact this exception, many works of appropriation art could fit within this provision. Furthermore judges would be able to expand on and find workable definitions of 'caricature', 'parody', and 'pastiche' which take account of artistic practices. However, given the approach of the U.K. judiciary towards parody, there is little guarantee that this exception would benefit appropriation artists.

The following part of this essay examines the Supreme Court decision in *Campbell*,[lxxi] a musical parody case, which indirectly, overruled much of *Koons*, by its criticisms of the Sixth Circuit decision in *Campbell* (which followed the *Koons* decision).[lxxii] The decision in *Campbell* goes some way towards accommodating appropriative practices, and this author makes suggestions as to how the fair use factors can be applied in cases involving appropriation art.

III. Fair Use after Campbell [lxxiii]

In May 1989, the group 2 Live Crew recorded a rap version of the Roy Orbison song, *Oh Pretty Woman*. 2 Live Crew used the opening line from the Orbison song, as well as the song's meter, 4/4 drum beat, and bass riff, with the intent to create a parody. 2 Live Crew claimed that doubling the length of the original's bass riff and changing the lyrics served to heighten the comic effect of their parody.

In July 1989, 2 Live Crew wrote to Acuff-Rose, the publisher of *Oh Pretty Woman*, and offered to pay a fee for the parody and to give full credit to the song's writers. Acuff-Rose refused permission to release the parody, but 2 Live Crew released the song anyway. In June 1990 Acuff-Rose sued for copyright infringement, but the District Court dismissed the action, ruling that 2 Live Crew's parody was a fair use.[lxxiv] However, the Sixth Circuit reversed the decision, finding that 2 Live Crew's song was not fair use as a matter of law.[lxxv] Key factors in the Sixth Circuit's decision were the court's reliance upon the commercial motive of the 2 Live Crew and the harm to Acuff-Rose's market.

The Supreme Court, in reversing the decision, stated that a judge's task is not to be simplified by bright-line rules because the fair use doctrine calls for case-by-case analysis and recognised that every work of intellectual property is to some extent derivative, as all works necessarily borrow and use that which preceded them.[lxxvi] The court's analysis of the fair use factors is set out below. Whereas in *Koons* the court relied on the decision in *Sony* for finding that the commercial nature of the copying by Koons militated against a finding of fair use, the Supreme Court in considering the first fair use factor explained that the decision in *Sony* stands for the proposition that:

> [The] fact that a publication [is] commercial as opposed to non-profit is a separate factor that tends to weigh against a finding of fair use.... But that is all, and the fact that even, the force of that tendency will vary with the context is a further reason against elevating commerciality to hard presumptive significance. [lxxvii]

The Supreme Court also pointed out that the investigation under this factor is 'whether the new work merely 'supersede[s] the objects' of the original creation... or instead adds something new, with a further purpose or different character, altering the first with new expression, meaning or message; it asks ... to what extent the new work is 'transformative'.[lxxviii] The Supreme Court stated that, though not determinative of fair use, the goal of copyright was furthered by the creation of transformative works and 'the more transformative the work, the less will be the significance of other factors, like commercialism, that may weigh against a finding of fair use.'[lxxix]

This emphasis on altering the original work and adding new stylistic elements before a secondary use can be considered transformative will weigh against appropriation artists who make a literal copy of a copyright protected image, although a work which includes a copyright protected work along with other images is more likely to be found to be a fair use. The Supreme Court did not over-rule the narrow definition of parody in *Koons*, in that it stated that where a paro-dist uses an author's prior works to create a parody, the parody must in part comment upon the parodied work.[lxxx] Justice Kennedy was clearly sceptical of the parodic content of 2 Live Crew's work, and in his concurring opinion stated the importance of keeping parody within narrow limits:[lxxxi]

> The parody must target the original, and not just its general style, the genre of art to which it belongs, or society as a whole . . . . This prereq-uisite confines fair use protection to works whose very subject is the original composition and so necessitates some borrowing from it . . . . If we allow any weak transformation to qualify as parody, however we weaken the protection of copyright.[lxxxii]

Although the Supreme Court did distinguish between satire and parody and noted that whilst parody needs to mimic an original to make its point, satire does not,[lxxxiii] the basis on which it made its distinction is not justifiable. The court sug-gests that parody is of greater public benefit than satire because it sheds light on an earlier work and creates a new work.[lxxxiv] Satire, though, does create new works, and even if no light is shed on the copied work, comment is made on society and its values which must be at least of equal benefit to society as parody. The court, how-ever, did recognise that very often parody 'shades into satire' and stated that the key to determining whether a derivative work no longer sufficiently targeted an original to qualify as a parody depends on the market harm to the original.[lxxxv]

The court also stated that 'the new work's minimal distribution in the mar-ket' might be a factor in affording protection to derivative works even where they loosely target the original. Thus, appropriation art that is produced in limited quantities and is parodic or satiric may be considered a fair use,[lxxxvi] and the court in *Koons*, who were doubtful that Koons' work constituted a parody, could have found that Koons' work was a fair use because he only sold three copies.

Unfortunately for appropriation artists, the court failed to resolve the issue of whether a derivative work must either use an original that is already well-known or must at least expressly acknowledge the original work in order to consti-tute a parody of the original as opposed to being a satire of society as a whole.[lxxxvii] It is submitted that this first factor is best understood when the purpose and char-acter of the original work relative to the secondary work are analysed. A presump-tion in favour of fair use can then be made when the purpose and character of the two works are so dissimilar that economic substitution will not occur. Courts should not be seeking to determine under this factor whether the defendant was able to realise more money than the claimant,[lxxxviii] but whether the use by the defendant intended to exploit the *commercial* success of the original work because invariably all parodies are produced for profit.

In *Campbell*, the Supreme Court agreed with the lower courts that the nature of the original work was creative and, thus, central to the core of copyright protection. However, the court ruled that because parodists generally copy well-known, creative works, the second fair use factor is not as important in fair use analysis of parody cases as in other cases. In cases involving appropriation art, courts should bear in mind that whereas a writer may quote or paraphrase a literary text and capture the ideas contained within the text without taking the expression, very often a visual artist cannot quote or paraphrase an artistic work in the same manner without taking the expression. Creative works should only receive more protection than factual works where the use is designed to compete with the original or when the use exploits the original's success. This approach will favour appropriation artists for whom the point very often is to take the expression from an original work which is invariably creative, whereas those that take from factual works do not necessarily need to take the expression of the original work.

In *Campbell*, the 2 Live Crew copied the first line of the original lyrics and significantly changed the lyrics thereafter. The bass riff from the original was repeated during the parodic version, but otherwise the music had also been changed. The Supreme Court noted that copying a quantitatively significant amount weighs against fair use, whereas, on the other hand, to be effective, a parody must imitate 'the original's most distinctive, and memorable features, which [he] can be sure the audience will know.'[lxxxix] The court remanded the case for the lower court to evaluate 'the amount taken, in light of the song's parodic purpose and character, its transformative elements, and considerations of the potential for market substitution.'[xc]

The court failed to give guidance on instances when too much of an original work is taken. This author suggests that, subject to the other fair use factors, where the amount copied from the original image is such that a substitution is not likely to occur, a finding of fair use is appropriate. In terms of policy, this fair use factor can be viewed as allowing and encouraging appropriation artists to use images for the creation of their works, though not to the extent that the incentive to produce original works is diminished. If artists are only allowed to copy non-substantial parts of images, it will surely stifle creativity, and if the reason for the appropriation is to comment upon or criticise a work, the appropriation would be pointless where the artist could not appropriate enough of the work for it to be recognisable.

In assessing the likelihood of market harm the Supreme Court in *Campbell* stated:

> When a commercial use amounts to mere duplication of the entirety of an original, it clearly 'supersede[s] the objects,' of the original and serves as a market replacement for it, making it likely that cognizable market harm to the original will occur . . . But when, on the contrary, the second use is transformative, market substitution is at least less certain, and market harm may not be so readily inferred.[xci]

Therefore, where an appropriation artist's use of a work is sufficiently transformative, because the two works will serve 'different market functions,'[xcii] market substitution cannot simply be presumed. In this respect, it is highly unlikely that the market for Koons' art is the same as the market for the picture postcards of Rogers. It would not be surprising if the controversy surrounding this legal dispute increased sales of Rogers' postcard.[xciii] Notably, the court failed to address the fact that Koons only produced four sculptures.

Every fair use, by definition, involves a loss of potential royalties to the copyright owner because the defendant is seeking to use something for which he has not paid.[xciv] However, not every effect on potential licensing revenues is appropriate for analysis under this factor since there is no impact on potential licensing in situations where, for example, the copyright owner would not license the use of the image. The Supreme Court in *Campbell* stated that, 'the market for potential derivative uses includes only those that creators of original works would in general develop or license others to develop.'[xcv] By virtue of the statute, a use cannot be declared an infringement unless (assuming the other factors are also in the defendant's favour) there is a market to be harmed.[xcvi] Given the importance accorded to this factor by the Supreme Court in *Campbell*, it would be very tempting for courts to weigh this factor against a defendant even where there is an insubstantial loss of revenue, with the consequence that this factor would never weigh in a defendant's favour. However, evaluation of this factor should be a matter of degree and not depend on whether an adverse market impact exists, but contingent on the surrounding circumstances. 'Market harm is a matter of degree, and the importance of this factor will vary . . . with the amount of harm.'[xcvii] Copyright does not just protect the interests of copyright owners; it also protects the interests of users. Courts have found that prejudice to the interests of copyright owners does not always occur whenever copyright material is copied. The Supreme Court and legal commentators appear to agree that the copier's use must cause a 'substantially adverse impact' on the owner's market.[xcviii]

It has been suggested that because copyright is set in a social context more general considerations of fairness may be considered in influencing the decision.[xcix] Some judicial decisions indicate that the propriety of the defendant's conduct is a factor that is considered,[c] and may weigh against a defendant who has evinced a tendency towards laziness.[ci] For appropriation artists, therefore, it is important that their critical strategies are understood and not simply regarded as a lazy approach to creating art. 'Good faith' was considered in *Campbell*,[cii] where the plaintiff argued that the fact that the defendant had requested and been denied permission to use the plaintiff's composition, should be weighed against a finding of fair use. The Supreme Court pointed out that 'the offer may simply have been made in a good faith effort to avoid this litigation. If the use is otherwise fair, then no permission need be sought or granted. Thus, being denied permission to use a work does not weigh against a finding of fair use.'[ciii] Because of the questionable legal status of some forms of appropriation, this point may prove very important to appropriation artists who have used copyright protected images despite being refused permission to do so.

Section 107 of the Copyright Act 1976 does not state what weight should be given to the individual fair use factors. In *Campbell*,[civ] the Supreme Court weighed the factors equally. The statutory language suggests that all four factors should be considered and no single factor should be treated as dispositive of the issue. To achieve the necessary flexibility that Congress desired in order to accommodate current and developing technologies, different weight could be given to each factor depending on the facts of the case, a view endorsed by Judge Leval who has stated:

> The importance of the fourth factor should depend on the analysis produced by examination of all the factors. If the other factors clearly indicate that the secondary use should be considered fair use, then the copyright owner's deprivation of royalty revenue might play very little role in the analysis.[cv]

As a guiding principle, when balancing the fair use factors, judges should focus on whether the secondary work is a potential substitution for the original work by using the statutory factors and also, for greater consistency, where relevant, the courts could consider the additional factors mentioned above. Although a case-by-case analysis does not increase the certainty in the law, it does increase the flexibility of the doctrine, which was the intention of Congress. This flexibility will generally enable the courts to deal with new challenges to copyright law, technological or otherwise, thereby providing greater access to copyright protected works with greater opportunity afforded to create derivative works. Rather than expect Congress to change the scope of fair use, courts should remember that the fair use doctrine should be applied where rigid application of the law stifles the very creativity it is designed to foster and courts should also bear in mind that copyright law was enacted 'not primarily for the benefit of the author, but primarily for the benefit of the public.'[cvi]

IV. Licensing

If a defendant is unwilling to risk litigation over the appropriation of a copyright-protected work, an alternative is to seek a licence for use of the work. The final part of this essay focuses briefly on the licensing of works and considers the suitability of licensing from the point of view of the user and the right-holder.

Direct licensing between the parties is the most flexible form of licensing and has distinct advantages for right-holders who can control the circulation of their works themselves. Where artists incorporate several copyright-protected images into a single work, licensing can create considerable overheads in terms of time and money, having to locate and negotiate with right-holders. The variability of prices for licensing works and the inequality of bargaining power can make this form of licensing prohibitively expensive. Right-holders could refuse a licence where their work is to be parodied, or demand an exorbitant price for the use of their work. This form of *ad hoc* direct licensing is not only unpredictable, it is also disadvantageous to appropriation artists, with the possible consequence that it could unnecessarily inhibit the production and development of appropriation art. Even if authorisations could be readily obtained, their cumulative price may prove to diminish the cost effectiveness of the production of the new work. High transaction costs might be reduced by collective administration and the establishment of statutory controls and compulsory licensing.

Collective administration is a system of copyright administration whereby right-holders authorise collecting societies to administer their rights, that is, to monitor the use of the works concerned, negotiate with prospective users, issue licences for designated fees, and collect payment for the right-holder in addition to distributing the fees. This form of collective administration originates from the nineteenth century, when public performances of musical compositions required the enforcement of copyright. The widespread use of copyright-protected images in new works makes it extremely difficult for right-holders not only to identify and issue a licence for every use of their work, but also to effectively enforce their rights. If they were able to do so, the costs would be disproportionate to the royalty received.

The Design and Artists Copyright Society Limited (DACS), established in the U.K. in 1983, is an example of a collective administration organisation. DACS acts as a copyright and collecting society for visual artists. DACS licenses reproductions of its member's works on an individual basis and administers and protects copyright on behalf of the creators that it represents.[cvii] DACS issues standard licences, and its fees are charged according to a scale that is not based on the standing of the artist.[cviii]

DACS has reciprocal representation agreements with visual arts collecting societies throughout Europe and the rest of the world, enabling it to represent, in the U.K., the copyright interests of artists worldwide, and which in turn is reciprocated by its international affiliated organisations. This is important from a user's point of view, as DACS has to rely on the voluntary transfer of rights by its members. The reciprocal arrangements effectively mean that a collecting society can control the rights worldwide for a large percentage of copyright-protected works, which represents an enormous advantage to users who are saved extra transaction costs trying to locate foreign right-holders.

The work of a collecting society like DACS can essentially be seen as a balance between the interests of the right-holders and the needs of users. DACS relies on members to transfer their rights voluntarily for administration. If a user, however, wishes to licence a work but it is not administered by DACS, he has to revert to direct negotiation with the right-holder. In certain circumstances, the legislature may intervene and force the right-holder to license the work for a fee. This type of licence is known as a compulsory licence. In the music industry, problems experienced by practitioners of digital sampling, regarding licensing samples and the consequences of failure to so license, have led several commentators to call for the implementation of a compulsory licence scheme to ensure that these artists can develop their art without fear of being, as one commentator put it, 'unfairly dominated by strong players in the industry.'[cix] Similarly, with appropriation art, commentators have called for the implementation of a compulsory licence scheme to ensure that appropriation artists can further their art.[cx]

Compulsory licences[cxi] are classic examples of what have been termed 'liability rules,' so called because they allow use of a copyright owner's work without permission, provided adequate compensation is paid.[cxii] The compensation that is paid should reflect the sum the parties would have agreed upon through private negotiations. Compulsory licences are usually adopted as a compromise in revising and developing copyright legislation in two situations. Firstly, compulsory licensing is offered when technology has created new uses for which the author's exclusive rights have not been clearly established.[cxiii] Second, compulsory licensing is used when technology has made old licensing methods for established rights ponderous or inefficient. Barbara Ringer, the former U.S. Registrar of Copyrights, viewed compulsory licensing as a possible solution when technology advances to a state where it is impossible to balance copyright owners' and users' rights. Ringer described the evolution of compulsory licences as an 'inexorable historical process:'

> First you have a copyright law that was written at a particular point in the development of communications technology, and without much foresight. Then you have technological developments, which create whole new areas for the creation and use of copyrighted works. Business investments are made and industries begin to develop. The law is ambiguous in allocating rights and liabilities, so no one pays royalties. A point is reached where the courts simply stop expanding the copyright law and say that only Congress can solve the problem by legislation. You go to Congress but you find that you have hundreds of special interest groups lobbying for or against the expansion of rights, and the legislative task is horrendous. So Congress, looking for a compromise, turns to compulsory licensing.[cxiv]

Compulsory licences have four distinct purposes. First, compulsory licences remove the copyright owner's power to refuse to deal with a prospective user. Second, usually some form of revenue collecting body is established which helps to reduce transaction costs by reducing the cost of finding information regarding ownership, availability, and cost of the licence. Third, compulsory licences stop the copyright owner from preventing transformative uses. Fourth, compulsory licenses are often perceived as the only way to compensate authors where uses cannot be monitored or where the cost of doing so would be prohibitive.[cxv]

Whilst there may be some advantages to a system of compulsory licensing for images, it is unlikely that such a system could be currently adopted, as it runs contrary to U.K. and U.S. obligations to the Berne Convention,[cxvi] is contrary to copyright's overall free market philosophy and deprives the right-holder of the right to strike a bargain for the use of his work.

Conclusion

Without in any way suggesting that the legislature become expert in subjects such as postmodernism and appropriation practices, an understanding of the cultural and artistic practices of appropriation art could prove decisive in determining whether the art form is allowed to develop organically rather than in a manner dictated by copyright legislation. It is clear that modernist conceptions of the artist as the creator of a stable work do not sit easily with postmodern practices, and though there has been much debate recently concerning the ability of copyright law to protect right-holders in the digital environment, and subsequent proposals for the reform of the law, copyright law should be flexible enough to respond to non-technological artistic and cultural developments.

It is clear that there is a distinction in the law between the visual and the literary. Whilst writers can convey the exact expression of ideas contained in quoted or paraphrased text, visual artists cannot quote or paraphrase images in the same manner to convey the expression of the ideas contained within images. The judiciary needs to understand the processes of creative authorship and the culturally transformative nature in which copyright-protected works are used, otherwise it will continue to privilege right-holders over transformative users, who are themselves creative authors in their own right. This does not mean that the law should cater to particular movements or styles, particularly as these movements may prove 'too ephemeral for the pace of law.'[cxvii]

The case for modernisation of current copyright legislation, as regards appropriation art, is based on the premise that private ownership of mass culture is somewhat of a contradiction in terms.[cxviii] To understand appropriation as transcending reuse or plagiarism, it is necessary to understand that our social environment is increasingly determined by simulated signs. The semiotic basis of postmodern art is what makes appropriation both central to, and unavoidable in, contemporary representation. The referent in postmodern art is no longer nature but the closed system of fabricated signs that make up our environment.[cxix] It would therefore be unfortunate if, as one commentator points out, intellectual property laws focusing on private property interests deprive us of the optimal cultural conditions for dialogic practice. By objectifying and reifying cultural forms – freezing the connotations of signs and symbols and fencing off fields of cultural meaning with 'no trespassing' signs – intellectual property laws may enable certain forms of political practice, but more harmfully constrain others.[cxx]

i   With thanks to Professor Lionel Bently

ii   Schwartz, Hillel: *The Culture of the Copy: Striking Likenesses, Unreasonable Facsimiles* (New York: Zone Books, 1996) 248.

iii   The use of the term 'appropriation' in this essay refers to the practice of using without the consent of the copyright owner part or all of an existing copyright protected image in the creation of a work of visual art by a person other than the copyright owner.

iv   Buskirk, Martha: 'Appropriation Under the Gun', *Art in America*, June 1992, pp.37, 39.

v   See 17 U.S.C. ss.102-103; in the U.K., see s.1 CDPA 1988.

vi   See 17 U.S.C. ss.101, 106; in the U.K., see ss.16-21 CDPA 1988.

vii   See 17 U.S.C. ss.107-120; in the U.K., see ss.28-75 CDPA 1988.

viii   The terms fair use and fair dealing are used synonymously in this Essay (except where indicated to highlight differences between the two doctrines).

ix   960 F.2d 301 (2d Cir. 1992).

x   Directive of the European Parliament and of the Council on the Harmonisation of Certain Aspects of Copyright and Related Rights in the Information Society, Directive 2001/29/EC (22nd May 2001) ('Information Society Directive').

xi   127 L Ed 2d 500 (1994).

xii   The focus on parody in this essay serves as a metaphor for the artistic and critical transformative use of works protected by copyright.

xiii   It has been suggested that the whole history of art, not just the collages of Cubists, Dadaists and Surrealists, is a history of sampling. Leo Steinberg, writing in 1978, stated that borrowing images was vital to 'the abundant spiritual intercourse between artists and art', and 'there is as much unpredictable originality in quoting, imitating, transposing, and echoing, as there is in inventing.' See Steinberg, Leo: 'The Glorious Company (of Horse Thieves)' introduction to Lipman, Jean and Marshall, Richard: *Art About Art* (New York: Dutton, 1978) 25 as cited by Schwartz, Hillel: op.cit., p.309. The origins of appropriation as a definitive aspect of modern art can be traced back to Manet's 'Olympia' in 1865, which is itself based on Giorgione's 'Sleeping Venus'; see Carlin, J: 'Culture Vultures: Artistic Appropriation and Intellectual Property Law', 13 *Colum.-Vla J.L. & Arts*, (1988) pp.103, 108.

xiv   Wolfram, E. *The History of Collage* 14, as cited by del Peral, S: 'Using Copyrighted Visual Works in Collage: A Fair Use Analysis', 54 *Alb. L. Rev.* (1989) pp.141, 146.

xv   Digital sampling is a process which involves the recording, encoding, and storage of one or more sounds from external sources for replay on command, see Moog, Robert A: 'Digital Music Synthesis', *Byte*, June 1986, 155, 165. Musicians who engage in the art of sampling are at once involved in the process of deconstruction (in that they are engaged in taking apart musical compositions) and recontextualisation (as they create new meanings within the whole for the component parts they have taken). On 'recontextualisation', see Gann, Kyle: 'Noises of Fate: You Don't Need A Sampler to Recontextualise', *The Village Voice*, July 24, 1990, p.92.

xvi   Fellner, C: *Industrial Design Law* (London: Sweet & Maxwell, 1995) p.78. Arthur Baker, a pioneer of the 'electro' sound of rap music which relied heavily on the use of synthesisers and early programmable machines, has been quoted as saying: 'Sampling is a new form of music, just like collages . . . if you like a sound you can have the sound,' see Miller, 'High-Tech Alteration of Sights and Sounds Divides the Arts World', *Wall St. J.* 1 Sept., 1987, 1, col.1.

xvii   For example John Cage in music, Naum June Paik in video, Jean Luc Godard, and Bruce Conner in film, Richard Foreman and Robert Wilson in theatre and William Burroughs in literature, see Carlin, J: op.cit., p.106.

xviii   Mamiya, Christin J: *Pop Art and Consumer Culture* (Austin: University of Texas Press, 1992) p.158.

xix   Ibid., p.160.

xx   Adler, Amy M: 'Post-Modern Art and the Death of Obscenity Law', 99 *Yale L.J.* (1990) pp.1359, 1364.

xxi   Appropriation art is said by one commentator to present 'the most radical challenge to copyright laws to date,' see Greenberg, Lynne A: 'The Art of Appropriation: Puppies, Piracy and Post-Modernism', 11 *Cardozo Arts & Ent L.J.* 1 (1992); McLean, W.F: 'All's not Fair in Art and War: A Look at the Fair Use Defence After Rogers v. Koons', 59 *Brook. L. Rev.* 373 (1993) (where the author claims that appropriation undermines copyright laws and its modern ideas of authorship and originality). *Cf.* Sherman, B: 'Appropriating the Postmodern: Copyright and the Challenge of the New', 4 *Social and Legal Studies* 31 (1995), where the author argues that the claims that are made about post-modern art 'opposing' and 'undermining' originality are based on a number of unexamined and, on the whole, unsubstantiated assumptions.

xxii   960 F.2d 301 (2d Cir. 1992).

xxiii   Buskirk, Martha: op.cit., pp.37-39.

xxiv   See Anderson, Peter: 'On the Legal Limits of Art', *A & E.L.R.*, October 1994, 70, 73.

xxv   Ibid.

xxvi   Ames, K.E: 'Beyond Rogers v. Koons: A Fair Use Standard For Appropriation', 93 *Colum. L.Rev.* (1993) pp.1473, 1477-1478. Appropriation is not the only technique employed by post-modern artists in their work. See Solomon-Godeau, A: 'Photography After Art Photography', in Wallis, B (ed.): *Art After Modernism: Rethinking Representation* XVII 62, 80 where the use of various post-modern techniques to refute or subvert the concepts of modernist aesthetics is discussed, as cited by McLean, W.F: op.cit., n.66, p.385.

xxvii   Badin, Roxanna: 'An Appropriate (d) Place in Transformative Value: Appropriation Art's Exclusion From Campbell v. Acuff-Rose Music Inc.', 60 *Brook. L.Rev.* pp.1653, 1660.

xxviii   One commentator has suggested that this is probably because of the uncertainty as to the legal standard a court would apply, see Ames, K.E: op.cit., 1484. Interestingly this characteristic also used to be found in digital sampling suits. It appears that it was in the interests of record companies and music publishers to exploit the doubt over the legal status of sampling so that they could maximise their profits by licensing samples.

xxix   Morris, Gay: 'When Artists Use Photographs: Is it Fair use, legitimate transformation or rip-off?', *ARTnews*, January 1981, pp.102, 103-104.

xxx   Ibid., p.104.

xxxi   960 F.2d 301 (2d Cir. 1992).

xxxii   *Rogers v. Koons* 751 F. Supp. 474 -476 (S.D.N.Y. 1990).

xxxiii   See Ball, H: *Law of Copyright and Literary Property* 260 (1944) as cited in *Harper & Row Publishers, Inc. v. Nation Enters.* 471 U.S. 539, 549 (1985).

xxxiv   *Stewart v. Abend* 495 U.S. 207, 236 (1989) (quoting *Iowa State Univ. Research Found., Inc. v. American Broadcasting Cos., Inc.* 621 F.2d 57, 60 (2d Cir. 1980)).

xxxv   The six illustrated examples of fair use are not presumptively fair, and balancing of the fair use factors must be applied. The statute by use of the words 'shall include' clearly indicates that the four specified factors are non-exclusive. By virtue of 17 U.S.C. s.101 the terms 'including' and 'such as' are illustrative and not limiting. Congress has suggested other possible fair uses, such as 'use in a parody of some of the content of the work parodied,' see The House Report on the Copyright Act of 1976, p.65.

xxxvi   *Rogers v. Koons* 751 F. Supp.474, 479 (S.D.N.Y. 1990).

xxxvii   See Jaszi, P: 'On the Author Effect: Contemporary Copyright and Collective Creativity', in Woodmansee and Jaszi (eds.) *The Construction of Authorship* (Durham, NC: Duke University Press, 1994) pp.29, 41-48 (where the author argues that the decision reflects the ideology of romantic authorship and serves to sideline artists who use existing copyright protected works by denying 'that they might have an equally important role to play in the continuing process of cultural transmission by which texts are reformulated and elaborated'), see ibid., p.41.

xxxviii 17 U.S.C. s.107.

xxxix   As illustrated by *Harper & Row Publishers, Inc. v. Nation Enters.* 471 U.S. 539 (1985) where the presumption that news reporting was a presumptive fair use was rebutted because the other fair use factors weighed against such a finding.

xl   960 F.2d 301, 309 (2d Cir. 1992). Koons made four copies of his 'String of Puppies,' three of which were sold for a total of $ 367,000, and the fourth copy he kept, Ibid., 305.

xli   464 U.S. 417, 449 (1984). The legislative history of the Copyright Act 1976 does not make such a clear distinction militating against commercial uses, see House Report 1976, 66 which states that: 'the author's consent to a reasonable use of his copyrighted works has always been implied by the courts as a necessary incident of the constitutional policy of promoting the progress of science and the useful arts, since a prohibition of such use would inhibit subsequent writers from attempting to improve upon prior works and thus . . . frustrate the very ends sought to be attained'. Furthermore, the uses listed in the preamble to 17 U.S.C. s.107 are generally conducted for profit.

xlii   See House Report 1976, 65.

xliii   *Berlin v. E.C Publications, Inc.*, 329 F.2d 541 (2d Cir. 1963).

xliv   960 F.2d 301, 309 (2d Cir. 1992).

xlv   Rogers' photograph is even described by the court as a typical American scene, see Ibid., 303.

xlvi   Ibid., 309.

xlvii   Ibid., 310.

xlviii   Ibid., *Cf.* the position in the U.K. where the audience plays no role in the parody inquiry.

xlix   In a later infringement action, Koons had made a sculpture incorporating the well-known cartoon figure Odie, once again his defence of parody was rejected by the court, because the parody was of society at large, rather than of the cartoon character, and the appropriation would have been too much even if the court had decided Koons' work was a parody, see *United Feature Syndicate v. Koons* 817 F. Supp. 370, 383-384 (D.N.Y. 1993).

l   *MCA v. Wilson* 677 F.2d 180, 182 (2d Cir. 1981).

li   471 U.S. 539, 563-564 (1985).

lii   960 F.2d 301, 310 (2d Cir. 1992).

liii   *Sony Corp. of America v. Universal City Studios, Inc.* 464 U.S. 417 (1984); *Williams & Wilkins Co. v. United States* 487 F.2d 1345 (Ct. Cl. 1973).

liv   Defendant's Brief at 53.

lv   960 F.2d 301, 311 (2d Cir. 1992).

lvi   See n.xlvi and and accompanying text.

lvii   *Harper & Row Publishers, Inc. v. Nation Enters.* 471 U.S. 539, 568 (1985).

lviii   Ibid., 566. In *Sony*, the Supreme Court reasoned that 'a use that has no demonstrable effect upon the potential market for, or the value of, the copyrighted work need not be prohibited in order to protect the author's incentive to create', see 464 U.S. 417, 450 (1984).

lix   960 F.2d 301, 312 (2d Cir. 1992).

lx   Ibid., 310.

lxi   The court stated that: 'there is simply nothing in the record to support a view that Koons produced 'String of Puppies' for anything other than sale as high-priced art', see Ibid., 311-312.

lxii [1972] 2 Q.B. 84, 94.

lxiii See *Williamson Music Ltd v. The Pearson Partnership* [1987] F.S.R. 97, 103 (where Judge Paul Baker Q.C. acknowledged that a parody could constitute fair dealing under s.30(1) CDPA 1988). Parody in the U.K. is treated very differently by the judiciary than in the U.S. U.K. judges look to see whether the parody infringes the copyright in the parodied work, i.e. there is no departure from normal copyright principles and the courts treat parody as an issue of substantiality.

lxiv *Cf. Pro Sieben Media A.G. v. Carlton U.K. Television Limited* [1999] 1 W.L.R. 605 where the Court of Appeal ruled that sufficient acknowledgement did not require that the author be identified by name, any other form of identification which the author may be accustomed to identify himself, may be adopted.

lxv   See e.g., *Schweppes Ltd v. Wellingtons Ltd* [1984] FSR 210; *Williamson Music Ltd v. Pearson Partnership* [1987] F.S.R. 97. Appropriation artists may also infringe the moral rights of the author who has the right not to have his work subjected to derogatory treatment, see s.80 CDPA 1988.

lxvi Article 5.1, Information Society Directive, provides for an exception to temporary copying.

lxvii Ibid., Article 5.5.

lxviii Ibid., Article 5.3(k).

lxix See Article 122-5-4 French Intellectual Property Code and similarly Article 22, s.1, 6 of the Belgian Copyright Act 1994.

lxx   Article 39, Copyright Act 1996.

lxxi 127 L Ed 2d 500 (1994).

lxxii 972 F.2d 1429 (6th Cir. 1992).

lxxiii 127 L Ed 2d 500 (1994).

lxxiv 754 F.Supp. 1150 (M.D. Tenn. 1991)

lxxv 972 F.2d 1429 (6th Cir. 1992).

lxxvi 127 L Ed 2d 500, 513-514 (1994). Literary theorist, Linda Hutcheon, notes that the distinction between parody and plagiarism can be a very fine one since the intention to imitate with critical irony and the intention to imitate in order to deceive are very hard to distinguish, see Hutcheon, Linda: *A Theory of Parody* (New York and London: Methuen, 1985) p.32.

lxxvii 127 L Ed 2d 500, 519 (1994). See also *Harper & Row Publishers, Inc. v. Nation Enters.* 471 U.S. 539, 562 (1985), where the court explained that the crux of the profit/non-profit distinction 'is not whether the sole motive of the use is monetary gain but whether the user stands to profit from exploitation of the copyrighted material without paying the customary price.'

lxxviii 127 L Ed 2d 500, 515 (1994). See also *Basic Books Inc. v. Kinko's Graphics Corp.* 758 F. Supp. 1522 (S.D.N.Y. 1991)where the District Court defined a 'transformative use' as one that 'must employ the quoted matter in a different manner or for a different purpose from the original.' This is in sharp contrast to a purely commercial use that simply repeats the copyright material in its original form and is unlikely to constitute a fair use, see Ibid., at 1530-1531, citing Leval, P: 'Toward A Fair Use Standard', 103 *Harv. L. Rev.* 1105, 1111 (1990).

lxxix 127 L Ed 2d 500, 515-516 (1994).

lxxx Ibid., 516.

lxxxi   Ibid., 527.

lxxxii   Ibid., 528.

lxxxiii   Ibid., 516-517.

lxxxiv   Ibid.

lxxxv   Ibid., 516 n.14.

lxxxvi   *Cf.* Ibid., 517 n.16 where the court states 'The only further judgment, indeed, that a court may pass on a work goes to an assessment of whether the parodic element is slight or great, and the copying small or extensive in relation to the parodic element, for a work with slight parodic element and extensive copying will be more likely to merely 'supersede the objects' of the original.' *Cf.* Ibid., 524 n.24.

lxxxvii   The court did though suggest that the second fair use factor 'the nature of the copyrighted work' is not likely to be helpful in separating 'the fair use sheep from the infringing goats in a parody case' because parodies almost always copy publicly known, expressive works. Ibid., 520.

lxxxviii   Note that in *Rogers v. Koons* 960 F.2d 301 (2d Cir. 1992) the court was very aware of the fact that the plaintiff, Rogers, was paid $ 200 for the photograph 'Puppies,' whereas Koons received $ 367,000 for the sale of three of his sculptures.

lxxxix   127 L Ed 2d 500, 521 (1994).

xc   Ibid., 522

xci   Ibid., 523 (citations omitted). This represents a marked shift from the Supreme Court decision in *Sony* where a fair use analysis based upon productive use was rejected, see 464 U.S. 417, 455 n.40 (1984).

xcii   127 L Ed 2d 500, 523 (1994).

xciii   It is interesting to note by way of analogy that in the field of music, new recordings that feature samples from old records often serve to make consumers aware of or reactivate interest in the sampled source. James Brown is a prime example of an artist whose back catalogue had long since been deleted, but due to his popularity with sampling artists, he witnessed a resurgence in popularity and his back catalogue was re-issued and repackaged to meet the new demand.

xciv   However, Judge Pierre Leval has stated the importance of market impairment being reasonably substantial, see Leval, P: op.cit., 1124-1125. See also Fisher, W: 'Reconstructing the Fair Use Doctrine', 101 *Harv. L. Rev.* 1659, 1672 (1988) where the author suggests that courts must estimate the *magnitude* of the market impairment caused by privileging the defendant's conduct; merely ascertaining the *existence* of adverse impact will not suffice.

xcv   127 L Ed 2d 500, 524 (1994).

xcvi   As recognised by Jacobs J. in his dissenting opinion in *American Geophysical Union v. Texaco Inc.*, there is a circularity to the problem in analysing the impact on potential licensing revenues, see 60 F.3d 913, 937 (2d Cir. 1994).

xcvii   *Campbell v. Acuff-Rose Music, Inc.* 127 L Ed 2d 500, 523 n.21 (1994).

xcviii   Ibid., 524. See also Leval, P: op.cit., 1125 (where the author states that: 'the market impairment should not turn the fourth factor unless it is reasonably substantial').

xcix   Weinreb, L: 'Fair's Fair: A Comment on the Fair Use Doctrine' 103 *Harv. L. Rev.* 1137, 1152. *Cf.* Leval, P: op.cit., 1125-1130 (1990) (where the author suggests that the four factors in section 107 are the pertinent factors and any other factors are false factors that divert the inquiry from the goals of copyright. Leval suggests that these 'false factors' may have a bearing on the appropriate remedy or on the availability of another cause of action, but not on the fair use inquiry).

c   See, e.g. *MCA, Inc. v. Wilson* 677 F.2d 180, 183 (2d Cir. 1981) where the court noted that: 'The court may also consider whether the paraphrasing and copying was done in good faith or with evasive motive.' Note also, *Grand Upright Music Ltd. v. Warner Bros. Records, Inc.* 780 F. Supp. 182 (S.D.N.Y. 1991) the first digital sampling case to come to trial where the court ruled that the defendant's conduct in sampling the plaintiff's work after being denied permission, exhibited callous disregard for the rights of others and warranted criminal prosecution.

ci   *Schroeder v. William Morrow & Co.* 566 F.2d 3 (7th Cir. 1977).

cii   127 L. Ed. 2d 500 (1994).

ciii   Ibid., 520 n.18. *Cf. Grand Upright Music Ltd. v. Warner Bros. Records, Inc.* 780 F. Supp. 182.

civ   127 L Ed 2d 500 (1994).

cv   *American Geophysical Union v. Texaco Inc.* 802 F. Supp. 1, 21 (S.D.N.Y. 1992).

cvi   See H.R. Rep. No.2222, 60th Cong., 2nd Sess.7 (1909).

cvii   See www.dacs.co.uk for further details. In the U.S., see the Artists Rights Society, www.arsny.com.

cviii   *Cf.* collective administration organisations such as the Copyright Clearance Center in the U.S. which provides licensing systems for the reproduction and distribution of copyrighted materials in print and electronic formats, where right-holders maintain maximum control over the use of their works and individually negotiate remuneration for the use of their works.

cix   Note: 'A New Spin on Music Sampling: A Case for Fair Play', 105 *Harv. L. Rev.* 726, 742 (1992). The commentator suggests a compulsory licensing scheme as a fallback for those unable to arrive at a negotiated agreement. See e.g., Baroni, M.L: 'A Pirate's Palette: The Dilemmas of Digital Sound Sampling and a Proposed Compulsory License Solution', 11 *U. Miami Ent. & Sports L. Rev.* 65 (1993); and 'They Don't Make Music The Way They Used To': The Legal Implications of 'Sampling' in Contemporary Music', *Wis. L. Rev.* 1941 (1992).

cx   See e.g., Hamilton, Marci A: 'Appropriation Art and the Imminent Decline in Authorial Control Over Copyright Protected Works', 42 *J. Cop'r. Soc'y.* 93 (1994); See Meeker, Heather J. 'The Ineluctable Modality of the Visible: Fair Use and Fine Arts in the Post-Modern Era' 10 *U. Miami Ent. & Sports L. Rev.* 195; Quentel, Debra L: 'Bad Artists Copy. Good Artists Steal:' The Ugly Conflict Between Copyright Law and Appropriationism', 4 *UCLA Ent. L. Rev.* 39 (1997).

cxi   The term 'compulsory licence' is used in a general sense to refer to non-voluntary licences both statutory and compulsory. A 'statutory licence' is one where the terms of the licence and the rights of the licensee under it are set out in the statute that establishes the licence.

cxii   See Calabresi and Melamed: 'Property Rules, Liability Rules, and Inalienability: One View of the Cathedral', 85 *Harv. L. Rev.* 1089 (1972) where the authors describe all legal entitlements as protected by either 'property rules', or 'liability rules'.

cxiii   Ringer, Barbara: 'Copyright in the 1980s', 23 *Bull. Cop'r. Soc'y.* 299, 303 (1975).

cxiv   Ibid., 306.

cxv   An example of this form of statutory remuneration where right-holders would otherwise receive none, is the Audio Home Recording Act 1992 ('the AHRA 1992') which was enacted in response to concerns over private copying of digital audio. The AHRA 1992 was not drafted by Congress but by twelve lawyers representing the interested parties. The interested parties were the music industry (record producers), songwriters and music publishers and the consumer electronics industry.

cxvi   Under Article 9(2) of the Berne Convention there is the scope for Member States to provide compulsory licences to the extent that they do not conflict with the normal exploitation of the work and do not unreasonably prejudice the interests of the author. The limitations under Article 9(2) indicate that compulsory licenses with regard to reproductions will only be permitted in special circumstances. It must be doubtful whether it genuinely could be said that special circumstances exist for enacting a compulsory licence specifically for appropriation art.

cxvii   Meeker, Heather J: op.cit., p.230.

cxviii See e.g., Buskirk, Martha: op.cit.; Ames, K. E: op.cit.; and McLean, W.F: op.cit.; French, Robert. A: 'Copyright: Rogers v. Koons: Artistic Appropriation and the Fair Use Defence', 46 *Okla. L. Rev.*175 (1993).

cxix   Carlin, J: op.cit., pp.103, 110 (1988).

cxx   See Coombe, R.J: 'Objects of Property and Subjects of Politics: Intellectual Property Laws and Democratic Dialogue', 69 *Tex. L. Rev.* 1853, 1866-1868 (1991).

Public Access to Art, Museums, Images, and Copyright: The Case of Tate

Naomi Korn and Peter Wienand

Great works of art 'are not the product of single and solitary births; they are the product of many years of thinking in common, of thinking by the body of the people, so that the experience of the mass is behind the single voice'. The same may be said of great institutions.[i]

F. Spalding, quoting Virginia Woolf

The internet and the increasing commercial activities of museums and galleries mean that copyright has increasing importance in the art world.[ii]

S. Stokes

Museums and Copyright

In this chapter, we examine the particular tensions that face museums and galleries in dealing with copyright. Such tensions arise because the law, as it stands, does not allow (except in some very limited circumstances) any gateway through the restrictions of copyright to permit museums to freely reproduce and disseminate images of their holdings.

Museums exist to give people an opportunity to engage with the creations of their own and other societies, and perhaps to find inspiration and enjoyment in that engagement. They can be imagined as guardians of cultural memory. Human memory, as current theories of brain function tell us, is selective and creative. Inevitably, the collections of museums are selective rather than comprehensive, but museums today are acutely conscious of this and seek to use their collections as creatively as possible.

The legal protection of works of art, including photographs and images recorded in other media, is at root a form of property rewarding the investment of effort and resources in creativity. Copyright protects original works and its policy justification is partly to offer an incentive to create original works and partly to dissuade plagiarism. Unlike other forms of intellectual property rights,[iii] however, it does not exist to protect ideas. The criterion for copyright protection is not novelty but originality. The system recognises that creativity is fuelled by the contemplation and experience of other works.

It follows that there are points of contact between the role of museums and copyright law, since both are concerned in the broader sense with creativity. However, serious reflection about the relationship between the activities of museums and the effect of copyright law has only begun recently, fuelled by a number of factors:

· First, is the realisation of the increasing relevance of copyright, which has resulted from the greater scope of museum publishing and the advent of new technologies, most notably the Internet;

· Second, are the changes in the law, notably the increase in the period of copyright protection (bringing larger swathes of museum collections within the ambit of copyright)[iv] and in relation to non-infringing uses of copyright works – specifically the uses that can be permitted by law on public policy grounds[v] and which have been a subject of considerable recent debate;

· Third, the perception arising from these developments that museums and museum professionals need greater guidance in relation to copyright, a perception which resulted with the foundation in 1996 in London of the Museums Copyright Group.[vi]

Reflection on the relationship between the activities of museums and the effects of copyright law suggests that, by and large, copyright law makes insufficient allowances for the educational and non-commercial uses of images by museums. Museums are actually disfavoured in comparison with schools, universities, and libraries, a situation which undoubtedly reflects a now-outdated view of what museums do, as well as the success of rights holders lobbying to prevent any extension of 'fair dealing' categories.

But the relationship between museums and copyright is really quite complex, and copyright is a means for museums as rights holders to generate much-needed revenue. Indeed, the significant shrinkage in real terms of government funding has meant that museums and galleries need the revenue generated from copyright to meet the costs of core activities, as well as to fund investment in new ventures designed to bring their collections before new audiences. The exploitation of photographs of the works in museum collections, where the copyright in the photographs will often belong to the museums or their trading subsidiaries, is a particularly significant instance of such revenue-generating activity. This is an aspect of museum activity that has recently encountered challenge, potentially threatening images as a source of revenue.[vii]

Of course, copyright in the original work as well as copyright in the photograph may be brought into play. Where copyright still protects the original works, museums must engage in negotiation with rights holders (such as artists, artists' estates, or their representatives). A good way of considering these issues in context is to study the practice of a particular institution. Since its collections of modern art are largely protected by copyright, Tate is an example *par excellence* of the balancing act that museums have to perform in relation to copyright.

Tate: a History

An understanding of the founding of Tate, the nature of the organisation's development, and the relationship and interaction with the Government in power and the public, are crucial to examining its dual roles as a guardian of works and a consumer of images. The organisation now known as Tate began life in 1897 as the National Gallery of British Art, in the building on Millbank, London, that is now Tate Britain. It was the result of growing public opinion that a national gallery was needed to showcase the achievements of the British School. The building itself and its foundation collection were provided by the sugar refiner and collector Henry Tate, and the gallery was popularly known from the start as the Tate Gallery, though this did not become its official name until 1932.

Tate was administratively part of the National Gallery until it became independent in 1954. In 1917, it was given additional responsibility for forming a national collection of international modern art. Despite the ambivalence towards the arts of successive governments, and the fact that Tate only began to receive a grant for acquisitions in 1947, the collection grew rapidly. It now comprises approximately sixty-four thousand works, encompassing over five hundred years worth of British art, including around thirty-seven thousand works of the Turner Bequest and over fifteen-thousand contemporary British and foreign works still in copyright. In order to show more of the collection and to reach out to the regions, Tate Liverpool and Tate St. Ives were created in 1988 and 1993. Acute space problems continued, however, the solution of which was the creation in London of Tate Modern, designed to house the international modern collection. Following this, the Millbank building, then reverted to its original function as a national gallery of British art, or Tate Britain, thus finally fulfilling Henry Tate's dream.

Free public access to the Collection was fundamental to Tate since its foundation. Until 1947, a charge was made on students days, but otherwise access to the national collection was and remains free except at Tate St. Ives, where there is an admission charge. With over 5.25 million visitors to Tate Modern in its first year,[viii] the Tate family of galleries is now one of the most popular public attractions in the country, despite a reported 8% drop in visitor figures throughout Britain in the arts and culture from 1993 to 1999.[ix]

There is now a fifth Tate site, which, though virtual in nature, has the potential to reach the largest audience of all. The 1998 launch of the Tate website, www.tate.org.uk, saw the achievement of the ultimate ambition of Tate: the potential to provide unlimited and free access to the entire Tate collection in one virtual space online. The site not only generates interest in art and provides educational and interpretative insight into the Tate collection (the virtual leading to the real), it also initiates a live stream of conferences and talks (webcasting), exhibitions online, and events listings that provides the virtual visitor with a value-added experience. It is anticipated that the entire Tate collection will be digitised by the summer of 2002, and in keeping with its philosophy of public access, the public is encouraged to view images and download them for their personal use or private research. However, in order to prevent inappropriate reproductions, images are reproduced on the web in low resolution and copyright holders are credited.

Museums and Education

Museums and galleries see their mission as more than warehousing a collection of old objects. They are educational institutions in the widest sense.
    P. Wienand [x]

A greater emphasis on the need to communicate information and ideas relating to the Tate collection has also resulted in the development of education departments. Professional educators and creators work in conjunction with current exhibitions and works on permanent display in order to interpret artworks and raise an awareness of art through a variety of educational activities, involving schools, adults, the local community and disadvantaged groups. In this, Tate is not unique. All museums are deeply concerned to explore the educational potential of their collections and activities.

Tate's education departments, as in the case of all education departments located in museums and galleries, benefit only to a limited extent from the 'permitted acts' provisions of the U.K. copyright law.[xi] The reproduction of works for the purposes of instruction might cover copying in the course of lectures or preparation for lectures, provided that this did not involve multiple copying.[xii] Equally, students would be permitted to make single copies of works for the purposes of private study or research. However, though museums are engaged in educational activities, the provisions in copyright law that apply to 'educational establishments' and 'prescribed libraries' do not apply directly, because museums and galleries fall outside the definitions of 'educational establishments' and 'prescribed libraries' (though some museums do administer libraries that qualify as prescribed libraries).[xiii]

As a result, Tate's educational role has found itself in an uncomfortable dilemma. While, on the one hand, Tate has built up close working relationships with artists and strives to protect their moral rights, on the other hand, works will need to be reproduced and images may need to be cropped or edited during the course of creating exciting activities for the community. One such example includes the drastic alteration of images for visually-impaired students as a means of assisting their comprehension of the works. In every instance where a work in copyright needs to be reproduced, permission has to be requested from all rights holders, and sometimes charges are incurred.

Images for Revenue

As Tate strives to fulfil its philosophy of promoting its collection and enabling as many people as possible to experience the world of art, financial constraints have meant that Tate has been forced to look to means of generating income beyond its public funding. In particular, the Tate shop at Millbank, established in 1972, was the first permanent Tate outlet to sell postcards, posters, and products made from reproducing works in the Tate Collection. In 1996, a limited company, Tate Gallery Publishing, entirely owned by the Trustees with all its profits going to Tate, was established to increase revenue from retail and marketing.[xiv] In 2001, it was renamed Tate Enterprises. Recently, an application was made to register TATE as a trademark to increase the international scope of the promotion of the gallery's products line, and during the last year, a partnership has been formed with the DIY giant B&Q to market a range of branded Tate paints.

Like most museums and galleries, Tate operates as a repository of images of works. The Tate Picture Library provides third parties with the facility to reproduce from transparencies of works in the Tate Collection. However, the increasing need for self-funding and the instigation of these new business initiatives have created a conflict: 'between the duties and responsibilities, both legal and professional, of museums and galleries to encourage the public to participate freely in the cultural and scientific life of the community and the importance of self-funding to allow for this'.[xv]

Thus, the public is encouraged freely to enjoy the art works, but once they wish to own a reproduction of a work, they are charged for these specific services and products. In this, Tate is not unique. Image licensing in its various forms is a significant activity of museums and galleries, helping to fulfil the objective of wider dissemination, while also contributing revenue. This gives museums an opportunity to exploit items in their collections even if they are out of copyright. Some have suggested that this is somehow immoral, amounting to an attempt by museums to remove from the public domain representations of works which are themselves no longer protected by copyright.

This is, however, to misconstrue the position adopted by museums. As we have seen, museums have a duty to disseminate information about their collections. New technologies massively increase the demand for such information and, hence, the investment required to enable museums to meet the expectations stoked by the technologies. Museums, therefore, must ensure both that high quality, accurate images are disseminated, and that the funds are available to create and, where necessary, digitise them. Copyright has a dual significance here: it protects the investment of skill and labour in high quality images and digitisations, and it gives museums the basis on which to charge licence fees and royalties.

Reference has been made earlier in this book to the *Bridgeman v. Corel* decision.[xvi] While this case would apparently undermine the licensing of photographic images by museums and indeed others, there are many grounds for believing that the decision is incorrect. Certainly the view taken by leading U.K. commentators suggests that it would not be followed by the U.K. courts.[xvii] It has also been suggested that the case may be of doubtful authority in the U.S., not least because of the plaintiff's presentation of the case (as noted in some remarkably forceful *dicta* by Judge Kaplan in his ruling).[xviii]

In April 2002, the European Commission published a draft directive on public sector information based on a consultative Working Document[xix] containing proposals that would apply to 'documents' made available by 'public sector bodies'. At the core of the proposals is a suggestion that public sector bodies should make documents available on a cost-recovery and non-exclusive basis only. Most museums and galleries would fall within the category of 'public sector bodies'. The term 'document', as defined in the Working Document, would have a very wide meaning and could apply to all manner of materials created in the course of a museum's activities, including photographs, audio-visual works, matter created for exhibitions, text for publication in book form or on-line, and so on. If the proposals were implemented in the form put forward in the Working Document, this

Douglas Gordon, *Déjà Vu*, 2000 (still)

would remove the ability of museums and galleries to generate profits from image licensing and related activities, which could in turn undermine their ability to invest in other core activities. This was made clear in many of the responses to the proposals,[xx] but it remains to be seen whether these responses will be reflected in any draft directive.

Public Access to Art

Technological developments, financial necessity, and the desire to provide the public with a value-added art experience have further tested the relationship between Tate and copyright. It has created a situation whereby Tate may have acquired the work and provides free public access to it, yet at the same time has to exert control over its reproduction and request permission accordingly. In this way, Tate sits in the dual position as the owner of artists' works and custodian of artists' rights, as well as the consumer of images of these works.

For example, a number of works have now been acquired by the Tate, among them, Douglas Gordon's *Déjà Vu* (2000), a vastly slowed down film[xxi] made from other artists' films. Its very creation has tested the fundamental concepts embodied in the earliest laws protecting artistic works from unauthorised copying,[xxii] but in this case, not only was the artist required to gain permission from the original filmmakers to create this work, and thus for Tate to display it, but Tate also must have Gordon's permission to reproduce any part of it.

Works encompassing multiple images, such as collages and montages, exemplify superbly artistic endeavours that exploit elements of existing artistic works. In this way, while borrowing from other artists, they also crucially demonstrate the skill and artistic judgement that are requirements for copyright protection. Video works may also include both imagery that has been borrowed from other artists, as well as a variety of audio content whose inclusion may be less prominent within the final piece but will still require copyright clearance. The recently commissioned work by Peter Blake for the Tate Century Development is a fine instance whereby the entire work was created out of the most popular works on display at Tate Britain. As in the case of Gordon, permissions were required from all the rights holders of those works in copyright prior to the realisation of the project. Future reproductions of Blake's work would not only require his permission as the final artist, but also reproduction permission from the copyright holders whose works are included in the piece, as well as the moral rights of each of the artists.

Copyright is not the only issue that needs careful attention. The manipulation or reproduction of artworks may infringe the moral rights of the artist who created the original work. In particular, any treatment or manipulation of works that is 'derogatory' will infringe the moral right of integrity of the artist,[xxiii] while the failure to identify an artist whose right to be identified has been asserted will infringe the moral right of paternity.[xxiv]

Naturally, the advent of the Internet has inspired its own form of art – Net Art – which exists purely in cyberspace. An example is *Uncomfortable Proximity* by the collective group of artists known on the Tate website as Mongrel and which 'mirrors the Tate's own web-site but offers new images and ideas collaged from their own experiences.'[xxv] Although the images were selected deliberately because copyright (and hence also any moral rights) had expired in the works used, the copyright existing in the photographs of the works meant that their exploratory manipulation could only be performed if the original works were part of the Tate Collection and were not on loan to the Tate.

There is no doubt, as this article's epigraph by Virginia Woolf suggests, that great works are inspired by each other. Indeed, the history of Western art, particularly since the Renaissance, is a history of artists' borrowings. However, Tate's role in promoting contemporary art has recently raised important copyright issues. Since 1984, Tate has promoted the Turner Prize – an art award of excellence equivalent to the Booker Prize for literature.[xxvi] The Prize has provoked and inspired intense media interest and propelled the nominees into the public spotlight. The shortlist selection for 2000 included Glenn Brown's *The Loves of Shepherds (after*

Double Star by Tony Roberts) 2000, which became the subject of a media campaign focusing on the appropriated nature of his work. Brown's paintings are based on images from popular culture, in this particular case the cover design of a science fiction paperback. Debates in the media as well as recent publications[xxvii] have not only focused upon whether Brown's painting was an original work but, moreover, have questioned the very nature of art itself.

Guardian of Works and Consumer of Images

With its large collection of contemporary and modern art taken with recent technological and cultural changes, Tate is continually involved in the reproduction of images and their copyright implications. Tate has a responsibility to secure the permission of all copyright holders prior to the reproduction of works. This has largely been achieved through the creation of the post of Copyright Officer and the implementation of departmentally focused copyright workshops in which Tate staff are educated about the importance of copyright clearance. The Copyright Officer is also responsible for overseeing the processes of copyright across the organisation. These include the reproduction of works in the Tate Collection; clearing rights for the Tate website; negotiating copyright licences with individual rights holders and copyright clearing houses; and securing reproduction rights and/or copyright permissions for works that are lent to the Gallery for temporary exhibitions. In this way, Tate can actively fulfil its responsibilities to artists, copyright holders, and the public while continuing along the path described by Frances Spalding as 'a complex, constantly changing entity, which in the course of its first hundred years has frequently been the subject of heated debate. Both its critics and its admirers attest to the fierce, possessive affection it arouses, while it continues to occupy a central role within our cultural life'.[xxviii]

The Strange Absence of Collective Licensing Schemes

In many industries which are heavily reliant on copyright works, and which therefore require streamlined, effective, and equitable copyright clearance mechanisms, licensing schemes have been administered by collecting societies.[xxix] U.K. law regulates the operation of such collecting societies and provides a framework within which the licence fees charged may be challenged, in principle preventing the abuse of the quasi-monopoly position that collecting societies may acquire.[xxx] The advent of new technologies and government policies that aim to encourage the dissemination of museum images via the Internet[xxxi] makes the adoption of such schemes highly desirable. The sheer quantity of material that can be disseminated means that the task of seeking clearance may become prohibitively expensive, consuming a large part of project budgets. The European Commission has indicated its view that, in relation to online activities, licensing is to be preferred to reliance on 'permitted acts' exceptions.[xxxii] And even more conventional museum activities in the educational and commercial spheres would be assisted by the existence of a fair licensing regime.

What is remarkable about the museum sector as a whole is the absence of large scale licensing schemes geared to facilitating the use of artworks by museums. There are collecting societies that could play a role here, notably the Design Artists Copyright Society (DACS), which has begun to provide services that are similar to the museum's in collecting art for use.[xxxiii] However, it would appear that there have been no serious initiatives to explore the possibility of an umbrella licensing scheme, regulated under the provisions of U.K. copyright law, to address the needs of museums in relation to their online activities. Individual institutions have had to negotiate on a case-by-case basis, and there is evidence that some, at least of the licensing bodies in question, are currently adopting a very rigid attitude to licensing online activities.

This would seem to undermine the validity of the European Commission's contention that licensing is the proper means by which copyrighted works can legitimately be disseminated online.[xxxiv] It was principally on the basis of this contention that the provisions to allow museums (along with other public access institutions, including public libraries and educational establishments) the use of copyrighted works in the context of their non-commercial activities (contained in the recently adopted Directive)[xxxv] were limited to analogue uses of such works and do not apply to public exposure of works by means (*inter alia*) of the Internet. At present, this issue is of largely theoretical significance, since the relevant provisions are not among those which must be implemented by Member States.[xxxvi] Nevertheless, it suggests that legislators may have been given assurances by rights holders and their representatives that are not being borne out in all industries, casting a shadow over the validity of the policy underlying the legislation in question.

While this is clearly a matter of concern and disappointment to the museum community, it also appears to be short-sighted on the part of those organisations purporting to represent rights holders. Concerns as to on-line piracy and loss of control have been addressed by the provisions in the Directive requiring legal protection against circumventing encryption and other technological methods of copy protection and against tampering with rights management systems.[xxxvii]

A carefully negotiated umbrella licence covering the on-line activities of museums, perhaps subject to annual review, would surely do much to win legitimacy for the relevant collecting societies and, more importantly, considerably extend their market. As the experience of Tate has shown, museums and galleries are as keenly interested in safeguarding copyright in artists' works as they are in using images to provide an educational experience.

i F. Spalding, *The Tate: A History* (1st edn., 1998) 9; quoting Virginia Woolf, *A Room of One's Own*.

ii S. Stokes, *Art and Copyright* (1st edn., 2001) p.1.

iii Such as patents.

iv In Europe, as a result of Council Directive No 93/98/EC of 29 October 1993, harmonising the term of protection of copyright and certain related rights.

v In relation to the provisions of Article 5 of the Directive 2001/29/EC of the European Parliament and of the Council of 22 May 2001 on the harmonisation of certain aspects of copyright and related rights in the information society.

vi Which may be contacted via the authors of this chapter, c/o 66 Lincoln's Inn Fields, London WC2A 3LH.

vii The view held in some quarters that it is somehow wrong for museums to assert copyright in photographs of out of copyright works received support from the decision in *The Bridgeman Art Library Ltd v. Corel Corporation*, 36 F. Supp. 2d 191 and 25 F. Supp. 2d 421 (S.D.N.Y., 1998), although see the section on 'Images for Revenue' later in this chapter. The European Commission DG Information Society's recent proposals for a Directive on public sector information (which at the time of writing had not yet been published) could also undermine the ability of museums to generate profitable revenue from image licensing.

viii *The Art Newspaper*, No.116, July-August 2001.

ix *Evening Standard*, 25th July 2001.

x P. Wienand, A. Booy and R. Fry, *A Guide to Copyright for Museums and Galleries* (1st edn., 2000) p.2.

xi See the Copyright, Designs, and Patents Act 1988, Chapter III (as amended).

xii Copyright, Designs and Patents Act 1988, s.32(1).

xiii See Copyright, Designs and Patents Act 1988, ss.32 to 36 (educational use) and ss 37 to 43 (copying by librarians and archivists).

xiv F. Spalding, *The Tate: A History* (1st edn., 1998) pp.193, 248.

xv P. Wienand, A. Booy and R. Fry, *A Guide to Copyright for Museums and Galleries* (1st edn., 2000) p.75.

xvi Note 7 above and S. Stokes 'Copyright and Photography, from Graves' Case to Bridgeman v. Corel', in Part 1 of this book.

xvii S.Stokes, and the press release of the Museums Copyright Group at http://www.mda.org.uk/mcopyg.htm, referring to the opinion provided to the Group by Jonathan Rayner James QC.

xviii B. Hoffman, 'Protecting art images' (1999) *The National Law Journal* Vol. 22, No. 9.

xix Published on-line on the Cordis website by DG Information Society on 21 January 2002, but subsequently taken down.

xx See http://www.cordis.lu/econtent/psi/psi_reuse_consultation_replies.htm.

xxi D.O.A. (AKA Dead on Arrival) produced in 1950 and directed by Rudolf Mayer.

xxii Fine Arts Copyright Act 1862, 25 & 26 Vic c68.

xxiii Copyright, Designs and Patents Act 1988, s.80.

xxiv Copyright, Designs and Patents Act 1988, s.77.

xxv S. Nairne, www.tate.org.uk/webart/mongrel/home/default

xxvi F, Spalding, *The Tate: A History* (1st edn., 1998) pp. 227-228.

xxvii S. Stokes, *Art and Copyright* (1st edn., 2001) p.134.

xxviii F. Spalding, *The Tate: A History* (1st edn., 1998) p.9.

xxix Such as the music industry, where schemes are administered by the Mechanical Copyright Protection Society (MCPS) and Performing Right Society Ltd (PRS).

xxx Copyright, Designs and Patents Act 1988, Chapter VII.

xxxi For example, the projects funded by the New Opportunities Fund (NOF), and Culture On Line.

xxxii Recital (26) of Directive 2001/29/EC (see note 5 above) refers to on-demand broadcasts, but the principle applies more widely.

xxxiii Such as, for example, the Bridgeman Art Library.

xxxiv See note 29.

xxxv See note 5 above and Recital 42 and Articles 5(2)(c) and 5(3)(n) of the Directive.

xxxvi Indeed, it is now clear that the U.K. Government has no intention of implementing any of the non-mandatory provisions of the Directive (including Article 5(2)(c)) at this stage.

xxxvii Articles 6 and 7 of the Directive.

After Digitopia:
The Internet, Copyright and Information Control

Gregor Claude

Media convergence has become an Internet mantra: everything that can be digitised will be. Increasingly, cultural products like texts, sound, still and moving images, can be put in digital formats. And once something is digitised – converted into a string of ones and zeros – it can be reproduced and distributed cheaply, fast, and in whatever quantity desired. Implementing this technology as a global network has undermined the stability of intellectual property. Yet it has also opened up rich new possibilities for artistic practice.

But another tendency is being asserted online: an increasing control of information – not through the application of copyright law – but through digital systems that can control access to the content of digital objects, including digital cultural works. Imagine a book that won't open if you lend it to one-to-many friends, or a film that self-destructs after it has been viewed, or a photograph with an expiry date. This kind of control is enabled by sophisticated encryption technologies that 'wrap' a digital object in a kind of protective code that can control the manner of access and the use of the content inside. Developed on behalf of the big culture industries – the recording, film, and publishing industries that hold their assets as copyrights – this technological control is a new form of information governance that in many ways supersedes the legal control afforded by copyright without bearing any of its standard limitations, such as that of fair use. In the U.S. and Europe, these digital wrapping techniques have now received the backing of the law. Caught between technological and legal control, artistic and cultural experimentation with digital media may be squeezed out of exploiting this new technology.

Two snapshots of cyberspace will serve to highlight the differences among these divergent tendencies. First, the digitopia of the mid-1990's and, second, the more recent copyright crackdown on the Internet. Next, we go on to examine today's emerging forms of Internet governance. Understanding a little about how the technology of the Internet works is the key to grasping the significance of these new forms of governance. Too often the uses of technology are seen as an inevitable, merely technical phenomena that are difficult to understand and really only of concern to engineers. To avoid this kind of technological determinism we take a peek inside the 'black box' of technology to draw out its possibilities and explain why digital media is different. We then move on to some details of the control solutions that aim to deal with the ease of copying from the Internet. With this in mind, we can assess the implications and consequences of this technology for culture and the arts, and the narrowing that today's forms of Internet governance threaten to place on the realm of creative freedom.

Snapshot: Digitopia, b. 1993 d. 2001

The future of the Internet seemed vastly different only a few years ago. Stewart Brand's injunction that 'information wants to be free' was repeated so often that it seemed everyone had heard it but nobody could remember where. When John Gilmore, co-founder of the Electronic Freedom Foundation, said 'the Net interprets censorship as damage and routes around it', he was highlighting this new communications tool (originally developed by the military to ensure the survival of a communications infrastructure in the event of nuclear war) as one that had irreversibly transformed into an uncontrollable free flow of information to anyone with a PC and a telephone line.

Soon the implications, for copyright, were discussed with either unconstrained excitement or panicked terror. If the Internet was an untameable space of the free flow of information, how could existing intellectual property controls possibly be effective? In 1994, John Perry Barlow wrote 'The Economy of Ideas', an influential essay on the Internet's consequences for intellectual property that was to become a manifesto for the new economy: 'Everything you know about intellectual property is wrong', he told us.

> If our property can be infinitely reproduced and instantaneously distributed all over the planet without cost, without our knowledge, without its even leaving our possession, how can we protect it? How are we going to get paid for the work we do with our minds? And, if we can't get paid, what will assure the continued creation and distribution of such work? [i]

Copyright has always protected the physical expression of an idea (a book or a painting) rather than the idea itself, but on the Internet, argues Barlow, the expression of ideas in digital media isn't a physical expression, just 'voltage conditions darting around the Net at the speed of light'. It simply can't be controlled or protected. Nevertheless Barlow and the other Internet pioneers were optimistic for the future of the arts. The end of copyright would free the creatives from the cynical agents and businesses who are only in it for the money. Creativity could be financed in both old and new ways: through patronage, or by charging for interactivity with the client. Somehow the creatives were seen as only winning out in these new relationships. Esther Dyson explains, 'Creators will increasingly be paid for working, rather than their work. As individuals, they often won't have the means to protect their copyrights or to exploit them. Starting out, creators may even want to give their work away in order to get enough of a reputation to get a job or sell performances or services . . . The rewards will go to the creator who keeps creating, rather than to the person or corporation that might own the rights to the product'.[ii] Barlow was less businesslike in his enthusiasm, writing at the end of 2000, 'Behold DotCommunism. And dig it, ye talented, since it will enrich you'. [iii]

These sentiments all had one thing in common: the belief that the Internet exists in the absence of the law. Permanently outside of any particular state's jurisdiction, the Internet had transcended law through technology.

Snapshot: the Copyright Crackdown

In the late 90's, 'cyberia' was a space of openness and possibility, a new frontier for information homesteaders. The term 'cyberia' was famously invented by novelist William Gibson to describe this new, indeterminate, and chaotic info-space. But for some, these newcomers encroached on space they had already come to dominate. For large copyright holders like the culture industries, the words 'information wants to be free' sounded an awful lot like 'we'll take everything you've got'. The Net was the embodiment of the copyright holders' worst nightmares.

The Napster case brought by the Recording Industry Association of America (RIAA) of 2000-2001 brought the new realities of digital copyability to the attention of the world, and is an example with implications not just for music but for all digital media. Napster, a program that helped Internet users find and download digital music, launched in 1999. At its peak in February 2001, Napster had 20 million users; that month they downloaded 2.8 billion songs.[iv] For the first time in years some of the most commonly used terms on search engines were associated not with porn but with music. The predictions of info-anarchy, it seemed, had been borne out.

But Napster spent almost the entirety of its short active life in litigation, and on March 6, 2001, Judge Marilyn Patel issued an injunction ordering Napster to stop the exchange of copyrighted music, calling it a wholesale infringement of copyrights. By May, songs downloaded via Napster had fallen nearly 90% as all copyrighted material was removed from their servers. With the RIAA's shutdown of Napster, digitopia died. Napster alternatives continue today, and some like Gnutella have a decentralised form that means there is nobody in particular to sue, unless you sue all users individually (though some say this is only a matter of time). But none of the alternatives have (yet) come close to the convenience that Napster provided, and the sheer volume of traffic it enabled.

In fact Napster itself still exists. In what seems like a bizarre twist, Bertelsmann, one of the big five music industry firms, bought Napster during the case. The most important message from the Napster case is not the chaos of the Internet, but the consolidation of the recording industry. Industry consolidation is the classic response to crisis. Currently Bertelsmann, AOL Time Warner, and EMI are joining to create an online music distribution platform called MusicNet, which may be based on the Napster model. The remaining two music giants, Vivendi and Sony, have formed a rival alliance and will develop an online distribution network called Pressplay. MusicNet will be promoted among AOL subscribers, and Pressplay will be marketed through a deal with Yahoo!.

Napster was a lesson to all the culture industries, and they have learned not to underestimate the Internet or lose control of their information. They believe they will not make the same mistake again. Currently both MusicNet and Pressplay are seeking to use technological controls to 'tether' the music they distribute to PC's by restricting user's ability to duplicate the files they receive or burn them onto CDs.[v] Whether or not this is the final form their services take, the point is clear: from now on they will be the ones in control of the music. The law had returned, and this time it too would be armed with technology.

What is different about Digital Media?

Digital media is different. Convergence, mentioned briefly in the introduction to this essay, is a way to describe what happens when different media digitise. Convergence means the Internet is the universal media platform: it encompasses all others. Within digital media, all forms of culture are at one level just information to be stored, processed and transmitted by computers, and made available on the Internet. Following in the logic of the snapshots above, we now turn to look at two different and often contradictory aspects of digital media technology: copyability and control. These two tendencies go some way to explaining what's behind both the Internet-libertarians and the culture industry controllers.

Copyability

Digital media is fertile: it reproduces easily. Reproducing a book or photograph is difficult, tedious, and relatively expensive; reproducing a painting may be impossible. But copying a file on a computer is as easy as clicking 'copy' and 'paste'. This copyability is the most important difference about digital media. It is the key element of the Internet that transforms the reproduction and circulation of the digital cultural object. It is no more difficult to make thousands of copies of a digital image than it is to make one. Further, each copy is a perfect copy, and can reproduce, as would the original. Arguably there are only copies and no originals on the Net.

Copying is the core functionality of computers. The technological architecture that make up these machines – the software code and hardware – are designed to carry out three basic information operations: the storage, transmission, and processing of data. Each of these operations requires copies of information to be made. Simply running a program or opening a file means making multiple copies and storing them in various parts of the computer. Open an Internet browser, for example, and you will hear the computer whiz into action while the program opens. One of the first things your computer must do in order to run that program is transmit a copy of it from its storage site on your hard drive into the random access memory (RAM). There, your computer's processor can act on the instructions it receives. When you type a web address into your browser to visit a website, you are interacting with the copy of the program your computer has just made, not the program as it exists on your hard drive. On quitting the program, the RAM copy is erased from memory and ceases to exist, while the copy on your hard drive sits until instructed to make another usable copy of itself. In this way, you never use the same program twice. This process applies just as much to images or text files or any other form of digital media.

So it's not just that copying is easier with digital media, it's unavoidable and intrinsic. And when computers are networked into the Internet, this copying is transformed from a slow, local, access-controlled process to a fast, global, open process. The Internet is a worldwide, distributed, unregulated, decentralised copy machine.

For the man who designed the original protocols of the World Wide Web in 1989, this was exactly the point. The Web – that segment of the Internet that we are most familiar with today – was designed by research physicist Tim Berners-Lee in order to facilitate the academic culture of freely sharing papers and research. Writing in 1998, he recalled:

The Web was designed to be a universal space of information, so when
you make a bookmark or a hypertext link, you should be able to make
that link to absolutely any piece of information that can be accessed
using networks. The universality is essential to the Web: it loses its
power if there are certain types of things to which you can't link.[vi]

With hyperlinks (and today, search engines), accessing information or media
seems less like 'getting a copy' and more like 'going to a site'. But it is a copy of a
website that appears on our screens; Berners-Lee could equally have said the Web
'loses its power if there are certain types of things which you can't copy'.

Copyability gives digital media a somewhat different economics from ordinary objects. The schoolbook economics of arriving at price from supply and
demand are no good here. If everything is copyable, then everything is in a permanent glut. Where there are bottlenecks, they are caused by lack of capacity in terms
of a low band-width or not enough storage space. This is not an economy of
scarcity, but superfluity. You can't envy your neighbour's Internet when you've got
exactly the same one. Furthermore, the usefulness or value of information often
increases the more widespread it is. The peculiar reproductive economics of
information create the conditions for the slogan 'information wants to be free'.

Information Control

Cybernetics is the science of systems control. Norbert Wiener, the maverick math-
ematician and information theorist, coined the term from the Greek for 'governor'
to describe the new science of the systems of information control that he and his
colleagues were developing in the late 1940's.[vii] In contrast to William Gibson's
'cyberia', its root term 'cybernetics' had a very different connotation (though also
utopian in its own way). The irony is rich: 'cyberia', the realm of new, unlimited,
and invigorating freedoms, translates literally as 'control space'.

Digital media is uniquely conducive to information control. Indeed control
is as essential to computers as copying, and just as those three basic information
operations – the storage, transmission, and processing of data – all require copying, they also require information control. A computer program, for example, is
essentially a series of commands and feedback mechanisms arranged in logical
sequence. Digital media are created with those programs according to a program's
commands. And digital media exist in file formats that make them readily manipulated by these programs.

Today's control systems use programs to control not just information itself,
but access to that information. These access control programs range from the

password prompt we get to check our email to the encryption technology that enables secure transactions to take place on the Internet. Another kind of control system, Digital Rights Management, has emerged over the last few years. This is the software mentioned above that can 'wrap' digital media to control the way and by whom it is used. As the name implies, they are offered by their developers as a technological solution to the problem of controlling intellectual property rights.

The problem that digital rights management aims to solve is closely related to the discussion above about the fertility and reproducibility of digital media. Engineers describe their computers as 'universal machines'. By this they mean that the only constraints on computers are that they are machines to store, transmit, and process data. What that data represents or how it is processed is limited only by the ingenuity of the programmer and the physical capacity of the machine (as in memory storage capacity, transmission speed, and processor speed). Another feature of the universal machine is that it can represent or simulate any other machine. Anything that can be described as series of logical sequences or algorithms can be programmed into a computer.

All these features are the opposite of a purpose-built machine. A DVD player and a Walkman, for example, are both information machines that store, transmit, and process information, but only for very limited purposes. The information architecture of these devices – both the hardware and software (if any) – determine very strictly how they operate. Digital rights management uses encryption technology in both hardware and software to shape universal machines into something a bit more like purpose-built machines and to facilitate the control of digital content by rights holders.

The latest digital rights management developments have been named 'trusted systems', so called because rights holders can trust them to enforce those rights. These systems use hardware and software to manage access to and use digital media. Mark Stefik, the chief proponent of trusted systems and head of research at Xerox's Palo Alto Research Centre, explains:

> A trusted system is aware of the rights associated with a digital work because the rights come with the work. Every approach to digital property rights requires a means of expressing rights. They can be attached to the work itself or can be stored in a database. Digital rights fall into several natural categories. For example, transport rights include the rights to copy, transfer, or loan. Render rights include the rights to play and print. Derivative work rights include the rights to extract, embed, and edit.[viii]

The U.S. culture industry's trade associations have co-ordinated several attempts to build reliable and trusted systems. For example, the Motion Picture Association of America has undertaken multiple lawsuits to protect its 'Content Scrambling System' that encrypts all its DVDs; the Recording Industry Association of America is developing its 'Secure Digital Music Initiative'; and the Association of American Publishers are working on their 'Open Ebook Publishing Standards Initiative'.

One of the most ambitious recent copy-control programs was revealed by the IT news website, *The Register*, in December 2000. They detailed the plans of a consortium of computer hardware manufacturers lead by IBM to develop control systems that included components built into a computer's hardware. The scheme, known as Content Protection for Recordable Media (CPRM), would have provided a secure way to control certain media formats by bypassing the computer's own operating system and communicating directly with the disk drive.[ix] By collaborating with T.13, a technology committee of the American National Standards Institute and the organisation that sets the standards used by most disk drives and CD-ROMs, CPRM was intended to be included on almost all new consumer computers. This initiative was an explicit attempt to reconfigure the computer from a universal machine into a device for delivering media. *The Register's* revelation caused such an outcry that in February 2001 IBM announced they had withdrawn the proposal. This response demonstrates one of the limits of control. As Stanton McCandlish from the Electronic Frontier Foundation put it, 'People are not going to buy crippleware'.[x]

There are other limits to trusted systems. Anything you can encrypt, we can crack, say the hackers. The Secure Digital Music Initiative (SDMI) was the most recent example. In September 2000, the SDMI announced a $10,000 prize for anyone who could crack its protection code. The prize was boycotted by much of the hacker community; why help the music industry devise even greater protection to protect its monopoly, they argued. The music industry boasted that they didn't expect to be paying out prize money anytime soon in any case, but even without many of the world's best hacker minds publicly at work on the crack, it was less than a month before a solution was announced.

Once a crack is made, the Internet itself facilitates its spread.[xi] It might take an expert to crack an encrypted format for the first time, but the crack can then be made into an automated program, distributed online, and put to use by ordinary users. Like anything else that is digitised, hacking is ubiquitous. Control of this sort initiates a kind of arms race between copy and control, with copy-protectionists seeking new ways of restricting access and info-liberationists (or pirates, depending on your point of view) developing new ways to foil them.

The Return of the Law: Copyright and Information Control

The arms race, however, has been disrupted by the intervention of the law. Old copyright regimes may have been undermined, but the latest copyright legislation, such as the 1998 Digital Millennium Copyright Act (DMCA) in the USA or the 2001 European Union Copyright Directive (EUCD), attempts to re-impose the effectiveness of copy control for digital media. In particular, their so-called 'anti-circumvention' provisions make it a crime to attempt to circumvent any digital rights management scheme. As a result, trusted systems that specify the manner of use and access of their content grant copyright holders what could be called an exclusive prerogative over the content they own.

With this prerogative, copyright material is just like any other commodity: whoever owns it enjoys exclusive control over it and may determine the manner of its use. The position that copyright should be treated as any other kind of property has argued in the past that fair use provisions of copyright law amount to a tax on the copyright holder, as if public access to knowledge or culture is provided as a benevolent gift (or under duress). Legal prohibition on the circumvention of digital copy control schemes, without equivalent restrictions on the deployment of trusted systems, is like granting the culture industry lobby yet another tax break or legal loophole.

These anti-circumvention provisions highlight a novel element in the latest copyright regimes. By endorsing the private control enabled by digital rights management, the law has in effect delegated a lawmaking function to copyright owners. This creates a new kind of jurisdictional authority that is exercised privately. In this case, jurisdiction, the authority of the state to apply the law in a specified area, has become the authority of the copyright holder to control the segments of knowledge and culture that they own. It is a kind of techno-jurisdiction where what the digital object says, goes. What once was public and legal in form can now be private and technological in form. For the first time, a work can be published and circulated with privately determined, but legally enforceable, restrictions on the manner of its use.

It is worth noting briefly the wider context of this privatised law. The phenomenon of the state delegating or devolving its functions, whether to private corporations or regulatory bodies and quangos accelerated in many areas throughout the 1990's and continues today. Another example in the realm of information technology is ICANN, the Internet Corporation for Names and Numbers, a private corporation with the massive authority of controlling the Internet's addressing protocols. The decisions ICANN makes determine the structure of the Internet in substantial ways. What different examples of this sort of delegation have in common is that they are seen as a way of developing technical solutions to technical problems. The result is a form of technocratic governance removed from the realm of democratic accountability. One critic of this 'policy laundering' approach wrote recently about ICANN, 'They came, they bored, they conquered'.[xii]

Information Control and Creative Freedom

The Internet opens up new possibilities for artistic practice. It constitutes a new creative medium in its own right, and a new fertile space for the circulation and viewing of art in new ways. I do not want to suggest what digital art might be; it is a particularly indeterminate category. A recent report by two jury members of the transmediale.01 art festival in Berlin, Germany in 2001 recounts the difficulty of trying to pin down what digital art is and isn't.[xiii] Here, another possibility is of concern: the ability of the digital artist to borrow, appropriate, and re-use other works in new ways.

The raw material of culture is culture. Creativity always appropriates the results of past creativity. New culture continually re-purposes already existing culture, making it into something new. Digital media, in addition to allowing more perfect control, also allows more perfect appropriation. Precursors of a kind of perfect appropriation could be found in Duchamp's readymades or Heartfield's photomontages. And just as readymades or photomontages transform the meaning and significance of their constituent components, digital appropriation in the arts will too.

The situation Walter Benjamin describes in 'The Work of Art in the Age of Mechanical Reproduction' is deepened with the possibilities opened up by digital reproduction.[xiv] Benjamin contrasts the nineteenth-century 'auratic' work of art with twentieth century non-auratic photography and film that is stripped of aura. In doing so, he problematises the idea of 'the original'. The end product of making a film, for example, is not its final print, but its exhibition in cinemas around the world. The digital work of art of the twenty-first century, whether music, a movie, a website, an image, or a text, is fully reproducible and malleable for anyone with a standard PC. There are no originals on the Net – everything you view on your terminal is always already a representation of a prototype. Each work is at the same time a copy of the original it was made from, and the original from which further copies can be made. Each copy is fully malleable, open to appropriation, re-purposing, and what Benjamin called 'reactivation'.[xv]

For Benjamin, the auratic art object was something that resisted the viewers' attempts to understand and appropriate its meaning. It was as if the auratic art object gazes back at the viewer and keeps its distance. Digital media objects that are protected by trusted systems don't gaze back, but they certainly do resist attempts at access or appropriation. They may or may not have the aura that Benjamin talked about, but they do have power. There is nothing mysterious about this power; it is simply what information control and encryption allow. This is the power that was one of the goals of cybernetics: systems control at a distance. Such protected objects are the projection of the power of the owner over an item of property. The digital media object, encased in trusted systems encryption, is its own law and its own policeman; the owner of that digital media object is its lawgiver.

Duchamp and Heartfield caused outrages in their day by their appropriations, but nobody ever suggested their work was illegal. But just as digital media and the Internet open up new avenues for artistic experimentation, trusted systems backed by the force of law threaten to disable them. Today, bodies like the MPAA and the RIAA vigorously use legal threats, harassment, and litigation to police the new privileges granted by the DMCA.[xvi]

Information control is not the opposite of creative freedom. As discussed, information control is essential to the functioning of computers. Creative freedom in digital media is not a technological issue but a social one. Currently, that social issue is dominated by panicked culture industry copy-protectionists seeking to protect their assets. Of course, it is crucial that creators can be compensated adequately for their digital work. Importantly, some proposals to deal with copyright issues through technology, including some forms of 'micropayments' and metering, hold out promising potential. On the Net there is good copy and bad copy, good control and bad control. There's nothing in digital media technology that forces us to use it in one particular way or another. The independent variable in this equation is people. It is the sum of the actions of the culture industries, governments, media creators, software engineers, hackers, and users who will determine the future of digital media and copyright. But right now, the culture industry's technological initiatives and the laws they have lobbied for are at the forefront, and they have put a squeeze on culture.

Even if trusted systems and digital rights management don't work, it doesn't matter. Even if it is a losing battle for the copy-protectionists, the result of the technological and legal apparatus being created to control proprietary culture will be the same: a narrowed terrain for experiment. Piracy cannot be eliminated; trusted systems can never offer perfect protection. Even hard-wired protection like CPRM that make computers more like playback machines can be dismantled by determined pirates.[xvii] But the culture industries developing these technologies have simultaneously lobbied and achieved legislation that places the force of law behind even the weakest digital rights management scheme, making it seem that they are well aware of their cyber-vulnerability. Their 'copyright grab'[xviii] seeks to protect their assets held in the form of copyrights, but the consequence of their digital and legal strategy is to foreclose on the public realm of culture, disable the computer as a formidable and fertile creative tool, and as a consequence, restrict the creative freedom of all artists.

i   John Perry Barlow, 'The Economy of Ideas', *Wired* 2.03, March, 1994.

ii   Esther Dyson, *Release 2.0: a Design for Living in the Digital Age* (Viking, 1997) 155-6.

iii   John Perry Barlow, 'The Next Economy of Ideas', *Wired* 8.10, October, 2000.

iv   'Big Music Fights Back', *The Economist*, June 16, 2001.

v   John Borland, 'Revolutionaries Press the Mute Button', *CNET News.com*, July 13, 2001.

vi   Tim Berners-Lee, 'Realising the Full Potential of the Web', www.w3.org/1998/02/Potential.html.

vii   Norbert Wiener, *Cybernetics: or Control and Communication in the Animal and the Machine* (MIT Press, 1948) p.11.

viii   Mark Stefik, 'Shifting the Possible: How Trusted Systems and Digital Property Rights Challenge Us to Rethink Digital Publishing', *Berkeley Technology Law Journal* 12:1, Spring, 1997.

ix   Bruce Schneier, *Crypto-gram* newsletter, February 15 2001. See www.counterpane.com/crypto-gram.html.

x   Andrew Orlowski, 'IBM withdraws CPRM for hard drives proposal', *The Register* 22 February, 2001.

xi   Schneier, 'The Natural Laws of Digital Content', Digital presentation, February, 2001. See www.counterpane.com/literature.html.

xii   JJ King, 'They came, they bored, they conquered', *Mute* 20, July, 2001.

xiii   Florian Cramer and Ulrike Gabriel, 'On Software Art', in the Rhizome mailing list, 28 September, 2001, http://rhizome.org/archive/digest/msg00038.rhiz.

xiv   Walter Benjamin, 'The Work of Art in the Age of Mechanical Reproduction', *Illuminations*, (Fontana, 1992).

xv   For a discussion of reactivation see Celia Lury, *Cultural Rights: Technology Legality Personality*, (Routledge, 1993).

xvi   See http://www.eff.org/ for an archive of the Felten and Sklyarov DMCA cases.

xvii   Schneier.

xviii   Pamela Samuelson, 'The Copyright Grab', *Wired* 4.01, January, 1996.

Part 3
Authorship

Who's Painting Copyright's History? [i]

Kathy Bowrey

Some beauties yet no precepts can declare,
For there's a happiness as well as care.
Music resembles poetry, in each,
Are nameless graces which no methods teach,
And which a master-hand alone can reach. [ii]

True ease in writing comes from art, not chance,
As those move easiest who have learn'd to dance. [iii]

Alexander Pope (1688-1744)

The history of copyright has overwhelmingly been concerned with literature and not art. Most writings have focused on the economic and legal relations of the book trade, publishers, and authors in the eighteenth and early nineteenth centuries. In most accounts, copyright protection was gained by the passing of subject-specific legislation throughout the nineteenth century, including for the fine arts and some decorative arts. This occurred only after legal cases involving literary property rights had already established the general nature of the legal right. From this perspective, it may be thought that art, as a relative late-comer in the legislative scheme, had little bearing on the origins and development of copyright law.

Today, we are accustomed to media-specific classification of cultural production in copyright law. The discriminations we tend to make between kinds of works are based upon reference to the technology or production techniques used. For example, literature involves written expressions made with pen and ink on paper or on a word processor; art involves forms of pictorial representation by means of paint and brush, charcoal, or other substances marked on a surface. However, as a matter of history, there is a problem in separating cultural production into discrete media-specific categories, and especially where literature is separated from art. This way of classifying works had little resonance with how cultural production was classified and valued from the Renaissance into the Romantic period of the late eighteenth and nineteenth centuries. As the above quotation from Pope shows, inferences as to whether a work, as a technological artefact, was a literary or an artistic creation mattered far less than judgements made about the conditions of its execution and cultural reception. Artists and poets were distinguished from mere artisans and scribes. What was relevant was whether a work was by a master; whether it was sublime, original, expressive; whether it was the act of a God-like creator. Or was it merely a useful work; a likeness produced to order; a servile copy; an effort deserving no more than the anonymous attribution due to any other skilled worker?[iv]

Although copyright historians have primarily focused on the realm of literature, writings consistently question the importance of the creative subject to the law in broad terms familiar to those with an interest in art and literary theory. Most copyright writers have been driven to discount the influence of the creative personality, and particularly the Romantic subject, on the law. Nonetheless, this theme has long influenced how the copyright story is told. Questions that have loomed large in postmodern theory about reading the status, significance, and value of works have also framed many recent approaches to copyright as a subject of legal history. The challenge of understanding this area of legal history is to understand how questions about the cultural specificity of the subject privileged by law have come to define the telling of the origins of copyright, even though writers are nearly always trying to show the absence of any universal subject or value being embodied in the law.

What follows is an overview of influential writings on the history of copyright dating from the late 1960s to the present. Works are categorised thematically, rather than strictly sequentially. Although 'art' is not the primary concern of the writers, works in each grouping address different attitudes towards the creative subject and the law.

I. Copyright and the Rise of the Modern Author

In the late 1960s, within a year of each other, two American legal scholars, Benjamin Kaplan[v] and Lyman Ray Patterson,[vi] published two key works. Thereafter, 'publisher'[vii] and 'author'[viii] perspectives on the history of copyright emerged throughout the seventies and, through the enormous output of John Feather,[ix] continued to flow in the nineties.

In these early writings about copyright's history, the primary concern was to explain why the priority of the law was not concerned with protecting the author's private property rights in the text. Although modern copyright law developed at the same time as the rise of the professional author and the birth of the modern romantic author, the law was relatively unsympathetic to either of these changes to the writer's social status. For example, John Feather's research unearthed an enormous amount of detail about the nature and diversity of British printing practices from the fifteenth to the twentieth century. Because of his deep understanding of the history of the printing trade and, in particular, of the close ties between the large London printing establishments and some Parliamentary quarters, Feather does not show much surprise or alarm about the inconstant consideration of the concerns of 'Grub Street'. Rather than judge copyright with reference to the presumed interests of authors, Feather evaluates copyright with reference to local circumstances; personal and political relationships; parliamentary instrumentalism; and in this environment, the inability to achieve political consensus. Given this context, we should not expect copyright to reflect any *one* party's hopes or desires.

The writers here emphasise the impact of political organisation, lobbying, and petitioning Parliament on the 'development' of copyright law. There is a tendency to presume that society is better served when the law addresses the 'needs' of publishers and/or authors, however, these works actually say very little about the impact of the copyright regime on society. Many of these early works present copyright as a subject of history or as an unfinished project. Although it is not necessarily stated, they read as if the law's destiny would be fulfilled were copyright to better serve the poets, and it could then also better reward the scribes.

Michel Foucault's work 'What is an Author?'[x] redresses these literary politics. Foucault interrogates the philosophical presuppositions related to the 'rise of the author', including the juridical and institutional system that placed the author and her or his text in a system of property relations. The work has had a major influence on the telling of copyright's history. Many conferences were held in the 1980s and early 1990s to explore the relevance of Foucault's work and literary theory more generally to copyright law.[xi] This marks a new stage in reading the history of copyright, seeking to refocus the relationship between law and authorship.

Mark Rose's paper 'The Author as Proprietor'[xii] was one of the first to deal with the history of British copyright following Foucault's lead.[xiii] This paper centres on a discussion of the late eighteenth-century case, *Donaldson v. Beckett*.[xiv] In this decision, the court addressed the question of the origins of copyright law and specifically the argument that the author was a proprietor – a claim justified by Locke's theory of labour and Romantic theory.

Donaldson v. Beckett was just one in a series of cases pursued by publishers in the eighteenth century, when exclusive rights to publish literary works started to expire under the limited terms of the first copyright law, The Statute of Anne, 1710[xv]. Publishers fashioned themselves as the time-honoured guardians of the author, whom, it was claimed, had always 'owned' their texts:

> Authors have ever had a property in their Works, founded upon the same fundamental maxims by which Property was originally settled, and hath since been maintained. The Invention of Printing did not destroy this Property of Authors, nor alter it in any Respect, but by rendering it more easy to be invaded.[xvi]

Lockean discourse concerning real property was translated to the cause of literary property. Every man was entitled to the fruits of his labour, they argued, and therefore it was self-evident that authors had an absolute property in their own works. This property was transferred to the bookseller when the copyright was purchased, and thereafter it continued perpetually, just like any other property right.[xvii] It was also argued that:

> Style and sentiment are the essentials of a literary composition. These alone constitute its identity. The paper and print are merely accidents, which serve as vehicles to convey that style and sentiment to a distance. Every duplicate therefore of a work, whether ten or ten thousand, if it conveys the same style and sentiment, is the same identical work, which was produced by the author's invention and labour.[xviii]

Texts had exclusive rights beyond those granted by statute law. These 'perpetual' property rights, originally owned by authors, were grounded in common law and natural law, and assigned via contracts to publishers.

In *Millar v. Taylor* (1769),[xix] publishers had some success. The majority of the court found that there was an author's perpetual property right to their texts. However, when the defendant initiated an appeal to the House of Lords, 'the booksellers prevented this appeal from going forwards by coming to term with him'. Rose argues that the booksellers were keen to prevent an appeal because the Lords, including peers, lawyers, and laymen alike, were judged to be unsympathetic to their cause. Parliament was also judged as against anything that looked like a monopoly in the book trade.[xx]

Donaldson v. Beckett was essentially an appeal of *Millar v. Taylor*, dealing with disputed rights to the same work: James Thomson's *The Seasons*. A poem in blank verse, it comprised four books and a final hymn that was first published from 1726 to 1730. It was a popular work that some claim inspired reflections on Nature by Turner, Wordsworth, and Coleridge.

The majority of the *Donaldson* court failed to find any authoritative legal precedent in support of the perpetual right of authors. The principle speaker for the Lords, Lord Camden, rejected such a view:

> I find nothing in the whole that favours of Law, except the term itself, Literary *Property*. They have borrowed one single word from the Common Law. . . Most certainly every Man who thinks, has a right to his thoughts, while they continue to be HIS; but here the question again returns; when does he part with them? When do they become *public juris*? While they are in his brain no one indeed can purloin them; but what if he speaks, and lets them fly out in private or public discourse? Will he claim the breath, the air, the words in which his thoughts are cloathed? Where does this fanciful property begin, or end, or continue?[xxi]

Camden rejected the claim that the common law had ever recognised such a right. This was in line with Lord Mansfield's thoughts in *Millar v. Taylor*, which states that it could not have existed as a right from time immemorial, since there was no record of it prior to the invention of the printing press. He then proceeded to discuss if it *should* recognise such a right, concluding that:

> Knowledge has no value or use for the solitary owner; to be enjoyed it must be communicated . . . Glory is the reward of science, and those who deserve it, scorn all meaner views . . . It was not for gain, that Bacon, Newton, Milton, Locke instructed and delighted the world . . . Some authors are as careless for profit as others are rapacious of it; and what a situation would the public be in with regard to literature if there were no means of compelling a second impression of a useful work . . . All our learning will be locked up in the hands of the Tonsons and Lintons of the age, who will set what price upon it their avarice chuses to demand, till the public becomes as much their slaves, as their own hackney compilers are.[xxii]

A dissenting judgement by Justice Ashhurst endorsed the view of Lord Mansfield in *Millar v. Taylor* that such a right was warranted by the principles of 'natural justice and solid reason'.

> Making an Author's intellectual Ideas common, means only to give the purchaser an Opportunity of using those Ideas, and profiting by them, while they instruct and entertain him; but I cannot conceive that the Vendor, for the Price of Five Shillings, sells the Purchaser a Right to multiply Copies, and so get Five Hundred Pounds.[xxiii]

Donaldson v. Beckett was significant for it's finding that there was no common law literary property right. This left the power to define (and limit) copyright exclusively with Parliament. Statutory rights could not be beefed up in the interest of authors and publishers by way of legal reference to rights that might be claimed as existing according to 'natural law'. Although the Law Lords had discredited the case for a common law literary property, the significance of this was not so clear at the time. There was confusion surrounding the reasoning behind the decision, there being no official case report and incomplete and anonymous copies of judicial speeches in public circulation. Rose argues that though 'the London booksellers failed to secure perpetual copyright . . . the arguments did develop the representation of the author as a proprietor, and this representation was very widely disseminated'. He goes on to note that 'the Lords' decision did not touch the basic contention that the author had a property in the product of his (sic) labour. Neither the representation of the author as a proprietor, nor the representation of the literary work as an object of property, was discredited'. [xxiv]

Rose is interested in *Donaldson v. Beckett* because the decision demonstrates 'the historicity of the seemingly 'solid and fundamental unit of the author and the work'. [xxv] That is, the case shows that there is no necessary connection between authors and texts. Such a relationship was only constructed in the eighteenth and nineteenth century. However, the view of 'the author as proprietor' has been so widely circulated since then that it is often assumed to be a universal, timeless truth. Uncritical histories such as Bonham-Carter's *Authors by Profession* [xxvi] continued to advertise the 'author myth'. Rose's work tries to redress this ahistoricism, and in doing this, Rose made a valuable contribution to the copyright story.

What is troubling about his work is that, though it raises fundamental questions about the nature of the legal order, it fails to take them very far. If property arguments were so dominant in the late eighteenth century, why was the majority of the court in *Donaldson v. Beckett* so unmoved by them? Rose suggests that the problem was that whist Lockean ideas were current, Romantic conceptions of authorship were still relatively new to Britain. Failing to appreciate what was, to the Romantics, an essential difference between works of 'art' and works of 'industry', the Lords could not see why literary works should be treated differently than mechanical works. Mechanical works were protected by patents. So the court treated copyright as a kind of patent for literary works – hence it remained a statutorily limited property interest.

The problem with this is not what it says, but rather with the way the explanation leaves off at this point, implying that there was no acceptance of copyright as a natural right because the *Donaldson* court was basically a conservative one, imprisoned in their time and space, and thereby unable to appreciate the significance of the artistic movement coming their way. In reading 'The Author as Proprietor', one is left with the feeling that if the test case for a common law right had come just a little bit later, when there was broader acceptance of Romantic ideas, there may have been a different result. 'What if . . . ?' points are difficult to argue with: however, Rose's failure to link up here with an earlier point he made about the eighteenth-century ideal of an autonomous legal order causes some concern. If the importance of legal precedent was that it allowed law to rise above the rabble and their ever-changing fashions in ideas, giving law the authority that comes with 'objectivity', there is no reason to presume a different result would follow a decade or so later, even though a romanticised civil society may have wanted it. To be caught by the past was no mere historical accident; it was an established strand of the politics of the common law courts.[xxvii] *Donaldson v. Beckett* was not just a decision about the author's right to copyright, it was also about the authority of law and its relationship to society. Rose's account, however, is so preoccupied with the former issue, it fails to do justice to the latter.

Rose expanded upon this article in his book *Authors and Owners*.[xxviii] Here Rose ties his critique of Romantic notions of authorship to a critique of Lockean possessive individualism. He argues that this period was marked more by relations of *propriety* than *property*. Whilst authors were paid for their work, payment symbolised honour, virtue and reward for the writer, not recognition of ownership of the text.

This propriety/property distinction can create some confusion for the reader familiar with the history of property theory. Rose treats 'property' as if it is fixed to a particular idiom of trans-historical relevance, derived from CB Macpherson's influential interpretation of possessive individualism.[xxix] It leaves sixteenth – to mid-eighteenth-century literary property in a no man's land of 'pre-property'. This is unsatisfactory in a book that purports to map the links between economic and political theory and the realm of cultural production.

Whilst Rose is generally careful in his treatment of Locke, he tends to merge Locke's views on literary property with Blackstone's inventive reinterpretation of them in the literary property cases of the eighteenth century. This marginalises the significance of the enlightenment philosopher's empiricist's views. Whilst Locke's ideas contributed to the social construction of the author, he was uncertain about how far the private property right that belonged to the author of a work should extend. The exercise of extensive private ownership rights could conflict with the pursuit of truth.[xxx] This created a philosophical impasse for Locke, however Rose treats it more as an oversight. It is precisely the coincidence of the need for both public and private rights in a text that makes copyright a peculiar and indeterminate subject of private property, as was recognised in *Donaldson v. Beckett*. Much of the objection to acknowledging in law the social importance of 'good works', by defining copyright as the natural right deserved by the creator of expressive works, related to concerns over the educational implications of this for society. The law that respected the natural property right of the author was also a law creating a 'tax upon knowledge'. There were competing social goals at stake in the literary property debates. This complexity should not be confused with the law's lack of development. Because of historical, philosophical, and jurisprudential reasons, there could only be a very loose and uncertain connection between the Romantic notion of authorship and possessive individualism.

David Saunders' book, *Authorship and Copyright*,[xxxi] is in a sense, a scholarly response to the work of Rose. His main purpose is to distinguish the author as a legal subject from the author as a cultural construct. Saunders wants to show that Anglo-American copyright, unlike the French, is not *organised* by the aesthetic figure of the 'whole' human being and, hence, to save it from postmodern criticisms like Rose's, that he views as being 'preoccupied' with the text and the subject. The French model was based on a natural right of personality, whilst the Anglo model developed out of trade regulation of booksellers and publishers. He cites the works of Patterson and Feather as authority. He suggests that because of this, though Anglo-American law can in places reflect aesthetic concerns, such occurrences are simply 'fortuitous' historical accidents.[xxxii] So far as copyright is a body of law, aesthetics don't touch its heart. In fact, as a body that emerged from a myriad of pragmatic considerations, Saunders questions whether it follows any particular direction at all.

Although the Anglo-American legal world holds the received wisdom that copyright is an economic right rather than a right of personality, if you move beyond concerns for legal form (the origins of the law), Lockean and Romantic conceptions of property are clearly evident and intermingling in the substance of copyright cases. However, Saunders fails to appreciate this because he only considers British case law in any depth up to the decision in *Donaldson v. Beckett*. His main preoccupation is with the early *legislative* period and so, though Saunders' discussion of 'authorship' is quite broad, his analysis of law is quite narrow.

Catherine Saville's more recent work, *Literary Copyright Reform In Early Victorian England*,[xxxiii] also focuses pretty much exclusively on copyright as defined in legislation, and her work picks up where Rose left off. Although the modern author may not have been accorded great respect in the literary property debates of late eighteenth century, surely by the 1840's the prospects for a more favourable legal right must have improved. What happened to author's rights with the passage of The Copyright Act 1842? Saville considers why efforts to reform copyright law in the interest of professional authors, supported by literary elders like William Wordsworth and sponsored in Parliament by Serjeant Talfourd, were compromised. Her reading is influenced by Feather's approach, and however given her subject is to the legislation, she focuses much more on Parliamentary politics than the politics of the printing trade, degrees of influence in the House, party pragmatics, and more philosophical perspectives that affected legislative decision making. This combination of factors led to important concessions, such as an extension of the copyright term for authors, but as with Saunders, it is not concerned with the adoption of any coherent rationale for copyright protection.

In theme, *all* these works are preoccupied with authors and their claims to own texts in law. They are engrossed in literary property legislation. Where case law figures, it is only considered in relation to how the courts interpreted The Statute of Anne, 1710. Why the story of literary property legislation is presumed by many as the model for all copyright law is not explored. There was quite diverse subject matter protected in early nineteenth century legislation similar to the literary property acts, however these are left for others to chronicle. It is presumed that the copyright story is primarily about the legal meaning of 'literature'.

Literary culture was never exclusively concerned with 'literature', that is, the printed word. In her seminal text, *The Printing Press as an Agent of Change* [xxxiv], Elizabeth Eisenstein points to the links between the rise of the artist and the development of printing press. Before the printing press, great works of art, so far as they were considered to be earthly creations, were most clearly identified with the noble patrons that had sponsored the work. The presses allowed art works to be recorded and distinguished in the form of books with engravings of paintings and sculptures, and publishers quickly realised the commercial value of the printed image. Eisenstein argues that this form of publication allowed the development of sustained dialogues about art and arts practice, and by recognition of the great Masters, a separation of the 'true' artists from mere artisans. Biographies of artists and engravings of their portraits helped individualise the creative identity behind the work. Artists took their place as a subject of literary culture (even though the arts professional was not necessarily accepted in gentlemanly circles) and valued for their expressive contribution. The artisan/craftsperson was identified with maintaining oral traditions, with competency judged in terms of technical mastery and not expressive input.

It became common for painters to assign to particular printers the exclusive rights to make engravings of their works. The second copyright Act of 1734, the Engraving Copyright Act, also known as 'Hogarth's Act', was legislative recognition of the economic value of engravings to book publishing. Hogarth was an established painter at the time of the Act, which reputably followed the piracy of his popular series of images that satirised moral and social abuses in a style 'similar to representations on the stage', such as *A Harlot's Progress* (6 scenes, c. 1731). Hogarth was also an engraver and from 1720 had run a business engraving book plates and painted portraits. The Engraver's Copyright Act protected the rights assigned between artists and publishers of engravings, and publishers of engravings from piracy in the same manner as The Statute of Anne. It was not a law inspired by recognition of the engravers' artistic rights per se. A distinction remained, in practice, between 'artist' and 'artisan' engravers. It was Hogarth's worth as a creative and inventive subject that warranted protection, not his talents as an engraver. For the most part, though engravers were often required to exercise a high degree of skill and independent judgement in making engravings, they were considered scribal employees exercising at best a 'secondary' claim to creativity – mere technical interpreters of another's vision.

Whilst copyright law expanded to incorporate new reproductive technologies and protect the investments in the works produced by these means, there was not necessarily an associated rise in respect for the new skills and artistic practices related to technological 'progress'. Engravers generally lacked the social standing to reap great benefits from copyright law unless they were also noted as 'artists'. They struggled for acceptance in the Royal Academy of the Arts during the nineteenth century. In similar battles with the French Academy, it was claimed: 'If engravers have to be admitted to the Institute, then locksmiths will have to be admitted as well'.[xxxv] In part, the acceptance of engravers as artists was assisted by the arrival of another reproductive technology – photography. Engraving was favourably contrasted with the newer technique as 'photography is incapable of correcting the faults of a picture, bad drawing, want of keeping, etc., but copies all the *vicious* with the *good*'.[xxxvi] It was argued that the kind of labour engaged in engraving was closer to art than to the craft of photography.

Copyright law may be relatively quick to protect economic claims associated with new reproductive technologies, but the apparent technological history of the new works created generally led to a devaluation of the labour associated with these creations. The expansion of copyright's domain created new cultural struggles played out in society and in law for recognition of the talents associated with use of the new reproductive technologies. These are issues that are taken up in critical theoretical approaches to copyright's history.

II. Copyright in Theory

A second group of writing does not focus so narrowly on literature and focuses in much more depth on the nature of law and legal rights. Among them, Bernard Edelman's *Ownership of the Image*,[xxxvii] draws on Marxist theory, specifically the work of Althusser. In relation to owning the image, here specifically the case for photography, Edelman traces its reclassification from a process involving manual labour and incapable of sustaining a copyright, to a creative endeavour deserving protection. When photography was a craft practised by small trades-persons and amateurs it was seen as a mechanical activity. There was no labour involved capable of attracting a copyright. However, with the cinema industry attracting investment, particularly after the development of the talkies, the court changed the way it interpreted photographic activity. They 'corrected' the error of their previous classification and re-characterised photography as a creative endeavour. Edelman argues that the subject served by this was not the creative photographer because s/he automatically consented to the disposal of her/his rights in the image by way of a labour contract. It was 'capital' that copyright created and rewarded. Copyright reduced the risk to investors of a 'plagiarised' film competing with the 'original'. For Edelman, 'creativity' is celebrated in copyright law not out of respect for art, but because it is a tool that can serve the interests of capital.

Edelman's approach has influenced a number of works that offer political readings of the development and practice of intellectual property law, including Celia Lury's *Cultural Rights, Technology, Legality, and Personality*,[xxxviii] Ronald Bettig's *Copyrighting Culture: The Political Economy of Intellectual Property*,[xxxix] and Jane Gaines' *Contested Culture: The Image, The Voice and The Law*.[xl] These works tend to be ignored by mainstream copyright lawyers, with Lury and Gaines usually dismissed as being of greater relevance to cultural studies, than law. Although they are all scholarly and complex works, perhaps lawyers are nervous about seriously addressing what the writers say about the economy of copyright practice.

On one level, Brad Sherman & Lionel Bently's *The Making of Modern Intellectual Property*[xli] addresses similar political themes, but in terms of theory, it is written in the language of jurisprudence, which is more familiar to lawyers. This work discusses the origins of copyright with reference to a distinction between pre-modern and modern intellectual property laws. Pre-modern laws are characterised as subject-specific and geographically localised. Modern laws are abstract, forward looking, and are perceived as autonomous. The eighteenth-century literary property debates are cast as a pre-modern struggle over the nature and legitimacy of intangible property rights. It is argued that the law was unable to effectively determine the metaphysical dimensions of intangible property – there was no universal philosophy to which the law could be confidently tied. Following the eighteenth-century literary property debates, there was a jurisprudential shift away from a concern that the law reflects the 'natural' property in mental labour, to a 'consequential' analysis of the merits of granting a right. In the process, it has been left up to the autonomy of law, rather than to natural rights, to 'create' the intangible property.

With modern law-making, protecting creative efforts of many forms is accepted as legitimate. The main interest of law reformers is not with cultural questions about the meaning or significance of works, but with legal aesthetics – drawing simple, uniform, and precise laws. Legal simplicity does not come from reliance on definition in terms of philosophical essences or principles, but from a high level of legal abstraction in definitions. It is argued that these abstractions serve to include, but never clearly exclude, various objects from protection. The property at the heart of intellectual property rights is now only partially defined. It is mainly explained in terms of comparisons between different intellectual property rights. For example, copyright might still be cursorily distinguished from patents by reference to the essential creative activity at issue, patents cast as involving 'discoveries' rather than creation. However, the unique expression at issue in patents would only be legally defined with reference to the technical requirements of the patent specification and the conditions of its registration, and thereby patents are differentiated from a copyright expression that lacks these distinctions. The authors suggest that by the late nineteenth century any reference to creativity in intellectual property texts is superficial.

With the full modernisation of the law in the twentieth century, 'the law moved its focus away from the labour used to create, for example, a book . . . to focus instead on the book . . . itself'.[xlii] With echoes of Edelman's theoretical concerns, Sherman & Bently argue that rather than try to value the labour embodied in the book, modern law assesses value with reference to the (potential) macroeconomic value of the book as a commodity, and in the main, tries not to value the work at all. The subject matter of intellectual property is decontextualised – seen as a 'legal object', that is represented as property in law by indicia such as legally significant drawings and writings, and as circumscribed by policy.

These more theoretical works draw out the implications of looking for creativity in copyright's history. They are most conscious of tracking what is left out when an inquiry is too single-minded in pursuit of the creative subject in the law. Ultimately, they also lead to a questioning of the point of dwelling too much on reading copyright law with reference to its historically contingent origins. The law is too fluid, the legislators too creative, and the economic interests too powerful, to be caught by culture and the past.

III. Postmodern Histories

A third grouping of writings use a postmodern sensibility to inform their analysis of contemporary cultural and legal practice. Rosemary Coombe's *The Cultural Life of Intellectual Property*[xliii] and John Perry Barlow's 'The Economy of Ideas', and 'The Next Economy of Ideas'[xliv] explore the creativity inherent in cultural practices that confront intellectual property rights. Appropriating practices are considered as creative practices, often motivated by political objections to corporate power. The works are histories of the present, based on conclusions about copyright's past. The writers reflect on how particular social and economic relations and practices have been historically favoured by the law, and they discuss how others have been constrained.

Coombe's work adopts Foucault's insights into authorship and authority in her reading of contemporary cultural practices. She makes explicit the cultural specificity of the subject privileged by the law by examining postmodern and transgressive appropriations of corporate intellectual property and its legal consequences. Coombe argues that we live in a postmodern society, and our collective experience and memory is recorded with reference to mass-media signs and symbols. To express ourselves, we draw upon this experience. We treat it as our common heritage, and we use it individually to affirm our identities. We are not necessarily passive consumers of meanings produced by the author and marketed by a cultural and corporate elite. In viewing cultural texts, we can generate new, personally meaningful identities that resist manufactured culture.

From an intellectual property point of view, the reference points or cultural symbols we draw upon are privately owned, and therefore access can be prohibited. Coombe gives numerous examples of how corporate actors have used the intellectual property regime to ensure that only corporately appropriate (sanitised) messages circulate. She argues that this enables certain forms of political practice and constrains others; it permits the proliferation of 'benign' identities and silences others. For Coombe, copyright law is a great site for exploration of contemporary art and cultural practice, read in terms of production of, and resistance to, cultural power. She is also an acute observer of 'fringe' cultural practices in contest with the 'mainstream'. However, she treats creativity as a defining characteristic of those resisting the law. Mainstream copyright practice is not interested in sponsoring creative activity. It is preoccupied with commercial considerations. This is also a perspective she shares with Barlow's prophecy of the early 90s:

> Intellectual property law cannot be patched, retrofitted, or expanded
> to contain digitised expression any more than real estate law might
> be revised to cover the allocation of broadcasting spectrum ... Digital
> technology is detaching information from the physical plane, where
> property law of all sorts has always found definition.[xlv]

In analysing the concept of 'ownership', Barlow argues that the model of legal protection has changed since the Middle Ages in response to shifts in the economic base. He locates copyright law as part of the first and second waves of development, and argues, following Alvin Toffler's analysis, that we are now in 'The Third Wave' where information replaces land, capital, and hardware as the 'property' of value. Information is commodified differently to 'hard' goods: put simply, value is not necessarily generated by controlling its circulation. Barlow predicts that because of this, copyright will lose its popularity as a means of protecting information and innovation. It will largely be superseded by licensing contracts and encryption of programs, which are supported by a market ethics that rewards 'information (that) wants to be free', but not necessarily at zero cost. That is, the cyber-market is a place where consumers will loyally reward useful ideas and ease of access to the digital goods they desire and through this means a democratic kind of natural selection will advance manufacturers, inventors, and artists of merit. Barlow's update on the original article treats the massive appeal of Napster, as a mode for free digital delivery of music files, as proving his theory in practice. Peer-to-peer distribution technologies, such as Napster, will replace the 'artificial' reward structures established by copyright law, allowing for a more immediate and direct relationship and exchange between 'cultural producer' and 'consumer'.

Like Coombe, Barlow believes that intellectual property law has primarily constrained freedom of expression and creativity:

> It's captivating to think about how much more freedom there will be
> for the truly creative when the truly cynical have been dealt out of the
> game. Once we have all given up regarding our ideas as a form of
> property, the entertainment industry will no longer have anything to
> steal from us. Meet the new boss: no boss. We can enter into a conve-

nient and interactive relationship with audiences, who, being human, will be far more ethically inclined to pay us than the moguls ever were. What could be a stronger incentive to create than that?[xlvi] Unfortunately, Barlow fails to consider that entrepreneurial spirit is a force capable of undermining the development of an ethical community of technology users and consumers. He tends to assume that, once the tyranny of intellectual property rights is overcome, cyber-competition will tap into an ethical framework that involves a commitment to unrestricted, democratic exchanges between producers and consumers of technology. What is the basis for such faith?

He romanticises the potential of 'organic' reward structures. When Barlow distinguishes post-industrial society from earlier modes of production, he ignores the historical links between 'Second Wave' and 'Third Wave' markets. Such links impact upon chances for market success. They also affect one's ability to seek more favourable legislative rebirths of copyright law. Barlow's black and white treatment of law and economic history make an abstract argument easier to read, but to anyone with some understanding of either of these things, it is ultimately unsatisfying for the same reason. For one thing, he romanticises the appropriation of digital works. The motivation of users of peer-to-peer distribution services, like Napster in its original form, cannot universally be described as an interest in creative exchanges. At least for some, the attraction is the relative technological ease of obtaining works for free. Once copyright owners put in place stronger technological and legal obstructions to stem free uses, many of the people who had practised copyright 'resistance' will drop out of the picture. Can those who remain be expected to influence mainstream politics and ultimately the ongoing practice of the law?[xlvii] What of the claims of mainstream creative artists who have no desire to contest copyright law? Barlow's writing appropriates the cultural cache associated with claims to creativity exclusively to his own cause, ignoring that other's claims to creativity will continue to legitimate mainstream copyright law.

The recent work by Matthew Rimmer [xlviii] takes the form of microhistories of particular cultural disputes like Coombe's, but he does not presume creativity to be the exclusive tool of any particular cause. Rimmer's work, drawing upon a different postmodern sensibility, looks at all cultural production as collaborative activity. As the product of collaborative activity, any mass reproduced work at the heart of copyright is also a site of competing claims for artistic attribution and copyright ownership. He then accounts for how proponents advocate, contest, resist, litigate, and lobby – manipulating cultural discourse, most especially surrounding relative claims to 'creativity' – in order to achieve desired legal outcomes.

When viewed from this battleground, the law's mediations of creativity are complex and fluid. There is no creative subject universally favoured in law, nevertheless, there are numerous reasons that account for the success or failure of particular claims, such as historical privilege, money, professional organisation and support, access to and use of the media, effective legal counsel, political favour, and personality. Because postmodern histories are deeply involved in the richness of contemporary cultural practice, these works are potentially of interest to a broader audience than many of the more theoretical legal works.

IV. Conclusion

Over the past few decades, the history of copyright has seen several fashions in its writings. Many writers have sought to combine the concerns of earlier writings: to write about the law without assuming a linear direction; to account for the 'author affect' on the law and other social influences; to acknowledge localised resistances and politics; and to consider how the politics of the law and of law making might influence the ensuing legislation.

Most writers have felt bound to pursue the truth of creativity in law, as viewed through literature, literary theory, critical legal theory, and postmodern practice. They share a motivation to explain what might seem counter-intuitive to the uninitiated; to tell why copyright is not all that interested in honouring the creative subject; and to tell why it never has been. In law, creativity has a shady legal presence and a certain dullness of meaning, and though in each stage writers have appropriated at least some of the concerns of those before them, they have been at their most creative in reconstructing the concept of 'creativity'. In copyright's history, creativity is both a constant and a most unstable subject.

i   An earlier version of this paper was published as 'Who's Writing Copyright's History?' *European Intellectual Property Review*, 18:6, 1996, pp.322-329.

ii Alexander Pope, *An Essay on Criticism: Part One* (London: Lewis, 1711). (eds) D.F. Theall and I. Lancashire, Dept. of English (Univ. of Torontoand Univ. of Toronto Press 1997) lines 141-5.

iii Alexander Pope, lines 362-3.

iv This theme is further explored in K. Bowrey, 'Don't Fence Me In: The Many Histories of Copyright', SJD thesis, (Sydney University 1994).

v   Benjamin Kaplan, *An Unhurried View of Copyright*, (New York: Columbia University Press, 1967).

vi   Lyman Ray Patterson, *Copyright in Historical Perspective*,
     (Nashville: Vandebilt University Press, 1968).

vii   Ian Parsons, 'Copyright and Society', in *Essays in the History of Publishing*,
     (ed) A. Briggs, (London: Longman, 1974) p. 29.

viii   Victor Bonham-Carter, *Authors By Profession*, Volumes One & Two,
     (London: The Society of Authors, 1978).

ix   *The Provincial Book Trade in eighteenth century England*, (Cambridge: Cambridge
     University Press, 1985); *A History of British Publishing*, (London: Croom Helm, 1988);
     Publishing, Piracy and Politics: An Historical Study of Copyright in Britain,
     (London: Mansell, 1994).

x   In *Textual Strategies: Perspectives in Poststructuralist Criticism*, edited by J.V. Harari,
     (Ithica N.Y., Cornell University Press, 1979) p. 141.

xi   See for example, the conference proceedings published in (eds) Martha Woodmansee &
     Peter Jaszi, *The Construction of Authorship: Textual Appropriation in Law and Literature*
     (Durham, London: Duke University Press, 1994).

xii   Mark Rose, 'The Author as Proprietor: Donaldson v. Becket and the Genealogy of Modern
     Authorship', 23 *Representations*, (1988), 51. It was republished in Brad Sherman & Alain
     Strowel, (eds), *Of Authors and Origins: Essays on Copyright Law*, (Oxford: Clarendon
     Press, 1994) pp. 23-55.

xiii   Martha Woodmansee's article, 'The Genius and the Copyright: economic and legal
     conditions of the emergence of the "author"', *Eighteenth Century Studies*, 17 (1984) p. 425,
     predated Rose's work, however, it is primarily about copyright and the development of
     a class of professional writers in eighteenth century Germany.

xiv   4 Burr. 2408, 98 Eng. (1774) Rep. 257.

xv   For works published before the Act commenced the term was twenty-one years.
     For unpublished works the term was fourteen years plus a further term of fourteen
     years if the author was still alive after the expiration of the first term.

xvi   *The Case of Authors and Proprietors of Books*, as quoted in Rose (1988), supra n. 12, 57.

xvii   Ibid.

xviii William Blackstone, *Tonson v. Collins* (1760) quoted in Rose, p. 63.

xix   4 Burr. 2303, 98 Eng. Rep. 201.

xx   Rose(1988), supra n. 12, p. 67.

xxi   (ed) Stephen Parks, *The Literary Property Debate: Six Tracts 1764-1774*.
     (New York: Garland Publishing, 1975) F32.

xxii   Ibid., F34.

xxiii Ibid., E35.

xxiv Rose (1988), supra n. 12, p. 69.

xxv   Ibid., p. 78.

xxvi Supra n. 8.

xxvii Eighteenth century tensions over this tradition are discussed by Michael Lobban
     in 'Blackstone and the Science of Law', *The Historical Journal*, Vol 30, No 2 (1987) p. 311.

xxviii The full title is *Authors and Owners. The invention of copyright*,
     (Cambridge, Massachusetts. London: Harvard University Press, 1993).

xxix *The Political Theory of Possessive Individualism: Hobbes to Locke*,
     (Oxford: Clarendon Press, 1962).

xxx   See Bowrey, supra n. 4, pp. 80-90.

xxxi (London: Routledge, 1992).

xxxii Ibid., p. 237.

xxxiii (Cambridge: Cambridge University Press, 1999).

xxxiv The full title is *The Printing Press as an Agent of Change: Communications and Cultural Transformations in Early Modern Europe*, (2 vols), (Cambridge: Cambridge University Press, 1979).

xxxv Quoted in Gordon Fyfe, 'Art and Reproduction. Some Aspects of the Relations Between Painters and Engravers in London 1760-1850', in (eds) Jerry Palmer & Mo Dodson, *Design and Aesthetics*, (Routledge 1996) p.197.

xxxvi Engraver, George Doo, 201.

xxxvii The full title is *Ownership of the Image. Elements for a Marxist Theory of Law*, translated by Elizabeth Kingdom, (London: Routledge and Kegan Paul, 1979).

xxxviii (London: Routledge, 1993).

xxxix (Colorado: Westview Press, 1996).

xl (Chapel Hill: University of North Carolina Press, 1991).

xli (Cambridge: Cambridge University Press, 1999).

xlii Ibid., p.174.

xliii *The Cultural Life of Intellectual Properties. Authorship, Appropriation and the Law*, (Durham, London: Duke University Press, 1998).

xliv 'The Economy of Ideas: A Framework for rethinking patents and copyrights in the Digital Age', (1994), *Wired*, March, pp.84-89, 126-129. 'The Next Economy of Ideas: Will Copyright Survive the Napster Bomb?' 10 August 2000, *Wired*, pp.240, 242.

xlv 'The Economy of Ideas', supra n.31.

xlvi 'The Next Economy of Ideas', ibid.

xlvii For more on the politics of cultural resistance and activism (mainly in the vein of Coombe), see Naomi Klein in *No Logo. Taking Aim at the Brand Bullies*, (New York: Picador, 2000) and Kalle Lasn, *Culture Jam. The Uncooling of America™*, (New York: William Morrow, 1999).

xlviii See for example, 'Shine: Copyright Law and Film', *Australian Intellectual Property Journal*, Vol 12 (3) 2001, p.129.

Copyright, Art, and Objecthood

Anne Barron

Introduction

It is often claimed that the institution of copyright is fundamentally oriented towards the promotion of the arts, and in particular towards the protection of artists from unscrupulous 'pirates' who – but for the copyright system – would exploit art for commercial gain and leave artists themselves to 'starve in their garrets'. Indeed it is around this claim, paradoxically, that those who lobby in the political arena for copyright's continuing expansion converge with many of copyright's academic critics. It has become a commonplace of critical legal scholarship that copyright's primary social function is to give juridical form to a 'Romantic' aesthetic; that the key doctrinal features of copyright law – especially the concept of authorship – have been crucially shaped by this aesthetic; and that the law of copyright is centrally oriented towards promoting forms of cultural production that comply with the core values of the Romantic movement.

Copyright's proponents could readily agree with the critical legal scholar's representation of the copyright system. Romanticism, after all, is an ideology in which artists are held up as uniquely sensitive souls, valiantly transcending the prosaic routines and necessities of everyday life to express their 'genius' in works of the imagination: it follows that a copyright system informed by Romanticism must be one which offers protection to these exceptional but fragile individuals. But whereas pro-copyright activists would flaunt this supposed fact as a reason for celebrating the institution, the project of much recent critical legal scholarship around copyright has been to draw attention to the problematic aesthetic judgements that are implicated with copyright's commitment to Romantic ideology, and the ethical concerns that arise therefrom. In particular, copyright's critics have been anxious to identify that realm of creative endeavour which is negated or denied by Romantic ideology, and to show how copyright law reinforces the exclusive and exclusionary status of the individual genius.

In their 1996 article on 'the ethical reaches of authorship', for example, Peter Jaszi and Martha Woodmansee point out that 'With its emphasis on originality and self-declaring creative genius, this [Romantic] notion of authorship has functioned to marginalize or deny the work of many creative people ... Consequently, 'it should not surprise us to learn that [copyright] law tends to reward certain producers and their creative products while devaluing others'.[i] Although Jaszi and Woodmansee focus primarily on the way in which the Romantic conception of authorship embedded in copyright law devalues the creativity of indigenous artists working in traditional forms and genres, their diagnosis of the limits of copyright could equally explain the law's failure to recognise many forms and genres of contemporary Western art:

> no copyright can exist in a work produced as a true collective enterprise (rather than by one or more identifiable or anonymous 'authors'); a work cannot be copyrighted unless it is 'fixed' [which excludes body art, land art and performance art in general]; copyright does not extend to works that are not 'original' [which rules out the art of the readymade and appropriation art in general]; and copyright does not protect 'basic' components of cultural productions [and so radically limits the protection awarded to minimalist and conceptual art].[ii]

That copyright law cannot accommodate whole swathes of contemporary artistic production under its protective umbrella is clear. What is less clear is how and why this state of affairs could have come about – especially given that copyright tends to be justified as an instrument for *encouraging* the progress of the arts – and whether anything can or should be done about it. This chapter will focus more on the first of these questions than on the second. It aims to contest the notion that Romanticism has been responsible for the narrow (from the contemporary artist's perspective) range of subject matter protected by copyright law, and at the same time to offer an alternative framework for understanding the relationship between copyright and the practice and theory of art.

My target here is not the work of any particular copyright scholar – and certainly not the work of Jaszi and Woodmansee, who separately and together have provided highly nuanced and sophisticated accounts of copyright law's connection with the aesthetic domain.[iii] I focus more generally on an implicit and often unarticulated assumption that informs much critical scholarship on copyright and the arts: that the Romantic conception of authorship is to blame for this troubled and unsatisfactory relationship. Convenient though it may be to sum up copyright's inadequacies by reference to the Romantic author, unreflective Romantic 'determinism', it will be argued, cannot adequately explain the degree to which and the manner in which copyright law accommodates art (and in particular visual art), and processes ideas about art. First, as I argue elsewhere,[iv] it

Carl Andre, *Equivalent VIII*, 1966

misreads the history of copyright, overestimating the importance of aesthetic theory to the emergence and development of the institution, and downplaying other influences on the trajectory of legal change in this area – notably commercial pressures, technological change, and the internal conceptual logic of property law itself (of which the copyright system, crucially, is a branch). Second, as I argue in Part II of this essay, it tends to preclude other ways of understanding how art-theoretical concepts – in conjunction with these other influences – have been implicated in that process. This is because Romantic determinism has been sustained by an excessive focus on the category of authorship in copyright law – the 'subject' of copyright law – and a tendency to overlook the ways in which the protected work – the 'object' of copyright law – is defined for legal purposes.

I argue that it is the work, rather than the author, that has constituted the key site of intersection between copyright, art and art theory, because it is the manner in which copyright law defines the work, rather than the manner in which it defines the author, that exposes copyright's aesthetic prejudices (such as they are) most vividly. And when the focus turns to the work, it is if anything a modernist – not a Romantic – aesthetic that appears to be reflected there. It has not gone unremarked that copyright law assumes its object to be much the same kind of entity that modernist criticism across all the arts assumes *its* object to be: stable, fixed, closed, self-contained, and autonomous of its context and audience.[v] While reiterating this point here, my main concern is to explore the way in which copyright law also fragments this object into an elaborate list of species or types, and to identify parallels between this tendency and a similar – also modernist – tendency in thinking about the visual arts. The first section of the U.K. Copyright Act[vi] provides as follows:

s.1(1) Copyright is a property right which . . . subsists in the following
    descriptions of work:

  a original literary, dramatic, musical and artistic works

  b sound recordings, films, broadcasts or cable programmes, and

  c the typographical arrangement of published editions.

s.4 of the Act goes on to elaborate the legal meaning of the category 'artistic work' in the following way:

s. 4(1) . . . 'artistic work' means –

  a a graphic work, photograph, sculpture or collage, irrespective of
    artistic quality,

  b a work of architecture being a building or a model for a building, or

  c a work of artistic craftsmanship.

  (2) . . . 'building' includes any fixed structure, and a part of a building
    or fixed structure;

    'graphic work' includes –

  a any painting, drawing, diagram, map, chart or plan, and

  b any engraving, etching, lithograph, woodcut, or any medium
    on which an similar work;

    'photograph' means a recording of light or other radiation on image
    is produced or from which an image may by any means be produced,
    and which is not part of a film;

    'sculpture' includes a cast or model made for the purposes of
    sculpture.

I argue that there are clear affinities between the way U.K. copyright law dissects the genus 'work' for the purpose of delineating the possible objects of a *property* right and a tradition of thinking about the arts (much older and more entrenched than Romanticism) in which the separate arts are distinguished from each other and in which the essential components of each art carefully dissected for the purpose of identifying their *aesthetic* limits and possibilities. This tradition of aesthetic thought stretches from Aristotle to Alberti, through the work of Armenini to the rise of the Academies of Art in the 17th century; it emerges with renewed vigour in Jean-Baptiste Dubos' *Critical Reflections on Poetry and Painting* (1719) and arguably reaches its apogee in Gotthold Ephraim Lessing's *Laocoon* (1767).

Of course, the significance of developments in eighteenth-century aesthetics to the development of copyright law's 'Romantic' predisposition is often stressed by proponents of Romantic determinism: the eighteenth-century developments that paved the way for the Romantic movement were the elaboration of a unified conception of 'Art' in general as a unique and special arena of human activity, and the emergence of a distinct philosophical discourse which could provide an explanation of the nature and value of 'Art'. Yet the more or less contemporaneous efforts (by Lessing, Mendelssohn, Herder and others) to offer a systematic classification of the particular arts, and to demarcate the boundaries between the components of the system at the level of their distinctive modalities of expression, have been ignored.

Broadly, these efforts were oriented towards building an understanding of what is specific to each art: an account of the differences between the types of 'sign' each art employs ('natural' or 'arbitrary'); the sensory apparatus involved in the perception of these signs (e.g. sight, touch, hearing); and whether they are perceived in space or in time. Nor is this tradition of purely historical interest, for it re-emerges with a vengeance in the modernist art criticism and theory of the 1940s-1960s, and specifically in the work of Clement Greenberg and Michael Fried. In his classic essay 'Art and Objecthood',[vii] for example, Fried argues that the modernist arts are 'explicitly concerned with the conventions that constitute their respective essences'.[viii] Further, 'the concepts of quality and value and . . . the concept of art itself are meaningful, or wholly meaningful, only within the individual arts. What lies between the arts is theatre'.[ix] Fried proceeds to argue that the modernist sensibility finds theatricality 'intolerable', mainly because of this incapacity or refusal to be bounded by the divisions between the arts; but partly also because a theatrical work exists for, and is incomplete without, an audience, and because the sense that it addresses is above all else the sense of time. Modernist art, on the other hand, defeats time: it is wholly manifest immediately and at every moment.

It is precisely the status of these distinctions, hierarchies, and exclusions that is at stake in much contemporary art practice and criticism. As Douglas Crimp pointed out in 1979, it was theatricality, and with it temporality, that came to characterise much of the art that followed minimalism in the 1970s.

The mode that was thus to become exemplary during the seven
-ties was performance – and not only that narrowly defined activity called performance art, but all those works that were constituted *in a situation* and *for a duration* by the artist or the spectator or both together.[x]

And as Thierry de Duve has argued,[xi] this can be seen as part of a broader tendency towards the production of generic art, that is, 'visual' art that has severed its ties with the specific crafts and traditions of either painting or sculpture. This art has taken many forms, including those referred to by Crimp but also – in the 1980s and since – practices involving mixed media, video, and readymade objects. These postmodernist art practices have not only found themselves in conflict with the norms of Modernist art criticism: they are not easily accommodated, either, by the norms of copyright law, because the affinities between copyright's classificatory schemas and the categories that sustain Modernist critical conventions are striking. Copyright law (at least in the U.K.) has always been premised on the notion that all the arts can, for its purposes, be confined within a determinate list of mutually exclusive expressive forms, each with an essential character. Thus 'artistic works' are distinguished from 'literary works' because they are visually significant and meant to be appreciated by the eye, rather than written and intended to be read.

Within the category of 'artistic works', paintings, sculpture, works of architecture, photographs and so forth are separately listed and defined, and as the statutory formulation reproduced above shows, 'artistic work' has no meaning in law beyond this: 'artistic work' is simply the name applied to each element in this cluster of separately enumerated objects. It is because of its taxonomic approach to the characterisation of its protected objects – that is, because of its commitment to the *genus*, as opposed to the *genius* [xii] – that copyright law is now so frequently confounded by contemporary practices in the visual arts that exceed the categories of 'painting' and sculpture'. From the perspective of copyright law, the problem with these practices is that they do not conform to any of the species accommodated by the legal genus of 'artistic work'. If they are characterised as art by the art world, this is not because they can be described as paintings or sculptures, but simply because their making or doing is accompanied by the claim 'this is art' and calls for an aesthetic judgement on the part of the viewer. Yet copyright law in the U.K. has no category of 'art', and it does not demand of the objects it protects that they elicit an aesthetic response. Copyright law therefore cannot recognise whole swathes of contemporary practice in the visual arts as having any claim to legal protection as such.

The Genus and the Copyright

One of the most remarkable features of copyright's historical development has been the piecemeal and particularistic manner in which its reach has extended over time to accommodate new kinds of intellectual object. This is especially evident in relation to the visual arts. Beginning in 1735, a series of legislative measures, their form roughly modelled on that of the 1710 Act, awarded copyright protection to engravings (1735-1777); sculptures (1798-1814); and paintings, photographs and drawings (1862). These measures were codified in the form of the 1911 Copyright Act, which added works of architecture and works of artistic craftsmanship to the list. All of the entities protected by these early statutes continue to be legally recognised in the current U.K. Copyright Act as copyright works: 'engravings', 'sculptures', 'paintings', 'photographs' and 'drawings' are all listed in s.4 of the Act, together with 'collages', as belonging to the category 'artistic work'.

These legal developments have evidently not been motivated by systematic thinking about the arts in general, or the visual arts in particular: new categories of protected subject matter have not been derived by deduction from a broad concept of 'Art', or even 'Visual Art', but have been added incrementally by way of analogy with what had already received the protection of the law. Even when the term 'Art' has been used in legal discourse, as in the title of the 1862 Act (the 'Fine Arts Copyright Act'), it has exerted no independent force as a legal concept. Under this Act, no less than under the other legislation referred to above, the only issue of any relevance to the status of a given entity as a copyright work has been whether the entity belongs within a list of separately identified classes of protected object: in the case of the 1862 Act itself, the list included paintings, drawings and photographs.[xiii]

The 1911 Act codified the many copyright statutes that by then existed, and organised the many classes of protected object into four groups – literary, dramatic, musical and artistic works – which continue to be recognised in the current law. But these four groups were not (and are not) themselves systematised by reference to a broader legal concept of 'Art', and the group of works designated 'artistic' was (and is) simply a list. As has been pointed out already, the term 'artistic work' has never had any significance in law except as a label applied to some entity which qualifies for copyright protection on other grounds (e.g., because it is a 'painting' or a 'sculpture' – or indeed a 'map' or 'chart' – within the meaning of s.4 of the Copyright Designs and Patents Act 1988). Of course this still leaves open the question of how each of the classes of object in the 'artistic work' category is to be defined, and here the legislation has remained largely silent: significantly, all it says is that graphic works,[xiv] photographs, sculptures, and collages are protected 'irrespective of artistic quality'. Beyond this, it is up to the courts – whose task it is to interpret the statutory scheme – to tease out what is meant by each of these concepts. And as

I shall explain below, they have tended to do so by reference to the technical features that characterise objects assigned by ordinary language use to these categories, not in terms of whether these objects can claim the status of 'art'.

As far as the artist is concerned, two consequences flow from this way of thinking about the objects of copyright. First, it has resulted in their being disaggregated into a series of classifications and sub-classifications that appear highly anomalous from the perspective of the contemporary artist, whose practice can no longer be confined by the categories of painting, drawing, sculpture, collage, engraving, architecture or even photography. There is no specific sub-classification of the 'artistic work' category that could accommodate installation art, video art,[xv] environmental art, body art, performance art, mixed media works, or most conceptual art; nor is there a general overreaching category of 'art' that could accommodate the products of these practices instead. I would argue that this owes far less to deliberate aesthetic discrimination than to the peculiarities of copyright's legislative history: in particular, the manner in which techniques of legislative drafting have been deployed to manage the pressure exerted on the statutory framework of copyright law by the interest groups who have successfully pressed their claims in the political arena. Yet the *effect* of this taxonomic approach to defining the objects of copyright is certainly discriminatory, simply because the narrowness of the law's classifications causes it to fail to reflect the diversity of contemporary art. Second, the manner in which the privileged classifications of painting, drawing, sculpture, collage, engraving, architecture and photography are defined as a matter of copyright law has little to do with how contemporary practitioners of these arts would define their own practice. This is because the law, as shall be demonstrated below, defines each of these types of artistic work in terms of the differences between their compositional/creative and artefactual conditions and the modes by which they are perceived by the senses: differences which are supposed to be aesthetically neutral.

This myopic way of seeing the 'artistic work', as far as contemporary art is concerned, has nothing to do with Romanticism, though it is certainly analogous to other tendencies in eighteenth-century aesthetics. Historians of aesthetics generally pinpoint the eighteenth century as the site of a convergence of two very different attitudes to art.[xvi] One is a universalising trend towards imagining art, with a capital A, as a 'system' of the five major arts – painting, sculpture, architecture, music, and poetry – unified as a distinct arena of human activity under common principles supplied by the philosophical discourse of aesthetics. This approach produces the following kind of question: 'what is it that a poem and a picture, a musical piece and a statue have in common, although the media in which they are cast, the material nature of the products, differ so widely?' Romanticism, of course, answers this question with a general theory of artistic creation.

The second attitude, however, is preoccupied with how these kinds of work differ from each other: it is a particularising attitude, oriented towards demarcating the boundaries *between* the arts and identifying what is unique to each of them. Variants of this tendency can be traced back to antiquity: Aristotle's *Poetics*, for example, distinguished poetry from painting in terms of the media characteristic of these two arts (words, melody, and rhythm, as opposed to colour and drawing).[xvii] In a sense, the workshop literature of medieval Europe perpetuated this approach, though in an unreflective manner. This literature was comprised of 'how to' manuals by and for practising artists, characterised by their lack of systematic arrangement and their omission of any reference to the aim or function of the arts referred to, or to the values they embodied or served.[xviii] The technical orientation of these treatises necessarily led them to focus on specific arts and the materials and means involved in making specific examples of each art. Thus their authors 'strictly limited the scope of the subject matter they explored; they thought of and discussed only the conditions and processes of the production of a [specific] work of art . . . The only question the medieval artist asked . . . was: How is it done?'[xix]

During the Renaissance, humanist scholars speculated at a higher level of generality about the components of each of the visual arts (especially painting, sculpture and architecture), but even so, the *paragone* (comparison) literature of the time consolidated the tendency to focus on what distinguished these arts from each other rather than on what they shared: 'the specific nature of each medium, and . . . the particular processes required by working in each of them'.[xx] This particularising tendency exerted a powerful, if unacknowledged, influence on the thought of eighteenth-century aestheticians such as Lessing and Mendelssohn. And these early reflections on the 'specific nature of each medium' crystallised a set of ideas about the visual arts that are echoed in the 'medium-specific Modernism' developed by Clement Greenberg and his followers in the mid-twentieth century.

Although this attentiveness to the particularities of artistic methods, means, and materials has received far less attention from copyright scholars than the universalising attitude, it is here that the most interesting parallels between copyright law and aesthetic theory are to be found. For in eschewing the category of 'Art' and focusing instead on defining instances of 'artistic work' such as painting and sculpture in purely technical terms, legal discourse replays – in its own key – one of the oldest themes in the history of art theory. The implications of this paradox have only become obvious and important in the wake of the turn from specific to generic art: it is because copyright law assumes that 'Art' manifests itself only in a determinate array of species of object such as painting and sculpture that it cannot accommodate any artistic gesture that is not realised in one or other of these forms. Thus it is precisely in its blindness to 'Art', I would argue, that copyright law's discriminatory and exclusionary potential resides. Before proceeding to elaborate on this argument, however, it is necessary to confront the Romantic 'determinism' thesis outlined in the Introduction, because if true, this thesis directly contradicts the argument I want to advance in this essay. In the next section, then, I will trace the emergence of the universalising attitude to 'Art', show how the Romantic movement absorbed this attitude, and analyse the claim that copyright law, in its turn, reflects a Romantic aesthetic.

The Emergence of 'Art'

As Kristeller has convincingly shown, the universalising attitude emerges for the first time only in the eighteenth century.[xxi] Until the early modern period, the term 'art' was applied to all kinds of human activities which we would now call crafts or sciences. It designated any *techne* or skill which could be learned: 'a skill in making products, a skill in practical performance, and a skill in theoretical activities of the mind'.[xxii] The first of these meanings is the closest to the contemporary understanding of art as yielding 'works' of art, but before the emergence of a unified concept of fine art in the eighteenth century, 'the class of works of art included not just works imbued with 'aesthetic' value . . . but all utilitarian products of skilled or mechanical labour. Works of art were not sharply distinguished . . . from craft-products'.[xxiii] In the Middle Ages, for example, architecture, sculpture and painting tended to be categorised, along with other crafts, as 'mechanical' arts in contradistinction to the 'liberal' arts; music was considered a liberal art in the same company as mathematics and allied disciplines; and poetry, also a liberal art, was closely linked to grammar and rhetoric.[xxiv] Not even the Renaissance produced a formulation of a system of the fine arts or even a comprehensive theory of aesthetics, though it brought many important changes in the social position of art and the artist.[xxv] The visual arts of painting, sculpture, and architecture began for the first time to be theorised as a separate group and distinguished from the crafts during this period,[xxvi] but the attempt to dignify them with a special status sometimes proceeded by analogising them to poetry and music, and sometimes by representing them as sciences, which suggests that there was as yet no category of 'fine art' that was recognised as clearly distinct from the sciences.

Kristeller identifies the publication of Batteaux' *Les Beaux Arts Reduit à un Même Principe* ('the fine arts reduced to the same principle') in 1746 as a key moment in the crystallisation of the category: the fine arts (all of which are said to have pleasure for their end) are here rendered as music, poetry, painting, sculpture, and the dance; and the principle that is common to them all is said to be the imitation of beautiful nature.[xxvii] The *Encyclopédie ou Dictionnaire Raisonné des Sciences, des Arts et des Métiers*, published in Paris in 1751, put the finishing touches to Batteaux' system by including architecture among the imitative arts,[xxviii] and by 1762, British writers such as Lord Kames (Henry Home), the Scottish judge and aesthetician, were taking the 'system' of the fine arts for granted: the latter lists poetry, painting, sculpture, music, gardening, and architecture as 'fine arts'.[xxix] These French and British conceptions of the arts, however, were motivated more by critical than by philosophical concerns, and it was in Germany that the field of philosophical aesthetics took shape for the first time. Kant's *Critique of Judgement* (1790) is of such fundamental importance to the history of aesthetics precisely because it incorporated this new tendency to theorise about the 'system' of the arts into the most sustained philosophical treatment yet of the concept of beauty. At the same time, his analysis of beauty broke with the earlier association of beauty with imitation or mimesis: it paved the way for the Romantic conception of art as an expression of subjective feeling or imagination, and of value in art as linked with the intensity of the artist's feeling and the quality of his or her imagination.[xxx]

The exaltation of the artist's creative nature became evident first – from the 1760s – in literary theory and practice, and migrated from there to embrace the visual arts. This is significant, because as Barasch has pointed out in his treatment of the writings of a leading Romantic art theorist, Wilhelm Heinrich Wackenroder, there is a tendency in the literature of the movement to regard the work as merely a conduit to the artist's 'soul' and so to overlook its specificity:

> What the spectator looks for, and indeed finds, in a painting are not the material or formal components of the painting itself; the true subject of the spectator's vision, in Wackenroder's view, is the personality of the artist. The work of art, it turns out, is only a stepping stone to the artist, a medium through which we can meet him.[xxxi]

The desirability of 'meeting the artist' followed in part from the Romantic conception of genius as connoting a kind of spiritual superiority which was connected especially with artistic activity. The concept of genius already had a long history in art theory by the late eighteenth century, however. Barasch sees it at work in art theoretical writings of the High Renaissance (notably Zuccari's *The Idea of Painting, Sculpture and Architecture*, published in 1607[xxxii]), where it is sometimes invoked to question the received view that painting or sculpture is best effected by following institutionalised traditions and prescribed rules. The new emphasis placed on genius in the second half of the eighteenth century can thus be seen as the movement of an old but peripheral theme in art-theoretical writing to centre-stage. Now the artist is no longer regarded as one who must be guided by rules and inherited forms or styles in producing works of art, but is unequivocally seen as one who is equipped with an exceptional endowment (and not merely an exceptional skill or technique), which manifests itself in breaking rules, departing from traditions, effecting breakthroughs: that is, in originality.

Other key terms in the discourse of Romantic art theory – imagination, inspiration, expression – also echoed elements of older traditions of theorising about painting and sculpture, but as Osborne points out, like genius, these terms 'took on a new significance in the course of [the Romantic] movement and so revolutionised the theory of art'.[xxxiii] Imagination had previously signified the capacity to memorise visual impressions gleaned from experience and retain these in the mind as resources for later use, or the capacity to perfect the appearances encountered in nature by reference to the Ideal forms that arrive in the artist's mind through reflection and introspection; now it is the inventive or productive imagination – the ability to conjure up images which have no counterpart in nature and which therefore transcend the limits of experience – that is emphasised. The well-spring of original creative endeavour – inspiration – ceases to be seen as the effect of a (divine) force acting upon the artist from outside, and is conceived of as having its source in the unconscious part of his or her own being:[xxxiv] thus the real subject of every work of art is the artist, and the compulsion to express oneself comes to mark out the artistic sensibility.

Consequently, the meaning of 'expression' also shifts: whereas for the Classical tradition it referred to the facial or bodily attitudes by which the emotions of the figures depicted in painting or sculpture are signified, now it means the process by which the artist's *own* feeling is conveyed through the art work. The central importance now given to these ideas in conjunction with one another 'constituted a new attitude towards art with new concepts of its functions and new standards of assessment'.[xxxv] The art work was now supposed to be the medium through which less sensitive souls could commune with the artist's superior personality. It followed that it was acceptable to appraise the work of art by reference to the degree and complexity of imaginative invention contained within it, or the intensity of the emotions conveyed by it: 'Art should communicate shades and colours of feelings not otherwise accessible or enable the observer to experience standard emotions with fresh insight or vividness'.[xxxvi]

'Art' and Copyright

The law shows no sign of having been led by these developments in selecting out categories of intellectual creation for the very different kind of status entailed by copyright protection. As has been shown, copyright law knows no concept of art as such. And although the law now protects a list of art forms that includes all the components of the 'system of the arts', the history of its progress in this regard exemplifies a completely different evolutionary logic to that described by Kristeller. True to its title, the Fine Arts Copyright Act 1862 extended the protection of copyright law for the first time to paintings, and so added painting to a list of art forms – notably sculpture – whose products were already protected by other statutes. But this list included art forms that were excluded from the 'system of the arts' (e.g. engraving and photography); excluded art forms that were included in the system (notably architecture); and elided two of the (aesthetically) favoured art forms – music and poetry – under the general category of the 'book'.[xxxvii]

Whatever the logic underlying the array of protected subject matter in the mid-nineteenth century, it was not the same as that underpinning the emergence of the system of the arts and the concept of Art in general at the end of the eighteenth. Even when, in 1911, the list was reorganised to produce the four groups of protected works mentioned above – literary, dramatic, musical and artistic works – the new taxonomy bore only a superficial resemblance to the aesthetic categorisation of the five major art forms: architecture was included for the first time in the 'artistic works' category but took its place alongside such prosaic items as diagrams and charts, while poetry was not explicitly mentioned but (as a form of literary work) was implicitly placed in the same category as examination papers and railway timetables. The position today is broadly the same. More fundamentally, criteria of artistic merit have on the whole[xxxviii] been very deliberately excluded from playing any role in determining whether an entity falling into one of the designated categories qualifies for copyright protection. To this extent, the proposition that copyright law is the legal expression of a particular aesthetic theory is simply not sustainable.

This can be illustrated by reference to copyright law's own conceptions of 'authorship' and 'originality'. Authorship in law, first of all, is simply the description of a causal relationship between a human intentionality and a work: the

Copyright Act states nothing more than that 'author', in relation to a work, means the person who creates it'. [xxxix] The work, in turn, need not be of any particular nature or quality in order to gain protection: it must simply be attributable to some determinate person. It follows that the originator of the protected work need in no way be a 'genius' in the Romantic sense in order to acquire the status of author for the purpose of copyright law. True, some works of authorship – including artistic works – must be original if they are to obtain the protection of copyright, but the legal concept of originality has little in common with the Romantic notion of originality. A work is original in law if it can be shown that its author has expended some more than minimal conscious effort in its production: it is quite clear that imaginative effort is not required. And although the requirement of originality translates into the rule that a work must not be copied if it is to gain the protection of copyright,[xl] this rule cannot meaningfully be equated with Romanticism's antipathy to imitation. Because the rule excludes only slavish copies, copies which exemplify no 'material alteration or embellishment' of the work of another,[xli] the criterion of originality is no bar to the protection of a work which incorporates pre-existing material and is, to that extent, derivative. For all of these reasons, it is impossible to see in the legal concepts of 'author' and 'originality' a clear reflection of the ideas that were characteristic of the Romantic movement.

One further legal concept deserves some attention at this point, however, and this is the concept of the 'work' itself. For although copyright law avoids defining its objects in terms of an overreaching conception of 'Art', it does invoke an overreaching concept of the work.[xlii] What then is a 'work' in law? The concept is nowhere defined in the legislation, but case law shows that certain features are consistently predicated of every object that is deemed by the courts to be a copyright work – quite apart from and prior to the question of whether it qualifies as a particular *kind* of work (e.g., an artistic work).[xliii]

First, there can be no copyright work without some human author who can be said to originate it. To gain the protection of copyright law, an entity must be capable of being conceived of as the result of some (more than minimal) human intervention in the 'real', whether or not this intervention is mediated by mechanical or other technical means. Thus, a landscape or scene cannot itself constitute a copyright work, though a photograph or painting of the same landscape can. Second, a copyright work must be capable of certain definition. There are two means, in turn, by which copyright law ensures that its objects will have clearly delineated boundaries: through the principle that copyright extends only to the 'expressive form' that ideas assume and not to ideas as such; and by requiring that works must be manifest to the senses in some way, either because they are recorded, or fixed, in some material embodiment,[xliv] or because the process of their creation makes this inevitable.[xlv] In other words, copyright law demands both that a concrete expressive form be conceptually separable from an 'underlying' realm of general ideas attributable to some determinate author and that this (intangible) expressive form be perceptible to the senses.

There is no doubt that this way of thinking about the object of copyright operates now to deny or radically curtail protection for many contemporary practices in the visual arts, and a few examples will suffice to illustrate this point. The apparently uncontroversial principle that every protected work must be attributable to the creative efforts of some determinate author is of major significance here. It cannot comprehend the art of the readymade, which of course denies the necessity of the artist's hand; nor can it accommodate the site-specific art work – much less one that depends for its completion on the participation of the spectator – because the principle implies that every aspect of a work must be attributable to its creator. The requirement of embodiment or fixation is no less important: it has the consequence that any form of artistic endeavour which does not yield some tangible object, or some record of an event, performance or 'happening', cannot be or generate anything that constitutes a work in law. The notion that a work is an objectification, in a bounded expressive form of human creativity, is similarly crucial to the capacity of copyright law to accommodate contemporary visual art, for it excludes any art practice that resists its own reification: conceptual art, some of which liquidates the object entirely; and performance art, which yields an event unfolding in time rather than a spatially delimited artefact.[xlvi] Finally, the concept of the work also imposes constraints on the *kinds* of objects in which the work can appear: the object cannot be a human being as such;[xlvii] the object must arguably be reasonably permanent;[xlviii] and it cannot be liable to decay, disappearance, or continuous change.[xlix] The implications of all this for body art, installation art, environmental art, kinetic art, and any art which involves the use of organic or unstable components should be clear.

Does all of this justify the conclusion that the legal concept of the work reflects copyright law's commitment to a particular aesthetic theory? As I have argued elsewhere,[l] the answer to this question must be 'no', because the work concept has actually been generated by the copyright system's more fundamental commitment to the logic of property. Copyright law is a branch of property law, and the chief function of property law is to define the things which may be objects of exclusive private control and identify the persons in whom those rights of control may be vested. Because of their amorphous character, intellectual objects pose particular difficulties of identification and attribution, and the concept of the work is a response to those difficulties: in order to position an intangible entity as an object of property, the law must be able to see it as an identifiable and self-sufficient 'thing', attributable to some determinate author and perceptible to the senses through the physical medium in which it is recorded or embodied. So if copyright's 'way of seeing' the work has blinded it to many contemporary practices in the visual arts – and it clearly has – then this is not, I would argue, the effect of deliberate aesthetic prejudice, but simply a by-product of copyright law's pursuit of certainty, objectivity, and closure.

The same can be said of another, rather different, pattern within current legal thinking about the object protected by copyright. This also has serious reper-cussions for copyright's capacity to accommodate the art of today; and it also does not derive from Romanticism, though it closely parallels a quite different attitude towards the arts that long preceded the Romantic movement. I refer here to the law's tendency to define different *species* of work as significant for copyright pur-poses and to distinguish these by reference to the nature of their material carriers; the system of signification deployed within them; and the way they are perceived by those who experience them. This tendency also testifies to the difficulties posed for the law by the amorphous character of intangible entities because it answers to the need for objective and certain criteria for defining these entities in the process of singling them out for legal protection. To this end, the law dis-aggregates the category of 'artistic works' into a series of sub-classifications (painting, sculpture, drawing, and so forth), and explicitly avoids building criteria of aesthetic evalua-tion into the definitions of what these are for legal purposes – by ignoring issues of quality, subject matter, and content and focusing instead on the minimal technical conditions of their production.

Yet, it is precisely this way of thinking about artistic works – in terms of what art theorists would call their 'media' – that has striking parallels in art theory: the particularising trend in art theory that was outlined briefly above. In the next sec-tion I elaborate on how the entities listed in s.4 of the current Copyright Act as 'artistic works' are defined in law. In a subsequent section I examine the most important eighteenth-century exponents of the particularising approach to aes-thetic appreciation and consider how Clement Greenberg elaborated his credo of formalist Modernism from it in the mid-twentieth century. In the final section I summarise the parallels between Greenberg's pursuit of an aesthetic of 'truth to media' and copyright's ostensibly *anti*-aesthetic definitions of genres of visual art.

Medium-specific 'Artistic Works'

s.4 of the Copyright, Designs and Patents Act 1988 lists an array of entities as belonging to the category of 'artistic works' and thus entitled to copyright protection. The list includes paintings, engravings, sculptures, drawings, and collages, but the Act nowhere expressly defines or elaborates on what is meant by any of these terms, so it has been left to the courts to flesh out their meanings. Faced with the task of determining what is accommodated by a particular term within the 'artistic work' category, the courts have propagated a tried and tested strategy – familiar from the very earliest period of copyright's application to the visual arts – of focusing on the material embodiments through which visual representations of that type are 'normally' made manifest.[li] When confronted with the argument that make-up applied to a person's face yielded a 'painting' within the meaning of the copyright legislation, for example, one judge recently demurred, insisting that 'paint without a surface is not a painting'.[lii] A similar preoccupation with specific means and materials as definitive of the particular artistic media referred to in the legislation is evident in the case law relating to drawings, engravings, sculptures, and collages. In an early case on drawings, it was said of a very crude line drawing that it was 'not a pleasing, particularly accurate or tasteful representation upon paper of the object represented, nor does it appeal to imagination, affectation, memory, or association'[liii] but, being a 'representation on paper', it nonetheless acquired the protection of copyright. In the Australian case of *Greenfield Products Pty Ltd. v. Rover-Scott Bonnar Ltd.*,[liv] Pincus J. departed from the reasoning in *Wham-O MFG Co v. Lincoln Industries*[lv] in relation to engravings – where a mould which had been cut with a lathe from a steel die block to create the desired shape of a plastic frisbee was held to be an engraving – but offered an equally 'materialist', though narrower, definition of engraving instead:

> I do not well understand why the court [in *Wham-O*] thought that working at a lathe cutting into a rotating piece of metal with a tool is the work of engraving . . . it is not all cutting which is engraving; for example to cut a steel rod into lengths is not to engrave it . . . The term does not cover shaping a piece of metal or wood on a lathe, but has to do with marking, cutting or working the surface – typically a flat surface – of an object.[lvi]

In *Breville Europe plc v. Thorn EMI*,[lvii] Falconer J. accepted that a plaster cast of a sandwich made for the production of die-casting moulds for the heating plates of a sandwich toaster could be a sculpture under the 1956 Copyright Act. The word 'sculpture', he said, should be given its ordinary dictionary meaning – the art of forming representations in the round or in relief by chiseling stone, carving wood, modeling clay, casting metal or similar processes – and anything which is the result of one of these processes ought to qualify as a sculpture in law. It has also been suggested that where an object cannot have a permanent existence because of the material with which it is made, it cannot be a sculpture as a matter of law.[lviii] However, it is the treatment of collage in the case law that perhaps most exemplifies this 'materialist' tendency. In *Creation Records Ltd. v. News Group Ltd.*[lix] Lloyd J. said that 'collage' involves 'as an essential element the sticking of two or more things together. It does not suffice to point to the collocation, whether or not with artistic intent, of . . . random, unrelated. and unfixed elements . . .'[lx]

To the artist or art critic, all of this will seem astonishingly at odds with contemporary practices in the visual arts, although the judges themselves have not appeared to find this lack of fit particularly troubling. Thus, although it was pointed out by the plaintiff in *Creation Records* that the 1988 Act should not be construed to deny protection to the 'great variety of novel forms' of visual art as artistic works under s.4, Lloyd J. simply said that he did not consider it necessary or appropriate to concern himself with that issue. (Lloyd J. did regard it as significant that artworks such as 'Carl Andre's bricks . . . the stone circles created by Richard Long . . . Rachel Whiteread's house . . . the living sculptures of Gilbert and George and . . . installation art generally' are not 'intrinsically ephemeral'[lxi] because they are designed to last for a reasonable period of time, but whether this meant that they could in Lloyd J.'s opinion qualify as artistic works does not emerge clearly from his judgement. It is certainly very difficult to find a category in s.4 in which these artworks could be comfortably accommodated).

Thus far, the courts have been driven to confront two quite different problems that have emerged from their interpretation of s.4. The first is the problem of how to devise a principle by which to distinguish 'sculptures', or indeed 'collages', from manufactured three-dimensional objects in general. The second is the problem of how to distinguish 'artistic works' from the other categories of work protected by the Act, particularly literary and dramatic works. Both of these difficulties arise because of the lack of any overeaching definition of the term 'artistic' in the legislation, and the fact that the courts have been more or less disqualified from importing any criterion of aesthetic merit into their interpretation of s.4 – all of the items listed there, with the exception of works of artistic craftsmanship and works of architecture, being expressly stated to be protected 'irrespective of artistic quality'. The inclusion of this phrase in the Act reflects an assumption that aesthetic evaluations are necessarily subjective, as well as a legislative concern not to invite judges to become involved in subjective evaluations: 'no test . . . can have been entrusted to [the courts] unless it is one from which there are excluded any questions of taste, subjective quality, and personal opinion; it exceeds the functions of a court of law to adjudicate on these, indeed they are inconsistent with the very concept of the rule of law'.[lxii] Yet in seeking to pursue one set of legal values – objectivity; judicial impartiality – copyright law has compromised others to which it is also, necessarily, committed: notably the avoidance of monopoly and the achievement of definitional certainty.

This can be illustrated, first, in relation to the difficulties that have arisen over the meaning of 'sculpture' in copyright law. As long as the materials by which sculptures were 'normally' made and the 'normal' manner of their making distinguish them clearly from other kinds of object, the lack of a criterion referring to their artistic quality is not experienced as creating definitional problems. However, twentieth-century developments in sculpture (the shift from casting and forming to the construction of 'sculptures' using pre-fabricated materials) have made it possible to argue that prototypes for ordinary, industrially-manufactured objects of commerce are also sculptures, and so protected from copying by the manufacturer's trade rivals. As long as judges continued their past practice of invoking physicalist definitions of sculpture focusing on the character of the material object and the processes by which it was made, it was inevitable that industrial prototypes would gain the protection of copyright law.[lxiii]

Yet this conflicted with the well-established policy of *not* allowing manufacturers to avail of copyright to monopolise the shapes of objects –particularly functional objects – on the ground that otherwise, competition between manufacturers would be needlessly impeded.[lxiv] In *Metix Ltd. v. GH Maughan Plastics Ltd.*,[lxv] Laddie J. attempted to finesse this difficulty, by requiring a showing of artistic *intent* on the part of the maker of the object in issue in that case – a mould for a cartridge intended for industrial use. Considered in the light of this new test, the claim of copyright predictably failed. The manufacturers, Laddie J. found, did not consider themselves (nor did anyone else consider them to be) *artists* when they designed the moulds in issue; they devised the shape for the purpose of achieving a particular functional affect only. A sculpture, he went on, is a three-dimensional work made by an artist's hand.[lxvi] Now, clearly, without a further definition of what an 'artist' is, or what it would mean to have an 'artistic' intent in the making of something, this new formulation of what a sculpture means in law is somewhat circular. Yet it is interesting that Laddie J. thought it necessary to retreat to an aesthetic conception of sculpture (albeit that this was formulated in terms of a test of intention rather than quality) in the face of this attempt to 'abuse' the copyright system by claiming protection for something which 'has [no] independent significance outside a commercial production process'.[lxvii] Arguably, this testifies to a deep-seated ambivalence about copyright's relationship to both art and commerce, and a kind of strategic uncertainty about whether the line between protected and unprotected subject matter is in the same place as the line between art and commerce.

The absence of a definition of 'artistic' in law has been confronted from a different direction in cases where, although there is no doubt that the work in issue is protected by copyright, it appears capable of being categorised in more than one of the ways stipulated by the Copyright Act. It has been pointed out in a number of cases that circuit diagrams, for example, contain information about the components of a circuit and how those components are connected to each other, and that they convey this information in a form of notation, i.e., engineers' notation. Therefore, it is argued, they qualify as literary works within the meaning of s.3 of the Act – 'any work . . . which is written' in any form of notation or code – even though ostensibly they are diagrams, and so also artistic works within s.4. Jacob J. responded favourably to this argument in *Anacon Corporation Ltd. v. Environmental Research Technology Ltd.*,[lxviii] but conceded, as he did so, that an artistic work is essentially something which can be appreciated by the eye. Other cases, too, have confirmed – although this is nowhere expressly stated in the legislation – that what distinguishes artistic works from other categories of protected work is that they contemplate material which is 'visually significant'.[lxix] Of course, the same could be said of certain kinds of dramatic work – mimes, for example – but here the courts would invoke a further distinction between visual experiences that unfold in time, because they involve action,[lxx] and those that exist 'instantaneously', as it were, in space. The latter, presuming always that they are original products of an author in the sense outlined above, and fit within one of the items listed as artistic works in s.4, are artistic works; the former would be dramatic works. Against this background, one can only wonder about the legal status of pieces such as Cornelia Parker's *The Maybe* (1995), where the artist 'exhibits' the motionless form of actress Tilda Swinton as she lies asleep in a glass case.

Medium-specific Arts

This mode of thinking about artistic works in terms of what art theorists would call their 'media' has striking parallels with a certain tendency in art theory itself: what I have called the 'particularising' trend in aesthetic thought. Lessing's

Laocoon (1766) is perhaps the most important document in this tradition of theorising about the arts. Here Lessing, while acknowledging that poetry and painting are united in their common purpose of eliciting an aesthetic response through the (mimetic) representation of beautiful objects, followed Jean-Baptiste Dubos' earlier *Critical Reflections on Poetry and Painting* (1719) in sharply distinguishing these arts – and locating the identity of each – in the type of 'sign' they employed. Poetry arranges ('arbitrary') signs – sounds – in time; painting deploys ('natural') signs – colours and figures – in space, and 'from the difference of these means all the specific rules for each art are to be derived'. Within the category of natural signs, Lessing's contemporary, Moses Mendelssohn, further distinguished between audible and visible signs, a distinction that corresponded to the sense organs of hearing and sight to which these signs respectively appealed. Visible natural signs were further subdivided according to whether they were arranged successively in time or simultaneously in space, and the latter category was bifurcated yet again in terms of dimensionality: spatial forms were either two or three dimensional. Thus music deploys audible natural signs – and dance visible natural signs – in time; sculpture and painting each employ visible natural signs in space, the former in bodies, the latter on surfaces.[lxxi]

Lessing did not attempt a systematic classification of the arts, dealing only with painting and poetry but, like Mendelssohn, he prioritised the visual over the spatial in characterising the signs deployed by painting: indeed this is why he is able to elide sculpture under painting within his analysis of the plastic arts,[lxxii] thus neglecting to demarcate the former from the latter. Yet another of Lessing's German contemporaries, Johann Gottfried Herder, sets out specifically, in his *Plastik* (1778), to inquire into the basis of the differences between painting and sculpture. He answered: 'To sight belong only planes, paintings, figures of one plane, but bodies and shapes of bodies belong to touch'.[lxxiii] Herder's attentiveness to, and celebration of, the sense of touch was revolutionary for its time, and is notably absent from Lessing's *Laocoon*. As Wellbery argues, this is symptomatic of a broader tendency within Lessing's analysis towards the erasure of the materiality of the expression-plane – and with it, space experienced as 'tactile differentiation' – despite his explanation of 'painting' as characterised by the deployment of signs in space. 'It seems, rather, that the spatiality of the plastic arts is less important than their visibility. The concept of space is tailored to the concept of vision: it is . . . space as seen . . . the simultaneity of things within a synoptic view . . . their co-existence within a momentary vision'.[lxxiv]

It is this pure optical space that re-emerges in the 1960s in Clement Green-berg's and Michael Fried's writings as the space of painting alone, quite distinct from the three-dimensionality which is 'the province of sculpture'.[lxxv] Greenberg first acknowledges his debt to Lessing, however, in the title of an early essay, 'Towards a Newer Laocoon',[lxxvi] where his concern is to distinguish painting, not from sculpture so much as from literature, and so to contain the threat posed to visual art by those art movements that seemed bent on reproducing the effects of literature within painting. Here he appears to follow the eighteenth century prece-dent of linking the specificity of each art to the unique way in which its material of expression is perceived: each art, Greenberg seems to suggest, must articulate with the kind of perceptual experience involved in the apprehension of its charac-teristic products. In terms reminiscent of Herder, he argues that the avant-garde had discovered the key to art's self-preservation in the principle that each of the arts 'should be defined solely in terms of the sense or faculty which perceived its effect and by excluding from each art whatever is intelligible in terms of any other sense or faculty'.[lxxvii] What is 'new' in Greenberg's analysis relative to Lessing's, however, is his emphasis on the ways in which the media of artistic expression resist or channel the possibilities for communicating sensations. For Lessing, the materiality of the medium through which sensation is conveyed had constituted an obstacle to, as well as a vehicle for, the experience of the imagined aesthetic object that art strives to represent. 'What Lessing repeatedly urges for art is the transformation of matter into the immateriality of a mental representation, the elimination of every material residue which could burden or limit the movement of the imagination'.[lxxviii] For Greenberg, on the other hand, it is precisely in the recal-citrance of its medium that each art finds the key to its sovereign purity: 'it is *by virtue of* its medium that each art is unique and strictly itself. To restore the iden-tity of art, the *opacity* of its medium must be emphasised'.[lxxix] The medium of each art, that is, resists the unrestrained expression of artistic content, but precisely in its resistance, permits the distillation of the unique experience provided by each art.

'The arts . . . have been hunted back to their mediums, and there they have been isolated, concentrated and defined'.[lxxx] For Greenberg, medium, the key to each art's specificity, serves a number of related purposes. It demarcates an autonomous jurisdiction for each art: 'the unique and proper area of competence of each art coincide[s] with all that is unique to the nature of its medium'. It serves as a criterion by which each of the arts can be purified of anything extraneous to its nature, i.e. any effect that might be borrowed from the medium of any other art. And as such, it provides 'the guarantee of [each art's] standards of quality as well as of its independence'.[lxxxi] Greenberg's attentiveness to medium is particularly carefully elaborated in relation to painting. In 'Modernist Painting' he indicates that 'the limitations that constitute the medium of painting [are] the flat surface, the shape of the support, the properties of pigment', and later, in the same essay alights on 'flatness' as the most fundamental of these because it 'was the only condition painting shared with no other art'.[lxxxii]

By reference to norms derived from these physical properties – 'flatness and its delimitation' – Greenberg is then able to write *the* history of painting, locate its trajectory, and identify its canon. The key to his story is painting's suppression of the sculptural, carried on at first (in sixteenth-century Venice) in the name of colour, continuing more self-consciously from the mid-nineteenth century with the pictorial avant garde's 'progressive surrender to the resistance of its medium'[lxxxiii] and continuing through the abandonment of chiaroscuro by Manet, of linear perspective by Cezanne, of Euclidean space by the Cubists, and of figuration by the first abstractionists. In this way, Greenberg seeks to justify abstraction as the fulfilment of painting's inexorable historical destiny.

Formalism as an aesthetic doctrine therefore necessarily accompanies Greenberg's conception of medium-specific art, for if the history of painting simply *is* a history of the development of visual form, its only subject matter being the medium-related norms of painting itself, it can only be evaluated in terms of the visual characteristics of the works that comprise it. Greenberg thus identifies as 'the first and most important item upon [the] agenda [of the nineteenth-century avant garde] ... the necessity of an escape from ideas, which were infecting the arts with the ideological struggles of society. Ideas came to mean subject matter in general.... This meant a new and greater emphasis upon form...'[lxxxiv] It also involved, concomitantly, an assertion of the absolute autonomy of the separate arts, and in particular, an insistence on the entitlement of painting and sculpture – the central forms of visual art – 'to respect for their own sakes, and not merely as vessels of communication'.[lxxxv] Thus, as well as a separation of form from ideas, Greenberg's avant-garde observes a further distinction between visual art and literature, the field of the former being radically delimited from that of the latter. Referring with approval to the passing of art's subservience to literature after the seventeenth century, Greenberg writes that '[t]he arts lie safe now, each within its own 'legitimate' boundaries . . . Purity in art consists in the acceptance, the willing acceptance, of the limitations of the medium of the specific art'.[lxxxvi]

The tendency to essentialism that permeates Greenberg's analysis of the specificity of painting is only apparently at odds with its capacity to accommodate historicity and change. It is true that he purports to provide a history of painting by pointing to an evolutionary dynamic compelling successive generations of painters to 'test' the physically-determined norms of the medium for their indispensability and then refuse them, one by one, in order to affirm flatness (or two-dimensionality) as the norm that is unique to painting alone. This produces change at the level of visual form:

> Painting abandons chiaroscuro and shaded modelling. Brush strokes are often defined for their own sake . . . Primary colours, the 'instinctive', easy colour, replace tones and tonality. Line, which is one of the most abstract elements in painting since it is never found in nature as the definition of contour, returns to oil painting as the third colour between two other colour areas. Under the influence of the square shape of the canvas, forms tend to become geometrical – and simplified, because simplification is also a part of the instinctive accommodation to the medium. But most important of all, the picture plane itself grows shallower and shallower, flattening out and pressing together the fictive planes of depth until they meet as one upon the real and material plane which is the actual surface of the canvas . . .[lxxxvii]

Moreover, Greenberg seems to accept that the norms of painting themselves will continue to change historically as those currently accepted as fundamental, including 'flatness', are in their turn negated 'for the sake of new expression:'[lxxxviii] he acknowledges that 'this testing is by no means finished'.[lxxxix] But ultimately he represents the norms isolated by Modernist painting 'in its latest phase'[xc] (i.e., at the time of writing, 1960) as universal conditions of painting as such, grounded in/by the irreducible physicality of the flat canvas. As far as Greenberg is concerned, 'modern painters got rid of the *expendable* conventions of painting only in order to uncover an irreducible remainder consisting of its *essential* conventions'.[xci]

Quite apart from the problems attendant upon representing the history of an art practice as an entirely self-referential series of responses to the demands of the physical properties of that art's medium, all of this raises difficult issues concerning the ontological status of the art object that are never completely resolved within Greenberg's work. In particular, Greenberg oscillates between the physical and the perceptual in seeking to pin down the essence of painting. Thus he refers *both* to the physical characteristics of the materials of painting *and* to the kind of sensory experience involved in perceiving the effects of painting as somehow constitutive of this particular art. Further, the former is elided under the latter in Greenberg's confusing equation of 'the ineluctable flatness of the support' with 'two-dimensionality'.

The emphasis placed on the qualities of the support would seem to commit Greenberg to the physicalist position that the essence of painting is given by the material factuality of the stretched canvas. Two-dimensionality, on the other hand, is a feature not of the canvas as a material object, but of the space of the picture plane, a space amenable (at least as far as Greenberg is concerned) to a purely visual perception 'into which one can only look, can travel through only with the eye' and of which, therefore, only a purely optical experience 'as against optical experience modified or revised by tactile associations'[xcii] is possible. As Michael Fried subsequently points out, the physicalist position necessarily leads to the inference that the essence of painting lies in its condition of 'objecthood',[xciii] and for Fried as for Greenberg, objecthood is precisely the condition of 'non-art'.[xciv] Yet there are moments when Greenberg seems to steer perilously close to this position. Thus in 'Towards a Newer Laocoon', he asserts that 'purity in art consists in the acceptance, willing acceptance, of the limitations of the medium of the specific art.... The history of avant garde painting is that of a progressive surrender to the resistance of its medium'.[xcv] And in 'After Abstract Expressionism', we encounter the following cryptic announcement: 'the irreducible essence of pictorial art consists in but two constitutive conventions or norms: flatness and the delimitation of flatness; and . . . the observance of merely these two norms is enough to create an object that can be experienced as a picture: thus a stretched or tacked-up canvas already exists as a picture, though not necessarily as a *successful* one'.[xcvi]

This passage helps to clarify Greenberg's major themes, even as it threatens to undo his entire project by confronting, yet failing to resolve, 'the impossible dilemma raised by the blank canvas'.[xcvii] Pushed by the logic of his own position to accept that a blank canvas is a picture, he nonetheless recoils from this prospect – it is 'not necessarily a successful one' – a retreat which is completed by Fried's rewriting of his 'blank canvas' remark in the idiom of an uncompromising formalist aesthetics.[xcviii] Similar aporias attend Greenberg's analyses of art practices which seem *prima facie* only to continue the evolutionary dynamic that he himself identified. The monochrome painting seems utterly Greenbergian, observing to the letter the limiting condition of flatness, yet Greenberg hesitated before it, conceding, for example, that Frank Stella's black paintings were indeed paintings, but dismissing them as 'not good enough'.[xcix] As for the minimalists, who took Stella's work as a signal to finally break through the picture plane to the third dimension that lay beyond it, Greenberg's condemnation was unequivocal. Yet, as many commentators have noted, 'minimalism depends on Greenberg's doctrine, and all the more so since it rejected it'.[c]

Donald Judd directly *confronted* the specificity of painting rather than ignoring it, but for him painting had become a 'set form' permitting an ever narrower array of creative possibilities.[ci] Thus, by 1965, Judd could say that 'the main thing *wrong* with painting is that it is a rectangular plane placed flat against the wall', for this 'determines and limits the arrangement of whatever is on or inside it'[cii] to the point where what remained to be done within these limits could only be done with 'less strength and variation'. Painting had therefore exhausted itself, and 'the obvious response [was] to give up working on a single plane in favour of three dimensions'.[ciii] Though this strategy can plausibly be viewed as a fulfilment of the modernist project as described by Greenberg – the project of identifying limits only to transcend them – he himself regarded minimalism as an overstepping of the line beyond which 'a picture stops being a picture and turns into an arbitrary object'.[civ] This indicates that what Judd understood as just another 'conventional limit, literally a frame to exceed'[cv] if to do so would be 'interesting', Greenberg took to be essential to the viability of the medium and therefore capable of supersession only at the cost of ending up in the field of the arbitrary object, the field of non-art.

The difficulty Greenberg experienced in attempting to maintain the distinction between art and objecthood without lapsing into contradiction can be read as symptomatic of the more fundamental dilemma that haunted his early writings, if not his 'mature' work: how to hold the line between art and (commercialised, commodified) mass culture and so preserve the possibility of an oppositional art. Although he appreciated that the emergence of artistic modernism had depended on the birth of mass culture in the nineteenth century, and that it had always drawn on low cultural idioms and images in order to renew and reinvigorate itself, Greenberg could never accept that heterogeneity or transgression (of the high/low boundary) had any role to play in defining a modernist aesthetic. On the contrary, the confusion of the high with the low had to be denied if art was to retain any autonomy in an increasingly rationalised and administered society. In essays such as 'Avant Garde and Kitsch' and 'Towards a Newer Laocoon', for example, Greenberg justified his purism as 'the translation of an extreme solicitude, an anxiousness as to the fate of art, a concern for its identity'[cvi] in the face of the encroachments of the culture industry. Thomas Crow explains Greenberg's position as follows:

In search of raw material, mass culture had progressively stripped traditional art of its marketable qualities, and had left as the only remaining path to authenticity a ceaseless alertness against the stereotyped and the pre-processed. By refusing any other demands but the most self-contained technical ones, the authentic artist could protect his or her work from the reproduction and rationalisation that would process its usable bits and destroy its inner logic. From this resistance came modernism's inwardness, self-reflexivity, 'truth to media'. [cvii]

Yet, as Crow goes on to point out, the only possible audience for modernist art – an elite audience which disdained popular culture – 'endorsed, in every respect but its art, the social order responsible for the crisis of culture',[cviii] *viz.* the reduction of culture to a parade of mass-(re)produced consumer commodities. The possibility that his avant garde would be co-opted by the institutions of the art world – including the art market – and consequently lose its critical edge, was therefore built into Greenberg's medium-specific modernism from the start; and by the 1960s his position seemed to be that this outcome was actually to be welcomed.

Greenberg's postmodernist detractors – artists as well as critics – have challenged his conclusions by exploiting the tensions and contradictions in his writings, and have comprehensively rejected the rhetoric of aesthetic purity that accompanied artistic Modernism generally.[cix] One manifestation of this has been a widespread rebellion against the forced separation of art from mass cultural 'kitsch' through an open acknowledgement of art's reliance on popular and/or commodified practices and images: the appropriation art of the 1980s – in both its affirmative (e.g. Jeff Koons) and critical/disruptive (e.g. Sherrie Levine) modes – is the most recent sign of this rebellion, though it replayed strategies that had been anticipated by American Neo-Dada in the 1950s and Pop Art thereafter. The same anti-Modernist energy has fuelled a huge expansion in the range and diversity of recognised artistic 'media' – from painting and sculpture to photography, performance, conceptual propositions, installations, film, video, and hybrids of these. And as the categories of painting, sculpture, and the notion of an autonomous aesthetic have been attacked or deconstructed, the many other hierarchies on which Modernist discourse is founded have also been questioned and destabilised. If the Greenbergian analysis of *painting* relies on a belief in the capacity of the eye alone, abstracted from the phenomenological experience of viewing and without reliance on any form of 'decoding', to apprehend and therefore constitute the work as a self-sufficient entity, postmodernist *art* exploits the space occupied by everything that this analysis negates: its repression of tactility and of the corporeally situated quality of vision itself,[cx] its occlusion of the necessarily textual quality of visual no less than literary forms – the fact that they are read rather than merely seen – and its urge to banish all extraneous subject matter (ideas, including especially social and political commentary) as nothing other than a source of 'infection'.[cxi] Thus a leading contemporary art critic and theorist, Hal Foster suggests that all of these exclusions have 'returned' in one form or another within the art practices of the 1960s and after, motivated by an outright rejection of the purposes Greenberg identified medium-specificity as serving: the defence of art's autonomy, purity and immanent standards.

One of these counter-tendencies found expression in Conceptual Art, which problematised the assumption that art is purely and primordially visual.[cxii] Joseph Kosuth's word paintings, for example, 'asserted a strict identity between verbal concept and artistic form',[cxiii] offering written documentation to the 'viewer' instead of purely visual experiences. This was part of a broader tendency towards the dematerialisation of the art object: the production of art that yielded no object; or in which process, context-dependence, chance or randomness were prioritised over form, self-sufficiency, authorial control or intentionality.[cxiv] The genres encompassed by this tendency, in turn, have included Land Art[cxv] (whose 'works' are completed by the forces of nature, the landscape or the built environment); Body Art (where the body and/or its products are used as material for art-making); Installation Art (where the art is defined primarily by its spatial location and context rather than by the materials that constitute it); Performance Art; and Video Art (where the use of video, an essentially time-based medium, is apt to suggest a refusal of the instantaneity or simultaneity celebrated by Modernist critics such as Fried).

Conclusion

Thus far, it has been suggested that there are some striking affinities between the way Greenberg derives aesthetic norms for the separate arts, and the way the courts assess whether something counts as an artistic work for the purpose of determining whether it attracts a property right. Both critic and court search within the self-contained technical demands of the media of the established arts for a set of criteria that could ground their respective judgements. This has produced some remarkable similarities between Modernist critical conventions and the norms of copyright law insofar as these relate to the subject matter of legal protection. The idea/expression dichotomy recalls Greenberg's separation of idea from form, because copyright law cannot recognise ideas, as opposed to the visual forms in which they reside, as protected 'artistic works'. The definition of the 'artistic work' in terms of what is visually significant, and the strict demarcation of the artistic from the literary (as well as the dramatic and the musical), calls to mind Greenberg's insistence that 'visual art should confine itself exclusively to what is given in visual experience, and make no reference to anything given in any other order of experience'.[cxvi] The legal requirement that a 'painting' must, if nothing else, have a 'surface' – preferably a flat surface – is uncannily similar to Greenberg's identification of the flat surface as the key limiting condition of painting as an art form. Examples could be multiplied. The net effect is that artistic Modernism and copyright law tend to favour some artistic genres, and some artistic gestures within those genres, over others.

It has already been noted that these discriminatory tendencies are bound to appear anachronistic from the perspective of the contemporary artist. More fundamentally, however, they proceed from contradictions that are internal both to artistic Modernism, and to the copyright system's attempts to deal with artistic works. In both cases, the contradictions revolve around the relationship between art and objecthood. As we have seen, copyright law has been designed in such a way as to avoid giving judges licence to enforce their own subjective aesthetic preferences in the process of adjudicating in copyright disputes, and judges themselves have attempted to further this policy by defining artistic works in technical, 'materialist' or 'physicalist' terms. However the literal objectivity of this approach has had two peculiar consequences. On the one hand, it has led copyright law to include ordinary items which have little claim to creativity (which contradicts copyright's actual purpose of facilitating fair competition in markets for goods incorporating intellectual creations by defining limited property rights in those creations). On the other hand it has led copyright law to exclude some art forms from its protective remit completely (which contradicts the rhetorical claim that copyright's purpose is to encourage the progress of the arts). The result is that copyright law's conception of the artistic work now faces a crisis of credibility similar to that suffered by the 'medium-specific' artistic Modernism preached by Clement Greenberg and others in the 1960s – although for different reasons.

Greenberg's own attempt to walk the line between art and objecthood – the very line on which the blank canvas sits – was inspired, as we have seen, by a concern to defend art's autonomy from the depredations of commercial culture and so preserve the possibility of an oppositional art. Yet his insistence on 'truth to media' as the key to this project had two peculiar consequences of its own. On the one hand it led Greenberg to acknowledge that a blank canvas already existed as a painting (which contradicted his insistence that paintings are radically distinct from arbitrary objects). On the other hand his commitment to art's autonomy forced him to admit that a blank canvas would not necessarily be a *successful* painting (which contradicts his claim that nothing guarantees quality in painting apart from its observance of norms derived from the physical nature of the medium). The effect of this latter move, as de Duve has noted,[cxvii] was to cause Greenberg's *modernism* (consisting of a reflexive questioning of the specific conventions of painting), to yield to his *formalism* (the subjection of the results of this questioning to a judgement of their generic quality as art). In this way it was Greenberg, once the arch-defender of specific modernism, who himself opened the door to generic art by opting to commit to 'formalism' when the zero degree of painting finally beckoned.[cxviii]

Interesting though these convergences are, they are, however, simply that: convergences. As I have argued elsewhere,[cxix] the law's categories and procedures are best understood in their singularity: as products of copyright's legislative history, the 'peculiar reason' of the common law, and a logic of property that is simply not reducible to the logic of aesthetic judgement. This is by no means to suggest, however, that intersections ought not to be sought between copyright law's constructs and contradictions and the equally singular concepts and aporias prevailing in the domain of art theory and criticism. Nor is it to suggest that the identification of these connections ought not to prompt a rethinking of the ways in which law handles the task of 'encouraging the progress of the arts'. It is precisely those aims that have motivated the writing of this essay.

The author is grateful for the support provided by an Advanced Research Award from the Arts and Humanities Research Board, which assisted towards the writing of this essay.

i   Peter Jaszi and Martha Woodmansee, 'The Ethical Reaches of Authorship' (1996) 95:4 *South Atlantic Quarterly* 947-977, 948.

ii   Ibid.

iii   See especially Peter Jaszi, 'Towards a theory of copyright: the metamorphosis of 'authorship" (1991) *Duke L. Jnl.*, p.445; Martha Woodmansee, *The Author, Art and the Market* (New York: Columbia University Press, 1994), especially ch.2.

iv   Anne Barron, *Copyright and Culture* (forthcoming, London: Butterworths, 2003).

v   See generally on modernist criticism, and the postmodernist critique of modernism,
     Stephen Connor, *Postmodernist Culture* (Oxford: Blackwell) (2nd edn., 1997).
     On the affinities between the legal concept of the copyright 'work' and the 'reified aesthetic
     object' presupposed by literary criticism see Mark Rose, 'The Author as Proprietor:
     Donaldson v. Beckett and the genealogy of modern authorship' (1988), 23 *Representations*,
     p.51. On its affinities with modernist conceptions of the work, see Robert Rotstein,
     'Beyond Metaphor: Copyright Infringement and the Fiction of the Work' (1993) 68
     Chicago-Kent Law Review, p.725.

vi   Copyright Designs and Patents Act 1988 (hereinafter CDPA).

vii 'Art and Objecthood' in G. Battcock (ed.), *Minimal Art: A Critical Anthology*
     (New York: E.P. Dutton, 1968), pp.116-147.

viii Ibid., p.142.

ix   Ibid.

x   Douglas Crimp, 'Pictures' in B. Wallis (ed.) *Art After Modernism* (New York:
     New Museum of Contemporary Art, 1984) pp.175-188.

xi   Thierry de Duve, *Kant after Duchamp* (Cambridge, MA: MIT Press 1996).

xii Cf. Martha Woodmansee, 'Genius and the Copyright: economic and legal conditions
     of the emergence of the 'Author" in *The Author, Art and the Market* (*op cit.*, note 3), ch.2.

xiii Fine Arts Copyright Act 1862, s.1.

xiv Under the CDPA s.4(2), the category of 'graphic works' includes paintings, drawings,
     diagrams, maps, charts and plans; engravings, etchings, lithographs, woodcuts
     or similar works.

xv   The CDPA s.5B protects 'a recording on any medium from which a moving image may
     by any means be reproduced' – but as a film, not as an artistic work.

xvi See for example P. Kristeller, 'The Modern System of the Arts' in *Renaissance Thought
     and the Arts* (Princeton: Princeton University Press, 1990) pp.163-227; Mosche Barasch,
     Theories of Art: from Wickelmann to Baudelaire (London: Routledge 2000), Ch.3.

xvii Monroe C. Beardsley, *Aesthetics from Classical Greece to the Present*
     (New York: Macmillan 1966) p.55.

xviii Moshe Barasch, *Theories of Art: from Plato to Wickelmann*
     (London: Routledge 2000), p.74.

xix Ibid., p.86-7.

xx   Ibid., p.168.

xxi P. Kristeller, *op cit.*, note 16.

xxii Lydia Goehr, *The Imaginary Museum of Musical Works* (Oxford: Clarendon, 1992) p.149

xxiii Ibid., p.150.

xxiv P. Kristeller, *op cit.*, note 16, p.175.

xxv Ibid., p.178; M. Barasch, *op.cit.*, note 18, Ch.3.

xxvi P. Kristeller, *op.cit.*, note 16, p.182. This happened initially in sixteenth century Italy,
     and somewhat later in the rest of Europe (ibid.).

xxvii Ibid., p.199-200.

xxviii Ibid., p.202.

xxix H. Homes, *Elements of Criticism*, quoted in P. Kristeller, *op.cit.*, note 16, p.211

xxx   On the philosophical tradition of German Romanticism generally, see Andrew Bowie, *Aesthetics and Subjectivity: from Kant to Nietzsche* (Manchester: Manchester University Press 1990) and Frederick C. Beiser, *The Fate of Reason: German Philosophy from Kant to Fichte* (Cambridge: Cambridge University Press 1987). On the Romantic movement in the practice, theory and criticism of the arts (especially in literature), see generally M.H. Abrams, *The Mirror and the Lamp* (Oxford: Oxford University Press 1953). For an account of the links between the German Romantic philosophy and the Romantic movement, see D. Simpson, 'Introduction' in David Simpson (ed.) *The Origins of Modern Critical Thought* (Cambridge: Cambridge University Press, 1988).

xxxi   Moshe Barasch, *Theories of Art: from Wickelmann to Baudelaire* (London: Routledge 2000), p.295-6

xxxii   M. Barasch, *op.cit.*, note 18), p.295 ff.

xxxiii   Harold Osborne, *Aesthetics and Art Theory* (London: Longmans 1968), p.132.

xxxiv   Ibid., p.139.

xxxv   Ibid., p.132. For an extended analysis of these ideas in relation to the leading painters working in the period between 1800 and 1850, see William Vaughan, *Romanticism and Art* (London: Thames and Hudson, 1994).

xxxvi   H. Osborne, *op.cit.*, note 33, p.135

xxxvii   The Copyright Act 1842, which awarded copyright to 'books', defined 'book' in s.2 to include 'every . . . sheet of music'.

xxxviii   The exception here, of course, is the 'work of artistic craftsmanship': see *George Hensher v. Restawile Upholstery* [1976] AC 64. It has been suggested that 'works of architecture, like the subject matter falling within s.4(1(a), need not possess any 'fine art' attribute in order to qualify' (Hugh Laddie, Peter Prescott, Mary Vitoria, Adrian Speck and Lindsay Lane *The Modern Law of Copyright and Designs* (London: Butterworths) (3rd edn, 2000), p.194.

xxxix   CDPA, s.9.

xl   Peterson J. in *University of London Press Ltd. v. University Tutorial Press Ltd.* [1916] 2 Ch. 601, at 608-609.

xli   *Interlego v. Tyco* [1988] 3 All ER 949.

xlii   CDPA, s.1.

xliii   The features referred to here are in all essential respects the same as those alighted upon by the judges and commentators who debated the question of 'literary property' in the eighteenth century. I draw attention to them here because they have tended to be obscured by the exclusive concern with authorship that tends to accompany the focus on Romanticism; and because historically their elaboration was both highly controversial and absolutely fundamental to the maturation of the legal institution of copyright. See further M. Rose, *op.cit.*, note 5; Brad Sherman and Lionel Bently, *The Making of Modern Intellectual Property Law* (Cambridge: Cambridge University Press 1999), Ch. 1

xliv   This is the rule for literary, dramatic and musical works under the CDPA, s.3(1).

xlv   This would appear to be the case in relation to the 'artistic works' listed in the CDPA, s.4.

xlvi   At best, copyright law might be able to accommodate some forms of performance art as 'dramatic works' under the CDPA s.3(1), but again, only if there is some record of the performance (which could be a photograph or video): a 'happening', for example, of which no record exists, will get no protection.

xlvii   *Merchandising Corporation of America Inc v. Harpbond Ltd* [1983] FSR 32.

xlviii   *J & S Davis (Holdings) Ltd. v. Wright Health Group Ltd.* [1988] RPC 403;
         Creation Records v. News Group Newspapers [1997] EMLR 444. Cf.
         Metix Ltd. v. GH Maughan Plastics Ltd. [1997] FSR 718

xlix   *Komesaroff v. Mickle* [1988] RPC 204.

l   Anne Barron, 'No Other Law? Property, Authority and Aboriginal Art' in Lionel Bently
         and Spyros Maniatis (eds.) *Intellectual Property and Ethics*
         (London: Sweet and Maxwell, 1998), pp.39-87.

li   The early Acts relating to engravings described the object of protection as a 'print', made
         by a process of 'engraving, etching or working, in mezzotinto or chiaroscuro'. Again, the
         eighteenth and early nineteenth century Acts relating to sculptures referred to 'models'
         and 'casts' of busts, and 'statues' of human and animal figures.

lii   *Merchandising Corporation of America Inc v. Harpbond Ltd* [1983] FSR 32, at 46.
         Although he did not explain why a human face could not be a surface in the relevant sense,
         Lawton L.J. seemed to be troubled by the fact that make-up on a face, by its nature,
         is not designed to be permanent, and 'if the marks are taken off the face there cannot
         be a painting' (ibid.). It would seem that the difficulty Lawton L.J. is alluding to here
         is that of conceiving of the copyright work other than by analogy to, if not as, a physical
         object: hence 'a painting is not an idea: it is an object' (ibid.).

liii   *Kenrick v. Lawrence* (1890) L.R. 25 Q.B.D. 99.

liv   (1991) 95 ALR 275.

lv   [1984] 1 NZLR 641, [1985] RPC 127, Court of Appeal of New Zealand.

lvi   (1991) 95 ALR 275, at 284-5. Cf. *Talk of the Town v. Hagstrom* [1991] IPR 649.

lvii   [1995] FSR 77.

lviii   *J & S Davis (Holdings) Ltd. v. Wright Health Group Ltd.* [1988] RPC 403. Cf. *Metix Ltd.
         v. GH Maughan Plastics Ltd.* [1997] FSR 718.

lix   [1997] EMLR 444.

lx   Ibid., p.451.

lxi   Ibid.

lxii   H. Laddie et al., *op.cit.*, note 38, p.197

lxiii   *J & S Davis (Holdings) Ltd. v. Wright Health Group Ltd.* [1988] RPC 403 (dental
         impression tray); *Wham-O MFG Co v. Lincoln Industries* [1985] RPC 127 (prototype
         frisbee); *Breville Europe plc v. Thorn EMI* [1995] FSR 77 (sandwich toaster).

lxiv   See, for example, the discussion in *British Leyland v. Armstrong* [1986] 1 ALL ER 850.

lxv   [1997] F.S.R. 718.

lxvi   Ibid., p.722.

lxvii   Ibid., p.721.

lxviii   *Anacon Corporation Ltd. v. Environmental Research Technology Ltd.* [1994] FSR 659.

lxix   *Interlego v. Tyco*, *op.cit.*, note 41

lxx   *Norowzian v. Arks No.2* [1999] EMLR 67.

lxxi   D.E. Wellbery, *Lessing's Laocoon* (Cambridge: Cambridge Univeristy Press, 1984), p.86 ff.

lxxii   Ibid., p.116.

lxxiii   Quoted in M. Barasch, *op.cit.*, note 31, p.166

lxxiv   D.E. Wellbery, *op.cit.*, note 71, p.115.

lxxv   Clement Greenberg, 'Modernist Painting' in C. Harrison and P. Wood, eds.,
         Art in Theory 1900-1990 (Oxford: Blackwell 1992), pp.754-760, 756.

lxxvi   C. Greenberg, 'Towards a Newer Laocoon' in C. Harrison and P. Wood *op.cit.*,
         note 75, pp.554-560.

lxxvii   Ibid., p.557.

lxxviii D.E. Wellbery, *op.cit.*, note 71, p.116.

lxxix C. Greenberg, *op.cit.*, note 76, p.558 (emphasis added)

lxxx Ibid.

lxxxi C. Greenberg, *op.cit.*, note 75, p.755.

lxxxii Ibid., p.756.

lxxxiii C. Greenberg, *op.cit.*, note 76, p.558.

lxxxiv Ibid., p.556.

lxxxv Ibid.

lxxxvi Ibid., p.557-8

lxxxvii Ibid., p.558

lxxxviii C. Greenberg, *op.cit.*, note 75, p.757

lxxxix Ibid.

xc Ibid., p.756

xci Thierry de Duve, *Pictorial Nominalism* (Minneapolis: University of Minnesota Press, 1991), p.156 (emphasis added).

xcii C. Greenberg, *op.cit.*, note 75, p.757

xciii This is indeed the inference drawn by Thierry de Duve in one of his more tendentious readings of Greenberg: a stretched canvas is simply a readymade object; and if a stretched canvas is a painting, then any readymade object, including a tube of paint – or Duchamp's *Fountain* for that matter – can be a painting. See T. de Duve, *op.cit.*, note 91, Ch.7.

xciv M. Fried, *op.cit.*, note 7; C. Greenberg, C. Greenberg, *op.cit.*, note 75, p.758 ('a picture stops being a picture [when it] turns into an arbitrary object').

xcv C. Greenberg, *op.cit.*, note 76, p.558.

xcvi C. Greenberg, 'After Abstract Expressionism' in J. O'Brian, ed., *Clement Greenberg: The Collected Essays and Criticism Volume 4* (University of Chicago Press, 1993), pp.121-134 at 131-2. Fried anticipates de Duve's move (T. de Duve, *op.cit.*, note 93): if a stretched canvas could conceivably be a successful painting then indeed 'nothing more than the name [of painting] would remain' (M. Fried, *op.cit.*, note 7 at p.123 n.4). He escapes from this spectre of 'pictorial nominalism' by relocating the essence of painting in that which 'compels conviction' at a given historical moment (see note 98 below).

xcvii T. de Duve *op.cit.*, note 11, p.259

xcviii 'Seeing something as a painting in the sense that one sees the tacked up canvas as a painting, and being convinced that a particular work can stand comparison with the painting of the past whose quality is not in doubt, are altogether different experiences . . . Unless something compels conviction as to its quality it is no more than trivially or nominally a painting. This suggests that flatness and the delimitation of flatness ought not to be thought of as the 'irreducible essence of pictorial art' but rather as something like the *minimal conditions for something's being seen as a painting*; and that the crucial question is not what these minimal and, so to speak, timeless conditions are, but rather what, at a given moment, is capable of compelling conviction, of succeeding as painting. This is not to say that painting *has no* essence; it *is* to claim that that essence – i.e., that which compels conviction – is largely determined by, and therefore changes continually in response to, the vital work of the recent past. The essence of painting is not something irreducible. Rather, the task of the modernist painter is to discover those conventions that, at a given moment, *alone* are capable of establishing his work's identity as painting . . . The two questions – What constitutes the art of painting? What constitutes good painting? – are no longer separable; the first disappears, or increasingly tends to disappear, into the second'. (M. Fried, *op.cit.*, note 7, p.123-4, n.4).

xcix T. de Duve *op.cit.*, note 11, p.203.

c Ibid., p.218. See also Hal Foster *The Return of the Real* (Cambridge, MA: MIT Press 1996), Ch.2.

ci Donald Judd, 'Specific Objects' excerpted in C. Harrison and P. Wood *op.cit.*, note 75, pp.809-813.

cii Ibid., p.810 (emphasis added).

ciii M. Fried, *op.cit.*, note 7, p.118

civ C. Greenberg, *op.cit.*, note 75, p.758

cv H. Foster, *op.cit.*, note 100, p.44

cvi C. Greenberg, *op.cit.*, note 76, p.554

cvii Thomas Crow, 'Modernism and Mass Culture in the Visual Arts' in *Modern Art in a Common Culture* (New Haven: Yale University Press 1996), Ch.1, p.9.

cviii Ibid., p.11.

cix See generally, David Hopkins, *After Modern Art 1945-2000* (Oxford: Oxford University press 2000) Ch.2-7.

cx Martin Jay, *Downcast Eyes* (Berkeley: University of California Press, 1993) Ch.3.

cxi C. Greenberg, *op.cit.*, note 75.

cxii 'In conceptual art the idea or concept is the most important aspect of the work' (Sol LeWitt 'Paragraphs on Conceptual Art' (1967) in C. Harrison and P. Wood, *op.cit.*, note 75, pp.834-837, 834) and 'even if not made visual, is as much a work of art as any finished product . . . Conceptual art is made to engage the mind of the viewer rather than his eye or emotions', ibid., p.836.

cxiii D. Hopkins, *op.cit.*, note 109, p.177.

cxiv One intervention which expressed the mood of the time was 'Still and Chew' (1966). Here John Latham and a group of art students collaborated in chewing up the pages of a collection of Greenberg's essays which Latham had borrowed from the library at St. Martin's School of Art, where he taught. The pulp which resulted was then brewed and bottled – before being returned to the library.

cxv A well known example is Robert Smithson's disappearing *Spiral Jetty* (1970).

cxvi C. Greenberg, *op.cit.*, note 75, p.758.

cxvii T. de Duve, *op.cit.*, note 11.

cxviii Thus 'aesthetic judgement is still necessary. But the pressure that the conventions of painting had put on its practice is now nil, and one is forced to allow for an art that is no longer the outcome of its specific history, a generic art . . . The line passing between a picture and a successful one had to be redrawn between art and good art'. Ibid., p.222.

cxix A. Barron, *op.cit.*, p.51.

Portrait of the Artist as a Brand

Celia Lury

I think I've got phenomenal ability to base very important decisions totally on emotion. If it feels right, 100 per cent, I don't ask myself why. If I did ask myself why, I wouldn't be able to find out the answers, and I think that's why a lot of people get stuck. If it feels right, I just do it.
If I find out that what I've been doing isn't art, I don't really care.
　　Damien Hirst, *The Observer*, 1999[i]

Becoming a brand name is an important part of life. . . It's the world we live in.
　　Damien Hirst, *The Economist*, 2001[ii]

In these statements, the artist Damien Hirst proclaims that he just 'does' it, that what he 'does' might not be art, and that he does not really care whether it is or not. More than this, Hirst says that he is a brand name, and thus implies that what he 'does' should be protected by the laws of trademark as much as, or rather than, by those of copyright, the conventional recourse of artists who seek to protect intellectual property rights in their work. Indeed, the title of a recent book of Hirst's work, *Damien Hirst ® Pictures from the Saatchi Gallery*, makes this explicit. A trademark is a name, a sign or a symbol (indeed it may be anything represented graphically) that is used to identify and distinguish goods. By registering a trademark, the mark owner can obtain a monopoly in the use of the mark in relation to specified goods and services. The mark does not have to be original, but it must be distinctive. Alternatively, without registration, the law of 'passing off' can give protection to trademarks which have been used sufficiently to generate consumer associations. Moreover, unlike other forms of intellectual property, the period of the monopoly afforded by trademark can be unlimited, provided the registration is renewed and otherwise properly maintained (Trademarks Act, 1994). Hirst's statements thus seem to imply a novel relationship between the artist and the artwork, one in which he disavows artistic creativity and aligns himself explicitly with commerce, identifying his artistic practice in relation to a brand name protected by trademark and its common law equivalent, passing off. This identification is itself caught up in the making of the still-undecided entity, yBa (or YBAs or NBA),[iii] whose own acronymic titles are widely taken as an aspiration to global corporatism.

... Britain is developing macro-brands – whole industries where the word 'British' raises the value of the product. British film, British fashion, British art and British architecture are more fashionable than ever. Damien Hirst is a thriving brand whose name adds immense value to a product.

What's Hot

Vodafone, Manchester United, Virgin, Conran, WPP, Egg, Richard Rogers, Brit Art, Hussein Chalayan, Sky, First Direct, Orange, Royal Bank of Scotland

What's Not

Rover, Marks & Spencer, the BBC, British Airways, Laura Ashley, Mulberry, Liberty, British Telecom, Barclays [iv]

This chapter will consider the ways in which the name Hirst operates as a brand, and explore its relation to contemporary intellectual property law, in particular that relating to trademark.

The Author-function and Copyright

To explore the significance of Hirst's claims, let me start with a brief discussion of the author-function, since this provides a critical historical framework in which they may be evaluated. In his famous essay, 'What is an Author?' Michel Foucault establishes the author-function as a relationship that puts the unity and the coherence of an object (a work or set of works) into relation with the identity of a constructed subject (the author). This relationship is mutually constitutive, that is, it is a relationship in which the subject and object are mutually defined. On the one hand, Foucault is clear that there is a distinction between a person and the constructed subject, the author, to whom the object is attributed. The unity of the author-function as a principle for guaranteeing the coherence of the object can, for example, be assigned to several competing or co-operating people. On the other hand, the object that is constituted in the relationship of the author-function is only a selection of 'the millions of traces left by someone after his death'. The author-function provides the terms of the distinction between the essential identity of the work and the diversity of 'the mere accidents' which convey it. In sum, the author-function plays a fundamental role in the relationship through which 'an author' is constructed as the subjective principle of unity and as a singular font of expression manifest in the different forms given to the object, 'the work'. [v]

As Foucault makes clear, the author-function is not relevant to all texts or genres in all ages; rather it is the result of precise and complex historical procedures. Among these procedures, intellectual property law is generally acknowledged to have an important role. For example, Roger Chartier writes, 'it is only the Statute [of 1710, the first legislation in England concerning copyright] that allows the generalisation of the "author-function"'. [vi] As Chartier goes on to explain, in the legal rulings that followed this Statute, the assertion of the author's monopoly of the right to copy came to be based in a dual line of reasoning,[vii] both elements of which have had considerable bearing on the historical development of the author-function. The first was based on a theory of property derived from the political philosopher John Locke, which sustained that a man, as the proprietor of his own person, is also the owner of all the products of his labour. Since literary compositions are a product of labour, their authors have therefore a natural right of property in their works. The second line of reasoning draws on the aesthetic category of originality supposedly inherent in literary compositions that made them incompatible with the mechanical inventions that were subject to another branch of property law, that of patents. Consequently, literary compositions were not to be identified with any of their material forms; their identity was instead given by the irreducible singularity of the 'style', 'sentiment', and 'language' present in every copy of their work.[viii] This founding definition provided the basis for a series of judgements and further legislative revisions which consolidated the functioning of the author as not simply the owner of the product of his labour, but also as the source or (creative) origin of the artwork. The author is, 'the figure that, at least in appearance, is outside [the work] and antecedes it'.[ix]

This account can necessarily only touch on the many procedures that shaped the author-function at any particular moment. What is important for a consideration of Hirst's claims is the sense that the artwork exists in relation to a constructed subject within the larger space of a set of operations, including those of the law. Thus, it has been suggested that copyright law constitutes the author as the (prior) origin of the artwork, with the consequence that the artwork is seen to exist in relation to a subject that precedes it and that this relationship is an important part of what constitutes the integrity and originality of the work. However, this is not simply to say the artwork as object is situated in a complex set of processes. Rather the artwork itself – in its relation to the constructed subject, the author – comprises a set of operations with their own effectiveness. Indeed, during the twentieth century there emerged a large and growing body of artistic practice that makes explicit, in various ways, the artwork as perpetually in a state of becoming. Some of this work draws attention to the historically changing relation between the work and the constructed subject, the author. In these processes, the conditions of the integrity and originality of the work – in artistic and legal terms – have been variously deconstructed and reconstructed.

The example of the artistic practices of Marcel Duchamp has a special importance in this regard, because of the ways in which his position as an author has come to be recognised through a series of deferrals. These include the specification of the necessity of a rendezvous between subject and object for the emergence of a readymade as well as Duchamp's reproduction (and revision) of his earlier work, as is exemplified by *Green Box*. As Thierry de Duve puts it:

> An exemplary instance indeed: the readymade is a kind of rendezvous. It is born of the encounter of an object and an author. Object and author are nothing but the conditions of their encounter, nothing further being supposed about them. It is necessary and sufficient for them to exist to be able to meet. The object is a given; it exists somewhere, no matter where, available mentally...The author is likewise a given. The note from the *Green Box* doesn't grant him or her any talent, any interiority, or motivation. He or she has no truth to declare, only a speech delivered on no matter what occasion but at such and such an hour. [x]

More generally, there has been, in many artistic practices, a move away from the specific to the generic, for example, from painting to art in general, with the consequence that there is a growing loss of specificity in the relation between the subject and the object. In relation to the author-function, the consequence of these and other practices has been that the author has lost the privileged position of originator.[xi] Instead 'the act that founds the work is on an equal footing with those that bring about its future transformations; this act becomes in some respects part of the set of modifications that it makes possible'.[xii] But at the same time, the author-function does not disappear, but remains. It becomes no more and no less than a relation of assertion.

Thus, at the same time as 'the Duchamp effect' [xiii] is acknowledged in much contemporary art practice, the field in which the assertion of the author-function occurs has itself been vastly expanded. This is in part a consequence of the proliferation of museums, galleries, and art publications in the latter part of the twentieth century, but it is also a result of the speed and intensity of the flows of mediation (and of immediacy) that characterise contemporary culture. Indeed this latter expansion is both the context of, and a resource for, contemporary artistic practice.

As Rosalind Krauss puts it, we live in the post-medium condition, a situation in which the (popular) media and (artistic) mediums co-exist. And what is significant for the argument being put forward here is that the co-existence of mediums and the media mean that subsequent transformations of the act of founding the work are inevitable, but cannot be specifically determined in advance, thus further transforming the possibilities of the author-function.[xiv] It is the combination of the developments outlined here that make it possible to speak of Hirst as a brand name.

This is not, of course, to suggest that Hirst is the first or the only artist to challenge the terms of the author-function: the work of many artists has disturbed the legitimacy of any claim of originality in artistic practice. Nor is it to deny the special significance of Andy Warhol (who set up his own business – Andy Warhol Enterprises – together with an industrial workshop he called 'The Factory' that produced pictures of consumer goods) or that of postmodern artists such as Jeff Koons, much of whose work presents itself as a commodity,[xv] and is its own publicity (as is true of the commercial product brand). Indeed in a 1992 article that discusses the work of Jeff Koons, Martha Buskirk had already identified some of the factors discussed here [xvi] as providing the circumstances in which the author-function might be subsumed by brand loyalty.[xvii] Thus she suggests that the successful artist is increasingly able to establish 'his or her sole right to a particular style or method – a 'trademark' style – and others who attempt to use the same means are dismissed as mere imitators'.[xviii] But while acknowledging the importance of Buskirk's argument, I want to suggest that Hirst's practice comprises a novel manipulation of different codes of authorship, and that his work marks a further step in the development she outlines. To develop this argument, however, it is necessary to say a little more about the brand.

Brand Loyalty and Trademark Style

Historically, the brand was a mark of ownership intended to create trust in the consumer as a guarantor of the quality of particular products. As such it was a mark typically claimed by manufacturers of products, although the law has long accepted that the 'origin function' can include selection rather than or as well as manufacture. Trademark law was the means to secure a monopoly on the use of that mark with the dual purpose of protecting the owner from unfair competition and the consumer from 'confusion' as to the origin of the good. However, the brand is also – and increasingly this is its primary function – the mark of a relationship between products, a relationship that is the site of systematic intervention, subject to the rapidly changing pressures of intensive mediation and the practices of commercial calculation. Think of *Nike*: what defines it as a brand is more the relationship between products, between one generation of *AirMax* and the next, for example, and less that between producer and products. Indeed, as is well known, *Nike* does not make shoes at all; it sub-contracts its manufacturing to factories in (shifting locations in) East Asia. The CEO, Phil Knight, describes *Nike* as a marketing company.

> For years, we thought of ourselves as a production-oriented company, meaning we put all our emphasis on designing and manufacturing the product. But now we understand that the most important thing we do is market the product. We've come around to saying that *Nike* is a marketing company, and the product is our most important marketing tool.[xix]

In this and other cases, the brand is a multiply-mediated set of referrals between products, in which one product refers to another – through a set of highly charged, intensive associations – across a discontinuous time and space. It is neither the source nor the effect of referrals, but simply the mark of deferral and referral. Indeed, at any one time, the brand as a set of transformations includes both what one might call protentions and retentions:[xx] referrals forward and back in time. In this regard, the brand is both unitary and multiple, invariant and dynamic: it is a set of possible or legitimate transformations that have a unity and integrity but do not have an origin. And it is in this sense that it is possible to consider Hirst as a brand name, and to identify a Hirst 'trademark style'.

> On the one hand, in occupying the author-function as a relation of assertion, a subject such as Hirst, while understood to prime action (to be just doing it), need have no necessary interiority, no biography, not even a life, but only a name (or names). As Hirst himself puts it,

> I said the other day ... that I feel a bit like I don't want to be Damien Hirst, and it's too late to do anything about it. I don't like being 'Damien Hirst', I've decided. But you can't avoid it.[xxi]

The brand is a name that may be detached not only from an individual's life but even from the indexical form of the signature; it is the name as a taxonomic function alone.

> The 'Name', when one abstracts it from the signature which indicates it and 'contains' it, loses its 'index' character and becomes a 'trademark'. Indeed, like the trademark, the name is of a symbolic order. Thus the name 'Degas' abstracted from its index the signature is

something like 'Ford' or 'Cadillac'. It does not mean that the artist, Mr
Degas, was *there* any more than the name Ford means that Mr Ford
has taken part in the fabricating of the car which bears his name. [xxii]

On the other hand, in this relation of assertion, the object need only tenuously, if
at all, be an artwork in either of the senses that emerged in the extensions and
revisions of legal judgement following the copyright legislation of 1710. It is less
and less a matter of the labour of the author and less and less a matter of the irreducible singularity of 'style', or 'sentiment' with the consequence that originality
may not simply be renounced but rendered irrelevant. It was, for example, recently reported that,

> The artist Damien Hirst has agreed to pay an undisclosed sum to
> head off legal action for breach of copyright by the designers and
> makers of a £14.99 toy which bears a remarkable resemblance to his
> celebrated 20ft bronze sculpture *Hymn*, bought by Charles Saatchi
> earlier this year for £1m. ... The artist has also agreed to restrictions
> on future reproduction of the polychromatic bronze figure, described
> by one critic as 'a masterpiece' and 'the first key work of British art
> for the 21st century', which Hirst admitted was inspired by his son
> Connor's anatomy set. [xxiii]

Hirst had, it seems, anticipated such a course of legal action; that is, he acknowledged the work was copied. In a discussion of the work in a published interview,
he stated, 'I might even get sued for it. I expect it. Because I copied it so directly.
It's fantastic'. [xxiv] Similarly, he said on organising the show 'Some Went Mad, Some
Ran Away ...' at the Serpentine Gallery in 1994, that 'arranging a show is like
organising already organised elements'. [xxv] In occupying the author-function as
a relation of assertion, Hirst is not so much concerned with originality, as with
assemblages and reassemblages, with appropriations and incorporations:

> I don't want to say this is the new view of the world, because I don't
> believe that exists. The changes between things aren't the important
> thing. You want to make art work that is timeless and universal, so
> you don't want to be the new way of seeing the world really. [xxvi]

In sum, Hirst's proclamation of himself as a brand is one way of occupying the
author-function as a relation of assertion, a relation that is both more forceful and
less meaningful (less tied to notions of originality) than previous formulations. It
enables him to explore connections and the relations between things and claim
ownership of these relations. It also enables him to do so in a way that does not
have to be original although it must be distinctive. [xxvii]

How to spot a Trademark Style

Writing in 1992, Buskirk suggests that the collapsing of categories implied by the development of trademark styles is held 'in check' by 'the neo-avant-garde's situation within the institutional network of the art world'.[xxviii] But a number of developments have transformed the conditions in which it operates since the time at which she was writing, including ongoing changes in the legal regulations surrounding the art world and the terms and conditions of participation in the institutions of the art world. In what follows I want to suggest that such changes have helped produce a situation in which trademark becomes an increasingly appropriate framework within which the developments in the author-function described here may be supported.

First, there have been a number of changes in trademark law that have encouraged a more widespread use of trademark in relation to the products of the culture industry as a whole. Most obviously perhaps, as a consequence of recent legislation, a trademark may now be established on the basis of nothing more than a relation of assertion. Thus, the Trademarks Act 1994 no longer insists upon the period of prior use and consumer recognition that was required in previous legislation for the owner to be able to call upon legal protection of a mark. Instead, initially at least, all that is required to acquire protection for ownership of a mark – if it can be shown to have appropriate characteristics – is for the mark to be registered. The Act also includes the removal of the prohibition on 'trafficking' in trademarks contained in the 1938 Act, and the facilitation of multi-class applications. Moreover, there has been a growing judicial acceptance of more expansive trademark rights over the last twenty or so years. This expansion comprises a movement away from a 'confusion' definition of infringement (as to the origin of the product) toward a broader 'dilution' definition, which precludes all unauthorised uses that would lessen (or take advantage of) the mark's distinctiveness.[xxix] Thus it used to be the case that trademark infringement would only be found where the use of a protected mark by someone (X) other than its owner (Y) was likely to cause consumers to be confused as to the origin of the product to which the mark was attached. The issue was whether consumers would think that X's product actually came from Y. Now it is increasingly being suggested – with varying degrees of success – that if X's use of Y's signs on its product causes consumers to be reminded of Y on seeing X's product, even while knowing that X and Y are distinct traders, infringement has occurred. In other words, creating associations between products by means of (visual, olfactory, aural, etc.) signs – that is, organising a set of deferrals and referrals – is becoming established as the exclusive prerogative of the trademark owner, while associations created by other producers can be legally prevented. Moreover, this is a protection that does not have to rely on evidence of a calculation of trade source or origin by the consumer/viewer, but rather on the memory of distinctive sensation or effect.[xxx] In this regard, it seems as if there is an emerging legal basis for the protection of art as a trademark style as defined here. (However, it should be noted that there is as yet no legal authority that suggests that the imitation of an artist's style amounts to passing off in the U.K.).

Second, consider the relation between art and popular culture. Buskirk's discussion of the conditions contributing to the potential eclipse of copyright by trademark include both the rise of the celebrity artist within the art world and the routine appropriation of mass-produced cultural products by artists. But it does not include a serious consideration of the reverse movement – the appropriation of art works in popular culture – other than to suggest that it must involve a degree of naivety on the part of advertisers.[xxxi] But it is now increasingly clear that such reverse movements – that is, the use, naive or otherwise, of art works in mass cultural forms – have to be acknowledged. Moreover, such two-way movements are not simply incidental, but actually constitutive of the art world. This is especially clear in relation to the circulation and valuation of Hirst's work because of the patronage of Charles Saatchi, whose reputation in the advertising world preceded his entry into the art world as a collector. While Saatchi's motives in the purchase and display of the work of Hirst and other so-called young British artists is the focus of much discussion (so, for example, there have been a number of disputes relating to the supposed 'copying' of art works owned by Saatchi in advertisements made by his advertising company), it is clear that the boundaries of the art world are not simply leaky but functionally permeable. All this is not to suggest that a distinction between the art world and popular culture can no longer be drawn, but rather that the terms of this distinction are now being made visible as the result of a system of (asymmetrical, but two-way) movements. Indeed, this is precisely the situation that Krauss describes as the post-medium condition.

Consider Hirst's so-called spot paintings. In all the paintings of this series, 'The gaps between the spots are the same size as the spots. That's one constant factor. The spots are painted with household gloss. That's another'.[xxxii] In an interview in 1999, Hirst said he eventually wanted to stop the spot paintings,[xxxiii] but then in 2001 *The Economist* recorded him saying 'I think I'll always make them'.[xxxiv] Then again he has said, 'I want them to be an endless series, but I don't want to make an endless series. I want to imply an endless series'.[xxxv] In each of these paintings, a static pattern vibrates; as Hirst himself puts it, the paintings 'are full of life'.[xxxvi]

Damien Hirst, *Cetyltrethylammionium P-Toluenesulfonate*, 1996

Each individual painting is simultaneously present and absent, referring forward and backward, caught up both in their own internal movement and in the movement of the series of which they are a part.

As is well known, the spot paintings are not the product of Hirst's own labour. They are currently made by (sub-contracted to) assistants in a studio in Leyton, East London. Hirst tells his assistants what size he wants the paintings to be and they make them. In 1999, the assistants had painted about 300; by 2001 about 400 to 500 had been produced. Nor do the spots, the basic elements of the paintings appear to have a clear beginning or end, and this limitlessness means that the paintings cannot be understood in relation to any origin. 'Imagine a world of spots', Hirst says. 'Every time I do a painting, a square is cut out. They regenerate. They're all connected'.[xxxvii] Thus the series itself is an assembly of units characterised by their manipulation of speed, variability and the viewer's experience of any particular painting or work is affected by those preceding and following them. This is precisely the experience of television as theorised by Raymond Williams. The gap or interval between each painting is not simply the mark of the division of discrete works, but part of a flow. A flow, in which the 'true sequence' is not the official, or chronological series, but a (multiple) series of differently related units, some larger and some smaller than each painting. However, while the series offers the experience of flow in its own right, a further consequence of the intense mediation of Hirst's work is the multiplication of the possibility that the flow will be 'accessible, in several alternative sequences, at the flick of a switch'.[xxxviii] Or, as *The Economist* puts it, 'for those with smaller budgets, signed photographic prints of a spot painting entitled *Valium* are being sold for $2500 in an edition of 500 from Eyestorm.com'. The consequence of this is that there is a radical indeterminacy to the sequencing of the series.

While this indeterminacy cannot be understood in terms of originality – since each switch is not intended and could not be considered as the outcome of the instructions by which they were made – neither is it extraneous to the work – considered either as individual paintings or as the series. Rather, it is a function of the relations of openness in the (multiple) series, or set of possible and legitimate transformations, of deferrals and referrals, that is marked by the assertion of the brand name Hirst. And, as in the case of commercial product brands, such relations are the basis of the distinctiveness of what Buskirk calls a trademark style. In short, the case of Hirst does not imply that the imminent collapse of categories identified by Buskirk is either complete or inevitable. Rather it suggests that the interdependence of the categories may be made visible and productive of a particular position for the author. Or to put this another way, occupying the author-function as a relation of assertion enables Hirst to challenge the distinction between art and life, while sustaining a categorical difference between art and commodity culture in a post-medium condition. Indeed, it may also enable him to challenge the distinction between art and science.

Art, Life and Science

To illustrate this final claim, let me return to the notion of the brand as the mark of deferral and referral. As noted above, many contemporary brands operate as a system of products in which the relations between products are the site of intense affective mediation, not only intended but also unintended, planned, and unplanned. Think once again of *Nike*, and then of *Niketowns* and the high profile sponsorship of sports events and individuals by *Nike* in which the values of individuality, competitiveness and achievement are mobilised to name a set of deferrals and referrals between an open system of products. Then think of Hirst, his vitrines, his self-promotional organisation of shows, his media appearances, his links with restaurants, and his participation in Fat Les, the trio of performers whose song 'Vindaloo' became the unofficial English team anthem for the World Cup in 1998.[xxxix] In each case, the strategies by which such values are mobilised may be considered somewhat experimental in that some variables are reduced to a minimum while others are intensively and systematically manipulated.[xl] And Science is indeed the name of Hirst's company:[xli]

> People believe science, but they don't believe art, which to me is stupid. I remember looking in a drugstore window in a bad part of London and seeing all these people looking like shit, queuing up to get their pills. Everything looked clean and perfect except the people. But there's this massive confidence in the ability of pharmaceuticals to give immortality. I thought, 'I wish people would believe in art like they believe in this'. Eventually I just said fuck it, and I put it back on the wall. It's a piece called *Pharmacy*.[xlii]

But very often such manipulation or experimentation spills over into an event; indeed this is part of what is recognised as a crucial component of the Hirst brand name. As Hirst describes the show 'Some Went Mad, Some Ran Away ...':

> ... the exhibition will be about that kind of dealing with life when things are, in a way, out of control, where there is this over-layering and over-lapping of meaning giving this intense activity which is like life to me, like a writhing pit of snakes.[xliii]

In short, it is the event-like nature of the relations described here that sustains the quality of this-ness, the presence and directness, that is so frequently commented on in relation to Hirst's work. In the event 'a global surplus of effect, a kind of booster-effect'[xliv] transforms the situation of exhibition – the field of assertion – into one of (un)control'.[xlv] This quality is the direct presentation of a lived relationship – 'see it, be surprised, live it and like it (or not)'. It is an openness of connection, of interaction – 'a global excess of belonging-together enabled by, but not reducible to, the bare fact of having objectively come-together'.[xlvi] As Hirst himself puts it, when describing the exhibition, 'Some went mad, some ran away ...',

> It's like there is a lot of energy when the aeroplane explodes and there is a lot of death after it has exploded but it is at the point when it is exploding, and I quite like it on that level. [xlvii]

Such events are, some commentators suggest, the way science is done.[xlviii] The slogan *Life/Live* [xlix] may thus not only be an appropriate statement of the distinctiveness of the Hirst brand, indicating something of the quality of the relations between works so named, it may also be a way of acknowledging that the author-function described here is coming close to that of the scientist as described by Foucault.

Brand Management

In sum, the claim by Hirst that he is a brand name can be seen as a transformation of the author-function in which the relation between subject and object is no more, and no less, than a relation of assertion. And this relation of assertion can also be seen to have become 'proprietary' (in a trademark sense) when coupled with actual or anticipated public recognition. This transformation thus enables Hirst to secure a position in which his work need be neither original nor be the product of his own labour, but may still be recognised as art (and perhaps science). Moreover, it ensures that he may claim authorship of his work in the post-medium condition. Nevertheless, the contracted-yet-expanded occupation of the author-function as a brand name does not mean that everything that Hirst just does will be successful. (Un)control is not simply the opposite of control. Managing a brand has its own distinctive problems. On the one hand, the repetition of the name is unlikely to sustain the brand identified by the name Hirst because it does not make possible (un)control:

> It's ridiculous for me to make Damien Hirsts. I'm constantly getting calls from people who want to buy medicine cabinets, or butterfly paintings, or things I've already done. I think you've just got to pull away, try to ignore it and work on other things.[l]

On the other hand, diversification may undermine the brand; as he says: 'I think there's a bit of a joke in me in some ways, because I've diversified so much away from art'.[li] He says he opened the restaurant, *Pharmacy*, because it 'was a great way to take the gallery into a new realm' but came to the view that his participation in this and the restaurant *Quo Vadis* were not entirely successful:

> It just wasn't art at the end of the day. You end up getting involved in fucking aprons, knives and forks, pots and pans, all the shit of life that you don't really want to get involved in. Stocks and shares, ties, boots, Blu-Tack, glue, string.[lii]

In the interview with Leith, Hirst says 'he's avoided pitfalls, but that he's also made mistakes – such as the 'barbecue with little plastic tables and chairs'. He says he has 'been working on things very tentatively for the past two years'. In the same interview, he says that he,

> is trying to rearrange his life so he can have ideas in his own time. He is fixing up an 8,000 sq ft studio in Gloucestershire. He wants galleries to come to him, rather than work to the galleries' deadlines. He has just turned down a chance to exhibit at the Venice Biennale. 'I realised that you can control the pace', he says. It is a question of 'trying to convince yourself that you've got all the time in the world'.[liii]

Hirst may be able to convince himself this is so, but the referrals and deferrals of the distributed system of products that his name now marks has its own rhythms, switches, and stoppages to which he has contributed, but which he does not – and cannot – (un)control. For this reason, Damien Hirst – the person, not the constructed subject of the attenuated author-function described here – may be interested to know that brands are separable, transferable assets.

The author would like to thank Anne Barron for her comments and for information relating to trademark law.

i   Leith, W., 'Avoiding the Sharks', *Observer*, Sunday February 14, 1999.

ii   'Portrait of the Artist As a Brand', *The Economist*, February 10, 2001.

iii   According to Simon Ford in 'Myth Making', *Art Monthly*, 1996, no.3, pp.3-9, the earliest usage of 'young British artists' was for the British Pavilion of the 1996 Venice Biennale. He also records other names for the grouping including the 'neo-conceptual bratpack' by Sarah Greenberg, *Artnews*, September, 1995, 'The Brit Pack' by Patricia Bickers, *The Brit Pack: Contemporary British Art, The View from Abroad*, (1995) and the 'Britpop' artists by Waldemar Januszczak, *The Sunday Times*, December 3, 1995.

iv   Arlidge, J., 'Britannia's Brand-new Start', *Observer*, Sunday May 14, 2000.

v   Foucault, M., 'What is an Author?' in *Aesthetics, Method and Epistemology*, ed. J. Faubion, (London: Penguin, 1998) pp.187-204

vi   Chartier, R., 'Foucault's Chiasmus: Authorship Between Science and Literature' in T. Yamomoto, (ed.) *Philosophical Designs for a Socio-Cultural Transformation Beyond Violence and the Modern Era*, (Boulder: Rowman and Littlefield, 1998) p.124. See also Frow, J. 'Repetition and limitation: computer software and copyright law', *Screen*, 29, 1, 1988, pp.4-20; Rose, M. *Authors and Owners: The Invention of Copyright*, (Cambridge, Mass.: Harvard University Press, 1993); and Lury, C. *Cultural Rights*, (London: Routledge, 1993).

vii   Whether these two lines of reasoning are present in the Statute itself or emerged in the debates of the 1760s and 1770s over literary property at common law, is a controversial issue.

viii   Chartier, R. (1998), pp.123-5.

ix   It is important to bear in mind, however, that the rights of reproduction have always been vested in copyright holders rather than authors as such, thus placing special importance on the terms of the contract between an author and his or her publisher.

x   de Duve, T. 'Echoes of the Readymade: Critique of Pure Modernism' in M. Buskirk and M. Nixon (eds.) *The Duchamp Effect* (Cambridge, Mass. and London: The MIT Press, 1996) pp.93-130.

xi   As Martha Buskirk points out, however, while the appropriations made by Duchamp violated traditional notions of art, they did not infringe on established copyrights and patents: 'In the readymades . . ., it is no apparent violation of legal strictures – then or now – to display a factory-produced item such as a bicycle wheel or a urinal' (1992) p.98.

xii   Foucault, M. (1998), p.218.

xiii   Buskirk and M. Nixon (eds.), *The Duchamp Effect* (Cambridge, Mass. and London: The MIT Press, 1996).

xiv   Krauss, R., 'A Voyage on the North Sea', *Art in the Age of the Post-Medium Condition*, (London: Thames and Hudson, 1999).

xv   See Buskirk, 1992, for a discussion of Koons' work in relation to the shift she describes from author function to brand loyalty.

xvi   Among the factors Buskirk identifies as relevant to this development are: the emergence of both copyright and trademark principles in the nexus of judgements regulating the art world; a set of unwritten understandings and agreements that extend beyond the bounds of the purely legal; and the increasing recognition accorded to artistic styles based on a more conceptual working method.

xvii   See also Lury, 1993, in which I suggest that the second half of the twentieth century saw a shift in the culture industry from that of a regime of rights associated with copyright to one organised in relation to the brand and trademark.

xviii   Buskirk, M., 'Commodification as Censor: Copyrights and Fair Use', *October*, no.60, 1992, pp.82-109.

xix   Knight, P., 'High Performance Marketing: An Interview With Nike's Phil Knight', by G.E. Willigan, *Harvard Business Review*, July-August, 1993, pp.90-101.

xx   Gell, A., *Art and Agency. An Anthropological Theory* (Oxford: Clarendon Press, 1998).

xxi   Burn, G., 'The Knives Are Out', *The Guardian*, Monday April 10, 2000.

xxii   Gandelman, C. 'The Semiotics of Signatures in Paintings: A Piercian Analysis', *American Journal of Semiotics*, 3, 1985, pp.73-108.

xxiii   Dyer, C., 'Hirst Pays Up for Hymn That Wasn't His', *The Guardian*, Friday May 19, 2000.

xxiv   Burn, G., 'The Knives Are Out'.

xxv   Wilson, A., 'Out of Control', *Art Monthly*, no.177, 1994, pp.3-9.

xxvi   Wilson, A., 'Out of Control'.

xxvii   Such distinctiveness is necessary if the assertion of a brand name is to be seen as a transformation of the author-function rather than a sign of its dwindling significance, since, as Foucault puts it, 'the name as an individual trademark is not enough when one works within a textual tradition',1998, p.214.

xxviii   Buskirk, M. 'Commodification as Censor: Copyrights and Fair Use', *October*, no.60, 1992, p.108.

xxix   Shaughnessy, 1997, quoted in Frow, J. 'Signature and brand' in J. Collins (ed.) *HighLow* (New York and London: Macmillan, 2001).

xxx   I am grateful to Anne Barron for the information in this paragraph relating to changes in trademark law.

xxxi   Thus she says, 'But subtle or implied criticism is something that advertisers and others in the mass media are capable of overlooking. This tendency is demonstrated by the number of advertising endorsements that Warhol was asked to do', (1992) p.108.

xxxii   Leith, W., 'Avoiding the Sharks', *Observer*, Sunday February 14, 1999.

xxxiii   Leith, W., 'Avoiding the Sharks'.

xxxiv   'Portrait of the Artist As a Brand', *The Economist*, February 10, 2001.

xxxv   *Damien Hirst. No Sense of Absolute Corruption*, 1996. Interview by Stuart Morgan, New York Gagosian Gallery.

xxxvi   *Damien Hirst. No Sense of Absolute Corruption*, 1996.

xxxvii   *Damien Hirst. No Sense of Absolute Corruption*, 1996.

xxxviii   Williams, R. (1974) *Television: Technology and Cultural Form*, London: Fontana.

xxxix Nike is notorious for ambushing sponsored sporting occasions (as when its advertising featured prominently in the English cities in which Euro '96 played, although they were not an official sponsor). Something similar is suggested in the description of Vindaloo as a hi-jacking of football 'for our own purposes' by Keith Allen, another member of Fat Les.

xl Massumi, B. 'Too-blue: Colour Patch for an Expanded Empiricism', *Cultural Studies*, 2000, 14 (2), pp.177-226.

xli As Michael Corris ('Damien Hirst', *Artforum*, January, 1992, p.96) notes, 'Hirst's ostentatious recapitulation of insect behaviour [*A Thousand Years*] might also seem to burlesque the scientific method, to be a subtle indictment of the ideology of science, with its grotesque logic of induction and its equally grotesque 'controlled' animal experiments on the order of 'What would happened if we smashed a primate's skull in with a hammer?'. Alternatively, the name of the company can be seen to indicate a desire by Hirst for his work to operate in the field of discourse in a way that science does.

xlii '"*Brilliant!" New art from London*',1995, Damien Hirst interview with Marcelo Spinelli.

xliii Wilson, A., 'Out of control'.

xliv Massumi, B., 'Too-blue: Colour Patch for an Expanded Empiricism'.

xlv Not many consumer product brands are as open to (un)control as Hirst. Nike perhaps comes closest.

xlvi Massumi, B., 'Too-blue: Colour Patch for an Expanded Empiricism'.

xlvii Wilson, A. 'Out of control'.

xlviii Stengers, I. 'Who is an author?' in *Power and Invention. Situating Science* (Minneapolis: University of Minnesota Press, 1997); Rabinow, P. (1998); Massumi, B. (2000).

xlix This is the name of an exhibition held in Paris in 1996 featuring work from many of the artists associated with YBA including Hirst.

l Leith, W. 'Avoiding the sharks'.

li Leith, W. 'Avoiding the sharks'.

lii Burn, G. 'The knives are out'.

liii Leith, W. 'Avoiding the sharks'.

Art and the Making of Modern Copyright Law

Lionel Bently*

Looking through the lists of statutes that appear at the front of the leading books on U.K. copyright law, such as *Copinger* or *Laddie, Prescott & Vitoria*, a reader is confronted with a strange chronology.[i] The earliest copyright statute appears to be the Statute of Anne of 1710, an instrument which provided the authors and proprietors of 'copies' of books with the right to control the printing and reprinting of those books.[ii] This Act is followed by a 1735 'Act for the Encouragement of the Arts of Designing, Engraving, and Etching historical and other prints',[iii] a 1787 Act to protect the Designers of Calico Prints,[iv] and a 1798 Act to protect sculptures.[v] In the first half of the following century, special laws were developed for the protection of dramatists, lecturers, and musicians,[vi] recognising that such works were frequently exploited by public performance rather than reproduction. It is not until 1862 that an Act appears for the protection of 'fine arts' – the Copyright (Works of Art) Act – which declares:

> The author . . . of every original painting, drawing, and photograph . . . shall have the sole and exclusive right of copying, engraving, reproducing and multiplying such painting or drawing, and the design thereof, or such photograph, and the negative thereof, by any means and of any size, for the term of the natural life of such author, and seven years after his death. [vii]

The incremental development of the law seems strange to the modern eye, for at least two reasons: first, while we are not surprised to find the regulation of the printing of books at the start of the list, most readers carry the assumption that copyright law protects, at its core, works of art as well as literature, and might thus expect works of art to have been protected for as long as books. Yet paintings and drawings were left unprotected for over 150 years. Second, a modern reader almost certainly would be surprised to see that engravings received legislative protection one hundred-and-twenty-seven years before paintings and drawings. After all, if copyright is about authorial creativity, surely paintings and drawings would be more deserving of protection than such reproductive arts as engravings?

The aim of this piece is to sketch the context of the 1862 Act, the first Act specifically to protect painters. Although the 1862 Act can be seen as the outcome of a host of societal and cultural influences,[viii] the emphasis will here be placed on three elements: a coincidence between cultural understandings of writing and painting; the emergence of a modern concept of copyright as art and literature; and the destabilisation, prompted by the spread of photography, of the existing arrangements between artists, engravers, and print-sellers.

The Romantic Authorship Thesis and the Equivalence of Painting and Literature

Perhaps the most obvious reading of the Act is as an example of the legal reflection of romantic aesthetics. A number of writers have implied that the history of copyright law is a tale of gradual alignment of law with a specific emanation of aesthetic theory: the romantic author.[ix] According to this account, while in its earliest form copyright law was concerned with regulating the book trade, over time the philosophical foundation of copyright shifted to the provision of legal rights to individual creators, which enabled these creators to control the uses of their intellectual productions. More specifically, copyright law incorporated notions of creativity drawn from aesthetic theory, both in defining the sphere in which protection was extended to works of 'art and literature' and in ascribing rights to the 'authors' of those works. The 1862 Act can be viewed as one of the key examples of this shift, in that the rhetoric surrounding its introduction draws heavily on romantic aesthetics for its understandings of the equivalence of painting and writing. Painting was as deserving of the protection of law as writing, precisely because their production involved similar processes of creation.

There can be little doubt that the passage of the 1862 Act depended on the widespread acceptance of the equivalence of painting and writing. As the Attorney General argued, during the second reading of the first Copyright (Works of Art) Bill of 1861, the justification for the legislation was that 'The artist . . . ought to be put in the same category with the [writer]'.[x] This equivalence of writer and artists was, in fact, so frequently taken for granted that the law's omission to protect painting was taken as exceedingly anomalous in the 1860s. For example, barrister William Marshall remarked in 1863 that,

> I cannot help thinking that it was a singular anomaly in our law, that, notwithstanding the refinements to which it had attained, in the recognition of the rights of property, there should have been no recognised property in the design and composition of a picture . . . Upon what ground should the privilege be granted in the one case, and denied in the other?[xi]

While the treatment of the writer and painter as equals may have seemed natural to contemporaries, even within the prevailing thought of the time there were plenty of other ways of looking at the relationship between art and literature which denied their equivalence. More specifically, it was perfectly possible to distinguish paintings from literature in terms of ontology, the senses, technology, economics of production, mode of production, relationship with nature, ownership of physical property, and interpretation. The currency of these distinctions in earlier years, goes some way to explaining the failure of the law to protect works of fine art, and even after the passage of the Act, would operate as the premises for arguments, of both those opposed to copyright protection of paintings [xii] and those who wanted a system of copyright for paintings that was better attuned (than the 1862 Act) to the specific needs of such artists. [xiii] However, for most of those involved in the political processes surrounding the 1862 Act, these understandings were marginalised, and the equivalence of the painter and writer was taken to be self-evident.

The basis of this equivalence lay in the aesthetic understandings of how the works were produced: in at least the typical or ideal case, both literature and paintings were widely considered to be equivalent because both were the emanations or expressions of the ideas of a creator. And they were equally works of genius and imagination that added to the cultural richness of mankind. [xiv] As the President of the Royal Society of Arts in his annual address of 1862 wrote:

> Is it not strange that, until the present year, our laws should have given no protection to artists in the enjoyment of *works of the highest genius and the most brilliant imagination*; and that, although we acknowledged the natural and undisputed right of the rudest industry to the enjoyment of its productions, we disregarded the claims of men whose labours have afforded mankind some of *the highest and purest pleasures*? [xv]

The same ideas pervade the Attorney General's speech in Parliament when promoting the 1861 Bill, which goes further by tying the theory of art to a theory of property: [xvi]

> It is admitted that everyone should have a property in that which is the work of his hands, but how much stronger becomes his vested right *when that work is the conception of his mind embodied in a painting or statue*. Are we going to deprive the artist of his just and proper protection, and that which is, after all, the highest and the noblest property in the world?

Again, the work of the artist is not imitation, but expression of the conception of the mind.[xvii] The foundation of copyright is that it protects such creations from imitation. He continued, 'The principle of protection is established with respect to the author, and it is high time that the artist should also taste its advantages . . . Art and literature spring from the same source and stand on the same foundation.' Importantly, this equivalence of art and literature should be recognised as one which is neither timeless nor universal. It is based upon a specific aesthetic, which can be traced back into the eighteenth century. The equivalence of painting and writing seems to have been grounded in the development of the idea of fine arts (separate from the mechanical arts) which has been seminally described by Kristeller.[xviii] As the fine arts in turn became refashioned in the context of the romantic movement, the central definitive criteria were transformed from 'imitation' and 'beauty' to 'authorship', 'creation', and 'expression'.

The Idea of Copyright

The realignment of painting and writing as both expressions of individual creators, then, underpinned the rhetoric surrounding the artists' claim to protection in 1859-62. However, this aesthetic equivalence of painting and writing as 'works of the mind' was, of itself, only one component of the rhetorical claim to copyright in painting. The parity of painting and writing in aesthetic theory only had political and legal power once it was (or could be) accepted that copyright was about 'authorship' and 'writing'. The aesthetic parity would have had little rhetorical force if the basis for the regulation of the book trade, print selling, and design by the existing laws had not been reconceived as concerned with the protection of works of authorship.

During the eighteenth century, while there were the particular legislative enactments described above, there was no law of Copyright. In this period the term copyright was hardly ever used (the prevailing term in relation to books at least being 'literary property'), but when the term 'copy-right' *was* used, it tended to be with either of two meanings. In the early eighteenth century, the term 'copy-right' seems to relate to rights in 'copies', i.e., manuscripts. Later in the century – for example in the Sculpture Act of 1798 – 'copyright' was understood as referring to a category of right, the right to control copying. Importantly, 'copy-right' was not conceived as an area of law. The concept of 'copy-right' did not take on its modern meaning as a branch of law until the middle of the nineteenth century, when these various enactments came to be seen as forming a 'Copyright law'.[xix]

This transition from 'copy-right' to 'Copyright law' was a product of multiple and complex processes in the making of modern intellectual property law which have been considered at length elsewhere.[xx] In part, the transition was worked out judicially through the lengthy debates over whether there was a common-law, perpetual, right over literary property in the period from 1759-1774.[xxi] While the book publishers' claim to the common law right failed in *Donaldson v. Beckett*,[xxii] the link between authorship and the Statute of Anne, and the very legitimacy of literary property was established in the public mind. Moreover, while the literary property debate may have failed to establish a perpetual common law right for authors, the decision of the House of Lords in *Donaldson v. Beckett* left room for the recognition of such rights as regards unpublished works which were not touched by the Statute of Anne. In this context, the judiciary began to piece together a domain for the common law right, namely that it be 'the property in an author or composer of any work, whether of literature, art, or science, such work being unpublished...'[xxiii]

The crystallisation of a modern category of 'Copyright law' as a distinct and recognisable branch of law was not just effected through the courts, but in various other arenas as a response to a whole range of forces. This process of categorisation – selection and necessarily exclusion – was not one dictated by any philosophical logic, but an exercise informed by pressing practical concerns (such as the need to describe the law to others at home and abroad). For example, the mid-nineteenth century spawned a host of legal textbooks, each of which had to define, organise, and explain its own domain. The construction of these textbooks prompted an engagement with the aesthetics of law – the shape the law itself took – requiring justification for the inclusion, exclusion, or levels of coverage and attention paid to the various enactments or systems of legal protection (such as engraving and the printing of designs on calico). Not surprisingly, from 1820 to 1850 there were a variety of competing suggestions as to how the law should be categorised; whether as a law of printing, a law of fine art, a law of industrial art, a law of form, or a law of copyright.[xxiv] Similar concerns with the form of law (reflecting a new-found desire for the law to be arranged in an abstract and forward-looking manner rather than as discrete subject-specific responses to specific problems) arose as attempts were made at legislative reform (such as Talfourd's activities in the 1830s)[xxv] and the government began to negotiate international bilateral arrangements from the late 1830s onwards.[xxvi] But undoubtedly the most significant emanation in this context was the International Copyright Act of 1844, which empowered Her Majesty to give protection to the authors of books *and works of art* first published in a foreign country, including drawing, painting, sculpture, engraving, lithography and 'any other works whatsoever of Literature and of the Fine Arts'.[xxvii]

As a result of these 'codifying' activities, in the 1850 and 1860s 'Copyright law' became an area of law with a specific identity,[xxviii] an abstract law which extended to 'all works of literature and art in the widest sense'. This was a self-image or identity that was not neutral but had important consequences, for, as has been stated, British law did not give protection to painters prior to 1862, and yet the image of copyright presupposed just such protection. In fact, the image became a standard or ideal which begged that the legislature pass a law to protect paintings and drawings.[xxix] By 1862, a claim to copyright for paintings had purchase with the legislature precisely because a new and modern concept of Copyright had emerged, one in which the self-image of Copyright was at least in part aesthetic. In turn, the 1862 Act was perceived as an important step in the perfection of the law – the approximation of the positive law to its own self-image, the submission of the law to its own logic.[xxx] For example, the barrister E.M. Underdown described the Act as 'another and most important step towards the completion and perfection of the series of parliamentary enactments on the subject of artistic copyright'. He remarked that the legitimacy of the artists' claims to such rights, already established 'in the abstract' had prior to 1862 only been 'very partially recognised' by the law.[xxxi]

The Demand for Regulation

In many ways, the 1862 Act marks a point at which the modern concepts of 'art' and 'copyright' coincided, and this coincidence provided a logic that rendered the claims of painters to protection difficult to resist. But perhaps the most remarkable aspects of the 1862 Act relate to the circumstances that forced the relationship between copyright and art onto the legislative agenda. It is through an understanding of these particular circumstances that we learn most about the contingency under which copyright law (in general, and more specifically for painting) came into existence and appreciate something about the limits of the romantic account of copyright law's history.

Legislative attention was first drawn to the issue of copyright protection for painting and drawing by the Society for Arts. In practical terms, there were a whole host of matters that prompted the Society of Arts in the 1850s to seek copyright.[xxxii] Among the many factors were concerns over the status of artists, forgery, the making of replica works, the importation of pirate copies of engravings from abroad,[xxxiii] the copying of works in the expanding numbers of art galleries, and the unauthorised alteration of existing works.[xxxiv] However, probably the key to understanding the moves for the 1862 legislation is to be found in the way in which the emergence of photography was threatening to destabilise certain reasonably well-established economic relations between artists and the print trade.

The domestic market for prints had existed for centuries, but a notable expansion can be dated roughly to the mid-eighteenth century and the emergence of a 'consumer society'.[xxxv] As the print trade expanded during the late-eighteenth and early-nineteenth centuries, painters came to realise that they controlled an asset of value to the print-sellers: fresh material in the form of newly painted canvases. Following the huge commercial success of William Woollett's engraving of Benjamin West's *The Death of General Wolfe*, published in 1776, the previous relation of interdependence between painter and publisher (whereby the painter benefited from the publicity given to their works by reproductive engravings) was transformed into a dependence of print-sellers on painters for a continuous supply of new works worth publishing. This competition among print-sellers gave painters the bargaining power to pick and choose who published prints of their paintings.[xxxvi] Furthermore, a painter was able to sell the 'right' to engrave the painting while it was still in the artist's possession prior to its delivery to the commissioner or new owner.[xxxvii]

Some art historians have suggested that fees were being paid as early as the 1760s; more concrete evidence exists, however, showing that the Scottish painter of 'narratives', Sir David Wilkie (1785-1841), received £50 from the print-seller Alderman John Boydell for the right to engrave *The Blind Fiddler*, which had been exhibited at the Royal Academy in 1807,[xxxviii] and £1200 from Moon, Boys, and Graves for the right to engrave *The Chelsea Pensioners*, a picture of soldiers outside a pub receiving news of the Battle of Waterloo (exhibited in 1822).[xxxix] In the 1820s, Sir Thomas Lawrence (1769-1830) (who was largely a portrait painter as well as President of the Royal Academy from 1820) entered a written agreement with print-sellers Robinson and Hurst, under which Lawrence was to be paid £3000 p.a. for the exclusive privilege of having plates engraved from his pictures.[xl] It seems that artists of certain subjects could get half their incomes from these 'copyright' fees.[xli] There is certainly good evidence that this was so for Edwin Landseer (1803-73) in the 1840s,[xlii] and it is clear that J.M.W. Turner prospered as a result of the income he gained from the 800 different prints made from his paintings during his lifetime.[xliii] In a similar vein, William Powell Frith (1819-1909) sold copyright in his extraordinarily popular picture of a crowd scene at the Epsom races, *The Derby Day*, exhibited in 1858, to the publisher Ernest Gambart

William Powell Frith, *The Derby Day*, 1856-58

for £1,500, the same price Jacob Bell had paid for the painting [xliv]. Gambart, in turn, had it engraved by Auguste Blanchard in Paris, and when it was published in 1862, it sold over 5,000 copies.

More remarkable still, were the dealings surrounding Frith's next blockbuster, *The Railway Station*, a crowd scene at Paddington Station, first exhibited in 1862. Commissioned by a dealer named Flatow, who paid £4500 for the painting and its copyright, the painting was engraved by Francis Holl in 1862, and the next year Flatlow sold both painting and copyright to Henry Graves and Company for £16,300.[xlv] Finally, the pre-Raphaelite, William Holman Hunt (1827-1910) – having received £200 in 1856 from Gambart for copyright of his religious composition, *The Light of the World* (exhibited in 1854), (which was engraved by W.H. Simmons, published in 1860, and became 'one of the best selling engravings of all times') [xlvi] – obtained the astonishing fee of £5,500 from Gambart for *The Finding of Christ in the Temple*, a painting exhibited in 1860, with the engraving by August Blanchard being published in 1867.[xlvii]

Looking back, it seems remarkable that print publishers were prepared to pay such fees when it was clear that they had no legal protection if the picture were to be engraved independently [xlviii]. The existing laws concerning copyright in engravings gave the print-seller some security against the copying of the engraving itself (at least by mechanical means),[xlix] and contracts with painters and engravers contained what lawyers would now call 'boiler-plate' to ensure, as far as possible, that those rights were secured.[l] The vulnerability of the print-seller to independent engravings is illustrated by the case of *De Berenger v. Wheble*.[li] Here the plaintiff had purchased from painter Philip Reinagle [lii] the privilege of engraving prints from two pictures painted for Reinagle's own use, and which Reinagle owned. The plaintiff employed an engraver, Thompson,[liii] who in addition to making the two engravings for the plaintiff, had taken two sketches for his own use. From these, he made two prints for the defendant, who published them in *The Sporting Magazine (or Monthly Calendar of the Transactions of the Turf, the Chase and Every other Diversion Interesting to the Man of Pleasure, Enterprise and Spirit)*. The court of King's Bench rejected the claim for infringement of copyright in the engraving, since the defendant had not copied the engraving, but the original work. Abbott L.C.J., a judge revered for his common sense, stated that were the Engravings Acts to be interpreted as the plaintiff proposed, it would extend the monopoly to the painting itself, and this 'would destroy all competition in the art'.[liv]

In the absence of a copyright, the arrangement between painter and publisher was precarious because it would not impose any obligation on the painting's owner to forbid further engravings being made that could compete with the print-seller's. When arrangements were made for the engraving to be done prior to first sale of the canvas,[lv] in theory, the publisher could have increased the security of his position by obliging the painter not to part with the painting unless he required the purchaser-transferee to undertake not to allow its engraving. But there is little evidence that any such arrangements were made [lvi]. In other cases, the print-seller could buy the picture – and the supposed 'copyright' – from the painter, only disposing of the picture after the engraving had been published, and thus having the advantage of not needing a third party's permission during the often lengthy engraving process. In general, however, the print-sellers simply took risks. The explanation for the generous fees paid to the likes of Wilkie, Frith, Hunt, and Landseer, must be found in the high size of their profits compared to the risk involved – Gambart made at least £8000 profit from his dealings with Hunt's *The Light of the World* and at least £5000 with *Finding of Christ in the Temple*.[lvii] The extent of that risk was, however, rapidly changing after the 1840s.

The 1862 Act can be seen, in many ways, as an attempt to formalise these (increasingly lucrative) practices, to turn expectations into rights, powers into assignable properties, and thereby to remove the uncertainties which artists, engravers, and print-sellers faced.[lviii] In part, the artists resented the fact that the power to authorise engraving *in reality* lay with the owner (or possessor) of the artwork rather than the artist[lix]. This was because it was the owner of the personal property in the picture who had the legal power to decide whether to loan or provide access to the canvas, and for many engravings this was required for lengthy periods – sometimes a number of years. The result bore no consistency in practice: sometimes owners recognised the moral claim of the artist [lx] and at other times would keep the fee for themselves. [lxi] For example, Mr. Jos J. Jenkins, Secretary of the Old Watercolour Society, commented that:

> Some few of my drawings have been engraved by the proprietor of the drawings. In respect of two of them, it came to my knowledge that the possessor received a money consideration for the copyrights. In none of the instances was I consulted . . . or received any remuneration whatever for the copyrights. [lxii]

The impact of these varying practices on painters was not merely financial: where permission to make the engraving had been granted by the artists, contracts would often provide for the artists' supervision of the engraving process and touching of proofs (to the mutual benefit of all concerned). [lxiii] However, in cases where engravings were made from pictures loaned by owners, the painter had no control over the quality of the engraving. [lxiv]

Yet, the 1862 Act was not sought merely to provide order, consistency, and legitimacy to a series of practices that had developed as an adjunct to an artist or owner's ability to control access to a work. Rather, the Act was a response to a number of changes, which were seen as likely to threaten those practices. One such change was the gradual expansion in public galleries exhibiting works of living artists to the general public – a practice which threatened to undermine an artist's hope that ownership of the painting would act in practice as a control over access and reproduction. [lxv] For example, one engraver complained: [lxvi]

> I purchased from the artist, Mr. Turner, the copyright of the Temeraire and had the picture engraved. This picture forms one of the bequests to the National Gallery, and upon hearing that several water-colour drawings were in progress to engrave from, I wrote to the trustees on the subject, informing them of my right in the copyright of that particular picture; their reply to me was to the effect that they could not recognize any copyright I might have in the picture.

Another, much more significant threat to existing relations, was the development of photography, or as Charles Landseer put it, 'foe-to-graphic art'. [lxvii] In the lengthy evolution of photography that can be traced back to the eighteenth century, an important marker was William Stirling's *Annals of the Artists of Spain*, published in 1847, which contained a series of calotype reproductions of works of art. [lxviii] Further improvements took place in the 1850s, [lxix] and the photographic process increasingly came to be used to reproduce art works.

For the time being, the threat posed by photography was not in terms of its ability to replace engraving as the primary mode of reproduction of paintings: [lxx] the processes were not yet developed enough to do that (though it did not stop it from becoming a long term concern).[lxxi] Rather, photography provided a means by which engravings could be reproduced quickly and cheaply by pirates.[lxxii] It was no longer necessary for a pirate to employ an engraver to imitate the original engraving. A pirate copy could be produced which was the same quality as the original.[lxxiii] Photography thus threatened the profitability of engraving rather than its function.

Clear evidence exists of widespread photographic reproduction of engravings in the 1860s. Gambart, the print-seller who paid generous fees for the right to engrave paintings, was particularly aggrieved[lxxiv]. In a letter to *The Times* he wrote [lxxv]

> I have been suing the photographers for years. I have not always suc-
> ceeded in getting my costs, but I always got a verdict when we went to
> trial. I did not always go to trial. They usually apologise, and say they
> won't do so again. I mean to prosecute in every case where my engrav-
> ings are photographed. I must do so, or give up my business. It is of no
> use to me to go on publishing my engravings if the moment I publish
> I am to be knocked out of the field by piracies.

One such case appears in the Law Reports, *Gambart v. Ball*.[lxxvi] In this case (like many cases which did not reach the Law Reports), the defendant had copied engravings (including those of Holman Hunt's *The Light of the World*; and Rosa Bonheur's *The Horse Fair*) on a very reduced scale by means of photography.[lxxvii] Gambart sued, arguing this was an infringement of copyright in the engravings (particularly under the 1777 Act).[lxxviii] The 1777 Act gave the owner the exclusive right to control 'engraving, etching or working' of the protected design and copying 'in any other manner'. The defendant argued that this phrase should be given a narrow interpretation, namely one that was *ejusdem generis* with the preceeding examples, all of which were limited to purely mechanical modes of reproduction.[lxxix] Finding for Gambart, the Court of Common Pleas held that the right to control copying covered 'any process by which copies may be indefinitely multiplied', and thus covered photographic copies (even though the process did not exist when the 1777 Act was passed and was at least partially chemical rather than mechanical in nature). Byles J. observed that 'it is plain that a photographic copy may excite in the mind of the beholder the same pleasurable emotion as would be communicated by a copy of any other description' so that the value of the engraving rights 'would be sensibly diminished if the multiplication of copies by means of photography were held to be lawful'.[lxxx] The opinion of Keating J. testifies to the extent of the threat that photographic reproduction posed to print-sellers. He said,[lxxxi] '[i]n order to be satisfied that a multiplication of copies by means of photography would seriously invade that property, one need only look at the beautiful array of photographic copies which meets the eye at every turn.'

The advent of photography also threatened to disrupt the practices of the print-selling trade in other, less direct, ways. In the early nineteenth century, engravings were attributed value not merely as representations of original paintings but also in themselves. In part, this value derived from the scarcity of prints, which in turn was a consequence of the fact that plates were expensive to manufacture and had a limited life.[lxxxii] Print collectors began to differentiate between different qualities of print, attributing particular value to proof versions.[lxxxiii] As technological developments in the nineteenth century (in particular steel plates and electrotyping of copper plates) enabled the making of tens of thousand copies, print-sellers had adopted some of the categories developed in the context of these collecting practices to their own ends: for example, claiming that editions were limited, plates destroyed, issuing copies signed by artist or engraver, or both, as well as specifically marketing 'artist's proofs'.[lxxxiv] After some controversy, a system of 'authentication' was developed by print-sellers to reinforce consumer confidence in the artificial rarity of particular prints. More specifically, in 1847, the leading firms of print-sellers had established the Printsellers Association, which required its members not to sell any print for over one-and-a-half guineas unless it had been stamped with the Association's mark. In turn, before the Association would stamp a print, the seller had to declare the size of the editions. Moreover, the Association regulated the identification of different types of proofs, such as 'artist's proofs' and 'proofs before letters'.[lxxxv]

In this environment of regulation to maintain artificial scarcity and, ultimately, profits, the emergence of photography could only be viewed as an unwelcome, destabilising influence. Further replication by pirates had the potential not just to diminish the value of the original painting but also the value of the different type of prints, or at least so the print-sellers believed. In a remarkable exchange between the editor of *The Athenaeum* and print-seller Ernest Gambart, in 1862, Gambart responded to the journal's criticisms of the system of differentiating between various proofs. Given that with electrotyping any number of flawless copies could be made, the journal asserted that the false claims to difference in quality amounted to 'chicanery' intended to inflate prices.[lxxxvi] Gambart's response firstly denied that the new techniques had the consequences suggested, pointing out that even when utilising steel (rather than the softer copper, as had been the practice since the 1830s, and which gave significantly fewer impressions), there remained clear differences in the qualities of the copies.[lxxxvii] The print-seller went on to argue that even with these techniques, selling the prints more cheaply would have an undesirable impact. As a consequence of his experiences, he averred 'the cheap issue would destroy the sale of the dearer original' and that 'it is the duty of the publisher not to diminish by acts of his own volition the value of the engravings which he has sold. Collectors who pay large prices for choice engravings do not care to see them sold at one tenth or one hundredth part of the price . . .'.[lxxxviii] In Gambart's view, 'prints are luxuries which must remain costly and are not expected to be in everybody's reach'.[lxxxix]

The threats from photography to print-sellers were indirectly threats to both engravers and artists[xc]. Print-sellers became reluctant to pay copyright fees without the assurance that their efforts would not be undermined and their profits reduced. Even if the risk to the publisher was difficult to assess, it could still be used to bargain the painter's price down. For example, in Gambart's negotiations with Holman Hunt over copyright in *The Light of the World*, Gambart's position was:[xci]

> that there was the chance of the public not liking the print, and then no-one would divide his loss, while if it became popular, photographers throughout England would pirate his work, and the prosecution of each would cost L70; the only penalty to them would be the loss of a simple camera.

In 1868, Landseer refused to allow photographers to copy his works, writing that[xcii] 'Mr Graves is now the only publisher who consents to give large sums for the loan of important pictures for the purpose of Engraving, and as you know considers his bold speculations greatly injured by photography'. It is clear from this that the impact of photography on print publishers had an indirect effect on artists' copyright fees; an effect that even the enactment of the 1862 law was unable to curtail.

Conclusion

Giving protection to artists, as the 1862 Act did, could not halt the threat posed by photographic reproduction. Although in providing protection against 'copying, engraving, reproducing, and multiplying such painting or drawing, and the design thereof . . . by any means and of any size', the Act explicitly granted greater protection than had been accorded to engravings, it was clear after *Gambart v. Ball* that small photographic copies of engravings infringed even the engraving copyright. The 1862 Act therefore added little extra to the legal armoury of artists and print-sellers in their attempts to stifle the proliferation of photographic reproductions. Rather, the achievement of the 1862 Act was to register a concern, anticipate a longer term threat (direct photographic reproduction of paintings), and institute what was seen as the ethically and aesthetically appropriate ordering of rights: one in which the claims of artists were acknowledged alongside the long accepted claims of engravers.

The 1862 Act, too, marked a significant development in the making of modern Copyright law. The protection of paintings and drawings by copyright utilised a number of different concepts from those, which had been used in the previous legislation. For example, protection of paintings and drawings arose on creation rather than first publication, but only if the works were 'original', and the protection extended beyond 'reprinting' to cover reproduction in a variety of different media. Over the following half century, as lawyers, politicians, reformers, and interest groups attempted to produce a single legislative Copyright code, these three ideas would come to be a central focus for debate, and ultimately, in 1911, to form key principles of a codified Copyright law.

---

*   Lionel Bently expresses thanks to Lucy Peltz of the National Portrait Gallery, London

i   G. Davies, K. Garnett, and J. Rayner James (eds.), *Copinger & Skone James on Copyright* (14th edn., Sweet & Maxwell, 1999) lxxxiii-iv; H. Laddie, P. Prescott, M. Vitoria, A. Speck, L. Lane (eds.) *The Modern Law of Copyright* (3rd. edn, Butterworths, 2000).

ii   1710, 8 Anne, ch.21.

iii   1735, 8 Geo. 2, ch.13; 1767, 6 Geo. 3, ch.38 (extending duration of engravers' rights to 28 years, and scope of Act to cover 'reproductive' as well as 'original' engravings); 1777, 17 Geo.3, ch.56 (giving action on the case for damages).

iv   27 Geo.3, ch.38 (1787); 29 Geo.3, ch.19 (1789); 34 Geo.3, ch.23 (1794).

v   An act for encouraging the art of making new models and casts of busts, and other things therein mentioned, 38 Geo. III. ch.71 (1798); 1814, 54 Geo. 3, ch.56.

vi   1833, 3 & 4 Will. 4, ch.15.; 1835 5 & 6 Will. 4, ch.65; 1842, 5 & 6 Vict., ch.45 s.20.

vii   25 & 26 Vict., ch 68 `An Act for Amending the Law relating to Copyright in Works of the Fine Arts, and for repressing the Commission of Fraud in the Production and Sale of such Works'.

viii   Some of the influences not touched on in this paper include: changing geographical locations of artworks, the spread of museums, the growth of a picture buying public, increasing valorisation of the uniqueness of art works, widespread beliefs in the civilising value of art works, changing conceptions of property and the strategic ability of certain groups to form politically-influential alliances.

ix   See D. Saunders, *Authorship and Copyright* (Routledge, 1992), reviewing and providing critique of such accounts.

x   162 *Parl. Deb. (3d. ser.)* 1637 (1861). Hansard mistakenly puts 'painter' instead of writer.

xi   W. Marshall, 'Copyright in the Fine Arts', (1863) 2 *Juridical Society*, pp.722-723. Further examples exist. Underdown in his commentary on the law of art copyright published in 1863 commented that the legislature 'had strangely omitted the rights of Painters as such': E. Underdown, *The Law of Art Copyright* (Crockford, 1863) 5. See also P. Burke, *The Law of International Copyright Between England and France* (Sampson & Low, 1852) viii; Anon., 'Property in Art' (1849) *Art Journal*, pp.133-134 (omission from copyright statutes a 'matter of surprise to many').

xii   E.g., Fitzjames Stephens, *Report of the Commissioners appointed to make inquiry with regard to the Laws and Regulations relating to Home, Colonial and International Copyright* (1878) c.2036 in 24 *Parliamentary Papers* (1878).

xiii   F. Leighton, 'Government and the Artists – I', (1879) 6 *Nineteenth Century* 968; Wells, 'Government and the Artists – II', (1879) 6 *Nineteenth Century* 969; 'The Copyright Consolidation and Amendment Bill, 1879, In Its Relation to the Fine Arts', (1880) *Athenaeum* 25; Report of the Select Committee on Copyright Bill [H.L.] and Copyright (Amendment) Bill [H.L.] Rep. No.189 (1898) (recommending separate treatment of 'artistic copyright').

xiv   P. Burke, *op.cit.*, note 11, p.x.

xv   (1862) 11 *J.Soc'y. Arts*, 21 Nov., p.13 (emphasis added).

xvi   Second Reading. (1861) 9 *J.Soc'y Arts*, 10 May, pp.471-472 (emphasis added).

xvii   This was also the view of the Society of Arts. See (1862) 11 *J. Soc'y Arts*, 22 Nov., pp.12-13: 'It ought no longer to continue the law of this country that from the moment the conceptions of the artist are embodied on canvass or sculptured in the marble, they cease to belong to their author, and may be pilfered by men who, when they cannot even imitate, can at least disfigure works which a lofty genius may have inspired'.

xviii   P. O. Kristeller, 'The Modern System of the Arts' (1951) 12 *Journal of the History of Ideas*, pp.496-527; (1952) 13, *Journal of the History of Ideas*, pp.17-46. See, M. Woodmansee, *The Author, Art, and the Market: Rereading the History of Aesthetics* (Columbia, 1994).

xix   B. Sherman & L. Bently, *The Making of Modern Intellectual Property: The British Experience, 1760-1911* (Cambridge University Press, 1999).

xx   *Ibid.*

xxi   These have now received considerable academic attention. See Sherman & Bently, ibid., Chs. 1-3; J. Feather, *A History of British Publishing* (Routledge, 1988); M. Rose, *Authors and Owners: The Invention of Copyright*; R. Deazley, *On the Origin of the Right to Copy: Charting The Movement of Copyright Law in Britain Throughout the Eighteenth Century (1695 -1775)*, Ph.D. (Queens University, Belfast, 2000).

xxii   (1774) 17 *Parliamentary History* col.953.

xxiii   *Prince Albert v. Strange* (1849) 1 Hal & Tw 1, 21; 47 E.R. 1302, 1310; 1 Mac & G 25, 42; 41 E.R. 1171, 1178 (Cottenham LC).

xxiv   Sherman & Bently, op.cit., note 19, pp.95-99.

xxv   These started ambitiously with an attempt at codification in a Bill of 1837 but culminated in the Literary Copyright Act 1842 (5 & 6 Vict. c.45). For background to the Act, see C. Seville, *Literary Copyright Reform In Early Victorian England: The Framing of the 1842 Copyright Act* (Cambridge University Press, 1999).

xxvi   Sherman & Bently, *op.cit.*, note 19, pp.111-118.

xxvii   International Copyright Act 1844 7 & 8 Vict. c.12).

xxviii   Sherman & Bently, *op.cit.*, note 19, 119-125.

xxix   *Ibid.*, pp.126-128.

xxx   While the ideological rhetoric was certainly important in the passage of the legislation, it would be wrong to see the 1862 Act as signaling the reduction of copyright law to a logic of romanticism The Act, after all, did not only protect art works which fell within the romantic philosophy: it also granted copyright protection to photographs, which was not seen as being a `creative' activity.

xxxi   *Op.cit.*, note 11.

xxxii   On Society of Arts, see D.Hudson & Luckhurst, *The Royal Society of Arts 1754-1954* (Murray, 1954).

xxxiii   See *Gambart v. C. & A. Lewis* (1859) *Art Journal*, p.195 (reproduction of etchings in Germany).

xxxiv   See evidence of Charles Landseer as to the alteration of *Eve of the Battle of Edge Hill* in Underdown *op.cit.*, note 10, p.178.

xxxv   N. McKendrick, J. Brewer & J. Plumb, *The Birth of a Consumer Society–The Commercialization of Eighteenth Century England* (Europa, 1982); J. Brewer, *The Pleasure of the Imagination: English Culture in the Eighteenth Century* (Harper Collins, 1997) pp.449-463.

xxxvi   T. Clayton, *The English Print 1688-1802* (Yale University Press, 1997) p.190. The print was published by Woollett, Boydell and Ryland. Other versions of *The Death of General Wolfe* were made later including one by T. Beech for the Art Union in 1860.

xxxvii   The Attorney General commented in the Debate on the Second Reading of the 1861 Bill that 'In many cases the remuneration of the artists arose from the power of engraving his picture, and it was quite clear that he could reserve that power if the purchaser did not choose to buy it along with the picture'. See 9 *J.Soc'y Arts*, p.471 (10 May 1861).

xxxviii   A. Griffiths, 'Two Contracts for British Prints', 9 *Print Quarterly* 184 (1992). The painting was owned by Sir George Beaumont, but the agreement was with Boydell and the engraver Mr. John Burnet. See also Clayton *op.cit.*, note 36, p.194 and n.50, p.302.

xxxix   Like *The Blind Fiddler*, this was engraved by John Burnet. See J. Burnet, 'Autobiography of John Burnet' (1850) *Art Journal*, 275-7. The engraving was published by Moon, Boys and Graves. The contract can be viewed in the Graves Manuscripts at the British Museum, Add. MS. 46, pp.140.

xl   J. Pye, *Patronage of British Art, An Historical Sketch* (Longman, 1845) 243, n.52; J. Hogarth in Underdown, *op.cit.*, note 10, at 194. See also Clifford, A. Griffiths & M. Royalton-Kisch, *Gainsborough and Reynolds in the British Museum* (British Museum, 1978), 38; R. Godfrey, 'Conclusion: The Early Nineteenth Century', in D. Alexander & R.T. Godfrey, *Painters and Engraving – The Reproductive Print from Hogarth to Wilkie* (Yale Center for British Art, 1980) p.69.

xli   Godfrey, *ibid.*, 69. However, for some artists the market was erratic. See J. Dustin Wees, 'The Printing and Publishing of John Martin's Plates' in M.J. Campbell, *John Martin: Visionary Printmaker* (Campbell Fine Art, 1992) p.9.

xlii   R. Ormond, *Sir, Edwin Landseer* (Philadelphia Museum of Art, 1982) p.12 (more than half Landseer's income came from copyright fees on engravings). Note also J. Maas, *Gambart- Prince of the Victorian Art World* (Barrie & Jenkins, 1975) p.30; A. Dyson, 'Images Interpreted: Landseer and the Engraving Trade', (1984) 1 *Print Q.* pp.29, 39; C. Fox, 'The Engravers' Battle for Recognition in Early Nineteenth Century London' (1976) *The London Journal*, pp.2-3.

xliii L. Hermann, *Turner Prints:The Engraved Work of J.M.W. Turner* (Phaidon, 1990) 9, p.248. Many of Turner's dealings are related in J. Gage (ed.), *Collected Correspondence of J.M.W.Turner* (Clarendon, 1980).

xliv See W. Frith, *My Autobiography* (Richard Bentley, 1887) Ch.21, esp.p.273; J. Maas, *Holman Hunt and the Light of the World* (Scholar Press, 1984), p.66.

xlv The engraving was published on October 1, 1866. It bears the words 'copyright registered', a reference to the registration of the Frith painting under the 1862 Act.

xlvi L. Hermann, *Nineteenth Century British Painting* (London: de la Mere, 2000) 243; Maas (1984), *op.cit.*, note 44, p.68. The copy in the holdings of the Victoria and Albert Museum bears the signatures of artist and engraver and the stamp of the Print-sellers Association.

xlvii Maas (1975), *op.cit.*, note 42, p.120.

xlviii This was clear from early on. See Sergeant Talfourd, 38 *Parl. Deb.* 872 (1837): 'At present, an engraver or publisher, who has given a large sum for permission to engrave a picture, and expended his money or labour in the plate, may be met by unexpected competition, for which he has no remedy'.

xlix The 1735 Act (8 Geo. 2, ch.13), known as Hogarth's Act, was rather limited, conferring protection only to engravings which were engraved by their 'inventor or designer' or at his/her instigation, and in *Jefferys v. Baldwin* (1753) 1 Amb. 164; 27 E.R. 109, this was held to be limited so that no right arose in favour of a person who employed an engraver to make prints of busses of the British Herring Fishing Society. See also *Blackwell v. Harper* (1740) Barn. C.210, 27 E.R. 616 (engravings of plants fell within statute but engravings from existing prints or drawings would not be protected). The 1767 Act (6 Geo. 3, ch.38) extended such protection to 'any other print or prints whatsoever' and in *Newton v. Cowie* (1827) 4 Bing. 234; 130 E.R. 759, Best CJ held that this meant what it said, so that an engraving based on a drawing in a patent specification was protected. The effect of these two pieces of legislation seems to have been that a print-seller could obtain rights over an engraving either by way of assignment from an artist who had arranged for the engraving of his work, or by assignment from the engraver. Actions against distributors of pirate copies under the 1735 Act required the plaintiff to demonstrate that the defendant knew he was dealing with infringing copies, but this was removed by 17 Geo. 3, ch.56: *Gambart v. Sumner* (1859) 5 H. & N. 5, 157 E.R. 1078.

l For example, the contract between Graves and Wilkie over *The Chelsea Pensioners* required Wilkie to assign 'all his copyright or right in the nature of copyright of and in a certain picture...entitled and known as *The Chelsea Pensioners'*– even though no copyright then existed in a published painting. See Graves Manuscripts, *op.cit.*, note 39, p.20. The *Art Journal* criticised such practices, observing that 'To talk of a 'copyright' in pictures . . . is to speak loosely and without meaning. In legal language, the term as applied to pictures, is unintelligible': 'Property in Art' (1849) *Art Journal*, pp.133, 136.

li (1819) 2 Stark 548; 171 E.R., 732.

lii (1749-1833). The 1817 volumes include three engravings after Reinagle: New Series, Volume 1, between p.32 and p.33, contains the print *Grouse Shooting* but the engraving is attributed to William Nicholls; (1817) vol.50 (Old Series), at p.113, contains *Puffin Shooting at the Back of the Isle of Wight* (engraved by Nichols) p.205, and *Spearing the Otter* (with no attribution of the engraver, but stated to be from a picture by Philip Reinagle 'by his permission'.) The 1816 Volume 48 at p.53 also contains another engraving by W. Nicholls after Reinagle's *Partridge Shooting*.

liii Possibly Charles Thompson (1791-1843) or John Thompson (1785-1866).

liv   Op.cit., note 51 pp.549, 732.

lv   Engravings could take a very long time to produce, and this could delay delivery of the painting to its purchaser for years. Sometimes artists would make available unfinished paintings to engravers so that the latter could undertake preliminary work.

lvi   James Duffield Harding (watercolourist, 1797-1863) (attempts to reserve copyright easily frustrated); Frederick Goodall (1822-1904) gave evidence that 'I sold a picture to a dealer, expressly reserving the copyright; he gave me a letter agreeing to those terms. It subsequently passed from his hands, and a publisher is now having it engraved without my consent'. See Underdown, *op.cit.*, note 11, 180; Anon, 'Property in Art' (1849) *Art Journal*, pp.133, 136 (on sale purchaser gets all rights and is not bound by any prior contract between painter and seller). Cf. Delabere Roberton Blaine, *Artistic Copyright (Report prepared for SEAMC)* (1858) 10 ('contracts are often made by artists with the purchasers of such pictures, by which contract the Engraving Copyright is secured to the artist. Such contracts are constantly avoided by the purchaser selling the picture to a third person without notice of the artist's contract as to the copyright. He is thus defrauded of this property and his fame as an artist is exposed to serious injury'.) It is interesting to note that the period saw the first moves towards recognition of contractual arrangements over property which were capable of binding purchasers thereof: *De Mattos v. Gibson* (1848) 4 De. G. & J. 276, 45 E.R., 108.

lvii With respect to the *The Light of the World* Gambart's expenses were £2000, and sales in the first year of publication £10,000 (1863) *Athenaeum* April 11 (No 1850) 495. As regards *Finding of Christ in the Temple*, he paid £ 5,775 for the painting and its copyright but collected £ 4,000 in exhibition fees, £ 5,000 in profits on the engraving, and sold the picture for £1,500. See G. Reitlinger, *The Economics of Taste – The Rise and Fall of Picture Prices, 1760-1960* (Barrie & Rockliff) vol x, 147. However, only a few artists such as Wilkie, Landseer, Hunt, Frith, and Millais could guarantee these sorts of returns, and not surprisingly these were favoured by the publishers, who competed fiercely to obtain the right to engrave their works: M. Tedeschi, *How Prints Work: Reproductions, Originals and Their Markets in England 1840-1890* (Ph.D. Dissertation, Northwestern University, 1994).

lviii In his speech praying leave to introduce the 1837 Bill, Talfourd had remarked: 'At present, great uncertainty prevails . . . as to the right of engraving from original pictures'. 38 *Parl. Deb.* 872 (1837).

lix   Frank William Topham (1838-1904) complained that '[s]everal years since I sold a drawing without anything being said about copyright. I know that the person to whom I sold it called upon a publisher and offered to sell the copyright for his own emolument'. See Underdown, *op.cit.*, note 11, p.181. Amongst the Graves manuscripts, *op.cit.*, note 39, p.223, there is an example of a contract made by Graves in 1852 with Benjamin Windus, the owner of two Turner drawings, for a loan to have engravings made. There is also a rather strange contract in 1833 between Moon, Boys and Graves and Caroline Lane by which the latter assigned copyright as regard her deceased husband (Theodore)'s painting, *Mathematical Abstraction*, 'the Copyright of which is rightfully vested in me by consent of Lord Northcote, the proprietor of the picture...': *ibid.*, p.36.

lx   See the evidence of Thomas Mogford (painter of portraits and landscapes, 1800-1868) in *ibid.*, p.197 (fee shared by possessor and artist). In many cases the engraver would indicate who owned the painting: see e.g., the engraving of Lawrence's Duke of York by Charles Turner (1821) which refers to the original picture being in the possession of Major General Sir R Brownrigg.

lxi   John Fredrick Lewis (1805-76, President of Water Colourist Society from 1855-7)
        in Underdown, *op.cit.*, note 11, p.174; Sir William Boxall (1800-79, portait painter) in
        ibid., p.175; Frank Topham (1838-1924) in *ibid.*, p.181; Charles Branwhite (Bristol
        landscape painter and watercolourist, 1817-80) in *ibid.*, p.181; C. R. Leslie in
        ibid., p.182. Frith relates one instance where Bell bought a picture (*Sherry, Sir?*) from
        him, sold `copyright' for 40 guineas, and presented Frith with the copyright money;
        however in another cases (e.g., *Pope and Lady Mary*) the owner proceeded to arrange
        for the pictures engraving without consulting Frith and the owner retained the hundred
        guineas he received. See 1 Frith, *op.cit.*, note 44, p.219 ff. However, formal written
        agreements were made by Frith with Flatow in 1860 and Gambart in 1863: these are
        detailed pp.328 and 338. Cf. D. Blaine, *On the Laws of Artistic Copyright and their
        Defects* (John Murray, 1853) pp.39-41.

lxii   Underdown, *op.cit.*, note 11, p.184.

lxiii   See e.g., Moon, Boys and Graves's contract with the painter David Wilkie and engraver
        James Stewart over *The Scottish Wedding*, requiring that Wilkie supervise the progress
        of the engraving and touch proofs: Graves Papers, *op.cit.*, note 39, p.25.

lxiv   J. Hogarth in Underdown, *op.cit.*, note 11, 194 (explaining that one unauthorised engraving
        of Lawrence's portrait of George IV was so poor that 'the public, judging of the picture by
        the print, so estimated it that the picture acquired a very indifferent reputation'.)

lxv   Samuel Palmer (1805-1881) in *ibid.*, p.174 (copying at Royal Academy Exhibition); John
        Linnell (1792-1882) *ibid.*, p.177; George Lance (1802-1864) *ibid.*, p.190; Mr. J. Hogarth
        ibid., p.195. See also Lance, *ibid.*, p.190 ('I know of cases where copies of my works must
        have been made during the time of their exhibition') and Mogford, *ibid.*, p.196, ('I saw an
        artist making a facsimile of Landseer's *Peace* in the Vernon Gallery, and other pictures by
        living artists in the same collection being copied'.) In 1860, the problem of copying in art
        galleries was referred to in the Journal of the Society of Arts: (7 December 1860) 9 *J.Soc'y
        Arts* p.44. A debate ensued, see 9 *J.Soc'y Arts* pp.82, 92, 101, (21 December 1860,
        28 December 1860, 4 January 1861).

lxvi   Underdown op.cit, note 11., *The Fighting Temeraire* was exhibited at the Royal Academy
        in 1839 and Hogarth's gallery in 1844. It was engraved by J.T. Willmore and the engraving
        was published in 1845. It was later re-engraved on steel by Willmore for the series,
        The Turner Gallery, (1859).

lxvii   See 1 Frith, *op.cit.*, note 44, p.212.

lxviii W. Ivins, *Prints and Visual Communication* (M.I.T. Press, 1969), p.124.

lxix   T. Fawcett, *The Rise of English Provincial Art – Artists, Patrons, and Institutions outside
        London, 1800-1830* (Clarendon, 1974) p.192.

lxx   On limitations affecting the ability of photography to satisfactorily reproduce paintings,
        see T. Fawcett, 'Graphic versus Photographic in the Nineteenth Century Reproduction'
        (1986) 9 *Art History* pp.185-212. Photomechanical techniques of reproduction really began
        to replace engraving in the 1880s: A. Griffiths, *Prints and Printmaking: An Introduction
        to the History and Techniques* (2nd edn., British Museum, 1996) 56;
        W. Ivins, *op.cit.*, note 68, p.93.

lxxi   Cf J. Ford, *Ackermann 1793-1983, The Business of Art*, p.147 (Ackermann, 1983)
        (arguing that photography 'was beginning to challenge engraving and lithography
        as a means of reproducing images, bringing with it a sense of quickening change and
        unease to traditional print-makers').

lxxii   E. Gambart, *On Piracy of Artistic Copyright* (Tegg, 1863) pp.5, 7. Pirate copies were produced within one hour of the publication of the original art work, and for as little as one shilling. The (1872) *Art Journal*, p.208 stated that photography's 'finest works are reproduction of engravings . . .' See also Underdown *op.cit.*, note 11, p.11:'now that the methods of reproduction by means of photography and chromolithography have reached such perfection, and facsimiles can be so easily made, this protection and recognition have become far more necessary than before, indeed the right of multiplying copies is in many cases more valuable than the original work itself'

lxxiii   *Ibid.*, 7. Lithographic techniques could be used to make colour reproductions.

lxxiv   See *Gambart v. Hamilton & Bewley* (1859) *The Athenaeum* 9 July (No 1654); *Gambart v. Palmer* (1862) *The Athenaeum* 15 November 15, 630 (failed), (1862) *The Athenaeum* 20 December (No 1834), 806 (£10 damages); *Gambart v. Powell & Pipere* (1862) *Art Journal* (December) p.241; *Gambart v. Sclater* (1863) *The Athenaeum* 11 April (No 1850) p.495, (1863) *Art Journal*, p.106 (£100 damages); *Gambart v. Mayne* (1863) 14 C.B. (N.S.) 320, 143 E.R., 469 (attempt to get retrial where initial action had failed). For an assessment, see Maas (1975), *op.cit.*, note 42, p.112.

lxxv   Cited in Maas (1975), *op.cit.*, note 42, p.159.

lxxvi   14 C.B.(N.S.) 306, 143 E.R. 463 (1863). Also described in (1863) *The Athenaeum* Jan 24 (No.1839) p.121; May 9 (No 1854); (1863) *Art Journal*, pp.210-11.

lxxvii   Apparently Gambart paid Bonheur £1600 for the painting and its copyright, and spent 800 guineas on its engraving, but made £29,000 from sales of the print. See Tedeschi, *op.cit.*, note 57, p.26.

lxxviii   The 1777 Act, 17 Geo.3, ch.57, gave the proprietor of an engraving a special action upon the case against infringer with a possibility of damages and recovery of double the costs of suit. The 1735 Act, 8 Geo.2, ch.13; had only given a right to obtain forfeiture of infringing plates and copies and penalties of 5 shillings per print. 1767, 6 Geo.3, ch.38; Byles J., *op.cit.*, note 76, pp.319, 408, observed that 'the confusion of words in these statutes is great, but I think no-one will say that they fail for want of words'.

lxxix   The International Copyright Act 1852 15 & 16 Vict. ch.12, s.14, had extended the scope of the Engravings Acts 'to include prints taken by lithography or any other mechanical process by which prints or impressions of drawings or designs are capable of being multiplied indefinitely'.

lxxx   *Op.cit.*, pp.317, 468.

lxxxi   *Op.cit.*, pp.319-20, 468-9.

lxxxii   Tedeschi, *op.cit.*, note 57, 31 (copper plates rarely produced more that 500 impressions, but steel plates could produce 30,000.) For the latter figure see J. Burnet, *op.cit.*, note 39, p.276.

lxxxiii   E. Chambers, *An Indolent and Blundering Art: The Etching Revival and the Redefinition of Etching in England 1838-1892* (Ashgate, 1999) Ch.3.

lxxxiv   Gambart's practice with respect Holman Hunt's *The Finding of Christ in the Temple* illustrates this perfectly: Gambart planned to sell between 1000 and 2000 'artist proofs' at 15 guineas, 1000 'proof before letters' at 12 guineas, 1000 proofs at 8 guineas and 10,000 prints at 5 guineas. See M. Tedeschi, *op.cit.*, note 57, p.58.

lxxxv   Chambers, *op.cit.*, note 83.

lxxxvi   (1862) *The Athenaeum* 17 November (No 1829) p.630. See also 20 December (No 1834) 806 (referring to 'false and vicious' system of proofs and arguing that photographs did not harm sales and could provide publicity.)

lxxxvii   E. Gambart (1862) *The Athenaeum* 6 December (No 1832) pp.736-737.

lxxxviii E. Gambart (1862) *The Athenaeum* 27 December (No 1835) p.847.

lxxxix E. Gambart (1862) *The Athenaeum* 22 November (No 1830) p.663.

xc 1 Frith, *op.cit.*, note 44, at 212, commented that 'I have suffered so dreadfully from translation of my pictures by photogravure, that I hold the method in absolute abhorrence'.

xci J. Maas (1984), *op.cit.*, note 44, p.67.

xcii See A. Dyson, *op.cit.*, note 42, p.39.

Copies and Translations

Richard Shone

As a practice at the very centre of the Western tradition of art, making copies has assumed a multifarious variety of forms and uses. At one extreme, it means the manufacture of a minute replica of another artist's work as a marketable object; at the other, a free variation of a work in which the value lies in imaginative transformation rather than in verisimilitude.

Of course, no replica can be exact. No matter how hard the young studio apprentice tried to imitate and please his master, his copy was inflected by his own sensibility, by his innate rhythms and sense of emphasis, even when attempting to suppress them. This was usually more apparent if the student was destined to become an artist of consequence. Degas' drawings after the old masters, for example, are wonderfully respectful but, knowing his later work, we are able to recognise certain inflections and minute alterations as inescapably his. In the same way, no matter what liberties one artist takes with the work of another in a free variation, an echo of the original source remains. The greys and blacks of Manet's habitual palette, for example, retain their presence in Jasper Johns's *Catenary (Manet-Degas)* of 1999, a painting that, at first glance, appears to have little relation to its source, the fragments of Manet's *Execution of Maximilian* in the National Gallery, London. But a work such as the Johns, complex as it is, does not raise the questions and problems that inevitably occur when direct copies are under consideration.

A good deal of the bricks and mortar of art history has involved the making of distinctions between an autograph work and a replica (by the same or a different hand). Sorting out productions by studio assistants from those by close imitators and deciding what is a contemporary and what a later copy. This establishes an *œuvre* and sets the parameters for a monograph or a *catalogue raisonné*. Such connoisseurship is rarer now than it once was, but it is still meat and drink to the salerooms where huge sums of money depend on such attributions. In 2001, for example, Christie's in Rome offered what was catalogued as a nineteenth-century copy of a work by the Dutch seventeenth-century artist, Jan van de Capelle; it was withdrawn just before the auction and placed in Christie's prestigious London sale of old masters in December 2001 as an autograph winter scene by Van de Cappelle with an estimate many times that given in Rome. It sold spectacularly for over three-quarters of a million pounds and is a perfect example of the supreme value set on originality. There are also distinctions to be made between an original painting and re-workings done much later, in which an artist or restorer, perhaps a century or two afterwards, has altered the work to bring it within the orbit of contemporary taste and expectations. Fig leaves or convenient draperies have been introduced, family crests painted out, religious sentiment increased by a new upturn of the eyes or a more abject or appealing gesture of the hands, or the framing and background have been altered to suit current decorative style (famously seen in Lorenzo di Credi's alterations to Fra Angelico's San Domenica altarpiece in Fiesole). Here one can run into the problem of a work by a competent artist given a new lease of life by a much more interesting one.

A direct copy of another work is, of course, quite distinct in intention from a deliberate forgery. The latter may well contain elements lifted from the work of the artist being forged, but the end result will be passed off as a 'new' work by that artist. Forgery is the result of a technically adroit hand and a mind usually devoid of any personal originality but one that is magpie-like in its appropriation of a salient autograph style. Persuasive pastiche is its hallmark. The cunning rests in giving people – experts and the general public alike – something they want to see and to believe in. The most famous example is that of Hans van Meegeren, a disappointed Dutch artist who developed highly elaborate technical procedures to forge the work of his historic countryman, Vermeer. He artfully chose Vermeer's early period and filled in the apparent gaps in the Delft artist's development, beginning with a *Christ at Emmaus* in 1937. So expert is its handling, it took in the great historian and critic Abraham Bredius and proved to be the first step of Van Meegeren's course of revenge on an artworld that he felt had not given him his due when he had exhibited his own paintings. Several further Vermeers were produced, but he was eventually caught, tried, convicted of fraud, and died a few weeks after his trial in 1945. His forgeries now, of course, have a value of their own: they are original Van Meegerens, and his brilliance is recognised as residing not in the forgeries themselves but in supplying works at a moment when the romance of Vermeer's obscurity and the rarity of his paintings fuelled an unprecedented commercial demand.

Deliberate forgery such as this takes us perhaps too far from the time-honoured and fruitful practice of copying. Copies were crucial to the continuously evolving language of art. Like babies learning to speak by imitation, one generation of artists handed down its grammar and syntax, expanded or retracted, to the next. It would be a mistake, however, to think that copying virtually died out in the late nineteenth and early twentieth centuries. There are instructive examples of accurate copies by more recent artists in which the exercise has helped them to forge their own original style. There was the young Balthus, whose 1926-27 copies of Piero della Francesca, made in Arezzo, determined both the chalky aspects of his characteristic colour as well as the disposition of figures in some of his best-known early paintings, such as *La Rue*. Henry Moore in Italy during the 1920s found frescoes rather than sculpture a more fruitful source, remarking that 'Giotto's painting is the finest sculpture' he encountered in Italy; but his most accurate copy was an ink study after a drawing attributed to Jacopo Bellini, which he made from an Alinari photograph. More recently, Bridget Riley made a painstaking replica in 1959 of Seurat's painting *The Bridge at Courbevoie* (Courtauld Institute Gallery, London), helping her to understand aspects of colour contrasts and masses at a critical moment in her career.

Examples such as those given above were highly personal transactions. Most copies in the past were widely used to disseminate knowledge of famous works and were made by professional copyists. Apart from painting, engraving became the popular medium for this kind of copying. It is comparatively cheap, easily transported and, in relation to oil on canvas or panel, is less labour intensive. The engraved version of Raphael's *Judgment of Paris*, made by Marcantonio Raimondi, is the most celebrated example of an influential source, for it lies behind Manet's *Déjeuner sur l'herbe*, 1862-63 (Musée d'Orsay, Paris), which in turn provoked Picasso's great series of variations (in several media) a century later (see Karsten Schubert's essay).

This brings us to the translation of one artist's work by another, a meeting at the half-way house between minute replica and deliberate forgery. This is by far the most interesting aspect of 'copying', for it adds sometimes significant works to an artist's *œuvre* and can refresh our appreciation of past art. As Roger Fry wrote: 'Each generation, almost each decade, has to remake its Old Masters. If we did not continually go on revaluing and remaking them, they would be not merely old, but dead'. Here artists are attracted to the singling out of certain qualities for emphasis or elaboration. These might include the overall design, colouristic aspects, elements of the subject matter itself, any or all of which chime with the interpreters' own interests and practice, sometimes at a profound, even subconscious level.

Take, for example, Matisse's *La desserte*, which the artist copied in 1893 from a still life by Jan Davidsz de Heem in the Louvre. The Dutch painting is a luxurious tumble of fruit, flowers, and vessels, a mandolin, and a white napkin hanging from the table top, all projecting from a dark surrounding interior. Matisse's copy emphasises the rhythmic complexity of the original, its echoing verticals and elipses. Here we see Matisse the spatial designer rather than the inventive colourist; even so, it is essentially a copy rather than a work of originality. But in 1915, Matisse returned to the de Heem, and while he retained many of the compositional features of the still life, he painted an unmistakable Matisse. Filtered through his own immediately preceding paintings influenced by Cubism (such as the 1914 *Goldfish and Palette*, Museum of Modern Art, New York), the result is a magnificent, elaborate translation. When we look at a typical later interior by Matisse, such as *Still Life With a Sleeping Woman* (1939-40, National Gallery, Washington), the spatial sequence across the canvas is undoubtedly informed by his early study of the Dutch still life.

With the increasingly widespread supply of photographs in the nineteenth century, the commercial need for copies and engravings abated. But there was one artist who made vivid use of prints from the works of earlier artists. Vincent van Gogh made copies after Rembrandt, Delacroix, Millet, Doré, Daumier, and others, nearly all from etchings and wood-engravings. He gave various reasons for making this body of work, mostly carried out when he was recovering from his mental breakdown in the asylum at Saint-Rémy. He could paint figures without recourse to models ('I shall not lose sight of the figure, even though I have no models at the moment' he wrote to his brother Theo on 19 September 1889). He found consolation and pleasure in such work: 'I let the black and white by Delacroix or Millet ... pose for me as a subject. And then I improvise colour on it ... searching for memories of *their* pictures'. Van Gogh thought of his copies as translations into another language, and he was not unaware that copying might seem old fashioned but, rather, at this particularly fragile moment in his life, he obviously found reassurance in turning to the work of his heroes. However, he was not without scruples when carrying out such copies, feeling he might be accused of plagiarism. He once forwarded to his friend John Peter Russell a batch of prints his brother had sent to him in order not to be tempted to make further translations. The last of the series is a version of Millet's celebrated *Sower*, carried out in February 1890. There followed two months of crippling mental illness, but when he resumed painting on his move to Auvers-sur-Oise, the emphatic linearism that had become evident in his copies was now intensified in his Auvers landscapes, along with the development of an even more arbitrary palette partly induced by his need to invent colour when working from black and white sources.

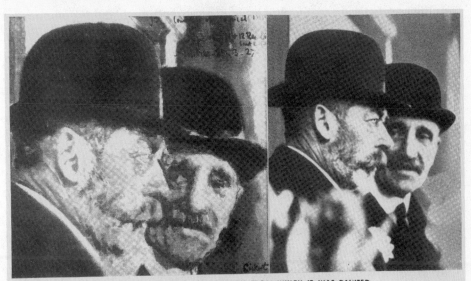

SICKERT PORTRAIT OF THE KING AND THE PHOTOGRAPH FROM WHICH IT WAS PAINTED

Mr. Richard Sickert's finely impressionist study in oils of the King (on left) to be shown privately at the Lefevre Galleries, King Street, St. James's, and, on right, the newspaper photograph from which the portrait was painted. The King was photographed talking to Major Fetherstonhaugh, his racing manager, during a Grand National at Aintree

In the twentieth century, photographs of works of art have been the most common source for copies and translations, as well as those elements of appropriation and extrapolation that frequently occur in collage and silkscreen printing (as in, for example, Robert Rauschenberg's 1964 *Tracer*, which is dominated by a Rubens nude Venus seen from the back). But it would be mistaken to think that this use of photographs was an especially modernist practice. In the nineteenth century, they were welcomed by academic and conservative figurative artists who took from them particular poses or gestures for incorporation into their own work. We know too that, although they were not always happy to reveal their sources, painters as distinct as Gustave Moreau, Thomas Eakins, and Franz von Stuck relied on photographs, chiefly of the human figure, that were either purchased, especially commissioned, or taken by the artists themselves. In the twentieth century, artists have appropriated photographic images of every kind, especially from newspapers and magazines (most famously used by Picasso for *Guernica*) right up to digitally enhanced images of a projected future.

One of the most extraordinary bodies of work based on photographs is that of Walter Sickert. What is remarkable here is that his embrace of the medium as a source occurred in the late years of his life, from the 1920s to his death in 1942, after he had gained his earlier reputation for a spontaneous handling of paint and immediate reactions to his subject following impressionist procedures. In fact, his spontaneity was nearly always mediated through the time-honoured practice of careful preparatory studies. Later on, the photograph took the place of these drawn and elaborately notated, squared-up studies. Some of these photographs he took himself, others were taken by assistants under his direction; but the most famous works of his late years relied on newspaper photographs recording people and events of the day, subject matter of which Sickert had little or no personal experience. He usually produced such works very swiftly while the person or event was still newsworthy. This was the case with his transcription of the arrival in England of Amelia Earhart after her solo transatlantic flight, a painting exhibited on 30 May 1932, exactly seven days after its photographic source had appeared on the front page of the *Daily Sketch*. Occasionally Sickert blatantly acknowledged the commercial source of his image on his canvas: one of the best of these, showing George V and his racing manager at Aintree, has inscribed in Sickert's hand at the top: 'By Courtesy of Topical Press Agency/11 and 12 Red Lion/Court E.C.4/Aintree - 25.3.27'. This caused considerable surprise when the work was shown in 1931, so much so that the picture was refused when offered as a gift to the Glasgow City Art Gallery and again when offered to the Tate Gallery. Some press photographers were indignant at Sickert's borrowings, seen as an infringement of their copyright. At the same time, when Sickert had recommended the use of photographs to students at the Royal Academy Schools in the 1920s, the press got hold of the story and disparaged the artist's unconventional advice. For them, it undermined the idea of originality in art, whereas we can now see it as one of Sickert's most innovative contributions. In fact, his work of the 1930s was prophetic of much photo-based painting of later decades, and parallels have justly been drawn between his work and that of such artists as Warhol, Bacon, Kitaj, and Richard Hamilton.

We have moved a long way from the laborious copy, carried out by a student or apprentice, with nail-biting fidelity, but while aspiring artists today rarely make copies in the same spirit, the art of an earlier age still has universal appeal for current practitioners – from profound homage to jocund pilfering. It is perhaps the variety of ways and consequent multiplicity of meanings in which the past surfaces in the present that distinguishes our own time. In previous centuries, artists would appropriate figures or passages from art history to be subsumed in their own productions. Originality of subject and even composition was less important than impact of vision and personal handling of a theme. Today, flooded with information and the daily torrent of visual images from the press, film, television, and the internet, artists are more likely to appropriate from other art in a much more self-conscious way, often reading old images through the spectacles of new agendas and placing the past in quotation marks. We have had Polke making paintings after Goya; Salle including a Hobbema landscape in a multi-image painting; Cy Twombly raiding Turner and Richter's unfocused versions of Titian. None of their works would have been made with the originals immediately to hand.

Other artists have recreated works of the past as *tableaux-vivants* in order to photograph themselves in an assumed role: Cindy Sherman and Yasumasa Morimura are notable practitioners in a line that goes back to the narrative situations influenced by the old masters in Julia Margaret Cameron's photographs in the 1860s. The recreation in three-dimensional terms of a specific painting is less common, but we have recently seen Anthony Caro's sculptural expositions of works by Duccio and Van Gogh; and Gavin Turk's 'self portrait' as Marat in his bath after Jacques-Louis David. In these examples, all the works that have provided the sources were safely out of copyright. To quote or re-interpret work by living or recently dead artists occupies a murky middle-ground between influence and appropriation. The painter Glenn Brown, well known for his replicas of reproductions of works by Dalí and Auerbach, ran into trouble when he took the cover design, by Anthony Roberts, of a paperback sci-fi novel for children as the basis for his painting, *The Loves of Shepherds (After Double Star by Tony Roberts)* 2000. The designer's attention was drawn to the work when it was shown at Brown's Turner Prize display at Tate Britain in 2000. The title explicitly refers to Fragonard's famous series of decorations *The Loves of Shepherds* more commonly known as *The Pursuit of Love* (1771-72, Frick Collection, New York) with their airy, sensuous images of youthful ardour, pursuit, and declarations. The frolicsome fantasy of these decorations haunts Brown's painting, combining, as it does, references to traditional pastoral (and earlier works by Boucher) and a now somewhat outdated sci-fi fantasy. It is highly indicative of the complexities of creativity that Brown's work should now be the subject of a case of infringement of copyright.

The author wishes to thank Caroline Elam and Bart Cornelis of *The Burlington Magazine* for help in the writing of this essay. The quotation from Roger Fry is taken from his catalogue preface to an exhibition of *Copies and Translations* held at the Omega Workshops, London, in 1917. For Van Gogh and copying see, among others, Ronald Pickvance *Van Gogh in Saint-Rémy and Auvers*, (exhibition catalogue, Metropolitan Museum of Art, New York, 1986). For further discussion of Sickert and his sources, see the present writer in *Sickert: Paintings* (edited by W. Baron and R. Shone), Royal Academy of Arts, London, 1992.

Richard Shone is an Associate Editor of The Burlington Magazine, and the author of several books on nineteenth and twentieth century art.

Raphael's Shadow: On Copying and Creativity

Karsten Schubert

The verb 'to copy' means very different things to different people. In an accusatory legal context, 'to copy' describes an act of intellectual trespassing, often clandestine and performed for base motives, an act to be discouraged and punished whenever possible. The negative terms it is here given imply an objectionable lack of imagination, intellectual rectitude, and moral sense.[i] For artists, on the other hand, 'to copy' carries completely different connotations. When asked by André Warron about the issue of copying, Pablo Picasso replied:

> They said that when I began in Paris I copied Toulouse-Lautrec and Steinlen. Possible, but never was a painting by Toulouse-Lautrec or Steinlen taken for mine. It is better to copy a drawing or painting than to try to be inspired by it, to make something similar. In that case one risks painting only the faults of the model. A painter's atelier should be a laboratory. One doesn't make a monkey's job there: one invents.[ii]

In the laboratory of the artist's studio, the copy is allocated a place of special importance and honour, something not simply helpful, but central and indispensable to the creative enterprise. We can illustrate what Picasso meant by looking at a specific group of works in his oeuvre, a group that its self forms part of what is one of the most sustained and substantial sequences of copying and counter-copying in Western art. It is a sequence that reads like a roll call of European painting.

The protagonists are Raphael, the etcher Marcantonio Raimondi, Edouard Manet and Picasso himself, with Giorgione, Titian, Watteau, Courbet, Cezanne and many others on the sidelines. At the beginning of this 500-year sequence stands a drawing by Raphael, at the end, Picasso's 1959-61 series of paintings after Manet's *Le Déjeuner sur l'Herbe*. What happened in between – and why it happened – is the subject of the following overview.

Raphael

Raphael's lost drawing, *The Judgement of Paris*,[iii] is a tour-de-force illustrating his ability to draw together different sources to create a homogenous composition: two Roman sarcophagi (one at the time in the Villa Medici, the other in the Villa

Marco Dente da Ravenna, *The Judgement of Paris (after Raphael and Raimondi), 1520/27*

Pamphili) have been identified as sources, and in the figure of Paris we can detect the *Torso de Belvedere*. All the other figures are based on antique sources as well – if not directly, at least by way of allusions. These allusions would not have been lost on Raphael's highly educated audience. According to Vasari, Raphael's composition was held in high esteem by much of the artistic community of Rome. It is easy to understand why: it was in effect a one-sheet pattern-book, supplying artists with a wide range of inspirations based on some of the most celebrated antiquities known at the time, succinctly summarising contemporary preoccupations with particular antique models. The drawing became so famous, it was soon chosen as a subject by Marcantonio Raimondi,[iv] the great exponent of early Italian printmaking.[v]

Raimondi was at the time in the employment of Raphael, who may have been the first artist to understand the importance of having his images disseminated as widely as possible. In fact, much of Raphael's early influence could arguably be attributed to Raimondi's etchings.[vi] So large was the demand for *The Judgement of Paris*, for example, that Marco Dente da Ravenna made a slavish copy a few years later [vii] of Raimondi's print, clearly with the intention of deceiving buyers into thinking that *his* was the original.[viii]

In the chain from Raphael to Picasso, the Raimondi copy is the most straightforward link, constituting as it does an absolutely faithful rendering of Raphael's composition for general distribution, allowing artists who were not able to see Raphael's original to learn from it. The correct credits were given in the inscription and added with the artist's consent (and probably financially benefited him as well). Raimondi's etching is also a reminder of the important role copies play in art history: with Raphael's original lost, Raimondi's etching is the only first-hand record of the work known to us.

Raphael/Manet

Three hundred and fifty years later, when Manet turned to the Raimondi print[ix] for inspiration, the artistic agenda was much less clear. No longer was the goal a workmanlike, reliable copy of the source. Although certainly interested in the compositional potential of the Raphael, Manet was clearly also focusing on what Raphael had come to represent in the intervening time. The choice of a lost Raphael work allowed the reference without inviting direct, distracting comparison. Although *Le Déjeuner sur l'herbe* summarises an entire raft of influences and references by way of direct quotation, pastiche, and allusion, it is the specific Raphael source I will focus on.[x]

In the nineteenth century, Raphael was universally considered the greatest painter of all time, an artist whose position was unassailable. Manet invoked this status for his own purposes, paying homage to his source, while at the same time claiming similar status (that of a masterpiece) for his own work.[xi] He achieved this complex goal by turning *The Judgement of Paris* into an anti-model for his own activity and in the process recontextualised and updated the composition. By making a figurative group at the periphery of Raphael's composition the centre of his own, and by recasting Raphael's mythological subject matter into a scene from contemporary life, Manet stripped the image of its original meaning. All that remains are the poses and the gaze – a gaze melancholic and gentle in *The Judgement of Paris*, but scandalously challenging and provocative in *Le Déjeuner*. The great liberty Manet took with Raphael's composition, and the degree to which he transformed it, only further underlined the magnitude of his own achievement.

When Manet's *Le Déjeuner* was first shown in the 1873 Salon des Refuses, it caused an outcry, the echoes of which have long reverberated through the history of art. The painting outraged the public: for the majority of contemporary observers, it was shocking subject matter painted in an even more shocking manner. Of course, Manet's painting has since taken a central place in the history of modern art, partly because with hindsight we now understand Manet's intentions, and partly because of what has since accrued to *Le Déjeuner*. Its status today is such that it is difficult to look at it with any degree of objectivity. *Le Déjeuner* has become obscured by its own mythology.

In spite of its status as the first great masterpiece of modern art, *Le Déjeuner* can seem tentative because of the irresolvable contradictions and tensions it contains. There is the tension between the perceived realism and the self-conscious and decidedly anti-realistic handling of paint and pictorial space. The 'rude' realism of the scene is also countered by the fact that the composition is not as casual as at first glance it may seem but is in fact based on classical sources. Besides referring to *The Judgement of Paris*, Manet quotes from *Le Concerte Champetre* (Louvre) – a painting at that time attributed to Giorgione, but today accepted as being by the young Titian. There are other, less obvious derivations: the background landscape recalls Courbet, and there are echoes of Watteau's Arcadian scenes – which in their turn were influenced by Giorgione. Thus Manet's canvas, rather than marking a complete breach with the past, pays fulsome homage to the great tradition of Western painting. That a work so revolutionary should be steeped so firmly in history only added to contemporary puzzlement.

Much has been made of the almost Greenbergian quality of *Le Déjeuner*, that is to say its utter flatness and denial of pictorial depth. The figures resemble cut-outs, held in place between sheets of glass.[xii] The similarity of scale between the main group of figures and the bather in the background only underlines this spatial claustrophobia. The landscape is sketchy and vague, almost an afterthought or listlessly painted backdrop. In *Le Déjeuner*, Manet essays through most genres of painting as practised at the time: landscape, still life, mythology, and portraiture. At a stretch, one could even interpret the odd bird in mid-flight at the top of the canvas as a nod to religious painting. And there is the strange tension between the outdoors and the posed studio air of the composition. Using unheard of juxtapositions, Manet imploded the stifling conventions of genres, and the unnerving realism so many contemporaries commented on is the outcome of this strategy. Perhaps the reason for the great shock Manet's contemporaries felt when they saw *Le Déjeuner* for the first time also lies here: nudity and sexuality had always been a staple of painting, and of Salon painting in particular, but in the Salon, these subjects were carefully crouched in mythological or historical guises. Manet does away with this safety net: the nude in profile, though taken from Raphael, is no longer nude in the way that mythological nudes are. Rather, they are *naked*, as is made blatantly clear by the still life of hastily removed clothing in the foreground, implying the woman has only just undressed. She stares at the onlooker in the most nonchalant manner, if not quite challenging, then neither perturbed in the slightest by the realisation that she is being observed. Her gaze is unapologetic, and to the contemporary public, used to the presentation of woman

Edouard Manet, *Le Déjeuner Sur l'Herbe*, 1862-63

as meek and submissive (unless they came in the guise of goddesses), this assertiveness must have read like a great provocation.[xiii] Mirroring the ambiguity of the subject matter, Manet's handling of paint caused equal consternation. *Le Déjeuner* is characterised by a disunity of style, space, location, and narrative, a narrative we, the viewers, have disrupted.

Le Déjeuner is not unresolved (as is often claimed)[xiv] but irresolvable, permanently in a state of intended dialectical flux. Its miracle is to achieve equilibrium between parts and genres that over time have lost their validity. Here, each genre, tired from overuse and thoughtless application, is given a new lease on life, though forever pitched on the knife's edge. *Le Déjeuner* is a self-conscious, unqualified hymn to the craft of painting. It is a painted manifesto, a declaration of what is possible after decades of stagnation. Much of what it contains is now commonplace in the Modernist canon. Its declarative nature has become part of art history in the same way that manifestos have become staples of Modernism. Even the eclat *Le Déjeuner* caused in 1873 has become part of the avant-garde gambit, a benchmark for artistic dissent and the fury it can unleash.

Manet's painting is both a blueprint for modern painting and its first realisation, and in this respect it has remained very much a painter's painting. Picasso's
attitude toward it confirms this, but I shall argue that in his case there is a further
dimension that links him much more deeply and personally to Manet's masterpiece.
Manet and *Le Déjeuner* held a special place in Picasso's mind. The *Le Déjeuner*
paraphrases of 1959-61 were by no means the first (or indeed the last) time Picasso
engaged with the painting, but they remain his most sustained comment on Manet
and his work, and they had the most profound effect on Picasso for the rest of his life.

Manet and Picasso

On his first visit to Paris in 1900, the nineteen-year-old Picasso had a rare opportunity to see *Le Déjeuner* in the exhibition of nineteenth-century French painting
that was included in the Exposition Universelle. Although the scandal it had
caused at the Salon des Refuses in 1873 was not forgotten, the work's importance
in the evolution of Modern French art was now recognised. Unfortunately, Picasso's immediate response to the canvas is not recorded, but one only needs to look at
his portrait group, *The Soler Family* of 1903,[xv] with its awkward composition,
harsh, even lighting, and strange flat figures, to see that *Le Déjeuner* had made an
impact on the young painter. Taking Manet's strategy a step further, Picasso placed
the members of the Soler family against a pale blue ground, thereby underscoring
the painting's lack of spatial depth.[xvi]

We find the next reference to *Le Déjeuner* in a letter written by Andre Souares
to the couturier and great collector, Jacques Doucet in March 1924. The occasion
was Doucet's acquisition of Picasso's *Demoiselles d'Avignon* (1907):[xvii]

> I am amazed that you have managed to become the owner of the most
> lasting work we have today ... *Les Demoiselles des Avignon* could not
> be anywhere but at your house, while waiting for the museum where
> it will eventually go. I think in it Picasso has shown the full reach of
> his capabilities. It is his *Card Players* [Cezanne]. As with the other
> painters of our time, with the exception of Gauguin, what he lacks is
> thought. In this painting, however, he has put all the brains he has.
> His admirable touch and miraculous sense of values did the rest. Did
> I say The *Card Players*? What I should have said is that these *Demoi-
> selles* are Picasso's *Déjeuner sur l'herbe*. He did, moreover, have this
> secretly in mind.[xviii]

He did, moreover, have this secretly in mind. Souare's reference is as tantalising as
it is frustrating, because we have no further proof that what he claims is true. This

is not to say that we should automatically mistrust or discount him, but there is no other confirmation, either from Picasso himself or from a third party in his inner circle. There are nevertheless a great many parallels between the two paintings and enough circumstantial evidence to back up Souares's assertion that Picasso intended *Les Demoiselles d'Avignon* as a manifesto painting, modelled after *Le Déjeuner* both in spirit and ambition. Manet saw himself as the Baudelaerian painter of modern life, and it is highly likely that Picasso, three decades later, understood his own role in a similar way. It would therefore be only natural for the young painter to turn to a historic precursor with whom he shared an agenda of comparable radicalism and programmatic ambition. Why Picasso kept to himself the fact that he considered *Les Demoiselles* his *Déjeuner* is understandable. It would have been very difficult at that time for an unknown painter to make such an outlandish claim. Modesty forbade a public declaration of his intentions. There is, nevertheless, one direct reference to *Le Déjeuner* in Picasso's painting: the still life in the foreground of Manet's canvas occupies a similar place to the one in *Les Demoiselles*.

As time passed and *Les Demoiselles d'Avignon* itself acquired iconic status – becoming for twentieth-century art history what *Le Déjeuner* is for the nineteenth century – many of the parallels between the two works became more obvious. These are not so much formal-stylistic parallels – though they could be and have been construed as such. Like *Le Déjeuner*, *Les Demoiselles* is characterised by a series of stylistic fissures and inconsistencies. In Picasso's case, the question has been raised as to whether *Les Demoiselles* is actually unfinished.[xix] Picasso always skirted the issue when asked about its finished or unfinished status, but his unwillingness to answer the question may indicate that in a modernist context the answer was no longer of consequence.[xx]

As far as the respective histories of the two paintings are concerned, there are uncanny similarities: for all their fame, they both remained remarkably invisible until the 1940s. *Le Déjeuner* was in private hands until it was acquired by the Louvre in 1934, but only publicly displayed in 1947 at the Jeu de Paume. Before this, it had been exhibited on only a handful of occasions: in 1863, as already mentioned, during the Exposition Universelle of 1900, and as part of the Manet retrospective at the Orangerie des Tuileries in 1932.[xxi] It is very likely on that occasion Picasso wrote on the back of an envelope: 'When I see Manet's *Déjeuner sur l'herbe* I say to myself trouble in store for later'.[xxii]

If *Le Déjeuner* was rarely on public view, *Les Demoiselles* had received an even lower profile:[xxiii] though known and discussed in avant-garde circles, it was first exhibited nine years after Picasso painted it. It was then that the picture was seen by Jacques Doucet, who finally acquired it from Picasso in 1924. A few years after Doucet's death, his widow sold it in 1937 to the Museum of Modern Art in New York, and it was there that the public 'career' of *Les Demoiselles* began. Alfred Barr, the museum's founding director, allocated it a central place in his emerging narrative of modern art. To this day *Les Demoiselles* stands firmly at the heart of an institution that itself takes up the most commanding place in the history of twentieth century art.

From mythological invisibility to central placement in the Jeu de Paume and the Museum of Modern Art respectively, both paintings eventually attained iconic status. By mid-century, Picasso could finally admit the connection between *Le Déjeuner* and *Les Demoiselles*. Yet, other than in a few unremarkable drawings in 1954, no further references to Manet appeared until 1959, when Picasso began his *Dejeuners* series [xxiv] – twenty-eight paintings, about one-hundred-and-fifty drawings, a series of related sculptures, and linocuts – a project that was to occupy him for the better part of two years until August 1961. But why did Picasso choose Manet and why *Le Déjeuner*? Why respond to Manet's masterpiece so obsessively? And why did he embark upon such a project from 1959 to 1961 – during the later stages of his career?

Manet was by no means the only artist Picasso paraphrased during those years, but this particular dialogue is distinguished for being the most extended, productive, and tightly focused. Picasso's paraphrases of the old masters had begun in 1955 with the *Women of Algiers* series (after Delacroix), an exercise that was followed by the 1957 *Las Meninas* set after Velazquez. Another, smaller and more sporadic series after Holbein (also 1957) was inspired by a book on the German Renaissance painter Picasso had been given by his long-time dealer and friend, Daniel-Henry Kahnweiler. That same year Picasso also turned to Rembrandt, and the series of paraphrases came to a close in 1962 with the *Rape of the Sabines* variations after Poussin. Each series touched on a wide number of concerns that interested Picasso, yet on every occasion it is possible to identify one central motivation: for example, the Delacroix variations are Picasso's homage to Matisse (who had died the previous year), and *Las Meninas* were a reflection on Picasso's Spanish origins. The final series in the sequence, after Poussin's *Rape of the Sabines*, is a musing on French (and Picasso's own) classicism.

This preoccupation with the old masters during the second half of the 1950s may seem to indicate a conscious opting-out of contemporary discourse. It cannot have escaped Picasso during this period that for the first time in his life he was no longer at the forefront of contemporary art. In the mid-1950s, his pre-eminence was challenged by a generation of younger artists for whom he had become an anachronism. To make matters worse, Picasso's sense of artistic impotence was mirrored by dramatic changes in his private life. In 1954, Francoise Gilot had left Picasso with their two young children, Claude and Paloma. Their relationship had been deteriorating gradually,[xxv] but Gilot's final departure nevertheless came as a great shock: here, for the first time, it was his mistress who took the initiative. A sense of failing strength descended on Picasso, mixed with fear of old age, loneliness and artistic and physical impotence – in short, everything he had always dreaded. It took him nearly five years to regain a sense of equilibrium (the arrival of Jacqeline Roque, his companion and wife for the remainder of his life, helped greatly).

It was against this background that Picasso began work on the *Déjeuner* series. Addressing Manet at this point allowed Picasso not only to engage in a dialogue with a painting that he had always hugely admired, but that he had also referred to at the moment when he took his greatest personal gamble artistically. If Picasso in 1907 talked covertly about *Le Déjeuner*, he now talked covertly about himself at the time of *Les Demoiselles*. To invoke his own past directly would have been an admission of defeat.

So, on 23 June 1961, Picasso drew the following scene: a dramatically foreshortened woman bending forward and gathering up her chemise, a suited man with hat and walking cane, seated in profile against a tree. Drawn in outline, without any shading or added colour, the image is as reduced as possible. The composition's source is nevertheless obvious.

In the drawing, Picasso has simplified Manet's composition not only by use of economic draftsmanship and by reducing it to the point of caricature, but also by halving the number of protagonists: there is now one couple instead of two. The drawing is akin to a pictogram *of Le Déjeuner*, as if Picasso were trying to determine how little he needed to quote before his source became unintelligible. It is also like a jigsaw puzzle, with each individual component – the man, the woman, the tree, and the space between them – precisely delineated, and everything fitting together without gaps. The seemingly effortless fluidity and confidence of the drawing suggests that it stands at the end of a series of gradual reductions and simplifications of Manet's original composition. As a matter of fact, though it loosely picks up from where Picasso had left off a few days before, it is without precursor or follow-up in any conventional sense.

Its seeming randomness makes *Les Dejeuners* different from all the other series of paraphrases Picasso undertook.[xxvi] *The Women of Algiers* or *Les Meninas*, for example, are characterised by a sense of direction, where the first canvas in

Pablo Picasso, *Le Dejeuners (After Manet)*, 1961

the sequence is the most literal, most obviously quoted, while the final one is the most abstract and furthest removed from the source. In *Les Dejeuners* on the other hand, no sense of direction in any conventional sense can be detected. If anything, Picasso's strategy here can be described as a non-strategy. Taking Manet's built-in ambiguity literally, Picasso subjects *Le Déjeuner* to a series of narrative, pictorial, and painterly transformations while adding and subtracting from the number of protagonists; changing the setting from forest clearing to beach; running the narrative gauntlet from caricature to Arcadia and back again; switching styles and pictorial grammar from canvas to canvas, from drawing to drawing, and sometimes even half-way through a particular work.

The discourse with Manet had a profound effect on Picasso's work, helping him to effectively overcome the sterility and mannerism that had characterised so much of his output in the late 1940s and 1950s and replacing them with the pictorial and painterly strategies that were to become the hallmarks of his work from then on. The concentration on mostly two-figure groups; the prevalence of mythological, nature and nude subjects; the possibility of multiple styles, not just from canvas to canvas but within a single picture: all this was first formulated in the *Les Dejeuners* series.

'Copying' Manet in 1959-61 set in motion the train of Picasso's late work, the most productive decade of his entire career.

Epilogue

Record, exercise, homage, parody, quotation, paraphrase, exorcism, caricature, metamorphosis, transformation, catalyst: at its simplest, a copy is a way of recording a work of art. At its most complex, it establishes a dialogue across generations, cultures, and centuries.[xxvii] Copying can be a way of familiarising oneself with another artist's work, whereby the source is deconstructed mentally and reconstructed in the copy. Degas' early drawings after Italian Renaissance paintings are a case in point, and so are Cezanne's many drawings after old master paintings in the Louvre.[xxviii] Copying is a way of establishing affinities and preferences, and of acquiring technical skills and fluidity. Cezanne's drawings after the old masters, for example, supplied him with a repertoire of poses from which he was to draw for the rest of his life.

Yet however faithful a copy may be, its objectivity is compromised from inception: a process of transformation and adjustment inevitably removes it from its original source. The choice of one work over another, and the way a copy emphasises certain aspects of a work at the expense of others, betray the copyist's own preferences and intentions. The copy always tells us more about the copyist than about the original. Once an artist leaves the realm of faithful copying, the possibilities are endless. The initial impulse can set off a transformation of such magnitude that no trace of the source remains: in certain of his *Dejeuners* drawings, for example, Picasso leaves Manet's realm altogether behind him.

What is interesting is the conceptual ambiguity of so much creative copying: Manet quoting Raphael in *Le Déjeuner* is both a rejection of Raphael's status and an affirmation in the same way that Picasso's *Les Dejeuners* are both a respectful homage to, and a caricature of, Manet. This ambiguity is not accidental but conscious: it is the mechanism by which precedent is simultaneously invoked and overcome. From an artist's point of view, ambiguity is both the goal and hallmark of a successful copy.

Copying in the studio has many parallels with the image of a scientist working in a laboratory: taking the research of one's predecessors and subjecting it to all kinds of new tests and theories until the original thesis either crumbles or transmutes into something wider, altogether more inclusive. However great this transformation, or however ironic and farfetched, the copy ultimately affirms the status of the source in a quite unexpected way: never again, for example, will we be able to look at Raimondi's etching without thinking of *Le Déjeuner*. Instead of standing at the end of the creative chain, the copy is located at the very centre of the artistic enterprise. It allows artists to define and declare their affinities and locate their own position in relation to the past and their contemporaries. Without copying art history and the discourse that defines it, culture would become mute, imprisoned in a meaningless present, disconnected from both the past as well as the future. This is the most important thing to keep in mind, especially today, when copyright has become such a contentious issue, and when more and more artists seem to run into legal trouble over it.

To deny artists the right to copy is to deny their right to be creative.

i   Copying and copyright have become such contentious issues because a gulf has sprung up between post-Duchampian, postmodern artistic practice and a still fundamentally Modernist–Romantic interpretation of copyright. The postmodern notion that an image can be transferred from one context to another, without any noticeable transformation taking place, sits uncomfortably with the expression-idea dichotomy entrenched in current (modernist) legal models of authorship and originality. In the pre-Duchamp past, the use of an existing image went hand in hand with a corresponding transformation. This transformation, it could be said, was the external marker of the conceptual shift that underlay it. The two, until Duchamp, always went in tandem. Duchamp's radical work of 1914-21 forever separated them, and by 1980, his gesture had become common cultural currency.

ii   See Dore Ashton, *The Atelier of La Californie* in: Picasso, Las Grandes Series, exhibition catalogue (Madrid: Museo Nacional Reina Sofia 2000), p.563.

iii   Little is known about the work. Probably a presentation drawing, it can be dated to about 1515-17.

iv   Bartsch XIV no 197.

v   A very readable, if fanciful account of Raimondi's life and career can be found in Giorgio Vasari, *Lives of the Artists*, vol 1, (London: Everyman 1996).

vi   For an overview of the role prints played in the Raphael reception see: *Raphael et la seconde main*, exhibition catalogue (Geneva: Cabinet des Estampes and Musée d'Art et Histoire 1984).

vii   Bartsch XIV no 198.

viii   That this should have happened is not without irony. It was Albrecht Dürer who brought a case against Raimondi in 1506 for copying his etchings, probably the earliest recorded instance of copyright violation *avant le lettre*. Dürer only partly succeeded: Raimondi was permitted to copy his compositions, though he was no longer allowed to affix the Dürer monogram.

ix   It is unclear if Manet had access to the Raimondi print or the Ravenna copy.

x   Manet's sources were first convincingly analyzed in Michel Fried's 1969 essay 'Manet's Sources', which the author later incorporated in his book *Manet's Modernism* (Chicago and London: University of Chicago Press 1996).

xi   Raphael/Raimondi's etching was widely known in nineteenth-century Parisian artistic circles. Courbet had used elements from it in at least two of his paintings. By quoting *The Judgement of Paris*, Manet not only bows (however ironically) to the past but also pointedly engages in the artistic battles of his own time.

xii   This cut-out and collaged quality also characterizes the Raphael/Raimondi etching.

xiii   If we are looking for parallels of this in literature, it must be Emile Zola's *Nana*, who likewise comes across with unprecedented directness and offers no excuses for her actions and behaviour.

xiv   See footnote 19 below.

xv   *The Soler Family* 1903, oil on canvas, 150 x 200 cm. Museé des Beaux Arts, Liege (Zervos XXX).

xvi   In one of those strange flukes of history, Sabastia Junyer Vidal, a close friend of Picasso at the time, sketched in a landscape, creating the same disjointedness between figures and background as in *Le Déjeuner*. When Picasso's dealer Kahnweiler acquired the painting ten years later, Picasso insisted on painting out Vijar's landscape and reinstating the original background.

xvii   *Les Demoiselles d'Avignon* 1907, oil on canvas, 244 x 234 cm. Museum of Modern Art, New York (Zervos XXX).

xviii   See the chronology by Judith Cousins and Helene Seckel in Rubin/Seckel (eds): *Les Demoiselles d'Avignon, Studies in Modern Art*, volume 3 (New York: Museum of Modern Art, 1994), p.179.

xix   The assertion that *Le Déjeuner* is likewise unfinished cannot be correct: Manet would not have shown an incomplete canvas in the Salon des Independents.

xx   See William Rubin, in Rubin/Seckel.

xxi   To this day the painting has actually never left Paris.

xxii   Archives Picasso, quoted after Marie-Laure Bernadac, Picasso 1953-1972: 'Painting as Model', in: *Late Picasso*, exhibition catalogue (London: Tate Gallery 1988), p.70. The envelope is postmarked 1929.

xxiii   For a summary of the painting's reception history see Judith Cousins and Helene Seckel, pp 179ff

xxiv   The paintings and drawings are reproduced in Douglas Cooper, *Les Dejeuners* (London: Thames and Hudson 1963).

xxv   See Francoise Gilot (with Carlton Lake), *Life with Picasso* (London: Virago 1990).

xxvi   For a long time *Les Dejeuners* were not appreciated. The great Picasso collector, Victor Ganz, for example, considered the series a failure. Only much later, and with hindsight, did its significance become clear.

xxvii   The most comprehensive overview of the field was given in the exhibition *Copier Creer*, held at the Louvre in Paris in 1993. See Jean-Pierre Cuzin, *Copier Creer: De Turner A Picasso – 300 œuvres inspirees par les maitres du Louvre* (Paris: Reunion des Museés Nationaux 1993).

xxviii   *Copier Creer*, cat nos.50-77.

'This is Not by Me.' Andy Warhol and the Question of Authorship

Andrew Wilson

I like Andy Warhol. I like Andy Warhol. I like Andy Warhol.
I like Andy Warhol. I like Andy Warhol. I like Andy Warhol. I like
Andy Warhol. I like Andy Warhol. I like Andy Warhol. I like Andy
Warhol. I like Andy Warhol. I like Andy Warhol. I like Andy Warhol.
I like Andy Warhol. And that is why I like Andy Warhol.
　　Joe Brainard, 'Andy Warhol: Andy Do It' [i]

During a 1966 interview, Andy Warhol turned to his interviewer and asked, 'Why don't you ask my assistant Gerard Malanga some questions? He did a lot of my paintings'.[ii] When Warhol started painting again after 1968, he often said that Brigid Polk now made his paintings. Earlier, a factory person, Alan Midgette, was used by Warhol to impersonate him at openings or on the college lecture circuit. Edie Sedgwick, a Factory Superstar, was also similarly used by Warhol (her hair and Warhol's wig could at times look similar). At a film screening, Warhol once introduced Malanga as Warhol, who then proceeded to sign autographs as if he really was Warhol. In a 1971 interview with Malanga, Warhol pointedly suggested that 'I suppose you could call the paintings prints, but the material used for the paintings was canvas . . . Anyone can do them'.[iii]

Indeed, in 1965, Warhol lent some of his screens to Elaine Sturtevant so she could make her work (simulations or appropriations of his), and as early as 1963 he had told the critic Gene Swenson that 'I think somebody should be able to do all my paintings for me. I haven't been able to make every image clear and simple and the same as the first one. I think it would be so great if more people took up silk screens so that no one would know whether my picture was mine or somebody else's'.[iv] However, Warhol also got uptight about the idea that perhaps Malanga had, after leaving his employ, forged a number of his 'Flower' paintings. In his diary for June 11, 1978, Warhol said, 'I decided I won't sign the fake ones that're turning up all over Europe – the ones that people told us they bought from Gerard.

Maybe I should do new ones and make good on the fakes in Europe. I don't know. I'll see'.[v] Near the end of his life, Warhol visited Sotheby's to authenticate some paintings, 'one of them was one of those fake "Electric Chairs", the ones Gerard denies doing. A blue one. It wasn't stretched right. The people get greedy and they want a bigger picture, so it's got a border on it'.[vi]

The paradox and contradiction that is made apparent by these anecdotes defines much of the art of the last 50 years; art that has found itself by questioning authorship, authenticity and identity. It's a questioning that ranges across many issues: the authority and meaning of the signature; the use of found source material as copy or theft; the adoption of a strategy of simulation within the conception of the work; a re-questioning in those terms of the status and usefulness of the Duchampian readymade that itself refers directly, through the act of nomination, to the role of the signature; the definition of the copy in terms of the relationship to a primary source that has been lifted to new use, the repetition of such an act, or even the representation of the act of repetition as a form of copy. For Roland Barthes, for example, the act of repetition takes its place beside his understanding of the disappearance of the author and signals the rediscovery of the double as 'a Copy, not a Shadow: *beside*, not *behind*: A flat, insignificant, hence irreligious Double'. Warhol's repetition also registered for Barthes 'the destruction of art' and an access to 'a new temporality', which, in fixing and freezing life, was ultimately concerned with death.[vii]

Within this semantic whirlpool, questions of identity and authorship can become mired on the opposition of what has come to be termed 'High' and 'Low' culture, as a way of explaining the act of copying as a culturally creative force – lifting up an image taken from a commonly held culture towards a point of creative transformation by a detached artist to reveal some truths about the world – the act of copying from 'Low' culture being permitted by its very transfer into the world of 'High' culture. This point of view is deeply flawed. As Rosalind Krauss has persuasively argued, such a sublimation model disregards the notion that mass cultural forms often position themselves as a point of resistance to the mechanics of the sublimation model – that is to say, if you question whether or not 'mass-cultural material constitutes a set of "sources" comparable to the resources on which artists have traditionally drawn', and the answer is in the negative, then the question for these other analyses is whether mass culture itself is not an historically specific phenomenon that cannot be assimilated into the art-historical model without overlooking this historical specificity. The work of the Frankfurt School (Theodor Adorno) and of Walter Benjamin was consecrated to rethinking culture through the lens of mass culture, a lens whose historical and material consequences must transform the very definition of art. Some, although by no means all, of the other models that have arisen as a consequence of such arguments could include: the simulation model (Jean Baudrillard); the desublimatory model (Roland Barthes); the culture-political model (the Birmingham School); and the reappropriation model (Michel de Certeau).[viii]

In the early 1950s, those British artists, architects, and critics who formed the Independent Group – such as Peter & Alison Smithson, Richard Hamilton, Ian Henderson, Eduardo Paolozzi, Reyner Banham, and Lawrence Alloway – provided evidence of a similar distrust of the sublimation model in their meetings, events, exhibitions, and work. Their thinking was close to that of Adorno and Benjamin in that they held to the belief that such mass cultural material had to be understood critically rather than just lifted and used, beliefs that can be recognised in writings such as the Smithsons' 'But Today We Collect Ads' of 1956 or the definitive text by Alloway from 1959, 'The Long Front of Culture'. Within such a framework, the copy becomes not an issue of theft, but one of use, legitimated not only as representation, but also as a critical enquiry that asks questions of the identity and uniqueness of art itself.

In New York in the early 1960s, Warhol was not isolated in positioning these issues at the heart of his work. His fellow Pop artists built on the lead given by Jasper Johns and Robert Rauschenberg in using pre-existing material not just as the source for their work but as providing its actual physical material. Warhol's use of the silk screen process after 1962 was not directed at constructing a repertoire of images that could be deployed in many different combinations, as it was in Rauschenberg's case. For Warhol, the screen allowed him to copy repetitively images that had themselves been mechanically – that is repetitively – reproduced in the mass media (or were, at least, available for such reproduction). If the other Pop artists were concerned with a realist treatment of their source material, Warhol's work revolved as much around a critical engagement with issues of authorship and identity as it did with the nature of the source material he was copying and the content of the resulting representations. In Warhol's eyes, these two approaches were inextricably linked. In the early 1960s, the emerging Pop Art countered the pretensions of an Abstract Expressionism – culturally pure and psychologically charged – whose work's value resided in the supposed authenticity of its expression. Pollock's statement, 'I am nature', is contradicted and shown to be hollow by Warhol's rejoinder, 'I want to be a machine'. This difference is given even greater weight when seen in the context of Warhol's profession as a commercial artist, rather than as an artist communicating supposedly eternal truth. Furthermore, as recent research has shown,[ix] in the early 1960s, Warhol was also closely involved with a number of writers and poets, including his assistant Gerard Malanga, whose work was founded on a similar attitude to that held by the Pop artists with regard to the originality, authorship and content of their work.

Joe Brainard's 1963 poem quoted above, 'Andy Warhol: Andy Do It', not only plays with Warhol's use of repetition and permutation in his image-making, but was also created within a culture of literary copying of which Warhol would have been only too aware. Brainard, alongside Ron Padgett, Ted Berrigan, and Gerard Malanga, were all poets whose work used lines and forms written by each other and other poets, creating a vertiginous culture of reference.[x] Here, however (and in other contemporary poems by Brainard, such as the end of a 1964 essay on Warhol's film *Sleep*, that repetitively states 'I like *Sleep*', twice on each line), the copied reference is to Warhol's own pictorial instance of self-copying as repetition. If the repetitive silkscreens of press images was increasingly identified as Warhol's signature style, he was not just repeating an image each time the screen is moved over the canvas, he was copying himself (or, at the very least, re-inscribing himself), and by so doing, making himself more evident (if also more removed). In this sense, Warhol's act of repetition also identifies the degree to which narcissism sits at the heart of his practice – the canvas bearing repeated images becoming a blank or mirror.

What this entails is that the signature exists in a state of stress where its authority and meaning, if essentially unstable, is absolute. Warhol might have inferred that anyone could (and, in certain cases, probably did) make his work – even though the choices of image, use of colour and composition, were his decisions to make – and yet the copying of his own work was rigidly policed against. In the early 1970s, fakes were made of two print portfolios by Warhol – *Marilyn Monroe*, 1967, and *Flowers*, 1970 – which were issued in a different size and colours.[xi] Each fake print was stamped on the back 'published by Sunday B Morning' and 'fill in your signature', and occasionally these can be found signed by Warhol: 'This is not by me. Andy Warhol'. At the same time that Warhol is here acknowledging his ownership of the copied images, he is also stating them as not being 'by me'. The signature becomes a form of certification of creative activity as well as of ownership, and that this should take place in the context of copying and the making of fakes burdens the signature even more: it says what the work is, as much as it hides from what it is not. The signature affirms a work to be by Warhol and denies authorship from the creator of the source image. For example, Warhol

Andy Warhol. *Flowers*, 1964

may indeed write on the back of a Sunday B Morning *Flowers* print 'This is not by me. Andy Warhol'. But in doing so, he is also writing (in silence) that it is also not by the original photographer of the image, Patricia Caulfield – the presence of her signature has effectively been erased.[xii]

Just as repetition underscores the meaning of Warhol's work – its fecundity both apeing and criticising the American dream – the use of his signature was promiscuous. In 1966, Warhol put an advertisement in *The Village Voice* in which he used his name – and by extension his signature – to promote a particular range of goods: 'I'll endorse with my name any of the following: clothing AC-DC, cigarettes small, sound equipment, ROCK 'N' ROLL RECORDS, anything, film, and film equipment, Food, Helium, Whips. MONEY!! love and kisses ANDY WARHOL EL 5-9941'.[xiii] He did not own these things, he had not created them, but they were given life by his name and their value could be enhanced by the addition of his signature. By the time that this ad was published, Warhol's practice had turned a corner, as he increasingly deployed his signature as a producer might.

In 1963, along with his wish to be a machine, Warhol started using a machine as a surrogate recording device that linked stillness with repetition. A fixed film camera, at first a motorised Bolex loaded with a 100 foot, 3-minute film magazine, would be switched on once the subject had been arranged or chosen and the magazine would then be left to run out. The camera would be loaded with another magazine and the process repeated with no camera movement and very few zooms. With his film *Sleep*, each time the magazine was changed, the camera position would also alter slightly. In 1965, Warhol described making the film, recalling that 'it started with somebody sleeping and it just got longer and longer and longer. Actually, I did shoot all the hours of the movie, but I faked the final film to get a better design'.[xiv] The faking was achieved by using the camera/projector as a doubled copier – the source is not just repetitively copied onto each frame of film, but then each of the edits is repeated to stretch and slow down the film out even more. Here, in microcosm, is a central aspect of Warhol's practice revealed as a highly developed concern with processes of duplication and what they might mean – that ranges from the camera as such to the media industry as a whole.

Warhol's engagement with filmmaking also points to a fundamental change in emphasis in the conception of his work and in terms of his authorial stance. By 1966, Warhol's film production was becoming increasingly industrialised and, as David James has cogently analysed, 'Warhol delegated more and more responsibility until in some of the late films he was no more than a name attached to a product completed essentially without participation on his part other than the marshalling of production expenses and the publicity. In the expansion of his activity from being the operator of a camera to being the operator of an industry, his erasure of authorship – his most characteristic authorial gesture – was recontextualised',[xv] and it was as a producer rather than an author that Warhol increasingly situated himself in films, painting and all the other activities of Andy Warhol Enterprises. As he later admitted, 'I read very carefully every review of everything that I produce – that is, everything that has my name on it. When I used to do the work myself I never read any reviews or any of my own publicity. But then, when I sort of stopped *doing* things and started *producing* things, I did want to know what people were saying about them because it wouldn't be anything personal'.[xvi] However, what Warhol describes here had to a degree been his way of working since he was a commercial artist in the 1950s, when he had started using assistants to help him make his work. This was also the situation in which he used his mother to sign, title, and letter many of his early drawings. It is not so much that there was a split between artist and producer, but that Warhol was as much an artist as a producer.

It is tempting to see Warhol's discomfort when confronted by fakes or copies of his work as just the flip-side of his own use of other artists' images as sources for his work. One of Warhol's most pointed appropriations was his re-presentation of cardboard Brillo boxes as wooden silkscreened boxes for his solo show at the Stable Gallery in 1964 – the design for the boxes having been created by the little-known Abstract Expressionist James Harvey.[xvii] The opposition between the Pop sensibility and an earlier, purer Abstract Expressionist sensibility being put into high relief by this act of theft. And yet Warhol did not so much steal as use and transform.

Warhol was not as distanced from his work as was often made out at the time; rather, he exerted an extreme control over his work through the choices he decided to follow. Patricia Caulfield's photograph used by Warhol for his *Flowers* paintings is almost unrecognisable when placed beside his finished works (and it is not just the difference between a photograph, reproduced in a magazine becoming the source for a series of paintings on canvas in a wide range of sizes). However, Elaine Sturtevant's paintings of Warhol's *Flowers*, made with the use of the original screens, are virtually indistinguishable from Warhol's original. Just as Warhol has used but not copied the Caulfield, Sturtevant has used but not copied the Warhol. Nevertheless, the intention behind Sturtevant's gender-determined simulation of works by male Pop artists since 1965 (she also, for example, mounted a full-scale facsimile of Claes Oldenburg's *Store*) is a world away from the repetitive emptiness of Warhol's New Realism.[xviii]

The positioning of Warhol's usage of a destabilised notion of originality and authorship within the 'High/Low' debate is perhaps best recognised in the number of paintings he produced after the works of other artists. In 1963, following the U.S. tour of Leonardo da Vinci's *Mona Lisa*, Warhol completed a series of paintings on the subject – the whole painting and details of the head and shoulders or the folded hands. The resulting paintings are essentially a portrait of a celebrity; the image is as much an icon (and derives from the same image-bank) as his portraits of Elvis Presley, Marlon Brando, Liz Taylor, and Marilyn Monroe. In Warhol's eyes, there is little difference between these contemporary icons and the most famous of Renaissance portraits. In effect, he does not paint or copy the portrait but delivers an image that shows it to be a ghost – and a very different thing to the painted object hanging behind bullet proof glass in the Louvre. For one thing, again the image is repeated, not so that it is devalued as such, but in absolute recognition of its value as a box office draw (*Thirty Are Better Than One*, being the self-explanatory title of one of his 'Mona Lisa' paintings[xix]). Furthermore, *Multicolored Mona Lisa*, 1963, in which the images are repeated and overlapping in black, yellow, blue, and red, suggests nothing less than printer's waste from the proofing process of a high speed four-colour printer; the *Mona Lisa* becomes imaged as a celebrity souvenir found in a cheap magazine.

In 1982, Warhol used the work of another Italian artist, Giorgio de Chirico, for his source material. This was an intelligent choice given that de Chirico had since the 1920s consistently copied his paintings from his earlier metaphysical period. There had been a de Chirico retrospective at MoMA, New York, in 1982, and though few works were exhibited that were dated after the 1920s, the catalogue did dramatically raise the issue of de Chirico's practice of copying by reproducing in a grid eighteen versions of *The Disquieting Muses*, which the artist had painted between 1945 and 1962. This painting was among those by de Chirico that Warhol chose to re-present. In an interview with Achille Bonito Oliva, Warhol refers to the catalogue image of the 18 versions of *The Disquieting Muses* before asking also, 'What about Morandi? Didn't he repeat himself? Most artists repeat themselves throughout their lives. Isn't life a repetition of events . . . I just like to do the same thing over and over again. Every time I go out and someone is being elected President or Mayor or something, they stick their images all over the walls and I always think I do those . . . I always think it's my work . . . All my images are the same . . . but very different at the same time . . . Isn't life a series of images that change as they repeat themselves?' [xx]

In de Chirico, Warhol had found his alter ego, for not only did Warhol's process mean that each painting had inscribed within it its own repetition, but that he had also copied his own works, whether it was remaking the *Brillo Boxes* in 1968 for an exhibition at the Stockholm Moderna Museet, or his series of *Reversal* paintings from 1979, in which paintings from the 1960s were repainted in negative as a form of retrospective gesture. *Big Retrospective Painting (Reversal Series)*, 1979, is one such example, including, left to right, repeated images of 'Flowers', 'Kellogg's Corn Flakes' (originally used for a 1964 box), 'Marilyn Monroe', 'Car Crash', 'Cows', 'Mao', 'Campbell's Soup Can', 'Electric Chair', and 'Self-Portrait'. The critic David Bourdon has written of these paintings that they reveal the extent to which Warhol preferred to make 'a pastiche of his former subjects, which he now arbitrarily juxtaposed as if to contradict their earlier significance'.[xxi] However, more to the point, is Warhol's realisation that in copying his own work, he was strengthening the currency of the original work from the 1960s, which had long since taken its place within the mass-cultural image-bank. The 'Reversals' were testimony to the power of these earlier paintings.

The 'Reversals' were also mimicry of the highest order, something that he also investigated in his 'Camouflage' paintings of 1986. Camouflage both tries to be something else and disappear at one and the same time. Warhol intended the paintings to be understood as a form of abstract painting (like his 'Piss' paintings and 'Rorsach' paintings) which might be understood as coloured pattern or, again like camouflage, the simplification of a given image. The use of the camouflage motif can also be taken as a signifier for Warhol's practice in terms of the 'High/Low' debate, for which copying and mimicry provided a critical bridge in much the same way that J.G. Ballard suggested camouflage both hides and is meant to reveal: 'The camouflaged battleship or bunker must never efface itself completely, but confuse our recognition systems by one moment being itself, and the next not itself. Many impersonators and politicians exploit the same principle'.[xxii]

The 'After de Chirico', 'Retrospectives', and 'Reversals' series do mark a shift in Warhol's art. In the 1960s, the subject-matter of his work was concerned with questions of authenticity and authorship, mechanical reproduction, mass culture, repetition, and detachment, but the work's content engaged with the contemporary American landscape as understood through the lens of glamour and death – the flip-side of the American dream. The mechanical copying of mass-cultural source material alongside his use of repetition created a matrix in which supposed detachment and the emptying out of emotion clears the stage for the normalisation of everyday horror. By the late 1970s, subject-matter and content had come closer together as he became more concerned, like younger artists Sherrie Levine and Jeff Koons, primarily with destabilising the notion of authorship and stretching the limits of originality. In the 1960s, the different critical awareness Warhol manipulated – what was being painted and how it was being painted – fed into each other, but by the 1980s these different positions had come closer together. It is in this way that Warhol, following Marcel Duchamp's embrace of nomination in his creation of the Readymade, paved the way for contemporary artists who have increasingly challenged the extent to which a copy of something has to be understood as much on its own terms as in terms of its source.

i C, A Journal of Poetry, No.1, New York, December 1963/January 1964.
ii Nat Finkelstein, 'Inside Andy Warhol', Cavalier Magazine, September 1966, p.88.
Furthermore, referring to Andy Warhol's Index (Book) of 1967, Malanga has disclosed that 'Andy said in the Andy Warhol-Random House book, "Gerard signs all of my paintings", which is true'. See Patrick S Smith, Andy Warhol's Art and Films, (UMI Research Press, Ann Arbor, Michigan, 1986) p.414. These statements would come back to haunt Warhol. In 1967, Malanga went to Rome and while there, 'running short of money, forged a series of "Warhols" – silkscreened images based on a news photograph of the dead Cuban leader Ché Guevara. He made two phoney paintings, gave one to a girlfriend and offered the other for sale – priced at $3,000 – through a Rome gallery; in a February 1968 exhibition at that gallery, he also showed, signed and numbered silkscreen prints from an edition of fifty, priced at fifty dollars each. When the dealer sought to verify the provenance of the "Warhol" Guevaras, Malanga wrote to Warhol, explaining that if the works were not authenticated, the poet would be "denounced – Italian style" and thrown into jail. Malanga enclosed a

newspaper review of the show, commenting, "Andy, this is the *first* time that your art work has been praised by the Communist press." "What nerve!" Warhol remarked. Not one to be outwitted, he wired back, authenticating the paintings but stipulating that all moneys were to be sent directly to him as "Mr Malanga was not authorised to sell the artwork." David Bourdon, *Warhol*, (Harry N Abrams, New York, 1989) p.291.

iii   Gerard Malanga, 'Conversation with Andy Warhol', *Print Collector's Newsletter*, No.1, January/February 1971, p.127.

iv   Gene Swenson, 'What is Pop Art?', *ARTnews*, November 1963, p.26.

v   Pat Hackett (ed.), *The Andy Warhol Diaries* (Warner Books, New York, 1991) p.142.

vi   Ibid., p.631.

vii   Roland Barthes, 'That Old Thing, Art …', Stephen Henry Madoff, *Pop Art, a critical history* (California University Press, London 1997) p.371.

viii   Rosalind Krauss, 'Introduction', *October* #56 (*High/Low A Special Issue*) Spring 1991, p.4.

ix   Reva Wolf, *Andy Warhol, Poetry and Gossip in the 1960s* (Chicago University Press, 1997). These poets and writers included John Ashberry, Ted Berrigan, Joe Brainard, Ron Padgett, and Rene Ricard.

x   For an exhaustive analysis of the work of these poets in terms of copying, theft, and their relationship to Warhol, see ibid., pp.81-123.

xi   For more information see Frayder Feldman & Jorg Schellmann (eds.), *Andy Warhol Prints* (Abbeville Press, New York, 1989) Appendix 2, p.134.

xii   As a result of being sued for using the Patricia Caulfield image, Warhol became more careful about the images he used and, as Ronnie Cutrone, his assistant in the 1970s remembered, 'So, basically what I do is photograph anything that's not people, and in this way he doesn't get *sued* from magazines if he cuts pictures out and things like that'. Patrick S Smith, *Andy Warhol's Art and Films*, op.cit., p.277.

xiii   Ad in *The Village Voice*, February 10, 1966, reprinted in Wayne Koestenbaum, *Andy Warhol* (Weidenfeld & Nicolson, London, 2001) pp.99-100.

xiv   Stephen Koch, *Stargazer, Andy Warhol's World and His Films* (Calder & Boyars, London, 1974) p.37.

xv   David James, 'The Producer as Author', in Michael O'Pray (ed.), *Andy Warhol, Film Factory* (British Film Institute, London, 1989) p.138.

xvi   Andy Warhol, *From A to B and Back Again, The Philosophy of Andy Warhol* (Picador, London, 1976) p.162.

xvii   This was, however, probably unintended. He had sent Nathan Gluck to the supermarket to find suitable boxes that could be used as sources, but ended up having to go himself 'in order to exchange Gluck's "arty" choices for a plainer set consisting of Heinz tomato juice, Kellogg's corn flakes, Mott's apple juice and two versions of Brillo soap pads'. See Marco Livingstone, 'Do It Yourself: Notes on Warhol's Techniques', *Andy Warhol: A Retrospective* (Museum of Modern Art, New York, 1989) p.72.

xviii   To this one should also add Mike Bidlo's 1980s recreations of Warhol's work (and as that of other artists) such as his *Campbell's Soup Can* paintings, as well as the recreation of Warhol's *Factory* in 1984, also the strategies enacted by Sherrie Levine in her series of photographs after Walker Evans, Rodchenko, and other photographers, and her watercolours after images in books of works by Schiele, Mondrian, Klee, Miro, and others.

xix   Towards the end of his life, Warhol completed a huge series of paintings derived from da Vinci's *Last Supper*, one of which – *Sixty Last Suppers*, 1986 – revisits *Thirty Are Better Than One*.

xx   Industrial Metaphysics – Interview with Andy Warhol by Achille Bonito Oliva',
     Andy Warhol (After de Chirico) (Waddington Galleries, London 1998) p.9.

xxi David Bourdon, *Warhol*, op.cit., p.380.

xxii J.G. Ballard, 'Project for a Glossary of the Twentieth Century', in Jonathan Crary and
     Sanford Kwinter (eds.), *Incorporations* (Zone, New York, 1992) p.277.

Part 4
Bridging the Gap

Justifying Copyright

Michael Spence

Visual artists are both the creators and the users of material protected by copyright. An individual artist may benefit or be burdened by the regime. It all depends upon the ways in which she creates and appropriates. For this reason it is difficult to weigh the various justifications that have been offered for the system. The most that can be hoped is that, in the majority of cases, a legal regime both derived from a system of royal censorship and sometimes heralded as a bulwark of free speech, does more to empower artists than to silence them.

The justifications usually offered for copyright fall into two groups. First, there are those that stress the economic advantages of the system. Second, there are those that stress its deontological legitimacy. In broad terms, arguments of the former type have been more popular in the United States, where the constitutional validity of the copyright legislation depends upon the goal of promoting 'the Progress of Science and useful Arts'. Arguments of the latter type have tended to be more popular in mainland Europe, where it has been stressed that creators 'ont mérité au moins deux récompenses: d'une part, rester les maîtres de leur création, fruit de la conjonction de leur intelligence et de leur sensibilité; … d'autre part, ils méritent, comme les autres catégories de travailleurs, d'assurer leur subsistance, en conférant la jouissance de leur œuvre au public, moyennant rémunération.'[i] This regional difference, though its importance it is often exaggerated by commentators, helps to explain much about copyright history and politics.

This essay will consider each of these types of justification in relation to the specific field of the visual arts. None of the arguments considered here is without difficulty. However, collectively, they do seem to provide some type of justification for copyright protection in at least some circumstances. The difficult question that is left to policy-makers and courts, is just how strong that protection ought to be and when it ought to be available.

Economic Justifications for Copyright

The economic justifications for copyright focus on the need to provide incentives for the creation and dissemination of creative works. For economic theorists, the intended beneficiary of the copyright system is the community as a whole, which demands the production of, and access to, as many creative works as possible. It is assumed that, in perfect conditions, the market will ensure the production of goods and those goods will be allocated to the party who values them the most. There will be incentive to produce goods because their selling price will allow a producer to recoup both the costs of production and the benefit of the goods to a purchaser. But creative works are said to be 'public goods' in that it is difficult to exclude non-purchasers from their enjoyment. Because of the difficulty of excluding non-purchasers, there will be no incentive to create and to disseminate works. They will be under-produced unless the law intervenes to cure this 'market failure'. Even assuming that the rights given to the copyright owner constitute some type of 'monopoly' and entail the dead-weight loss associated with all monopolies, the advantages of the copyright system in curing this market failure are said to outweigh those losses. Other potential methods of curing the relevant market failure, such as systems of state or private patronage, are seen as less desirable in that they involve the centralisation of decisions about which types of work will be produced.

It is clear that, in relation to some types of creative work, this theory holds some merit. An author might be less inclined to a write a novel, or a publisher less able to produce it, if a rival can produce a cheap edition of the novel bearing none of the costs associated with the creation of the work. And creating a market for the novel by, at least temporarily, excluding the rival publisher, seems to have at least three advantages. First, it seems more democratic than having a patron or the state chose which novels to finance. Second, not only is it more democratic, the creation of such markets may be an essential corollary of a commitment to free speech. By creating a competitive private market for works, copyright may create the conditions in which individuals are given an effective opportunity for their opinions to be heard. Third, the market mechanism will ensure a steady flow of creative work, not subject to the varying commitment of a patron or the state to the funding of the arts. It is far less clear, however, that the theory applies to all of the creative work protected by copyright and, in particular, to much of the visual arts. The problem with the economic justification of copyright is that: (i) there is much which copyright protects that would be produced and disseminated even without the incentive effects of the copyright regime, and (ii) it is difficult to structure copyright such that the monopoly losses associated with the regime are no greater than those required to ensure the production and dissemination of a given category of work, especially given the wide range of subject matter that copyright protects.

Works of visual art that have significant value as physical objects offer a good example of works that may well be produced and disseminated even without the copyright incentive. The public goods problem does not arise if the object of value that has been created is, not the image, but the original work itself. Of course, there might still be a disincentive to create and to disseminate works in the possibility that they could be reproduced on a wide scale. The artist might so resent the possibility of her work being used to decorate postcards and tea towels that she chooses not to create at all. The owner of the original work may so resent the idea of poor quality reproductions being made of it, that she locks it up and never makes copies of it from which other copies could be made. In the absence of a system of droit de suite, it might also be necessary to rely upon reproduction rights to recoup the costs of producing works whose value has not been realised at the time of their first sale. However, as long as there is a lucrative market for a work as a physical object, there will usually be sufficient financial incentive for the artist to produce it. There will usually also be sufficient financial incentives for the owner of the original work to disseminate copies of it. The artist will be able to make a profit from the sale of the original work itself and, given the low cost of reproduction, the owner of the original work will usually be able to make a profit from selling copies of it, even if those copies can themselves be reproduced. The importance of copyright in providing an incentive for the production and dissemination of artistic works is therefore going to depend upon the relative commercial importance of dealing in the work as a physical object and of licensing reproductions of it.

The protection of visual art also demonstrates the difficulty of shaping copyright so as to ensure an adequate incentive for the production and dissemination of works, but no more. Whatever monopoly losses copyright might entail are justified only to the extent that degree of control over the work it affords is optimal for inducing the creation and dissemination of works. The extent of that control is determined by the range of uses of the work reserved to the copyright owner, the range of available defences to copyright infringement and the period of protection. The extent of the control afforded the copyright owner is also determined by the important rules that protection extends to a 'work' but not its underlying 'ideas' and that a copyright owner can only prevent the use of a 'substantial part' of a work. These last two rules are, at best, very vague. They depend for their precise application upon the judge deciding a particular case and her failure to achieve the appropriate level of protection may well unnecessarily exacerbate dead-weight monopoly losses. But these rules are particularly difficult to apply, and therefore the risk of dead-weight losses high, in the field of the visual arts. This is because the idea in an earlier work upon which a later work might wish to build is normally a visual idea and it is particularly difficult to allude to a visual idea without repro-ducing a substantial part of the expression by which it is constituted. Allusion to an earlier work will, for a visual artist, often require the use of a substantial part of the work itself. Of course, that can also be true in some contexts involving written texts, such as parody, but it seems particularly true in the context of the visual arts.

Thus there may be little to gain, and a lot to lose, from the operation of copy-right in at least those sectors of the visual arts in which the physical object of the work has sufficient economic value to provide an incentive for production. This will often be true in the field of 'fine' arts. An economically efficient system might therefore refuse copyright protection in such circumstances, and yet afford it in others in which the importance of reproduction to the economic value of the work was greater and the risk of dead-weight loss less. It might refuse copyright protec-tion for 'fine' art and yet afford it to drawings on greeting cards and calendars. The difficulty with such an approach is that it would entail distinctions of even greater uncertainty than those, that currently define the scope of copyright, such as that between 'fine' art and other kinds of visual art. The cost of the system, and its potential dead-weight loss, would increase as uncertainty increased the cost of policing its boundaries. Cases such as *Hensher v. Restawile Upholstery (Lancs)*[ii] regarding the category of works of artistic craftsmanship found in United King-dom copyright law, reveal the very great difficulty of drawing such distinctions at least in the court room, if not elsewhere. Thus the economic justification of copy-right has some merit, but it cannot entirely account for our copyright system, especially as that system applies to certain types of visual art.

Deontological Justifications for Copyright

The economic arguments for copyright assume that the regime exists to serve a public purpose. But it may be that regime exists, not to advance the common weal, but to give force to certain ethical obligations owed to creators.

The strength of these ethical obligations has been fiercely contested. At one extreme, post-modern critics have claimed that no individual can have a claim over a work because no individual can claim responsibility for its creation. At the other extreme, some have claimed that these ethical obligations are so strong that they give rise to 'human rights'. Article 27(2) of the Universal Declaration of Human Rights proclaims that 'Everyone has the right to the protection of the moral and material interests resulting from any scientific, literary or artistic pro-duction of which he is the author'. But neither of these extreme positions is likely to have much impact in shaping the future of copyright law.

Two more modest lines of argument will be considered in this essay. First, there are two arguments that parallel those often used to underpin the law of obligations. Second, there are four arguments that parallel those often used to underpin the legal institution of property. In considering these arguments, the difficult question of whether they might apply when a corporation, a *legal* rather than a *natural* person, is the first owner of copyright, shall be put to one side.

I. Arguments parallel to those commonly found in the Law of Obligations

Of the arguments that parallel those commonly justifying obligations, two have been most important. These are: first, an argument from the harm done to a creator by the unauthorised use of her work; and second, an argument from the unjust enrichment constituted by the unauthorised use of a work. An over-riding difficulty with both these arguments is that, even if either can be sustained, it is not clear why the remedying of harm or the reversal of an unjust enrichment might require the grant of a property right, such as copyright, and not merely to the recognition of a legal obligation such as those known to the law of tort or restitution. But, in any case, each of these arguments is somewhat problematic.

a. The Argument from Harm

This argument commonly consists in two parts. It is claimed that the unauthorised user causes harm to the creator of work simply by her use of the work. It is then claimed that the creator of the work does a would-be user of the work no harm by excluding her from its use. Therefore, the law prevents harm to the creator, and does the would-be user no wrong, by preventing unauthorised use. There are three problems with this argument.

First, it is not at all clear whether the unauthorised use of a work does its creator any harm. In assessing such harm, we should count only the extent to which the creator of the work is worse off because of the unauthorised use *per se* and not the extent to which she might be better off were that use prohibited. It would be circular to include the loss of any profit that might flow from the exclusive use of the work, because the question of whether the creator is entitled to exclusive use is essentially the question of whether copyright is justified. It is at least arguable that a creator can suffer harm of the relevant type by the unauthorised use of her work. A creator may suffer harm by unauthorised use if the work is thereby changed in a way that renders it no longer useful to her. This may be the case with any work that has an expressive purpose. Imagine that a visual artist creates a particular image to promote affirmative action on the grounds of race. If that image is appropriated by a neo-Nazi group, it may no longer have value for the artist. Even without their altering the actual image, its use by the neo-Nazi group may change its meaning, may render it liable to be read differently by an anticipated audience. From the perspective of the creator, this may do the image such damage that she can no longer use it herself, even if it is clear that the creator has no association with the unauthorised use. Such an argument depends, however, on the contested claim that the meaning of a work can change through use, a claim that will obviously be more convincing in some contexts than in others. The more usual assumption is that no harm is caused to the creator by the unauthorised use of her work. This is because works are considered to be not 'crowdable': that is, use of the work by one person or in one way will not prevent its use by another person or in another way. The first assumption underpinning the argument from harm is at best a highly contentious one.

Second, the other assumption of the argument from harm, that the creator of a work does a would-be user no harm in excluding her from its use, is also high- ly contentious. In assessing such harm, we should count only the extent to which the would-be user is worse off in a world in which the work has been created and she is excluded from its use than she would be in a world in which the work had never been created. This is because the usual assumption is that, without the efforts of the creator, the work would not have existed, and so there can be no harm to the would-be user in exclusion from its use. It is unclear, however, whether this will always be the case. In particular, when a work becomes an important part of a community's social or cultural life it may be that exclusion from the use of the work does a would-be user real harm. This might occur in two circumstances. First, use of the work might be necessary effectively to comment upon the work itself. If the would-be user is excluded from commenting effectively upon a work that has become an important part of the culture in which she operates, she might be worse off than she would have been had the work never been created. The copyright law of most countries thus includes a defence to infringement to cover this type of use. Second, use of the work might be necessary because it has become so important to the culture that it constitutes a shorthand for a range of meanings for which no adequate alternative means of expression exist. In these circumstances, use of the work might be necessary either to contest, or to invoke, the range of meanings for which it is a cipher. The parodic use of iconic works of visual art offers an example of activity that can be prevented in some copyright systems, and is privileged with a special defence to infringement in others. But the situations in which it might be necessary to use a work to contest, or to invoke, a particular range of meanings do not all involve parody. And it is arguable that excluding the would-be user from the work in all such situations is effectively to silence her. She may well be worse off in a world in which the work has been created and she prevented from using it, and thereby contributing to the discourse of her culture, than she would have been had it never been created. Thus both the assumptions underpinning the argument from harm seem somewhat problematic.

Third, even assuming that a creator can show harm from the unauthorised use of her work, and the would-be user can show no harm in her exclusion from its use, it is not axiomatic that this is harm of a type that the law ought to remedy. The state does not, and should not, intervene to prevent all types of harm, even deliberately inflicted harm. It may be that the state should protect the creator from harm caused by the alteration of the meaning of her work through unauthorised use, at least where that use constitutes a misrepresentation as to the creator's intended meaning. This degree of control over the meaning of expressive works may even be seen as entailed in the right to free speech. In First Amendment cases such as *Hurley v. Irish-American Gay, Lesbian and Bisexual Group of Boston*,[iii] the Supreme Court of the United States has affirmed that a speaker ought to have control over the content of her self-expression at least to the extent of not being forced – even by quite tenuous implication as in the case *Boy Scouts of America v. James Dale*[iv] – to express views with which she would disagree. However, there have been critics of this position. Harm from the unauthorised use of a work is of a type to which all expressive acts are subject – all our words are constantly being read and misread – and it is arguable that the state ought not to intervene to prevent use of this type. This objection would be particularly strong where the unauthorised use did not imply any defamatory claim about the creator's intended meaning. It may be that the right approach to the reading and misreading of the creator's work is simply to encourage her to produce more work that makes her meaning clear. It may be that the right to free speech entails no control over how our words will be received, except the control achieved by more speech, by explanation and clarification. These are difficult issues, but it is clear that those who would rely upon the argument from harm to justify copyright have considerable work to do in explaining why the relevant harm is of a type that the state ought to remedy. The argument from harm seems to be of some, but limited, assistance in justifying copyright.

b. The Argument from Unjust Enrichment

The argument from unjust enrichment is that the unauthorised user of a work receives a benefit from its use and thereby 'reaps where she has not sown'. This behaviour of 'reaping without sowing' is assumed to be morally reprehensible. The phrase is biblical and assumes much of its rhetorical power from that resonance, although its equivalent biblical usage occurs in a New Testament parable in which the behaviour is neither condoned nor condemned. This principle, and the corresponding argument from unjust enrichment, are even more problematic than the argument from harm to the creator.

First, it is clear that the principle against reaping without sowing is not absolute. We all reap without sowing, and regard ourselves as justified in doing so, even without the consent, implicit or explicit, of those upon whose efforts we build. For example, the pioneer of a new style or technique in the visual arts might establish an artistic language and educate a public to understand it. The pioneer may wish to preserve the style or technique she develops for her own use, or for the use of those within her circle. But subsequent creators will imitate, adapt and expand that style or technique. And they may well do so, not only without the permission of the pioneer, but against her objections and to challenge her authority as the first practitioner of the style or technique. Imitation – authorised and unauthorised – is a vital part of ongoing artistic discourse. To condemn all reaping without sowing would be to condemn all imitation and to stifle the development of artistic traditions. It would be to condemn us to live in a world of self-sufficiency mitigated only by agreement, a world in which few of us either could, or would want to, live.

Second, the principle against reaping without sowing is not an independent principle that can be used to justify entitlements to the exclusive use of a work. It is relevant, if at all, only once such an entitlement has been established. Given that the principle is not absolute, the question upon which its application depends is precisely when, if ever, it is wrong to reap without sowing. The answer implicit in the principle is that it is wrong to reap without sowing if someone else, and in particular the sower, has a stronger claim to that which is reaped. But this, of course, assumes that the sower does have a claim to that which is reaped and that its strength can be assessed. This assumption cannot be justified on the basis of the principle itself. In the copyright context, whether a particular unauthorised use constitutes an *unjust* enrichment depends upon whether, and how strongly, a creator's claim to exclude others from its use can be justified. But that is exactly what the various justifications for copyright are seeking to determine. So the principle against reaping without sowing turns out to be one that can only apply once it has been determined on other grounds that a creator ought to be able to exclude others from the use of her work. It adds nothing to the substantive justification of the law of copyright.

II. Arguments parallel to those used to underpin the Institution of Property

We turn, then, from two arguments used to justify copyright that parallel those found in the law obligations to arguments more frequently used to support the institution of property. There are four such arguments. They are; the argument from creation; the argument from desert; the argument from person-hood and the argument from personal autonomy.

a. The Argument from Creation

The intuition that we are entitled to control that which we create seems fundamental. It is given expression, for example, in the claim of the monotheistic religious traditions that the Creator God is owed obedience by His creation. When asked to justify the claim to copyright, many creators simply point out that they were responsible for bringing a particular work into being. Although this argument is not made in any of the academic literature discussing copyright, it is included here because it is so frequently encountered in the claims of creators themselves.

The weakness of this argument as a justification for copyright can be seen by contrasting it with the theological claim that it seems to parallel. First, unlike the God of the monotheistic religions, no human being creates *ex nihilo*. Every work, even leaving aside the claims of the post-modern critics, is in some part creation and in some part imitation. It at least draws upon the traditions of the genre in which it is working. Distinguishing precisely what an individual creator contributes and what she borrows can be almost impossible. Yet the argument from the fact of creation requires that such distinctions be drawn.

Second, and more importantly, while the theological claim has to do with the relationship between the Creator and His creation, the argument for copyright from creation concerns the relationship between the creator and third parties. We have already established that being prevented from using a work can do a would-be user harm. Later on, we shall see that being prevented from using a work may also unduly restrict a would-be user's personal autonomy. The important question is why the fact of creation gives the creator a normative claim against these third parties, particularly one that trumps their claim that he ought not to do them harm or to restrict their liberty in situations in which preventing them from using the work would do so. It is a logical mistake to argue that the fact of creation can ground such a normative claim. Those who point to the fact of creation as a justification for copyright, seem implicitly to be making the normative claim that the unauthorised use of a work harms a creator, robs her of her just deserts or affects her person-hood and the recognition of her personal autonomy. Given that these are each independent justifications of copyright, it seems that the argument from creation, properly understood, simply collapses into these other arguments. Like the argument from unjust enrichment, the argument from the fact of creation makes no independent contribution to the justification of copyright.

b. The Argument from Desert

It is a claim frequently made that the creator of a work 'deserves' control over its use. There are two ways in which such a desert claim may be established. First, a creator might deserve control over the use of the work as a reward for her efforts in producing it. Second, a creator might deserve control over the use of the work as a reward for the contribution that it makes to her culture. In outlining the difficulties that arise with these arguments, we should put to one side the general philosophical difficulties raised by the concept of desert. Desert is an uncertain concept that has only recently become the subject of rigorous philosophical analysis. But, even assuming that the concept of desert can be clearly expounded, it proves a difficult basis for the justification of copyright. This is for three reasons.

First, there is no direct correlation between a creator's effort or contribution and the works which copyright might be expected to protect. If it is effort that is deserving of reward, then the question arises what the minimum threshold of effort might be for a work to be deserving of protection and whether works that required little effort should be protected. Copyright would be in danger of protecting only the perspiring, and not the inspired, creator. If it is contribution that is deserving of reward, then the question becomes what level of contribution is deserving. We have already seen that every work is in some part creation, and thus potentially a contribution to a community's cultural life, and in some part imitation. But even that part of a work which is genuinely creative and thus potentially a contribution to a community's cultural life, may actually detract from it. Take the example of a violent and pornographic motion picture. It seems peculiar to claim that even the creative parts of such a work make a contribution to our culture which is deserving of reward.

Second, even if the creator of a work can establish her desert there may be good reasons for not recognising her claim to control the use of the work. She may already have been rewarded in other ways. Imagine, for example, that the creator of an visual image has been paid for its production. She may have been amply rewarded in the payment she receives and copyright protection might be more than she deserves. Further, whenever a would-be user can show that exclusion from use of a work will do her harm or unduly restrict her personal autonomy, the question arises as to why the creator of the work ought to be rewarded at the expense of the would-be user.

Third, there is no reason why, even if the creator of the work deserves something as her reward for effort or contribution, it ought necessarily to be the control over the use of the work that copyright affords. We reward those who work hard to establish world peace and thereby contribute to our public life, with gratitude, praise and, perhaps, a Nobel prize. It is hard to see that the creator of an artistic work expends more effort, or contributes more, than such people. In particular, the reward that many creators seek has nothing to do with copyright protection, but rather with the type of protection afforded by moral rights regimes: that is, the ability to prevent their work from being distorted and the ability to be identified with their work. The concept of desert seems once again to express a persistent intuition that creators ought sometimes to be able to control their work but is, in itself, unable to provide a satisfying justification of the copyright system.

c. The Argument from Personhood

This argument is that a work is an embodiment of the personality of the creator. Control over the work is essential to secure the creator's control over her own personality. This view has been wrongly attributed to both Kant and Hegel, but parallels the work of the modern American philosopher Radin regarding the general justification of property rights. There are two principal difficulties with this approach.

First, it is questionable just how many works constitute, or are intended to constitute, an embodiment of the creator's personality. The concept of personality is itself problematic. More seems to be intended than the concept of reputation protected by the law of defamation. What might be intended is the author's self-presentation, including her self-expression. Her personality may be, not how she is perceived by others, but how she wants to present herself. But it is unclear how much art is intended by its creator to constitute even such self-expression, let alone some even broader notion of personality. The poet T.S. Eliot famously thought art an escape from personality rather than its incorporation. It may be that an individual artist embodies her personality in her work, but it may also be that she would be appalled by such a Romantic conceptualisation of the relationship between the artist and her work.

Second, even assuming personality to mean something as discernible as self-presentation, it is unclear precisely how much control over her self-presentation a creator ought to be afforded. It has already been suggested that such control might be appropriate in contexts in which there is a threat that unauthorised use will change the meaning of the work in a way that does the creator harm. But that she ought to have control over her self-presentation to the extent of being able to prohibit the reproduction or publication of her work in a way which is perfectly faithful to its meaning though, perhaps, at a time or by someone not of her choosing, is far more questionable. If a case can be made that the creator should have such control, it must have something to do with the need to grant her a sphere of personal autonomy, an alternative justification for copyright which is considered below. As a justification for copyright in visual works, the argument from personhood seems, without more, to have little to recommend it.

d. The Argument from Personal Autonomy

This attractive argument flows from the intuition that valuing personal autonomy must involve granting an individual at least some control over those things with which she is most closely associated: to allow her to carve out an area of individual dominion. If a creator can show a close association with a particular work, then respect for her personal autonomy may require that she be given at least some degree of control over its use. This type of argument has often been built upon the justifications for private property offered by Locke in *Two Treatises of Government* and Hegel in *Philosophy of Right*.

Locke argues that every person has a property in her own person and thence her labour; which property seems to amount to a conception of personal liberty. When a person labours on an object which is not owned by anyone else, she joins that object with her labour and thereby makes it hers. Thus if a creator has joined her labour with an artistic work the only way in which to respect her property in her person – her liberty – might be to afford her property in the work.

Hegel argues that private property helps individuals to develop as autonomous persons by allowing them to interact with external objects in a way which facilitates the 'supersession of the pure subjectivity of personality'.[v] The precise meaning of this claim, and the extent to which Hegel's work constitutes a variant of person-hood theory, is a matter of considerable contention. But the best reading of the relevant passages of *Philosophy of Right* seems to be that property helps individuals to develop as autonomous persons by carving out an area over which they can exercise their will. It does this by enabling them to make choices about taking possession, using and alienating things in the external world. While for these purposes Hegel argues that 'mental aptitudes, erudition, artistic skill, ... inventions, and so forth'[vi] do not themselves count as objects capable of constituting property, they may become capable of constituting property by being embodied in 'something external'[vii]. Hegel specifically anticipates that copyright can constitute property on this basis.

Without attempting a detailed critique of the work of Locke or Hegel, at least two difficulties with arguments from personal autonomy as justifications for copyright should be outlined.

First, none of the usual arguments from personal autonomy can establish a nexus between the creator and her work such that recognition of her right to control the work is essential to recognition of her personal autonomy. As for arguments built upon the work of Locke, it has been pointed out: (i) that a person may not own herself, even though she is free, because it may be impossible to own a person; (ii) that the concept of 'mixing labour' is incoherent because labour, as a series of actions, is incapable of being mixed with something that could become the subject of a property right; and (iii) that there is no necessary reason, even though she is free, why the labourer ought to gain the resultant mixture rather than simply to lose her labour. This last objection would be particularly compelling in the situation in which a work is more the product of a moment of inspiration than a long period of labour. As for arguments built upon the work of Hegel, it is not clear why Hegel sees property as essential to the attainment of freedom, rather than merely as an institution which expands an individual's range of choices and thereby increases her autonomy. A possible solution to this problem has been offered by Waldron who emphasises that a person's actions in relation to an object may change it, 'registering the effects of willing at one point of time and forcing an individual's willing to become consistent and stable over a period.'[viii] This effect would be lost if others were allowed to alter the object after the initial registering of the individual's will and some type of continuing control over the object is therefore essential to the development of the individual as an autonomous person. This reading of Hegel has been criticised by those who point out that Hegel seems to conceive of autonomy as the condition in which an individual can operate as a 'choosing agent', rather than as a particular psychological state. But, even if it can be accepted, Waldron's reading may still mean that the work of Hegel provides only limited support to the claim that copyright is essential to the recognition of personal autonomy. This is because, as we have already seen, the usual assumption is that works are not crowdable in the sense that their use by one person will not change them for use by another. It might only be in the context in which the use of an expressive work does significantly alter it that this justification of copyright could be relied upon.

Second, against the claim that control over a creator's work is essential to the protection of her personal autonomy, must be set the claim that the grant of such control is a limitation of the autonomy of those who would seek to use the work without her permission. It is therefore necessary to demonstrate that the impact on the creator's personal autonomy of refusing her control over the work, would outweigh the impact on the would-be user's autonomy of granting the creator such control. Again, there are hints, but only inconclusive hints, as to how this issue might be handled in the work of Locke and Hegel. Locke argues that the labourer only has a right to appropriate the fruits of her labour if there is 'enough and as good left in common for others.' This proviso has, of course, been the subject of extensive philosophical commentary. But at least one commentator claims that it preserves the autonomy of the would-be user in all situations in which 'use of the [work] is essential to the use of his rational and creative faculties.'[ix] If that is true, then the argument would only justify a far more restricted version of copyright law than that currently in force in any part of the world. Hegel addresses the problem of the autonomy of the would-be user directly. He acknowledges that given that 'the purpose of a product of mind is that people other than its author should understand and make it the possession of their ideas',[x] it must sometimes be legitimate for others to take the ideas which underpin that valuable intangible and embody them in a different form. Indeed, so much might others take on those ideas that they might embody them in something external in a way that might give them as strong a claim to those ideas as has the original creator.[xi] In other words, preventing them from using a work will sometimes be an unjustified restraint on their autonomy. Hegel argues that the question of when preventing the use of a work is justified cannot be finally settled either in principle or by positive legislation.[xii] He says that 'copyright legislation only attains its end of securing the property rights or author and publisher only to a very restricted extent',[xiii] but claims that determining precisely what that extent should be is a fruitless task. The argument from personal autonomy seems to support some type of copyright regime, but knowing what precise shape that regime ought to take is exceedingly difficult.

Conclusion

It can be seen that none of the arguments outlined above offers a knock-down justification for the law of copyright in any particular form, far less in the precise form in which it is increasingly being harmonised at an international level. The history of the law of copyright is a history of disputes between three groups each represented by powerful lobbies: the creators of copyright material such as authors and visual artists, the producers of copyright material such as publishers and printers and institutional users of copyright material such as educational institutions and libraries. Each of these groups relies upon the type of arguments outlined in this essay to secure legislative change in particular contexts. The interests of non-institutional user groups have been barely represented in copyright policy discussions. In that creators have benefited from such negotiations, they have benefited most when their interests coincide with the interests of producer groups. They have benefited least when, as users themselves of copyright material, their interests have coincided with those of the non-institutional users of copyright material. If it is accepted that cumulatively these arguments constitute some type of case for granting creator's control over their work, the really interesting discussion is at the level of detail and concerns precisely when and how that control ought to be granted. Creators need actively to participate in this discussion and, to do so, they need to be armed with the arguments outlined in this essay. For it is with the weaponry of those arguments that important battles over the detail of the copyright system will be fought and, perhaps, won or lost.

    i Gautier, P., *Propriété littéraire et artistique*, 3rd edn,
        (Presses Universitaires de France, Paris, 1999) at 29.

    ii [1976] A.C. 64

   iii 515 U.S. 557, 132 L. Ed. 2d 487, 115 S. Ct. 2338

   iv 530 U.S. 640, 147 L. Ed 2d 554, 120 S. Ct. 2446

    v Hegel, G. W. F., *Philosophy of Right* tr. with notes by T. M. Knox (Clarendon Press,
        Oxford, 1967) at 235

   vi *ibid* at 40

  vii *ibid* at 41

 viii Waldron, J., *The Right to Private Property* (Clarendon Press, Oxford, 1988) at 373

   ix Gordon, W., 'A Property Right in Self-Expression: Equality and Individualism in
        the Natural Law of Intellectual Property' (1993) 102 Yale L.J. 1533 at 1576.

    x Hegel, G.W.F., *Philosophy of Right* tr. with notes by T. M. Knox (Clarendon Press,
        Oxford, 1967) at 55.

   xi *ibid* at 55-56.

  xii *ibid* at 56.

 xiii *ibid* at 56

Appropriating the Postmodern: Copyright and the Challenge of the New

Brad Sherman

The academic energy dissipated in chronicling the various changes in copyright law has been formidable. Indeed, the problems that new subject matter poses for the law, have become a prime focus for many commentators. For example, we are reminded that copyright law is unable to accommodate 'new' forms of cultural creation such as Aboriginal art, databases, and digital sampling in music, film, and video.[i] While the challenge of the new is a theme that continues to dominate the literature, there has been a change in the way that copyright law is presented. Instead of merely outlining the problems posed by a new technology or subject matter, commentators discuss the demise of copyright law,[ii] the irrelevance of its modernist assumptions,[iii] and the way in which central ideas of copyright law, such as authorship and originality, are being currently undermined. Drawing upon developments in adjacent fields, these range from post-structuralist arguments about the death of the author, to examinations of the impact of Romanticism and related notions such as personality and genius on copyright law.[iv] While these critiques raise many issues, which impinge upon our understanding of copyright, the most interesting and challenging dilemmas have been reserved for the theory-informed genres of appropriation art and postmodern 'painting'.[v]

Appropriation art, said to represent 'the most radical challenge to the copyright laws to date',[vi] is the process by which artists borrow images from other sources and assimilate them into their own work.[vii] Although postmodern representational practices cannot easily be accommodated within accepted artistic categories, appropriation art usually takes the form of open and direct copying, montage, collage and simulation. Given its roots in Dada, Surrealism, and Pop Art,[viii] and the fact that appropriation art covers a wide range of activities, it is unsurprising that the extent to which images are appropriated (or 'copied'), and the uses to which they are put, varies between different artists. For instance, the act of appropriation often involves the artists reproducing an original work and attributing the copy to themselves.[ix] Other artists copy an original work, but make minor changes or additions to it. Examples of this include Marcel Duchamp's famous addition of a moustache to a replica of the *Mona Lisa*. More recent examples are an entire series of Mike Bidlo's full-sized copies of paintings by Cezanne, Matisse, Pollock, Lichtenstein, and Picasso, to which Bidlo attaches his signature and renames them, as in the latter case, *Not Picasso*. Some artists copy an original work, but alter the medium in which it is represented,[x] while others mix subjects or areas that are classically separated.[xi] In this way, post-modern artistic practices frequently entail movement across boundaries: most notably mixing high and low art; the artistic and the obscene; and the visual and the verbal.

While for some people, postmodernism offers a 'value-free, decorative, de-historicized quotation of past forms', for others it 'is a value-problematizing form of acknowledging the history and, ironically, the politics of representation'.[xii] By intentionally reproducing images taken from other works of art and claiming authorship of the new product, appropriation artists raise questions about copying and plagiarism. They also highlight the precarious position occupied by artists in relation to the traditions they work in and, in so doing, remind us that 'the uniqueness of a work of art is inseparable from its being imbedded in the fabric of tradition'.[xiii] By placing a well-known object such as the American flag, a painting by Picasso, or an advertising logo in a new context,[xiv] the appropriation artist aims to denaturalize it and, thus, to provide the borrowed object with a new meaning or vocabulary.[xv] Such practices, frequently force us to reconsider the way we think not only of the object in question, but also about art more generally. For example, appropriation artists often caricature and mock traditional artistic criteria such as originality and authorship,[xvi] questioning whether it is any longer possible to speak of 'original' works of art, and whether it is sensible to attribute a work of art to an isolated, individual – the artist. By openly copying images, appropriation artists emphasise how the environment they represent is made up as much by advertising logos, trademarks, and media images protected by copyright law, as it is by landscapes, mountain ranges, and forests.[xvii] In so doing, they aim to bring attention to the role that laws governing intellectual property play in policing that landscape.[xviii]

It has been suggested that appropriation art stands 'opposed to the concepts of originality and expression that form the foundations of copyright law'.[xix] We have also been told that 'post-modernist art critiques the very attributes that copyright law uses to define art: namely, artistic creativity and originality'.[xx] Like post-modern theory, appropriation art is said to represent 'the most radical challenge to the copyright laws to date. Indeed, appropriation art virtually renders the Copyright Act's insistence on creativity and originality obsolete'.[xxi]

Andy Warhol, *Gold Jackie*, 1964

It is the aim of this essay to examine the claims made about the effects of postmodern artistic practice on copyright law. More specifically, we will explore the way appropriation art is said to 'challenge', 'critique', and 'oppose' the legal notion of *originality*. Within this context, two questions will resound: (1) To what is appropriation art said to be opposed? (2) What does it mean to say that copyright law is challenged by appropriation art and how is it challenged? In answering these questions, it will be argued that the claims made about postmodern art 'opposing' and 'undermining' originality are based on a number of unexamined and, on the whole, unsubstantiated assumptions. These include the idea that in highlighting semantic indeterminacy the law will somehow collapse and the related assumption that the activities of the artistic avant-garde (and what is written about them in law journals) have a direct and corresponding impact upon copyright law. In highlighting these claims, I hope to explain why it is that 'despite the rhetorical force of much that has been said and done in the name of 'appropriation' over the past decade, it has produced few changes in the way that the law deals with artistic property'. xxii

Opposing Originality

Originality operates in copyright law as an evaluative concept that distinguishes works that are given legal protection from those which are not. There are a number of ways in which the work could be evaluated so as to satisfy the exclusionary function performed by the originality examination. One option would be to focus upon the work in isolation from any external points of reference and to judge the work in terms of its own mode of being, or its inherent attributes. Another possibility would be to adopt a more subjective approach which concentrates upon some intuitive or emotional reaction from the observer of the work. In turn, the work could be evaluated in terms of its relationship with some external point of reference, such as the artist or audience.[xxiii] While there is a degree of overlap between these different approaches, it is via the latter method that the originality of the work is determined in copyright law. More specifically, this decision is made with reference to the relationship between subject and artefact or, to use more conventional legal language, between author and work. Originality is, as Whale says, 'the word used to describe the causal relationship between an author and the material form in which the work is embodied'.[xxiv]

One consequence of using the author/work relationship as the framework within which originality is determined, is that there is little concern in copyright law as to whether or not a work is novel. That is, the meaning given to originality in copyright law differs from its conventional meaning, now carrying with it the meaning of being distinguished by 'genius',[xxv] and therefore not a mechanical act. Given that the originality examination does not depend upon the novelty of the work, it is meaningless to speak of the problems created for copyright law by the fact that in the age of mechanical reproductions there are very few originals.[xxvi] Indeed, rather than being undermined, copyright law should be seen as dependent upon and, in part, the product of mechanical reproduction.

Although decisions as to the originality of the work are set within the artist/work relationship, this should only be seen as providing the framework within which the examination proceeds. Scrutiny of the way in which the framework is used reveals that copyright law only recognises certain types of relationships (or labour) as giving rise to the necessary qualities that enable us to label a work 'original'. That is, the author/work relationship is treated as a necessary, but not sufficient, condition for establishing the originality of copyright works. There have been a number of attempts to outline and describe the particular situations beyond the author/work relationship, which provide the requisite conditions of originality. These include the idea that in order for a work to be original, it must not be copied.[xxvii] A variation on this is the idea that the work must originate from the author.[xxviii] Another approach sees originality in terms of the 'skill, labour, and effort'[xxix] that goes into the creation of the artefact, to which there is sometimes added the requirement of a minimum level of creativity. Yet another approach states that, where the work has been copied, mere 'skill, labour, and effort' is insufficient to establish the originality of the work. Instead, what is needed is that there be a material embellishment of a visually significant kind.[xxx] Most recently, and more controversially, the U.S. Supreme Court said that for a work to be original, it must be 'creative' (and not merely involve the exertion of sweat, labour, and effort).[xxxi]

A number of commentators have remarked upon the differences that exist between the various tests used to describe that 'something irreducible' which distinguishes the original from the non-original work.[xxxii] In part, the diversity of these tests reflects the multi-faceted nature of copyright law and the range of the subject matter protected. More importantly, however, it reflects the fact that since originality is an evaluative (evidential) concept, it is very difficult, if not impossible, to describe that 'something special' which enables copyright law to label a work original.

Despite these difficulties, there have been numerous attempts to rationalise and order the different tests used to distinguish the original from the non-original work. The ambiguity of the various tests, and the way in which this ambiguity is most frequently resolved, can be seen in the following: 'Conflicting claims have arisen because of the admitted ambiguity of "originality"' . . . 'but what I want to show is that these [different conceptions of originality] grow out of the same philosophical root: property in the person'.[xxxiii] More specifically, we are told that in copyright law, 'original' means 'that the particular work owes its origin to the author'.[xxxiv] Put another way, 'authorship as origin is . . . the most fundamental category of copyright law, in relation to which all other categories are secondary'.[xxxv] While there are differences between these various approaches, they have in common the fact that the central point of their discussion is the *author* of the work. That is, the technique used to order and rationalise the various tests determining whether a work is original or not, is to focus on the role of the *subject* or *author* in that process. The more extreme versions of this approach (as in *Feist*[xxxvi]) share the idea that the subject, as the central voice of creation, must always be present in, and have an impact upon, the production of the artefact. Without this, the work cannot be said to be original.

While it may be possible, on the surface, to suggest that the author acts as the central organising principle of the originality examination, this is only made possible by ignoring a number of other important questions. That is, the attempt to collapse the originality examination into the subject is only achieved by suppressing other aspects of the examination. One of the most important factors suppressed as a result of the preoccupation with the subject, is the idea of the *work* and of the prominent role this concept plays in copyright law.[xxxvii]

While many commentators have focused on the problematic nature of the author, few if any have focused on the equally problematic notion of the work.[xxxviii] Even if we accept the subject as a focal point of examination, the answer to the question of whether an author has exhibited the necessary degree of control, choice, or input in the production of the work, or has exerted the requisite degree of 'sweat, labour, and effort', depends on a number of different factors such as the type of work in question, how that work as a genre is interpreted, and the decision as to when and where a copyright work begins and ends. Such ontological problems about the nature and existence of the work are exasperated in many jurisdictions by the absence of formal registration requirements such as exist in patent, design, and trademark law.

One of the consequences of using the individual as the basis for explaining the originality examination is that the work tends to be treated as a stable, coherent unity – it is sprung shut and rendered determinate.[xxxix] The idea of the work as a closed and stable entity is reinforced by the fact that most copyright works have a number of well-defined features such as cover, title, signature, and frame, which provide an apparent totality, coherence, and unity. However unified and coherent the legal notion of the copyright work may appear to be, upon closer scrutiny, it transpires that the copyright work is inherently unstable. There are numerous situations where one can see this instability and fluidity, and perhaps the best example is in relation to the idea-expression dichotomy: in the attempt by copyright law to stipulate the site upon which this elusive notion of originality must be located.

The idea of the copyright work as a stable, fixed entity, which is assumed in many of the discussions on copyright and postmodern artistic practices, is further undermined when we acknowledge that the meaning given to the copyright work is dependent upon and shaped by the particular legal category in which it is placed. The circular nature of this relationship can be seen if we attempt to answer the question of whether or not appropriation art is eligible for copyright protection.

Since appropriating practices clearly borrow from identifiable sources, the usual reaction to appropriation art is that the work had been copied. While the act of copying clearly involves the exertion of sweat, labour, and effort, in order to gain copyright protection, there must be material embellishment of a visual nature.[xl] Although the distinguishing variation may, as Posner says, 'inhere in a detail, a nuance, a shading too small to be apprehended by a Judge',[xli] it is unlikely that it will also extend to the meaning of, or the information relayed by, the work. The reason for this is that the originality of the copyright work is shaped by the category of work in question: artistic works are judged in terms of artistic criteria,[xlii] and literary works in terms of literary criteria.[xliii] In short, artistic copyright is concerned with the visual image, whereas literary copyright is said to protect the written communication of instructions, information, and ideas.[xliv]

The problem confronting the postmodern artist in these circumstances is that there is very little, if any, physical/visual difference between the appropriation art and the source from which the images are appropriated.[xlv] While copyright law focuses on the material embellishment, that is, the physical change introduced to the object, the distinguishing feature of appropriation art lies not in its physical or material nature, but in the meaning that is given to the image embodied in the painting. Thus, while copyright law ignores the meaning of the artistic work and focuses on its surface appearance, appropriation art inverts this process by focusing on the meaning of the work at the expense of its 'visual' appearance.[xlvi] If we step back from this examination, we see that the appropriation artist's difficulties arise from the fact that the work will be judged as an artistic work, and not as a literary one. In other words, the problems confronting the appropriation artist can be traced both to the categories used by copyright law when it evaluates originality, and to the rigidity with which these categories are interpreted.[xlvii]

While an examination of the likely fate of postmodern artistic practices in copyright law highlights the importance of the way in which the subject matter is categorised, it also enables us to glimpse some of the blind spots and the circularities of copyright law. In particular, it highlights the unstable nature of the copyright work by reminding us not only that the idea is unsettled when its dependence upon expression is recognised, but also that the expression is further undermined when we acknowledge its circular relationship with the category of work in which it is embodied.

So far, this examination has focused on what could be referred to as the structures or frameworks of the originality examination. However important these structural constraints may be, they only provide us with a partial picture of that process. The reason for this is that the question of the originality of a particular work not only depends upon the structure or relationship within which the questions are asked, but also upon the specialised traditions, practices and codes of knowledge which shape the concretion of that structure. The influence of these factors not only extends to decisions on whether a particular work is original or not but, more importantly, to the question of whether a particular category of 'objects' falls within the scope of the copyright protection. This can be seen, for example, in relation to the question of whether the art of the indigenous Australians is susceptible to copyright protection. While the situation is now changing, there were a number of factors which were influential in shaping the belief that Aboriginal art was not creative and, therefore, for the purposes of copyright law, not original. These ranged from the fact that Aboriginal 'art' was displayed in ethnographic museums where it was defined in functional, rather than aesthetic, terms to the belief that, as a form of primitive art, Aboriginal art was timeless and, therefore, authorless.[xlviii]

Despite the important role that cultural, social, and practical factors play in shaping decisions about whether or not a work is original, in all but a few instances they are ignored. While this can be seen as yet another feature that copyright law shares with the legal tradition in general, there are a number of factors peculiar to copyright law which reinforce this loss. This stems in part from the attempt by copyright law to distance itself from perceived problems in aesthetic judgement, which in turn reflect the modernist's anxiety of contamination: the fear of art being tainted by politics, morality, or other social judgements.[xlix] Indeed, modern copyright law has so doggedly attempted to separate itself from aesthetic and cultural questions, it seems to have adopted Malraux's notion of the museum without walls, in which 'the whole of known culture is defined according to a neutral and negative institutional equality, divorced from all function, meaning, human use, and social dimension'.[l] Whatever advantages there may be in this cultural and aesthetic agnosticism, the belief that aesthetic considerations play no role in copyright law has reinforced the denial of the 'interpretive dimension', and of the impact that the cultural, social, and political factors play in the originality examination.

This indicates a fundamental confusion exists between the rejection of any attempt to evaluate the work in terms of its artistic merit and the cultural factors which shape and influence decisions – those things that tell us what constitutes a painting or a literary work in the first place. Another influential factor in the suppression of aesthetic and cultural interpretation is the sense in which the preoccupation with the creator of the work – and the individualisation of the work that this emphasis promotes – leads to the isolation of the work from the contextual factors that situate and constitute it as an entity. When combined and set within the framework of the Anglo-American legal tradition, these factors have, in Bourdieu's words, the 'gradual effect of masking, through the inculcation of things arbitrary, the arbitrariness of things inculcated' with the result that 'culture . . . becomes nature', in other words, 'culture is realised by denying itself as such, that is as something both artificial and artificially acquired'[li].

While the impact of these social and cultural practices and prejudices differs from work to work, the most important consequence of recognising their existence is the further undermining of the stability that is so often attributed to the copyrighted work. Given the positive enabling role that such prejudice plays in interpretation, there can be no end to the interpretative process and, as such, no end to the meanings that are given to copyrighted works. The presumed stability of the copyrighted work is further undermined when we recognise that the meaning of a particular work not only changes according to the cultural prejudice that confronts it, but also that these influences are ubiquitous and fragmented; change over time; differ from work to work; and even differ within a particular genre of works. When we add to this the ontological problems that surround the copyrighted work, the difficulties that the law has in separating the idea of a work from its expression, and the circular relationship that exists between expression and the category in which the work is placed, it becomes apparent that it is not some unified, coherent object that copyright law deals with, so much as it is a fluid and open-ended set of concepts. The consequence of this is, as the work is sprung open – in effect, rendered indeterminate – we are reminded of an earlier era when the work was seen not as the product of a producer, but rather as something which was transpersonal and in flux.[lii]

The stability of the originality examination, which is taken for granted in the material on copyright and postmodernism, is further undermined when we acknowledge that the examination is only made possible because it is situated within and based upon other conceptual frameworks. Investigations into these frameworks reveal that they too are based on other ideas and concepts. That is, as the originality examination is unpacked, we are presented with a set of concepts, questions, and ways of thinking that are themselves open-ended, fragmented, and contradictory.

Taking with us this particular interpretation of the originality examination, it is now possible to return to the question posed at the beginning of this section: What does it mean to suggest that originality is opposed or undermined by appropriation art? If the open-ended, de-centred, and dispersed view of originality is accepted, the answer to this question must be that it is both unhelpful and problematic to speak of appropriation art as being challenged by, or opposed to, originality. More specifically, it reveals that in order to be in a position to reach these conclusions, it is necessary to see originality (and indeed appropriation art) as coherent, unified structures. The reason for this is that given the frameworks within which the arguments proceed, and the fact that there seems to be little desire to embrace more extreme forms of radical indeterminacy, the only way in which one can say appropriation art undermines copyright law is to believe that in its natural or proper state, copyright is based upon fixed and stable ideas.

What does it mean, for example, to say that, as a result of recent controversies in literary theory – like that stating we can no longer say that an author's work is original – 'one of the fundamental supports for copyright law comes crashing down'? [liii] Implicit within this argument is the idea that if one is able to highlight inconsistencies in copyright law, the system will collapse. As with many of the more conventional approaches to the subject, faith in the unity and coherence of copyright law underlies such an argument, as does the belief that its constituent elements are (and should be) unified in a common theme or aim. Accordingly, it is felt that if any one area were to fail, the whole edifice would also fail. These arguments also share the idea that copyright law does and should speak with one voice, be it as the basis for criticism or exegesis. In this sense, many of these postmodern writings reveal themselves to be archetypically modern, particularly in so far as theirs is a project that attempts to locate (or rescue) the metanarratives of copyright law, or to argue that postmodern artistic practices challenge and undermine these metanarratives.

Another consequence of recognising the open-ended nature of the originality examination is that we are forced to accept that much of the literature on copyright and postmodernism is based on a selective reading of copyright law: that it ignores and suppresses aspects of the originality examination. To concede as such leads us to ask a further question: Why should we accept the picture of copyright law upon which these arguments are grounded? Given that it is possible to agree with an interpretation, which highlights the open-ended nature of copyright law, this question has made it all the more pressing to disagree with the conclusions that are said to follow from it. It is possible to argue, for example, that however indeterminate or open-ended the concepts of originality and idea-expression may be, this does not deny the fact that they continue to play a central role in copyright law. That is, it is possible to accept the open-ended nature of the originality examination without necessarily agreeing that this means that copyright is undermined or even challenged. Likewise, it is possible to accept that although postmodern artistic practices raise important questions about authorship, originality, and plagiarism, they will have little impact on the way that copyright law operates as a practice.

The fact that little consideration has been given to these issues is indicative of more fundamental problems. This can be seen in the fact that nowhere is it spelled out how and why appropriation art is said to oppose or challenge copyright law; why it is the function of judgement – the role of discrimination, taste, or political choice – that necessarily leads to the demise of copyright; or why the activities of the avant-garde, challenging as they are, should have any necessary impact upon copyright law. Hand in hand with the absence of any explanation as to why appropriation art challenges or undermines copyright law is the unquestioned assumption that there is a direct link or correspondence between law and culture.[liv] That is, there is a belief in the universality of art, and that the questions raised by appropriation art have a corresponding effect upon legal practice. While it is possible to suggest that postmodern artistic practices may prompt us to reconsider the way we think about originality and authorship, it is more problematic to suggest that these practices will necessarily have a corresponding impact in law.

Such conclusions also reveal that though these recent writings on copyright and postmodernism pose many important challenges to our understanding of the law, there are many points shared in common with the more traditional approaches to the subject. It is this, which explains why, on reading these commentaries, there is more a sense of continuity and deja-vu than of the demise or death of copyright law. That is, while there is a sense in which the recent postmodern writings on copyright law attempt to distance themselves from the more orthodox literature, if we step back from these discussions we see that there are, despite the implicit claims to the contrary, many points shared in common. The main reason for this is that much of the recent literature has taken all too seriously what could be referred to as the grand narratives of copyright law. Even the most critical of commentaries have tended to adopt the language, ideas, and ways of seeing which they seek to criticise, and by following a familiar style of legal scholarship, they apply ideas to law but layer them on surfaces which are neat, ordered, and complete.

While it may not be possible to talk of appropriation art as being opposed to originality, and it is highly unlikely that the legal system will grind to a halt because of the work of a Sherrie Levine or a Jeff Koons, this does not mean that we cannot speak of originality. Nor utilise some of the insights that appropriation art and postmodernism offer for our understanding of copyright law. Indeed there are a number of different options available. One possibility is to explore the various strategies and techniques adopted to avoid the uncertainty and flux that characterise not only the originality examination, but also copyright law more generally. In response to appropriation art, it may be interesting to examine the role that boundaries play within copyright law, how and when they are made transverse, and the problems they then generate. Another possibility arises when we recognise that despite the problems often associated with the idea of the 'subject', it cannot be denied that the author acts, at least on the surface, as a central organising principle in copyright law.

As such, rather than focusing on the imaginary character of the author, a better approach might be to account for the role played by the subject in the way we think of and organise copyright law. Yet another approach would be to shift the focus of attention away from copyright law's dependency on the author, to an examination of the extent to which the author is constituted by copyright law. In turn, we could outline the imagination and skill that has been exercised in the attempts to reconcile new forms of authorship – such as companies[lv] and computers – to the idea of individual authorship that prevails in copyright law. Alternatively, as many now argue, we could replace the subject as the centre of analysis and focus on the factors which promote and hinder the circulation of copyright works, or upon the variety of practices which help constitute the copyright work as an entity.

Perhaps the most important task of all, however, is casting a disbelieving eye over the picture that has been painted and so readily accepted of copyright law. While there are numerous ways in which this could be done, a good starting point is to move the focus of attention away from merely lamenting the modernist features of copyright law and, instead, recognise that copyright law is made up of a mixture of the modern and the postmodern. Indeed, in its preoccupation with surface, its recognition of the intertextuality of works, and its constant refusal to distinguish works of high and low authorship, copyright law is perhaps among the most postmodern of all legal subjects.[lvi]

Reprinted from *Social & Legal Studies* (SAGE, London, Thousan Oaks, CA and New Delhi), vol.4 (1995).

i Thanks to Lionel Bently and Alain Pottage.

ii See N. Turkewitz, 'Authors' Rights are Dead' (1990) 38, *Journal of the Copyright Society of the USA*, p.41.

iii See E. Wang, '(Re)Productive Rights: Copyright and the Postmodern Artist' (1990) 14, *Columbia-VLA Jl of Law and the Arts*, p.261; J. Carlin, 'Culture Vultures: Artistic Appropriation and Intellectual Property Law' (1988) 13, *Columbia-VLA Jl of Law and the Arts*, p.103; P.Kreig, 'Copyright, Free Speech and the Visual Arts' 93, *Yale LJ* (1984), p.1565; L. Greenberg, 'The Art of Appropriation: Puppies, Piracy, and Post-Modernism' (1992) p.11, *Cardozo Arts & Entertainment Law Journal*, 1; M. Buskirk, 'Commodification as Censor: Copyrights and Fair Use' (1992), *October*, 92. A. Adler, 'Post-Modern Art and the Death of Obscenity Law' (1990), *Yale LJ*, p.1359.

iv   See E. Earle, 'The Effect of Romanticism on the 19th Century Development of Copyright law' (1991) 6, *Intellectual Property Journal*, p.269.

v   L. Hutcheon, *The Politics of Postmodernism*, London: Routledge (1989), p.44.

vi   Greenberg, above, n.3, p.33.

vii   See Wang, above, n.3; Greenberg, above n.3.

viii   See A. Bonnett, 'Art, ideology, and everyday space: subversive tendencies from Dada to postmodernism' (1992) 10, *Society and Space*, p.69.

ix   Marzorati, 'Art in the (Re)Making' (1986), *Art News*, p.90, (quoted in Wang, above, n.3, p.261, n.5). See also B. Kruger, '"Taking" Pictures: Photo-texts by Barbara Kruger' (1982) 23, *Screen*, p.90.

x   For example, as part of the 'Banality Show', Jeff Koons displayed a sculpture which had been reproduced from a photograph taken by Rogers (*A String of Puppies*). The main differences between the two being that the sculpture was larger than life and that Koons had made some minor visual changes (such as adding flowers and altering the colours).

xi   By incorporating phrases onto their photographs, artists, such as Sherrie Levine, juxtapose the written and the visual. Other artists achieve similar results by transposing objects from one context into another.

xii   Hutcheon, above, n.5, p.94.

xiii   W. Benjamin, 'The Work of Art in the Age of Mechanical Reproductions', in H. Arendt (ed), *Illuminations*, tr. Harry Zohn, New York: Fontana (1968), p.223.

xiv   Duchamp's *Readymades* offer a well-known illustration of the application of the idea that a new meaning is given to an image or an object (such as a urinal) when it is relocated in a new environment (such as an art gallery).

xv   Jeff Koon's said of his appropriation of the *Puppies* photograph: 'It was only a postcard photo and I gave it spirituality, animation, and took it to another vocabulary'. Quoted in Greenberg, above n.3, p.23. Speaking of Sturtevant's appropriation of Jasper John's *Flag*, Cutler said 'Sturtevant shifts the reference from Johns to herself, giving the flag a fresh perspective. In this new context the flag becomes, once again, controversial'. Sturtevant Drawings at Bess Cutler, quoted in John Henry Merryman, 'Counterfeit Art' (1992) 1 *Intl Jl of Cultural Property*, 71, n.75.

xvi   See Carlin, above n.3, p.108.

xvii   The 'referent in post-Modernism is no longer 'nature', but the closed system of fabricating signs that make up our environment'. Carlin, above, n.3, p.111.

xviii   Sherrie Levine, 'Five Comments', in B. Wallis (ed), *Blasted Allegories: An Anthology of Writings by Contemporary Artists* (Cambridge, Mass, 1992.), p.92.

xix   Wang, above n.3, p.264.

xx   Greenberg, above n.3, 1. Appropriation art . . . 'also function(s) as direct attacks on the primacy of originality as a definitional tool in defining works of art, on the integrity of the masterpiece, and on the line between mischievous copying and artistic breakthrough'. Ibid., p.14.

xxi   Greenberg, above, n.3, p.33. See also J. Gaines, *Contested Culture: The Image, the Voice and the Law*, London: BFI (1991), p.65.

xxii   P. Anderson, 'Copyright: Post-Modernism and Appropriation' (1989), *National Association for the Visual Arts Newsletter*, pp.3-5.

xxiii   See M. Abrams, *The Mirror and The Lamp: Romantic Theory and the Critical Tradition*, London: OUP (1973).

xxiv   R. Whale and J. Phillips, *Whale on Copyright*, Oxford: ESC Publishing (1983), p.39.

xxv The idea of 'genius' (which is used here in the sense of an individual having genius, rather than being a genius), and the role that it plays in copyright law is clearly problematic. See D. Saunders, 'Dropping the Subject: protocol for a positive history of authorship and the law of copyright' in B. Sherman and A. Strowel (eds), *Of Authors and Origins: Essays on Copyright Law*, Oxford: Clarendon Press (1994).

xxvi See Wang, above n.3, p.264; D. Quint, *Origin and Originality in Renaissance Literature*, New Haven: Yale UP (1983).

xxvii *University of London Press v. University Tutorial Press* (1916) 2 Ch 601.

xxviii Ibid.

xxix *Ladbroke v. William Hill* (1964) 1 WLR, p.273.

xxx In relation to artistic works. *Interlego v. Tyco* (1988) RPC 343.

xxxi *Feist Publications, Inc v. Rural Telephones Services Company, Inc* 111 Sup. Ct. 1282 (1991); 113 L. Ed (2d) p.358.

xxxii In order for a work to be original, it must exhibit 'that something irreducible, something which is one man's alone'. Holmes J., *Bleistein v. Donaldson Lithographing* 188 U.S. 239 (1903).

xxxiii Gaines, above n.21, p.58.

xxxiv Frank J., *Alfred Bell & Co., Ltd. v. Catalda Fine Arts, Inc.*, 191 F2d 99 (2d Cir 1951), 102. In another context it has been said: 'the idea of originality reveals itself as a direct witness to the unique individuality of an author. Originality symbolises the mystery of *principum individuationis*, which in its most idealized form is the concept of the soul; ultimately that it is its only function' Thomas McFarland, *Originality and Imagination*, Baltimore: John Hopkins U. Press (1985), p.85.

xxxv J. Frow, 'Repetition and Limitation: Computer Software and Copyright Law' (1988) 29, *Screen* 3, 9.

xxxvi *Feist Publications, Inc v. Rural Telephones Services Company, Inc*, above n.31.

xxxvii A factor which assists and reinforces the suppression of the work is that by focusing upon the individual subject, copyright law falls back upon the tautological relationship between author and originator. This arises from the response to the question, 'what is an author?', to which copyright law answers, 'an author is an originator'. When asked, 'what is an originator?', copyright law replies, 'an originator is an author'. 'The work of art stems from the artist, so they say. But what is the artist? The one who produces works of art. The origin of the artist is the work of art, the origin of the work of art is the artist, "neither is without the other"'. J. Derrida, *The Truth in Painting*, tr. Bennington and McLeod, Chicago: Chicago Uni Press (1987), pp.31-32. Or, as the U.S. Supreme Court said: an 'author' is 'he to whom anything owes its origin: originator; maker'. *Burrow-Giles Lithographic Co v. Sarony*, 111 U.S. 53 (1884), p.58.

xxxviii Cf P. Jaszi, 'Towards a Theory of Copyright: The Metamorphosis of Authorship' (1991) *Duke LJ*, p.455.

xxxix T. Eagleton, *Literary Theory*, Oxford: Blackwell (1983), p.138.

xl *Interlego v. Tyco* (1988) RPC, p.343.

xli *Gracen v. Bradford Exchange*, 698 F. 2d 300 (7th Cir. 1983).

xlii *Interlego v. Tyco* (1988) RPC 373-374; *Rose Plastics GmbH v. William Beckett & Co (Plastics) Ltd* (1989) FSR 113, p.123.

xliii *Exxon v. Exxon Insurance* (1982) RPC 69.

xliv 'What is protected is the plaintiff's "artistic work" and as such, not any information which it may be designed to convey'. Buckley LJ, *Catnic Componets v. Hill and Smith* (1982) RPC 183, pp.222-223.

xlv   It was said that one of the reason why Koons lost the copyright action (*Rogers v Koons*, above n.59) against him was that the court ignored the formal and contextual differences between Roger's photograph of the puppies, and Koons (self-consciously sophisticated) copying of the work. See Greenberg, above n.3, 1263. That is, the court said that the aesthetic appeal of the two works was identical. See Smith, above n.56.

xlvi   There is, in effect, a reversal of the idea-expression dichotomy: the expression is the same, it is the idea which is different. The problems that are likely to confront the postmodern artist are exacerbated by the absence of visual quotation marks, or some equivalent thereof. See M. De Grazia, 'Sanctioning the Voice: Quotation Marks, The Abolition of Torture, and the Fifth Amendment' (1992) 10, *Cardoza Arts & Entertainment Law Journal*, pp.545, 553-554.

xlvii   One possible basis for protection would be if the appropriation art was 'read' rather than 'viewed'. That is, if it were evaluated as a literary work and not as artistic work: *Bilhöfer v. Dixon* (1990) FSR 105, p.122. Equally important is the standpoint of interpretation adopted. As to the question, who was the appropriate person to interpret an exhaust pipe as an 'artistic work', Hoffman J. said it would not be the 'visitor observing the exhaust pipe mounted on a plinth at the Tate Gallery but to the engineer wanting to make an exhaust which would fit under a Marina'. Ibid.

xlviii   See B. Sherman, 'The Myth of Primitivism' (1992) 2 *Intl. Journel of Cultural Property*, p.423. Cf Australian Law Reform Commission, *Designs: Issues Paper 11*, Sydney (1993) p.59.

xlix   A. Huyssen, *After the Great Divide*, Bloomington: Indiana Uni Press (1986), p.vii. For an application of these ideas within law see B. De Sousa Santos, 'Towards a Postmodern Understanding of Law' in *Legal Culture and Everyday Life*, Onati IISL (1989) p.113.

l   K. Coutts-Smith, 'Some general observations on the problems of cultural colonialism' in Susan Heller (ed), *The Myth of Primitivism*, London: Routledge (1991) p.29.

li   P. Bourdieu and A. Darbel, *L'Amour de l'art: Les musées d'art européens et leur public*, Paris: Editions de Minuit (1969), pp.162-163. Cambridge: Polity Press (1991).

lii   M. Foucault, 'What is an Author?' (1979) *Screen*, 19, 20. For a critical examination of the argument that the work is a set of ideas which have no bounds or marks whatsoever see F. Hargraves, *An Argument in Defence of Literary Property*, 2nd edn, London (1774) pp.6-7.

liii   C. Aide, 'A More Comprehensive Soul: Romantic Conceptions Of Authorship and the Copyright Doctrine of Moral Rights' (1990) 48 *Toronto Faculty of Law Review*, pp.211, 220.

liv   P. Karlen, 'Legal Aesthetics' (1979) 19 *British Journal of Aesthetics*, 95. Cf M. Price, 'The Author in Copyright: Notes for the Literary Critic' (1992) 10 *Cardoza Arts & Entertainment Law Journal*, pp.703, 705.

lv   *Le Monde v. Microfor*, JCP 1988 II 20932, Court of Cassation, Plenary Assembly, Decision of Oct.30, 1987.

lvi   See Gaines, above n.24, pp.63-64.

'Hiroshige vs. Van Gogh': Resolving the Dilemma of Copyright Scope in Remedying Infringement

Paul Edward Geller [i]

To say that copyright is 'property', although a fundamentally unhistorical state-ment, would not be baldly misdescriptive if one were prepared to acknowledge that . . . in practice the lively questions are likely to be whether certain consequences ought to attach to a given piece of so-called property in given circumstances.[ii]

I. A Thought-Experiment

In the latter half of the nineteenth century, European literati and artists became captivated by Japanese art, especially prints. When in Paris, Vincent van Gogh, a collector of Japanese prints himself, painted the *Portrait of Père Tanguy*. Tanguy had an art-supply shop in which he often displayed the works of avant-garde painters. The background of the *Portrait of Père Tanguy* is covered with Japanese prints.[iii]

In the Fall of 1887, Van Gogh painted his *Japonaiseries*.[iv] The most notable are based on a pair of works by Utagawa Hiroshige from the series *One Hundred Views of Famous Places in Edo*.[v] Hiroshige, in his wood-block prints, composed in clearly delineated levels of space and subtly gradated colours; Van Gogh, in his oil paintings, pushes and pulls our vision with agitated brush-strokes and boldly opposed colours. In the first exhibit to this Article, we see one of Hiroshige's pair of prints, *The Plum Garden at Kameido*; in the second, Van Gogh's study of that print, *The Tree*.[vi]

How would Hiroshige have responded had he known what this foreign enthusiast, Van Gogh, had made of his works? It might be a mistake to attribute to Hiroshige our litigious impulse to dispute Van Gogh's decision to make studies of his graceful prints in viscous oils.[vii] While traditional Oriental culture might have demanded that a student acknowledge a master for creating models worthy of imi-tation, it did not threaten the student with legal sanctions for copying such mod-els, even badly. Hiroshige might have thought, like the Chinese scholar Shen Zhou before him, 'if my poems and paintings, which are only small efforts to me, should prove to be of some aid to the forgers, what is there for me to grudge about?'[viii]

Utagawa Hiroshige, *The Plum Tree (Teahouse) at Kameido*, 1857

Vincent van Gogh. *Japonaiserie: The Flowering Plum Tree (After Hiroshige)*, 1887

Assume that Hiroshige's prints were protected by copyright in France towards the end of the nineteenth century.[ix] Suppose, more hypothetically, that one of Utagawa Hiroshige's heirs, holding his rights, then sued Vincent van Gogh for making studies of the prints and Vincent's brother Theo, or another of his heirs, for offering these studies to the public. This hypothetical suit is not posited to test the state of French copyright law over a century ago, but rather as a thought-experiment to elucidate the dilemma which arises with the basic question: What is the proper scope of copyright? Since this dilemma is common to all copyright laws, the attempt to resolve it here will make use of comparative legal analysis.[x]

II. The Dilemma: Copyright Scope

The field of copyright has distinct dimensions. On one dimension, authors create works. Here a court has to ask: Is copyright in one work infringed by another work? On the other dimension, works are disseminated to the public. Here the question becomes: What remedies should the court grant against the dissemination of an infringing work? Our dilemma will be considered on both dimensions.

a. The Rate of Cultural Feedback

These dimensions, though distinct in theory, are intertwined in practice. Creators elaborate works in communicating with colleagues and critics, patrons and promoters, and larger publics.[xi] Technology has progressively globalized the communication networks into which creators have fed, and feed, their works. To assess this progress, start with the fact that, two millennia ago, the Roman Empire and the Han Dynasty of China did no more than sporadically trade with each other. Only later did Greek art forms, previously brought by Alexander to the frontiers of India, filter into the Far East over the Great Silk Road.[xii] Still later yet, Chinese inventions essential to globalisation, such as the magnetic compass and paper, reached the West.[xiii]

Creations are thus fed back into communication networks at varying rates. To take an example closer to our time, the art worlds of modern Japan and Europe initially learned of each other's rapidly developing styles with significant delays. The Japanese art of the 'floating world' had already produced such greats as Utamaro in the eighteenth century, but it most notably synthesised Oriental and Western models of landscape art in the work of Hokusai and Hiroshige in the early nineteenth century.[xiv] While Europe had only fragmentary contacts with the full range of artistic developments in Japan before the middle of the nineteenth century, European access and response to this art had expanded greatly by the time Van Gogh reached Paris in 1886.[xv]

This rate of feedback is critical to the rationale of intellectual property. Farmers would be reluctant to market produce that was promptly stolen once it went on sale. But the law recognises property in the fruits of the farmers' labour and polices the marketplace for thieves. Authors and inventors would lose incentives to release their products of mind to the world if, in the process, they found such public goods pirated by free-riders.[xvi] Instead, armed with intellectual property, they are supposedly induced to feed more works and inventions back into communication networks, in turn further stimulating culture and technology. As the rate of feedback increases, so do the chances that new ways to create, for example, new plot lines, musical harmonics, artistic techniques, etc., come to light.[xvii]

Such feedback helps to achieve policies that motivate intellectual property. The Constitution of the United States speaks of promoting 'the Progress of Science and useful Arts'.[xviii] Starting in the French Revolution, Continental European doctrine posited authors' rights as 'sacred' natural rights, but the Revolutionary legislators understood full well that such rights had to be codified with an eye to enhancing culture.[xix]

b. Infringement Analysis or Exceptions?

Our hypothetical case squarely raises questions of copyright scope. Should the law entitle Hiroshige or his heirs to stop Van Gogh from making studies of Hiroshige's prints? To stop Van Gogh's heirs from feeding resulting new works back into world culture? To impose liability for making or exploiting these works? Such questions lead into the following dilemma:

If, on the one hand, creators had no legal control over the fate of their products of mind, they would lose reasons to input such public goods into communication networks. On the other, with too much control, they could stop others from elaborating on their creations and from releasing still further products of mind to the world. If the rules on point are too lax, copyright becomes ineffectual for accelerating the feedback of new works. If the rules are too stringent, copyright becomes counter-productive by burdening such feedback.[xx]

This dilemma may be reconceptualised in doctrinal terms. Copyright arises out of creative acts: Hiroshige has copyrights in the prints he creates, and Van Gogh has them in the studies he creates. In principle, copyrights, so-called properties, entitle creators to dispose of their respective works at will; however, in our hypothetical suit, such rights could well conflict. That is, Hiroshige's right in a print, if given force without regard to other creators' rights, could lead to stopping Van Gogh or his heirs from exercising this later creator's right to dispose of his study of that print. But the fact that Hiroshige's work comes first ought not be decisive for the simple reason that, unlike patent law, copyright law does not favour works or authors because of priority in time. The follower, Van Gogh, may further invoke freedoms of creation and expression.[xxi]

Courts, when faced with such dilemmas or conflicts, want to find equitable and just solutions. They are like Goldilocks who, in the home of the three bears, wanted porridge that was neither 'too hot' nor 'too cold'. While acknowledging Hiroshige's work as calling for protection, a court might sympathetically hear counter-arguments. Van Gogh could claim that his works are only private studies, or his heir could argue that his works ought not be kept from the public. The court may well ask: Does any equitable or policy-based defence, sometimes a provision setting forth an apparent exception, excuse arguable infringement? In the United States there is the doctrine of fair use, and Germany allows transformative uses under the narrower doctrine of free utilisation (*freie Benutzung*).[xxii] Other jurisdictions permit such transformative uses as parody under specific exceptions, while still others subject such uses to general infringement analysis.[xxiii] But in hard cases, it often becomes difficult to distinguish fair uses, or even specifically exempted uses, from those which are arguably infringing.[xxiv]

True dilemmas are never fully resolved by Goldilockean compromises. Rather, courts have to resolve our dilemma consistently with basic copyright rationales. Unfortunately, the judicial manoeuvre of seeking *ad hoc* compromises can scramble the lines between true exceptions and infringement analysis and, at the same time, make a muddle of underlying rationales. In a seminal case in the United States, suit was brought for abridging George Washington's writings, and the Supreme Court asked whether this arguably transformative use was 'a justifiable use of the original materials, such as the law recognises as no infringement of the copyright'.[xxv] It is symptomatic of subsequent confusion that the Court's decision is now seen as significant for the evolution of the so-called exception of fair use, even though the decision merely upheld a finding of infringement.[xxvi] One of the four criteria set out in the statutory provision for fair use continues to invite courts in the United States to re-test infringement by asking: Does the copying in question lack 'substantiality'?[xxvii] It also remains unclear in German and Swiss law whether the doctrine of free utilisation serves as an exception or does anything other than limit infringement analysis.[xxviii]

Most importantly, infringement analysis is common to all copyright laws. By contrast, such doctrines as fair use and free utilisation are idiosyncratic to particular copyright laws, and specific exceptions vary considerably between all these laws. In approaching the common dilemma of copyright scope, only infringement analyses common to the major copyright systems will here be considered: no further analytic tools will be used.[xxix] It should be stated upfront: it will not suffice to clarify criteria for determining when copyright infringement does or does not take place. For purposes of resolving the dilemma of copyright scope, such all-or-nothing determinations will prove to be too crude. Rather, as explained in the next step of the argument here, courts need to reach more finely differentiated findings of infringement. After that, it will be a matter of calibrating such findings with the different remedies available for infringement.[xxx]

III. Creating Works: Infringement?

Asking when infringement takes place engages analysis along the dimension of creation. It focuses on pairs of works: on the one hand, the work of a prior creator, in our case Hiroshige; on the other hand, the work of a later alleged copier, in our case Van Gogh. In such a case, infringement analysis compares the prior and later works.

a. Complementary Doctrines for Hard Cases

Our hypothetical suit poses a hard case of infringement to dramatise our dilemma. Let us start by sorting such hard cases out from easy cases and by broaching the complementary doctrines that help courts to decide hard cases. Such doctrines, developed in different copyright systems, guide the analysis of protectability and, after that threshold issue, of infringement itself.

i. Sorting Out the Hard Cases

Courts avoid our dilemma in easy cases, where they are faced with only literal or close copies. Such copies, displaying little or nothing new above and beyond the works copied, cannot in themselves enrich the creativity that feeds culture. The dilemma becomes acute, however, when prior works are admitted to be the bases of later works that are therefore alleged to be infringing.[xxxi]

In the eighteenth century, copyright was instituted to deal only with easy cases, the pirate reprinting of books or re-staging of plays. At the start of the nineteenth century, courts typically found no infringement in what leading French commentary called '[t]he transmutation of form that the translator causes the original to undergo'.[xxxii] But in the course of that century, as trade in books became increasingly globalized, authors and publishers started to claim rights to stop translations in foreign markets. Ultimately, the right of translation was subsumed under the more general right to control the making and exploitation of derivative works. The scope of copyright was effectively expanded beyond protecting prior works against substitution by later works in the markets that the prior works targeted. Copyright reached new markets in new media, for example, as literary works were adapted to the stage or film.[xxxiii]

In hard cases, plaintiffs allege that defendants have derived works from their own. In such cases, courts often resort to complementary doctrines to limit copyright scope. These doctrines operate on theoretically distinct levels of analysis that tend to come together in practice.[xxxiv] On the level of determining what is protectible, there is the principle that courts may not protect 'ideas' or 'facts', but rather only 'expression' or 'forms'. On the level of finding infringement, courts ask whether plaintiff's work is copied in defendant's 'substantially' similar work or whether 'essential' or 'characteristic traits' of one work are taken in the other. But such notions as 'ideas' defy ready definition, and equally metaphysical notions of 'substance' suggest that works of the mind are things like tables and chairs, consistently perceived by all audiences, but none of these doctrines by itself guides courts to consistent decisions.[xxxv]

For example, in the United States, the holder of copyright in the novel *Gone with the Wind* brought suit for infringement by the novel *The Blue Bicycle*. But the suit went no further than the court's refusal to grant a preliminary injunction once it found similarities only between idea-determined materials such as stock 'characters' and 'scenes and the sequence of events'.[xxxvi] In the French case involving the same novels, the court of first instance found infringement in similarities between just such 'intrinsic elements', while the intermediate trial court held that such materials, notably characters and plot, could not be protected.[xxxvii] Although the highest French court of appeal overturned that intermediate judgement for insufficiently specified findings, the court on remand found that the materials in question had been so creatively transformed that no actionable similarities remained.[xxxviii]

The right to control derivative works and any limiting doctrine, such as the idea-expression distinction, tend to struggle with each other, like a pair of overly oiled wrestlers. Unfortunately, whether the right or the limiting doctrine wins all too often depends on a momentary false step rather than any consistently balanced judgement from case to case. It is relatively easy to ascertain when copyright may be invoked to prevent copies from substituting for a specific work in a given market, but it becomes more difficult to determine when to stop protecting a prior work against later works in other markets that the prior work does not address.[xxxix] Courts and commentators have refined doctrines limiting copyright scope in this regard, but they have done so largely in case-by-case analyses. Basic refinements in major jurisdictions will be touched on schematically here.

ii. Creative Options and Protectability

In the case of the play *Abie's Irish Rose*, Judge Learned Hand formulated these classic, cautionary words concerning the distinction between ideas and expression:

> Upon any work, and especially upon a play, a great number of patterns of increasing generality will fit equally well, as more and more of the incident is left out. The last may perhaps be no more than the most general statement of what the play is about, and at times might consist only of its title; but there is a point in this series of abstractions where they are no longer protected, since otherwise the playwright could prevent the use of his 'ideas', to which, apart from their expression, his property is never extended.[xl]

In hard cases, courts sort out 'ideas' and 'expressions' with diverse tests and criteria. All these judicial devices will be generically considered here under the rubric of *creative options*. This term will indicate the range of expressions potentially available to elaborate a given work. Courts in the United States apply the so-called merger test to measure whether sufficient creative options are present. To the extent that an idea can be realised in only one or a small set of expressions, there is merger between the idea and the expressions that, accordingly, are not protected.[xli] Continental European doctrines comparably lead courts to grant or withhold protection to the extent that underlying ideas do or do not allow for sufficient creative options to elaborate original works. French jurisprudence refuses protection when 'an automated or constraining logic' dictates how the author's mental input (*apport intellectuel*) is given form, while German doctrine speaks of a more or less open 'room for the play' (*Spielraum*) of creativity.[xlii]

As a corollary, courts may be said to 'filter' some expressions, such as *scènes à faire*, functionally determined software modules, etc., out of the scope of protection.[xliii] For example, in one French case, a researcher sued a writer for taking expressions from his scholarly works on Cajun culture to use in a novel set in a Cajun locale. But the trial court found no infringement in the use of such culturally typical expressions that it considered to be indispensable to giving the novel 'a minimum of verisimilitude'.[xliv] Moreover, to the extent that there is only one way, or very few ways, to convey facts accurately in compilations such as lists, charts, etc., resulting expressions may not be protected. Obviously, there can be just one correct spelling and numbering for each listing in a telephone directory and only a few conventional schema or signals for situating sites on maps.[xlv] To put the matter more generally, whether idea-determined materials may be protected against copying will turn on how they fare under tests or criteria to which doctrines of creative options lead in the cases. For example, in *Romeo and Juliet* or *Abie's Irish Rose*, there were only so many ways that a family feud might have served as background for the particular tragedy or comedy into which each play cast its young lovers.[xlvi]

All these doctrines do not always dictate precise tests or criteria. Courts often glibly assume that we all know ideas when we see them. However, the term 'idea' often evokes only evanescent Platonic flashes of insight or mental will-of-the-wisps.[xlvii] As a result, courts often have difficulty specifying at what point a set of creative options is too restricted to allow for protection, that is, how coarsely or finely to filter out idea-determined materials. For example, in one case in the United States, copyright was asserted in a so-called pitching form into which such baseball statistics as game times, betting odds, pitchers' performances, etc., were compiled. But one judge on appeal went to the heart of the matter, effectively asking: What is the 'proper level of abstraction' for formulating such categories of data, more generally, for grasping 'the ideas which underlay' the expression in the work at issue?[xlviii] Logically, without knowing just how to focus on any idea against which merger or creative options might be measured, it becomes impossible to say when there are too few ways to express that idea to protect corresponding expressions. The ambiguity of the term 'idea' also obscures the borderline between copyright law, in which ideas are not protected independently of expression, and patent law, in which they are not protected independently of utility. [xlix]

In response to these definitional vagaries, consider the sense of 'idea' in the statutory terms of any 'procedure, process, system, [or] method' for generating works and thus 'embodied' in works.[l] Classically, Aristotle explained the idea of tragedy in such operational terms: have a hero commit an act of *hubris*, and have him fall and discover his own fall, to accomplish a catharsis of pity and fear in the audience.[li] Contemporary aesthetic analyses have unpacked entire systems of comparable formulae for elaborating different plot lines that appear in genres starting with folk tales and extending to modern stories.[lii] Of course, works differ in how they incorporate procedures or methods: for example, a musical score instructs performers on how to play the musical work it represents, in what key, with what timing, etc. In video games, audio-visual displays are run by interactive software procedures, while paintings embody methods of composition, colouration, etc.[liii]

iii. The Sliding-scale Analysis of Infringement

In easy cases, courts find infringement in the full reconstruction of plaintiff's work in a literal or close copy. In hard cases, the question remains open: *How much* of the creative fabric of a work must be re-generated before there is infringement? Judge Hand warned against responding to this question once and for all: 'Nobody has ever been able to fix that boundary, and nobody ever can'.[liv] Hard cases are endemically subject to such line-drawing exercises that may well start at the threshold stage of analysing protectability, but that all too often slip unnoticed into the stage of analysing infringement itself. Before tightening up analysis, it will be useful to survey how it tends to shift from stage to stage.

Since creativity is protean, standards of protection, such as 'originality' or 'creativity', are satisfied to varying degrees from case to case. In the United States, the Supreme Court indicated that a minimally creative compilation of facts would attract 'thin' protection against literal or close copies.[lv] By implication, a more creative work would call for 'thicker' protection, not merely against literal or close copies, but against translations, adaptations, or other derivative works. Continental European doctrines, typically predicating degrees of creativity that can vary from work to work, comparably allow for the sliding-scale analysis of infringement.[lvi] Courts in diverse jurisdictions may then adjust the scope of protection in the light of the respective creativity of plaintiff's and defendant's works.[lvii]

Unfortunately, judicial penchants can at times push and pull such sliding-scale analysis ambivalently. Consider, for example, a pair of cases in Germany where copyright law, in principle, has traditionally set the ostensibly high standard of protecting only 'personal intellectual creations'.[lviii] In one case, the courts, generous to a plaintiff, seemed to short-circuit that standard by indulging the premise that industrial-drafting techniques of perspective, shadowing, etc., allowed for introducing sufficient personal creativity into a simple technical drawing to protect it against close copying.[lix] In another case, judicial sympathies favoured the defendant: the image of a female nude ingeniously posed by the innovative fashion photographer Helmut Newton was at issue, but a painting which creatively transformed that image, albeit recognisably, was found not to infringe Newton's copyright.[lx]

Realistically viewed, courts can at times be generous toward plaintiffs who face close or literal copies and, at other times, tolerant toward defendants who transform prior works. Professor François Dessemontet notes the opening for possibly inconsistent results: 'The outcome in a given case might well be that, while the plaintiff's work could be protected against outright piracy by a third party, it does not receive protection as against defendant's work that incorporates parts of it less obviously or more creatively than any slavish copy'.[lxi]

b. Reframing the Doctrines into more coherent Analysis

To reconcile such judicial approaches, doctrines of creative options will here be more tightly tied into the sliding-scale analysis of copyright infringement. Hopefully, as it is made more coherent, such analysis will guide courts more consistently with underlying copyright rationales. But analysis is here re-framed only experimentally; other attempts to pull it together might work as well or better.

i. The Spectrum from Copying to Creation

Our operational definition of 'ideas' encompasses a wide range of procedures and methods for generating works.[lxii] At one end of this range, distinguish as *routines* those information-processing procedures so fixed and detailed that they leave little or no room for creative options in themselves. Moving forward from that starting point, distinguish the following processes along a spectrum from copying to creation.[lxiii]

a. At the start of the spectrum, *rote copying* results from applying a single set of Aidentified routines to a work. For example, to copy a text literally, with the same wording, we might change fonts, using as many routines as there are printing symbols, plus some others to reformat the text. Or, to copy an image closely, we might trace it out on transparent paper, or we might photocopy it, laying it into the photocopy machine, setting the desired number of copies and other parameters, and pressing the button. Either way, a given set of identified routines suffices to obtain our copy.

b. There are many different processes in the middle of the spectrum. The rubric of *knowledgeable reworking* seems to cover most of them. Such processes use routines that are generally known, but not necessarily all identifiable. Nor need the set of such routines used in a given case fully suffice to determine the entire work generated in that case. Consider translating a French cookbook into English: it is necessary to rely on lexical and syntactic routines known, sometimes only implicitly, by bilingual speakers. For example, while French usage regularly places adverbs between verbs and direct objects, English-speakers most often relocate the adverbs, usually to the beginning or end of clauses. In any event, a straightforward cookbook, if not almost every work-a-day text, is susceptible of only a slightly variable set of translations likely to be acceptable to bilingual speakers. As other examples of mid-range processes, consider selecting and organising facts into a compilation, or excerpts into an anthology, or recontextualizing a work, as in appropriation art.[lxiv]

c. At the far end of the spectrum, there is *innovative recasting*. Here, no known set of routines suffices for moving from one work to another or even to comparable works. Consider the enterprise of translating James Joyce's *Ulysses* into French: at hundreds of thousands of points, the translators had to make choices that linguistic rules alone could not have dictated.[lxv] The saxophonist Charlie Parker provides another example: starting from the chords of the tune *Cherokee*, which an accompanying guitarist had inverted just 'to keep a beat going', he moved into an entirely new mode of jazz improvisation.[lxvi]

At the start of the spectrum, rote copying can be automated. When a photocopy machine copies an image, a microprocessor in the machine executes a complex set of routines. Rote copying comes about for the simple reason that, before formalising these procedures in any computer algorithm, the programmer must have identified them all. Imagine a more complex case: a computer, digitally recording audio input, for example, a musical work, converts all the sounds of that work into video output, which is screened as moving visual patterns. The computer program effectively reprocesses the musical work, its rhythms, melodies, chords, timbres, etc., visually by playing these materials out as lines, light and dark, colours and values, etc., all moving in space and time, apparently as an abstract cinematic work. Assume, too, that the algorithm used here is in an off-the-shelf program, which the party making the conversion does not creatively supplement, say, through interactive input. That is, without such input, this party makes a rote copy.[lxvii]

Moving further along the spectrum, mid-range processes such as knowledgeable reworking can only be partially automated. For example, an expert system can be used to help with the translation of a text, but the routines of such systems succeed with variable confidence factors in translating all but the simplest texts. These factors represent the probabilities that the expert system will translate given passages to the satisfaction of bilingual speakers, and they can vary depending on the difficulty of any given passage and the languages in question. Such variability will arise even in using an expert system to translate a work-a-day text like our hypothetical cookbook from French to English, both closely related languages that share largely common roots. It will every so often prove necessary to call upon the implicit knowledge of bilingual speakers to decide between proposed translations that are arguably acceptable or equally debatable.[lxviii]

At the far end of the spectrum, innovative recasting largely defies automation. Suppose that a text to be translated, like our example of James Joyce's *Ulysses*, breaks systematically with most cultural precedents. As Umberto Eco emphasises, such a work can challenge us 'to rethink the whole language, the entire inheritance of what has been said, can be said, and could or should be said'.[lxix] Innovative recasting is needed to translate Joyce's novel into French, since no bilingual consensus provides rules to guide translation at most points in this seminal English text. Of course, run-of-the-mill works can also be innovatively recast, as when popular tunes became fodder for modern jazz.[lxx]

A word of caution is called for at this point. Infringement analysis need not look to the actual genesis of the works in question. It is rather a matter of ascertaining to what extent there were routines available to move from plaintiff's to defendant's work at the time of the later work.[lxxi] To the extent that available routines did not suffice, it may be inferred that the allegedly infringing work arose thanks to processes that ranged from knowledgeable reworking to innovative recasting. The computer metaphor, just used, provides merely one way to think about such a determination. Expert testimony will often be helpful in making the requisite findings.[lxxii]

ii. Application to Literary and Artistic Works

Our framework of analysis ostensibly applies no matter what type of work is at issue. But, once again, there is a difficulty that arises from protean creativity, which manifests itself in the ever-proliferating diversity of media and genres. Indeed, some commentators suggest that infringement analysis changes radically from one type of work to another, for example, from literary to artistic works.[lxxiii] Let us then test our framework of analysis by asking whether it can be cogently applied to diverse types of works.

On the one hand, literary works are coded in discrete terms, such as words and phrases, arranged pursuant to grammatical rules. On the other, artistic works are embodied in continuously variable materials such as line, space, light, and colour, configured in space. In computer terms, a literary work can be generated using a lexicon like the ASCII code and a sequencing or syntactic program, while an artistic work can be more or less faithfully bit-mapped. The same distinction can be reconceptualised as applying between works repeatably readable from texts and works uniquely embodied in objects.[lxxiv]

This distinction admits of both border-zone and hybrid cases.[lxxv] For example, a musical work is more like a literary work when it is written down in a score, but it moves into a border zone, where it becomes more like an artistic work, when it is performed.[lxxvi] Chinese poetry forms a hybrid case when written in calligraphic form: no translation into an alphabetic language, no matter how creative, can render the resonance of such a poetic text with its visual form.[lxxvii] How can a court assess where works fall along the spectrum of creative processes, given that works tend to be so diversely situated relative to the basic distinction between literary and artistic works?

In a literary work, like a novel, it is a matter of analysing, most notably, how the text is sequentially translated into another language or sequentially adapted into another medium or genre. For example, Dashiell Hammett's detective story *The Maltese Falcon* was made into John Huston's film by dramatising it into dialogue, acting instructions, etc., and by visually elaborating it into sets, action, camera work, etc. Making Hammett's text into a screenplay required knowledgeable cuts and adjustments to fit the story into the time, censorship, and cinematic constraints of the motion picture.[lxxviii] Huston's filming of the story moved up the spectrum toward innovative recasting in the ways the motion picture was shot, paced, and edited.

By contrast, it is often a subtle matter to analyse how one artistic work is transformed into another. The materials of such a work, for example, graphics, light and shade, colours and values, etc., can be so packed together, its visual signals so saturated, that they become inextricable to the untrained eye. Nelson Goodman, whose philosophical analysis is seminal here, gives the example of a print by Hokusai, in which '[a]ny thickening or thinning of the line, its color, its contrast with the background, its size', would change the entire impact of the work.[lxxix]

Look at the exhibits to this Article, reproducing a pair of works in question in our hypothetical suit. Of necessity, Hiroshige's *Plum Garden* reappears in Van Gogh's *Tree*, since the prior print is the subject matter of the later study. Furthermore, the bare similarity of their patterns neither proves rote copying nor disproves knowledgeable reworking or innovative recasting.[lxxx] To compare the earlier and later works in this regard, it is necessary to disentangle differences far more tightly woven into their expressive fabrics than overall similarities.

iii. Illustration in our Hypothetical Case

Recall the test for sorting out creative processes: Can any one set of known routines suffice to move from a prior to a later work? [lxxxi] To the extent that routines do not suffice, knowledgeable reworking or even innovative recasting might be at work. Now apply this approach to Hiroshige's *Plum Garden* and Van Gogh's *Tree*, which we already contrasted briefly at the start.[lxxxii] Here is how Klaus Berger, a leading expert on 'Japonism' in Western art, focuses on the movement from one work to the other:

> . . . the bright orange framing strip and the added, entirely random
> Japanese characters point in a new direction that lies beyond both
> Western and Eastern traditions. The exaggeration of the graphic
> arabesque, and the dense, ungradated masses of paint, combine to
> destroy the Japanese equilibrium between drawn framework and
> rhythmic colour . . . The gnarled black bough screams aloud; the
> scattered blossoms are trapped between those fateful black
> tracks and the red wall of the sky. Whereas in the Japanese work
> everything expands into space, here it is confined, shut off, dramati-
> cally exaggerated. The curves and verticals seem to fight each other,
> and the green configuration below thrusts against the upper red
> quarter, conveying the suspense of a conflict that still hangs in the
> balance.[lxxxiii]

Starting from Oriental models, Hiroshige's space hints at classic Western perspective and anticipates Impressionism as well.[lxxxiv] His print *The Plum Garden* moves the eye back from more intensely coloured foregrounds to paler backgrounds, while Van Gogh's study *The Tree* scrambles all such inherited visual signals, for example, drawing our eye under the red sky and bursting yellow blossoms into a constricted space punctuated by angular tree trunks. Our expert is categorical about the revolutionary step Van Gogh is taking beyond the Impressionism which formed the background for his mature work: 'The result is a kind of explosion that opens the way to Expressionism'.[lxxxv]

Contrast another pair of works not in the exhibits: Hiroshige's print *Sudden Shower over the Great Bridge near Atake* with Van Gogh's study *The Bridge*.[lxxxvi] The older artist clearly blocks out a simple Spring shower which falls on passers-by who are walking across a solid bridge planted in a placid river. The younger artist brushes in driving rain, a bridge uneasily suspended on moody pilings, and a turbulent river, all with the tensions of a raging storm. Our expert wonders 'what the unfortunate people in the picture have done to deserve such an elemental onslaught'.[lxxxvii]

Is Hiroshige's copyright infringed by Van Gogh? On the spectrum starting at rote copying and including knowledgeable reworking, Van Gogh ultimately reaches the stage of innovative recasting. It would nonetheless oversimplify matters to declare in the abstract, which of these processes infringes copyright and which does not. To resolve the dilemma of copyright scope, it will prove necessary to distinguish more finely between the consequences that a court may give to these processes.

IV. Disseminating Works: Remedies?

It is time to change from the dimension of creation to that of dissemination. If the court orders Van Gogh to stop painting his studies, it nips dissemination in the bud. If it orders Van Gogh's heir not to display these studies, it stops dissemination in its tracks. The impact of awarding money to Hiroshige's heir will depend on the amount of the award.

a. Property versus Liability Remedies

It is helpful at this point to distinguish between property and liability regimes.[lxxxviii] When a court is ready to order you off someone else's land, whenever you set foot on it, a property remedy is available. When the court merely holds you liable to pay money after you have already trespassed, a liability remedy is imposed. As Professor Jerome Reichman explains, the optimum mix of property and liability remedies will vary according to the branch of intellectual property and the case.[lxxxix]

Our dilemma arises precisely because Hiroshige may claim property, not merely in the prints he created, but in the later studies Van Gogh created of those prints. Hiroshige's property claim would be most decisively implemented in an injunction to preclude Van Gogh or his heirs from exercising any further property claim to dispose of his later work freely. As already pointed out,[xc] however, not only does copyright law not contain any principle, as does patent law, favouring any initial creator because of priority in time, but it is subject to freedoms of creation and expression. In reaching an appropriate mix of remedies, it will be argued, a court may resolve our dilemma in the case before it, while avoiding conflicts between prior and later creators' claims.[xci]

Typically, under copyright law, the mix of remedies has erratically varied from case to case.[xcii] This variation has in part arisen because the doctrines limiting copyright scope, such as the idea-expression distinction and substantiality criteria of infringement, have been neither uniform in meaning nor coherently articulated.[xciii] Furthermore, in considering remedies, courts have to take account of equitable considerations that change from case to case, for example, the force of the parties' initial showings, the eventual impact of proposed remedies on the parties' respective positions, etc.[xciv] It is submitted that courts should fashion and coordinate property and liability remedies within a framework of analysis such as that proposed here. In particular, they would do well to situate where works fall along the spectrum from rote copying to innovative recasting.[xcv]

The following guidelines are proposed to tighten up present copyright law, with due regard for equitable considerations present in any given case:

1. No injunction or other coercive remedies should be issued against whoever makes a solitary copy exclusively for private enjoyment or study.

2. Courts should (a) always be ready to enjoin and otherwise provide coercive relief against rote copying for the public, (b) exercise discretion in granting injunctions and other coercive remedies concerning works generated by mid-range processes such as knowledgeable reworking, and (c) refrain from enjoining innovative recasting, as well as the dissemination of the new works thus generated, absent strong equitable reasons for stopping them.

3. Courts may (a) impose the full range of monetary awards, including statutory or other special damages used for punitive or deterrent purposes, in cases of rote copies, especially when these are marketed with scienter, but (b) adjust actual or statutory damages, or reasonable royalties or profit shares, to the market interests at stake in any other case.

How would these guidelines apply to our hypothetical suit? Assume that the court finds that Hiroshige's prints are innovatively recast in Van Gogh's *Japonaiseries*.[xcvi] First, no order would be issued to stop the making of these studies privately; second, no order would lead to seizing these studies or enjoin publicly displaying or marketing them. Third, a money judgement could still be obtained for such marketing, and it would be measured by considering how Hiroshige's prints contributed to the appeal that Van Gogh's studies would hold for relevant audiences. Our dilemma would be resolved: neither creativity nor feedback into cultural networks would be blocked, while both prior and later creators' rights would be protected on the marketplace.[xcvii] Having glanced at how our guidelines come together in our hypothetical case, let us now look at how they may apply more particularly in other hard cases.

b. Applications to different Remedies

Works of authorship display different creative processes in endlessly variable combinations and permutations. As a result, the guidelines just proposed would still lead to different mixes of remedies from case to case, although hopefully with more rhyme and reason than before. Some comments are in order on how to reach optimum mixes in complex cases.

i. Injunctive and Related Relief

At the level of injunctions and other coercive remedies, there is an obvious difficulty. A framework has been proposed for the sliding-scale analysis of infringement. But how does it help in making all-or-nothing decisions, notably whether to enjoin or not? Of course, courts should try to tailor remedies to the cases before them as closely as possible.[xcviii] But all too often, judges are confronted by hard choices, with no Solomonic compromise possible. The guidelines proposed here are clear and bright in some of these cases, but call for refinement in others.

Regarding private copies, a French commentator already explained at the turn of the century: 'A copy made as a [private] study is exempt from remedies for infringement'.[xcix] Courts and legislators have to avoid invading privacy, whether of creators or of end-users of works. Refraining from coercive relief against private copying avoids the risks both of intimidating the timid muse that inspires creation in private and of violating constitutionally protected privacy interests. For example, the law does not stop computer programmers from making private copies of programs to discover methods and codes underlying these programs.[c] Privately made studies are also indispensable for younger artists who conduct research into artistic methods in copying older works. They need to get the knack of such methods manually as well as in inspecting the works visually.[ci]

Faced with public dissemination, courts have to decide whether or not to grant injunctions or other coercive remedies. Courts protect copyright owners' markets by stopping copying, by seizing hard copies, or by preventing sales or showings. It has been proposed that discretion to issue such orders be exercised with an eye to where plaintiff's and defendant's works fall along the spectrum of creative processes.[cii] Courts are most ready to enjoin or seize rote copies, that most obviously threaten markets the copied work targets but that bring nothing new into the marketplace. In mid-range cases, where knowledgeable reworking generates translations, adaptations, etc., discretion has to be exercised to balance the risk of allowing harm to protected markets against the risk of obstructing the feedback of new content.[ciii] For example, the Ninth Circuit thought it inappropriate to enjoin the exploitation of the film *Rear Window* when that work turned out to be subject to renewal rights in the short story on which it had been based. Such an injunction would not have advanced the right-holder's market interests, and it made little sense to deny 'the public the opportunity to view a classic film for many years to come'.[civ]

Of course, how discretion is exercised may vary according to procedural options available in a given legal system. For example, a judge may be more ready to grant a preliminary injunction pending an expedited determination on the merits than the long preparation of a jury trial.[cv] At the far end of the spectrum, where a prior work is innovatively recast into a truly different work, there tends to be less risk that markets properly reserved to the prior work might be prejudiced by the later work. At the same time, the argument for declining to enjoin the different and later work becomes all the stronger to the extent it represents new expression to release to the world.[cvi]

ii. Damages and other Awards

The difficulty at the level of monetary awards is not so obvious. It would seem that such awards can be easily adjusted within our framework of sliding-scale analysis. After all, the court can award more or less money to plaintiff depending on how massive or marginal defendant's taking is found to be. But the issue is not so simple, since the measures of monetary awards are diverse: some are granted for punitive or deterrent purposes; some, to compensate plaintiff for usurped markets or other damages; some, to recover defendant's undue gains.[cvii] The proposed guidelines suffice to co-ordinate such measures in simple cases, but they call for refinement in more complex cases.

For punitive or deterrent purposes, many courts may assess monetary awards, especially statutory or other special damages, at levels beyond the market interests at stake in the cases before them.[cviii] There is no risk that the prospect of paying such extraordinary damages might discourage the release of new creations to the world when they are levied against rote copies, for the simple reason that such copies feed nothing creative into communication networks. Quite the contrary, incentives to release original works run the risk of being blunted unless the unauthorised marketing of rote copies as substitutes for original works is discouraged.[cix]

But there is the risk that awards out of proportion with market stakes might burden the feedback of new content in cases where reworked or recast works are found to be infringing. Such cases call for purely compensatory awards, notably damages, royalties, or profits, or else statutory damages granted in lieu of such awards.[cx]

The amount of any compensatory award has to be gauged in the light of the relative impacts of plaintiff's and defendant's works on the marketplace. It is easy enough to measure damages in a case where plaintiff's work finds itself forsaken because defendant's work merely serves as a substitute for this prior work on the markets it addresses. It is then a matter of measuring losses, such as lost sales of copies or of tickets, other lost payments to access or show the work at issue, lost royalties accruing from such uses, or even arguably lost good will.[cxi] In other cases, plaintiff might not yet have put the work at issue on the market or might not have had any market success, or the work might be transformed by defendant into a derivative work that addresses different markets, for example, as when a novel is adapted to film. In neither event has plaintiff had damages in any actual market, so that reasonable royalties or shares of defendant's profits seem to be the only workable forms of monetary compensation. But it cannot be assumed, in conclusory fashion, that plaintiff is entitled to royalties or profits from all the new markets to which defendant's derivative work appeals. That issue turns on the very scope of the copyright which is here in question.[cxii]

The key here lies in apportioning compensatory awards to the extent to which plaintiff's work contributes to the appeal of defendant's on the marketplace.[cxiii] To start, in terms of our spectrum, the court can ascertain the extent to which plaintiff's work is routinely copied, knowledgeably reworked, or innovatively recast in defendant's work.[cxiv] Suppose, for example, quite hypothetically, that no license had been obtained from Dashiell Hammett to film *The Maltese Falcon*, as John Huston did knowledgeably and to some extent innovatively.[cxv] Not only would it not be equitable, but it would undermine incentives to make and release the film, if the writer were accorded all the film profits that would be otherwise attributable to talented stars, cinematic direction and production, promotion, etc. But the court may award Hammett reasonable royalties or shares of profits for Huston's rather thorough-going use of his story, which partially accounts for the abiding appeal of the resulting classic *film noir*, even while the court factors out creative filming, etc., also contributing to that appeal.[cxvi] It is not only a matter of the quantity of the materials taken from plaintiff's work, but of the qualities of these materials that contribute to their market appeal, even after defendant reworks and recasts them.[cxvii]

Finally, there remains the issue of including court costs and attorney's fees in monetary awards. For example, judges might well impose such litigation expenses on pirates selling rote copies without consent but excuse them for parties who sought to obtain licenses for transforming the works at issue. Such options are not easily co-ordinated with our guidelines, for one thing because legal systems differ considerably in their approaches to litigation expenses. Some might deal with them in their copyright statutes, and others in purely procedural laws.[cxviii]

iii. Proof: the Audience Test

In the United States, juries may find facts, while other systems largely rely on judges for that task. Of course, juries do not decide on injunctive and other equitable remedies that remain the judges' responsibilities. If called in the United States, juries find whether infringement takes place and assess monetary awards if they do so find.[cxix] Judge Jerome Frank left us with the following conventional wisdom on point:

> The proper criterion on that issue is not an analytic or other comparison of the respective musical compositions as they appear on paper or in the judgment of trained musicians. The plaintiff's legally protected interest is . . . in the potential financial returns from his compositions which derive from the lay public's approbation of his efforts. The question, therefore, is whether defendant took from plaintiff's works so much of what is pleasing to the ears of lay listeners, who comprise the audience for whom such popular music is composed . . .[cxx]

Perhaps, all triers of fact are tempted to act as test audiences when hearing infringement cases. Judges in non-jury systems, given their discretion to choose the best methods for finding facts, may at times consciously apply audience tests in such cases.[cxxi] Nonetheless, whether applied by judges or juries, audience tests give rise to a pair of related problems: first, not all triers of fact are sure to emulate accurately the responses of the relevant audiences; second, it is not always obvious who should constitute the relevant audience. To take an example of the first problem, imagine a case in which a poem is allegedly translated: to ascertain whether there is translation, much less how the appeal of the original poem finds its way into the translation, the trier of fact must itself be bilingual or hear testimony from an expert who knows the languages of both texts. As to the second problem, it brings us back to the issue of copyright scope: the extent of the markets reserved to plaintiff, along with the markets open to defendant, will depend on just this issue. But collapsing all criteria of relevant audiences into some notion of undifferentiated audience response only obfuscates the issue.[cxxii]

An imaginary case, introduced above, dramatises the problem of emulating audience response: a computer converts audio input into video output.[cxxiii] The computer reprocesses plaintiff's musical work, its rhythms, melodies, etc., into what appears to be an abstract cinematic work, namely moving and coloured patterns played out in real time on screen. Since the algorithm running the conversion is assumed to be pre-fixed without regard to the work at issue, the defendant who mechanically uses it to reprocess that work engages in rote copying that should trigger a full panoply of remedies.[cxxiv] Nonetheless, the average judge or jury might not hear, and in turn not see, much similarity in appeal between plaintiff's musical work and defendant's ostensible cinematic work, even though the algorithm maps one work onto the other, virtually point by point. As a result, a test merely asking the trier of fact to find infringement on the basis of some lay listener's and ordinary observer's response, but without the benefit of any analytic or expert comparison, might not lead to any finding of infringement at all, much less damages.[cxxv] Return, for a moment, to the example of the allegedly translated poem: there a bilingual expert could explain to the trier of fact how linguistic rules do, or do not, account for moving from plaintiff's text in one language to defendant's in another.[cxxvi] Similarly, in this imaginary case, an expert could focus the trier of fact on how the conversion algorithm generates, from plaintiff's musical work, the full fabric and potential appeal of defendant's ostensible cinematic work.[cxxvii]

Consider a real case which illustrates the problem of selecting relevant audiences. The artist Jeff Koons instructed an art studio to make a sculpture, in a number of copies, of a photograph of a couple holding a string of cute puppies. The sculpture, Koons claimed, critiqued kitsch sentimentality typified in the photograph, but no defence of fair use was allowed on that basis, and infringement was found on summary judgement.[cxxviii] But from whose perspective would Koons' sculpture so obviously constitute an actionable copy of the photograph, and whose markets would it usurp, if any, for purposes of assessing damages? In the eyes of other artists, Koons' coloured, three-dimensional sculpture slyly recontextualized, that is, in our terms, knowledgeably reworked, the black and white, two-dimensional photograph at issue.[cxxix] Still, the court, anticipating on the jury's emulation of an ordinary observer's response, felt compelled to make a 'black and white' finding of infringement, thus setting the stage for sweeping remedies.[cxxx] However, as Robert Rotstein acutely points out, such an audience test unavoidably involves a host of tacit premises about the markets that plaintiff and defendant might be respectively addressing.[cxxxi] In the *Koons* case, such premises seemed to blind the courts to differences between the photograph and the sculpture possibly significant for the art circles constituting one of these markets.[cxxxii]

In the imaginary case of the audio-to-video conversion, expert analysis of the conversion algorithm could explain how plaintiff's musical work was reprocessed into defendant's ostensible cinematic work.[cxxxiii] In the *Koons* case, did the instructions for 'copying' the photograph as a sculpture amount to such a fully determinative algorithm, or did they leave open enough creative choices to put infringement, or at least the measure of damages, into question? Even if 'enough' must ultimately be construed in this context with reference to some audience, it remains to be seen which audience was relevant in the *Koons* case: plaintiff's popular audience or defendant's artistically sophisticated audience? Plaintiff's popular audience was not relevant to the extent that no significant evidence indicated it to be lost as a market, but defendant's sophisticated audience could be, according to the appellate court, a source for an apportioned award.[cxxxiv] Following the reasoning outlined above, it would then have made sense in the *Koons* case to ignore plaintiff's photograph to the extent that it did not account for the appeal of defendant's sculpture on the art market.[cxxxv] An expert might well testify that Koons could have appropriated any equally banal image for that purpose. On that basis, only his audience would be relevantly plugged into the compensatory equation.[cxxxvi]

V. A Caveat and Conclusion

We started with a hypothetical suit. At issue were Hiroshige's wood-block prints. Relief was sought against Van Gogh's studies in oils of these prints. This case dramatises the dilemma implicit in all cases where prior works form bases for later works. On the one hand, denying relief would ignore copyright rationales altogether; on the other, overly stringent remedies could betray these rationales. This dilemma has become all the more critical as copyright has been expanded, for example, with rights to control derivative works and with ever-longer terms.

We have here reframed infringement analysis with an eye to resolving this dilemma. But our framework is not definitive, but merely an attempt to pull together various strands of infringement analysis in diverse copyright systems. Furthermore, all infringement analysis has to look to current culture for its premises concerning creative processes, aesthetic perceptions, and economic realities. Indeed, as a creature of our culture, copyright law can only proceed critically from just such premises in the light of its own basic rationales.[cxxxvii] No doubt, future aesthetic and economic insights will help to reconceptualise infringement analysis in new and better forms.

With that caveat in mind, a pair of points should be stressed in concluding. On the level of theory, courts need better analytic tools than shifting sets of vague and disparate tests and criteria of protectability and infringement. The attempt to bring underlying doctrines together into some coherent framework of analysis at least helps to debug corresponding tests and criteria and to optimise infringement findings and remedies in the cases. On the level of practice, courts ought not content themselves with simply finding infringement *vel non* but, in hard cases, would do well to discern more finely how plaintiffs' works are reworked or recast into defendants' works. In that light, it is submitted, they could grant remedies more consistently with copyright rationales.

i   Attorney, Los Angeles; Adjunct Faculty, International Intellectual Property, University of Southern California Law School: www-bcf.usc.edu/~pgeller/. This article, initially published in the *Journal of the Copyright Society of the USA*, vol.46(1), 1998, p.39, expands on a paper given at the interdisciplinary workshop *Creating Intellectual Property* which the Annenberg Center for Communication at the University of Southern California held on 26-27 September 1998. For their insightful comments on prior drafts, I thank Jeanne d'Andrea, Lionel Bently, Lorin Brennan, François Dessemontet, Jay Dougherty, Thomas Dreier, Bernard Edelman, Ysolde Gendreau, Paul Goldstein, Marci Hamilton, Ulrich Loewenheim, Jerome Reichman, Mark Rose, Robert Rotstein, Alain Strowel, and David Vaver. Copyright © Paul Edward Geller 1999

ii   Benjamin Kaplan, *An Unhurried View of Copyright* (New York: Columbia University Press, 1967), p.74.

iii   See Ingo F. Walther and Rainer Metzger, *Vincent van Gogh: The Complete Paintings*, trans. Michael Hulse (Cologne: Benedikt Taschen, 1993), vol.1, p.282.

iv   See ibid., pp.282-85 (also including *Oiran*, after Kesaï Eisen).

v   See Matthi Forrer, *Hiroshige, Prints and Drawings* (Munich: Prestel, 1997), prints 93-95.

vi   These exhibits reproduce transparencies provided by the Van Gogh Museum (Vincent van Gogh Foundation) in Amsterdam.

vii   However, Van Gogh himself did have 'scruples of conscience' that his elaborating on prior artists' works 'might be plagiarism'. Ronald de Leeuw, ed., *The Letters of Vincent Van Gogh*, trans. Arnold Pomerans (London: Penguin Books, 1996), p.477.

viii   Quoted in William P. Alford, *To Steal a Book is an Elegant Offense: Intellectual Property Law in Chinese Civilization* (Stanford: Stanford University Press, 1995), p.29.

ix   For the state of relevant French copyright law in the nineteenth century, see Alain Strowel, *Droit d'auteur et copyright: Divergences et convergences* (Brussels: Bruylant, 1993), pp.141-42, 598-99.

x   Analysis will here focus on economic rights that vary far less in scope from system to system than do moral rights, which raise a comparable, but more acute dilemma. For further analysis, see Paul Edward Geller, 'Must Copyright be For Ever Caught Between Marketplace and Authorship Norms?', in Brad Sherman and Alain Strowel, eds., *Of Authors and Origins: Essays on Copyright Law* (Oxford: Clarendon Press, 1994), pp.159, 194-98, abridged and revised in Paul Edward Geller, 'Toward an Overriding Norm in Copyright: Sign Wealth', *Revue Internationale du Droit d'Auteur (RIDA)*, issue 159, 1994, pp.2, 73-93.

xi See George Kubler, *The Shape of Time: Remarks on the History of Things* (New Haven: Yale University Press, 1962), pp.94-95, 115-16; Howard S. Becker, *Art Worlds* (Berkeley: University of California Press, 1982), chs.7, 8, 10 passim.

xii See Ernest F. Fenollosa, *Epochs of Chinese and Japanese Art*, 2d ed. (1913; reprint, New York: Dover Publications, 1963), vol.1, chs.5-6; Aurel Stein, *On Ancient Central-Asian Tracks*, ed. Jeannette Mirsky (New York: Pantheon Books, 1964), pp.17-33, 55-56, 79, 106-11, 194-96.

xiii See Joseph Needham, *Science and Civilisation in China* (Cambridge: Cambridge University Press, 1954), vol.1, ch.7; Lucien Febvre and Henri-Jean Martin, *L'apparition du livre*, 2d ed. (Paris: Éditions Albin Michel, 1971), pp.40, 102-09.

xiv See Sadakichi Hartmann, *Japanese Art* (1904; reprint, New York: Horizon Press, 1971), ch.4; Matthi Forrer, *Hokusai, Prints and Drawings* (London: Royal Academy of Arts, 1991), pp.17-19; Forrer, *Hiroshige, Prints and Drawings*, pp.19-21.

xv See Hartmann, *Japanese Art*, ch.5; Klaus Berger, *Japonisme in Western Painting from Whistler to Matisse*, trans. David Britt (Cambridge: Cambridge University Press, 1992), pp.6-34 passim, 48-49, 66-111 passim, 125-30, 184-89, 333-34.

xvi See generally Ejan Mackaay, 'Economic Incentives in Markets for Information and Innovation', *Harvard Journal of Law and Public Policy*, vol.13, 1990, pp.867, 873-85, 890-96 (indicating that free-riders need to be excluded to provide incentives for creation and dissemination). But see William Kingston, *Innovation: The Creative Impulse in Human Progress* (London: Calder, 1977), ch.3 (questioning whether economic incentives are always indispensable for creation).

xvii For further analysis, see Geller, 'Copyright Between Marketplace and Authorship Norms?', pp.188-90; Geller, 'Sign Wealth', pp.59-63.

xviii United States, Constitution, art. I, § 8, cl.8. See also United Kingdom, Statute of Anne, 8 Anne, c.19 (1710) (positing, in its title, the statutory goal: 'the Encouragement of Learning').

xix For historical background, see Strowel, *Droit d'auteur et copyright*, pp.89-91; Jane C. Ginsburg, 'A Tale of Two Copyrights: Literary Property in Revolutionary France and America', *Tulane Law Review*, vol.64, 1990, pp.991, 1005-22.

xx See Ejan Mackaay, 'An Economic View of Information Law', in Willem Korthals Altes, et al., eds., *Information Law Towards the 21st Century* (Deventer: Kluwer, 1992), pp.43, 57-61 (pointing out that the default position, absent intellectual property, is the free flow of information).

xxi For further analysis, see François Dessemontet, 'Copyright and Human Rights', in Jan J.C. Kabel and Gerard J.H.M. Mom, eds., *Intellectual Property and Information Law: Essays in Honour of Herman Cohen Jehoram* (Deventer: Kluwer, 1998), pp.113, 116-20.

xxii Compare Pierre N. Leval, 'Fair Use or Foul?', The Donald C. Brace Memorial Lecture, *Journal of the Copyright Society of the USA*, vol.36, 1989, pp.167, 170-75 (arguing that fair use properly excuses transformative uses), with Ivan Cherpillod, *L'objet du droit d'auteur* (Lausanne: CEDIDAC, 1985) pp.143-81 passim (comparing the German doctrine of free utilisation with other approaches to transformative uses).

xxiii   Compare, e.g., Alain Strowel, 'Belgium', § 8[2][a][v], in Paul Edward Geller, ed., *International Copyright Law and Practice* (New York: Matthew Bender, 1998), vol.1, pp.BEL-48 to BEL-49 (noting that Belgian law excuses parody and like uses under an exception if they comply with 'fair practice'), and André Lucas, 'France', § 8[2][a][iii], ibid., vol.1, pp.FRA-121 to FRA-122 (explaining that French law exempts 'parodies, pastiches, and caricatures' if they fall into an exception specific to 'this genre'), with Mario Fabiani, 'Italy', § 8[2][a], ibid., vol.2, pp.ITA-59 to ITA-60 (indicating that Italian law subjects such uses to general infringement analysis).

xxiv   See, e.g., *Cambell v. Acuff-Rose Music, Inc.*, 510 U.S. 569, 598-600 (Kennedy, J., concurring) (noting difficulty of distinguishing parody as fair use from 'just any commercial takeoff'); the French *Autumn Leaves* decisions, TGI Paris, 3e chambre, 7 Oct. 1992, *RIDA*, issue 155, 1993, p.222, *reversed*, CA Paris, 1re chambre, 11 May 1993, *RIDA*, issue 157, 1993, p.340 (disagreeing about whether the French parody exception applies to a takeoff without obvious comic intent); the German *Asterix Persiflagen* and *Alcolix* decisions, BGH, 11 March 1993, *Gewerblicher Rechtsschutz und Urheberrecht (GRUR)*, 1994, pp.191 and 206, respectively translated in *International Review of Industrial Property and Copyright Law (IIC)*, vol.25, 1994, pp.610 and 605 (analysing how the German doctrine of free utilisation applies to takeoffs on cartoon characters in different cases).

xxv   *Folsom v. Marsh*, 9 F. Cas. 342, 348 (1841).

xxvi   See Lloyd L. Weinreb, 'Fair Use and How it Got that Way', The 1998 Donald C. Brace Memorial Lecture, *Journal of the Copyright Society of the USA*, vol.45, 1998, pp.634, 637-38.

xxvii   See United States, Copyright Act, 17 U.S.C. § 107(3) (1998). But see Paul Goldstein, *Copyright*, 2nd ed. (Boston: Little Brown & Co., 1998), vol.2, § 10.2.2.1.c, pp.10:42-10:44, § 10.2.2.3, pp.10:54-10:58 (arguing that the 'nontransformative' character of a use need not preclude finding it to be a fair use and that 'substantiality' need not be the same in infringement and fair-use analyses).

xxviii   See Eugen Ulmer, *Urheber- und Verlagsrecht*, 3rd ed. (Berlin: Springer-Verlag, 1980), pp.275-78 (distinguishing the free use of public-domain materials from free utilisation so transforming plaintiff's protected materials that these 'fade away' [*verblassen*] in defendant's work). See also Switzerland, Loi fédérale sur le droit d'auteur et les droits voisins du 9 octobre 1992, RS 231.1, as amended effective 1 July 1995, ROLF 1995 1776 (deeming non-infringing the use of 'existing works for the creation of parodies or other analogous versions of the work' under article 11(3), but doing so outside the 'limitations on copyright' set out in chapter 5).

xxix   Purely local analyses, for example, guiding courts in only one or few U.S. circuits or other isolated jurisdictions, will not be considered. See, e.g., David Nimmer and Melville B. Nimmer, *Nimmer on Copyright* (New York: Matthew Bender, Dec. 1998), vol.4, § 13.03[A][1][c]-[d], pp.13-36 to 13-44 (critiquing criteria of certain U.S. circuits, such as 'total concept and feel' and 'structure, sequence, and organization'). Furthermore, not only doctrines such as fair use, but more basic constitutional principles remain outside the analysis undertaken here.

xxx   It is assumed here that both tasks, analysing infringement and fashioning remedies case by case, remain judicial rather than legislative responsibilities in all copyright systems. See Paul Edward Geller, 'Legal Transplants in International Copyright: Some Questions of Method', *UCLA Pacific Basin Law Journal*, vol.13, 1994, pp.199, 221-23.

xxxi   By hypothesis, in this universe of cases, there is always access to plaintiff's prior work, which is posited as consciously taken by defendant as a basis for a later work. See generally Alan Latman, '"Probative Similarity" As Proof of Copying: Toward Dispelling Some Myths in Copyright Infringement', *Columbia Law Review*, vol.90, 1990, pp.1187, 1204-14 (distinguishing criteria of access from criteria of infringement proper).

xxxii   Augustin-Charles Renouard, *Traité des droits d'auteurs* (Paris: Chez Jules Renouard et Cie., 1838-39), vol.2, p.37. See also Lionel Bently, 'Copyright and Translations in the English Speaking World', *Translation: FIT Newsletter*, vol.12, 1993, pp.491, 496-99 (explaining that the translation right was not clearly recognised in Anglo-American law until the mid-nineteenth century).

xxxiii For further background, see Paul Goldstein, 'Adaptation Rights and Moral Rights in the United Kingdom, the United States and the Federal Republic of Germany', *IIC*, vol.14, 1983, p.43.

xxxiv   Compare Kaplan, *An Unhurried View of Copyright*, pp.9-74 passim (analysing Anglo-American case law), with Cherpillod, *L'objet du droit d'auteur*, pp.59-108 passim (comparing French and German doctrines).

xxxv   For a critique, see Robert H. Rotstein, 'Beyond Metaphor: Copyright Infringement and the Fiction of the Work', *Chicago-Kent Law Review*, vol.68, 1993, p.701.

xxxvi   *Trust Company Bank v. Putnam Publishing Group, Inc.*, 5 U.S.P.Q. 2d 1874, 1878-79 (C.D. Cal. 1988). Note that Margaret Mitchell was herself sued, without success, for taking incidents in *Gone with the Wind* from a prior history of the Ku Klux Klan. For an account, see Alexander Lindey, *Plagiarism and Originality* (New York: Harper & Brothers Publishers, 1952), pp.108-09.

xxxvii TGI Paris, 3e chambre, 6 Dec. 1989, *Cahiers du Droit d'Auteur*, May 1990, p.21, *reversed*, CA Paris, 1re chambre, 21 Nov. 1990, *RIDA*, issue 147, 1991, p.319.

xxxviii Cass. 1e civ., 4 Feb. 1992, *RIDA*, issue 152, 1992, p.196, *on remand*, CA Versailles, chambres réunies, 15 Dec. 1993, *RIDA*, issue 160, 1994, p.255.

xxxix   But see Paul Goldstein, 'Copyright', The Donald C. Brace Memorial Lecture, *Journal of the Copyright Society of the USA*, vol.38, 1991, p.115 (ostensibly giving the benefit of the doubt to expanding copyright owners' protection 'to every market in which consumers derive value from their works').

xl   *Nichols v. Universal Pictures Corp.*, 45 F.2d 119, 121 (2d Cir. 1930), *cert. denied*, 282 U.S. 902 (1931).

xli   See Goldstein, *Copyright*, vol.1, § 2.3.2, pp.2:31-2:37.

xlii   The French *Pachot* decision, Cass. ass. plén., 7 March 1986, *RIDA*, issue 129, 1986, p.136 (using the quoted phrase 'constraining logic'). Compare André Lucas and Henri-Jacques Lucas, *La propriété littéraire et artistique* (Paris: Litec, 1994), pp.97-104 (concluding that the scope of protection turns on potentially creative, rather than functionally determined, choices), with Ulrich Loewenheim, 'Das Werk', in Gerhard Schricker, ed., *Urheberrecht: Kommentar* (Munich: Beck, 1987), pp.85, 97 (indicating cases where room for creativity is restricted by technical and related considerations).

xliii   See David Nimmer, et al., 'A Structured Approach to Analyzing the Substantial Similarity of Computer Software in Copyright Infringement Cases', *Arizona State Law Journal*, vol.20, 1988, pp.625, 635-48.

xliv   TGI Paris, 1re chambre, 16 Jan. 1991, *RIDA*, issue 148, 1991, p.180, *affirmed*, CA Paris, 1re chambre, 14 Jan. 1992, *RIDA*, issue 152, 1992, p.198 (plaintiff cannot claim an 'exclusive right to linguistic and cultural materials').

xlv   See Paul Edward Geller, 'Copyright in Factual Compilations: U.S. Supreme Court Decides the *Feist* Case', *IIC*, vol. 22, 1992, pp. 802, 804-06.

xlvi   See Rotstein, 'Beyond Metaphor', pp. 760-76.

xlvii See Gunnar W. G. Karnell, 'The Idea/Expression Dichotomy: A Conceptual Fallacy', *Copyright World*, 1989, no. 7, p. 16; Leslie A. Kurtz, 'Speaking to the Ghost: Idea and Expression in Copyright', *University of Miami Law Review*, vol. 47, 1993, pp. 1221, 1241-51.

xlviii *Kregos v. Associated Press*, 937 F.2d 700, 714 (2d Cir. 1991) (Sweet, J., dissenting), *summary judgement granted*, 795 F. Supp. 1325, 1329-35 (S.D.N.Y. 1992), *affirmed*, 3 F.3d 656, 664 (2d Cir. 1993) ('there are a limited number of statistics generally considered outcome-predictive by those familiar with the sport'), *cert. denied*, 510 U.S. 1112 (1994).

xlix   See *State St. Bank & Trust Co. v. Signature Financial Group*, 149 F.3d 1369, 1372-76 (Fed. Cir. 1998) *cert. denied*, 142 L. Ed. 2d 704 (1999) (rejecting prior tests for filtering out 'abstract ideas' in applications for software patents, but not fleshing out any new test beyond invoking the general patent criterion of a 'useful result').

l   United States, Copyright Act, 17 U.S.C. § 102(b) (1998). Based on this reading of 'ideas' as processes rather than representations, this Article not only expressly reinterprets the 'abstraction' analysis of infringement, but implicitly rejects the 'pattern' and 'total feel' tests. For glosses, see Nimmer, *Copyright*, vol. 4, § 13.03[A][1], pp. 13-31 to 13-40.

li   See Aristotle, *Poetics*, trans. Ingram Bywater, in Richard McKeon, ed., *Introduction to Aristotle* (New York: The Modern Library, 1947), pp. 624, 631-50 passim.

lii   See Roland Barthes, 'L'introduction à l'analyse structurale des récits', in *L'aventure sémiologique* (Paris: Éditions du Seuil, 1985), pp. 167, 168 (referring to Aristotle in introducing new analyses).

liii   See, e.g., *Micro Star v. FormGen Inc.*, 154 F.3d 1107, 1111-12 (9th Cir. 1998) (comparing musical scores to programs driving video games). For further analysis of basic differences between types of works, see below text accompanying notes 73-79.

liv   *Nichols v. Universal Pictures Corp.*, 45 F.2d 119, 121 (2d Cir. 1930), *cert. denied*, 282 U.S. 902 (1931).

lv   *Feist Publications, Inc. v. Rural Telephone Service Co.*, 499 U.S. 340, 349 (1991).

lvi   Compare Lucas, *La propriété littéraire et artistique*, pp. 101-02, 225-27 (explaining how criteria such as *apport intellectuel* [mental input] imply infringement analysis *à géométrie variable*), with Loewenheim, 'Das Werk', pp. 98-99 (explaining that criteria such as *Gestaltungshöhe* [level of formal elaboration] are inevitably satisfied to variable degrees).

lvii   See generally Thomas Dreier and Gunnar Karnell, 'Originality of the Copyrighted Work: A European Perspective', *Journal of the Copyright Society of the USA*, vol. 39, 1992, pp. 289, 291-99 (explaining Continental European sliding-scale analysis against the background of post-*Feist* U.S. law). Exceptionally, British copyright may eschew limiting doctrines that tend to lead to any sliding-scale analysis. See, e.g., *Ibcos Computers v. Barclays Mercantile*, [1994] Fleet Street Reports 275 (shying away from analysing possible merger, etc.).

lviii See Loewenheim, 'Das Werk', pp. 90-91. But see ibid., pp. 99-100 (explaining how German jurisprudence adjusts this standard, along with corresponding tests of protectability, as creative options diminish, for example, in cases of what in German is called the *kleine Münze* [small change] of copyright); Gunnar W.G. Karnell, 'European Originality: A Copyright Chimera', in Kabel and Mom, eds., *Essays in Honour of Herman Cohen Jehoram*, p. 201 (questioning whether E.C. directives introducing ostensibly different standards for software and other works ought to change the law).

lix The *Explosionszeichnungen* decision, BGH, 28 Feb. 1991, *GRUR*, 1991, p.529. See also Adolf Dietz, 'Germany', § 2[2], in Geller, ed., *International Copyright Law and Practice*, vol.2, p.GER-25 (noting the fictive character of this premise of the case, in the light of limitations of German copyright in the designs portrayed in technical drawings).

lx The *Power of Blue* decision, OLG Hamburg, 12 Oct. 1995, *Zeitschrift für Urheber- und Medienrecht*, 1996, p.315.

lxi François Dessemontet, 'Switzerland', § 8[1][a], in Geller, ed., *International Copyright Law and Practice*, vol.2, p.SWI-63.

lxii For this definition and examples, see above text accompanying notes 50-53.

lxiii For analyses on which these distinctions are based, see Kubler, *The Shape of Time*, pp.39-53, 62-82; Roland Barthes, 'Écrivains et écrivants', in *Essais critiques* (Paris: Éditions du Seuil, 1964), p.147; Umberto Eco, *A Theory of Semiotics* (Bloomington: Indiana University Press, 1976), pp.217-76 passim; George Steiner, *After Babel: Aspects of Language and Translation*, 2nd ed. (Oxford: Oxford University Press, 1992), pp.266, 447-49.

lxiv For an example of appropriation art, see below text accompanying notes 128-36.

lxv For background, see Richard Ellmann, *James Joyce*, rev. ed. (New York: Oxford University Press, 1982), pp.561-64, 600-04; Jacques Derrida, *Ulysse gramophone; Deux mots pour Joyce* (Paris: Galilée, 1987), pp.99-100, 121. For the observation that translating a classic work from its original into another language, for example, Shakespeare from English into German, can creatively enrich the language into which the translation is made, see Steiner, *After Babel*, pp.270-80.

lxvi See Ira Gitler, *Swing to Bop: An Oral History of the Transition in Jazz in the 1940s* (Oxford: Oxford University Press, 1985), pp.69-72 (quoting the guitarist Biddy Fleet). See also Nat Shapiro and Nat Hentoff, *Hear me Talkin' to Ya* (New York, Dover Publications, 1955), p.337 (quoting Dizzy Gillespie on parallel origins of bebop at Minton's in Harlem in the early forties: '[O]n afternoons before a session, Theolonius Monk and I began to work out some complex variations on chords and the like, and we used them at night to scare away the no-talent guys. After a while, we got more and more interested in what we were doing as music, and, as we began to explore more and more, our music evolved'.).

lxvii For counter-examples, namely of interactive conversions, including the reworking of Van Gogh's studies of Hiroshige, see Lillian F. Schwartz, 'Computers and Appropriation Art: The Transformation of a Work or Idea for a New Creation', *Leonardo*, 1996, no.1, p.43.

lxviii Of course, as software improves, it can accomplish more and more routines, allowing interactively participating authors to focus more and more on creative input. For further issues, see below note 124.

lxix Eco, *A Theory of Semiotics*, p.274. See also Derrida, *Ulysse gramophone*, pp.106-07, 137-43 (waxing ironic over a hypothetical project to computerise Joyce studies world-wide).

lxx See, e.g., Gary Giddins et al., liner notes to Charlie Parker, *The Complete Birth of the Bebop* (Stash Records CD, 1991) (indicating some of these tunes).

lxxi See Goldstein, *Copyright*, vol.1, § 2.3.2.1, pp.2:33-2:35 (proposing to analyse merger in terms of options available at the time of the later work).

lxxii For further analysis, see below text accompanying notes 121-36.

lxxiii See J.H. Reichman, 'Goldstein on Copyright Law: A Realist's Approach to a Technological Age', *Stanford Law Review*, vol.43, 1991, pp.943, 963-64 (critiquing any unified theory of infringement and contemplating only practically distinct standards).

lxxiv See generally Nelson Goodman, *Languages of Art: An Approach to a Theory of Symbols*, 2nd ed. (Indianapolis: Hackett Publishing Co., 1976), pp.113-22 (distinguishing between 'allographic' and 'autographic' works).

lxxv   For further analysis and examples, see Gérard Genette, *L'Œuvre de l'art: Immanence et transcendance* (Paris: Éditions du Seuil, 1994), vol. 1, pp. 129-81 passim.

lxxvi See Nicholas Cook, *Music, Imagination and Culture* (Oxford: Clarendon Press, 1990), pp. 71-83, 122-52 passim (explaining that scores provide necessary, but not sufficient, instructions for musical performances).

lxxvii See Arthur Cooper, 'Introduction', in *Li Po and Tu Fu: Poems*, trans. Arthur Cooper (London: Penguin Books, 1973), pp. 76-100 passim. See also Osvald Sirén, *The Chinese on the Art of Painting: Translations and Comments* (1936; reprint, New York: Schocken Books, 1963), pp. 44, 90 (quoting Sung art treatises: 'There is no difference between the study of painting and the study of calligraphy'. 'Poetry and painting follow the same laws'.).

lxxviii Compare, e.g., Dashiell Hammett, *The Maltese Falcon* (New York: Alfred A. Knopf, 1930; New York: Vintage Crime/Black Lizard 1992), pp. 40-41, 112-16, 195-97 (having the hero in the novel, Sam Spade, meet face-to-face with his lawyer, once in an ethically dubious conversation, and later force the heroine to strip naked to see if she was hiding stolen money on her person), with *The Maltese Falcon* (Warner Brothers 1941) (replacing meetings with telephone calls to the lawyer and deleting the strip scene).

lxxix Goodman, *Languages of Art*, p. 229.

lxxx   For example, manually faking art works might well entail knowledgeable reworking. For further analysis and authorities, see Richard Price and Sally Price, *Enigma Variations* (Cambridge, Mass.: Harvard University Press, 1995), pp. 67-88, 160-61. For the basic reason for rejecting any 'pattern' test, see above note 50.

lxxxi See above text accompanying notes 63-72.

lxxxii See above text accompanying notes 5-6.

lxxxiii Berger, *Japonisme in Western Painting*, pp. 131-32.

lxxxiv See Forrer, *Hiroshige, Prints and drawings*, pp. 21-22.

lxxxv Berger, *Japonisme in Western Painting*, p. 131. See also Schwartz, 'Computers and Appropriation Art', p. 45 (noting that, in 'appropriating Japanese woodcuts', Van Gogh changed his 'style of painting').

lxxxvi See Ingo F. Walther and Rainer Metzger, *Vincent van Gogh: The Complete Paintings*, pp. 282-85.

lxxxvii Berger, *Japonisme in Western Painting*, p. 132.

lxxxviii See Guido Calebresi and A. Douglas Melamed, 'Property Rules, Liability Rules, and Inalienability: One View of the Cathedral', *Harvard Law Review*, vol. 85, 1972, pp. 1089, 1091-93, 1106-10.

lxxxix See J.H. Reichman, 'Legal Hybrids Between the Patent and Copyright Paradigms', *Columbia Law Review*, vol. 94, 1994, pp. 2432, 2504-58 passim. It has been argued that rights to injunctions, rather than damages, form the optimal framework for negotiating licenses. See, e.g., Robert P. Merges, 'Of Property Rules, Coase, and Intellectual Property', *Columbia Law Review*, vol. 94, 1994, p. 2655 (making this argument, albeit with caveats). Counter-examples abound, however, showing that reliable prospects for judicial remedies are but some of the miscellany of factors on which any readiness to license might depend. See, e.g., Peter C. Grindley and David J. Teece, 'Managing Intellectual Capital: Licensing and Cross-Licensing in Semiconductors and Electronics', *California Management Review*, vol. 39, 1997, p. 8 (examining one field in the context of technology licensing over the century).

xc   See above text accompanying note 21.

xci   At the time of the French Revolution, when the legislators spoke of author's rights as 'sacred' property rights, it was not admitted that any injunction based on such property could lie against derivative works. See above text accompanying note 32. Thus these Revolutionary legislators ignored the doctrinal conflict raised here in its remedial consequences, and their legislative record indicates that they recognised copyright mainly to assure authors of 'some fruit of their labours', that is, monetary rewards. See Le Chapelier, *Le Moniteur universel*, 15 Jan. 1791, quoted in Strowel, *Droit d'auteur et copyright*, p.90.

xcii See, e.g., Lindey, *Plagiarism and Originality*, chs.9-15 passim (giving a wealth of examples from U.S. case law in the first half of the twentieth century); Marci A. Hamilton, 'Appropriation Art and the Imminent Decline in Authorial Control over Copyrighted Works', *Journal of the Copyright Society of the USA*, vol.42, 1994, pp.93, 115-25 (analysing different mixes of property and liability approaches in recent U.S. case law).

xciii See above text accompanying notes 34-61.

xciv For further analysis, see David Vaver, *Intellectual Property: Copyright, Patents, Trade-marks* (Toronto: Irwin Law, 1997), pp.255-68.

xcv   See above text accompanying notes 63-71.

xcvi This assumption benefits from hindsight. More recent transformations might require closer scrutiny. See, e.g., Schwartz, 'Computers and Appropriation Art', pp.45-47 (reworking Van Gogh's study by computer).

xcvii For the dilemma, see above text accompanying notes 19-30.

xcviii See, e.g., *Kepner-Tregoe, Inc. v. Carabio*, 203 U.S.P.Q. 124 (E.D. Mich., 1979) (allowing the release of defendant's work with certain portions redacted after close comparison with plaintiff's work).

xcix Eugène Pouillet, *Traité théorique et pratique de la propriété littéraire et artistique et du droit de représentation* (Paris: Librairie Générale de Jurisprudence, 3rd ed., 1908), p.601.

c   Compare *Sega Enter. Ltd. v. Accolade, Inc.*, 977 F.2d 1510, 1520-30 (9th Cir. 1992) (judicially allowing research copies as fair use), with Council Directive 91/250 of 14 May 1991 on the Legal protection of Computer Programs, 1991 J.O. (L 122) 42 (requiring, in article 6, statutory provisions to exempt decompilation).

ci   Compare Mai-mai Sze, *The Way of Chinese Painting: Its Ideas and Technique* (New York: Random House, 1959), pp.54-63, 115 (explaining Chinese tradition: 'Copying is a proved way of acquiring the necessary technical means of expression and, for many, a helpful steppingstone to creative results'), with Egbert Haverkamp-Begemann and Carolyn Logan, *Creative Copies: Interpretative Drawings from Michelangelo to Picasso* (New York: The Drawing Center, 1988), pp.16-21 (explaining European tradition from Renaissance to modern, 'more inventive forms of imitation').

cii   See above text accompanying notes 95-97.

ciii Compare Goldstein, *Copyright*, vol.2, § 11.0, p.11:2 (contemplating such orders to stop 'wholesale piracy' but not infringers who 'borrow a few protected elements' to make 'original' works of their 'own'), with Lucas, *La propriété littéraire et artistique*, p.608, n.68 (noting French orders to seize copies in cases of 'flagrant' infringement).

civ   *Abend v. MCA, Inc.*, 863 F.2d 1465, 1479 (9th Cir. 1988), *affirmed*, 495 U.S. 207, 236 (1990) (leaving untouched the appellate court's remedial analysis).

cv   See, e.g., Herman Cohen Jehoram, 'Netherlands', § 8[5][a][i], in Geller, ed., *International Copyright Law and Practice*, vol.2, p.NETH-77 (noting expedited Dutch *kort geding* procedure).

cvi   See generally Mark Lemley and Eugene Volokh, 'Freedom of Speech and Injunctions in Intellectual Property Cases', *Duke Law Journal*, vol.48, 1998, p.147 (arguing that overriding rights of free expression may preclude preliminary injunctions in many U.S. copyright cases).

cvii Remedies for the violation of moral rights, which lay beyond the scope of the analysis proposed here, require quite different perspectives than do remedies for the economic interests considered here. For further analysis, see Stig Strömholm, *Le droit moral de l'auteur en droit allemand, français et scandinave avec un aperçu de l'évolution internationale: Étude de droit comparé* (Stockholm: Norstedt, 1967), vol.II:1, pp.9-53 passim.

cviii For examples, see Miguel A. Emery, 'Argentina', § 8[5][a], in Geller, ed., *International Copyright Law and Practice*, vol.1, pp.ARG-56 TO ARG-57; James Lahore, 'Australia', § 8[5][a], ibid., vol.1, pp.AUS-108; David Nimmer, 'United States', § 8[5][a][i], ibid., vol.2, pp.USA-165 TO USA-166.

cix   For the suggestion that the TRIPs Agreement requires special damages to 'constitute a deterrent to further infringements', ostensibly in cases of just such piracy, see Thomas Dreier, 'Damages for Copyright Infringement in Germany', in Kabel and Mom, eds., *Essays in Honour of Herman Cohen Jehoram*, pp.134-36.

cx   For examples, see David Vaver, 'Canada', § 8[5][a][ii][B], in Geller, ed., *Internationa Copyright Law and Practice*, vol.1, pp.CAN-123 TO CAN-124; Joshua Weisman, *Israel* § 8[5][a][ii], ibid., vol.2, pp.ISR-32 TO ISR-34.

cxi   Compare Goldstein, *Copyright*, vol.2, § 12.1.1.1, p.12:7 (distinguishing between U.S. measures of actual losses in markets already occupied by claimant and of royalties or profits in other markets), with Dreier, 'Damages for Copyright Infringement', pp.130-133 (critically analysing comparable German measures).

cxii See above text accompanying notes 33-39.

cxiii See, e.g., *Peter Pan Fabrics, Inc. v. Martin Weiner Corp. Corp.*, 274 F.2d 487, 489 (2d Cir. 1960) (Hand, J.) (speaking in terms of the 'aesthetic appeal' of the works).

cxiv See above text accompanying notes 63-71.

cxv   See above text accompanying note 78.

cxvi See, e.g., *Sheldon v. Metro-Goldwyn Pictures Corp.*, 106 F.2d 45, 50-51 (2d Cir., 1939), *affirmed*, 309 U.S. 390 (1940) (granting plaintiff only that portion of defendant's profits due to adapting protected parts of his play into a film, but not profits due to exploiting purely cinematic parts of the film).

cxvii *Quaere* how to disentangle essentially copyright-related from publicity-right and trademark-related contributions to market appeal, for example, making and showing the work at issue from advertising well-known authors, stars, etc.?

cxviii Compare United States, Copyright Act, 17 U.S.C. § 505 (1998) (authorising awards of litigation expenses in copyright statute), with Germany, ZPO, § 91 (authorising them in general procedural code).

cxix See generally *Feltner v. Columbia Pictures Television, Inc.*, 523 U.S. 340 (1998) (holding that juries also assess statutory damages).

cxx   *Arnstein v. Porter*, 154 F.2d 464, 473 (2d Cir. 1946). But see ibid., p.480 (Clark, J., dissenting) (warning that the majority was substituting 'chaos, judicial as well as musical', for prior precedents). See also Latman, '"Probative Similarity" As Proof of Copying', pp.1191-92 (noting that *Arnstein* was one of a series of unsuccessful infringement actions brought by the same composer); Lindey, *Plagiarism and Originality*, pp.267-71 (critiquing Judge Frank's opinion for lowering the barrier of summary judgement to the then-current wave of 'plagiarism racketeers' holding up successful authors with meritless suits).

cxxi   See, e.g., Vaver, *Intellectual Property*, pp.80-82 (noting that Canadian judges may apply audience test); Loewenheim, 'Das Werk', pp.134-36 (indicating that German judges may refer to the perspective of 'the average observer' [*Durchschnittsbetrachters*] in the relevant 'circle' [*Verkehrskreise*] for fact-finding purposes in appropriate cases).

cxxii   See, e.g., Goldstein, *Copyright*, vol.2, § 7.3.1, pp.7:32-7:34 (noting that finders of fact tend to ignore doctrines limiting copyright scope, such as the idea-expression distinction, in attending only to average audience response).

cxxiii   See above text accompanying notes 66-67.

cxxiv   *Quaere* whether the author of the conversion algorithm may be deemed to transform the work at issue creatively, albeit indirectly? For further analysis, see Jerome H. Reichman, 'Electronic Information Tools: The Outer Edge of World Intellectual Property Law', *IIC* vol.24, 1993, pp.446, 468-72.

cxxv   See, e.g., *Dawson v. Hinshaw Music, Inc.*, 905 F.2d 731, 737-38 (4th Cir.), *cert. denied*, 498 U.S. 981 (1990) (holding it improper to submit recordings to lay-listener test, without benefit of expertise, in case of written scores of specialised music).

cxxvi   See above text accompanying notes 121-22.

cxxvii   See Goldstein, *Copyright*, vol.2, § 12.1.2.2, p.12:25 ('In cases where the defendant's work literally copies the copyrighted work and adds nothing original of its own, to permit the copyright owner to recover all of the defendant's profits gives the copyright owner no more than its due.').

cxxviii   *Rogers v. Koons*, 751 F. Supp. 474 (S.D.N.Y. 1990), *amended, on rehearing*, 777 F. Supp. 1 (S.D.N.Y. 1991), *affirmed*, 960 F. 2d 301 (2d Cir. 1992), *cert. denied*, 506 U.S. 934 (1992).

cxxix   See Martha Buskirk, 'Appropriation Under the Gun', *Art in America*, vol.80(6), 1992, p.37. *Quaere* who knowledgeably reworked the photograph, Koons and/or the personnel at the art studio? This issue, of course, does not affect infringement analysis.

cxxx   Injunctive relief was granted, and plaintiff claimed defendant's profits in six figures. *Rogers v. Koons*, 751 F. Supp. 474, 480-81 (S.D.N.Y. 1990).

cxxxi   See Rotstein, 'Beyond Metaphor', pp.779-88. See also Alfred C. Yen, 'Copyright Opinions and Aesthetic Theory', *Southern California Law Review*, vol.71, 1998, pp.247, 290-97 (also analysing the audience test in the light of recent critical theory).

cxxxii   The appellate court continued to restrict the audience to that without 'any special skills other than to be a reasonable and average lay person'. *Rogers v. Koons*, 960 F. 2d 301, 308 (2d Cir. 1992).

cxxxiii   See above text accompanying notes 123-27.

cxxxiv   However, once it realised that both royalty and profit measures might leave plaintiff with a negligible award, the appellate court jumped remedial tracks, approving the trial court's order to turn over defendant's sculptures and proposing 'enhanced statutory damages'. But it gave no thought to the risk that taking the sculptures off the market might undercut any award of royalties or profits, much less that such remedies might burden access to new art. *Rogers v. Koons*, 960 F. 2d 301, 312-14 (2d Cir. 1992).

cxxxv   See above text accompanying notes 113-17.

cxxxvi   See, e.g., the German *Alcolix* decision, *GRUR*, 1994, p.208, translated in *IIC*, vol.25, 1994, p.609 (holding that plaintiff's comic strip should be compared to defendant's parody from the perspective of readers with 'the necessary intellectual understanding' to appreciate the parody).

cxxxvii   See Rotstein, 'Beyond Metaphor', p.804; Yen, 'Copyright Opinions and Aesthetic Theory', pp.298-302.

The Future of the Copyright Exceptions

Robert Burrell

A number of commentators have noted that copyright seems to have lurched from one crisis to another over recent years. It now appears that the next major disputes are likely to centre around the copyright exceptions, that is, around the 'defences' or 'permitted acts' or 'users' rights' that all modern copyright systems provide so as to privilege certain acts that would otherwise amount to an infringement of copyright.

One reason why the exceptions look set to become the next fiercely contested aspect of copyright law is that this represents the next stage in the ongoing debate about the future of copyright in the light of recent technological advances. Now that the argument that the digital environment should be entirely unregulated by copyright law has been lost,[i] those opposed to the operation of copyright in cyberspace have turned their attention to ways of ensuring that copyright is applied in as narrow a form as possible. Attention has tended to focus on the exceptions rather than on the term of protection, the other traditionally important limitation built into the structure of copyright, in part because the international trend is clearly toward the lengthening of the copyright term. In addition, however, there appears to be a growing consensus that arguments over whether copyright should expire, say, 20 years after a work has been created rather than 70 years after the author's death miss the essential point. In particular, for those wishing to facilitate the 'transformative use' of copyright material, the key question is, what uses can be made of a work immediately, while it is still current and still in the public eye. On this view, lengthy, perhaps even perpetual, copyright protection might be unobjectionable provided that the copyright owner is not able to use its monopoly to prevent the creation of derivative, socially useful, works.

A second reason why the copyright exceptions seem set to become the next major battleground in copyright is that the process of international and regional harmonisation of the exceptions has now begun in earnest. Although the various international instruments relating to copyright have long contained some provisions dealing with this aspect of copyright law, for the most part, national governments and legislatures were left with a free hand in this area. Unsurprisingly, this led to 'bewildering differences in national copyright Acts in the area of exemptions and limitations'.[ii] More recently, however, the GATT-TRIPs Agreement has attempted to limit the circumstances in which a Member State may provide for an exception. The key provision of TRIPs is Article 13, which provides, 'Members shall confine limitations or exceptions to exclusive rights to certain special cases which do not conflict with a normal exploitation of the work and do not unreasonably prejudice the legitimate interests of the right holder'. While this provision has it origins in Article 9(2) of the Berne Convention,[iii] the enforcement mechanism of the TRIPs Agreement means that this wording is being transformed from a general statement of principle[iv] into a detailed three-stage test. A test capable of being used to determine whether any given exception is in conformity with international copyright norms.[v] As a result, Member States are being forced to treat the TRIPs provision as creating a significant limit on the circumstances in which they may provide for an exception.

At a regional level, the European Union became interested in the exceptions as part of its drive to harmonise aspects of copyright law. As it relates to the information society: the concern being that marked differences between national laws, as regards exceptions to copyright, might slow the development of pan-European information products. This, since a producer who relied on a particular exception under their national copyright law to incorporate part of a copyright work in their product would have no guarantee that they would not infringe copyright elsewhere in Europe. The Information Society Directive,[vi] therefore, sets out an exhaustive list of the grounds on which a Member State may provide for an exception, albeit in fairly general terms. The gestation period of this legislation led to consideration being given to the functions of copyright exceptions and attempts being made to categorise existing provisions.[vii] Interest in Europe seems set to continue as debate shifts to the question of whether the Information Society Directive is *intra vires* [viii] and, if so, the way in which the Directive should be implemented.

A third reason why so much attention has become focused on the copyright exceptions is that, in the U.K. at least, interest in such provisions has happened to coincide with developments in other areas of the law. Most notably, increased interest in the exceptions has coincided with the coming into force of the Human Rights Act. Not only has this created general interest in the intersection between copyright and the fundamental rights and freedoms guaranteed under that Act (in particular, freedom of speech), it has also furthered interest in the question of the extent to which limitations and exceptions can be found outside copyright law. That is, the circumstances in which human rights law, competition law, or the general principles of the common law might operate to place a limit on the rights granted to copyright owners.

The three factors that are creating unprecedented interest in the copyright exceptions have tended to lead to debates which have their own terms of reference and which are therefore at least partly isolated from one another. The starting points and motivations of those who are writing about the exceptions also vary to such an extent that it is not possible to summarise these debates in a way that does justice to the nuance and range of positions that commentators have adopted. Indeed, to a certain extent debates about the proper scope of the copyright exceptions provide merely another opportunity to discuss the fundamental questions of the justifications for, and the proper role of, a copyright system. Even if starting with the potential users of copyright works, rather than the potential owners of copyright, tends to cast these familiar questions in a new light.

If it is impossible to summarise adequately the entire spectrum of positions that have been taken in relation to the copyright exceptions, it is possible to identify certain key issues. Issues that raise both practical and theoretical difficulties and which can therefore be used to illustrate what is at stake when the scope of the copyright exceptions is being discussed, as well as some of the ideas and understandings of copyright which inform current debates. Two such issues will be identified and discussed in the remainder of this essay: namely, the relative merits of general as opposed to more specific exceptions. And secondly, the extent to which the availability of licences ought to be taken into account when deciding whether the defendant's actions fall within any given exception.

General or Specific Exceptions

Broadly speaking, it is possible to identify two approaches that can be taken to the provision of copyright exceptions. The first approach is to provide a small number of generally worded exceptions. Exceptions of this type might, for example, encompass 'private use' or, more generally still, 'fair use'. The second approach is to provide for a larger number of much more specific exceptions, encompassing carefully defined activities such as recording a broadcast so as to allow a programme to be watched at a more convenient time or using an extract from a work for the purpose of reporting current events. Whilst no copyright system corresponds exactly to these models, the United Kingdom leans heavily toward the second approach. Thus Chapter III, Part 1 of the Copyright, Designs, and Patents Act 1988 consists of some 57 sections which set out, often in great detail, a wide range of acts which will not infringe copyright. With the benefit of hindsight, it is possible to point to the Copyright Act 1911 as first laying down this approach. This is significant because the 1911 Act was an Imperial measure.

Although most former colonies have now had their own copyright legislation for a considerable number of years, for the most part this legislation has tended to follow the Imperial model developed in 1911. Thus Australia,[ix] Canada,[x] India,[xi] Ireland,[xii] New Zealand,[xiii] and Singapore[xiv] delineate the limits of copyright protection by way of an exhaustive list of specifically defined exceptions. The most generous of these provisions are the various fair dealing provisions. Whilst there are some significant differences of detail between different countries within the Commonwealth tradition, at a general level it is possible to say that these fair dealing exceptions allow works to be utilised for a limited range of purposes, such as research or private study. It must be emphasised that fair dealing exceptions will only apply if the work is used for one of the approved purposes. Other types of use will not come under the aegis of these provisions no matter how 'fair' they may be. In contrast, the United States has a general fair use defence which renders any use which the court deems to be 'fair', non-infringing, with further guidance being given by a set of non-exclusive policy factors which the court should take into account.[xv]

From time to time the wisdom of the Commonwealth approach has been called into question. For example, in the U.K., the 1977 Whitford Committee Report[xvi] recommended that the United Kingdom adopt a general defence of fair use. Similarly, in Canada, a 1984 report for the Department of Consumer and Corporate Affairs and the Department of Communications recommended that Canada adopt a fair use defence modelled along U.S. lines.[xvii] Whilst both these recommendations were rejected, and whilst subsequent back bench attempts to get a fair use defence incorporated into U.K. and Canadian law were unsuccessful, interest in moving toward the U.S. system remained. With the recent attention that has been given to the copyright exceptions, this interest has become more sustained across several Commonwealth jurisdictions. Most significantly, the Australian Copyright Law Review Committee has recommended the introduction of a general fair use defence[xviii] (though it again appears that this recommendation will not be acted upon in the foreseeable future). Similarly, a number of commentators have indicated that they believe that a fair use defence would have a number of advantages over the current Commonwealth approach.[xix] Unsurprisingly, this interest in moving toward the U.S. system has come almost exclusively from commentators who believe that an overreaching copyright law imposes unnecessary costs on consumers of copyright works, that it may stifle creativity, and that it could impact negatively on other socially important goals, rights, and interests.

It is only natural that such commentators should look toward the more generous provisions that already exist elsewhere. Especially as interest in a fair use defence has been further heightened by a related concern amongst this group; namely, that users are prejudiced under the current Commonwealth system whereby rights are described in open-ended and technologically neutral terms. And where exceptions are defined by reference to specific acts and specific technologies of reproduction and representation. Significantly, this latter concern was a factor cited by the Australian Copyright Law Review Committee as a reason for its decision to recommend the adoption of a U.S. style fair use defence.

Calls for introduction of fair use defence have met opposition from two very different quarters. Predictably, opposition has come from industry representatives and from commentators who are untroubled by the dangers of an overreaching copyright law and who believe that copyright needs to be strengthened in the light of recent technological advances. For such commentators, a fair use defence would undermine the position of right holders by introducing a highly unpredictable factor at a time when many copyright owners already face considerable uncertainty. Indeed several would go further and argue that many of the existing exceptions should be further restricted or repealed altogether. These arguments which, as will be seen, tend to be reinforced by the suggestion that the existing exceptions and defences can only be justified insofar as they relate to circumstances in which market failure is likely. Perhaps more surprisingly, opposition to the introduction of a more general defence has also come from commentators who are broadly supportive of the aims of those calling for the introduction of such a defence, but who are sceptical about what a fair use defence might achieve. Or those who emphasise that such a defence might also have a number of drawbacks.[xx] Someone coming to debates about the relative merits of a fair use defence for the first time will therefore be faced with two very different sets of arguments: Firstly, about whether the exceptions should be expanded or contracted and, secondly, amongst those who believe that the exceptions need to be expanded (or that at the very least the existing 'balance' needs to be preserved) there is disagreement about whether this aim is best achieved by providing general or specific exceptions.

This author is firmly of the view that an overreaching copyright law must be avoided, though space does not allow for a detailed defence of this position. The author also shares the view that there needs to be a fundamental overhaul of the permitted act provisions in the U.K. in outline because, in their current form, the exceptions make it impossible for a court to adopt a flexible response to technological developments or new artistic practices. Moreover, many of the existing exceptions are very poorly drafted, at least in part, because the draftsman has been forced to spell out the circumstances in which an exception is intended to apply in an inordinate amount of detail. In some cases the drafting is so bad as to make the provisions virtually worthless and, in other cases, renders the provisions so complex that it is difficult to imagine anyone ever seeking to rely on them.

The question, which arises, is how should the U.K. reform its laws? The problem with the existing debate between pro-user groups regarding the relative merits of a fair use style defence is that it has tended to focus on a narrow range of issues. In particular, much of the debate about the merits of a general defence has focused on the familiar themes of flexibility and certainty: a fair use defence is said to offer flexibility at the expense of certainty, the current approach is said to offer certainty but is very rigid. As with most flexibility/certainty debates, underpinning the respective positions are different attitudes toward judicial discretion and different attitudes toward the respective roles of the legislature and the judiciary. While this debate is undoubtedly important, there has been a tendency to gloss over a number of important issues.

More specifically, defenders of the *status quo* have for the most part failed to deal with the criticism that the existing provisions do not provide certainty to potential users and, hence, the strongest justification for the existing approach rests on an illusory foundation. The failure of the current permitted acts to provide certainty is partly a result of the poor drafting that dogs many of the existing provisions. In addition, it results from the fact that while the broad categories of behaviour that are covered by an exception are clear, the question arises whether an exception will be available if the precise circumstances are extremely difficult to predict. For example, while the question of whether a particular type of use can fall within the fair dealing provisions is *relatively* predictable, the question of whether any given act will fall under the aegis of one of the fair dealing exceptions will still ultimately depend on the way in which a court chooses to apply the inherently unpredictable test of 'fairness'. Indeed, it can be argued that the way in which the criterion of fairness is likely to be applied is marginally more certain in the U.S. because the American Act contains a list of factors which a court must take into account when deciding whether any given taking is fair. The group which is perhaps most adversely affected by a lack of certainty are the institutional users of copyright material, such as universities and libraries, who need to know exactly how much can be legitimately copied so they can structure their own copyright policies around a certain guaranteed minimum. By contrast, the U.S. provides users with a greater degree of certainty, since U.S. provisions are supported by a complex web of understandings, agreements, and policy statements that help to lay down minimum standards for fair use.[xxi]

On the other hand, those advocating the introduction of a fair use defence have failed to address the question of how judges in the U.K. and elsewhere would be likely to react to the introduction of a fair use exception. This criticism was first raised by Fitzgerald, in the context of Australian law, who argued convincingly that the fair use defence in the U.S. is closely bound up with constitutional guarantees of free speech, deep respect for a private sphere of home and family life kept relatively free from regulation, and vigorous notions of free competition underpinned by antipathy towards monopolies.[xxii] Supporters of a fair use defence must, therefore, think carefully about how a fair use defence would be likely to operate in a legal environment in which the principles which underpin and reinforce the fair use defence in the U.S. do not enjoy the same prominence. Moreover, this author has argued elsewhere that the history of the copyright exceptions in the U.K. shows that, if judges are unable to protect users at present, this is, in large partly because they have divested themselves of a series of tools. Tools that could have been used to keep copyright protection within more appropriate bounds.[xxiii]

In particular, the available evidence suggests that Parliament did not intend the introduction of the fair dealing provision in 1911 (which replaced the common law fair use defence that judges had developed in the U.K. prior to the passage of the 1911 Act), to mark the start of a more restrictive and less flexible approach to the copyright exceptions. More recently, judges have restricted the scope of the public interest defence, thereby increasing the risk that copyright will act as a restriction on freedom of expression and a right of access to information.[xxiv] Having ended special treatment for parodies, without there being evidence that Parliament was unhappy with the more liberal approach that courts in earlier cases had developed. Therefore, any proposal that focuses solely on the need for legislative reform should be treated with caution, since without a change in judicial attitudes any new defence may soon become as inflexible as the current arrangements.

Proposed reforms therefore need to be judged against a number of criteria. It should be recognised that the existing approach, whereby an attempt is made to define precisely every possible situation in which an exception might apply, is unsustainable, as it prevents courts from responding flexibly to technological advances and changes in artistic practices. Furthermore, such an approach will almost inevitably lead to poor drafting, while rarely if ever creating the 'certainty' that the defenders of this approach claim for it. A move towards a much more open system is therefore imperative. However, merely transposing a U.S. style fair use defence might be counterproductive, given that such a defence might operate very differently in another legal environment. A better approach would be to look at the Information Society Directive as providing an opportunity for fundamental reform. Thus far, pro-user commentators have tended to be opposed to the Directive, in large part because the initial proposals for an Information Society Directive would have been very restrictive of users' rights.[xxv] However, the final version of the Directive adopts a more liberal approach, such that it would be possible to follow the wording of the Directive closely and introduce a new range of flexible, but not entirely open-ended, exceptions. For example, under the terms of the Directive it would be possible to provide exceptions covering use 'for the purpose of caricature, parody, or pastiche', 'for the purpose of illustration for teaching or scientific research', 'for the purpose of public security', and 'for purposes *such as* criticism and review'. Provided such provisions were supplemented by minimum standards around which institutional users could safely structure their copyright policies, this approach could represent the beginnings of a much better deal for users. In addition, pro-user commentators must strive to ensure that their vision of a limited copyright comes to be accepted by the legislature, the judiciary, and the majority of commentators. It will be particularly important for pro-user commentators to meet the argument that an exception should only be available in circumstances where licences are unlikely to be agreed.

Exceptions, Licences and Market Failure

As has already been indicated, one argument that is frequently used to support a maximalist vision of copyright is that copyright exceptions should only be available in the absence of appropriate licensing arrangements. In other words, if someone wishes to make use of a work they should first and foremost expect to have to pay for it: use should only be free if it would be impossible, or at least impractical, to obtain a licence in the particular circumstances in question. This 'licensing' argument is often encountered in the context of discussions about legislative reform. However, many commentators would also like to see courts taking the availability of licences into account when applying the existing exceptions. In particular, it has been said that the availability of licences should be taken into account when considering whether the defendant's actions were 'fair' for the purposes of fair use/fair dealing exceptions. For example, Goldstein has argued that a distinction should be drawn between cases where a work itself is parodied and cases of satire, in which a part of a work is used to provide a critique of individuals, institutions, or society in general, arguing that it is only cases of parody that should fall within the fair use defence because, 'the copyright owner who is not willing to license a parody of his work may be more than willing, at a reasonable price, to license use of his work as a vehicle for social comment'. [xxvi]

From a formalistic legal perspective, the question of the relationship between the availability of licences and the provision of an exception is entirely circular, except in cases where the Act specifically provides that an exception is not to be available if the owner has made licences available.[xxvii] Since, of course, users whose actions are covered by an exception do not need to seek a licence. It is, therefore, important to appreciate that the licensing argument invariably forms part of an economic analysis of copyright in which the exceptions are treated as legitimate; only insofar as they are designed to overcome market failure, that is, circumstances in which the parties are unlikely to agree to a licence. For example, it is often said that this may occur because the transaction costs of negotiating a licence may outweigh the value of that licence.

The more traditional and most influential economic rationale for copyright protection is that copyright acts as an incentive for the creation of certain types of cultural product. The underlying premise of the incentive theory is that a work will only be created if the expected revenues exceed the cost of expression and the cost of making copies. In addition, the price of a successful work must compensate for the risk of failure.[xxviii] Copyright acts as a necessary incentive because creating a copyright work is often a time consuming and expensive business, but once a work has been produced it can usually be reproduced quickly and cheaply. This is said to create an almost classic public goods problem; for in the absence of copyright protection, non-producers would be tempted to take a free ride indefinitely, with either potential purchasers copying the work for themselves or with rival publishers emerging. They could undercut the author and publisher by not having to cover the cost of expression or bear the risk of failure if they waited until after a work proved its success. Without copyright protection, no one would bother to create or publish copyrighted works, or at the very least, the market would become skewed toward cheap production and faddish works, from which authors and publishers might be able to recoup their investment by relying on lead-time alone.[xxix]

Incentive theorists who support the licensing argument do so on the basis that it is in cases of market failure that there is the least danger that incentives will be eroded.[xxx] The more recent approach to copyright economics, sometimes referred to as the 'neo-classical' approach, sees copyright not only as providing incentives for the creation of works, but also as a mechanism which facilitates the exchange of rights and ensures that works become transferred to actors who value them most highly, thereby perfecting the market for copyright works. As such, it is said that the owner's rights should extend to all economically valuable uses of a work.[xxxi] Advocates of this maximalist vision of copyright insist not only that the exceptions be confined to cases of market failure, but also that even where it appears that transaction costs might lead to market failure, copyright owners must be given the opportunity to develop collective licensing or similar arrangements that will reduce transactions costs.[xxxii] Thus, they tend to favour a model in which exceptions are confined not merely to cases of likely market failure, but also to cases where a defendant can prove actual market failure on the facts.[xxxiii]

Aside from the specifics of the licensing argument, it is perhaps also worth drawing attention to the hostility toward state intervention, which underpins much economic analysis. From this perspective, overriding private property interests as a means to further broad social goals such as increasing access to information or lowering the cost of education is always objectionable, as Posner makes clear in his famous analogy:

> As we do not suppose that writers should be allowed to steal paper and pencils in order to reduce the cost of satire, neither is there a compelling reason to subsidise social criticism by allowing writers to use copyright materials without compensating the copyright holder.[xxxiv]

Opposition to the licensing argument has for the most part come from commentators who are opposed to economic analysis of copyright more generally or who are critical of the essentially conservative conclusions that most advocates of economic analysis draw. As has been seen, this is because disputes over the scope of the copyright exceptions are often little more than a veneer disguising more fundamental disputes about the functions of, and justifications for, a copyright system. It is therefore impossible to separate objections to the licensing argument from objections to economic analysis of copyright as a whole. Opposition to economic analysis of copyright has taken a variety of forms, though in the space available here it is not possible to adequately summarise the range of positions that commentators have adopted. Nevertheless, it is possible to identify three broad lines of attack that have been adopted by those opposed to the dominant economic models of copyright.

One line of attack has been to build alternative models of copyright with a view to demonstrating that copyright is not primarily about markets and wealth maximisation, but rather that it is a recognition of the natural right that authors have over their creations. That copyright also provides the underpinnings of institutions necessary for a healthy democratic civil society; and that it provides the best mechanism for striking a balance between our desire to reward authors whilst safeguarding other important interests. Or, that it is a result of lobbying pressure, which is defended by an elite that 'has reason to support legal rules that reinforce the premise that rewards in a market system mirror intelligence, education, and effort'.[xxxv] The precise role that the exceptions are said to play and the circumstances in which it is said that an exception ought to be available vary dramatically according to which of these alternative justifications or explanations is adopted; but generally speaking advocates of these alternative justifications and explanations would recognise that many of the exceptions are a reflection of some overriding non-monetary interest. Such interests might include free speech, privacy, access to information, efficient public administration, and the preservation and extension of cultural resources. From this perspective the defences are best thought of not as 'exceptions' that represent a deviation from the marketplace norm of full property rights, but as 'users rights' that are an integral and fundamental aspect of copyright law.[xxxvi]

A related approach adopted by some opponents of economic analyses of copyright has been to draw on objections to economic analyses of law in general. In particular, critics have focused on the wealth-maximisation principle on which economic theories of law rest, that is said to 'offer an essentially cold, hard, and, in consequence, inordinately narrow vision of human nature'.[xxxvii] Whilst an economic analysis of intellectual property rights may be less counter-intuitive than an analysis of adoption laws that treat children as commodities,[xxxviii] it cannot completely satisfy anyone who accepts that 'at its most serious, this is a branch of law which protects some of the finer manifestations of human achievement'.[xxxix] Thus it has been doubted whether an analysis of copyright law that takes wealth maximisation as its only value can properly respect artistic freedom and creativity.[xl]

A third, and in some respects most ambitious, approach has been to attack economic analysis on its own terms. At its most general, this attack has come from commentators who have criticised the nature of the research that has been conducted in this area. In particular, it has been pointed out that most of the economists working in this field have failed to conduct the empirical research needed to support their arguments. But, without such research, economics is little more than 'applied moral philosophy'.[xli] Nor is this simply an argument for economists to change their methodology, since it has been said 'the empirical information necessary to calculate the effect of copyright law on the actions of authors, potential defendants, and consumers . . . is probably uncollectable'.[xlii] Moreover, even if this data could be collected, it has been argued that this would not solve the problems of economic analysis. The difficulty is that unlike an economic analysis of other areas, such as criminal law, where there is an agreed goal (that crime should be reduced), there is no agreement on the appropriate trade off between production and dissemination of copyright works.[xliii]

Other critics have focused on the idea that copyright is necessary to provide incentives for the creation of copyright works, arguing that there are many types of work that are currently protected by copyright that would be created in the same numbers even in the absence of copyright protection. Thus, it has been said that works of fine art would still be created both because such works are often created for non-economic reasons and because the creators of such works have the possibility of selling the original, sometimes for large sums.[xliv] Similarly, it has been argued that there is no need to provide copyright protection for commissioned photographs, architectural works,[xlv] or for works created by salaried academics.[xlvi] In reply, it is sometimes said that even if authors often do not require an incentive to create works, publishers and other distributors will still need an incentive to distribute these works to the public. However, it has also been said that this has no application to those types of artistic work that are not principally communicated to the public through the distribution of copies or to photographs which are valued for their news content. Moreover, one prominent commentator has suggested that even in other cases the history of copyright suggests that publishers might be able to cover the cost of expression by relying on their lead-time and by developing various other strategies to maximise their revenue.[xlvii] At the very least, it is arguable that for all but the most expensive works (such as large budget feature films), sufficient incentives could be provided to distributors through a much more limited set of rights than copyright law currently provides.

A rather different critique of the incentive argument is that proponents of this justification for copyright have failed to explain the mechanism by which copyright acts as an incentive to authors and publishers given the widespread ignorance as to the nature and scope of copyright protection. As Jessica Litman puts it:

> Much of the literature repackaging copyright in theoretical terms
> proceeds from the assumption that authors' creation of works is

influenced by their awareness of the intricacies of the system. For those theorists who model the copyright law in economic or utilitarian terms, the assumption inheres in their approach: It is difficult to speak of the incentives supplied by a legal regime without relying on the convention that those whom the law seeks to prod are aware of the goodies that it offers as a bribe.[xlviii]

There is certainly room for argument about this claim, at the general level, of whether copyright acts as an incentive to creation. However, when we turn to the claim that too much fair use / fair dealing will undermine incentives and therefore the exceptions should only be available in cases of market failure, we can see that it is a serious flaw in the licensing argument; to leave unexplained how an expansive reading of the exceptions (which will pass unnoticed except by a handful of copyright lawyers) will come to act as a disincentive to the creation and dissemination of works.[xlix]

Still another line of attack comes from commentators who have emphasised the gulf between what an economic analysis of copyright purports to offer and what it can deliver in practice. The attraction of an economic analysis of copyright is that it purports to offer certainty by providing us with definite criteria against which we can judge the effectiveness of our existing levels of copyright protection. Vague talk of balancing rights and interests can be replaced by a single criterion of effectiveness, namely, do our existing provisions maximise economic efficiency? In practice, however, economic theorists have often leaned toward a maximalist vision of copyright, ignoring the barriers to creation thrown up by an overly broad copyright, or to the extent that they have tried to take account of other interests by coming 'dangerously close to the mushy balancing analysis from which economics was supposed to provide surcease'.[l] This inability of copyright law to provide greater certainty than other models of copyright perhaps also explains why many economic analyses have tended to lend strong support to existing arrangements. As Boyle notes, 'it also makes one a little sceptical to note that [economic analyses] tend to track the existing case law with surprising fidelity'.[li]

An attempt has been made in this section to explain the relationship between the licensing argument and a particular set of justifications for copyright law. Pro-user groups will have to confront the licensing argument and its economic foundations head on in the near future, as copyright maximalists insist that automated licence agreements and other technological innovations can lower transaction costs and hence will render the exceptions increasingly unnecessary. It is to be hoped that sufficient material has been presented here to demonstrate that the economic justification for copyright is far from uncontroversial and that there are other, equally plausible, explanations for copyright in which the exceptions are conceptualised as having a very different, sometimes even central, role. This should not, however, be taken to indicate that any one of these alternative explanations is by itself satisfactory. All too often copyright theorists of all persuasions have applied their preferred visions of copyright much too mechanistically, ignoring the increasingly accepted insight that there needs to be an interaction between our ethical principles and our observations of the world and its complexities.[lii] A closely related failing is that many copyright theorists write as if we were designing a copyright law in a state of nature, rather than against the backdrop of an existing copyright law that has created a series of expectations around which a variety of actors have structured agreements, understandings, and practices. This is not to suggest that our current arrangements are sacrosanct or that particular fundamental reforms are not desirable, but it does mean that all reforms, including reform of the exceptions, must be judged against the disruption they would create as well as against more concrete standards.

i   Compare, most famously, Barlow, 'Selling Wine Without Bottles: The Economy of Mind on the GlobalNet', in Ludlow (ed), *High Noon on the Electronic Frontier* (Cambridge, Massachusetts: MIT Press, 1996).

ii   Hoeren, *Copyright in Electronic Delivery Services and Multimedia Products* (Luxembourg: European Commission, 1995) p.12.

iii   But whereas that article only applies to the reproduction right, Article 13 applies to all of the exclusive rights of the copyright owner.

iv   See Heide, 'The Berne Three-Step Test and the Proposed Copyright Directive' [1999] EIPR 105.

v   See, in particular, WT/DS160/R (15 June, 2000) and note the subsequent arbitration proceedings: WT/DS/160/12 (15 January, 2001). For analysis see Ginsburg, 'Toward Supranational Copyright Law? The WTO Panel Decision and the 'Three-Step Test' for Copyright Exceptions' (2001) 187 RIDA 2.

vi   Directive 2001/29/EC of the European Parliament and the Council of 22 May 2001, on the harmonisation of certain aspects of copyright and related rights in the Information Society.

vii   Most notably, see Hugenholtz, 'Fierce Creatures. Copyright Exceptions: Towards Extinction?' (1997) paper delivered at Imprimatur Conference, available at: www.imprimatur.net/ IMP FTT/fier.pdf

viii   See Hugenholtz, 'Why the Copyright Directive is Unimportant, and Possibly Invalid' [2000] EIPR 499, drawing an analogy with the Tobacco Advertising Directive and arguing that the Information Society is invalid because it 'does not harmonise national rules, does not facilitate the free movement of goods or the freedom of services, and does not remove distortions to competition'.

ix   Copyright Act 1968, ss.40-73.

x   Copyright Act, R.S.C. 1985, ss. 29-30.9.

xi   Copyright Act 1957, ss.52(1)(a)-(y).

xii   Copyright Act 1963, ss.12, 14.

xiii   Copyright Act 1994, ss.40-92.

xiv   Copyright Act 1987, ss.35-74.

xv   17 U.S.C., s.107: 'In determining whether the use made of a work in any particular case is a fair use, the factors to be considered shall include (1) the purpose and character of the use, including whether such use is of a commercial nature or is for non-profit educational purposes; (2) the nature of the copyrighted work; (3) the amount and substantiality of the portion used in relation to the copyrighted work as a whole; and (4) the effect of the use upon the potential market for or value of the copyrighted work.

xvi   *Report of the Committee to Consider the Law on Copyright and Designs*, 1977 (Cmnd 6732) and see, in particular, paras.676-677.

xvii   *From Gutenberg to Telidon: A White Paper on Copyright* (Ottawa: Department of Consumer and Corporate Affairs/Department of Communications, 1984) and see, in particular, pp.35-49.

xviii   See Copyright Law Review Committee, *Simplification of the Copyright 1968, Part 1: Exceptions to the Exclusive Right of Copyright Owners* (Canberra, 1998) and see, in particular, paras.6.07-6.08.

xix   For example, see *Laddie*, 'Copyright: Over-Strength, Over-Regulated, Over-rated?' [1996] EIPR 253; Griffiths, 'Preserving Judicial Freedom of Movement–Interpreting Fair dealing in Copyright Law' [2000] IPQ 164; *Okpaluba, Digitisation, Culture and Copyright Law: digital sampling, a case study* (Thesis: (PhD) University of London, 2000); de Beer, 'Canadian Copyright Law in Cyberspace: An examination of the Copyright Act in the Context of the Internet' (2000) 63 Sask. L. Rev. 503; Fewer, 'Constitutionalizing Copyright: Freedom of Expression and the Limits of Copyright in Canada' (1997) 55 U.T. Fac. L. Rev. 175; Coombe, *The Cultural Life of Intellectual Properties* (Durham, North Carolina: Duke UP, 1998), Longdin, 'Shall We Shoot a Messenger Now and Then? Copyright Infringement and the On-line Service Provider' in Rickett and Austin (eds.), *International Intellectual Property and the Common Law World* (Oxford: Hart, 2000); Oliver, 'Copyright, Fair dealing, and Freedom of Expression' (2000) 19 *New Zealand Universities Law Review*, p.89.

xx   See Ricketson, 'Simplifying Copyright Law: Proposals from Down Under' [2000] EIPR 537; Bently, 'Copyright's Futures: To Expand or Contract' (1999) 1(2) *Digital Technology Law Journal* (online); Doherty and Griffiths, 'The Harmonisation of European Union Copyright Law for the Digital Age' [2000] EIPR 17; Macmillan, 'Adapting the Copyright Exceptions to the Digital Environment' (1999) 1(2) *Digital Technology Law Journal* (online).

xxi   The most important and best known of these 'external' influences on fair use is the Agreement on Guidelines for Classroom Copying in Not-for-Profit Educational Establishments with Respect to Books and Periodicals which attempts to lay down minimum standards for educational fair use and which was included in the final House of Representatives' report on the 1976 Copyright Act. Other educational guidelines exist in relation to sheet music and off-air recording of broadcasts. See further, See Crews, *Copyright, Fair Use, and the Challenge for Universities: Promoting the Progress of Higher Education* (Chicago: Chicago UP, 1993).

xxii   Fitzgerald, 'Underlying Rationales of Fair Use: Simplifying the Copyright Act' (1998) 2 *Southern Cross University Law Review*, p.153.

xxiii   Burrell, 'Reining In Copyright Law: Is Fair Use The Answer?' [2001] *IPQ*, p.361.

xxiv   Burrell, *ibid.*, and see Burrell, 'Defending the Public Interest' [2000] *EIPR*, p.394.

xxv   For criticism of some of the earlier proposals see, for example, PriceWaterhouseCoopers, *Final Report Study on Consumer Law and the Information Society* (17 August, 2000), pp.128-129; Heide, *supra* n. iv; Wing and Kirk, 'European / U.S. Copyright Law Reform: Is a Balance Being Achieved?' [2000] *IPQ*, p.138; Bently and Burrell, 'Copyright and the Information Society in Europe: A Matter of Timing as Well as Content' (1997) 34 CMLRev 1197.

xxvi   Goldstein, *Copyright: Principles, Law, and Practice* (Boston: Little, Brown, 1989, Supplement 1993), para. 10.2.1. Other commentators have adopted a very similar position, for example, see Posner, 'Parody as Fair Use' (1992) 21 *Journal of Legal Studies* 67. But for a strong attack on this distinction from an economic perspective see Merges, 'Are You Making Fun of Me? Notes on Market Failure and the Parody Defence in Copyright Law' (1993) 21 *American Intellectual Property Law Association Quarterly Journal*, pp.305, 311: 'a parodist's choice of a particular 'weapon' as embodying something else that is the ultimate 'target' is not accidental. Indeed, a successful parody might often be expected to parody both a copyrighted work and the values it represents. Surely, for example, a parody of 'Gone With the Wind' might use the movie as a weapon to parody romanticised notions of the Civil War and southern 'gallantry', while successfully mocking some of the overdone aspects of the film itself. The second problem with Posner's 'weapon'/'target' distinction is his assumption that a copyright holder will normally license parodies of the first sort, but not the second. This seems wrong, at least in those cases where the 'target' of the parody is a set of values or cultural assumptions deeply cherished by the copyright holder or at least widely held by the segment of the public loyal to her'.

xxvii   The U.K. Act does contain a limited number of exceptions of this kind. See CDPA 1988, ss.35-36, 60.

xxviii   The terminology employed here has been taken from an article by Landes and Posner that remains the single most important article on the economics of copyright law. See Landes and Posner, 'An Economic Analysis of Copyright Law' (1989) 18 *Journal of Legal Studies*, p.325.

xxix   See Landes and Posner, *ibid.*, p.332.

xxx   See, in particular, Gordon, 'Fair Use as Market Failure: A Structural and Economic Analysis of the Betamax Case and its Predecessors' (1982) 82 *Colum. L. Rev.*,1600.

xxxi   For example, see Merges, *supra* n. xxvi, p.306: 'And it is important to point out, the literature has passed beyond the point where a crude 'incentive' story passes for analysis in every case'. An excellent summary of the neoclassical position is provided by Netanel, 'Copyright and a Democratic Civil Society' (1996) 106 *Yale L.J.*, p.283.

xxxii   See Goldstein, 'Pre-empted State Doctrine, Involuntary Transfers and Compulsory Licensing: Testing the Limits of Copyright' (1977) 24 UCLA L. Rev. 1107. This is also implicit in the approach adopted by Smith, 'Collective Administration of Copyright: An Economic Analysis' in Palmer (ed.) (1986) 8 *Research in Law and Economics* 137. More generally, see Merges, 'Contracting into Liability Rules: Intellectual Property Rights and Collective Rights Organizations', (1996) 84 Cal. L.Rev. 1293. For discussion see Netanel, *supra* n. xxxi, pp.320-321.

xxxiii   See Merges, *supra* n. xxvi.

xxxiv   Posner, *supra* n. xxvi, p.73.

xxxv   Sterk, 'Rhetoric and Reality in Copyright Law' (1996) 49 *Mich. L. Rev.*, pp.1197, 1248.

xxxvi   For example, see Vaver, *Copyright Law* (Toronto: Irwin Law, 2000), p.190.

xxxvii   Duxbury, *Patterns of American Jurisprudence* (Oxford: Clarendon, 1997), p.397. Also
see West, 'Authority, Autonomy and Choice: The Role of Consent in the Moral and Political
Visions of Frank Kafka and Richard Posner' 99 Harv. L Rev. 384 (1985), in particular,
p.388, arguing: 'Posner's actors, despite the ordinariness of the situations in which they
find themselves, are not recognisable as ourselves or our neighbours. His wealth
maximising, racially discriminating employer, his wealth-maximising criminal who decides
how best to use his opportunity time and his burglar's tools, and his wealth-maximising tort
victim who is compensated ex ante for an accident uncompensated ex post do not resemble
the bigoted bosses, petty thieves, or the impoverished and paraplegic accident victims we
may work with, know or be. The inner lives of Posner's characters, although engaged in such
familiar situations are strikingly unrecognisable. They are not we, and their stark inner lives
are not ours'.

xxxviii Cf. Landes and Posner, 'The Economics of the Baby Shortage' (1978) 7 *Journal of Legal
Studies*, p.323, for example, p.327 where they argue: 'The thousands of children in foster
care . . . are comparable to an unsold inventory stored in a warehouse'.

xxxix   Cornish, *Intellectual Property* 4th ed (London: Sweet & Maxwell, 1999), p.3.

xl   See Yen, Restoring the Natural Law: Copyright as Labour and Possession' (1990) 51 *Ohio St.
L.J.*, pp.517, 542.

xli   See Priest, 'What Economists can Tell Lawyers about Intellectual Property' in Palmer (ed.),
(1986) 8 *Research in Law and Economics*, pp.19, 22. Also note the following claim:
'I do not believe that it is unfair to say that the entire literature . . . of which I am aware has
consisted of little more than assumptions. As a consequence, this literature has taught U.S.
almost nothing, nor has it guided research or thinking so that an approach with a firmer
empirical approach could be developed', p.20.

xlii   Yen, *supra* n. xl, p.543.

xliii   See Priest, *supra* n. xli.

xliv   See Gifford, 'Innovation and Creativity in the Fine Arts: The Relevance and Irrelevance
of Copyright' (2000) 18 *Cardozo Arts & Ent. L.J.* p.569.

xlv   See Sterk, *supra* n. xxxv, in particular, pp.1213-1214, 1225-1226.

xlvi   Cf. Landes and Posner, *supra* n. xxviii, p.331.

xlvii   See Breyer, 'The Uneasy Case for Copyright: A Study of Copyright in Books, Photocopies
and Computer Programs' (1970) 84 *Harv. L. Rev.*, p.281, but cf. Landes and Posner,
supra n. xxviii; Tyerman, 'The Economic Rationale for Copyright Protection for
Published Books: A Reply to Professor Breyer' (1971) 18 UCLA L. Rev 1100 and see
n. xxix and accompanying text.

xlviii   Litman, 'Copyright as Myth' (1991) *University of Pittsburgh Law Review*, pp.235, 241.

xlix   Cf. Gordon, *supra*, n. xxx.

l   Boyle, *Shamans, Software and Spleens* (Harvard University Press, 1996), p.39.

li   *Ibid.*, p.219.

lii   Cf. Glover, *Humanity: A Moral History of the Twentieth Century* (London: Pimlico, 2001),
in particular, 6, developing Rawl's idea of the 'Reflective Equilibrium'.

Art Crimes

Anthony Julius

Introduction

'When Benvenuto Cellini crucified a living man to study the play of muscles in his death agony,' remarked Oscar Wilde, 'a pope was right to grant him absolution. What is the death of a vague individual if it enables an immortal work to blossom and to create, in Keats's words, an eternal source of ecstasy?'[i] Few would concur with such a statement, and if pressed to explain why, some such principle as 'aesthetic ends do not justify criminal means' would probably be offered. This principle seems intuitively right and hardly demands amplification, let alone more formal defence. But let me take Wilde seriously, which entails treating his observation as a provocation rather than as a proposition demanding immediate, unqualified assent.

Cellini's offence was, of course, indefensible. If it was preparatory, say, to creating his great statue *Perseus*, reckoned to be one of the glories of Florentine art,[ii] then it would have been better if that statue had never existed. (Arguably, indeed, it ought to be melted down, in an act of reparative iconoclasm; at the very least, should we not refrain from exhibiting the result of Cellini's findings, just as we refrain from exploiting the medical findings of the Nazi doctors at Auschwitz?). Walter Benjamin's aphorism, that every work of civilisation is also a work of barbarism, has in such a context, a more literal truth than ordinarily acknowledged.[iii]

But must art always subordinate itself to law (it is the illegality of Cellini's act, rather than its immorality, that interests me here)? The example of Cellini is too unproblematical in its extreme wickedness; a general response to this question must address more taxing, less obvious instances. Cellini's case is easy to decide, and easy cases make bad jurisprudence.

Art can be, very often is, offensive. And when it offends, it does so against one or more of the following regimes: it violates the law; it violates morality; it violates social sentiment. Art does this, and artists do too. When the British sculptor Anthony-Noel Kelly, for example, took body parts in order to create sculptures, he succeeded in violating all three regimes. He committed an offence under the Anatomy Act; he betrayed his colleagues ('a gross breach of trust', according to the trial judge);[iv] he failed to show proper respect for the dead (once used, the parts were buried in a hole in the ground, without even a container). Following his conviction, he handed over the casts to the Royal College of Surgeons, the owners of the stolen heads, torsoes, and limbs. While he had limited aesthetic success, another criminal artist, Harald Nägeli (known, because of his prolific graffiti art as the 'sprayer of Zurich'), was both pursued, arrested, convicted, and jailed, and yet also was sponsored, collected, and defended by artists and art institutions. In 1987, a Heidelberg town employee charged with cleaning the fronts of buildings destroyed 'by mistake' two of Nägeli's sprayed drawings because (it was reported) 'he had not noticed that they were works of art.'[v]

The contingent nature of art's relation to law, morality, and social sentiment, and the positive delight that art takes in the ethically transgressive, are two, albeit contradictory, commonplaces of aesthetics.[vi] They are also, however, a continuing affront to received, non-philosophical opinion (which generally still expects art to be lawful, educative, benign). Contrast, for example, the public responses to, and the art world's defences of, the Royal Academy's 1997 'Sensation' exhibition. The public recoiled, while attending in record numbers (but, in the main, as if visiting a freak show); the curator celebrated as 'trangressive' the art on display.[vii] The two sides may be taken to have agreed on the affront, while disagreeing on its value. Art alarms as it pleases. Just when we wish to celebrate it, it troubles us. It bites the hands that applaud it.

But art can also be, often is, uplifting. Not in the cheap, Biedermeier,[viii] sense of offering easy pleasures, but rigorous, exacting, clarifying, engaging, challenging – a bracing alternative to, in Hardy's phrase, 'smugger things.'[ix] Crimes against art works are thus assaults not just on private property but also on certain collective values and goods, that is, the pleasure that we all take in art, the way it enhances our lives, its implicit celebration of the power and gifts of the imagination. Such crimes therefore cause particular dismay (hence our horror at certain acts of iconoclasm). Art works both explain the world to us and make us at home in it; to destroy an art work is an unusual act of dispossession, leaving desolate not just its owner but a much wider circle of admirers. It is destruction, of course, but it is also desecration.[x]

So if art offends, it is also offended against, and when offended against, the offence is against us too. Sometimes, the same art work both inflicts and suffers injury (sometimes the second, in consequence of the first). How, then, may we define art crimes (by 'art' I include literature; by 'crime' I include torts)? There are three kinds: (1) crimes against art works (2) crimes committed in the creation of art works (3) art works which are also crimes. The purpose of this essay is to outline these three kinds of art crime. Law and aesthetics offer rival accounts of art; classifying art crimes is a good way of probing the most contentious aspects of this rivalry, one which arises in part because law and aesthetics each has something to say about art, and in part because law seeks to regulate art.

Of course, writing of 'law' and 'aesthetics' as if each was univocal elides the competing voices, speaking up for different interests, which comprise both. Take copyright law, for example. Itself compromised by its unstable compromise of the claims of its various constituencies (authors, readers, publishers, and others), it is also in conflict with legally sanctioned principles of freedom of speech.[xi] Aesthetic doctrines, however ostensibly general, usually privilege one kind of art work, and argue for the revaluation of other art works. Purporting to describe all art, they restrict their definitions, discriminating as they describe, their embrace, however wide, inevitably also exclusionary.

The aesthetics of the artist, of the philosopher, and the art work itself, should also be distinguished. The *spontaneous* aesthetics of the artist amounts to no more than the claim that what he has produced is art and is of aesthetic value. He wants his work to be protected, but not otherwise interfered with. The *theoretical* aesthetics of the philosopher has more general pretensions. It engages with law usually only to the extent of debating the relation between art and morality. (Of course, the artist's aesthetic is not wholly particular, nor the philosopher's wholly general, because just as the former's commitment to his own work entails a commitment to other, like work, so the latter's commitment to art in general shrinks down to a commitment to certain art forms over others. The artist cannot ignore other work without falling into inconsistency; the philosopher cannot embrace all work without lapsing into vacuity. Thus E.M. Forster comes to the defence of D.H. Lawrence at the *Lady Chatterley* trial,[xii] and Aristotle derives his theory of tragedy from Sophocles and Euripides).[xiii] And there is the *implicit* aesthetics of the art work itself, that is to say, it indicates by implication both the class of art work to which it belongs and the kind of interpretation which makes most sense of it as an art work. Flaubert had something of this in mind, I suspect, when he observed that every work of art has its special poetics by which it is made and subsists.[xiv]

It follows from this that when I write below of 'law' or 'aesthetics' I simplify.

I. Art Crimes

One means by which art crimes of the first kind may be classified is by distinguishing between those crimes committed against art works which have regard to the works' aesthetic properties or status, and those which do not. Collateral damage during military bombardment, and assaults on statues of unpopular politicians, are instances of the second; burning books, and paint thrown at pictures that are contrary to the offender's notion of what counts as 'art,' are familiar instances of the first. Theories of iconoclasm, for example, often depend on just such a distinction; they make the intention of the offender paramount.

A better classification, however, divides art crimes into two complementary groups: offences of reproduction and offences of destruction. This approach pays less attention to the offender's intention, more to the effect on the art work of his crime. It also acknowledges the family resemblances both between the first and the third kinds of art crimes, and between art crimes of the first kind and certain lawful artistic practices. Thus:

> *Offences of reproduction* are at the terminal point of a passage which begins with an original work, and then passes through pastiche, then plagiarism, then breach of copyright, misattribution of authorship, and passing off, and forgery.
>
> *Offences of destruction* are at the terminal point of a passage which begins with an original work, and then passes through adaptations, then parody, then breach of moral rights,[xv] trespass, suppression or other breach of speech rights, and criminal damage.

The first passage concludes with mere copying, the second, with mere erasure. The one replicates, the other extinguishes. The first is an attack upon a work's uniqueness, the other on its existence, but both thereby attack its economic value. These passages move through forms of derivative art, or 'literature in the second degree' (Genette),[xvi] and then leave art's boundaries altogether in a descent through civil wrongs toward criminality. In each case the destination is jail. What begins in the studio or the study ends in a prison cell and we may thus imagine two kinds of solitariness: the isolation of creativity, the isolation of iniquity.

We may further imagine a boundary dividing the artist from the criminal, art from crime, instances of the supererogatorily good from instances of quotidian evil, the originating from the parasitic (whether duplicative or destructive). Cross this boundary and one ceases to be an artist and becomes merely an offender. The boundary is the means both by which art is protected and true artists distinguished from bogus ones. Positing such a boundary, however, immediately raises two questions. First, is a *wholly* original work possible? To which the answer is: no, but no matter. Second, how porous is the boundary? To which the answer is: so porous as to render it practically useless. It is a juridical boundary to which artists are, in the main, indifferent.

L.H.O.O.Q.

Marcel Duchamp, *L.H.O.O.Q.*, 1917

Offences of reproduction do not tend to injure the art work itself, while offences of destruction self-evidently may do. Unlawful copying of a poem does not harm the poem; on the contrary, it may enhance its reputation by making it more generally available. Vandalising a picture, by contrast, takes it out of circulation. This helps make the point that art works do not in themselves have circulation. This helps make the point that art works do not in themselves have rights. While the crime itself may be committed against the art work, the rights violated by this act are the artist's, or the work's owner, or some other third party. This is not, of course, to deny that damaged art works have a certain pathos: during the First World War, such works were exhibited in Paris as 'Assassinated Art'; during the Second World War, Italians faked evidence of damage to art by the Allies, and characterised the Liberation campaign as a war against art.[xvii] However, it is artists, and not their works, that suffer persecution.[xviii]

While there may indeed be objections to the ordering of the sequences, and their composition, and while other arrangements could be defended (and certainly imagined), the essential point, that the law exists to protect art, artist, and collector (though by no means with equal commitment), and must therefore adjudicate on certain critical aesthetic questions – specifically, determining what is art and what is non-art – holds good. Law claims to be art's friend, even though the protection it offers is often deficient (consider the case of the Parthenon marbles).[xix]

a. Offences of Reproduction

Pastiche is to be distinguished from plagiarism. Pastiche is open homage; plagiarism is secret indebtedness. Pastiche is a literary exercise ('I will now compose in the style of . . .'), a test of technique, a study in virtuoso ventriloquism, sometimes a fusty academicism, sometimes a commentary on the imitated work,[xx] sometimes a display of mimetic talent,[xxi] related in certain respects to the 'art' of translation. Plagiarism is akin to that, but invariably (though not always) written or composed under the sign of fraud. It practices a deception; the skills it requires are those of the confidence trickster. (Of course, pastiche is not itself always honest: when accompanied by a false signature, it is the art of the forger).

Art, however, muddies these distinctions. Consider, for example, the cento and the collage. The cento, a poem made up of lines or verses by other writers, and the collage, in which photographs, news cuttings, and all kinds of objects are arranged and pasted on the painting ground, are examples of art forms which both appropriate *and* originate. That is to say, in their constituent parts, they merely do the former, while in the specific combinations which they effect, they do the latter.[xxii] Each is an independent composition, and not a mere digest or abridgment. There are, of course, differences between the two, in part attributable to the differences in medium. While the cento reproduces, the collage lifts; in the one case, the source remains, in the other, it is transferred onto the new work. The cento is duplicative; the collage is substitutive.

Plagiarism is not just another word for copyright infringement, though there is considerable overlap in meaning. Acknowledged but unpermitted copying infringes without plagiarising; unacknowledged copying of works out of copyright plagiarises without infringing. A distinction should also be made between, on the one hand, plagiarism and copyright infringement, and on the other, the related, statutory tort known as misattribution of authorship (*s.84 Copyright, Designs and Patents Act 1988* – hereafter *CDPA*). A person has the right not to have a literary, dramatic, musical or artistic work falsely attributed to him as author. (The 18th century poet Chatterton was guilty of an unusual kind of misattribution, one to a fictional person of his own creation).[xxiii]

The *s.84* wrong is both the converse of copyright infringement and an instance of it. It is the *converse*, because while a copyright infringee complains that the infringer has stolen his work, a *s.84* plaintiff complains that someone else's work has been attributed to him. The infringee has something taken away from him which he wants to keep (or control); the *s.84* plaintiff has something given to him, which he wishes to repudiate. It is an *instance* of infringement, because an author's name is part of his work. His work gives his name brand value. Memoirists, for example, realise themselves in their work; they are their own literary creations. So both the s.84 tortfeasor and the infringer always claim the credit for something that's not their own – either a name or a work (or part of a work).

(There is an important economic aspect to this worth noting here. A novel written by a well-known author will attract greater sales than the same novel written by a tyro; the well-known author has an economic interest in maintaining his literary reputation. *S.84* protects that interest).

In contrast with the *s.84* tortfeasor, both the forger and the plagiariser pass off a copy as an original. In each case this deception entails the adopting of the work of another as one's own. And the commercial intention is often the same: to profit by a fraud. Although they may be characterised by their common absence of originality, five distinctions may be drawn between them which, when taken together, define the two offences.

i While the forger conceals his own identity, the plagiariser advertises
   it. The forger puts the true artist's signature in place of his own;
   the plagiariser does not. The plagiarist is the forger, but transformed
   by conceit. He wants the credit for the work, not just the profit.
   The forger will imitate a style, creating a new instance of it, and then
   pass it off as the work of the style's originator. Forgery thus elides
   the distinction between pastiche and plagiarism. It is a crooked

homage. The plagiarist seeks to pass off someone else's work as his own; the forger seeks to pass off his own work as someone else's.

ii Forgery is principally a crime of fine art; plagiarism tends to be a crime of literature. Forgery is usually, but not always, a visual offence; plagiarism is invariably a verbal one. It's difficult to plagiarise a painting (but not impossible – the patenting by the Neo-Dadaist Yves Klein of his colour IKB – 'International Klein Blue' – would make the unlicensed copying of, say, his painting *IKB 79* an offence of this kind); forgeries of literary works are relatively uncommon.[xxiv] Literary fraudsters tend to want recognition; art fraudsters are more interested in the money.

iii The economics of forgery and plagiarism are different. Forgery will be more profitable than plagiarism when greater value attaches to the author's name than to his work. So this is the choice that presents itself to the literary villain: do I make more money plagiarising a Dick Francis novel, or writing my own novel and passing it off as Francis'? My name plus his work, or my work plus his name? Within the literary market, plagiarism is not a serious problem – or only a serious problem when taken seriously (see below) – and forgery even less so. By contrast, in the art market, forgery is a huge problem: one expert 'fake-buster' has estimated that 40 per cent of art works currently in circulation are fakes.[xxv]

iv a plagiariser will admix his own work with the plagiarised work; the forger's work by contrast is both all his own work and wholly the work of the forged artist. A good forger must have qualities of empathy and humility; the plagiarist needs neither – just brazenness. A good forger may be an artist of considerable imitative skills; there is no such species of artist as the 'good plagiariser.' The art forger, David Stein, jailed for his forgeries, was allowed when incarcerated to continue to paint in the style of (other) artists, so long as the works bore his own signature. In 1970, a New York gallery advertised the exhibition of almost 70 Stein paintings with the notice 'Forgeries by Stein.'[xxvii] This blurs the distinction that the law makes between art and non-art: forgeries are mere 'simulated' art, and forgers are guilty of (in the language of the New York statute) 'criminal simulation.'[xxviii]

v forgery and plagiarism raise distinct questions about aesthetic value. Plagiarism challenges: isn't *all* literature derivative? Forgery challenges: why do we value a picture less when we discover its true provenance? Ask each question of the other, and the answer is obvious. Plainly, forgeries are derivative in a distinct, uninteresting way; equally plainly, plagiarisms, when discovered, devalue the plagiarising work as a whole (we can get the same – indeed, already have it – elsewhere).

b. Offences of Destruction

Just as pastiches are lawful imitations, and thus at the starting point of certain practices that become unlawfully duplicative, so adaptations are variations which open a series of possible interventions in an art work that conclude with its destruction. (One should distinguish adaptations from performances. Performances of a piece of music are not variations on it, but constitute it. The piece of music is the score plus a performance of it). Variations may comprise the reordering, supplementation, or deformation, of the work.[xxix]

Adaptations of certain kinds may breach copyright: translations, the converting of dramatic works into non-dramatic works (and vice versa), and pictorial versions of a copyrighted work's 'story or action' may all be infringements (*s.21 CDPA 1988*). They are different to the art work copied, but they are also duplicative of it and thus fall foul of the law.

One kind of adaptation is parody; its relation to the parodied work has been characterised as repetition with critical difference.[xxx] The satirist attacks the man, the parodist attacks his work;[xxxi] in this sense, as Nabokov put it, while satire is a lesson, parody is a game.[xxxii] Parody and pastiche each subordinate themselves to the copied work, but while the first does so in love, the second does so the better to attack. Each offers a tribute, the first in praise, the second in dispraise. Parody can also have readers rather than authors as its target. This is often the case when the parody is of a fashionable literary movement or school, teasing the public for the esteem in which the movement or school is held (as in the Ern Malley, and the Sokal, affairs).[xxxiii] But here the work only *becomes* a parody when its author's deception of his audience comes to an end (he is rumbled, or unmasks himself); until then, it is a hoax. In this limited sense, parody may be described as a context-specific form.[xxxiv]

The distinction between parody and hoax can have considerable legal significance. In 1997, the politician and diarist Alan Clark sued the London Evening Standard over diaries published by the newspaper and purportedly written by him but actually written by Peter Bradshaw. He said that readers were encouraged to believe that the diaries were his own (and therefore a *s.84* breach); the newspaper responded that they were obvious parodies. Clark won. The judge insisted that his judgment was 'no bar to publication of parodies'.[xxxv] This must be right: parodies do not need to be published under the name of the parodied author to be effective, and (evidently) *should* not be, if they are to be lawful. Max Hastings, the Evening Standard's editor, both made this point, and missed its significance, when he disclosed that Bradshaw was reluctant to write the diaries 'because he likes to write best in his own style *under his own name*' (my italics).[xxxvi] The reason Bradshaw (and his newspaper) got into trouble is because his work was closer to a hoax than a parody (that is to say, not quite either): however unintentionally, readers were led to believe that Clark was the author, not Bradshaw himself.

Parody can also be, indeed often is, plagiarism – but of a licensed kind. Parody requires readers to have the parodied work in mind to order to appreciate the joke; they must not be encouraged to believe that they are reading that work. Parodies lead readers to regard the parodied work in a new (and critical) light.[xxxvii] If the parodies themselves are read as further instances of the kind of work they parody, this point is lost. Therefore if a parody merely plagiarises, it fails as parody and becomes a candidate for infringement proceedings, a heavy punishment indeed for an aesthetic failure.

Intermediate between parody and physical injury to art works is the relocating of site-specific art works and the withdrawal from exhibition of other art works. (Sometimes, relocation leads to withdrawal, which in turn leads to destruction: when Richard Serra's site-specific sculpture *Tilted Arc*, was removed from its location in Federal Plaza, Manhattan, a new location could not be found and so it was dismantled and warehoused).[xxxviii] These are offences of destruction because they confound the work's *reason* for existence – to be viewed, or to be viewed in a particular place – even if they do not confound its *actual* existence. 'To remove the piece,' insisted Serra, 'is to destroy the piece.'[xxxix]

Just as we need to distinguish between the literary offence of plagiarism and the legal offence of copyright infringement, so we need to distinguish between iconoclasm and criminal damage. (The two discourses – the political-aesthetic and the juridical – overlap but are not identical here). Acts of criminal damage are not always iconoclastic; iconoclasts do not always damage the works of art that they attack. Iconoclasm is both enjoined and prohibited; in certain contexts it is a term of praise, in others, of opprobrium. Iconoclasts attack false idols; and there is a relation between modern art and destruction.[xl] Iconoclasts are thus truth-tellers and innovators. But also: iconoclasm is stigmatized (often correctly) as brutish, ignorant, mere vandalism; in the power it often attributes to mere images, it is also archaic. It is thus one thing, and its opposite. The iconoclast can be an artist or an enemy of art; sometimes, he can be both, and sometimes neither (as with the destruction of Stalin statuary in Eastern Europe).

The major cultural moments of iconoclasm are considered to be Byzantium, the Reformation, the French Revolution, and the Nazi persecution of 'degenerate art.'[xli] (To which I would add flag desecration in the United States in the last 30 or so years. For example, during the period of protests against the war in Vietnam, a New York artist exhibited a United States flag stuffed into the shape of a six-foot human form hanging by the neck from a yellow noose – a perfect instance of iconoclastic art)[xlii]. Banning or privileging art works are here the result of a particular struggle: between Catholics and Protestants, royalists and revolutionaries, nazis and modernists. Iconoclasm is thus often political in motivation; portraits of sovereigns, for example, will attract both reverence and hostility. Destroy the picture; unseat the monarch. During the French Revolution desecrating images contributed to the deligitimization of the King. It made it easier to kill him.[xliii]

Iconoclasm can be creative or it can be destructive; sometimes it can be both. The iconoclast may wish to substitute his own work for the work he damages, on occasions by adding to the damaged work (in which case, the 'new' work constitutes a kind of palimpsest). Iconoclasm directed at one art form can stimulate practitioners of other art forms: Reformation iconoclasm had precisely this impact on English poetry of the period.[xliv] If iconoclasm is a legitimate form of expression, as well as the means by which the expression of others is attacked, it is both the object, and an instrument, of censorship. Any legal system which denies the autonomy of art, and thereby seeks to bring it under a regime in which it may be called to account, is at least potentially iconoclastic. Just as art may be iconoclastic, then, so also may law.

Are art and law in a different kind of complicity too? Art is often implicated in crime, which leads to choices being made between prosecution and appreciation (unless it is possible to do both).

II. Art Crimes

By placing the crime in front of the art work, art crimes of the *second* kind reverse the narrative order of the *first*. In the *first* kind, an existing art work is copied or damaged; in the *second* kind, a crime precedes the art work. For example: a poet 'borrows' a boat in order to contemplate a late night scene, a sculptor misappropriates body parts, and a poem or a sculpture is the result.

In Book I of *The Prelude* Wordsworth tells the story of a row on a lake, late at night, on holiday from school:

> One evening . . .
>
> I went alone into a shepherd's boat,
>
> A skiff that to a willow tree was tied
>
> Within a rocky cave, its usual home.
>
> [. . .]
>
> No sooner had I sight of this small skiff,
>
> Discovered thus by unexpected chance,
>
> Than I unloosed her tether and embarked.
>
> [. . .]
>
> It was an act of stealth
>
> And troubled pleasure . . .[xlv]

The taking of the boat, that is. Still, he pushed on, and he writes with a restrained wonder about the experience of that evening. It was thrilling, and then it became terrifying, as he fancied the cliff that loomed over him a 'living thing.' At this point, he turned back, leaving 'my bark' (note the possessive – felonious – pronoun) 'in her mooring place.' During the days that followed, his 'brain / Worked with a dim and undetermined sense / Of unknown modes of being.' Lacking the perspective, he was unable to reflect on what had happened; he was instead possessed by intimations of 'huge and mighty forms, that do not live / Like living men.' They 'moved', he says, 'slowly through my mind / By day, and were the trouble of my dreams.'

The 'troubled' of the passage concerning the boat is thus picked up later on. The word, in one form, is used to describe the poet's response to his own unlawful act, and then, in another form, to describe the animating effect of the evening's experiences on his imagination. The hint is that the unlawful act was a necessary, initiating step toward the ultimate end, the poem which is *The Prelude* itself. Without the boat, the trip would have been impossible, or at any rate, that trip on that occasion.

Wordsworth's 'case' is an example of the second kind of art crime. Two points can now be made about it. First, the relation it establishes between crime and art work is a contingent one (one can imagine circumstances in which this passage in the poem could have been written without the prior unlawful act). Second, whatever the precise nature of its relation to that prior act, the art work has an existence independent of the crime which contributed to its creation. The crime is part of the work's pre-history, that is, the history of its creation. It is *not* part of its ontology, its mode of existence. The crime is not, that is, constitutive of the art work.

It is this double dislocation of art work from crime which allows prosecutors to insist in art crime cases of this second that their prosecutions have 'nothing to do with' art. This was precisely the claim of the prosecutor in the Kelly case.

III. Art Crimes

Art crimes of the *third* kind may be distinguished from the *second* kind by virtue of the fact that they make just such a prosecutor's claim difficult. This is because here the art work is the crime. These art crimes abandon the narrative structure of the *first* and *second* kinds. The crime is the art, the art, the crime. They are crimes of art.

Admit art crimes of this third kind and the jurisprudence of art becomes (in part, at least) a criminology. The following are examples of such art crimes: literary works indebted in certain proscribed ways to earlier literary works; certain kinds of iconoclastic art; parodies that amount to derogatory treatment of the art works they parody; graffiti; pornography. It follows that certain entire art forms, and not just particular art works, have a relation with crime which is enabling and creative. Transgression, of one kind or another, is esential to their composition. In its efforts to protect art in general, law will often outlaw particular instances of art, for example, works which contain a high degree of borrowed material.

I should distinguish between two different types of art crimes of the third kind. There are art works which are criminal in consequence of their relation to other art works, and there are those other art works which are unlawful for some other reason. The best examples of the first form are plagiarising works, parodies, and certain (other) kinds of iconoclastic art. These are all crimes *of* art which are also crimes *against* art – art preying upon art. Good examples of the second are graffiti, pornography, blaspheming literature, satires, defamatory novels,[xlvi] and art works censored for their political content.

The first form is the more interesting because here the law finds itself in the paradoxical position of proscribing one kind of art in order to defend another kind. Let me term the one form 'strong art crimes' and the other form, 'weak art crimes.' (Of course, certain art works can offend in both ways: blasphemous or pornographic parodies, for example).[xlvii]

The distinction derives from two different arguments between law and art. With strong art crimes, law tends to say: this is not art, and art to respond: yes, it is. With weak art crimes, law tends to say, it doesn't matter whether this is art, and art to respond: yes, it does.[xlviii]

Take the contrasting cases of plagiarising works and blasphemous works. With the former, an action for infringement may be met with the defence: this work borrows creatively, and though it may be derivative, it is original too. That is to say, it is a new art work, and not merely a replica of an existing one. With the latter, a prosecution for blasphemy may be met with the defence that the work's aesthetic status or merit entitles it to special protection.[xlix]

Law thus either refuses the work the status of art (strong art crimes) or is indifferent to its status as art (weak art crimes). Art may find itself either with the plaintiff or on both sides of the contest (strong art crimes) or on the side of the defence (weak art crimes).[l]

a. Strong Art Crimes

In certain plagiarism cases, and in certain 'moral rights' cases (on which more below), there is only *one* art work, and it is the victim. These cases concern works that merely replicate other works, and actions destructive of works, and they constitute art crimes of the first kind, *simpliciter*. (When merely the unacknowledged recycling of existing work, plagiarism is solely an economic, that is non-aesthetic, assault on art). In other plagiarism and moral rights cases, however, there are *two* art works, one is the victim, and the other, the aggressor. It is these cases that constitute strong art crimes. Works of 'appropriation art' – say, Sherrie Levine's rephotographed photographs by Edward Weston or her facsimiles of Mondrian's watercolours[li] – are good examples of what I have in mind here, but Shakespeare's work is the paradigm instance of the strong art crime. Were Shakespeare (and the authors of his 'sources') to be writing today, he could be prosecuted for copyright infringement.

I should first put the crime in its correct legal context. Copyright law is a settlement of two opposing principles. The first principle, expressed as a proposition, can be put thus: literary works are the property of their authors until alienated by them, and should be treated no differently from other forms of private property. And this is the second principle: literary works are written out of other literary works (writers in creative dialogue with their forebears), and are thus common property, part of the cityscape of the public domain. The first principle may be defended by a combination of arguments about the nature of private property and the nature of literary creativity. While the second principle may likewise be defended by a comparable combination, the tendency has been to emphasise the specifically literary arguments: there has been little support for arguments that would circumscribe – or, more radically, deny – the claims of private property in general.

These principles are, each one of them, persuasive and coherent. Copyright law, by contrast, is neither. Diminished by its embrace of both principles, faithful to neither, it leaves its constituencies – authors, publishers and readers – dissatisfied. If it is to be defended, it has to be on policy grounds. It represents a settlement, not a deduction. It is not derived from an examination of the question: what is the nature of literary creativity? but rather: how should the claim of the author to perpetual copyright and the claim of the public to instant and unrestricted access be balanced? There is thus no place in its final formulations for the triumphant declaration, quod erat demonstrandum!

One consequence of this is that copyright law is unstable and subject to revision. It is always going to be open to the objection that it gives undue weight to one or other competing interest. And in this passage from principle to interest, which is a decline in theoretical standing, the potential rationality of copyright law is sacrificed. Because copyright law is thus a *politically* rather than *intellectually* contested terrain, not grounded in one principle but in a plurality of incompatible principles, it tends not to attract the attention of jurists (compare contract law or criminal law). This is because it is in a mess and thus hardly conducive to jurisprudential inquiry – other than of a deconstructive kind in which its various incoherences are held up to critical scrutiny.[lii]

The history of copyright is thus the history of a struggle, each Act and reported case a battle won or lost by one side or the other. Authors complain that their interests are inadequately protected; audiences complain that their access to authors' work is unduly fettered. Authors both need, and are mistrustful, of their audiences. The relationship between authors and audiences is thus one of unhappy mutual dependence. Intellectual property law intervenes to institutionalise that unhappiness. Authors want to be read, but they also they want to be paid for what they write. And carry on getting paid. They want to control the terms on which their works are enjoyed, and they can't do this without the assistance of the State. The State helps – some would say, too much, others still argue, too little. Those who argue for the most extensive private rights are called maximalists; those who argue against those rights we might term minimalists. Not all authors are themselves maximalists; not all maximalists are authors – many, indeed, are entrepreneurs wishing to exploit the property rights assigned to them *by* authors. Authors, in fact, face both ways. They want both to exploit the work of other authors and to protect their own: 'We earn our money out of the stupid law but we hate it because we know that's a jive. What else can we do?'[liii]

The law is in particular disarray at present. Not only does intellectual property law fail satisfactorily to resolve the competing claims made on it by authors and audiences, it has also failed to keep abreast of their activities. It doesn't protect them; it doesn't altogether comprehend what they're doing. Intellectual property law no longer encompasses the field. It is thus *both* incoherent *and* incomplete, inadequate in two distinct senses. The 1911 Act did not address film; the 1956 Act did not address video. And the 1988 Act? It's adrift in cyberspace. Technology is outstripping the legal categories designed to contain it. And this is the only hope for the minimalists – that technology will simply make impossible the legal regulation of access to information.

And yet: what do these complexities have to do with the case of literary theft? A writes a poem; B copies it down and then claims it as his own: where's the difficulty? B is discredited; it's a scandal of reputation. And limited to that. The institution of literature itself is hardly implicated in the scandal. But what then of the paradoxical truth that novels, plays, and poems, can be *both* original *and* derivative: original *because* derivative, even. If we reject plagiarism do we also reject literature itself? It would be odd if we had to conclude that aspect of the institution of literature which most undermines it is yet also fundamental to its existence. Can plagiarism be *both* its poison *and* its nourishment?

It is usual to think of literary invention as taking place in the middle reaches of two extremes. At one end, we may imagine total originality, the impossible work written in new language addressing subjects never before addressed; at the other end, total derivativeness, the scandalous work, a mere transcription of an already existing literary work. Close to the one end, typically, we locate writers of genius, and we might put Shakespeare closest to that extreme of originality. At the other, ignominious, end, we place the cheats, the tricksters – thieves of the labour of others.

But what if Shakespeare himself were a plagiarist? Can a writer be, so to speak, at both ends of the spectrum at the same time? Both original and derivative? Both a creator and a thief? If the answer is 'yes,' then, at the very least, we need to rethink our understanding of literary merit. The 'greatest' just might *not* equal 'the most original'.

Of course, if Shakespeare's appropriations were adaptations, then it might be easier. But many are not: he just took whole passages and transcribed them. Does this make him a lesser playwright? Only if we could imagine someone else doing everything that he did but without taking those lines and plots from others. If we cannot imagine such an author, however, then we are on the brink of suggesting that the thefts were a necessary part of the creation. The truth is that most writers both steal and create; some of the more interesting ones create by stealing. It thus might be said that while a plagiarist most certainly a writer with a bad name, a writer with a *good* name is merely an *undetected* plagiarist. Under today's literary regime, he's lucky, but under other, earlier regimes, he'd be considered unlettered or mad.

But surely – the protest runs – plagiarism can no more be excused than any other kind of unpermitted appropriation. To hold otherwise is to sanction two wrongs: the depriving of one author of the benefit of his work, the conferring on another author of an undeserved reputation. The first is unjustly impoverished; the second, unjustly enriched. Indeed, if authors had no property rights in their work (or were unable to enforce those rights) they would not be able to secure royalties, and the amount of writing would drop, perhaps to zero, as they turned away from writing toward other, more profitable pursuits. The law of copyright, which protects authors from plagiarists, thus ensures the continuity of literature itself.

Or so it could be argued. But such an argument would not survive an encounter with the massive counter-example of Shakespeare, whose work suggests, as Richard Posner has conceded, that any copyright law, however narrow, inhibits literary creativity.[liv] Emerson confronted just this argument in his essay on Shakespeare. Great men, he wrote, are more distinguished by range and extent than by originality. No great man is original. The greatest genius is the most indebted man. Genius, indeed, consists in not being original at all, but rather in being wholly *receptive*. Shakespeare owed debts in all directions. He knew that tradition supplies a better fable than any invention can. In his times, our own petulant demand for originality was not so much pressed. The great poet comes to value his memory equally with his invention. He doesn't much mind from where his thoughts have been derived: from whatever source, they are equally welcome. It has come to be, Emerson rather scandalously proposes, practically a rule in literature that a man having once shown himself capable of original writing is thenceforth entitled to steal from the writings of others at his discretion. And then, pursuing his paradox to its terminal point, Emerson declares: Shakespeare is unique.[lv] Harold Bloom, a great Emersonian, holds likewise when he remarks that Shakespeare understood that literature and plagiarism were scarcely to be distinguished. Plagiarism, Bloom insists, is a legal distinction, not a literary one.[lvi]

Artists and writers themselves are divided on the subject of plagiarism. They defend themselves, while tending to acknowledge, in qualified terms, its general unavoidability. They certainly don't like it when their own work is ripped off;

Albrecht Dürer's inscription on a woodcut is representative: 'Woe to you! You thieves and imitators of other people's labour and talents. Beware of laying your audacious hand on this artwork.'[lvii] They don't like it when they are accused of ripping off the work of others; Paul Celan, for example, was devastated by the charge, and even years afterwards, a friend recalled that he would 'burst into sobs at the memory of a defamation he'd suffered.'[lviii] One plagiarised poet holds responsible 'the contemporary intellectual climate' for making plagiarism acceptable.[lix] He has a point: plagiarism has been defended (and defined) as 'contextual free play' or 'inter-art traffic,' and the most creative plagiarist in the English language this century, T.S. Eliot – a man who plagiarised Emerson when making his own defence of plagiarism – declared: immature poets imitate; mature poets *steal*.[lx] Freed of its slightly Raskolnikovian amorality – my literary superiority licenses my literary crimes – this has become a commonplace of a certain kind of avant-gardist aesthetics:

> Plagiarism is the conscious manipulation of pre-existing elements in the creation of 'aesthetic' works. Plagiarism is inherent in all 'artistic' activity, since both pictorial and literary 'arts' function with an inherited language, even when their practitioners aim at overthrowing this received syntax (as happened with modernism and post-modernism).
>
> At the beginning of the twentieth-century, the way in which pre-existing elements were used in 'artistic' productions underwent a quantitative leap with the discovery of collage. This development was pre-figured in the 'writings' of Isidore Ducasse (1846-70), who is better known by his pen name Lautreamont.
>
> In his Poems, Ducasse wrote: 'Plagiarism is necessary. Progress implies it.' This maxim summarises the use to which plagiarism has been put ever since. Two, or more, divergent elements are brought together to create new meanings. The resulting sum is greater than the individual parts.
>
> Plagiarism enriches human language.[lxii]

Though this statement is perhaps best regarded as a literary 'heresy' (in the sense defined by Eliot, that is, an attempt to simplify the truth by reducing it to the limits of our ordinary understanding),[lxiii] there is no doubt that plagiarism is indispensable to art, and chief amongst art crimes.

Let me now turn to parody. According to the 18th century rhetorician, Dumarsais, parody 'distorts in a mocking manner verses that were composed by someone else with a different goal in mind.'[lxiv] The French Code *de la propriété intellectuelle*, for example, protects this kind of disrespectful handling of another's work from infringement actions,[lxv] while in the United States parody is regarded as 'fair dealing' with the parodied work and thus not an infringement.[lxvi] The courts are thus willing to find that parodies do not infringe copyright, and to regard parodies as new works derived from the works that they parody.[lxvii] Likewise, trademark appropriation for the purposes of parody tends not to be regarded as infringement.[lxviii] However, as one would expect, law and aesthetics diverge in their characterisations of parody. For example: French law treats parody, pastiche and caricature as synonymous, relating the first to musical works, the second to literary works, and the third to works of art;[lxix] in one case, a distinction was drawn between parodies that were humorous and those which were spiteful, these latter parodies being unlawful; in another case, 'parody' and 'burlesque' were taken to be synonymous.[lxx]

If parody is safe from infringement charges, what of the integrity right of the author of the parodied work (see *s.80 CDPA 1988* – the so-called moral right to object to the derogatory treatment of one's work)? Most moral rights cases concern entirely non-aesthetic mutilations or distortions – the cropping of pictures, the dismantling of sculptures, and a recent example, the anthologising of a poem with a word missing from its first line.[lxxi] But parodies may also be 'distortions or mutilations of the work, or . . . otherwise prejudicial to the honour or reputation of the author' (in the phrasing of *s.80*). By defending the copyright or trademark case, do parodists thereby expose themselves to the moral rights case? If they do, then the lawyer's distinction between the 'take-off' and the 'rip-off'[lxxii] – the parodic first is permitted, the replicative second is not – ceases to offer the promise of an escape, and instead threatens two different routes, so to speak, to jail. Parody is an acknowledged literary genre; *s.80* might also make it, in certain instances at least, an unlawful one.[lxxiii]

b. Weak Art Crimes (and the Aesthetic Alibi)

Graffiti, especially when they take the form of unlicensed murals, are good examples of weak art crimes because while they are unlawful,[lxxiv] they do not offend against other works of art or, if they do, do so only contingently. Indeed, graffiti is invariably found in urban landscapes conspicuous for their lack of aesthetic quality (which is why graffiti is not iconoclastic). Blasphemous art works are another good example of such crimes because, as with graffiti, it is in the nature of their offence to strike against a non-aesthetic interest. Graffiti is an assault on property rights, blasphemy, an assault on ecclesiastical rights, such rights in each case sanctioned by the State. And as a final example, consider the literary satire, which is often defamatory of its target.

In prosecutions / civil actions in respect of such art crimes, artist-defendants invariably wish to argue that the criminal / tortious nature of their art work is trumped either by its artistic status and / or its artistic value. These are two versions – relating to ontology and value – of a defence which has been termed 'the aesthetic alibi.'

According to Martin Jay the alibi is deployed to make otherwise objectionable conduct acceptable when part of an aesthetic project. It transforms the proscribed into the permitted: 'what would be libellous or offensive in everyday life is granted a special dispensation, if it is understood to take place within the protective shield of an aesthetic frame.' We even, he adds, 'invent new categories like 'performance art' to permit behaviour that without its protection would in all likelihood threaten the perpetrator with immediate incarceration in a mental institution, if not a jail.'[lxxv] Artists themselves are alive to this, as are the defenders of practices the aesthetic status of which is contested, such as graffiti.[lxxvi] While 'this culture is horridly moralistic,' Kathy Acker observes, 'under the aegis of art, you're allowed to actually deal with matters of sexuality and other matters of plain old freedom.' But, she adds, this 'keeps the artist from fighting.'[lxxvii] The aesthetic alibi protects the artist, but at the price of neutralising her. Still, fall on the wrong side of the line, and one is a criminal; from the perspective of a writer convicted of blasphemy for his parodies of Scripture, the alibi 'turns a literary difference into a criminal offence.' If it is not literature it is a crime. Put more positively, 'literariness' thus 'grants rights', as Jess Marsh has noted in her work on the 19th century blasphemy trials.

In the rigour of its division between 'art' and 'non-art' the aesthetic alibi is thus a very specific variation on the general freedom of speech defence. In the United States, art has the protection of the First Amendment precisely because it is regarded as having communicative power on a par with that of the written or spoken word.[lxxviii] That is to say, art is protected because it is *like* (certain kinds of) non-art – social commentary, political propaganda, and so on. It is symbolic speech. By contrast, the aesthetic alibi pleads that art is to be protected because it is *un*like anything else, it is always and only its special self. First Amendment champions of art find safety for it as merely one kind of speech among other, protected kinds; aesthetic alibi advocates conversely find safety for art in its isolation from all other kinds of speech.

There is of course a striking difference between the legal and the aesthetic breadth of the aesthetic alibi. In English law, for example, it is only available in obscenity cases [lxxix] – the 'public good' defence in s.4 of the *Obscene Publications Act 1959* [lxxx] – while in aesthetics, it tends to be advanced against attacks on art from all quarters. (I simplify: certain works of art – parodies and satire – might also benefit from the aesthetic alibi, in the guise this time of the fair dealing exemption in *s.30 CDPA*, and thus be protected from infringement actions;[lxxxi] conversely, there are theories of art which do not shrink from anticipating the suppressing of works which fail to meet certain moral criteria – think of Tolstoy's *What is Art?*, for example).[lxxxii] But while obscene works thus enjoy a certain measure of protection, they also suffer a greater degree of exposure than other kinds of art work. This is because there is (in English law, at least) a public policy defence to copyright infringement where the plagiarised work is obscene, blasphemous or otherwise immoral.[lxxxiii] An obscene work thus may escape suppression only to suffer unhindered copying. Allowing for this rather unusual case, while law thus grants art certain privileges and protections, excepting it from certain penalties (or taxes – think of the U.S. Customs case regarding the Brancusi *Bird in Space*),[lxxxiv] and safeguarding it from certain dangers, it does not confer on art wholesale immunities. Art is by no means above the law.

Prosecutors / plaintiffs respond to the aesthetic alibi by: (i) denying that the contested work has artistic status, as in breach of copyright cases which assume that an art work which is not original is not an art work at all; or (ii) conceding the contested work's status, but denying its merit, as in pornography cases; or (iii) conceding both its status and its merit, but denying that either is relevant as a defence, as in hate speech cases and moral rights cases.

What the law refuses to recognise as art (or of sufficient artistic merit) may nonetheless be accepted within the art community as art (even, art of a high order). Law may therefore find itself making distinctions between art works refused by art itself, protecting some, prohibiting others. Sometimes, law will first prohibit and then protect – as in the case of Baudelaire's *Les fleurs du mal*, where a French Court of Appeal in 1949 reversed an 1857 decision condemning six poems for obscenity.[lxxxv]

The Kelly case is a good, recent example of the limitations of the aesthetic alibi in a juridical context. The prosecutor in the case insisted on the opening day of the trial that the case was not about art, nor was it even about outraging public decency.[lxxxvi] It was just, he said, about theft. He was wrong, of course; the theft was the least of it. Still, his misstatement was a strategic one. To admit art into the courtroom would have raised a difficult question. Should the use to which the defendant put the body parts be a defence? Does the aesthetic end justify the criminal means (the aesthetic alibi)?

As a defendant, Mr. Kelly was of little interest. He had his defences under the 1984 *Anatomy Act*, though they failed to get him acquitted. It was only as an artist – or someone who claims the privileges and status of the artist – that he was intriguing. And indeed he insisted that he was an artist. After a period of silence, he defended himself in a series of press interviews: 'I have never made money from this. This is about art.'[lxxxvii]

The Anatomy Act discriminates in favour of medical research and against the use by artists of cadavers. It recognises as legitimate a person's wish for his or her body to be used for anatomical examination. Yet if any person, during his last illness and in the presence of two witnesses, expressed the wish that his body be left to Mr. Kelly, or any other artist, the Act would not permit it. This seems objectionable for at least two reasons.

First, why shouldn't a person be free – public health considerations allowing – to dispose of his own body as he wishes? If he chooses to perpetuate his existence as a work of art, then why not? Who wouldn't prefer to gaze out at respectful gallery audiences, if the only alternative was gazing up at gagging (or bored) first-year medical students?

Second, the Act's prejudice against art and in favour of science exhibits a disregard for the claims of art, and artistic endeavour, typical of our culture. The Act is philistine. It only permits anatomical examinations when undertaken in the course of teaching, studying, or researching into, morphology. If Leonardo da Vinci were alive and working in England today, he too might therefore be at risk of prosecution under the Anatomy Act. Indeed, Mr. Kelly has been compared to da Vinci, and praised as 'a serious medical artist of considerable talent.'[lxxxviii] The human body has been an object of artists' attention since murals decorated our first dwelling places. If we want art, rather than kitsch, we have to let our artists take risks – with their subjects, as well as with our sensibilities.

For the moralists, the Kelly case presented no special difficulty. Respect for the dead is a necessary piety: if we cannot respect the dead, what prospect is there for teaching respect for the living? The violence done to corpses is often an aspect of the horror of war. Atrocities of the kind depicted by Goya in his great documentary work, *The Disasters of War*, are always and only occasions for deep dismay. They do not – or should not – be regarded as providing interesting opportunities for a certain kind of 'shock art.' They are degraded when they are treated merely as the means to some greater (though ultimately dubious) aesthetic end. As in war, so in peace. Bodies should indeed be left in peace. They should not be permitted to become the playthings of artists (or anyone else).

This sense that the dead have rights which artists may not violate is a powerful one, perhaps amounting to a taboo, and should not lightly be dismissed. It explains the widespread revulsion expressed by visitors to the exhibitions of artist Sue Fox's photographs of dead bodies in a Manchester morgue. It explains the equally widespread disgust generated by the Chapman brothers' three-dimensional version of Goya's *Great Deeds Against the Dead* shown in the recent Royal Academy 'Sensation' exhibition. And it explains the readiness of the jury to convict the artist who exhibited a sculpture of a mannequin's head wearing foetal earrings.[lxxxix] There is the sense that these art works violate their subjects, that they prey upon the dead, exploiting them in their passivity, their vulnerability.

Conclusion

Artists will always force the boundaries of what is held to be art; it follows that they will also force the boundaries of what is lawful. Just as aesthetics lags behind art, so law lags behind aesthetics. This does not mean that there is not an aesthetics implicit in law. Quite to the contrary. It is the existence of such an implicit aesthetics that both produces and then validates law's proscriptions. Graffiti, for example, is a crime which is (as Ferrell has argued) constructed out of the clash of alternative aesthetics;[xc] and though forgery likewise is a crime, it is not a 'natural' one, because it derives from historically specific notions of writing and authorship.[xci] Art law itself is predicated on categories of private property (including the author's own intellectual property)[xcii] and originality which artists, and thereafter theories of art, are bound to challenge. Indeed, little of what is termed 'art law' is worthy of the name. Art law (in this jurisdiction at least) does not so much protect freedom of artistic expression as property interests in art (including the author's). Certainly, when the two collide, the former is the invariable loser.

This leads, from the perspective of artists, to a certain disrespect for law, a qualified antinomianism: law has no place in art, because there should be no constraints on the imagination. (Artists usually make an exception of copyright infringement, because it does not appear to involve the inhibiting of artistic expression, only its parasitic replication). They would like a special 'First Amendment' right, one which prohibits any abridgement of freedom of artistic expression, and which is both stronger and narrower than the more general laws protecting speech. Stronger, because the special right would trump other rights (not to be defamed, for example); narrower, because it would relate only to art works. It is the sheer clumsiness of legal interventions in art that most exasperates its champions. Take, for example, the art critic Hilton Kramer's dismay at the

New York flag desecration trial: 'Suddenly, complicated questions of aesthetic intention and artistic realization – questions that require a certain specialized intelligence and taste even to be properly phrased, let alone answered – were cast into an alien legalistic vocabulary that precluded the very possibility of a serious answer.' [xciii]

From the perspective of moralists, however, artists deserve no greater license than any other citizen. Art – or rather, artistic status – excuses nothing. As prosecuting counsel in the *Madame Bovary* trial put it: 'Art without rules is no longer art: it is like a woman ready to take all her clothes off. Obliging art simply to respect the rules of public decency is not to enslave it but to honour it.' [xciv] The aesthetic alibi, to advocates of such a position, is already too strong; it should be withdrawn altogether. And for a person such as Catherine MacKinnon, for example, so far from art providing a saving qualification to the pornographic, it colludes with pornography, re-enforcing what is most objectionable about such representations of women: 'if a woman is subjected, why should it matter that the work has other value? Perhaps what redeems a work's value among men enhances its injury to women. Existing standards of literature, art . . . are, in feminist light, remarkably consonant with pornography's mode, meaning, and message.' [xcv] Moralists are not – or need not be (Mackinnon is a possible exception) – Platonists. They do not mistrust art; they merely hold that it should not have any special privileges. Art is a form of private property; as such it should be protected. Art is liable to offend against laws of decency, or whatever; when it does, it should be prohibited. And (a different point), if art's protection is to be secured by excluding certain of its instances from law's ambit, so be it. If art's inoffensiveness is to be secured by suppressing some of its instances, then so be it again.

These two positions, the artist's and the moralist's, cannot, I think, be reconciled. And there is no third position available to harmonise the contrary perspectives. We remain in the realm of discretion and contention: should this or that work be prosecuted? should this or that defendant be able to plead the aesthetic status of his work as a defence? should the class of offences in which the aesthetic alibi is a defence be extended, and if so, which offences (or torts) should be added? [xcvi] These questions remain inescapable; no grand synthesis will eliminate them. Law and art will remain in tension; the best that law and art (by which I include literature) studies can do is to describe the various aspects of their conflict.

© Oxford University Press 1999. Reprinted from Law and Literature: Current Legal Issues 1999, Volume 2 edited by Michael Freeman and Andrew D.E. Lewis (1999) by permission of Oxford University Press.

i   Quoted in Martin Jay, 'The Aesthetic Alibi', *Cultural Semantics* (Amherst, 1998), p.113.

ii   Harold Osborne, *The Oxford Companion to Art* (Oxford, 1970), p.212.

iii   Walter Benjamin, 'Theses on the Philosophy of History,' *Illuminations*, (London, 1973), p.258.

iv   Kathryn Knight, 'Sculptor jailed for theft of body parts,' 'The Times,' 4 April 1998, p.5.

v   Dario Gamboni, *The Destruction of Art: Iconoclasm and Vandalism since the French Revolution*, (London, 1997), p.328.

vi   See Anthony Julius *T.S. Eliot, anti-Semitism and literary form*, (Cambridge, 1995), pps. 119-120; and Joss Marsh *Word Crimes: Blasphemy, Culture, and Literature in Nineteenth-Century England*, (Chicago, 1998), p.12: 'The will to transgression and the urge to avoid it may be integral elements in all literary production . . .'

vii   'Artists must continue the conquest of new territory and new taboos': Norman Rosenthal, 'The Blood Must Continue to Flow,' *Sensation* (London, 1997): cf. Lawrence Durrell on Henry Miller, 'he had been forced to outrage the sensibilities of his contemporaries, to force the steel locks of the taboo . . . the art and the outrage march hand in hand' (Henry Miller, Lawrence Durrell, and Alfred Perlès, *Art and Outrage*, [London, 1973], pps. 8 and 54).

viii   'Biedermeier' is the term given to German and Austrian art in the period 1815-1848, which was solid, philistine, sentimental, familiar, accessible (see Osborne, op.cit). Arthur Danto contrasts Biedermeier art with the art of the avant-garde, as two ideal types, the one comfortable, the other quite the reverse, an art that 'will never become something that pleases the eye or enlivens the spirit' ('Why does art need to be explained? Hegel, Biedermeier, and the intractably avant-garde,' introduction to Linda Weintraub *Art on the Edge and Over*, [Litchfield, 1996], pps.12-16).

ix   'To a Lady Offended by a Book of the Writer's,' *The Complete Poems*, (London, 1976), p.65.

x   David Freedberg, *Iconoclasts and their motives* (Maarssen, 1995), pps.7, 35-6.

xi   Fiona Macmillan Patfield, 'Towards a Reconciliation of Free Speech and Copyright', in *The Yearbook of Media and Entertainment Law 1996* (Oxford, 1996), pps. 199-233.

xii   C.H. Rolph, *The Trial of Lady Chatterley* (London, 1961), pps.112-3.

xiii   Stephen Halliwell, 'Aristotle's Poetics,' in *The Cambridge History of Literary Criticism – Volume 1: Classical Criticism*, (Cambridge, 1993), pps.169-174.

xiv   'Chaque œuvre d'art a sa poétique spéciale en vertu de la quelle elle est fait et elle subsiste': quoted in René Wellek, *A History of Modern Criticism 1750-1950: The Later Nineteenth Century* (Cambridge, 1983), p.12. That is, so to speak, the ontological aspect of the art work's implicit aesthetics. Elsewhere, Flaubert addressed the hermeneutic aspect: 'Chaque œuvre à faire à sa poétique en soi, qu'il faut trouver' (op.cit., p.478).

xv   In the United States, of course, artists may rely on powerful First Amendment rights. 'Visual speech', according to the authors of an American art law textbook, enjoys 'constitutional protections virtually on a par with that of pure speech' (Ralph E. Lerner and Judith Bresler, *Art Law*, 2nd ed., [New York, 1998], p.668; see also pps.676-680).

xvi   Gérard Genette, *Literature in the Second Degree* (Lincoln, 1997).

xvii   Dario Gamboni, op.cit., p.43.

xviii   Gamboni, op.cit., pps.46-7.

xix   Illegally obtained, the Greek claim for their return is unenforceable: see Christopher Hitchens, *The Elgin Marbles*, (London, 1998).

xx   A pastiche, Genette observes (quoting Proust), may thus be 'criticism in action' (Genette, op.cit., p.8).

xxi   As in the *Chasse Spirituelle* affair. On 19 May 1949 'Le Mercure de France' put on sale a slim volume entitled *La Chasse Spirituelle*, attributed to Rimbaud. In fact, it was written by two actors who wanted to prove their competence in the Rimbaud idiom, a competence that had been challenged by experts a few months earlier (the actors had put on a dramatized version of *A Season in Hell*). They took in a number of Rimbaud specialists, for a while. Indeed, these specialists refused to accept that they had been duped, and insisted against the evidence of the actors' own manuscript that their work was truly Rimbaud's. For a fuller account of the 'affaire', see Genette, op.cit., pps.158-161.

xxii For the cento, see Margaret A. Rose, Parody: Ancient, Modern, and Post-Modern, (Cambridge, 1993), p.78, and the entries in Alex Preminger, ed., *The Princeton Encyclopedia of Poetry and Poetics* (New Jersey, 1974), J.A. Cuddon, *A Dictionary of Literary Terms*, (London, 1977); for collage, see Osborne, op.cit.

xxiii And his motives? An early biographer speculated: 'he hay have had a secret pleasure in hearing the poems, which he brought forward as Rowley's, so highly appreciated by the world, the consciousness that those works were the production of his own muse, must have filled him with exultation . . .' (John Dix, *The Life of Thomas Chatterton*, [London, 1837], p.51).

xxiv Shakespeare is a notable exception: see S. Schoenbaum, *Shakespeare's Lives*, (Oxford, 1991), passim.

xxv   Jonathan Jones, 'Forgery's Great Renaissance', 'The Guardian,' 25 April 1998.

xxvi Eric Hebborn, *Confessions of a Master Forger*, (London, 1997).

xxvii Lerner and Bresler, op.cit, p.206.

xxviii ibid., p.215.

xxix See Nelson Goodman and Catherine Z. Elgin, *Reconceptions in Philosophy & Other Arts & Sciences*, (London, 1988), ch.IV.

xxx   Linda Hutcheon, *A Theory of Parody*, (London, 1985), p.6.

xxxi For a careful account of the multiple differences between parody and satire, see Rose, op.cit., pps.80-86.

xxxii Quoted: Hutcheon, op.cit., p.78.

xxxiii Michael Heyward, *The Ern Malley Affair*, (London, 1993); Alan Sokal and Jean Bricmont, *Intellectual Impostures*, (London, 1998). This is the least interesting aspect of parody, the conservative ridiculing of artistic fashion's extremes (see Hutcheon, op.cit., pps.11, 77). For another example of a parody-hoax (or rather, what was first a hoax, and then a parody) see Martin Gardner, *The Night is Large*, (London, 1996), p.480. Gardner is writing about an earlier book of his, *The Whys of a Philosophical Scrivener*: 'In the book's chapter on aesthetics, I played a dirty trick on readers. I quoted what I said was a poem by William Carlos Williams and asked readers to compare it with a parody I had written of Williams's style. Actually, the parody was an authentic quote from one of Williams's poems, and what I said was by Williams was my parody. Naturally George Groth [a reviewer] was too dense to be aware of this sneaky switch.'

xxxiv See Rose, op.cit., pps.69-70, and Hutcheon, op.cit., pps.38-39.

xxxv *Clark v. Associated Newspapers Ltd* [1998] 1 All ER 959, at 972.

xxxvi Peter Bradshaw, *Not Alan Clark's Diaries*, (London, 1998), p.x.

xxxvii Parody 'is an intuitive kind of literary criticism, shorthand for what 'serious' critics must write out at length. It is Method acting, since a successful parodist must live himself, imaginatively, into his parodee. It is jujitsu, using the impetus of the opponent to defeat him': Dwight Macdonald, *Parodies: An Anthology from Chaucer to Beerbohm – and After* (New York, 1985), p.xiii.

xxxviii See Clara Weyergraf-Serra and Martha Buskirk, eds., *the Destruction of 'Tilted Arc': Documents* (Cambridge, Mass, 1991).

xxxix Quoted by Gamboni, op.cit., p.320.

xl Gamboni, op.cit., p.9.

xli ibid., p.10.

xlii Lerner and Bresler, op.cit., pps.707-8.

xliii Gamboni, op.cit., p.31.

xliv See Ernest B. Gilman, *Iconoclasm and Poetry in the English Reformation*, (Chicago, 1986).

xlv William Wordsworth, *The Prelude: A Parallel Text* (London, 1975), pps.54-56.

xlvi On some of the legal issues, see Eric Barendt, 'Defamation and Fiction,' in this collection; for some elaborated examples of 'literature as revenge,' see Louise DeSalvo, *Conceived with Malice*, (New York, 1994).

xlvii See Marsh, op.cit., pps.23-4.

xlviii The distinction is not absolute. Even though the sex film archivist and historian David Flint is used as a source by the British and American Film Institutes, 'that doesn't matter to the police,' he has explained, 'because they don't consider [his archive material] to be legitimate films … As far as they're concerned, *they're not real films, they're just criminal acts.*' ('The Guardian' 10 July 1998, Friday Review p.7, my italics). Likewise, consider Republican Senator Jesse Helms on Andres Serrano: 'I cannot go into detail about the crudeness and depravity of [his] art … I will not even acknowledge that it is art. I do not even acknowledge that [he] was an artist. I think he was a jerk' (quoted: Ronald K.L. Collins and David M. Skover, *The Death of Discourse*, [Boulder, Colorado, 1996], p.176). Laurie Adams has written well about 'the absurd confrontation between art and the law when the law tries to establish that something is or is not art (*Art on Trial* [New York, 1976], p.220).

xlix The argument will usually fail. In William Hone's 1817 trial in London, he defended his blasphemous parodies by reference to their substantial literary pedigree. The trial judge would have none of it: 'if the publication be profane, it ought not to be tolerated.' The trial was, Marsh comments, 'a moment of separation between literature and the subliterary' (see Marsh, op.cit., p.36).

l For a good account of some recent art controversies (including, where relevant, the litigation) in the United States, see Steven C. Dubin *Arresting Images: Impolitic Art and Uncivil Actions* (London, 1992).

li Robert Atkins Artspeak (New York, 1990), p.42. He describes her as an 'appropriator', and defines appropriation itself as 'the practice of creating a new work by taking a pre-existing image from another context … and combining that appropriated image with new ones. *Or, a well-known art work may be represented as the appropriator's own*' (my italics).

lii See, for example, Fiona Macmillan Patfield, 'Legal policy and the limits of literary copyright', in *Textual Monopolies: Literary Copyright and the Public Domain*, ed. Patrick Parrinder and Warren Cherniak, (London, 1997).

liii Kathy Acker, *Hannibal Lecter, My Father* (New York, 1991), p.12.

liv 'The more extensive is copyright protection, the more inhibited is the literary imagination. This is not a good reason for abolishing copyright, but it is a reason possibly for narrowing it, and more clearly for not broadening it': Richard Posner, *Law and Literature*, 2nd.ed., (Cambridge, Mass., 1998), p.403.

lv Ralph Waldo Emerson, *Emerson's Literary Criticism*, (Lincoln, 1995), pps.162-179.

lvi 'It shocks me increasingly to observe the vanishing of Freud's originalities in the presence of Shakespeare, but it would not have shocked Shakespeare, who understood that literature and plagiarism were scarcely to be distinguished. Plagiarism is a legal distinction, not a literary one, just as the sacred and the secular form a political and religious distinction and are not literary categories at all': Harold Bloom, *The Western Canon* (London, 1994), pps.74-5.

lvii Lerner and Bresler, op.cit, p.205. In the argot of graffiti writers, 'biting' means appropriating the style of another writer, and is very much deprecated: 'writers employ the notion . . . in much the same way that conventional art worlds negotiate and utilize more formal notions of forgery or copyright violation' (Jeff Ferrell, *Crimes of Style*, [Boston, 1996], p.87).

lviii Françoise Meltzer, *Hot Property*, (Chicago, 1994), p.65.

lix 'Some of my theory-minded colleagues . . . argu[e] that my insistence on ownership is a denial of the communal nature of art [. . .] While I doubt that Jones [the plagiariser] thought in these terms when he was copying down my work, I do believe he benefitted from the contemporary intellectual climate [. . .] In fact, had he underpinned his activities with theory, he might have found vigorous defenders among literary theorists': Neil Bowers, *Words for the Taking: The Hunt for a Plagiarist*, (New York, 1997), p.123.

lx See Hutcheon, op.cit., pps.5, 8.

lxi T.S. Eliot, *Selected Essays*, (London, 1951), p.206 (my italics). (For a discussion of this passage, see Julius, op.cit., pps.130-2). But there are limits to the extent to which writers will celebrate their own plagiarisms. The novelist Alasdair Gray, for example, makes a joke of his plagiarisms toward the end of his novel *Lanark*, but only once he has established it as a major and indisputably original work of fiction (London, 1985, p.485). And Kathy Acker, as a second example, begins an interview by confessing 'if I had to be totally honest I would say that what I'm doing is breach of copyright,' but then goes on to distinguish her practices from mere plagiarism, 'I had changed words, I had changed intentionality' (Acker, op.cit., 11-13).

lxii Stewart Home, *Neoism, Plagiarism and Praxis* (Edinburgh, 1995), p.51.

lxiii T.S. Eliot, *The Idea of a Christian Society and Other Writings*, (London, 1982), p.74.

lxiv Quoted by Genette, op.cit., p.16.

lxv 'Art L. 122-5. – Lorsque l'oeuvre a été divulgée, l'auteur ne peut interdire: [. . .] 4. La parodie, le pastiche et la caricature, comte tenu des lois du genre.'

lxvi *Campbell v. Acuff-Rose Music*, Inc., 510 U.S. 569, 114 S. Ct. 1164 (1994). But contrast the position in England, where 'such cases have usually been dealt with by asking whether an infringement has in fact occurred, rather than by considering the fair-dealing exemption [under s.30 of the CDPA]' (Patfield, 'Towards a Reconciliation', op.cit., p.229).

lxvii *Joy Music v. Sunday Pictorial Newspapers (1920) Ltd* [1960] 1 All ER 709.

lxviii Lerner and Bresler, op.cit., pps.712-18.

lxix Claude Colombet, *Propriété littéraire et artistique et droits voisins* (Paris, 1992), p.167.

lxx *Joy Music*, op.cit.

lxxi   The poet Ruth Fainlight reported, in a letter to the Times Literary Supplement, that Penguin had published her poem 'Handbag' in an anthology omitting a word from its first line: 'My mother's old bag' instead of 'My mother's old leather handbag,' thereby 'weakening the line, disrupt[ing] the metre as well as the pattern of assonance and alliteration through the entire poem.' This is a plain case of breach of s.80. ('Publish and be Damned,' TLS, 12 June 1998). Although she did not sue – or even threaten legal action – she could have done so, and Penguin would have had no defence.

lxxii   *Clark v. Associated Newspapers Ltd* [1998] 1 All ER 959, at 968.

lxxiii   However, if parodies *can* escape infringement claims, they will probably also be able to evade that it will also escape moral rights claims (often thrown in by authors just as a make-weight). The Asterix litigation in Germany is a good, recent example of how parodies fare in combined infringement / moral rights cases (the case is reported at [1995] 7 EIPR D-198). The defendant was the publisher of a comic book entitled 'ALCOLIX – the parody.' The owners of the exclusive licence in the Asterix series and characters sued, alleging both infringement and breach of moral rights (because the Asterix characters were associated by the parody with alcohol abuse and cruelty). The owners lost in the Federal Supreme Court. The parodist's creative effort was acknowledged. Though the parody necessarily contained adoptions, it achieved the appropriate interior distance from the parodied work by arguing with it. The question of infringement would be determined by applying the perspective of the reader who both knows the old, protected work and has the intellectual understanding demanded by the new work. This provides the working space needed for sophisticated art forms and artistic freedoms, guaranteed by art. 5(3) of the German Constitution. 'Art,' it declares, is 'free.'

lxxiv   Under New York's Penal Code, graffiti is defined as the 'etching, painting, covering, drawing upon or otherwise placing of a mark upon public or private property with intent to damage such property' (Lerner and Bresler, op.cit., p.711). For an examination of the 'criminal art' of graffiti see Susan Stewart, *Crimes of Writing* (Durham, 1994), ch.7. And for a similarly enthusiastic account – celebrating its 'creative lawbreaking' – see Jeff Ferrell, op.cit., p.29. According to Ferrell, graffiti 'threatens not only the legal boundaries of private property and public space, but the political and aesthetic boundaries of legitimate – even legitimately 'alternative' – art' (p.41).

lxxv   Jay, op.cit., p.111.

lxxvi   '. . . campaigners . . . employ the derivative phrase 'graffiti vandalism' to describe all forms of graffiti, whether murals, throw-ups, or tags. The effect, of course, is to lock graffiti into the context of vandalism, to tie it to activities like window smashing and cemetery desecration, *and to deny graffiti any special status as creative or artistic activity*' (Ferrell, op.cit., p.138, my italics).

lxxvii   Kathy Acker, op.cit., p.16.

lxxviii   Lerner and Bresler, op.cit., p.677. In the recent case of *Nelson v. Streeter* (16 F.3d 145 [7th Cir. 1994]), the court declared: 'It has been clear since long before 1988 that government officials are not permitted to burn books that offend them, and we do not see any difference between burning an offensive book and burning an offensive painting . . .' (quoted: Lerner and Bresler, op.cit., p.694). An artist had painted a satirical picture of the then recently deceased mayor of Chicago, Harold Washington.

lxxix   It is therefore not available, for example, in race hatred cases: see ss.18-22 Public Order
        Act (although s.20, which concerns public performances of plays, does require
        'the performance as a whole' to be taken into account. In any event, it is not impossible that
        certain productions, say, of 'The Merchant of Venice' could risk prosecution). In general,
        the position varies from jurisdiction to jurisdiction. In California, for example, where any
        unauthorised use of a deceased person's name, photograph or likeness for commercial
        purposes is actionable, there is a specific exception where such use is in connection with
        'single and original works of fine art' (CAL. CIV. CODE para 990 [West 1982 & Supp.1997];
        cited in Lerner and Bresler, op.cit., p.753).

lxxx   Available, that is, after a fashion. The aesthetic merit of the work is one only of a number
        of possible grounds for this defence: 'A person shall not be convicted of an offence . . . if it is
        proved that publication of the article in question is justified as being for the public good on
        the ground that it is in the interests of science, literature, art or learning, or of other objects
        of general concern.' Indeed, publication of an obscene work wholly without aesthetic merit
        might nonetheless be 'in the interests of literature' (see Geoffrey Robertson, Obscenity,
        [London, 1979], p.170; and see also Eric Barendt, *Freedom of Speech* [Oxford, 1987],
        pps.269-72). Compare, in any event, the current position in the USA, as expressed by the
        Supreme Court; 'At a minimum, prurient, patently offensive depiction or description of
        sexual conduct must have serious literary, artistic, political or scientific value to merit First
        Amendment protection' (*Miller v. California*, 413 U.S. 15, 93 S. Ct. 2607 [1973]; cited by
        Lerner and Bresler, op.cit., p.728).

lxxxi   'The use of copyright material in artistic works does not seem to be covered by any of the
        fair-dealing exemptions, unless it amounts to criticism, or possibly parody or satire . . . As at
        least some art may be considered to be appropriation of pre-existing work for purposes such
        as subversion or re-invention, this may be regarded as having a chilling effect on artistic free
        speech' (Patfield, 'Towards a Reconciliation,' op.cit., p.230).

lxxxii 'Not only should . . . no sacrifices be offered up to what among us is called art, but on the
        contrary the efforts of those who wish to live rightly should be directed to the destruction
        of this art, for it is one of the most cruel of the evils that harass our section of humanity':
        What is Art?, (London, 1994), p.197.

lxxxiii In the case of *Glyn v. Weston Feature Films*, the defendant film company was able to adapt
        Elinor Glyn's novel, *Three Weeks*, without infringing her copyright (see Patfield, 'Towards
        a Reconciliation,' pps.225, 232). Note also: 'so closely connected had the two crimes of
        blasphemy and obscenity become . . . that concepts which grew up around the one crime
        could shift with slippery ease to the other. Hence the arc of connection between the 1840
        Moxon-Shelley trial for blasphemy and D.H. Lawrence's posthumous arraignment for
        obscenity' (Marsh, op.cit., 209).

lxxxiv The importer of the Brancusi work successfully argued – against Customs opposition –
        that it was a work of art and thus exempt from duty: see Laurie Adams, *Art on Trial*,
        (New York, 1976), ch.2, and Gamboni, op.cit., pps.325-6.

lxxxv   E.S. Burt, "An Immoderate Taste for Truth:' Censoring History in Baudelaire's 'Les bijoux,'
        in *Censorship and Silencing: Practices of Cultural regulation*, ed. Robert C. Post
        (Los Angeles, 1998), p.111.

lxxxvi Kathy Marks, 'Artist stole dozens of heads, limbs, and torsos, court is told,' 'Independent'
        24 March 1998, p.1.

lxxxvii Quoted: Catherine Pepinster 'I am not a monster. I am an artist,' 'Independent on Sunday'
        13 April 1997, p.3.

lxxxviii Melvyn Howe, 'Body-snatch man wanted to be a Da Vinci,' 'Belfast Newsletter'
25 March 1998, p.5.

lxxxix Stephen White, 'Drawn and hung – or decently quartered?' 'The Times' 12 August 1997,
p.33.

xc Ferrell, op.cit., p.160.

xci Stewart, op.cit., p.27.

xcii 'ACKER: I sell copyright, that's how I make my living. LOTRINGER: You sell copyright?
ACKER: That's how writers make their money. Absolutely precisely. The work isn't
the property, it's the copyright' (Acker, op.cit., p.12).

xciii Quoted in Adams, op.cit., p.162. Of course, as far as the prosecutor was concerned,
'no exception [to the flag mutilation law] had been intended for sculpture' (p.149).

xciv Quoted in Nicholas Harrison, *Circles of Censorship: Censorship and its Metaphors in
French History, Literature, and Theory* (Oxford, 1995), p.49.

xcv Catherine A. MacKinnon, *Towards a Feminist Theory of the State* (Cambridge, Mass.,
1989), p.202.

xcvi Libel is an obvious candidate: see Barendt, op.cit., and also Posner, op.cit., pps.382-9.

List of Works Reproduced

lxxxviii Melvyn Howe, 'Body-snatch man wanted to be a Da Vinci,' 'Belfast Newsletter'
　　　　　25 March 1998, p.5.

lxxxix Stephen White, 'Drawn and hung – or decently quartered?' 'The Times' 12 August 1997,
　　　　　p.33.

　　xc Ferrell, op.cit., p.160.

　　xci Stewart, op.cit., p.27.

　xcii 'ACKER: I sell copyright, that's how I make my living. LOTRINGER: You sell copyright?
　　　　　ACKER: That's how writers make their money. Absolutely precisely. The work isn't
　　　　　the property, it's the copyright' (Acker, op.cit., p.12).

xciii Quoted in Adams, op.cit., p.162. Of course, as far as the prosecutor was concerned,
　　　　　'no exception [to the flag mutilation law] had been intended for sculpture' (p.149).

xciv Quoted in Nicholas Harrison, *Circles of Censorship: Censorship and its Metaphors in
　　　　　French History, Literature, and Theory* (Oxford, 1995), p.49.

　xcv Catherine A. MacKinnon, *Towards a Feminist Theory of the State* (Cambridge, Mass.,
　　　　　1989), p.202.

xcvi Libel is an obvious candidate: see Barendt, op.cit., and also Posner, op.cit., pps.382-9.

List of Works Reproduced

13 **Damien Hirst**, *Hymn*, 1999
2002 © Damien Hirst, all rights reserved
Photograph Stephen White, London, courtesy White Cube/Jay Jopling, London

28 **Sherrie Levine**, *After Walker Evans # 13*, 1981
2002 © Sherrie Levine, all rights reserved
Photograph courtesy Paula Cooper Gallery, New York

35 **Pierre Huyghe**, *2 Minutes out of Time*, 2000
2002 © Pierre Huyghe and Philipe Parreno, all rights reserved
Photograph courtesy Marian Goodman Gallery, New York

82 **Cai Guo Qiang**, *Rent Collection Yard* (Venice Biennale), 1999
2002 © Cai Guo Qiang, all rights reserved
Photograph courtesy Cai Guo Qiang, New York

165 **Glenn Brown**, *The Loves of Shepherds (After Double Star by Tony Roberts)*, 2000
2002 © Glenn Brown, all rights reserved
Photograph courtesy Patrick Painter, Santa Monica

177 **Marcel Duchamp**, *Fountain*, 1917
Collection Tate, London
2002 © Succession Marcel Duchamp/ADAGP, Paris and DACS, London
Photograph 2002 © Tate, London

202 **Art Rogers**, *Puppies*, 1986
2002 © Art Rogers, all rights reserved
Photograph courtesy Art Rogers/Pt. Reyes

203 **Jeff Koons**, *A String of Puppies*, 1988
2002 © Jeff Koons, all rights reserved
Photograph courtesy Sonnabend Gallery, New York

233 **Douglas Gordon**, *Déjà Vu*, 2000, (still)
2002 © Douglas Gordon, all rights reserved
Photograph courtesy Lisson Gallery, London

279 **Carl Andre**, *Equivalent VIII*, 1966
Collection Tate, London
2002 © Carl Andre/VAGA, New York and DACS, London
Photograph 2002 © Tate, London

322 **Damien Hirst**, *Cetyltrethylammionium P-Toluenesulfonate*, 1996
2002 © Damien Hirst, all rights reserved
Photograph Stephen White, London, courtesy White Cube/Jay Jopling, London

Index